THE
DICTIONARY
OF
DEMONS

ABOUT THE AUTHOR

M. Belanger is an occult expert, presenter, singer, media personality, psychic, and author of over thirty books on paranormal and occult topics. Belanger has been featured on TV shows including A&E's *Paranormal State*, *Paranormal Lockdown*, and the Travel Channel's *Portals to Hell*. Consulted for numerous documentaries and books, Belanger has also lectured on paranormal and occult topics at colleges and universities across North America. Belanger offers classes and weekend retreats on psychic development at Inspiration House in Oberlin, Ohio, a 150-year-old home with the coziest haunting you could hope to find.

To learn more about Belanger's work, start by exploring MichelleBelanger.com, where you'll find classes, books, music, and Inspiration House events. Follow Belanger on social media at twitter.com/sethanikeem or offer your support at patreon .com/haunted.

NAMES OF THE DAMNED

THE DICTIONARY OF

DEMONS

10th Anniversary Edition
Expanded & Revised
· · · · ·

M. BELANGER

Llewellyn Publications
Woodbury, Minnesota

Second Edition
Third Printing, 2022

Book design and format by Donna Burch-Brown
Cover design by Kevin R. Brown

For a complete list of art credits, see page 487.

Llewellyn is a registered trademark of Llewellyn Worldwide Ltd.

Library of Congress Cataloging-in-Publication Data
Names: Belanger, M., author.
Title: The dictionary of demons : names of the damned / by M. Belanger.
Description: Tenth anniversary edition. | Woodbury, Minnesota : Llewellyn
    Worldwide, [2020] | Includes bibliographical references. | Summary:
    "This premium-hardcover, limited edition of one the world's most
    important books on demonology has been expanded to include even more
    fascinating details about even more demons"— Provided by publisher.
Identifiers: LCCN 2020023460 (print) | LCCN 2020023461 (ebook) | ISBN
    9780738765365 (hardcover) | ISBN 9780738765495 (ebook)
Subjects: LCSH: Demonology—Dictionaries.
Classification: LCC BF1503 .B36 2020 (print) | LCC BF1503 (ebook) | DDC
    133.4/203—dc23
LC record available at https://lccn.loc.gov/2020023460
LC ebook record available at https://lccn.loc.gov/2020023461

Llewellyn Publications
A Division of Llewellyn Worldwide Ltd.
2143 Wooddale Drive
Woodbury, Minnesota 55125-2989
www.llewellyn.com

Printed in the United States of America

OTHER WORKS BY M. BELANGER

Nonfiction

Sumerian Exorcism

Summoning Spirits

Haunting Experiences

The Ghost Hunter's Survival Guide

The Ghost Hunter's Guide to the Occult

Walking the Twilight Path

Vampires in Their Own Words

The Vampire Ritual Book

Sacred Hunger

The Psychic Vampire Codex

The Psychic Energy Codex

Psychic Dreamwalking

The Watcher Angel Tarot Guidebook

House Kheperu Archives

House Kheperu Ritual Omnibus

Chasing Infinity

Wide World of Weird

Winding Path of Words

The Shadowside Series (Fiction)

Conspiracy of Angels

Harsh Gods

Resurrection Game

Other Fiction

This Heart of Flame

Immortal

These Haunted Dreams

One for the Ferryman

Fairytales for the Disenchanted

When Millie Comes Back

D Is for Demon

Wicked Kisses

Poetry

Darksong: Fantasies in Twilight

The Enchanted Wood

Soul Songs from Distant Shores

This Ritual of Me

This Trembling Flesh

Decks & Music

Psychic Aptitude Cards

Contemplation Cards

The Past Life Deck

The Watcher Angel Tarot

Blood of Angels

CONTENTS

ACKNOWLEDGMENTS

There are several people who helped me at various stages in the creation of this book. Some lent their expertise and insight. Others lent their artistic talents. Others simply lent their faith and support. All of them contributed things of value that I feel helped to improve upon the quality of this work. I cannot rate or rank their worth, and so in the spirit of this dictionary, I present them in alphabetical order: Father Bob Bailey, Christine Filipak, Clifford Hartleigh Low, Merticus, Dar Morazzini, Mykel O'Hara, and Joseph Vargo. I extend my warm and heartfelt thanks to each and every one of you. Your talents have been an immense help.

I must also extend a very special thanks to artist and traditional scribe Jackie Williams. Jackie was kind enough to design a demonic alphabet expressly for this dictionary. She also helped me through the long and sometimes arduous process of writing this book, assisting with scans, explaining the vagaries of medieval scribes, and—most importantly—reminding me to take a break and eat once in a while. Thanks also go out to the good people at Dover Publications who have generously allowed me to reproduce images from several of their books. And finally, I want to extend my gratitude to Joseph H. Peterson of EsotericArchives.com for both his dedicated scholarship and his generosity in making that scholarship freely available to all.

ACKNOWLEDGMENTS FOR THE
TENTH ANNIVERSARY EDITION

The *Dictionary of Demons* is an ambitious work and, with the tenth anniversary edition, I've striven to make it even more extensive. Without the support, talents, and inspiration of many excellent people, I could not have done that, especially not in the time frame I had. First and foremost, I want to thank Elyria Little. It is not easy to learn how to navigate the creative process of a writer, but I wouldn't get through any of it without your unflagging support. To Catherine Rogers, who has graciously put up with random three a.m. texts asking for drawings of obscure demonic sigils (and then drawn them by the next day), I can only hope the rest of the world comes to appreciate your talents and shining spirit the way I do. To Kirsten Brown for taking a chance and adding her talents to this massive undertaking. More eyes need to be on your work as well, and I hope I can help make that happen. To everyone at the Wellcome Collection for their swift response. You do the world a great service by making your extensive library of materials freely available to all. (Seriously, check out their online collection.) To Katrina Weidman for being that friend who always has my back even in some of the darkest (and coldest!) places in the country. To Jack Osbourne for his exuberant and open-minded curiosity no matter how strange our experiences may get. And, finally, to Ali A. Olomi: We have only met in virtual space, but your encyclopedic knowledge of the Jinn and other Islamic folk beliefs has vastly enriched my world. Thank you.

PREFACE
TO THE NEW EDITION

So many things have happened since I sat with these same files, these books scattered across every level surface of my home—but I've missed them. I'm not sure what it's like for other writers, but once a book of mine has been published, I avoid reading it. The urge to edit is just too powerful, and if I let myself read the book, I would realize that, even though it's published and out in the world, it's not finished.

They're never finished.

At best, a published book is as good as it can be at the time. But time changes things—it changes us, it changes the world and culture we live in, it changes the technology and the information we have available—and, hopefully, that also changes how we see and interact with all of those things. A book is this frozen moment, a kind of snapshot of where a person was during the production of the work. I don't go back and read my own books because, even if only a week has gone by since I finished the manuscript and sent it to the publisher,

I'm already not the same person who wrote that book. Ideally, I'm a better person, wiser, with opinions that have evolved as more information has become available. And I can't alter the book to reflect any of those things once it's out in the world—unless I get a chance to write a new edition.

That's what I've found so exciting about this process. Almost ten years have passed and so much has changed. So many more sources have become available—not only through the publication of new grimoires but also through old sources that nobody was looking at until just recently. These are texts that have deepened our understanding of the grimoiric tradition, changed timelines, reframed the development of several key aspects of this literature. It's exciting to come back to this project with these new perspectives, to add to, to refine, and in some cases to completely rewrite a few of the entries because the information available has evolved that much. For this new edition, I have been able to source a grimoire from Wales that was still being used by a cunning-man in the early 1800s and explore the Goetic demons in a French grimoire that predates Wierus's *Pseudomonarchia Daemonum*. I've learned that the *Grand Grimoire* and *Grimorium Verum* actually drew their demons from an older tradition, where before I had believed they were completely spurious, written only to capitalize on the sensationalism of demonic texts in their time. I even found evidence that pushed back the publication date of the *Testament of Solomon* to before the Common Era.

It's exciting to be able to make such changes—both to the text you hold in your hands and also to my understanding of its contents. And those are only a small taste of the updates. There was so much to explore for this edition. I know I didn't get it all—I cannot possibly get it all. The *Dictionary of Demons* is a book that will always have room to be revised, expanded, to evolve. That's the nature of the subject matter: demons are incredibly diverse, and humanity's approach to them spans art, literature, folklore, cinema, games, philosophy, and religion—not just the grimoiric tradition. Even narrowing the focus to include only those demons given proper names in the grimoiric tradition of Europe, there is still so much to cover.

This is a work that will never be completely finished. But, as I look back over what I have collected, changed, edited, and expanded over these past few months to bring you this tenth anniversary edition, I feel pretty good about the book in front of me.

It is as good as it can be at this time.

—M. Belanger
December 16, 2019

INTRODUCTION

This book had its genesis in a conversation with Father Bob Bailey. Some of you might recognize Father Bob from his appearances on the A&E television series *Paranormal State*. Father Bob and I were on a case together, and we had a little time to chat over tea. We'd never really had a chance to get to know one another, and this seemed as good a time as any.

For some of my fans, the idea of me hanging out in a hotel lobby with a Catholic priest might seem pretty strange. Father Bob and I come from very different worlds. He's an ordained priest with a parish in Rhode Island. He is also the co-founder of a group of paranormal investigators called the Paranormal Warriors of Saint Michael. I'm Pagan clergy, and I study everything from the occult to vampires. I'm the founder of a magickal society called House Kheperu. You would think that we would mix like oil and water, yet our shared interest in the paranormal guarantees that we have at least some common ground.

Because of the limits placed upon me as a psychic for the show, we could not talk about anything connected with the case. So, instead, we opted to talk about our different experiences with ghosts and spirits. Because Father Bob is often consulted on the topic of exorcism, inevitably demons came up. Father Bob was lamenting that there were no good resources out there that listed the names of demons, as names are seen as important in the process of deliverance. Although Father Bob cannot do full exorcisms without the sanction of the Catholic Church, he does get called in to do house cleansings and to perform blessings on people who feel that they are being haunted by something much darker than a simple human ghost.

In his line of work, the name of the demon is important. In the Catholic rite of exorcism, known as the Roman Ritual, this ties back to a story recorded in both the Gospel of Mark and the Gospel of Luke. Here, when Jesus is confronted by a possessed man, he very specifically asks the name of the demon before driving it out. The passage implies that the name has power over the demon. This concept itself ties back to very ancient beliefs from Babylon, Sumer, and Akkad—related cultures with a very lively demonology. Interestingly, in the biblical story, Jesus eventually drives out the demons into a herd of swine. In ancient Sumer, thousands of years before the Gospels were penned, one common method of exorcism involved transferring a possessing demon into an animal substitute—often a goat or a pig. In these rites as well, a powerful component was the demon's true name.

I joked with Father Bob about how great it would be if there were a real version of *Tobin's Spirit Guide*—the fictional book they used in the movie *Ghostbusters* to find the names of all the weird spirits that kept turning up in New York. And then I thought about it for a minute or two. *Tobin's Spirit Guide* might be a convenient plot device used in a funny movie, but there really are books out there that list the names of spirits—demons, angels, and everything else in between. They are called grimoires, and they are books of ceremonial magick written mainly between the twelfth and seventeenth centuries in Western Europe. Although the grimoiric tradition was not exclusive to Western Europe, they became a mainstay of Western European occultism throughout the Middle Ages and the Renaissance.

I'd long been collecting grimoires, and back in 2002 I'd even started a casual list of the names contained in these sometimes infamous books. The list of names was a personal reference for my creative efforts. I collected baby-name books for the same reason—I loved learning about the origin and meanings of names. Sometimes a particularly interesting or obscure name could inspire an entire tale. The grimoires were a good source of highly unusual names with extraordinary meanings—the sort you just couldn't find in your average baby-name book. Why not take that personal reference and expand upon it? My collection of names was already in a spreadsheet format, so it wouldn't be too hard to separate out all the demons, then expand each of them into full entries, like a dictionary . . .

As Father Bob and I sat sipping our tea in the quiet hotel lobby, my brain starting churning. It would be a lot of work to develop something definitive from the skeletal resource I had on hand, but since I knew where to look, it was a doable project. Maybe a little insane considering the amount of work it would require, but definitely doable.

"You want names to go with your demons?" I asked after thinking about it for a while. "Give me a little time, Padre. I might have a book for you."

WHAT'S IN A NAME?

Words had power in the ancient world, and few words were viewed with more fear than those that named the forces of evil. Among many ancient peoples, the names of demons and devils were thought to act as a kind of beacon, calling those beings up from the depths whenever their names were uttered. As a result, these names were often approached with superstitious dread. Some people in the modern era are still reluctant to pronounce the name of a demon out loud. In the Europe of the Middle Ages, this fear gave rise to a number of nicknames for Satan. Called Old Nick or Old Scratch, it was a common folk belief that these nicknames of the Devil had less power to draw his influence directly into a person's life when uttered out loud.

And yet, as far as the ancients were concerned, the names of devils and demons could do more than simply attract their attention. The names of spirits were thought also to compel them, control them, bind them, and banish them. In Jewish demonology, the many names of the night-demon Lilith were inscribed upon protective amulets because those names were thought to have power over her. Properly applied, they didn't attract her—they could drive her away. In the *Testament of Solomon*, King Solomon demands the names of a series of demons so he can then put them to work building the Temple of Jerusalem. By surrendering their names, one after the other, they acknowledge Solomon's power over them.

The *Testament of Solomon* and its related tradition had a tremendous impact on the European concept of demons. It helped to establish the belief that demons could be compelled and bound using the names of angels as well as magickal names of God. It presented demons as a very real—albeit largely invisible—force in the world, tormenting humanity with death, disaster, and disease. These concepts were already widely present in the demonology of other ancient cultures, from the Sumerians to the Egyptians to the Greeks, but with King Solomon in the story, the material became relevant to Christians, Jews, and Muslims alike. The book also helped to promote an idea that many demons were either fallen angels or the misbegotten progeny sired by those angels once they had come to earth—a concept that tied into even older traditions present in Jewish legends and hinted at within the first few books of Genesis.

Written some time in the centuries around the start of the Common Era, the *Testament of Solomon* likely started off as a Jewish text but it shows evidence of Christian redaction—changes and insertions that better reflect Christian beliefs. It is a pseudepigraphal text, which is to say that it was

not written by King Solomon himself, although it bears his name. It is named after him because it tells his story, and it is told from his perspective to lend that story more weight. This was a common practice in the time period during which the *Testament* was written, although it was equally common in that time (and for centuries afterward) to assume that the pseudepigraphal author really was the author of the text.

The *Testament of Solomon* is, by far, not the only extra-biblical tale that depicts King Solomon as a controller of demons. The legends that grew up around this Old Testament monarch are many and varied, from his escapades with the demonic Queen of Sheba, to the mystery of King Solomon's mines, to the years wherein the demon Asmodeus allegedly stole his throne. King Solomon's prowess as a wise man and magician also influenced Muslim legends: the stories of genies trapped in bottles like those found in the *One Thousand and One Arabian Nights* all tie back to the Solomonic tradition.

In order to understand the tradition influenced by this work, it's not necessary to believe that King Solomon somehow had demonic assistance in the construction of the Temple of Jerusalem, nor even that he had power over demons at all. The important thing to understand is that a great many people both in the ancient world and in Europe up through the Renaissance believed these things. And belief in Solomon's power was at least partly responsible for a complicated system of magick that revolved around spirit evocation. Names were a fundamental part of that system.

THE GRIMOIRIC TRADITION

The grimoires of medieval and Renaissance Europe are the direct inheritors of the Solomonic tradition as it appears in the *Testament of Solomon*.

They get their name from an Old French word, *grammaire*, which means "relating to letters." Letters, names, and the very process of writing are all integral to the grimoiric tradition. Some of these magickal books were viewed as possessing so much power in their words alone that if a passage were mistakenly read by someone not properly initiated into the mysteries, a master who understood the proper use of the book had to read a passage of equal length to negate the unwanted effects.[1]

Although no written line of descent currently exists to show us how concepts about demonic evocation recorded in the first few centuries of the Christian era survived to reemerge in the 1100s and beyond, the connection is unmistakable. King Solomon's name comes up again and again, and many of the grimoires are directly attributed to him. These are of course as pseudepigraphal as the *Testament of Solomon* itself, but that did not stop medieval writers and copyists from putting the old king's name on these forbidden tomes. Perhaps the two most famous are the *Clavicula Salomonis*—known as the *Key of Solomon*—and the *Lemegeton*, also known as the *Lesser Key of Solomon*.

The grimoires do not deal exclusively with demons. Many of the spirits in the grimoires are described as angels, elemental spirits, and beings known as Olympian spirits—intelligences tied to the seven planets and thus the seven celestial spheres. Given all the good spirits, bad spirits, and in-between spirits that were believed to be invocated by the rituals recorded in the grimoires, it can sometimes be difficult to tell what exactly is intended to be a demon. Certainly, the line separating demons from angels can get fuzzy in these works, particularly because many demons are pre-

Detail from an early sixteenth-century edition of the *Celestial Hierarchy* showing the seven planetary spheres in the scheme of Creation. Courtesy of the Merticus Collection.

sented as fallen angels, and they retain the traditional nomenclature of angels, with names ending in *-ael* or *-iel*.

However, as hazy as the identification of some of these spirits may at times be, there are also clear cases where the beings enumerated in the grimoires are described specifically as demons. Even

---

1. Richard Kieckhefer, *Forbidden Rites*, p. 8.

then, these beings are not necessarily presented as entities to be avoided. Instead, following in the tradition set down by the *Testament of Solomon*, the writers of these magickal texts seek to abjure, control, and otherwise coerce these demons into servitude by commanding them in the name of God and his angels.

This is probably one of the most striking things about the grimoiric tradition, and it often comes as a shock to both Christians and non-Christians who approach these books as forbidden bastions of black magick. The magickal system outlined in the grimoires is highly religious. Furthermore, this system is predicated on the existence of a supreme being, and that supreme being is very clearly the God of the Bible. There is no avoiding the influence of Yahweh or the Bible in these works. Even though many of the grimoires are devoted to the summoning and commanding of demons, the spells contained in these tomes frequently read like priestly orations uttered in a high Latin mass.

In part, this is because the magickal system in the grimoires was practiced mainly by members of the clergy. In the Middle Ages, priests and lay-brothers were some of the only individuals who had the literary expertise to write, read, and copy these tomes. Professor Richard Kieckhefer typifies the demonic magick of the grimoires as "the underside of the tapestry of late medieval culture."[2] This is, of course, interesting because at the same time that priests and lay-brothers were experimenting with demonic magick, most of Western Europe was swept up in a mania focused on witchcraft, sorcery, and pacts with the Devil. Folk beliefs about witchcraft and the very real tradition of the grimoires existed side by side and, in some instances, may have even fed into one another. However, even though it invoked demonic spirits, the magickal system of the grimoires was perceived as being distinctly different from the "Satanic" practices of witches—at least by its practitioners. This was primarily because of the ritual elements and invocations to God woven throughout the grimoires.

As curious as it may sound, given the frequent references to Christ and the Holy Trinity that appear in some of the grimoires, a lot of the priestly and ritual aspects of these books of magick were inspired by Jewish esotericism. The Jewish tradition known as the Qabbalah is a mystical path, but it also has practical magickal applications. Much of Qabbalistic magick revolves around the Tree of Life. This is a kind of mystic ladder that is seen as a map of reality. The Tree of Life contains ten *Sephiroth*—the plural of the singular *Sefira*, which may share a root with the Hebrew word *sefer*, or "book."[3] These Sephiroth are placed along pathways that move up the Tree of Life, from Malkuth, at the bottom, which represents the physical world, to Keter (also spelled *Kether*), at the top, which is the crown just beneath the Throne of God. In Qabbalistic magick, a trained individual seeks to ascend the ladder of the Tree of Life through rigorous practices that involve meditation, fasting, and ceremonial ritual. Encounters with demons and angels are a part of this mystic journey. The ultimate goal is a vision of the Throne of God, an experience believed to be powerfully transformational.

---

2. Richard Kieckhefer, *Forbidden Rites*, p. 13.

3. In the first edition, this section was informed erroneously by a nineteenth-century text identifying the root of Sephiroth as *sappir*, Hebrew for "sapphire." Thus, the line subsequently read: The Tree of Life contains ten *Sephiroth*—a word derived from a Hebrew term meaning "sapphire" or "jewel."

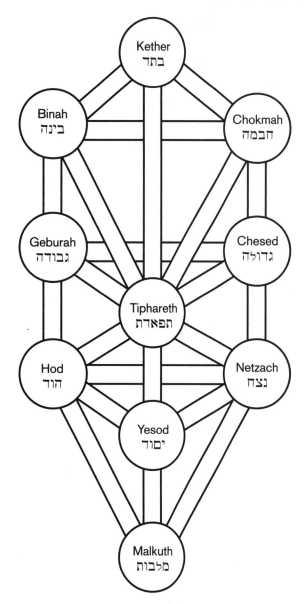

Tree of Life

the Angel Raziel—that have a long-reaching influence in later Christian grimoires. Another example of uniquely Jewish magick appears in the *Book of Abramelin*, also known as the *Sacred Magic of Abramelin the Mage*. Despite being written by a fourteenth-century Jewish scholar, this book had a significant impact on Christian ceremonial magick. In the modern era it remains one of the most influential texts in this tradition. Most of the Christian grimoires contain abjurations of the spirits that include a litany of names, many of which are titles of God in garbled Hebrew. They are not always accurately spelled and their true meanings don't always seem to be clearly understood by the Christian writers borrowing them, but their importance was recognized and retained within the system, albeit often by rote.

It would be possible to write another book entirely on the crossover between Jewish and Christian magick in the grimoiric tradition. The important point to be made for the purpose of this work is that the influence of Jewish magick ensured that the spells contained in European grimoires very closely resembled religious ceremonies. Hebrew names, and specifically Hebrew names of God, play a significant role, and the predominantly Christian authors of the grimoires then added Christian elements, such as references to Christ, the Trinity, and even the Virgin Mary. The result evolved into its own system, but it is clearly a system that stems from medieval Jewish magick as well as the Solomonic tradition, with roots stretching as far back as the hermetic magick practiced in the ancient Hellenic world. Demons and angels both play significant roles in this system, and rather than being controlled through black arts, demons were thought to be controlled only by those individuals holy enough and pure enough to

The grimoiric tradition borrows a lot from this Jewish mystical tradition. The ceremonial quality of Qabbalistic practice is adopted almost wholesale into the magick of the grimoires, as is the significance of Hebrew names—especially the secret names of God. There are several Jewish magickal texts—most notably, the *Sepher Raziel*, or *Book of* be able to convincingly command them with the many sacred names of God.

COMPILING THE NAMES

When I developed the concept for this book, the focus was on names. I knew it was possible to write an entire text on the practice of demonic magick as it appears in the grimoires, but that was not my goal. I simply wanted to create a resource of proper names attributed to demonic spirits, and the grimoiric tradition was the best place to start. As it turned out, I never had to stray far from the grimoires to produce an extensive list of names. Instead, I found that I had to set strict limitations for what would and would not be included in order to keep this book at a manageable length.

First, in order to be included in this book, the name had to be presented in the text as the *proper name* of a demon. It could not be a general name for a class of demon, like an incubus or a succubus. Aside from one lone exception, all of the names collected in this book were presented in their sources as the proper names of demons. The one exception is an entry on the Watcher Angels, a class of fallen angels. The belief in these beings had a significant if subtle influence on the demonology that underpins the grimoires, and I felt that this would best be covered in a separate entry that stands in addition to all of the individual entries on specific Watchers.

Second, the spirit being named had to be infernal. This meant that within its source text, the name was defined as one of the following: a demon, a fallen angel, or an evil angel. (A number of Jewish sources, such as the *Sword of Moses*, use the terms *wicked angel* or *evil angel* rather than *fallen angel*.) In some cases, the designation was hazy. I had originally sourced spirits named in the

Secret Grimoire of Turiel, but in the end I cut them all, because they were more properly Olympian spirits—intelligences believed to be tied to the seven planetary spheres—rather than fallen angels. In a few instances, when the grimoire itself does not make a clear distinction, I had to judge a spirit's status based on context. If the spirit is associated with malevolent magick or if its name appears in association with other known demonic spirits, and no effort is made to distinguish it from the demons, I have included that spirit's name in this book. Several spirits from the *Grimoire of Armadel* fall into this class.

As a result of these criteria for selection, you will find that I have sourced mainly the grimoires that stem from the Christian tradition of Western Europe. Christian clergy were hardly the only people producing tomes of demonic and spiritual magick in the Middle Ages and Renaissance, but they were certainly the ones who were most inclined to define certain spirits as demonic.

As we have seen already, these books had their genesis in Jewish mysticism, and there was a rich grimoiric tradition among Muslim writers as well. Some of these texts, like the Arabic *Picatrix* attributed to Al-Madjiriti, were excluded at the outset because they did not meet the most basic criterion for this work. The *Picatrix* has more to do with alchemy and astral magick—magick tied to the movement of the stars and planets—than with infernal spirits. Likewise, even certain tomes associated with the Christian grimoiric tradition were excluded because they did not contain named spirits specifically described as demons or evil angels.

An excellent example of this exclusion is the *Heptameron*, traditionally credited to Peter de Abano. This text, first published in Venice in 1496 but believed to have been written as many as two

The demon Belial at the gates of Hell. From the 1473 work *Das Buch Belial* by Jacobus de Teramo.

hundred years earlier, includes a section of seven groups of spirits with kings, ministers, and ruling intelligences. A number of these names are extremely similar to names that also appear in the *Sworn Book of Honorius*, a grimoire that is included in the bibliography of this book. In both texts, the spirits are associated with the seven planetary spheres. Their ranks and organization are nearly identical—but in the *Heptameron*, the spirits are specifically identified as *angels*. As a result, even though it is obvious that the *Sworn Book* was influenced by the *Heptameron*, I only included the versions of these names that appeared defined as demons in editions of the *Sworn Book*.

Although my primary aim was to source only proper names of spirits defined intratextually as infernal, I had another reason for sticking with the grimoires primarily associated with the Christian tradition of Western Europe: convenience. Works like the *Clavicula Salomonis* and the *Lemegeton* are some of the most widely available in the English language. Others, like the *Pseudomonarchia Daemonum* (a collection of names that actually appears as an appendix to a larger work by sixteenth-century scholar Johannes Wierus), are in Latin. I have a tolerable enough command of both Latin and French to understand the grimoires and contemporary works written in these languages. As a result, I can source these primary materials or compare them with modern English translations in order to achieve a more accurate reading of the demon names and functions. Although I have a decent grasp on Romance languages, I have little familiarity with Hebrew and even less with Arabic. This inability on my part to compare current translations against their source texts automatically ruled out a number of the more traditional Jewish and Muslim works of magick. In the case of several Hebrew names of Lilith, I reached out to Clifford Hartleigh Low of Necronomi.com. His command of the Hebrew language allowed me to transliterate these names for this book.

Multi-text referencing was necessary for a number of the names contained within this book. This was largely due to the very nature of the grimoires themselves. Many of these books were written prior to the invention of the printing press. This meant that they were handwritten manuscripts, copied from person to person, often furtively and in poor lighting. This method of transmission did not lend itself to accuracy—and in many of the grimoires, names are significantly different from one edition to the next. Even once the printing press came into the picture in the 1400s, only some of these magickal books made it into formal print. Others continued in manuscript form, hand-copied and hidden away for fear that their very presence in a scholar's library might lead the Inquisitors to come knocking at the door.

Modern translators have not helped to maintain consistency with these texts either. In some cases, a book by two different translators is hardly recognizable as the same text. In most cases, when names vary from edition to edition, I have simply compiled them into one entry, with notes on the variations and their sources. However, in the case of the *Sworn Book of Honorius* as translated by Joseph H. Peterson in 1998, and the edition of the *Sworn Book* produced by Daniel Driscoll in 1977, the differences in the names, functions, and descriptions of the spirits are so vast that I have chosen to give them all separate entries.

One of my secondary goals with this work was to present names that are new to people, or at least names that are rarely included in more standard reference works. Since the focus is on the proper names of demons connected with a largely Judeo-Christian system, however, I had to retread some familiar territory beyond the grimoires themselves. You will find all the old familiar names of demons from the Bible, primarily because these names are foundational to the demonology of medieval Christian Europe. As such, these names, or variations on them, appear in the grimoires over and over again.

I also felt it wise to branch out to several extra-biblical texts that contributed significantly to the medieval concepts of infernal beings. Jewish legends of demons like Lilith, Samael, and Azazel played their own roles in shaping medieval Christian demonology, and apocryphal texts cut from the early canon of the Bible, such as the *Book of Enoch* and the *Book of Tobit*, were also too influential to leave out. The focus remains on the grimoiric tradition, but names and themes from these related traditions are woven like threads throughout many of the European magickal books.

To summarize the criteria for the names included in this book:

- The names in this book are *proper names* of demons
- Names are clearly identified as belonging to demons, fallen angels, or evil angels in their source texts
- The names are drawn primarily from the Christian grimoiric tradition of Western Europe
- Some influential Jewish, biblical, and extra-biblical works are also sourced

The grimoires sourced in this book were written mainly during the Middle Ages and Renaissance. There are several works included that were written after this time, but they are either direct descendants of the grimoires or they became entangled with that tradition during the occult revival of the nineteenth century. The two main texts that might seem a little out of place based on the criteria outlined above are Charles Berbiguier's *Les Farfadets* and Collin de Plancy's *Dictionnaire Infernal*. These nineteenth-century French works are largely included because of an edition of the *Grand Grimoire* translated by A. E. Waite in his *Book of Black Magic and Pacts* and later reprinted by Darcy Kuntz. Waite gets material from both Berbiguier and de Plancy mixed up with the writing of Johannes Wierus. It was necessary to cite both French writers in order to put that information in context and to clarify its true origins.

Finally, it should be noted that this book, although extensive, is by no means an exhaustive collection of the demon names that appear in the grimoiric tradition. I have made a considerable effort to track down as many texts that fit my criteria as possible, but within the scope of this book it was neither feasible nor necessary to source every existing grimoire. There are simply

Fifteenth-century image of Satan and his demons. Early depictions of demons hardly compare to the modern image of a red-skinned man with a goatee. Courtesy of Dover Publications.

and even in the Renaissance to conserve book-making materials by cutting up old manuscripts to include in the binding or covers of later editions.

Any attempt to track down all of these books and study the information contained within would be the work of a lifetime, and perhaps several lifetimes. The variations on the demons named within these texts would be infinite, but perhaps that is simply the nature of demons.

In his nineteenth-century opus *Demonology and Devil-Lore*, Moncure Daniel Conway starts out with a story. Three friars have snuck out to the German mountains to witness the gathering of devils rumored to occur on Walpurgisnacht. One of the demons attending this event discovers them in the process of attempting to count the frolicking hordes of Hell. The demon behaves in a rather sympathetic fashion to the three fellows, suggesting that they leave off their counting and instead head to safety. For, he tells them, ". . . our army is such that if all the Alps, their rocks and glaciers, were equally divided among us, none would have a pound's weight."[4]

After having danced with the demons named in this book for quite some time, I know exactly how Conway felt when he quoted this tale.

ABOUT THIS BOOK

This book is not intended to be a how-to book on grimoiric magick, although if you read this book all the way to the end, you should come away with a basic knowledge of what grimoiric magick is and what it is not. This book is also not intended to be a definitive dictionary of the grimoires themselves. That is a subject that is far too vast, especially given the many different editions of each

too many different versions of the grimoires scattered throughout the libraries of Europe and far too many variations upon the names within those books. There are copies of copies of copies, each deviating slightly from a lost original. There are heretofore unknown versions of these books still lying unidentified in libraries and private collections. And there are grimoires that have been lost forever, either buried, burned, or partitioned into other books; it was common in the Middle Ages

---

4. Moncure Daniel Conway, *Demonology and Devil-Lore*, vol. 1, p. v.

grimoire—not to mention the amount of scribal error that twists and taints many of the texts. This is also not a book on types or species of demons. There are books like that elsewhere, and they have been done well by other researchers.

This is a reference book of names, first and foremost. However, it contains much more than simply the names of demons. It also contains ranks, affiliations, and powers traditionally associated with these entities. A rich tradition of demonology is woven within and throughout the European grimoires. Within this tradition, there is a pecking order in the infernal hierarchy. This pecking order is a dark reflection of the feudal society present in Europe at the time that many of the grimoires were first composed. Demons have titles and ranks like prince and king, duke and earl. Many of them serve superior spirits, and most also oversee whole retinues of their own. The spirits beneath each major demon arrange themselves in legions—a convention possibly influenced by the biblical passage recorded in Luke and Mark, in which a demon utters the phrase, "Our name is legion, for we are many."[5]

In addition to this, many demons have planetary and elemental associations. Some of these associations are likely the result of the influence of works on astral magick, like the *Picatrix*. There are grimoires that assign a demon or an angel to every planetary hour and every day of the week. Demons are also associated with the cardinal directions, and in at least one work, known as the *Ars Theurgia*, the demons enumerated within the text are tied to every conceivable point of the compass.

Demons are also assigned various functions, offices, and powers. The *Goetia*, a collection of

seventy-two infernal entities traditionally included in the larger work known as the *Lemegeton*, has some of the most elaborate descriptions. It portrays demons who teach language, demons who build castles and fortifications, and demons who reveal secrets about the past, present, and future. Other works, such as the *Testament of Solomon*, not only enumerate the powers that certain demons possess, but they also describe how to frustrate these powers. Typically, such texts include the names of angels believed to control and constrain the demons in question. A few of the grimoires include symbols, signs, and secret names of God that have power over the demons.

Whenever it is offered, I have included this information in each entry. If a demon's name is defined, that is also included in the entry. In several cases, the name is clearly derived from an existing word or even from the name of another demon; in these instances, the entry includes commentary on the likely origins and meaning of the name. Variations on the name, typically drawn from related texts, are included in the entry with a note on where these variations appear.

Nearly all of the fifteen hundred-plus entries in this book are the proper names of demons. There are a few exceptions. There are also entries for the most frequently sourced works. The books that have entries in this dictionary are by no means the only works cited throughout this work, but they are the most significant to an overall understanding of the tradition from which these names are drawn. In addition to entries on specific books, you will also find some entries on individuals. Most of these individuals are directly related to the significant sources cited throughout this work. Their entries also exist to give context to grimoiric magick and the related tradition of demonology

---

5. The Bible, Mark 5:9. See also Luke 8:30.

that influenced concepts about both angels and demons in Western Europe.

Throughout this book, you will also find a number of impact articles. These are short entries separate from the rest of the text that help to paint a broader picture about the beliefs, practices, and events in Western Europe that impacted religion, demonology, and the tradition of the grimoires. It is my hope that these extra articles will help provide context for the practice of demonic magick represented in the material in this book.

At the back of this book, I have collected lists of correspondences. These are from a spreadsheet I kept side by side with the entries in this text. These lists contain the names of the demons associated with a specific quality or power. The lists are alphabetized for easy reference. I have not included every single power, association, or ability connected with the demons in this text. Instead, I focused on the qualities I felt would be most useful to know. Use these for easy reference when you are looking for a demon specifically associated with topics like death, poison, or disease. Not all of the qualities are negative, because in the grimoiric tradition even spirits defined as demons could still be forced to be helpful.

Of course, the big question is: what on earth do you use a big book of demons for? This book is predicated on the idea that names have power. Many people still believe that even to say the name of a demon out loud is to summon that entity into their life. A great deal of fear surrounds the subject of demons, and I prefer to fight fear with knowledge. I think it is important to learn how the people who worked to summon demons actually believed they could be called up and compelled.

I also think it is important to understand that these infernal entities were not viewed as all-powerful. Although they were certainly presented as intimidating, the message of the entire Solomonic tradition underpinning the grimoires is that faith has power. Demons—whatever you think demons really are—are not invincible, and the best way to control and to combat them is by knowing their names.

The book you now hold in your hands contains over fifteen hundred names of power. Do not fear that power. Learn what it means and use it responsibly.

—M. Belanger, January 2010

AN OVERVIEW OF THE EXPANDED MATERIAL

As I neared completion of the manuscript in 2009, the original introduction to the *Dictionary of Demons* developed into a small book in its own right, one that explored (at times minutely) the roots of European demonology. Those roots stretch back through the development of Christianity to its predecessor, Judaism, and even further to the very seed of what we understand as Western culture in the ancient Middle East. There was a *lot* of ground to cover, and so the chapters explaining the various concepts, myths, and source texts from that milieu were extensive.

My editor at the time, Brett Fechheimer, very rightly encouraged me to trim this document, refining the focus to better introduce the specific names referenced throughout the text. For the sake of scope, these names were drawn mainly from a narrow selection of literature: books of magick in what is known as the Solomonic tradition. This was practiced primarily in Christian Western Europe throughout the Middle Ages and Renaissance and into the modern era.[6] That meant narrowing the topics covered in the introduction to the same slice of history, culture, and source texts in order to provide the best context for the real meat of the dictionary—all of the names. With this decision came the removal of several chapters' worth of information exploring biblical sources, pseudepigrapha, and demonology's Mesopotamian roots, not to mention mythological comparisons with a variety of world cultures, both modern and ancient.

For this new edition, I have resurrected the files culled from the original and reprinted the bulk of that original introduction here. However, the document is still dauntingly extensive, and in the interest in streamlining your journey to the main portion of this dictionary, I have separated large sections of the original introduction into individual chapters and

---

6. To reiterate from the previous section, this choice was one of academic practicality: I can read many of the languages of these primary materials, so I felt most confident with sourcing those texts.

placed these as appendices in the back of the book. Even so, this leaves us with a sizable document introducing the idea of the power of names, exploring the roots of demonology as our culture currently understands it, and delving into both biblical and extra-biblical works that have significantly shaped our beliefs of what constitutes a demon. There are a few small sections that inevitably echo what I salvaged for the edited introduction, but otherwise the vast majority of what follows will be new to those familiar with the original work.

I. ORIGINAL INTRODUCTION, WRITTEN (AND CUT) IN DECEMBER 2009

If there is one thing that myth and folklore love, it's demons—demons that haunt the night, demons that attack unwary travelers along lonely roads, demons that sit on the chest of a sleeper, tormenting that person with bad dreams till dawn. The further one goes back in time, the more the dark spaces of the world seem to be peopled with demons. Anything that was poorly understood and had unpleasant effects upon the mortal realm was typically assigned its very own demon—from dementia to disease, from famine to earthquakes, eclipses, and storms. As terrifying as the topic of demons may seem, people nevertheless fixate on these malevolent beings of misfortune. For every tale penned about the noble beings of the celestial realm, for every story told around the fire about the heroic deeds of the gods, there is an equal and opposite tale detailing in language both turbid and grim the exploits and dangers of the demons of our haunted world.

Perhaps the appeal of demons is merely the natural result of the allure that darkness holds for the human psyche. We are, as a species, fascinated with all those dangerous and evil things that lurk in the shadows. Consider the popularity of Dante's *Inferno*. Here is the classic tale of one man's journey through the Christian Hell. Dante devotes two additional books to otherworldly journeys, one to Purgatory and one to Heaven. Yet what do readers turn to again and again? The gruesome spectacle of the Underworld.[7] It's in our blood.

With our many advances in medicine and technology, we now understand that disease is caused not by demons but by germs (though medically-resistant staph infections may seem just as terrifying as any horde of angry devils). We know that earthquakes are the result of tectonic forces and the slippage of continental plates. Meteorological phenomena and climate change are the real demons behind weather shifts and increasingly destructive storms, and eclipses both solar and lunar are merely part of the inexorable cycle of time as it plays out in the dance of the heavens. Yet despite all this, we live in an age practically possessed by a fascination with demons. The Catholic Church still actively performs exorcisms—and it is no longer the only branch of Christianity to do so.[8] Demonic influence, possessions, and hauntings are all topics of books, movies, and television series. Even as the scientists at CERN pursue the Higgs boson particle and NASA sends robots to Mars, the popular imagination seems to stubbornly rebel against all the hard science. Demons are still believed by many to be the real force behind mass shootings,

---

7. Ian Thompson, writing in the *Irish Times*, identifies Dante's *Inferno* as "the most widely translated book after the Bible," and "for many, the greatest single work of Western literature." *Irish Times*, Sept. 8, 2018.

8. Leonardo Blair: "Rome Opens Up Exorcism Course to All Major Christian Faiths to Fight Rising Demonic Force." *Christian Post*. May 9, 2019.

private traumas, and the general discontent of our modern world.

Twisted Roots

For all the ink spilled on demons, fallen angels, and evil spirits today, few people fully understand where our beliefs in these beings stem from—never mind how those beliefs have been shaped and changed over the years. What we in the English-speaking world define as demons are beings grown in the fertile soil of Western European religion, mythology, and folk belief. In its own turn, the demonology of Western Europe developed from several key sources:

- Biblical sources (Old and New Testaments)
- Traditions of Jewish magick (Qabbalah)
- Hellenic magick via the humanist revival of Greek and Roman texts (curse tablets, magickal papyri, etc.)
- The mythology of the ancient Middle East

Jewish demonology itself, and thus the Christian demonology that grew out of it in the New Testament, was strongly influenced by the demonology of the Babylonians (who, in their turn, inherited most of their concepts from the Sumerians). Jewish demonology was so indelibly stamped by Babylonian beliefs that the ancient Israelites and the ancient Babylonians had many demons in common, almost all of which can be traced to originally Sumerian sources. The story of religion, mythology, and folk belief in the ancient world—particularly that region known as the Fertile Crescent, which gave birth to what we understand as Western civilization—is a story of cultural exchange and syncretism. Everyone shared every-

thing—and we've inherited the rich mythological stew that was the result.

In addition to the influence of the ancient Middle East on modern demonology, the impact of European humanists cannot be underestimated. It is through their efforts to reclaim and restore rare and vital works from the classical world that many of these works have come down to us at all across the gulf of ages. Many great thinkers—who defied the conservative views of the day (views that, incidentally, pretty much led to the Dark Ages)—were involved in this reclamation that lead directly to what we understand as the European Renaissance. The Florentine Medici were at the heart of this reclamation.[9] A number of ideas, techniques, and beliefs that would otherwise have been lost to the Dark Ages were rescued by their scholars, from artistic techniques to knowledge of mathematics and architecture.

Technical and philosophical knowledge were not the only legacies rescued by the Medici and other humanists from the ancient world. Hellenic society was profoundly steeped in magick, and a vast quantity of magickal scrolls and curse tablets survived. These *defixiones* and the texts that instructed in their use and design were among the rare books sought out and translated by humanist patrons. Although tracing a direct line of descent from the Greek and Roman magickal papyri to the magickal grimoires of the humanist period is beyond the scope of this work, the influence of Hellenic magick on the magick practiced in Europe from the thirteenth century onward is undeniable, and that magick was steeped in demons and related spirits.

---

9. Oliphant Smeaton, *The Medici and the Italian Renaissance*, pp. 18–20.

The Power of Names

Speak of the Devil and he will appear. At least, that's what our ancestors believed. Words had power in the ancient world, and few words were viewed with more fear than those that named the forces of evil. The names of demons and devils were believed to act as a kind of beacon, calling those beings up from the depths whenever they were uttered. Thus, in the past (and to some extent even now), all of these names were approached with a certain kind of superstitious dread. This gave rise to the many nicknames of Satan in use throughout Europe in the Middle Ages and beyond. It was a common folk belief that these nicknames, such as Old Nick or Old Scratch, had less power to draw his influence directly into a person's life.

And yet, as far as the ancients were concerned, the names of devils and demons could do more than simply draw their attention to a person; those names could also compel and control the minions of Hell. In Jewish demonology, the many names of the night-demon Lilith were inscribed upon protective amulets, for it was believed that anyone who bore these names would be safe from harm. The vast majority of Lilith amulets that have survived the passage of time were intended to protect newborns. Infants were perceived to be especially vulnerable to Lilith's predations in the first few weeks of their lives, as this demon was believed to be responsible for crib death.[10] Lilith's many names thus became apotropaics, talismans that kept her evil at bay, rather than inviting that evil into the world.

The Jews were not the only people to view demonic names as having talismanic power. Many of the cultures that grew out of the Fertile Crescent approached the names of demons in this fashion. Although those names certainly had the power to attract the demons' attention, when used in the proper context—and often by specially trained individuals—the names could also bind and banish the evil of these beings.

As far back as ancient Sumer, the names of demons were used in rituals of exorcism. The Sumerians had a rich and colorful demonology, and many aspects of Western demonology can be traced back to this ancient civilization. Lilith, for example, has her roots in the mythology of the Sumerians, where she appears most strikingly as the *ardat lili*, a maiden ghost who, having died a virgin, perpetually seeks out men at night in order to have sex with them. Her amorous attentions, however, are dangerous, if not fatal, and in this respect the ardat lili was a being greatly feared.[11] Numerous protective spells survive that are devoted to keep her at bay. Given the ardat lili's beautiful appearance and her lustful but dangerous embrace, it's easy to see how stories of this variety of Lilith demon may have eventually evolved into the succubus of medieval Europe.

Since so much of Western demonology is interconnected (especially once you dig down to its ancient roots), it can be fairly boggling to navigate at the outset. The Sumerians, as well as their cultural inheritors, the Babylonians and Assyrians, believed that demons were responsible for many of the evils in the world. There were demons of earthquakes and demons of storms, and these were frequently depicted as literally grinding the

---

10. B. Barry Levy, *Planets, Potions, and Parchments: Scientifica Herbarica from the Dead Sea Scrolls to the Eighteenth Century,* p. 89.

11. Reginald Campbell Thompson. *Semitic Magic: Its Origins and Development,* pp. 65–66.

earth to dust beneath the awesome fury of their power.[12] There were also demons of disease, and these were the demons that attacked humanity directly, rather than simply sowing disaster all around. Demons of illness were thought to grip hold of people, inhabiting their bodies and thereby causing the symptoms of their ailment. This belief forms the very foundation of the notion of demonic possession, and it gave rise to a fascinating variety of spells, prayers, and rites intended to drive the evil spirits out.[13]

Mesopotamian demon bowl, written in Mandaic script. Most of these items, intended to protect against demons and the afflictions they bring, date to the late Sassanid period (sixth to seventh centuries CE). Image courtesy of the Wellcome Collection, London.

The Sumerians had a demon for practically every ailment, and for demons, they had a specialized class of priest. Known as an *ashipu* priest or *ašipu* priest, these specially trained individuals were responsible for carrying out most of the rites and rituals related to exorcism. The rites of exorcism were part magick and part prayer, and they typically invoked specific deities from the Mesopotamian pantheon who were believed to have a par-

ticular skill for driving out demons. Among these were Ea, god of wisdom; Marduk, his mighty son; and Shamash, a solar deity connected to law and judgment.[14]

Rites of Exorcism

In Sumerian rituals of exorcism, the name of the demon possessing the afflicted individual was believed to be instrumental in driving that demon away. Oftentimes the name was not known, and so Sumerian exorcisms frequently included a litany of demonic names, working on the theory that if *all* of the demons that could possibly be responsible for the possession were named then at least one of those names would hit its mark. Many of the ancient rites of exorcism included a part where the exorcist demanded to know the name of the demon responsible for the possession. The demon was abjured in the name of various gods to give up the secret of its name so that it could be better controlled and dispelled by the exorcist.[15]

This technique should seem familiar to anyone who has read the biblical tale of the Gerasene demoniac. In Mark 5 and Luke 8, Jesus comes across a man so afflicted by the demons inside of him that he has abandoned human habitation to wander among the lonely tombs. Covered in rags and filth, he spends his days shrieking, crying, and doing harm to himself. In a famous exchange, Jesus demands to know the name of the demon possessing the man so that he can drive that demon out. The demon—several demons, actually—speak through the mouth of the afflicted man, saying, "My name is legion, for we are many."[16]

12. Thompson. 47–50.

13. Henry Frederick Lutz. *Selected Sumerian and Babylonian Texts.* University of Pennsylvania Press. Philadelphia, PA: 1919. pp. 35–40.

14. Lutz, pp. 57–59.

15. Lutz. pp. 51–53.

16. Mark 5:9.

The chilling significance of this statement is somewhat dulled if we forget that Jesus was living in a world of Roman occupation, and the main tool of the imperial war machine was the Roman legion. This was a collection of well-armed foot soldiers ranging in number between 5,300 and 6,000 men. In Jesus's time, Roman legions swept inexorably across the land, conquering whatever countries lay in their path and occupying them in the name of the emperor—who, by that time, was worshipped as a god. Thus, the response of the demon via the Gerasene man is chilling in two respects. For the authors who recorded this story in the gospels, the use of the word *legion* is inextricably linked with the brutal and unyielding soldiers of Rome. Further, it conjures images of a force so large as to be nearly uncountable in the ancient world. No wonder author William Blatty made such potent use of this biblical quote in *The Exorcist* and nearly every demon afterward is said to command not a battalion nor a phalanx of lesser devils but very specifically *legions*.

Aside from the "we are legion" comment, the story of the Gerasene man is important for another reason. Not only does Jesus demand the name of the demon, but he also then drives the demons out into a herd of swine. The swine go mad and charge to their collective deaths over a cliff, a detail that quite potently links the scene with tried-and-true methods of exorcism practiced in Jesus's day: the ancient Sumerians would frequently use an animal substitute for the possessed individual, transferring the demon through the power of its name into the animal. The demon was then bound to the animal with the power of its name—and with a little help from the gods whose names were also invoked to control and compel the demon.[17] With the demon thus trapped in this substitute flesh, the animal was then killed, an act which was thought to similarly kill the demon.[18]

While goats were sometimes used as the sacrificial substitutes in this procedure, another common animal used to draw the demon out of a human subject was a pig. Thus, the exorcism performed by Jesus on the Gerasene man conformed to all the familiar conventions that had come to typify exorcism in his day: he demands the demon's name, and he drives the demon into a substitute animal that is then killed to destroy the demon. The only real difference for those witnessing the act at the time would have been slight. Rather than abjuring the demon in the name of a variety of gods, Jesus invokes only the power of one god, God the Father, who acts through him to drive the demon away.

Not everyone reading this book is going to be comfortable with the idea of comparing Jesus's techniques of exorcism with those of the decidedly pagan Sumerians. But if we are to really understand the roots of demonology in the Western tradition, we cannot get sidetracked by the theological significance of stories about demons. Instead, we need to take a good, hard look at the socio-historical significance of these beliefs as taken within the context of their own cultural milieu. In simpler terms, there is a story behind Western beliefs about demons, and that story has been shaped by the beliefs and traditions of a variety of people—not just the people who wrote the

---

17. Henry Frederick Lutz, *Selected Sumerian and Babylonian Texts*, pp. 43–46.

18. Sometimes an inanimate object, such as a clay vessel, was used instead. Once the demon was transferred, the vessel was smashed. See Lutz, p. 50.

Bible. A lot of stories went into the development of demons as we know them, and it behooves us to understand them all—and how they changed and influenced one another.

Agents of the Damned

The very use of the word *demon* conjures images of a Judeo-Christian[19] worldview in which the damned are cast into Hell while worthy souls are rewarded with an eternity of bliss in Heaven. This is one of the primary reasons that most Pagans, Wiccans, and practitioners of other alternative faiths tend to shy away from the concept of demons. Modern Paganism acknowledges the existence of spirits, and spirits in the Pagan worldview can be both beneficent and malevolent, with many varying shades in between. And yet you will rarely encounter a Pagan who is willing to refer to a spirit explicitly as a *demon*. The term is too charged with its Christian associations. For the same reason, many Pagans also have trouble with the concept of angels—even though the angels shared by Christians, Muslims, and Jews are some of the most Pagan remnants of the Abrahamic faiths.[20] Angels and demons stretch back to the many polytheistic religions that proliferated throughout the ancient Middle East prior to the establishment of Jewish monotheism, and they are part of the rich cultural and mythological milieu from which the biblical tradition was born.

There is no denying that the word *demon* has come to possess strong associations with various iterations of the Christian faith, and yet demons as a class of beings are not exclusive to Christianity. Nearly every religion under the sun recognizes some class of being that can be interpreted as demonic. Hinduism has *devas* and *asuras*, which have strong comparisons to more familiar Christian ideas of angels and demons. There are demons in the Buddhist faith, and while they are more frequently depicted as conceptual beings representative of ideas and illusions, the shamanic Bön tradition native to Tibet fused with Buddhism to produce a cosmology rich in demons, gods, and hungry ghosts. As we have seen from our brief glimpse of the exorcisms of ancient Sumer, pre-Christian societies certainly had their versions of spirits that are more than ghosts and less than gods, and many of these are specifically malevolent in nature and antagonistic toward humanity. Furthermore, these evil spirits, which can be found in nearly every mythos the world over, are often depicted not only as malevolent entities that jealously attack humanity but also as beings capable of assuming control over their victims, up to and including full bodily possession.

Generally speaking (and certainly for the purposes of this book), demons are agents of disaster and chaos that willfully visit suffering and disease upon mortals. They are not exclusive to Christianity, nor is the concept of demonic possession exclusive to a Christian worldview. Demons are far older than Abrahamic religions, and many of our classic concepts of these antinomian beings have their roots in religious systems that were old before Christianity was even begun.

It is not the purpose of this book to delve into the theological implications of exorcism

---

19. A better and more inclusive term for *Judeo-Christian* is *Abrahamic* faith, particularly because the biblical tradition does not inform merely Christianity and Judaism but Islam as well. I have kept *Judeo-Christian* in this one instance as an accurate reflection of the original text cut in 2010. Henceforth in the text, it will be corrected to *Abrahamic*.

20. Karel Van Der Toorn et al., *Dictionary of Deities and Demons in the Bible*, pp. 50–51.

and demonology, whether these things are true or proper or right. Nor is it the intention of this book to address the question of whether or not demons are real. As far as this work is concerned, reality is secondary to belief. Regardless of their categorical reality, people from the ancient world onward have espoused a belief in demons, and this belief has had a tremendous impact on Western culture, from our literature to our theology to our magick and folk beliefs. Because of this impact, it behooves us to better understand where our ideas about demons originated and how those ideas have developed over the years. This book is my contribution to that process of understanding.

II. The Sources for the *Dictionary of Demons*

To place this book in context, we have traveled from the roots of the biblical tradition to ancient fragments of tales involving angels that did not fall from Heaven so much as they sauntered vaguely downward. From there, we found ourselves exploring the curious *Testament of Solomon* and the later tradition of European magick that merged concepts from the legend of Solomon with occasionally misunderstood techniques from medieval Jewish magick. Throughout all of this, we have seen how the concept of demons and fallen angels has grown and evolved over time, shaping and being shaped in turn by the very development of Western civilization. We have explored how demons have always been with us, from the very start of civilization, and how in at least some instances, they have been approached not as invincible enemies of humanity but as otherworldly tools to be exploited. Now it is time to consider precisely the books and other works that have

gone into the collection of demon names gathered in this tome.

The most obvious source for the demons of this book is the Bible. Despite the influence of earlier sources—notably the mythology of the Sumerians and Babylonians—on early Jewish and Christian demonology, the Bible remains one of the most significant texts in the formation of Western demonology. The stories recorded in the Bible gave rise to a vast and colorful tradition of folklore and extra-biblical writings, not the least of which is the whole Solomonic tradition.[21] To this end, I have also included a number of apocryphal sources that feature the names of demons. These lost books of the Bible were typically viewed at some point as genuine scripture but were then cut from the biblical canon in the first few centuries of Christianity. Apocryphal texts sourced in this book include *I Enoch*, the *Testaments of the Twelve Patriarchs*, and the *Ascension of Isaiah*. In addition to the biblical apocrypha, I have also sourced a variety of texts from traditions that are nevertheless tied to or inspired by the Bible. This includes Jewish Talmudic lore as well as some of the manuscripts recovered in the desert of Qumran. The Qumran texts, known popularly under the collective title of the *Dead Sea Scrolls*, include works such as the *Book of Giants*, the *War Rule*, and the *Testament of*

---

21. The tradition of King Solomon as a magician has ancient roots, and its early influence was extensive. Consider the bronze disc excavated at Ostia in 1918: "In 1918 Roman archaeologists excavated at Ostia a bronze disc, on one side of which was depicted Solomon as a magician, stirring with a long ladle some mess in a large cauldron. On the other side of the disc was a figure of the triple Hecate, who, like Solomon, was surrounded by mystic signs and magic characters." The disc remains on display at the museum at Ostia. Lynn Thorndike, *A History of Magic and Experimental Science During the First Thirteen Centuries of Our Era, Vol. II*, p. 279.

Amram (sometimes also called the *Dream-Vision of Amram* or simply *Vision of Amram*).

One of my goals when writing this book was to make each entry self-sufficient in terms of bibliographical references, and thus, whenever I source a particular work in the entry for a demon's name, I name that source directly in the entry. I also frequently cite some of the background information about the source itself, including its suspected author and the time in which it was thought to have been written. This may begin to seem redundant if readers go through the text alphabetically, perusing each entry, but this is a dictionary, and I felt it was far more likely that readers would skip around in the text, referencing names in various locations. With this usage in mind, I've made certain to include all the information you will possibly need within each entry so you will not have to flip back and forth between the entries and endnotes.

That being said, let me return to the list of works sourced for this dictionary. In addition to the biblical sources mentioned above, some names have come from miscellaneous scattered sources, such as the writings of clergymen who offered commentary on the beliefs in demons during their day (for example, Franciscan theologian Ludovico Sinistrari and Benedictine Dom Augustin Calmet) to dictionaries and encyclopedias written by demonographers like Collin de Plancy and Lewis Spence. Some of these works had to be sourced in their original language, notably Latin and French. Although translations of de Plancy's work exist in English, I found it more useful to read his entries in their original French, and when direct translations appear, they have been translated by my own hand. Any errors are strictly my own.

The most significant Latin work to provide a source of demon names for this text is *De Praestigiis Daemonum* (1564), with its famous appendix, the *Pseudomonarchia Daemonum*. This was written by the sixteenth-century humanist scholar Johannes Wierus (1515–1588). The *Pseudomonarchia* names a total of seventy-two demons, their ranks and powers, with details that reappear throughout the *Goetia*. It is sometimes called *De Officiorum Spirituum*, as it was from a similarly titled work that Wierus drew the names of his demons. It is likely related to, if not identical with, a text referenced by Johannes Trithemius as the *De officio spirituum*.

Trithemius (1462–1516) was a teacher once removed from Wierus: he had mentored Wierus's own instructor, Henry Cornelius Agrippa. Best known for his *Steganographia*, a coded work that contains nearly all of the spirits identified in the *Ars Theurgia*, Trithemius was an abbot as well as an occultist and avid collector of magickal texts.[22] In his *Antipalus Maleficiorum*,[23] a catalogue of the known books dedicated to the summoning of spirits, Trithemius includes a reference to *De officio spirituum*.[24] In his entry on this book, he records, *In hoc libro sunt secreto omnium artium:* "in this book are all secrets of the art." This statement has been echoed in several grimoires thereafter,

---

22. A serious comparison between the *Ars Theurgia* and the first book of Trithemius's *Steganographia* should be undertaken, as all of the names laid out upon the Theurgic compass appear in Trithemius's text. The descriptions of most of the spirits, including the numbers of their dukes and sub-dukes, are similar if not identical in these two texts.

23. Trithemius's *Antipalus Maleficiorum* was compiled in 1508, and as such, it establishes a date for the existence of a number of Solomonic manuscripts, including the *Claviculae Salomonis*, or *Little Keys of Solomon*.

24. Trithemius, *Antipalus Maleficiorum*, EsotericArchives.com.

and a number of subsequent texts have been given titles based on the *Book of the Offices of the Spirits*. Whether or not any of these are direct copies of the book itself or merely derivative of the material passed along through Wierus and others is unclear. At this point in time, no copies of the works initially referenced by Wierus or Trithemius are known to have survived.

Wierus's teacher, Henry Cornelius Agrippa (1486–1545), is most famous for his *Three Books of Occult Philosophy* (1509–1510). Although it does not add directly to this book, Agrippa's massive work influenced a great many of the subsequent texts in the grimoiric tradition, particularly with regard to magickal languages.[25]

Writing not long after Agrippa and Wierus, Englishman Reginald Scot echoed the list of seventy-two names in his 1584 work, *On the Discoverie of Witchcraft*. This work is ostensibly written in English, but given Scot's spelling and dated idiom, it very nearly needed its own translator. Scot's seventy-two Goetic demons will be familiar from Wierus and related works, with one or two minor exceptions that may be attributed to scribal error.

After these sources, the bulk of the names recorded in this volume are derived from the rich and extensive grimoiric tradition of Renaissance Europe.[26] The grimoires sourced in this book generally date between the fourteenth and seventeenth centuries, although some are thought to be older and a few were written as recently as the mid-1800s. The first series of names added from the grimoiric tradition came from the famous *Goetia*, and this, in fact, was the kernel around which my initial collection of demon names had coalesced. The *Goetia* is the first and probably oldest book of the *Lesser Key of Solomon*, and thanks largely to occultist Aleister Crowley, it is also the most well-known book in this grimoire.[27]

The *Goetia* contains the sigils and descriptions of seventy-two individual demons—a number by now of familiar significance. These demons are referenced in numerous works, and I have compared as many of these texts as I could find in order to compile the most accurate descriptions as possible. In doing so, I have combined references from Wierus's *Pseudomonarchia Daemonum* (1564) and Scot's *Discoverie of Witchcraft* (1584), as well as material on the Goetic demons found both in Dr. Rudd's *Treatise on Angel Magic* (sixteenth century) and his version of the *Goetia* as translated and produced by occultists Stephen Skinner and David Rankine.

Beyond the names from the *Goetia*, the lion's share of demon names came from two distinct works. The first, referred to as the *Ars Theurgia* in this text, is often listed as the *Theurgia-Goetia* in other writings. This is traditionally the second book of the *Lemegeton*, or *Lesser Key of Solomon*, a work firmly planted in the Solomonic tradition and dating back to approximately the seventeenth century. The *Lemegeton* is almost certainly derived

---

25. Sometimes a fourth book is attributed to Agrippa and appended to his work. Given the title *Agrippa's Fourth Book*, this text was in fact not written by Agrippa. Instead, it was written some thirty-five years after his death and given his name in an effort to lend validation to its contents. The *Fourth Book* expands upon Agrippa's information on the summoning of spirits, providing a list of spirits likely derived from *Liber Iuratus* (the *Sworn Book of Honorius*). Because this book was decried as spurious by Wierus, I have not included it as a source.

26. Primarily Christian and Western Europe, due to the nature of available published work.

---

27. Crowley published S. L. MacGregor Mathers's translation of the *Goetia* under the misleading title *The Lesser Key of Solomon*. Although the *Goetia* is a part of the *Lesser Key*, it is by no means the complete *Lesser Key*.

from older sources, but the oldest extant manuscripts are from a translation by Robert Turner produced in London in 1655.

The second is a curiosity unto itself. Known as the *Sacred Magic of Abramelin the Mage*, this work is powerfully steeped in Jewish esotericism. Aimed at achieving conversation with a heavenly being known as the Holy Guardian Angel, this classic text of ceremonial magick provides the names of literally hundreds of demons that are required to swear their subservience to the operator during the Holy Guardian Angel process. Attributed to a fourteenth-century Jewish scholar known as Abraham von Worms, the Abramelin material was translated into English by occultist Samuel Liddell MacGregor Mathers in 1898. Mathers was working from a fifteenth-century French manuscript that, at the time, was the only version of the Abramelin material available to him. Over the years, Mathers has received some criticism for his translation, but recently, Abramelin scholar Georg Dehn discovered that it was the manuscript, and not Mathers's translation, that was flawed. Dehn, in an exhaustive search for the real Abraham von Worms, has brought several other versions of the Abramelin material to light. These include a manuscript written in cipher and kept at the Wolfenbüttel Library in Germany, a manuscript dating to 1720 and kept at the Dresden Library, and finally a version of the Abramelin material published in 1725 by Peter Hammer in Cologne. In addition to these discoveries, Dehn claims to have traced Abraham von Worms—long thought to be a name crafted to legitimize the Abramelin story—to the very real Jewish scholar Rabbi Jacob ben Moses ha Levi Moellin, known in the fourteenth century as the MaHaRIL. Dehn's 2006 publication, *The Book of Abramelin*, has proven indispensable for its compari-

son of the surviving manuscripts, especially where the long lists of demon names are concerned.

Other works that serve as sources of names include the classic *Sworn Book of Honorius*, also known as the *Liber Juratus*. The oldest versions of this grimoire date to the fourteenth century, and it is considered to be one of the most influential grimoires. Many of the grimoires that came after it seem to have at least been inspired by its contents, if they have not directly borrowed portions of this book. I drew names from the 1977 Driscoll translation of the *Sworn Book*, published by Heptangle Press, as well as from the Joseph H. Peterson translation, which at the moment can only be found online at his extremely useful site, Esoteric Archives.com.[28] Of these two, the Peterson translation is by far superior, but then, Peterson has established himself as the definitive scholar of these antique texts. His research and commentary on all of the grimoires, not just the *Liber Juratus*, has been invaluable to the compilation of this book.

In addition to the classic grimoires, I have included several that some scholars believe to be spurious. The *Grimoire of Pope Honorius*, written in nineteenth-century France, yielded a few names, even though this book was most certainly never penned by the actual Pope Honorius III. Another large section of names came from Peterson's translation of the *Grimorium Verum*, a book that claims to have been written in 1517 but that most scholars date to the mid-1700s. Names taken from the *Grand Grimoire*, also known as *Le Dragon Rouge*, come from the Darcy Kuntz editions, which themselves come from translations by Arthur Edward Waite. These translations can be found in Waite's

---

28. After the publication of the first edition of the *Dictionary of Demons*, Peterson released a print copy of the *Liber Juratus* through Ibis Press in 2016. I highly recommend it.

1913 publication, the *Book of Black Magic*. All of these texts are clearly derivative of the grimoiric tradition, but their original sources are unclear. This, coupled with their authors' attempts to attain credibility by actively obscuring the origin and time period of the manuscripts, is why the tomes remain suspect. They are included because, spurious or not, their information nevertheless influenced later representations of the Solomonic material.

Although I have taken very little from it, another potentially spurious grimoire sourced tangentially within this text is the *Grimoire of Armadel*. Though it was translated by Mathers in the early 1900s, the earliest recorded mention of this book dates back to a bibliographical reference compiled by one Gabriel Naude in 1625. Author Aaron Leitch, in his book *Secrets of the Magickal Grimoires*, suggests that this book was less a legitimate grimoire and more a fabrication intended to feed an occult panic that gripped France between the years 1610 and 1640 CE. There were persistent rumors at the time of necromancy being practiced among the clergy, and the priestly tone of the *Grimoire of Armadel* seems constructed to feed these fears directly.

Some of the rarely sourced grimoires that have contributed names to this book include the *Munich Handbook* presented in Professor Richard Kieckhefer's excellent work *Forbidden Rites*. Translated and presented from a similarly academic standpoint are the *Liber de Angelis* and the *Liber Visionarum*. These are both amazing examples of the grimoiric tradition that I never would have encountered were it not for their inclusion in Claire Fanger's 1994 *Conjuring Spirits: Texts and Traditions of Medieval Ritual Magic*. The whole Magic in History series, from whence *Conjuring Spirits* comes, was tremendously helpful to this book, for it includes not only Profes-

sor Kieckhefer's *Forbidden Rites* but also Elizabeth Butler's *Ritual Magic* and *Fortunes of Faust*. If you are interested in expanding your own research beyond the curated material in this *Dictionary of Demons*, I highly recommend exploring these works.

Finally, related to both the grimoiric tradition and the Faust legends of Germany, I have drawn several names from the text known as *The Sixth and Seventh Books of Moses*. Attributed to Moses and intended to demonstrate how Moses was able to out-do the magicians of the Pharaoh with his own magickal tricks, this book circulated throughout Germany in the form of a variety of pamphlets in the 1800s. Eventually, it was compiled in 1849 by an antiquarian from Stuttgart by the name of Johann Scheible. This book is a blend of the grimoiric tradition, Talmudic lore, and the essentially German tradition of the *Faustbuch*, a magickal system that shaped and was shaped by the legend of Faust and his demon, Mephistopheles. Also attributed to Moses, but significantly more mysterious in its origin, is the *Sword of Moses*, published "from an unique manuscript," presumably in Hebrew, by one

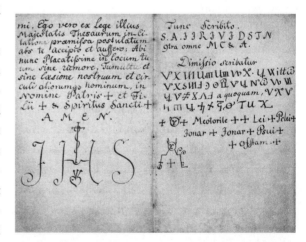

Interior pages of the *Clavis Inferni*, an eighteenth-century grimoire attributed to St. Cyprian. *JHS* is a Christogram derived from the first three letters of the name *Jesus* in Greek. Image courtesy of the Wellcome Collection, London.

Dr. Moses Gaster in London, 1896.[29] The full text of this book can also be found with commentary on Joseph H. Peterson's EsotericArchives.com.

All of the texts cited above comprise a massive body of work. I know that at least a few of my readers will now be wondering whether I left anything out in my exhaustive search for demon names (and whether I have a shred of sanity left after such a search!). In fact, there are a few traditional grimoires whose contents I chose to exclude from this book. One of these was the *Heptameron*. This influential work, traditionally attributed to Peter de Abano, was published at least two hundred years after his death in 1316 CE. For this reason, many scholars dispute the claim that Abano authored the text, although posthumous publications of grimoires are not entirely unheard of, especially in the case of magickal texts that might have proven dangerous to release in the author's lifetime.

The debate about the authorship of the fourteenth-century *Heptameron* was not the reason I left it out. The *Heptameron* clearly has some details in common with books like the *Sworn Book of Honorius* and, in fact, is echoed throughout much of the grimoiric tradition. For example, one of the "angels" said to reign on Friday in the *Heptameron* is called *Sarabotes*. This name is suspiciously close to the *Sworn Book*'s demon *Sarabocres*. But the *Heptameron* very specifically identifies all of the spirits presented in the text as angels. They are not described as being fallen—in fact, many of them are assigned to positions in one of the seven heavens. In a text devoted expressly to demons, this identification with angels precludes the inclusion of

these spirits as they appear in the *Heptameron*, even though they reappear as demons in later works.

For much the same reason that I left out the *Heptameron*, I did not source the sixteenth-century work known as the *Arbatel of Magic* (although you will find a few minor references to its magickal system). First published in Latin in Basel, Switzerland, in 1575, this grimoire is distinguished by its lack of infernal entities. It deals primarily with Olympian, or planetary, spirits, each assigned to one of the seven heavenly luminaries identified throughout Renaissance works. In this, it is a tome concerned primarily with celestial influences, and the spirits it describes are clearly separate from demons. Its concepts owe a great deal to the philosophy of Paracelsus (1493–1541). Although its contents are not relevant to our inquiry about demons, the *Arbatel* was nevertheless a significant work. Its influence can be seen in the *Secret Grimoire of Turiel* and *The Sixth and Seventh Books of Moses*. Perhaps best described as a tome of transcendental magick, it is notably the point of origin for the use of the term *theosophy* in the sense of occult knowledge.

Originally, I included the spirits listed in the related *Secret Grimoire of Turiel*. This text, unknown for many years, came to light only in the twentieth century. The material in this book is thought to date back to approximately the sixteenth century. However, it should be noted that since no extant copies exist beyond that discovered in 1927, there is a very real possibility that the grimoire was fabricated, much like the *Red Dragon Grimoire*.[30] The contents of the book seem far less calculated to shock or to play into the dark and mysterious

---

29. Joseph Jacobs et al., *Folk-Lore: A Quarterly Review*, p. 389.

30. Stephen Murtaugh, *Authentication of "The Secret Grimoire of Turiel" in Comparison with Frederick Hockley's "A Complete Book of Magic Science."*

reputation of the grimoires, and this alone argues for the probable legitimacy of the text. I ultimately cut from this book the material from the *Secret Grimoire of Turiel*, but not because of the disputed legitimacy of its contents. Instead, none of the spirits discussed in the *Secret Grimoire of Turiel* were identified explicitly as demons. Some are angels, but most are Olympic spirits, as with the earlier *Armadel*.

Another otherwise influential tome of celestial magick (or *astral* magick, from the Latin *astrum*, "star") that didn't make the cut for included material was the *Picatrix*. This Arabic text is said to date to the eleventh century, although a thirteenth-century date is more likely. While the *Picatrix* sometimes comes up in reference to demonic grimoires, the text itself adds little to the subject of demons. Instead, it deals primarily with astrological correspondences and the spheres of the heavens. The book also contains material on talismans, herbs, and philosophy. Trithemius includes a listing on the *Picatrix* in his catalogue of occult works. He notes that the edition he is referring to is a Latin text translated from an Arabic version in 1256. When it comes to the significance of time and planetary correspondences in ceremonial magick, the *Picatrix* and related Islamic traditions are foundational, but it is not a source of demonic proper names.

Finally, among those well-known and influential Solomonic texts left unsourced within this book is the *Ars Notoria*, sometimes called the *Notary Art of Solomon*.[31] A number of manuscripts bear this name, the oldest dating to the thirteenth century, although Joseph Peterson notes that the

Ars Notoria is closely linked to the *Liber Juratus* and that the *Liber Juratus* may in fact be dependent upon it.[32] Where the *Liber Juratus* contains a discussion of the spirits, including their names and offices, the *Ars Notoria* focuses on orations, prayers, and holy names of God. These are employed for the purpose of communion with the divine and achieving instant knowledge of all sciences.[33]

The *Ars Notoria* was well known, and not simply among a small subset of secret practitioners. Pope Benedict XIV, writing in his treatise on saints, observes, "There is a certain art, called *notoria*, by which, after certain prayers and other ceremonies having a show of piety, men learn all at once the liberal sciences."[34] Benedict XIV goes on to quote from the *Colloquies of Erasmus*, which reportedly contains an example of the *Ars Notoria*. Other books are cited as well, amply demonstrating the tremendous reach of this particular piece of the Solomonic tradition. A version of this book is included in Turner's translation of the *Lemegeton*, but I've left out both the *Art Pauline* and the *Almadel* from that work as well, since they either do not deal with spirits at all or deal expressly with angels. The same goes for the *Ars Notoria*.

New Sources in the Anniversary Edition

In the decade since the *Dictionary of Demons* was first published, writings about the Solomonic tradition have flourished. So many new grimoires have become available that it's been hard to keep

---

31. I have seen some misinformed websites represent this instead as the *Notorious Art of Solomon*, playing up an undeserved reputation as a manual of vile, forbidden magick.

32. See Peterson, *Ars Notoria: The Notory Art of Solomon*, http://www.esotericarchives.com/notoria/notoria.htm.

33. Notably, many of the spirits in subsequent grimoires function as the mediums through which this instant knowledge is obtained.

34. Benedict XIV, *Heroic Virtue: A Portion of the Treatise of Benedict XIV on the Beatification and Canonization of the Servants of God, Vol. III*, p. 122.

up. A number of factors have helped with this uptick in available work. Shifting attitudes in academia have led to a growing number of scholars who treat grimoires, magick, and the occult as a serious topic of inquiry in fields as widespread as literature, comparative religious studies, anthropology, sociology, psychology, and folklore. Changing technologies have also led to a proliferation of available texts: not only is it easier to publish and distribute a printed book, but social media has also allowed for people with specialized interests to connect in ways they really didn't have before. Another aspect of changing technology includes the ease with which a book can be digitalized and shared. Since the Google Books project, this has grown beyond merely scanning a text to make it available online. Organizations like the Wellcome Library in London have made their entire collections virtual, including high-resolution photo tours of many handwritten texts. These are so crisp, you can zoom in to see the stitching in the binding and all the varied textures on each vellum page. Finally, the uptick in scholarship is not limited only to the often exclusive halls of academia. Independent researchers and occultists have also been tirelessly working to transcribe and share these fascinating texts, and there is a reason the same handful of names appear again and again in these published manuscripts. Folks such as Joseph H. Peterson, Dan Harms, David Rankine, and Stephen Skinner have engaged in exhaustive exploration of the manuscripts in the Sloane collection, at the Folger Library, and at Wellcome. Over the past decade, they have brought into the public eye grimoiric texts that otherwise would have remained overlooked or entirely forgotten.

Between the academics, the online libraries, and the many new published grimoires, I almost couldn't keep up. As it was, I had to carefully limit what texts I sourced, focusing mainly on the ones that brought either a new perspective or a wealth of previously unknown names to the table. One of the heftiest new sources, the *Book of Oberon*, brought both.

Published by the team of Daniel Harms, Joseph H. Peterson, and James R. Clark, the *Book of Oberon* is drawn from a manuscript stored at the Folger Shakespeare Library in Washington, DC, under the title *Book of Magic, with Instructions for Invoking Spirits, etc.* Although the precise date of its creation is uncertain, the first date recorded in the work is 1577. In addition to having what is arguably a more complete list of the Offices of Spirits than many other works, the *Book of Oberon* stands out because its conjurations are not concerned merely with angels and demons; as its name implies, the grimoire contains spells for conjuring faeries as well. The text also contains a profuse number of demon names, many of which appear to be unique to this volume. Some of that uniqueness may come down to a matter of spelling and penmanship: the manuscript that became the *Book of Oberon* comprises several distinct works and shows evidence of multiple people's handwriting. At least one of these individuals was not well versed in Latin, and more than a few of the names recorded throughout this massive tome are inconsistently rendered from page to page. Some names change in their spelling even within the same line. A few, which otherwise appear to be representations of the familiar seventy-two Goetic demons, have spellings that suggest the person recording the name was taking written dictation and imperfectly rendered what they heard. Even with these obvious errors, however, the *Book of Oberon* is a landmark work, providing an unprecedented window into the working magick and folk beliefs of Shakespeare's England.[35]

Another exciting work made available through the tireless work of Joseph H. Peterson is the *Secrets of Solomon: A Witch's Handbook from the Trial Records of the Venetian Inquisition*, published in 2018. Known originally as the *Clavicula Salomonis de Secretis*, this is a grimoire that originated in Venice in 1636. It had originally belonged to Leonardo Longo, a former Dominican monk from Naples. He is likely the author of this grimoire, and he used it in his magickal practice. That practice earned him the scrutiny of the Venetian Inquisition. He was tried for witchcraft and ultimately executed. The confiscated book remained in the Archivio di Stato di Venezia.

The *Secrets of Solomon* is an exciting grimoire to see in print because it reveals a clear line of descent between the legitimate grimoiric tradition of the Renaissance and previously disputed grimoires such as the *Grand Grimoire* and the *Grimorium Verum*. The names of the demons, their powers, and their hierarchies are nearly identical in these works. Most of the differences are small spelling variations of the sort to be expected across a series of transcriptions. Although they still may have been penned in the 1800s, the *Grimorium Verum* and its related texts clearly derive from the material in the *Secrets of Solomon*.

Other rarely seen grimoires include several works in Rankine and Skinner's Sourceworks of Ceremonial Magic series. This is the same series that brought us *The Goetia of Dr. Rudd*, which provided some fascinating variations in the traditional

Pages from the eighteenth-century grimoire *Clavis Inferni*. The image on the left shows the Holy Spirit with seven stars and seven lights. Image courtesy of the Wellcome Collection, London.

seals of the seventy-two Goetic demons. The first of these, *The Grimoire of St. Cyprian: Clavis Inferni*, was published in October of 2009, and while I had wanted to include it in the first edition of the *Dictionary of Demons*, circumstances conspired to keep it out of my hands until after the manuscript had been turned in. The *Clavis Inferni* is a slim volume and the source text is a scant twenty-one pages in length. Filled with elaborate figures and illustrations, it manages to pack quite a lot into those pages. The original text is stored at the Wellcome Library in London, where it has been tentatively dated to the late eighteenth century based on its style of writing. A date within the manuscript reads, "MCCCCCCLLXVII," but, as Skinner and Rankine point out, "LL" is never used in Roman numerals.[36] The authors suggest that a careful examination of the letters reveals that the fourth letter from the end has been overwritten. From this, they posit a date of 1757.

---

35. These errors can be attributed to the Elizabethan authors of the book, to be clear. Harms, Peterson, and Clark have done an exemplary job of transcription, presentation, and providing context throughout.

---

36. Stephen Skinner and David Rankine, *The Grimoire of St. Cyprian: Clavis Inferni*, p. 25.

The *Clavis Inferni*, or *Key of Hell*, contains figures and sigils as well as brief prayers, conjurations, and bindings to summon and control demons. The only demons explicitly named in the text are the kings of the cardinal directions, but the text provides some interesting insight into elemental associations not typically seen in other grimoires. A vivid illustration of the four kings also suggests that there were animals associated with the demon-kings as well.

The second Skinner and Rankine text sourced in the new material is *The Keys to the Gateway of Magic: Summoning the Solomonic Archangels and Demon Princes*. Although the first print run of this book was produced in 2005, the text remained unavailable to me until it was reissued in 2011. This book is a composite of smaller Solomonic texts, and they are distinct enough that I have split the material relevant to this dictionary between two entries. The first text, entitled *Janua Magica Reserata*, is the document from which the book derives its name: it means *Keys to the Gateway of Magic*. Rankine and Skinner date this to the early to mid-seventeenth century.

The material comprising the *Janua Magica Reserata* is shared across several manuscripts, notably Sloane MS 3825 and Harley MS 6482. Most of this text is concerned with philosophical commentary on the nature of the soul, divinity, and angelic hierarchies. The section of interest to our purposes concerns a nine-tiered hierarchy of demons presented as the dark reflection of the traditional nine choirs of angels. A demonic prince is assigned to each, and several of these are ultimately echoed in a hierarchy presented by Francis Barrett in his nineteenth-century book *The Magus*. The line of descent, although oblique, given some of the distortions seen in Barrett's work, is interesting to note.

The second portion of the *Keys to the Gateway of Magic* identified and sourced in the *Dictionary of Demons* is entitled, appropriately enough, *Demon Princes*. This is represented in part of Sloane MS 3824, Sloane MS 3821, and Rawlinson D. 1363. *Demon Princes* is mainly concerned with the Kings of the Four Directions and their ministers, although, as in the Abramelin material, it places above them three very familiar demonic monarchs: Lucifer, Satan, and Beelzebub. I've used this text mostly in comparison with grimoires containing identical material, such as the *Book of Oberon*, adding entries only when *Demon Princes* demonstrated a significant variation.

Along the lines of variants, another new-to-this-edition source was an English translation of C. C. McCown's version of the *Testament of Solomon*. Most of the material widely published on the *Testament of Solomon* features the translation by F. C. Conybeare first released in the *Jewish Quarterly Review*, October 1898. After Conybeare, McCown produced a more complete translation in 1922, drawing upon a wider range of manuscripts. This was published as *The Testament of Solomon, Edited from Manuscripts at Mount Athos, Bologna, Holkham Hall, Jerusalem, London, Milan, Paris and Vienna*, and initially, the only version of this work I could track down was entirely in Greek. As McCown's translation is widely perceived to be superior to Conybeare's, I really wanted to compare them, especially given the number of lacunae in the source material Conybeare was working from. D. C. Duling has a translation of McCown's version published in volume one of *The Old Testament Pseudepigrapha* (1983). I finally got my hands on this for comparison, and where the differences are significant, I have noted them, expanding upon the old entries. The scholarship around McCown's work also pushes back the suggested date for the writing of the *Testament of Solomon*. Conybeare and his contemporaries had placed it at the first century CE. Current readings place it several centuries earlier.

Finally, in the course of cross-referencing some of the material in the *Book of Oberon* against known variations of the seventy-two Goetic demons, I discovered two gems, both of which were available to me only online. The first is a full transcription by Jean-Patrice Boudet of the French *Livre des esperitz*, or *Book of Spirits*. This sixteenth-century grimoire may at first appear to be a French translation of Wierus's *Pseudomonarchia Daemonum*, but upon closer inspection, it yields enough differences to indicate that it is a separate and distinct piece, almost certainly working from similar source material. The second gem, hosted in full on the website of the National Library of Wales, is an even rarer find. Known as the *Book of Incantations*, it is a working cunning-man's grimoire written by John Harries (1785–1839) and passed down to his sons so they could continue in the family trade. The first fifteen pages of the manuscript as it is currently bound contains a partial version of the *Goetia*, copied possibly from Scot or from the same text sourced by Scot in his *Discoverie of Witchcraft*.

These both were exciting and, although they largely only affirmed material already written in the entries devoted to the seventy-two Goetic demons, there were small variations. Harries's *Book of Incantations*, for example, shed light on the curious "Xenophilus" referenced obscurely by Scot, and the *Livre des esperitz*, which has no clearly identified author, named a couple of demons not seen in the *Pseudomonarchia* and derivative texts.

In researching these two texts, I became aware of another extant version of the infamous seventy-two, this time in mixed Latin and Italian. Called *Fasciculus Rerum Geomanticarum* and stored under the designation *Plut 89 Sup 38*, it is dated to the fifteenth century and at least part of it was copied in 1494. The reference to geomancy in the title is misleading, for the composite text actually includes excerpts from the *Picatrix*, orations connected to the seven planets and the Olympic spirits, a portion of the *Armadel*, and an additional Solomonic piece under the title *Salomon: De quatuor annulis*. The physical copy is stored in Florence at the Biblioteca Medicea Laurenziana. A full "holographic" version is available online, which involves high-resolution photographic images that you can freely explore. I was excited to compare the seventy-two demons in this fifteenth-century Italian text with those in the *Pseudomonarchia* and the *Livre des esperitz*, but the scribe's style of writing, combined with the erratic mix of Latin and Italian, foiled me. A lovely friend (with a much stronger background in Italian than I currently possess) offered to help, but the script on the rich vellum pages proved too much. Although I remain curious, I have, for the moment, given up.

In all, these sources generated approximately 30,000 words of new material that has been added to this tenth anniversary edition of the *Dictionary of Demons*. That's quite a lot, but it is important to note that there easily could be more. So many previously unpublished grimoires are being released now, such as Daniel Harms's *Of Angels, Demons & Spirits*, published at the beginning of 2019 and based on a seventeenth-century text kept in Oxford's Bodleian Library. Although I try to keep up on all of the latest papers and other releases, I failed to acquire this book in time to integrate its contents into my list of demons, evil spirits, and fallen angels. And Harms's book is one among many. The fact is, even working within the narrow boundaries set for the *Dictionary of Demons*, it is impossible to collect all of the names that are available. While this book is extensive and I have sourced each entry as accurately as I am able, there will always be limits.

The demons truly are legion.

Organization of the Text

As mentioned earlier, the entries in this dictionary are all self-referential, which means that they contain the source from which the name was derived as well as any useful background information on that source (or sources). In addition to all of the entries, you will find a series of breakaway articles scattered throughout the text. These are expansions of concepts covered within the text, and in many cases they elucidate a specific concept that is crucial to the understanding of several related entries. The text is also illustrated throughout with woodcuts, traditional demonic sigils, and modern interpretations of infernal beasts. The captions that accompany these illustrations will help give them context as you explore.

The dictionary itself should be self-explanatory: all of the demon names are presented in alphabetical order, from A to Z. There is a lot of ground covered between those two letters, and you're a tremendously dedicated reader if you try to plow through it all in one sitting. Instead, what I recommend is that you take some time to simply flip through the text, look over the illustrations, and read through the entries that catch your eye. If you're doing research of your own, then feel free to get straight to business. There are some appendices in the back that expand even further on the process of researching this book, the impact of scribal arts on the transmission of the grimoires, and the demonic traditions extant in the early Middle Eastern world.

There is also an extensive bibliography. Not all of the books are in print anymore, so I strongly suggest that if, like myself, you enjoy tracking down all of the books and articles referenced by a favorite author, you take a moment to look over books.google.com. Quite a number of the books sourced in this project are old enough to be copyright-free, and most of them are available for free download thanks to the Google Books project. Two other invaluable free sources are Esoteric Archives.com and Sacred-Texts.com. The Wellcome Collection (wellcomecollection.org) is freely accessible and contains a wealth of material, and the Sloane Manuscripts collection at the British Library (www.bl.uk/collection-guides/sloane-manuscripts) can be virtually explored as well.

Aariel: A demon granted the title of duke. Aariel serves in the court of the infernal king Asyriel. According to the *Ars Theurgia*, Aariel manifests only during the hours of the day. He is connected with the direction of the south and has twenty ministering spirits to serve him. See also *ARS THEURGIA, ASYRIEL.*

Abaddon: In the *Book of Job* and in *Proverbs*, Abaddon is mentioned as a place of destruction, possibly equivalent in concept with the modern notion of Hell. However, in Revelation 9:11, Abaddon is no longer the Abyss itself but is instead personified as the angel in charge of that Abyss. The name is translated in Greek to *Apollyon*, meaning "The Destroyer." Both Abaddon and Apollyon were integrated into demonology as powerful princes of Hell. In Francis Barrett's *The Magus*, Abaddon is associated with the seventh mansion of the furies, and he is said to govern destruction and wasting. Gustav Davidson, in his classic *Dictionary of Angels*, describes Abaddon as the "angel of the Abyss." In

An angel with the keys to Hell binds the Devil. From a twelfth-century miniature, courtesy of Dover Publications.

Crowley's edition of the *Goetia*, Abaddon is again mentioned, not as a being, but as a place in a binding. He appears in a hierarchy of evil spirits laid out in the *Janua Magica Reserata* where he is identified as prince of the Seventh Order. This order is otherwise known as the Furies, suggesting that Barrett had access to either this text or something related. See also APOLLYON, *GOETIA*, *JANUA MAGICA RESERATA*.

Abadir: Mathers suggests that the name of this demon means "scattered." Abadir appears in his 1898 translation of the *Sacred Magic of Abramelin the Mage*, where he is said to serve the infernal lord Asmodeus. The name is also spelled *Abachir*. See also ASMODEUS, MATHERS.

Abael: One of several demons who serve in the court of Dorochiel. Abael holds the rank of chief duke with four hundred lesser spirits at his command. According to the *Ars Theurgia*, he serves in the second half of the night, between midnight and dawn. See also *ARS THEURGIA*, DOROCHIEL.

Abahin: In the 1898 Mathers translation of the *Sacred Magic of Abramelin the Mage*, the name of this demon appears in a list of infernal servants to the arch-fiends Astaroth and Asmodeus. Mathers suggests that the name of this demon means "the Terrible One," from a root word in Hebrew. In another version of the *Abramelin* material, originally written in code and currently kept at the Wolfenbüttel library (the Herzog August Bibliothek), in Wolfenbüttel, Germany, the name of this demon is spelled *Ahabhon*. See also ASMODEUS, ASTAROTH, MATHERS.

Abalam: According to Wierus's *Pseudomonarchia Daemonum*, if the demon Paimon is summoned and given a sacrifice or other offering, this demon, along with his companion Beball, will also appear. Both Abalam and Beball are demonic kings who serve the Goetic demon Paimon. In the *Goetia*, their names appear as *Labal* and *Abali*. See also BEBALL, PAIMON, WIERUS.

Abariel: A demon in the hierarchy of the infernal prince Usiel. The *Ars Theurgia* describes Abariel as a chief duke who belongs to the hours of daylight. He has forty ministering spirits beneath him. Abariel has the power to conceal hidden treasure so that it may not be discovered or stolen. He can also reveal things that have been hidden, especially those items obscured through magick or enchantments. See also *ARS THEURGIA*, USIEL.

Abas: In the *Sacred Magic of Abramelin the Mage*, Abas is listed as a demon of lies and trickery. He can be called upon to assist the magician in matters dealing with illusion as well as spells of invisibility. This demon also appears in the Mathers translation of the *Clavicula Salomonis* with the same associations. According to Driscoll's edition of the *Sworn Book*, Abas is the king of the regions below the earth. His province includes the riches of the earth, and he is said to be able to locate and provide all manner of costly metals, including silver and gold. Additionally, he seems to be able to cause earthquakes, for it is said that he can pull down buildings and other structures and cause them to be destroyed. Finally, Abas and his minions can teach knowledge of the mixture of the elements, a possible reference to alchemy, although alchemical workings are not specifically described within the text. In the *Clavicula Salomonis*, the name of this demon is spelled *Abac*. See also *CLAVICULA SALOMONIS*, MATHERS, *SWORN BOOK*.

Abbnthada: Described as an agreeable, if somewhat jealous demon, Abbnthada appears in the hierarchy of Harthan, an infernal king who rules the element of water. According to the Driscoll edition of the *Sworn Book*, Abbnthada can be enticed to appear with the aid of appropriate perfumes. When he manifests, his body is large and has a mottled complexion. He has the power to swiftly move things from place to place, and he can provide darkness when it is required of him. He can also bestow strength in resolution, helping others to avenge wrongs. See also HARTHAN, *SWORN BOOK*.

Abdalaa: According to the *Liber de Angelis*, Abdalaa holds the rank of king in the hierarchy of Hell. He appears in connection with a compulsion spell guaranteed to procure the love of a woman. From the profusion of such spells in all of the magickal texts, it would seem that practitioners of the black arts had a very difficult time finding a date in the Middle Ages. To cure the medieval magician's lonely heart, this demon, along with his minions, were to be invoked and set upon the desired woman, at which point they would torment her horribly until she accepted her newfound mate. Note that Abdalaa is suspiciously close to the Arabic name *Abdullah*. This name means "servant of God" and is not generally associated with demons. See also *LIBER DE ANGELIS*.

Abech: A demon in the court of Amaimon, king of the south. The *Book of Oberon* identifies him as one of the twelve principal demons from that court. He is a teaching demon, with the power to instruct people in the sciences and all manner of languages. When he manifests, he appears like a king but shows only his head. His presence is announced by the sound of trumpets. See also AMAIMON, *BOOK OF OBERON*.

Abelaios: A demon who aids in spells of invisibility, Abelaios appears in Mathers's translation of the *Clavicula Salomonis*. He is said to answer to the demon Almiras, master of invisibility, and to Almiras's infernal minister, Cheros. This demon also appears in the Mathers translation of the *Sacred Magic of Abramelin the Mage*. See also ALMIRAS, CHEROS, *CLAVICULA SALOMONIS*, MATHERS.

Abezithibod: A demon who allegedly inhabits the Red Sea. Abezithibod appears to King Solomon in the extra-biblical *Testament of Solomon*. In this text, the demon claims to have actively worked against Moses during the parting of the Red Sea. He was trapped underwater after the parted sea came crashing back together again. Solomon puts the braggart demon to work, commanding him to uphold a massive pillar that must remain suspended in the air until the world's end. In his dealings with King Solomon, Abezithibod reveals himself as a rather prideful fellow, demanding special respect from the biblical monarch because he is the spawn of an archangel. He claims that his father is Beelzebub. This is one of the only places where Beelzebub is given archangelic status.

In his statement about his father Beelzebub, Abezithibod reveals the close connection between the *Testament of Solomon* and the tradition of the Watcher Angels. The *Testament of Solomon* most likely dates to a time when the Essene community at Qumran was writing extensively about the War in Heaven and the ongoing battle between the Sons of Darkness and the Sons of Light. These texts would later survive into the modern era among the Dead Sea Scrolls. This epic struggle of good versus evil is intricately tied in with the Watcher Angel myth that appears in the *Book of Enoch I*, where two hundred angels are said to have abandoned Heaven in pursuit of mortal wives. Through statements by Abezithibod and other demons in the *Testament of Solomon*, it is revealed that the author of this intriguing work believed that most of the demons that plagued humanity either were fallen angels themselves or were the misbegotten spawn of those angels, condemned forever to wander the earth and lash out at humanity. See also BEELZEBUB, SOLO-MON, WATCHER ANGELS.

Abgoth: In the fifteenth-century magickal text known as the *Munich Handbook*, this demon is summoned to assist with spells concerning the art of scrying. He is also called upon to discover the persons responsible for theft, so that justice may be done. He appears by name in the fortieth spell in the *Munich Handbook*. The same text includes the name *Abgo*, which, although presented as a separate demon, may well be a misspelling of this demon's name. See also *MUNICH HANDBOOK*.

Aboc: In the *Ars Theurgia*, Aboc is a demon who holds the rank of duke. He serves in the hierarchy of the north, and his immediate superior is the infernal king Baruchas. Aboc commands thousands of lesser spirits. He will only manifest in the hours and minutes that fall in the fifth section of the day, when the day is divided into fifteen portions of time. See also *ARS THEURGIA*, BARUCHAS.

Abracas: Listed as a demon in Collin de Plancy's 1863 edition of the *Dictionnaire Infernal*, Abracas is none other than *Abraxas*, a Gnostic deity who appears in the writings of Simon Magus. According to de Plancy, the demon's name derives from *abracadabra*, a word used widely in magickal talismans. This derivation, however, is highly suspect. Abraxas is often depicted as a composite being. He has a man's body, often armored, with legs like serpents and the head of a cock. He carries a whip in one hand and a shield in the other. His appearance is similar to that of a charioteer, and indeed, in some depictions, he appears riding a chariot pulled by four horses. The horses themselves represent the four elements. In Gnostic mythology, Abraxas is generally said to have a serpentine body surmounted by the head of a lion. He leonine head is surrounded with rays like those of the sun, an

Gnostic gems featuring images of the deity Abraxas. From the *Encyclopedia of Occultism*, by Lewis Spence. Courtesy of Dover Publications.

image that may hearken back to a Persian sun god said to share the same name. The rooster-headed image, however, remains the most recognizable, as it was commonly depicted on amulets, known as Abraxas stones, in the second century CE and thereafter. See also DE PLANCY.

Abriel: A demon serving in the hierarchy of the infernal prince Dorochiel. Abriel's name appears in the *Ars Theurgia*, where he is said to command four hundred subordinate spirits. He holds the rank of chief duke and manifests only in the hours between noon and dusk. Through Dorochiel, he is affiliated with the west. See also *ARS THEURGIA*, DOROCHIEL.

Abrinno: Also called Obymero. He is named in the *Book of Oberon*, where he appears in a spell with several other demons summoned by night to craft books. He and his fellows are capable of making tomes in a matter of hours, and they cover a variety of occult and forbidden topics, from alchemy to conjuration, nigromancy, and other magickal arts. Keep in mind that these book-making demons were working in a time before widespread use of the printing press, so books were rare and

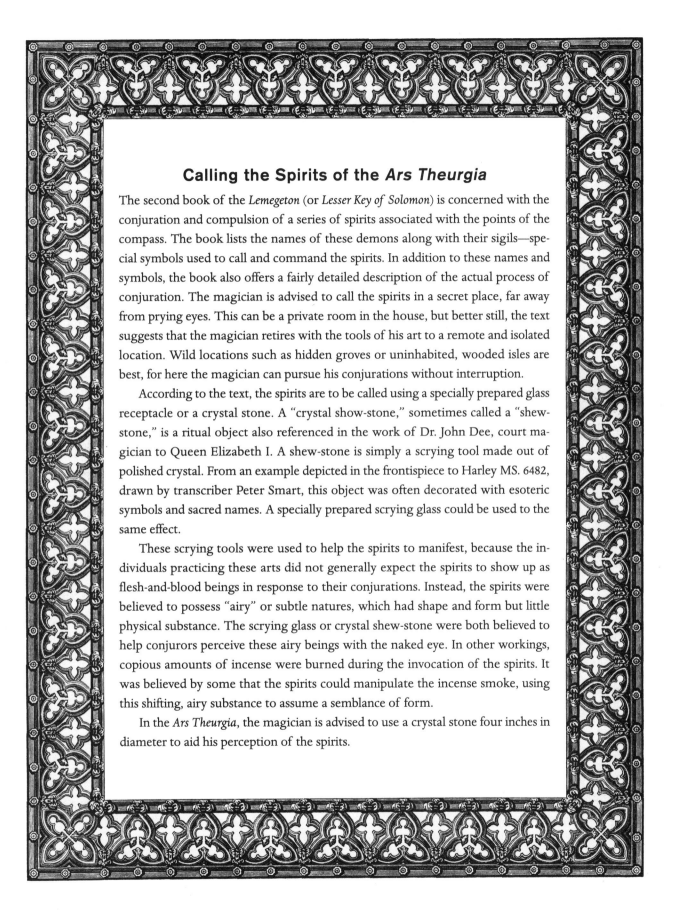

Calling the Spirits of the *Ars Theurgia*

The second book of the *Lemegeton* (or *Lesser Key of Solomon*) is concerned with the conjuration and compulsion of a series of spirits associated with the points of the compass. The book lists the names of these demons along with their sigils—special symbols used to call and command the spirits. In addition to these names and symbols, the book also offers a fairly detailed description of the actual process of conjuration. The magician is advised to call the spirits in a secret place, far away from prying eyes. This can be a private room in the house, but better still, the text suggests that the magician retires with the tools of his art to a remote and isolated location. Wild locations such as hidden groves or uninhabited, wooded isles are best, for here the magician can pursue his conjurations without interruption.

According to the text, the spirits are to be called using a specially prepared glass receptacle or a crystal stone. A "crystal show-stone," sometimes called a "shewstone," is a ritual object also referenced in the work of Dr. John Dee, court magician to Queen Elizabeth I. A shew-stone is simply a scrying tool made out of polished crystal. From an example depicted in the frontispiece to Harley MS. 6482, drawn by transcriber Peter Smart, this object was often decorated with esoteric symbols and sacred names. A specially prepared scrying glass could be used to the same effect.

These scrying tools were used to help the spirits to manifest, because the individuals practicing these arts did not generally expect the spirits to show up as flesh-and-blood beings in response to their conjurations. Instead, the spirits were believed to possess "airy" or subtle natures, which had shape and form but little physical substance. The scrying glass or crystal shew-stone were both believed to help conjurors perceive these airy beings with the naked eye. In other workings, copious amounts of incense were burned during the invocation of the spirits. It was believed by some that the spirits could manipulate the incense smoke, using this shifting, airy substance to assume a semblance of form.

In the *Ars Theurgia*, the magician is advised to use a crystal stone four inches in diameter to aid his perception of the spirits.

exceedingly time-consuming to create. Their service was a valuable one for sorcerers who relied on books for many of their spells and instructions. See also *BOOK OF OBERON*.

Abrulges: One of several demons named in association with Pamersiel, the first and chief spirit under Carnesiel, the infernal Emperor of the East. Abrulges holds the rank of duke, and he is reputed to possess a particularly nasty temperament. According to the *Ars Theurgia*, he is both arrogant and deceitful and he should never be trusted with secret matters. Despite this, however, his naturally aggressive nature can sometimes to be turned to good. Abrulges and all his fellow dukes can be used to drive off other spirits of darkness, especially those that haunt houses. See also *ARS THEURGIA*, CARNESIEL, PAMERSIEL.

Abuchaba: A demon tied to the west wind. Abuchaba functions as a servant of Harthan, the king of the spirits of the moon. His name appears in the Peterson translation of the *Sworn Book of Honorius*. According to this book, he has the power to change thoughts and wills. He can also call rains. The angels Gabriel, Michael, Samyhel, and Atithael all have power over him. See also HARTHAN, *SWORN BOOK*.

Abugor: A great duke who appears as a handsome knight. He can win the favor of kings, lords, and other powerful people. In addition, he knows the location of all things hidden in the earth. According to the *Livre des esperitz*, twenty-seven legions of spirits serve under him. He is likely the Goetic demon Abigor under a slightly different spelling. See also ABIGOR, *LIVRE DES ESPERITZ*.

Abutes: According to Mathers's translation of the *Sacred Magic of Abramelin the Mage*, this demon's name means "bottomless" or "measureless." Abutes appears in a list of demonic servitors who answer to the arch-demons Asmodeus and Astaroth. See also ASMODEUS, ASTAROTH, MATHERS.

Acham: A demon named in the Peterson edition of the *Grimorium Verum*. According to this text, Acham is a demon who presides over Thursday. He is also associated with Thursdays in the *Grimoire of Pope Honorius*. See also *GRIMORIUM VERUM*, HONORIUS.

Achol: A demon governed by the infernal king Symiel. Achol has sixty lesser spirits that minister to him. According to the *Ars Theurgia*, he is best summoned by day in a remote location or a private room of the house. Through his association with Symiel, Achol is connected with the direction north. See also *ARS THEURGIA*, SYMIEL.

Acquiot: In the *Grimoire of Pope Honorius*, this is the demon ruling Sunday. Acquiot may well be invented, as the *Grimoire of Pope Honorius* was a spurious grimoire intended to cash in on the reputation of the fourteenth-century *Sworn Book of Honorius*. See also *SWORN BOOK*.

Acreba: One of twenty dukes said to serve the demon Barmiel. According to the *Ars Theurgia*, Barmiel is the first and chief spirit of the south. Acreba serves his infernal master during the hours of the night and oversees the command of twenty ministering spirits of his own. See also *ARS THEURGIA*, BARMIEL.

Acteras: A duke of the demon Barmiel named in the *Ars Theurgia*. Acteras serves his infernal king during the hours of the day. He commands twenty lesser spirits and, through his affiliation with Barmiel, is connected with the south. See also *ARS THEURGIA*, BARMIEL.

Acuar: According to Mathers in his translation of the *Sacred Magic of Abramelin the Mage*, this demon's name is related to a Hebrew word meaning "tiller of the earth." Acuar is one of several demons who serve the four infernal princes of the cardinal directions: Oriens, Paimon, Ariton, and Amaimon. See also AMAIMON, ARITON, MATHERS, ORIENS, PAIMON.

Acuteba: A demon associated with the Moon. Acuteba serves King Harkam, together with the spirits Mylu, Byleth, and Bylethor. Able to appear either as a huntress or a bow-wielding king, this demon is tall, with skin the color of a storm cloud. He can conjure silver and transport objects, reveal secrets, and increase the swiftness of horses. When he appears, a great rainstorm is said to break out. See also *BOOK OF OBERON*, BYLETH, BYLETHOR, HARKAM, MYLU.

Adan: In the *Ars Theurgia*, Adan is a demon who serves in the court of the infernal prince Usiel. He is a revealer of secrets, and he also has the power to hide treasure so as to protect it from thieves. He serves only during the hours of the night, and he will only manifest during this time. He has forty lesser spirits that carry out his commands. See also *ARS THEURGIA*, USIEL.

Adirael: In his 1898 translation of the *Sacred Magic of Abramelin the Mage*, occultist S. L. Mathers presents this name as meaning "magnificence of God." Although this sounds like the name of an angel, Adirael is almost certainly fallen. According to the *Abramelin* material, Adirael is a servant of Beelzebub. See also BEELZEBUB, MATHERS.

Admirable History: A book published in 1613 by Sebastien Michaelis recounting his exorcism of a nun. According to Michaelis, during the process of this exorcism, the demon Berith explained to him the hierarchy of Hell. Berith also revealed the sins that were the special province of each demon as well as the holy adversary of that demon. The

adversary of the demon was typically a saint who had suffered the temptation of the demon's sin but did not fall. This armor of faith then gave the saint power to overcome the demon of that particular sin. See also BERITH.

Adon: A demon named in Mathers's translation of the *Sacred Magic of Abramelin the Mage*. Adon's name is almost certainly derived from Adonai, one of several Hebrew names for God. As a demon, Adon serves beneath Oriens, Paimon, Ariton, and Amaimon, the demonic princes of the four directions. See also AMAIMON, ARITON, MATHERS, ORIENS, PAIMON.

Adramelek: One of many demons named in Collin de Plancy's extensive *Dictionnaire Infernal*, published and republished throughout the nineteenth century. The name of this demon is actually the name of a Samaritan sun god sometimes rendered *Adramelech*. As such, he is one of the many foreign deities mentioned in the Old Testament that have been demonized with the passage of time. The early-nineteenth-century French writer, Charles Berbiguier, describes Adramelek as the Lord High Chancellor of Hell. In his book *Les Farfadets*, Berbiguier further asserts that Adramelek has been awarded the Grand Cross of the Order of the Fly, a supposedly demonic knightly order founded by Beelzebub. A. E. Waite, writing in his classic *Book of Black Magic*, repeats Berbiguier's attributions, although he incorrectly links them to the sixteenth-century scholar Johannes Wierus. Agrippa identifies him as an ancient king demonized over time. See also AGRIPPA, BEELZEBUB, BERBIGUIER, DE PLANCY, WAITE, WIERUS.

Afarorp: A demon whose name appears in Mathers's edition of the *Sacred Magic of Abramelin the Mage*, Afarorp is a servitor of the four infernal princes of the cardinal directions: Oriens, Paimon, Ariton, and Amaimon. See also AMAIMON, ARITON, MATHERS, ORIENS, PAIMON.

Afray: S. L. Mathers gives the meaning of this demon's name as "dust" in his 1898 translation of the *Sacred Magic of Abramelin the Mage*. According to this work, Afray serves the greater demons Asmodeus and Astaroth. See also ASMODEUS, ASTAROTH, MATHERS.

Agaleraptarkimath: One of two demons holding the rank of duke who serves directly beneath Prince Belzebuth. Ftheruthi is his fellow duke. Both demons are named in the seventeenth-century Venetian grimoire *Clavicula Salomonis de Secretis*. Compare to Agaliarept of the *Grand Grimoire*. See also AGALIAREPT, BELZEBUTH, FTHERUTHI, *SECRETS OF SOLOMON*.

Agaliarept: This demon appears in the *Grand Grimoire* and is named as a general of Hell. He is purported to command the Second Legion of Spirits for the glory of the emperor Lucifer and his Prime Minister, Lucifuge Rofocale. Agaliarept is a keeper of mysteries, and he is credited with the power to reveal any arcane or sublime secrets to the dutiful practitioner. Buer, Guison, and Botis, three beings traditionally included among the seventy-two demons of the *Goetia*, supposedly answer directly to him. See also BOTIS, BUER, GUISON, LUCIFER, LUCIFUGE, ROFOCALE.

Agapiel: One of fifteen demons who serve Icosiel, a wandering prince of the air. Agapiel holds the title of duke and oversees another two thousand two hundred ministering spirits. He is said to appear only during the hours and minutes that fall into the fifth portion of time when the day is divided into fifteen equal parts. In the *Ars Theurgia*, Agapiel and his cohorts are said to have a fondness for houses and are most likely to be found in private homes. See also *ARS THEURGIA*, ICOSIEL.

Agares: Named as the First Duke under the power of the east, Agares oversees a total of thirty-one legions of infernal spirits. According to Wierus's *Pseudomonarchia Daemonum*, he is very willing to appear when summoned. He takes the form of an old man riding a crocodile and carries a hawk on his fist. He has power over runaways and can fetch them back at the behest of the summoner. He can also compel people to run. He teaches languages and confers both supernatural and temporal dignities. He also has the power to cause earthquakes. He belongs to the Order of Virtues. According to the *Goetia of Dr. Rudd*, he is constrained by the angel Jeliel. Agares also appears in the sixteenth-century French grimoire *Livre des esperitz*, where his name is spelled *Agarat*. The *Welsh Book of Incantations* assigns him the ability to cause earthquakes in addition to his usual powers and says that thirty-one legions follow him. In the *Book of Oberon*, his name is spelled *Agaros* and he is one of twelve principal ministers to King Oriens. He has twenty-nine legions of lesser spirits beneath him. As with the *Book of Oberon*, most entries on Agares identify him as a subordinate of Oriens, king of the east. Other variations on his name include *Aharas* and *Acharos*. See also *BOOK OF OBERON, BOOK OF INCANTATIONS, GOETIA, LIVRE DES ESPERITZ, ORIENS, RUDD, WIERUS*.

Agasaly: One of several demons said to serve Paimon, one of the infernal princes of the cardinal directions. Agasaly is named in the *Sacred Magic of Abramelin the Mage*. In the 1898 Mathers translation of this work, drawn from a flawed French manuscript written in the fifteenth century, this name is spelled *Agafali*. See also MATHERS, PAIMON.

The Magick Word

The tools of the art of spirit evocation were often covered with esoteric symbols, names of power, and magick words. In the grimoiric tradition, the magician was generally expected to craft these items himself and to understand the significance of each inscribed symbol or image. One tool of conjuration was the ritual dagger. According to Scot in his *Discoverie of Witchcraft*, the magician must prepare this conjuring knife by writing or engraving special letters and figures into the blade. Four symbols go on one side of the blade, and on the other side the magician is to write the word *AGLA*. *AGLA* is an acronym commonly used in talismanic magick and it also appears in the protective amulets and summoning circles of a number of grimoires. The term is comprised of the first letters of the Hebrew phrase *Attah Gibbor Le'olam Adonai*. This phrase translates to: "Thou art mighty forever, O Lord."

Many Hebrew terms were adopted into the Christian grimoiric tradition, often without much recognition of their original meanings. AGLA, for example, finds its way into several demon names, despite its holy character. The same can be said of *Berith*, the Hebrew word for *Covenant*. In some cases, this demonization was accidental, but in others, there is intention behind the corruption of holy words. Just consider the anti-Semitism inherent in the descriptions of the Witches' *Sabbat*, which grew directly out of lurid accusations against Jews.

Conjuring knife with the magickal name *AGLA* from Scot's *Discoverie of Witchcraft*. Courtesy of Dover Publications.

Reminiscent of the Abramelin technique, a theurgist performs rituals to exercise divine powers on Earth. Nineteenth-century colored aquatint credited to William Charlton Wright. From the Wellcome Collection, London.

Agateraptor: In Peterson's translation of the *Grimorium Verum*, Agateraptor is listed as one of three demons who work as chiefs of Belzebuth, a variation on the name *Beelzebub*. In the *True Keys of Solomon*, this demon appears under the spelling *Agatraptor*. Along with his cohorts, Himacth and Stephanate, he is also said to serve the demon Beelzebub. See also BEELZEBUB, *GRIMORIUM VERUM*, HIMACTH, STEPHANATE, *TRUE KEYS*.

Agchoniôn: A demon of crib death mentioned in the *Testament of Solomon*. Agchoniôn appears with the head of a beast and the body of a man. In addition to suffocating infants in their cribs, he is said to lie in wait for men near cliffs. When a likely victim comes along, Agchoniôn creeps up behind him and pushes him to his death. This demon of suffering is number thirty-three from among the thirty-six demons associated with the decans of the zodiac. He can be driven away through the use of the name *Lycurgos*. In the later McCown translation, his name is rendered *Achoneôth*. He is given the title of *Rhyx*, meaning "king." The name that drives him away is spelled *Leikourgos*. See also SOLOMON.

Agei: A demon whose name appears in the Mathers translation of the *Sacred Magic of Abramelin the Mage*. Agei appears in the court of the demons Astaroth and Asmodeus, and he serves both of these infernal masters. According to another version of the *Abramelin* material kept at the Wolfenbüttel library in Germany, the name of this demon should be spelled *Hageyr*. See also ASMODEUS, ASTAROTH, MATHERS.

Agibol: A servitor of the demon-kings Amaimon and Ariton, Agibol appears in the 1898 Mathers translation of the *Sacred Magic of Abramelin the Mage*. Mathers suggests that this demon's name may stem from a Hebrew term meaning "forcible love," but that reading is tentative at best. See also AMAIMON, ARITON, MATHERS.

Aglafys: A demon said to serve Paimon, one of the four infernal princes of the cardinal directions. Aglafys appears in the *Sacred Magic of Abramelin the Mage*. Notably, *AGLA* is a word that commonly appears on amulets associated with the grimoiric tradition. It is also used in the invocation of spirits, typically occurring alongside "secret" names of God, such as *Shaddai* and *Sabaoth*. In the Mathers edition of the *Abramelin* material, the name of this demon is given as *Aglafos*. See also MATHERS, PAIMON.

Aglas: This being appears in the *Ars Theurgia* in connection with the court of the demon Gediel. Here, he is ranked as a duke who serves his infernal master by night. He commands a total of twenty lesser spirits. The name of this demon is probably derived from the magickal word *AGLA*. See also *ARS THEURGIA*, GEDIEL.

Aglasis: Appearing in the *Grimorium Verum*, this demon will destroy the enemies of the magician upon command. He also has power over travel and can instantly transport the magician to a location of his choosing. His name is likely another variation on the magickal word *AGLA*. His name can also be found in book 1 of the *Clavicle of Solomon*, dated 1709. This text is kept at the Wellcome Library in London and is related to the *Secrets of Solomon*, a grimoire seized by the Venetian Inquisition in the seventeenth century. According to this text, Aglasis is a demon of transport, carrying those who command him to any location in the world. He serves beneath Hael and Sergulaf, both high-ranking demons in the court of Duke Resbiroth. See also HAEL, RESBIROTH, *CLAVICLE OF SOLOMON*, *GRIMORIUM VERUM*, *SECRETS OF SOLOMON*, SERGULAF.

Agor: A chief duke serving beneath the demon Malgaras. Agor is tied to the powers of the day and has thirty lesser spirits to serve him. His name and seal appear in the *Ars Theurgia*, a seventeenth-century text that details an array of demons connected with the points of the compass. Through Malgaras, he is associated with the west. See also *ARS THEURGIA*, MALGARAS.

Agra: One of eight infernal dukes said to serve the demon-king Gediel during the hours of the night. Through his service to Gediel, Agra is associated with the southern point of the compass. According-

ing to the *Ars Theurgia*, he holds the rank of duke. Twenty lesser spirits exist to carry out his desires. See also *ARS THEURGIA*, GEDIEL.

Agrax: A demon serving beneath both Astaroth and Asmodeus, according to the 1898 Mathers translation of the *Sacred Magic of Abramelin the Mage*. In other versions of the *Abramelin* material, the name of this demon is spelled *Argax*. See also ASMODEUS, ASTAROTH, MATHERS.

Agrippa, Henry Cornelius: A Renaissance writer best known for his three-volume work *de occulta philosophia*, known widely as the *Three Books of Occult Philosophy*. Agrippa lived from 1486 until 1535 and studied briefly under the German abbot and occultist Trithemius. When his *Occult Philosophy* was first produced around 1510, he sent the manuscript to Trithemius to get his old teacher's opinion. Trithemius cautioned Agrippa to be secretive about the work because of its contents, and this may have inspired Agrippa to hold back on any formal publication of the book for nearly twenty years. Nevertheless, the work circulated widely in manuscript form, gaining a widespread reputation.

The *Three Books of Occult Philosophy* was Agrippa's attempt to revivify the art of magick as it had been practiced in the ancient world. He covers a wide range of topics, from natural magick to astrology, divination, and even necromancy. He draws upon a wide variety of sources, from the works of Greek and Roman philosophers to material drawn from Jewish mysticism and grimoires like the *Heptameron*. His book is probably one of the most influential works on Western occultism and esoterica. It is referenced frequently in the writings of Dr. John Dee. Many subsequent works, including a number of grimoires, integrate whole passages from the *Occult Philosophy*.

Sometimes Agrippa is acknowledged as the author of this material and sometimes he is plagiarized with gusto. One such instance involves *The Magus: or the Celestial Intelligencer*, produced by Francis Barrett in 1801. Barrett freely makes use of Agrippa's material without much mention of Agrippa himself. In a similar vein of capitalizing on Agrippa's work without his input, a *Fourth Book of Occult Philosophy* was produced thirty years after Agrippa's death. It is nevertheless attributed to Agrippa and pretends to include all of the demonic material and ceremonies originally cut from his work in order to appease its critics. Johannes Wierus, the famed student of Agrippa, categorically denounces this work as a forgery in his own book *De Praestigiis Daemonum*.

Agrippa's *Occult Philosophy* was finally produced in a printed form in 1533. Its denouncement by Dominican Inquisitor Conrad Köllin of Ulm as a work of heresy caused last-minute setbacks, leading to a quickly written retraction at the end of book three. See also WIERUS, BARRETT.

Aherom: A demon mentioned in the 1898 Mathers translation of the *Sacred Magic of Abramelin the Mage*. Aherom is listed among a vast number of other demons who serve the four infernal princes of the cardinal directions: Oriens, Paimon, Ariton, and Amaimon. See also AMAIMON, ARITON, MATHERS, ORIENS, PAIMON.

Akanef: In his 1898 translation of the *Sacred Magic of Abramelin the Mage*, occultist S. L. MacGregor Mathers suggests that the name of this demon is related to a Hebrew word for "wing." Akanef serves beneath the arch-demons Astaroth and Asmodeus and is summoned as a part of the Holy Guardian Angel working. See also ASMODEUS, ASTAROTH MATHERS.

Akesoli: A demon whose name means "the pain-bringer," at least according to occultist S. L. MacGregor Mathers. In his 1898 translation of the *Sacred Magic of Abramelin the Mage*, Akesoli is said to serve the demon-king Amaimon. Another spelling of this name is *Akefely*. See also AMAIMON, MATHERS.

Akium: Mathers takes this demon's name to mean "certainty." In his 1898 translation of the *Sacred Magic of Abramelin the Mage*, he lists Akium among the demonic servitors ruled by Beelzebub. *Akahim* is a variant spelling of this name. See also BEELZEBUB, MATHERS.

Akoros: A demon said to serve the infernal king Amaimon in the *Sacred Magic of Abramelin the Mage*. According to the Mathers translation of this work, Akoros comes from a Greek root meaning "overthrowers of authority." In the Peter Hammer edition of this work, the name of this demon is given as *Abarok*. See also AMAIMON, MATHERS.

Akton: A demon of disease who afflicts the ribs and lower back of mortals, tormenting them with aches and pains. He is one of thirty-six demons associated with the decans of the zodiac named in the pseudepigraphal *Testament of Solomon*. According to this text, Akton can be put to flight with the names Marmaraôth and Sabaôth. Although the origin and meaning of Marmaraôth is unclear, Sabaôth is one of the Hebrew names of God and means "Lord of Hosts." In the later McCown translation of the *Testament*, Akton's name is spelled *Aktonme*, and he is given the title of *Rhyx*, or "king." Curiously, this version says that the name that drives him away is *Marmaraoth of Mist*. The differences are a result of variations in the source material. McCown's sources are widely deemed the more accurate of the two. See also SOLOMON.

Alagas: In Mathers's 1898 translation of the *Sacred Magic of Abramelin the Mage*, the demon Alagas is said to have a name meaning "the Wanderer." Alagas and a host of other demonic entities appear in a lengthy list of beings who serve beneath Oriens, Paimon, Ariton, and Amaimon, the four demonic princes of the cardinal directions. Alagas is invoked as a part of the process of establishing a dialogue with an entity known as the Holy Guardian Angel. See also AMAIMON, ARITON, MATHERS, ORIENS, PAIMON.

Alan: Ordinarily a rather prosaic name, in the Mathers translation of the *Sacred Magic of Abramelin the Mage*, Alan appears as a demon who serves Astaroth. The name of this demon is given as *Alafy* in a version of the *Abramelin* material kept at the Wolfenbüttel library. The version kept at the Sächsische Landesbibliothek (Saxon State Library), in Dresden, Germany, spells the name *Alasi*. See also ASTAROTH, MATHERS.

Alastiel: A high-ranking spirit called upon to coerce a lesser spirit to inhabit a specially crafted ring. Alastiel is invoked to ensure that the demon in the ring will be cooperative, highly intelligent, and without deceit. This binding spell can be found in the Elizabethan grimoire known as the *Book of Oberon*. The goal is to provide a tutelary spirit that will serve the owner for the rest of their natural life. See also *BOOK OF OBERON*.

Alastor: A vengeance demon named in Collin de Plancy's *Dictionnaire Infernal*. In this text, de Plancy indicates that Alastor was known in the Zoroastrian tradition as the Executioner. Although the Zoroastrian connection is dubitable, in the tradition of the ancient Greeks, Alastor was indeed a spirit of vengeance. Zeus was known as *Zeus Alastor* whenever he assumed a vengeful form. In Waite's presentation of the *Grand Grimoire* from his 1910 *Book of Black Magic and Pacts*, Alastor is described as Hell's Commissioner of Public Works. He is also portrayed as an infernal judge. These attributions tie back to the work of Charles Berbiguier, a self-styled demonologist from the early nineteenth century. See also BERBIGUIER, DE PLANCY, WAITE.

Alath: A truly fearsome spirit whose name appears in the extra-biblical *Testament of Solomon*. Alath is a demon of illness said to attack children. He steals their breath, causing asthma, coughs, and other labored breathing. He is the twenty-first demon of those associated with the thirty-six decans of the zodiac, and he is said to have the body of a man with the head of a beast. According to the *Testament of Solomon*, he can be driven off by invoking the name *Rorêx*. In a later translation of this text by McCown, Alath is given the title of *Rhyx*, or "king." The angel constraining him is Rarideris. The two translations have several significant differences, because the later one was compiled using a more complete collection of source texts. See also SOLOMON.

Albewe: A demon of murder, mayhem, hatred, and discord, Albewe serves under the king of the spirits of Saturn, who is identified as Maymon in the *Book of Oberon*. When he manifests, it is in a monstrous form, with black, translucent skin. If compelled to take a more human shape, he may appear as an old man with a long beard or as an elderly woman leaning on walking sticks. See also ALDEE, *BOOK OF OBERON*, CHERASA, ETHEYE, MALYKE, MAYMON.

Albhadur: A chief duke in the hierarchy of Raysiel, an infernal king of the north. Albhadur has fifty lesser spirits that minister to him, and he is connected with the hours of the day. Described as an aerial spirit, Albhadur has a nature that is more subtle that physical, and he is not easily perceived with the naked eye. The *Ars Theurgia* recommends that he be viewed with the help of a stone crystal or scrying glass. See also *ARS THEURGIA*, RAYSIEL.

Albunalich: One of several demons said to serve beneath the infernal king Maymon. In the Joseph H. Peterson translation of the *Sworn Book of Honorius*, Albunalich is associated with spirits that have a tall and gracile appearance. Pale or yellow in color, they can summon snow and ice and also influence the emotions of anger, hatred, and sadness. They are connected with the planet Saturn and with the direction north. The angels Bohel, Cafziel, Michrathon, and Satquiel govern Albunalich and all demons connected with the planet Saturn. In the Driscoll edition of the *Sworn Book*, this demon appears under the name *Albunalith*, but his attributions are somewhat changed. In this version of the text, Albunalich is a king of the north who rules the element of earth. He is said to be able to impart knowledge of things to come and can also speak on things from the past. He has the ability to make people grow angry with one another, inciting rancor and causing the baring of swords.

On a lighter note, despite being a creature of earth, Albunalich is said to be able to bring temperate rains. He also takes great joy in wearing down and utterly frustrating anyone seeking treasures—presumably treasures that are buried in his domain of the earth. See also MAYMON, SWORN BOOK.

Alchibany: A demon named in Peterson's translation of the *Sworn Book of Honorius*. Alchibany is said to serve beneath the demon-king Maymon, who is connected with the direction north as well as the planet Saturn. Curiously, the text seems to also imply that Alchibany is subordinate to the southwest wind, although how this is reconciled with his service to an infernal king of the north is never made clear. Compare this demon's name to *Aliybany*, said to serve Albunalich, demon-king of the earth, in the Driscoll translation of the *Sworn Book*. See also ALIYBANY, MAYMON, *SWORN BOOK*.

Aldal: A demon specializing in tricks and illusions, Aldal can be conjured up to assist in any magick involving the deceit of the senses. Named in both the *Sacred Magic of Abramelin the Mage* and the *Clavicula Salomonis*, he is also recommended for invisibility spells. See also *CLAVICULA SALOMONIS*, MATHERS.

Aldee: Named in the *Book of Oberon*, Aldee is a particularly vile demon. He incites evil thoughts and tempts people toward chaos, murder, hatred, and

Lucifer devouring sinners. Medieval depictions of demons were monstrous and frequently featured extra mouths at the joints and at the privates. Courtesy of Dover Publications.

discord. His natural form is beaked and monstrous, with many faces and dark, translucent skin. He may also appear as a pig or an owl. If he wears a human guise, he looks like an old man or woman, often wearing black and carrying a cane or sickle. He serves Maymon, an infernal king who rules over the sphere of Saturn. He serves the interests of that king with four other demonic ministers. See also ALBEWE, ALDEE, *BOOK OF OBERON*, CHERASA, ETHEYE, MALYKE, MAYMON.

Aldrusy: A demon in the hierarchy of the wandering prince Uriel, at least according to the *Ars Theurgia*. Aldrusy holds the rank of duke and has six hundred and fifty lesser spirits to serve beneath him. He takes the form of a massive serpent with a human head. He is a troublesome spirit, dishonest and stubborn. See also *ARS THEURGIA*, URIEL.

Aleasi: A night-demon in the hierarchy of the north. According to the *Ars Theurgia*, Aleasi serves the demon-king Raysiel and holds the rank of chief duke. He appears only during the hours of the night and is reputed to have a very obstinate and evil nature. Forty lesser spirits serve him, carrying out his commands. See also *ARS THEURGIA*, RAYSIEL.

Aledep: In the Driscoll edition of the *Sworn Book of Honourius*, Aledep is one of three ministers said to serve directly beneath the demon-king Abas. Connected with the dark regions below the earth, Aledep and his compatriots know the location of all manner of precious metals and can be compelled to bring gold and silver in great quantities if appeased with the proper offerings. Aledep also seems to have some connection to earthquakes, for he is said to be capable of great destruction, causing buildings and other structures to be pulled down. He can confer positions of earthly power

as well, helping those he favors to gain influence and dignities in the world. See also ABAS, *SWORN BOOK*.

Alepta: According to the Mathers translation of the *Grimoire of Armadel*, Alepta is a demon who gives great riches. He can further exalt a mortal and make that person formidable to others. Finally, this demon has the ability to rescue those who call upon him from the hands of their enemies—although no indication is given of what the demon may demand in return for this service. See also MATHERS.

Alferiel: According to the *Ars Theurgia*, Alferiel is a demon in the hierarchy of Demoriel, the Emperor of the North. Alferiel is a mighty duke with eighty-four lesser spirits beneath him. His immediate superior is the demon Armadiel, who rules in the northeast. Alferiel is bound by both time and direction, and he will only manifest during very specific hours and minutes. If the day is divided into fifteen equal portions, the sixth of these is Alferiel's. (The Henson translation of the *Ars Theurgia* gives this number as fifteen. It was almost certainly intended to be twelve, but was copied incorrectly somewhere along the way.) See also ARMADIEL, *ARS THEURGIA*, DEMORIEL.

Alflas: One of several demons named in the court of king Maymon in the Joseph H. Peterson translation of the *Liber Juratus*, also known as the *Sworn Book of Honorius*. Maymon, and thus his servants, is connected with both the planet Saturn and the direction north—although Alflas is one of the demons in this list who is also specifically said to be subordinate to the southwest wind. Maymon and his court are described as tall, pale, and gracile. They can make it snow and they also have power to influence the emotions of anger, hatred, and sadness. Compare this demon's name with *Asflas*, said to serve Albunalich, demon-king of the earth, in the Driscoll translation of the *Sworn Book*. See also ALBUNALICH, ASFLAS, MAYMON, *SWORN BOOK*.

Algor: Appearing as a comely knight armed with spear and shield, Algor can grant the favor of princes and kings. He is named in the Elizabethan grimoire known as the *Book of Oberon*, where he is said to be one of twelve high-ranking servitors to Oriens, the reigning king of the east. See also *BOOK OF OBERON*, ORIENS.

Aliel: A demon named in the *Ars Theurgia*. Aliel serves in the court of the demon-prince Dorochiel where he commands forty lesser spirits of his own. He is said to have achieved the rank of chief duke, and he serves only in the first half of the night, between dusk and midnight. Through Dorochiel, he is associated with the west. His name appears again in the hierarchy of the demon Masiel. Here, Aliel is said again to serve during the hours of the night. He holds the rank of duke and has thirty spirits beneath him. He is also said to be a duke in service to the infernal king Maseriel. In this hierarchy, Aliel is connected with the direction of the south. He serves his master during the hours of the day and has thirty lesser spirits under his leadership. See also *ARS THEURGIA*, DOROCHIEL, MASERIEL.

Alingon: A courier-demon invoked to retrieve other spirits. Alingon is named in the *Book of Oberon*, where he (or she) works alongside two others in a spell to compel the demon Bilgall to appear. Alingon and their cohorts, Fortisan and Portisan, are immediate subordinates to Lucifer. See also BILGALL, *BOOK OF OBERON*, FORTISAN, LUCIFER, PORTISAN.

Aliybany: According to Driscoll's translation of the *Sworn Book*, this demon is connected to the element earth and the direction north. He serves the infernal king Albunalich. Like his master, he is said to have a fondness for gold and precious gems. He will greedily guard these, frustrating unworthy souls that seek the treasures of the earth. See also ALBUNALICH, *SWORN BOOK*.

Alleborith: A demon named in the *Testament of Solomon*, Alleborith is one of thirty-six demons associated with the decans of the zodiac. Alleborith is said to appear with the head of a beast and the body of a man. While most of his infernal brethren have the power of afflict humanity with terrible diseases, Alleborith has an unusual and very specific power: he can cause people to choke on fish bones. As demonic powers go, that's a pretty strange one. Perhaps because this ability is fairly minor in the grand scheme of things, no name is given, angelic or otherwise, that would put Alleborith to flight. One assumes that the Heimlich maneuver will work just as efficiently on demonically-inspired fish bones as not. In a later translation by McCown, which drew upon a more complete collection of source texts, Alleborith's name is spelled *Aleureth* instead. Most of his other details are identical, except he is given the title of king and assigned the thirty-first decan of the zodiac. In the earlier Conybeare translation, he is placed at the thirtieth. See also SOLOMON.

Allogor: An infernal duke named in the *Book of Oberon*, Allogor takes the form of a fair knight bearing a spear and a banner. He has insight into the doubts and fears held by those who summon him, and he can explain how these anxieties might come to pass—presumably so they can be avoided. A total of thirty legions of lesser spirits serve beneath him. Compare his name to Allocer in Mathers's *Lesser Key of Solomon* and also to Eligor in the *Pseudomonarchia Daemonum*. See also ALLOCER, *BOOK OF OBERON*, ELIGOR.

Alluph: The name of this demon may be derived from the word *aleph*, the first letter of the Greek alphabet. In the *Sacred Magic of Abramelin the Mage*, Alluph is said to serve all four infernal princes of the cardinal directions equally, and therefore equally partakes of their powers. Mathers parses his name as meaning either "duke" or "bull." "Bull" is far more likely, as the pictograph that ultimately became the letter aleph originally represented the head of a bull. See also AMAIMON, ARITON, MATHERS, ORIENS, PAIMON.

Almadiel: When this demon manifests, he takes the form of a monstrous serpent with a human head. He is bound to the hours of the night and he despises the day. He will only manifest when darkness has blanketed the land. He serves the wandering duke Buriel, and his name and seal appear in the second book of the *Lesser Key of Solomon*, known as the *Ars Theurgia*. Almadiel is hated by all other spirits, save for the others of his hierarchy. Within his own evil hierarchy, he commands a total of eight hundred and eighty lesser spirits. See also *ARS THEURGIA*, BURIEL.

Almasor: In the *Ars Theurgia*, Almasor is described as an infernal knight governed by the wandering demon-prince Pirichiel. According to that same text, Almasor is said to have no fewer than two thousand ministering spirits that attend him. See also *ARS THEURGIA*, PIRICHIEL.

Almesiel: One of the demons in service to Amenadiel, the infernal Emperor of the West. Almesiel's name and seal appear in the 1999 Henson translation of the *Ars Theurgia*. According to this text, Almesiel holds the rank of duke and commands three thousand eight hundred and eighty lesser spirits. See also AMENADIEL, *ARS THEURGIA*.

Almiras: In Mathers's translation of the *Clavicula Salomonis*, Almiras is described as the "Master of Invisibility." Together with a number of his infernal ministers, Almiras is invoked in a spell for becoming invisible. He appears in association with the same spell in Mathers's translation of the *Sacred Magic of Abramelin the Mage*. See also *CLAVICULA SALOMONIS*, MATHERS.

The identification of the wicked and their descent into hell. Engraving by A. Collaert. 17th century. Image courtesy of the Wellcome Collection, London.

Almodar: One of twelve infernal dukes who serve the wandering prince Soleviel. Half serve one year and the other half serve the next, thus spreading out the workload among them. Almodar commands one thousand eight hundred and forty lesser spirits of his own, and his name and seal appear in the *Ars Theurgia*, a magickal text that deals with spirits tied to the points of the compass. See also *ARS THEURGIA*, SOLEVIEL.

Almoel: A duke in the court of the demon-prince Usiel. Almoel commands twenty lesser spirits and has the power to reveal hidden things. According to the *Ars Theurgia*, where his name and seal appear, Almoel is connected with the hours of the night and will only appear to mortals during this time. See also *ARS THEURGIA*, USIEL.

Alocer: In the *Pseudomonarchia Daemonum*, Alocer is described as a great and strong duke. He appears first as a soldier riding a horse. He has a lion's face with fiery eyes. His skin is red and when he speaks, he has a loud and booming voice. Among his powers, he has the ability to teach astronomy and the liberal sciences. He can also provide familiar spirits. This demon appears in Scot's *Discoverie of Witchcraft*, where his name is spelled *Allocer*. He is said to have thirty-six legions of lesser spirits under his command. In the *Goetia*, he is called *Alloces* and he is said to have a red and leonine face. According to the *Goetia of Dr. Rudd*, he is governed by the angel Imamiah. His name also appears in the Welsh *Book of Incantations*. See also *BOOK OF INCANTATIONS*, *GOETIA*, SCOT, RUDD, WIERUS.

Alogil: A demon named in the *Sacred Magic of Abramelin the Mage*. Alogil is one of many demons who serve beneath Oriens, Paimon, Ariton, and Amaimon, the four infernal princes of the cardinal directions. There are several manuscripts that present the *Abramelin* material. In the fifteenth-century French manuscript translated by occultist S. L.

MacGregor Mathers in 1898, Alogil's name is given instead as *Plegit*. See also AMAIMON, ARITON, MATHERS, ORIENS, PAIMON.

Aloson: One of the demonic servitors ruled by the infernal lord Beelzebub. In the fifteenth-century French version of the *Sacred Magic of Abramelin the Mage*, the name of this demon is given as *Plison*. This spelling led translator Samuel Mathers to assume the demon's name was related to a Greek word meaning "to swim." See also BEELZEBUB, MATHERS.

Alpas: A demon whose name appears in connection with Oriens, Paimon, Ariton, and Amaimon. These are the four infernal princes of the cardinal directions as described in the *Sacred Magic of Abramelin the Mage*. Alpas serves beneath these four princes, answering to any of the four of them. See also AMAIMON, ARITON, MATHERS, ORIENS, PAIMON.

Alphasis: A demon who serves as a messenger or herald whenever the infernal kings of the four quarters of the world are invoked. Subordinate to the demon Paimon, he appears in the *Book of Oberon*, where his name is sometimes also spelled *Alphassis*. See also *BOOK OF OBERON*, EMLON, FEMELL, RODABELL.

Altanor: A demonic servant of Beelzebub, named in the *Sacred Magic of Abramelin the Mage*. In the fifteenth-century French manuscript sourced by Mathers for his translation of this work, the name of this demon is spelled *Alcanor*. See also BEELZEBUB, MATHERS.

Althes: A demon who appears by name in the fifteenth-century magickal text known as the *Munich Handbook*. Althes is summoned as part of a spell intended to allow the magician to reveal the identity of a thief. The demon is also called up in order to aid in divination. See also *MUNICH HANDBOOK*.

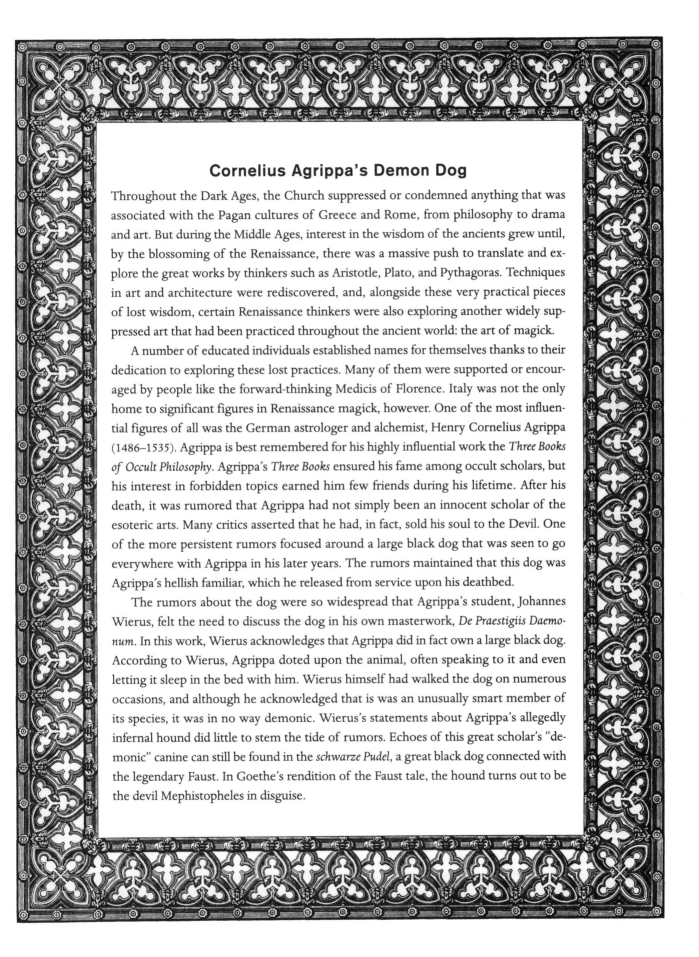

Cornelius Agrippa's Demon Dog

Throughout the Dark Ages, the Church suppressed or condemned anything that was associated with the Pagan cultures of Greece and Rome, from philosophy to drama and art. But during the Middle Ages, interest in the wisdom of the ancients grew until, by the blossoming of the Renaissance, there was a massive push to translate and explore the great works by thinkers such as Aristotle, Plato, and Pythagoras. Techniques in art and architecture were rediscovered, and, alongside these very practical pieces of lost wisdom, certain Renaissance thinkers were also exploring another widely suppressed art that had been practiced throughout the ancient world: the art of magick.

A number of educated individuals established names for themselves thanks to their dedication to exploring these lost practices. Many of them were supported or encouraged by people like the forward-thinking Medicis of Florence. Italy was not the only home to significant figures in Renaissance magick, however. One of the most influential figures of all was the German astrologer and alchemist, Henry Cornelius Agrippa (1486–1535). Agrippa is best remembered for his highly influential work the *Three Books of Occult Philosophy*. Agrippa's *Three Books* ensured his fame among occult scholars, but his interest in forbidden topics earned him few friends during his lifetime. After his death, it was rumored that Agrippa had not simply been an innocent scholar of the esoteric arts. Many critics asserted that he had, in fact, sold his soul to the Devil. One of the more persistent rumors focused around a large black dog that was seen to go everywhere with Agrippa in his later years. The rumors maintained that this dog was Agrippa's hellish familiar, which he released from service upon his deathbed.

The rumors about the dog were so widespread that Agrippa's student, Johannes Wierus, felt the need to discuss the dog in his own masterwork, *De Praestigiis Daemonum*. In this work, Wierus acknowledges that Agrippa did in fact own a large black dog. According to Wierus, Agrippa doted upon the animal, often speaking to it and even letting it sleep in the bed with him. Wierus himself had walked the dog on numerous occasions, and although he acknowledged that is was an unusually smart member of its species, it was in no way demonic. Wierus's statements about Agrippa's allegedly infernal hound did little to stem the tide of rumors. Echoes of this great scholar's "demonic" canine can still be found in the *schwarze Pudel*, a great black dog connected with the legendary Faust. In Goethe's rendition of the Faust tale, the hound turns out to be the devil Mephistopheles in disguise.

Althor: A servant of the infernal prince Dorochiel, Althor is named in the seventeenth-century magickal text known as the *Ars Theurgia*. Here he is listed, and a dozen demons given the rank of chief duke and said to appear in the hours before noon. Through Dorochiel, he is associated with the west. As a demon of rank, he commands forty ministering spirits of his own. See also *ARS THEURGIA*, DOROCHIEL.

Altramat: In the fifteenth-century *Munich Handbook*, Altramat is one of several demons said to guard the cardinal directions. He is named in a spell of divination that uses a young and virginal boy as the intermediary to the spirits. See also *MUNICH HANDBOOK*.

Alugor: According to the *Munich Handbook*, this duke of Hell has fifty legions at his command. When summoned, he appears as a knight. He is splendidly outfitted, and he approaches the magician bearing a lance, a scepter, and a banner. A martial demon, Alugor is especially skilled at providing warriors for protection or aggression. When requested, he can call knights to fight for the magician. He is also skilled at more subtle acts of conquest, for he can whisper in the ear of any knight, king, or marquis the world over and make them favorably disposed to the magician. In addition to all this, Alugor can also reveal the mysteries of the occult and foretell the outcome of duels. Compare his name and powers to those of the Goetic demon *Eligor*. See also ELIGOR, *MUNICH HANDBOOK*.

Alvedio: One of three ministers in the court of King Saba, ruler of the spirits of Mercury. He is named in the Elizabethan *Book of Oberon*, where he is said to help people win court cases, strike down the powerful, elevate the poor, and recover lost knowledge. He speaks with a beguiling voice and has an attractive appearance. If he is nearby, he causes people to shiver. He serves alongside the demons Hanyey and Yron, who work in a similar capacity to King Saba. See also *BOOK OF OBERON*, HANYEY, SABA, YRON.

Amada: A demon of prophecy, Amada gives answers about the past, present, and future. Named in the Elizabethan *Book of Oberon*, he is said to appear as a monstrous beast. His rank in the infernal hierarchies is that of duke, and forty-two legions of lesser spirits serve under him. See also *BOOK OF OBERON*.

Amaimon: One of the four kings of the cardinal directions. In most sources, he rules the spirits of the south. In the *Sacred Magic of Abramelin the Mage*, Amaimon is said to know the past, present, and future. He can cause visions and enable people to fly. He provides familiar spirits and can cause other spirits to appear and assume diverse forms. He can summon warriors for protection and revive the dead. The *Abramelin* material identifies him as one of eight sub-princes summoned to serve the magician as part of the Holy Guardian Angel rite. Mathers relates his name to a Greek root meaning "terrible violence and vehemence." According to both Mathers and Agrippa, Amaimon's equivalent in Jewish lore is the demon Mahazael. Scot's *Discoverie of Witchcraft* mentions that Amaimon is known for his dangerous, putrid breath and describes a technique of protection where conjurors wear a magick ring and hold this against their faces to ward away Amaimon's harm. The same technique is advised for the infernal king Bileth. Mathers also notes Amaimon's reputation for fiery or poisonous breath.

This demon appears in Wierus's *Pseudomonarchia Daemonum* under the name *Amaymonis*. Here he is a chief among evil spirits. He is mentioned in connection with both Asmodeus and Bileth, and he is tied to deception and abominable practices. Although he is associated with the south in the *Abramelin* material, Amaimon is listed as the "king of the east" in Dr. Rudd's *Treatise on Angel Magic*. Here, the name of this demon is rendered *Amaymon*. His name is spelled similarly in the Elizabethan *Book of Oberon*. According to this text, he appears as an old man with a long beard that bristles like horse's hair. He rides a fierce, roaring lion and carries a rod of command. Three lesser kings accompany him. He bestows titles and promotions and can also teach both philosophy and *ars notoria*. In the *Clavis Inferni*, his name is spelled *Maymon*. He rules in the south and is constrained by the angel Gabriel. His element is air and his animal is a bird. He has one foot that is of a cloven-hoofed beast. See also AGRIPPA, ASMODEUS, *BOOK OF OBERON*, BILETH, *CLAVIS INFERNI*, MA-HAZAEL, MATHERS, RUDD, SCOT, WIERUS.

Amalek: A demonic being named in the collection of Jewish lore known as the *Zohar*. According to this text, Amalek is the greatest impurity. He is credited with the ability to poison a person so thoroughly that he can bring about the death of the soul. In the *Zohar*, Amalek is equated to the fallen angel Samael. Although identified as separate entities, they are nevertheless presented as being the same essential being. Notably, Samael's name is sometimes translated as "poison of God." See also SAMAEL.

Amalin: A demonic servant in the hierarchy beneath the greater demons Astaroth and Asmodeus. Amalin's name appears in the Mathers 1898 translation of the *Sacred Magic of Abramelin the Mage*. See also ASMODEUS, ASTAROTH, MATHERS.

Aman: According to the Mathers translation of the *Sacred Magic of Abramelin the Mage*, Aman is a demonic servant of Astaroth. Both demons are invoked as a part of the Holy Guardian Angel ritual central to the *Abramelin* material. See also ASTAROTH, MATHERS.

Amandiel: A demon in the court of prince Usiel, whose name appears in the *Ars Theurgia*. Both Amandiel and Usiel serve the greater demon Amenadiel. Amandiel's name may be an intentional variation of *Amenadiel*, showing his fealty to this greater scion of Hell. Through his association with Amenadiel, Amandiel is connected with the west. Although the *Ars Theurgia* offers little on the origin or significance of his name, it does tell us that Amandiel is a demon connected with the hours of the day. He holds the rank of chief duke and has thirty lesser spirits to serve him. He excels at hiding away treasures so they may not be stolen, and he can also reveal treasure hidden away through magickal means. See also AMENADIEL, *ARS THEURGIA*, USIEL.

Amaniel: According to the *Sacred Magic of Abramelin the Mage*, Amaniel is part of the demonic hierarchy serving beneath the greater demons Astaroth and Asmodeus. In his translation of the *Abramelin* material, occultist S. L. MacGregor Mathers suggests that Amaniel is a fallen angel whose name means "nourishment of God." See also ASMODEUS, ASTAROTH, MATHERS.

Amasiel: A demon in the court of the wandering prince Menadiel. Amasiel is companion to the infernal duke Drasiel. According to the *Ars Theurgia*, Amasiel follows Drasiel in all things. As Drasiel may only appear in the third hour of the day, Amasiel must then follow in the fourth hour. See also *ARS THEURGIA*, DRASIEL, MENADIEL.

Ambolin: In the Mathers translation of the *Sacred Magic of Abramelin the Mage*, Ambolin is listed as one of several demonic servitors in the hierarchy beneath Astaroth and Asmodeus. According to Mathers's 1898 translation of this work, the name of this demon means "tending unto nothingness." See also ASMODEUS, ASTAROTH, MATHERS.

Ambri: One of twelve dukes specifically named in association with Caspiel, the infernal Emperor of the South. Ambri's name and seal appear in the *Ars Theurgia*, a book that teaches how to summon and compel a series of "aerial spirits" connected to the points of the compass. Ambri and his companions are reputed to be truculent and difficult to work with. If charged in the name of their direct superior, however, they can supposedly be bent to the conjuror's will. Ambri rarely manifests alone as he has two thousand two hundred and sixty lesser spirits under his command. See also *ARS THEURGIA*, CASPIEL.

Amchison: One of several demons mentioned in connection with the *Sacred Magic of Abramelin the Mage* whose name varies significantly between different versions of this work. In the version kept at the Wolfenbüttel library, the name is spelled *Arakison*. In the Peter Hammer edition, the name is *Arakuson*. And in the version of the *Abramelin* material kept in the Dresden library, the name appears as *Aracuson*. As all of these manuscripts are merely copies of a lost original, there is no way of knowing the proper spelling. Amchison or Arakuson is said to serve under the greater demon Magoth. See also MAGOTH, MATHERS.

Amduscias: This demon is said to first manifest in the form of a unicorn. According to Wierus's *Pseudomonarchia Daemonum*, he can also take the form of a man. He has the power to cause trees to bend and sway, and he can also conjure a host of musical instruments that will play invisibly on their own. In Scot's *Discoverie of Witchcraft*, he is accorded the rank of duke and is said to rule over a total of twenty-nine legions. He is one of the seventy-two demons of the *Goetia*; and in the *Goetia of Dr. Rudd*, he is said to be constrained by the angel Eiael. His name is alternately spelled *Amducias* and *Amdusias*. He also appears as a duke with twenty-nine legions in the Welsh grimoire knows as the *Book of Incantations*. See also *BOOK OF INCANTATIONS*, *GOETIA*, RUDD, SCOT, WIERUS.

Amediet: An infernal duke who has two thousand two hundred lesser spirits at his command. Amediet serves the demon Icosiel, who is described in the *Ars Theurgia* as a wandering prince of the air. Amediet prefers to manifest in houses, but he is bound to appear only during a specific time every day. If the day is divided into fifteen equal parts, then Amediet belongs to the hours and minutes that fall into the seventh portion of time. See also *ARS THEURGIA*, ICOSIEL.

Amen: In the *Ars Theurgia*, Amen is named as a demon in the hierarchy of prince Usiel. It is tempting to relate this demon to the ancient Egyptian deity Amen (also spelled *Amon*), but there is no indication in the text that the two are connected. Amen and his master Usiel both serve the infernal emperor Amenadiel, and Amen's name may relate more to this superior demon than to any ancient deities. Through Amenadiel, he is affiliated with the west. Regardless of the origin of this name, Amen is reputed to be a chief duke who holds sway over forty lesser spirits. He has the power to reveal hidden treasures and he excels at hiding things himself so they may not be discovered or stolen. He serves his master during the hours of the day. His name is sometimes spelled *Amon*, although the *Ars Theurgia* does not seem to relate him to the Goetic demon of the same name. See also AMENADIEL, AMON, *ARS THEURGIA*, *GOETIA*, USIEL.

Amenadiel: In the *Ars Theurgia*, Amenadiel is named as the primary Emperor of the West, and he governs that point of the compass with a massive retinue of loyal spirits. Amenadiel is said to have no fewer than three hundred great dukes and five hundred lesser dukes to carry out his commands, as well as a vast array of infernal ministers. He can be called in any hour of the day or night, and he appears in the *Ars Theurgia* along with the sigils and names of twelve of his dukes. As with all of the spirits named in the *Ars Theurgia*, Amenadiel possesses an airy nature and is best conjured into a scrying glass or crystal stone so that his true form can be seen. See also *ARS THEURGIA*.

Image of Amaimon, King of the spirits of the south as depicted in the *Clavis Inferni*. Note his cloven foot and problematic Black appearance. 18th century. Courtesy of the Wellcome Collection, London.

Ameta: A demon connected with the hours of the day, Ameta serves the infernal prince Usiel. Holding the rank of duke, he has forty lesser spirits beneath him. According to the *Ars Theurgia*, Ameta can find hidden things, especially those that have been magickally enchanted. He can also lay enchantments of his own, obscuring treasure and other items so they may not be discovered or stolen. See also *ARS THEURGIA*, USIEL.

Amiblel: A demon in the service of Demoriel, the infernal Emperor of the North. According to the *Ars Theurgia*, Amiblel has no fewer than one thousand one hundred and forty lesser spirits at his command. He holds the rank of duke and should be called only in the first two hours of the day. See also *ARS THEURGIA*, DEMORIEL.

Amiel: One of several chief dukes said to serve the demon Malgaras during the hours of the night. Through Malgaras, he is affiliated with the court of the west. He has thirty lesser spirits under his command. Amiel appears again in the same work under the rule of the demon Asyriel. Here, Amiel is depicted as a chief duke with forty lesser spirits who serve him. He is still connected to the hours of the night. Through Asyriel, this version of Amiel is connected with the south. See also *ARS THEURGIA*, ASYRIEL, MALGARAS.

Amitzrapava: A transliterated Hebrew name of the night-demon Lilith. According to Jewish lore, Lilith was the first wife of Adam, cast from the Garden for refusing to submit to her husband. She harbored an unnatural hatred for mothers in childbirth and newly born babes, and she was believed to roam the night, seeking to do harm. Scribing her names upon an amulet was thought to protect against her attacks, and a number of such amulets have survived to the modern day. Author T. Schrire, in his 1966 work *Hebrew Magic Amulets*, gathered together a number of Lilith's traditional talismanic names. Amitzrapava is only one of these many names. See also LILITH.

Amolon: A demon named in the *Sacred Magic of Abramelin the Mage*. Amolon is supposed to serve beneath the greater demon Beelzebub. Amolon's name appears in close proximity to that of another demon, Lamolon, and the similarities between the two may suggest that they are not separate demons but two variant spellings of the same name. See also BEELZEBUB, LAMOLON, MATHERS.

Amon: Also spelled *Aamon* and *Ammon*, this demon rules as a marquis over forty legions of devils. He appears as a wolf with a serpent's tale. In Wierus's *Pseudomonarchia Daemonum*, the wolf is said to vomit flame. In his translation in the *Discoverie of Witchcraft*, Scot changes this slightly, saying instead that the wolf only breathes fire. Amon can be commanded to assume the form of a man, but even in this case, his monstrous nature still shows forth. Here the texts diverge again. The *Pseudomonarchia* tells us that Amon's human form has dog's teeth and the head of a night hawk. Scot says he appears with dog's teeth and the head of a raven. The Welsh *Book of Incantations* agrees with Scot. The *Book of Oberon* agrees that his human form has the teeth of a hound but says nothing about the raven's head. The differences are slight but noteworthy. Both texts agree that this demon can speak of the past, present, and future. He also reconciles friends and foes and procures favor for those brave enough to call him up. He is named as the seventh of seventy-two demons in the *Goetia*. In the *Goetia of Dr. Rudd*, he is further said to bow to the power of the angel Achasiah. In the *Book of Oberon*, he is identified as one of the twelve principal ministers of King Oriens of the East. He is also named in the *Livre des esperitz*, a sixteenth-century French grimoire. See also *BOOK OF INCANTATIONS, BOOK OF OBERON, GOETIA, LIVRE DES ESPERITZ*, ORIENS, RUDD, SCOT, WIERUS.

Amoyr: A demon named in the *Ars Theurgia* from Henson's translation of the complete *Lemegeton*. Amoyr is identified as one of twelve infernal dukes who serve the demon-king Maseriel during the hours of the night. He has thirty lesser spirits at his command. He is connected with the direction of the south. See also *ARS THEURGIA*, MASERIEL.

Amriel: A demon ruled by the infernal prince Soleviel, a wandering spirit of the air. According to the *Ars Theurgia*, Amriel has one thousand eight hundred and forty lesser spirits at his command. He serves his infernal prince only one year out of every two. See also *ARS THEURGIA*, SOLEVIEL.

Amy: A great president who appears at first in the form of a flaming fire but after a while puts on the shape of a man. His office is to make one expert in astrology and all liberal sciences, give good familiars, and discover treasures that are kept by spirits. He rules over thirty-six legions of spirits. See also *BOOK OF INCANTATIONS*.

Anadir: The "flayer." Anadir is a servant of the demon Ariton named in the *Sacred Magic of Abramelin the Mage*. In the Mathers translation of this text, the demon's name is spelled *Anader*. See also ARITON.

Anael: A so-called "spirit of power" named in the Mathers translation of the *Grimoire of Armadel*. In this text, Anael is said to reveal all mysteries of the past, present, and future. He responds quickly to his invocation and can further teach the science of merchants. Anael also appears in the *Ars Theurgia* as a demon ruled by Gediel. According to this text, he is connected with the hours of the night and commands a total of twenty ministering spirits. See also *ARS THEURGIA*, GEDIEL.

Anagotos: One of several demons said to serve the infernal rulers Magoth and Kore. Anagotos appears in Mathers's translation of the *Sacred Magic of Abramelin the Mage*. In the *Abramelin* manuscripts kept at the Dresden and Wolfenbüttel libraries, the name of this demon is spelled *Anagnostos*, which might shed more light upon its original meaning. This name seems Greek in origin. *Gnostos* means "knowledge," and the Greek prefix *ana-* means "against." Thus, this name likely means "against knowledge" or "not knowing." See also KORE, MAGOTH, MATHERS.

Ananel: A fallen angel who chose to abandon Heaven in pursuit of a mortal wife. Ananel's name appears in the apocryphal *Book of Enoch*. He is listed among the "chiefs of tens" who served beneath Shemyaza and Azazel. These chiefs were essentially the lieutenants of the Watcher Angels, heavenly beings sometimes also known as the *Grigori*. See also AZAZEL, SHEMYAZA, WATCHER ANGELS.

Anatreth: According to the *Testament of Solomon*, Anatreth is a demon of disease. He is associated with the thirty-six decans of the zodiac. He torments humanity with pains in the belly, making it seem as if a person's entrails are being burnt and torn asunder. As with all of the zodiac demons named in the *Testament of Solomon*, Anatreth can be driven away with certain holy names. For this particular demon, the names Arara and Charara will cause him to flee. See also SOLOMON.

Andras: A violent demon reputed to be able to slaughter the master, servants, and all assistants in a household. This statement in Scot's *Discoverie of Witchcraft* is usually taken to mean that Andras is sent out to kill others. In the same text, Andras is said to take the form of an angel with the head of a black night-raven. He appears wielding a deadly sharp sword and riding upon the back of a fierce black wolf. He is given the title "Author of Discords." In the *Goetia of Dr. Rudd*, there is a slightly different entry on Andras. According to this text, the demon holds the rank of marquis. His purpose is to sow discord among men, but the statement about slaughter is written as a warning. Apparently, Andras has a particularly violent temperament, and those who are not careful when dealing with him run the risk of being killed along with everyone connected to them. Fortunately, the text provides the name of the angel that constrains Andras. That name is *Anarel*. Andras is also mentioned in Wierus's *Pseudomonarchia Daemonum* and the Welsh *Book of Incantations*. The *Book of Incantations* agrees that, if the exorcist is not wary, Andras will kill the exorcist and all companions.[37] Andras governs thirty legions of spirits. See also BOOK OF INCANTATIONS, GOETIA, RUDD, SCOT, WIERUS.

Andrealphus: A great marquis in the hosts of Hell, Andrealphus is said to take the form of a peacock. He can transform men into birds. In addition to this, he can teach geometry, astronomy, and any discipline dealing with measurement. He appears in both Wierus's *Pseudomonarchia Daemonum* and Scot's *Discoverie of Witchcraft*, where he is said to govern thirty legions. Andrealphus is also one of seventy-two demons listed in the *Goetia*. In the *Goetia of Dr. Rudd*, he is said to be constrained in the name of the angel Demabiah. The Welsh *Book of Incantations* says he can transform into a bird. See also BOOK OF INCANTATIONS, GOETIA, RUDD, SCOT, WIERUS.

Androcos: A demon named in the *Sacred Magic of Abramelin the Mage*. In his 1898 translation of this work, occultist Samuel Mathers suggests that this name means "orderer of men," from a Greek root. Androcos is said to serve the infernal prince Ariton. See also ARITON, MATHERS.

---

37. In many of the grimoires, the term *exorcist* is used interchangeably with *summoner*.

Seal of the demon Andromalius. Based on the design in the *Goetia of Dr. Rudd*. Ink on parchment, by M. Belanger.

Andromalius: The last of the seventy-two demons named in the *Goetia*. Andromalius is absent from both Wierus's *Pseudomonarchia Daemonum* and Scot's *Discoverie of Witchcraft*, books that otherwise contain the names and descriptions of the majority of the Goetic demons. No explanation for this omission is offered within the texts. According to the *Goetia*, Andromalius is a great and mighty earl. He has thirty-six legions of infernal spirits under his command, and he manifests in the form of a man holding a serpent in one hand. Andromalius is a demon of justice and revenge. He is said to have the power to punish thieves and other wicked individuals. He can bring a thief back to the place he stole from, and he can also bring about the return of the stolen goods. He reveals wickedness and underhanded dealings and can also uncover hidden treasure. According to the *Goetia of Dr. Rudd*, he is constrained with the name of the angel Mumiah. According to the Welsh *Book of Incantations*, he can find out all wickedness and underhanded dealing and punishes the same. See also *BOOK OF INCANTATIONS*, *GOETIA*, RUDD, SCOT, WIERUS.

Andros: A demon who often assumes the form of a many-headed dragon. Each of the heads on the dragon is that of a virgin with a soft and beauteous face. Andros serves as chief duke to the wandering prince Macariel as described in the *Ars Theurgia*. According to this text, Andros is not bound by any particular hour of the day but may make his appearance freely during the day or during the night. Andros is also a Greek word, meaning "man." Compare to the Goetic demon *Andras*. See also *ARS THEURGIA*, MACARIEL.

Andruchiel: A demon under the rule of the wandering prince Bidiel. According to the *Ars Theurgia*, Andruchiel is a great duke with two thousand and four hundred inferior spirits under his command. When he manifests he assumes a human shape, beautiful and radiant. See also *ARS THEURGIA*, BIDIEL.

Andyron: In the fifteenth-century *Munich Handbook*, Andyron is one of several demons summoned to assist in a spell of divination. Andyron can help a scryer see all manner of secret and hidden things. See also *MUNICH HANDBOOK*.

Aniel: A mighty duke in the hierarchy of the infernal prince Cabariel. He is affiliated with the west. Aniel has fifty ministering spirits that carry out his will. He is tied to the hours of the day and will appear between dawn and dusk. Aniel's name, as well as the seal that can bind and compel him, appears in the second book of the *Lesser Key of Solomon*, known as the *Ars Theurgia*. In this same book, Aniel also appears in the court of the demon Aseliel. Here, he holds the rank of chief president. He has thirty principal spirits who serve him and another twenty lesser spirits at his command. See also *ARS THEURGIA*, ASELIEL, CABARIEL.

Anituel: A demon named in the *Sixth and Seventh Books of Moses*. This magickal text, purporting to date to the days of the biblical Patriarch himself (but actually written in the 1800s), is fraught with inconsistencies, including the exact spelling of this demon's name. On his sigil, the name appears as *Aniouel*, while above the sigil the name is rendered *Antquelis*. The three vastly different versions of the demon's name, all presented together in the same manuscript, are somewhat baffling, and it is difficult to identify which name is strictly correct. Regardless of the quandary presented by its three different names, the *Sixth and Seventh Books of Moses* explains that this prince of spirits will appear as a serpent of Paradise when summoned, assuming much the same guise as the evil spirit that tempted Eve. Among his offices, Anituel oversees honors among men, conferring worldly fame or great wealth, as his summoner commands.

Annoboth: Also Annobath, Anaboth, and Annabath. He is a demon who teaches several magickal arts, particularly necromancy, geomancy, and chiromancy (palm reading). His name appears in the Elizabethan grimoire known as the *Book of Oberon*. As with many other demons named in that text, Annoboth reveals hidden treasure. Additionally, he will tell who owns the treasure and how best to acquire it. He can chase off any guardian spirits, but only if those spirits owe fealty to the north. Annoboth himself serves Egin, king of the north. He is both a lord and a governor who has mastery over eighteen legions of spirits. When summoned, he appears as a knight crowned with a double crown. He rides a pale horse and brandishes a warlike spear. See also *BOOK OF OBERON*, EGIN.

Anostêr: According to the *Testament of Solomon*, Anostêr is one of thirty-six demons tied to the decans of the zodiac. Specifically, he is number twenty-nine. All of the zodiac demons named in the *Testament of Solomon* are depicted as disease-bearing spirits that torment humanity with specific ailments. In Anostêr's case, he has the power to afflict his victims with infections of the uterine and urinary tracts. The text also holds him responsible for causing what it calls "uterine mania"—which seems to suggest that he is, in fact, the demon behind PMS. As great as the suffering Anostêr brings may be, he can be driven away from his victims through the use of the name *Marmaraô*. In the McCown translation, the constraining angel's name is instead spelled *Marmaroath*. See also SOLOMON.

Ansoel: A demon in the court of prince Usiel who serves in the hours of the night. Ansoel has the power to hide precious objects, protecting them from thieves. He can also reveal things that have been hidden away through similar magick. In the *Ars Theurgia*, he is said to hold the rank of duke with a total of forty subordinate spirits serving beneath him. See also *ARS THEURGIA*, USIEL.

Ansoryor: A particularly tricky demon who, if not properly bound, will freely lie. He also requires sacrifice to work with anyone who summons him. However, if the proper spells are known, he will help a person achieve mastery over a wide variety of topics in the span of only seven days. Ansoryor's specialties include pyromancy, hydromancy, nigromancy, and all the arts. Additionally, he teaches the secret properties of herbs, stones, and trees. When he manifests, it is in the form of a warlike knight who rides a pale donkey. On his arm, he carries a "viperous eagle," although whether this is an eagle with an ophidian look or some composite creature is unclear from the text. His name and description appear in the *Book of Oberon*, an Elizabethan manual of ceremonial magick. According to this tome, Ansoryor holds the rank of lord and commands twenty legions of lesser spirits. An alternative for his name is Antyor. See also *BOOK OF OBERON*.

Aonyr: A duke in the service of the infernal king Pamersiel. According to the *Ars Theurgia*, Aonyr is by nature both evil and false. He should never be trusted with secret matters. His aggressive nature can, however, be harnessed for good. Aonyr and all his fellows in the court of Pamersiel are useful for driving other spirits away from haunted houses. Through Pamersiel, he is affiliated with the east. See also *ARS THEURGIA*, PAMERSIEL.

Apelout: A spirit named in Peterson's edition of the *Grimorium Verum*. According to this text, Apelout is invoked in a spell intended to achieve invisibility. See also *GRIMORIUM VERUM*.

Apiel: This nocturnal demon is one of a thousand chief dukes said to serve the infernal king Symiel. He is part of the larger hierarchy of demons associated with the north, at least according to the *Ars Theurgia*. In that text, Apiel is described as possessing a very obstinate nature. He is reluctant to appear to mortals and, when he does appear, it is only at night. See also *ARS THEURGIA*, SYMIEL.

Apilki: A demon identified in the *Sacred Magic of Abramelin the Mage*. He serves beneath King Amaimon, one of four rulers of the cardinal directions. In the 1898 Mathers translation of this work, the name of this demon is translated "the misleader," from a Greek root. The name is also spelled *Apelki*. See also AMAIMON, MATHERS.

Apolhun: A servant of the princes Oriens, Paimon, Ariton, and Amaimon, Apolhun is mentioned in the *Sacred Magic of Abramelin the Mage*. In his

translation of this work, Mathers points out the similarity between this demon's name and that of *Apollyon*, a fallen angel mentioned in the *Book of Revelation*. Because of the similarities, Mathers suggests that the name of this demon means "the Destroyer." See also AMAIMON, APOLLYON, ARITON, MATHERS, ORIENS, PAIMON.

Apolin: A demon named in the fifteenth-century *Munich Handbook*. He is reputed to be an infernal instructor with the power to teach on any subject. He is called upon in a spell for increasing knowledge, where he is said to appear at night in dreams to impart everything he knows. The name of this demon is very likely derived from Apollo, a Greek solar deity, although it may also be related to Apollyon, Angel of the Abyss. See also APOLLYON, *MUNICH HANDBOOK*.

Apollyon: The so-called "angel of the Abyss." Apollyon is the Greek name for *Abaddon*, an angel named in the biblical *Book of Revelation*. In the grimoire known as the *Janua Magica Reserata*, or *Keys to the Gateway of Magic*, Apollyon is identified as one of nine princes in a hierarchy of evil spirits. Apollyon oversees the Seventh Order in this hierarchy, known as the Furies. The text states that the Hebrew version of this name is Abaddon. See also ABADDON, *JANUA MAGICA RESERATA*.

Apormenos: A demon named in the Mathers translation of the *Sacred Magic of Abramelin the Mage*. According to the text, Apormenos serves the demon Astaroth. See also ASTAROTH, MATHERS.

Apot: A demon who serves beneath Asmodeus and Magoth in the Mathers translation of the *Sacred Magic of Abramelin the Mage*. Mathers's source manuscript from fifteenth-century France is only one of two versions of the *Abramelin* material that contains this particular hierarchy. The other, a version from 1608 kept at the Wolfenbüttel library, gives a totally different spelling for this demon's name, to the point where it may well be a different demon entirely. The corresponding name in that text is *Sochen*. See also ASMODEUS, MAGOTH, MATHERS.

Aquiel: A demon said to preside over Sundays. Aquiel is named in Peterson's edition of the *Grimorium Verum*. See also *GRIMORIUM VERUM*.

Arach: The first of twelve demons said to serve the infernal king Maseriel by night. Arach holds the title of duke and has thirty lesser spirits under his command. He is named in the *Ars Theurgia*, where he appears in the hierarchy of the south. His name is very likely derived from a Greek word meaning "spider." See also *ARS THEURGIA*, MASERIEL.

Araex: A demon serving the infernal ruler Astaroth, Araex is named in the Mathers translation of the *Sacred Magic of Abramelin the Mage*. In the 1725 Peter Hammer edition of the same material, this demon's name is given as *Targoe*. In the 1720 version currently kept at the Dresden library, it is spelled *Taraoc*. There is a great deal of variation between the different *Abramelin* manuscripts. Much of it can be attributed to scribal error. See also ASTAROTH, MATHERS.

Arafos: A demon of the night who serves the infernal king Symiel in the hierarchy of the north. Arafos is attended by fifty ministering spirits. His name and seal appear in the *Ars Theurgia*. According to this text, Arafos is a stubborn and willful demon who is reluctant to manifest to mortals. See also *ARS THEURGIA*, SYMIEL.

Arakiba: A fallen angel named in the *Book of Enoch*. According to this text, Arakiba was one of the "chiefs of tens" of the Watcher Angels. These angelic chiefs led the Watchers, or *Grigori*, in their task to watch over humanity in the days before the Flood. Arakiba fell through sins of the flesh, taking a mortal wife when such a union between heavenly and earthly stock was forbidden. See also WATCHER ANGELS.

Araquiel: A fallen angel who guarded the secrets of the signs of the earth. Araquiel is named in the *Book of Enoch*, where he is said to have fallen after giving into the temptation of beautiful mortal women. One of two hundred Watcher Angels charged with overseeing humanity, Araquiel abandoned his heavenly duties to raise a family instead. Although the knowledge was forbidden, he taught the signs of the earth to humans, further breaking his trust with Heaven. See also WATCHER ANGELS.

Arath: This demon is called upon to assist in the discovery of thieves. He is also summoned so that he may lend his power to a spell for divination. He appears by name in the fifteenth-century *Munich Handbook*. See also *MUNICH HANDBOOK*.

Aratiel: A chief president in the hierarchy of the demon-prince Aseliel. Through his service to Aseliel, Aratiel is tied to the direction of the east. He holds the rank of chief president and has thirty principal spirits and twenty ministering spirits at his command. According to the *Ars Theurgia*, he manifests in a form that is courtly, courteous, and very beautiful to behold. He will only appear during the hours of the day. See also *ARS THEURGIA*, ASELIEL.

Aratron: A demon named in the Mathers translation of the *Grimoire of Armadel*. Aratron is said to reveal knowledge of the soul. He also possesses details abut the rebellion of the angels and the subsequent War in Heaven. There is a warning in the *Grimoire of Armadel* suggesting that it is unwise to spend too much time with any of this demon's familiar spirits. The name of this demon also appears in Rudd's *Treatise on Angel Magic*. Here, he is an Olympic spirit connected with Saturn. The name *Aratron* may be a variation on the demon *Ariton*. See also ARITON, MATHERS, RUDD.

Arayl: A servant of the demon-king Raysiel, Arayl holds the rank of chief duke. He has forty lesser spirits beneath him. Arayl is a demon of the night, and he will only appear during the hours between dusk and dawn. His name and seal appear in the *Ars Theurgia*, a book that deals with a variety of spirits connected with the points of the compass. Through Raysiel, he is connected with the direction north. See also ARS THEURGIA, RAYSIEL.

Arbatel of Magic: Sometimes also known as simply the *Arbatel*. This text, first published in Latin in Basel, Switzerland, in 1575, is distinguished as one of the few grimoires that deals exclusively with transcendent magick. The *Arbatel* deals primarily with planetary or Olympian spirits and has a distinct lack of demonic entities. It is not to be confused with either the *Almadel*, included in the *Lemegeton*, or the *Armadel*, frequently described as the *Grimoire of Armadel*.

Arbiel: A demon named in the *Ars Theurgia*. According to this text, Arbiel is one of twelve dukes in service to the infernal prince Hydriel. Hydriel governs no specific direction, and thus he and all the demons who serve him are said to wander through the points of the compass. Described as an aerial spirit, Arbiel has a subtle form and is best viewed in a crystal stone or scrying glass. When he manifests, he appears as a serpent with a woman's head and he has a fondness for places that are wet or swampy. See also ARS THEURGIA, HYDRIEL.

Archidemath: According to the fifteenth-century *Munich Handbook*, this demon is a guardian of one of the cardinal directions. He must be properly invoked as part of a divination for revealing the true identity of a thief. See also *MUNICH HANDBOOK*.

Arcisat: A duke of the demon Asyriel. Arcisat appears in the *Ars Theurgia*, where he is said to rule over twenty lesser spirits of his own. He is connected with the direction of the south and with the hours of the day. See also *ARS THEURGIA*, ASYRIEL.

Arcon: This demon's name likely derives from a Greek verb meaning "to rule." Arcon appears in the *Sacred Magic of Abramelin the Mage*, where he is said to serve the infernal lord Beelzebub. See also BEELZEBUB, MATHERS.

Arean: A demon in the hierarchy of the east, as outlined in the *Ars Theurgia*. Arean serves the infernal prince Aseliel in the capacity of chief president. He holds sway over thirty principal spirits and another twenty ministering spirits. He is tied to the hours of the day and will only manifest during this time. When he appears, he assumes a form that is courtly in manner and beautiful to behold. See also *ARS THEURGIA*, ASELIEL.

Arepach: One of several demons associated with the points of the compass, at least according to the *Ars Theurgia*. Arepach serves in the hierarchy of the demon-king Raysiel, who rules in the north. Described as having a particularly stubborn and evil nature, Arepach is a demon of the night, only manifesting during the hours of darkness from dusk until dawn. He holds the rank of chief duke, and accordingly has a twenty other lesser spirits under his command. See also *ARS THEURGIA*, RAYSIEL.

The Goat-Demons of Edom

Isaiah 34:14 talks about so-called "goat-demons" that greet one another in the ruins of Edom. These goat-demons are none other than the *Se'irim*, a class of beings from ancient Jewish demonology that were seen as hairy beasts often equated with goats.

The Se'irim also appear in Leviticus 17:7 and 2 Chronicles 11:15. The word itself translates roughly to "hairy demons," and it is often rendered as a satyr, a wild nature spirit from ancient Greek myth frequently depicted with the hairy legs of a goat. Interestingly, in the Greek myths, the goat-legged satyrs were often associated with orgiastic rites of wine and sexual indulgence. They were presented as the companions of Dionysius, the Greek god of wine and revelry, and in Greek art, satyrs were frequently depicted in the act of carrying off beautiful young maidens in order to ravish them in the wilderness in a frenzy of wine.

Azazel is said to be the chief of the Se'irim. In Leviticus 16:8, he is described as dwelling in the desert, haunting the same wild and waste places as the goat-demons themselves. There are indications that at least some of the primitive Semitic (most likely non-Hebrew) tribes offered sacrifices to the Se'irim. The Old Testament states that Jeroboam appointed priests for the Se'irim. But Josiah later destroyed the places of their worship, seeing them as an outrage against the faith of the Israelites. It is suggested that the practices accompanying the worship of these entities involved copulation of women with goats (a practice that once more calls to mind the Greek de-

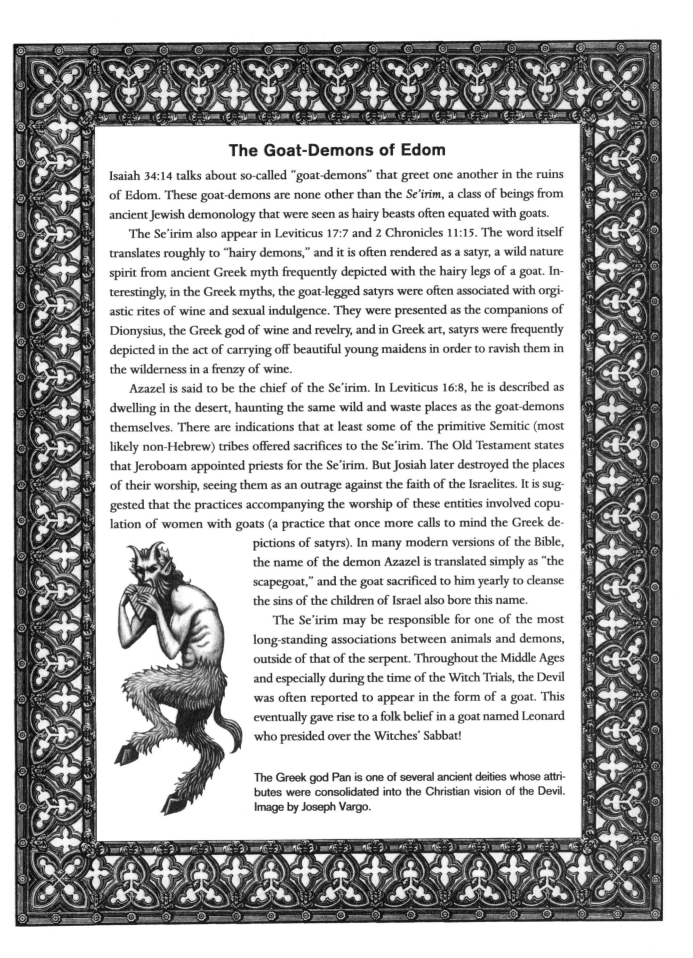

pictions of satyrs). In many modern versions of the Bible, the name of the demon Azazel is translated simply as "the scapegoat," and the goat sacrificed to him yearly to cleanse the sins of the children of Israel also bore this name.

The Se'irim may be responsible for one of the most long-standing associations between animals and demons, outside of that of the serpent. Throughout the Middle Ages and especially during the time of the Witch Trials, the Devil was often reported to appear in the form of a goat. This eventually gave rise to a folk belief in a goat named Leonard who presided over the Witches' Sabbat!

The Greek god Pan is one of several ancient deities whose attributes were consolidated into the Christian vision of the Devil. Image by Joseph Vargo.

A war between angels is brewing in Heaven. From Gustav Doré's illustrations for Milton's *Paradise Lost*.

Argilon: A demon said to serve the infernal ruler Astaroth. As a servant of Astaroth, Argilon wields all the same powers as his infernal master, including the ability to cause visions and to expound upon secret matters pertaining to the past, present, and future. Argilon's name appears in all four surviving manuscripts of the *Sacred Magic of Abramelin the Mage*. See also ASTAROTH, MATHERS.

Aridiel: In the demonic hierarchy connected with the points of the compass as outlined in the *Ars Theurgia*, Aridiel serves beneath the demon-king Caspiel, Emperor of the South. Holding the rank of duke, Aridiel is one of twelve demons of such rank given the honor of attending directly upon Caspiel. He has no fewer than two thousand two hundred and sixty ministering spirits under his command. See also *ARS THEURGIA*, CASPIEL.

Ariel: Appears as a treasure-finding spirit in the *Sixth and Seventh Books of Moses*. He is included among the Seven Great Princes of Spirits who, the text warns, include among their number some of the highest-ranking angels to have fallen from grace. In wider literature on angels and demons, Ariel appears among the fallen as well as those still loyal to the Throne of God. Ariel's name means "Lion of God," and this leonine aspect is often reflected in magickal texts—where he is frequently described as possessing the head of a lion.

Arifiel: A demon who serves Carnesiel, the infernal Emperor of the East. Arifiel holds the rank of duke and can be summoned individually or alongside his immediate superior. Both Arifiel and Carnesiel appear in an extensive hierarchy of demons associated with the points of the compass, as outlined in the *Ars Theurgia*. See also *ARS THEURGIA*, CARNESIEL.

Arioth: A demon said to be ruled jointly by both Magoth and Kore, at least in the 1898 Mathers translation of the *Sacred Magic of Abramelin the Mage*. In other versions of this text, Arioth serves only the demon Magoth. The name of this demon is likely a variation on the Hebrew name *Arioch*, which means "fierce lion." Arioch appears as a demon in several grimoires. See also KORE, MAGOTH, MATHERS.

Ariton: Sometimes also known as *Egin* or *Egyn*, this demon's name likely derives from the Greek word *arhreton*, which Mathers defines as meaning "secret" or "mysterious." In the *Sacred Magic of Abramelin the Mage*, Ariton is listed as one of eight sub-princes in an extended demonic hierarchy that includes such familiar faces as Beelzebub,

Asmodeus, and Astaroth. He is also named as one of the four demons who preside over the cardinal directions. Under his alternate name of Egyn, he oversees the north. According to both Mathers and Agrippa, Ariton's equivalent in Jewish lore is the demon Azael. In the *Abramelin* material, this demon is attributed with the power to discover hidden treasure. He knows the past, present, and future, and can cause people to have visions. He can make spirits appear and take any form, and he can also give familiars. In addition, Ariton is reputed to have the power to revive the dead. He reveals the identities of thieves, gifts people with the power of flight, and can make warriors manifest to protect his charges. Notably, a demon with the name *Aratron* appears as the spirit of Saturn in several works. See also AGRIPPA, ARATRON, AZAEL, EGYN, MATHERS.

Armadiel: A demon who rules as king of the northeast, Armadiel is third in rank beneath the great infernal Emperor of the North, Demoriel. Many demons who hold a similar rank have scores of lesser dukes serving beneath them. Armadiel, however, has only fifteen chief dukes who carry out his wishes. Their names and sigils can be found alongside his in the *Ars Theurgia*. Armadiel can also be found in a list of demons from Trithemius's *Steganographia*. See also *ARS THEURGIA*, DEMORIEL.

Armany: A demon associated with the eastern point of the compass, Armany serves in the hierarchy of Carnesiel, the infernal Emperor of the East. According to the *Ars Theurgia*, Armany holds the rank of duke. See also *ARS THEURGIA*, CARNESIEL.

Armaros: One of two hundred Watcher Angels said to have left Heaven in pursuit of mortal wives. Also known as the *Grigori*, or *Irin*, the tale of the Watchers appears in the *Book of Enoch* as well as in the Jewish Haggadah. In addition to their sins of the flesh, these fallen angels were said to have taught forbidden knowledge to humanity before the Flood. Armaros taught the resolving of enchantments. See also WATCHER ANGELS.

Armasia: One of several demons said to be ruled by the arch-fiend Beelzebub in the *Sacred Magic of Abramelin the Mage*. In the fifteenth-century French manuscript sourced by Mathers, the demon's name is spelled *Amatia*. Mathers suggests that this is derived from a Greek word meaning "ignorance." See also BEELZEBUB, MATHERS.

Armena: One of several chief dukes said to serve beneath the infernal king Raysiel. Armena is described as possessing an airy nature, and he does not easily manifest to mortals without the aid of a scrying glass or crystal. According to the *Ars Theurgia*, Armena has fifty lesser spirits at his command, and they minister to him during the hours of the day. Through his allegiance to Raysiel, Armena is connected with the court of the north. See also *ARS THEURGIA*, RAYSIEL.

Armesiel: An infernal duke, who has a total of one thousand three hundred and twenty ministering spirits to attend his needs. Armesiel himself serves the wandering prince Emoniel. According to the *Ars Theurgia*, Armesiel is free to manifest himself during the hours of the day as well as the night. He is drawn to woodlands. Armenadiel is also named in a list of demons from Johannes Trithemius's *Steganographia*, written around 1499. See also *ARS THEURGIA*, EMONIEL.

Arnochap: A demon tied to the west wind. According to the Peterson translation of the *Sworn Book of Honorius*, Arnochap functions as a servant of Harthan, the king of the spirits of the moon.

Among his powers, he is able to cause rains and to help people prepare for journeys. The angels Gabriel, Michael, Samyhel, and Atithael have power over him. See also HARTHAN, *SWORN BOOK*.

Aroan: A demon named in the Henson translation of the *Ars Theurgia*. According to this text, Aroan is a servitor of the demon-king Gediel, who rules under the infernal Emperor of the South. A night-demon, Aroan serves only during the hours of darkness. He holds the rank of duke and has twenty lesser spirits beneath him. See also *ARS THEURGIA*, GEDIEL.

Aroc: In the court of the demon Malgaras, Aroc serves as chief duke. Through Malgaras, he is connected with the direction of the west. According to the *Ars Theurgia*, Aroc rules over thirty attending spirits. He appears only in the hours of the night. See also *ARS THEURGIA*, MALGARAS.

Arogor: In his 1898 translation of the *Sacred Magic of Abramelin the Mage*, Mathers takes the name of this demon to mean "helper." Arogor is a servant of the arch-fiend Beelzebub. There is a strong likelihood that this demon's name was originally intended to be a palindrome, as several of the demons beneath Beelzebub have names that can be read the same backward and forward. This variation would be *Arogora*. The only way to be certain about this, however, would be to find the original manuscript from which all current copies of the *Abramelin* material stem. See also BEELZEBUB, MATHERS.

Arois: A chief duke of the day who commands ten ministering spirits. Arois is named in the *Ars Theurgia*, where he is said to serve the infernal king Malgaras. Through his allegiance to Malgaras, he is connected with the court of the west. See also *ARS THEURGIA*, MALGARAS.

Arolen: According to Mathers, the name of this demon means "strongly agitated" and is rooted in Hebrew. Mathers's translation of the *Sacred Magic of Abramelin the Mage* lists Arolen among the servitors of Beelzebub. See also BEELZEBUB, MATHERS.

Aron: This demon's name, also given as Aran, appears in the Elizabethan grimoire known as the *Book of Oberon*. There he is identified as a lord with command over forty-five legions of lesser spirits. Among his powers is the ability to tell about the past, present, and future. He knows the location of secret and hidden things and can acquire great dignities, favors, and promotions for those who know how to summon him. See also *BOOK OF OBERON*.

Arotor: A demon mentioned in the *Sacred Magic of Abramelin the Mage*. Arotor is said to serve the demon-king Magoth. In his translation of the *Abramelin* material, Mathers suggests that this demon's name means "ploughman" or "husbandman" (as in animal husbandry). In other versions of the work, the name is spelled *Arator*. This name may also have started out as a magickal palindrome. See also MAGOTH, MATHERS.

Arôtosael: A demon of illness and affliction, Arôtosael attacks the eyes, causing blindness and injury. His name is also spelled Artosael. According to the *Testament of Solomon*, Arôtosael can be put to flight by invoking the name of the angel Uriel. Notably, Uriel is identified as a demon in the *Ars Theurgia*. See also *ARS THEURGIA*, URIEL.

Aroziel: A night-demon loyal to prince Dorochiel. Aroziel appears in the *Ars Theurgia*, where he is said to hold the title of chief duke. Forty lesser spirits exist to carry out his commands. He is said to manifest only in a specific hour in the first half of the night. Through Dorochiel, he is connected with the west. See also *ARS THEURGIA*, DOROCHIEL.

Arpiron: Also known as *Harpinon*, this demon is said to serve beneath the arch-demon Magoth. Arpiron appears in Mathers's 1898 translation of the *Sacred Magic of Abramelin the Mage*. He is invoked as part of the Holy Guardian Angel working that is central to that text. See also MAGOTH, MATHERS.

Arrabin: One of several demonic servitors attributed to the rule of Magoth, Arrabin appears in the *Sacred Magic of Abramelin the Mage*. In the Mathers translation of this work, he is also said to serve the arch-fiend Kore. In other versions of the *Abramelin* material, the name of this demon is spelled *Arrabim*. See also KORE, MAGOTH, MATHERS.

Arrnoniel: A demon said to command two thousand and four hundred ministering spirits. Arrnoniel serves in the hierarchy of the infernal prince Bidiel, described as a wandering spirit of the air. A great duke in the *Ars Theurgia*, Arrnoniel reportedly manifests wearing a pleasing human form. See also *ARS THEURGIA*, BIDIEL.

Ars Theurgia: The second book of the work known as the *Lemegeton*, or *Lesser Key of Solomon*. The word *theurgia* comes from a Greek root meaning "sacramental rite" or "mystery." Theurgy itself is a type of magick that involves the invocation of beneficent spirits. It was originally practiced by the neo-Platonists. During the Renaissance, theurgy came to have the connotation of white magick, as opposed to the Goetic arts, which were generally viewed as black magick. The *Ars Theurgia* contains an extensive list of demons associated with the points of the compass. These demons are arranged in hierarchies, and each hierarchy is associated with one of the cardinal directions. An infernal emperor oversees each of the cardinal directions, and the demonic princes, kings, and dukes who serve beneath him are in turn associated with aspects of that direction, such as northwest and south by southeast. The demons of the *Ars Theurgia* that are associated with a specific direction are thought to rule over that portion of the compass and to be found in that direction when called. Their position is thought of as being fixed. In addition to these fixed points, the *Ars Theurgia* also contains the names of a number of wandering spirits, which it describes variously as princes and dukes. These wandering princes are tied to no specific point of the compass, but range with their courts from place to place.

The demons of the *Ars Theurgia* are presented as spirits of the air, and they are all thought to possess an airy nature that prevents them from being clearly seen with the naked eye. As a result, they are invoked into a scrying glass or a specially prepared crystal known as a "shew-stone." Notably, a crystal show-stone was also employed by Dr. John Dee in his work with the Enochian spirits. Although they are tacitly associated with the element of air due to their subtle natures, many of the spirits of the *Ars Theurgia* are also associated with other elements. They tend to be bound to the hours of either the day or the night, and most courts contain demons affiliated with each.

The exact date of the material contained within the *Ars Theurgia* is unknown. Within the *Lemegeton*, only the book known as the *Almadel* has an internal date establishing at least when it was copied. This fixes the writing of the version of the *Almadel* contained within the Sloane collection at the British Museum to 1641. Of the five books traditionally included in the *Lemegeton*, the *Goetia* is arguably the oldest, and there are strong connections that can be drawn between the material in the *Goetia* and that of the *Ars Theurgia*. Most significantly, both books employ the use of demonic seals or sigils in the invocation of their respective spirits. Notably, all of the major spirits in the *Ars Theurgia* appear in Johannes Trithemius's *Steganographia*. The descriptions of most of these spirits, including their directional affiliations and the numbers of their dukes and sub-dukes, are similar if not identical between these two texts. This places the establishment of this particular system of spirits to at least the end of the 1400s, if not earlier. See also *LEMEGETON*, *GOETIA*, TRITHEMIUS.

Artenegelun: A demon of disease, credited with the power to inflict fever, tremors, and weakness upon any target. Artenegelun is named in the *Liber de Angelis* as part of a spell designed to lash out cruelly at an enemy. Serving beneath the infernal king Bilet, when summoned this demon will go forth with his brethren and inflict great suffering and disease upon anyone that the magician targets. The only cure is for the magician to relent and bring an end to the spell. See also BILETH, *LIBER DE ANGELIS*.

Artino: One of twelve chief dukes said to serve the demon Dorochiel. He is connected with the west and with hours of the day. In the *Ars Theurgia*, he is said to be attended by forty ministering spirits. He will only manifest in the hours between dawn and noon. See also *ARS THEURGIA*, DOROCHIEL.

Artis: A great duke who appears wearing two crowns and wielding a sword in his hand. His office is to teach and answer all questions put to him. Additionally, he grants love and grace to all persons. Thirty-six legions of lesser spirits serve him. He can be found in the *Livre des esperitz*, a sixteenth-century grimoire in the French language. See also *LIVRE DES ESPERITZ*.

Asael: In the *Book of Enoch*, Asael appears as one of the Watcher Angels that chose to walk out of Heaven after swearing a pact with Shemyaza. The Watchers were divided into groups of ten, with each of these groups being led by one of their "chiefs of tens." Asael is counted among the chiefs of tens. Asael is also named in Conway's *Demonology and Devil-Lore* as one of four demons who personify elemental forces. His name may be a variant spelling of *Azael*. The other demons are Samael, Maccathiel, and Azazel. See also AZAEL, AZAZEL, MACCATHIEL, SAMAEL, SHEMYAZA, WATCHER ANGELS.

Asahel: One of several demons said to serve the infernal prince Aseliel during the hours of the day. According to the *Ars Theurgia*, Asahel holds the rank of chief president, and he has a collection of thirty principal spirits and twenty ministering spirits at his command. Through his affiliation with Aseliel, he is tied to the hierarchy of the east. See also *ARS THEURGIA*, ASELIEL.

Asbibiel: A servant of the demon-king Armadiel, Asbibiel holds the rank of duke. He has a total of eighty-four lesser spirits to minister to him. His name and seal can be found in the *Ars Theurgia*, where he is said to only appear in the thirteenth section of the day, if the day is divided into fifteen equal portions of time. He is affiliated with the north. See also ARMADIEL, *ARS THEURGIA*.

Asbiel: A fallen angel named in the *Book of Enoch*. Asbiel is said to have given evil counsel to the Watcher Angels. As a result of this counsel, two hundred of the Watchers chose to leave Heaven and succumb to the temptations of the flesh. See also WATCHER ANGELS.

Ascariell: Also spelled Askariell. A spirit conjured into a crystal to enchant it as a shew-stone or scrying glass. The demon, once present in the stone, can be used as a kind of messenger, calling forth other spirits to appear in the stone at the request of its owner. According to the *Book of Oberon*, As-

John Dee's crystal, or shew-stone, supposedly given to him in November 1582 by the angel Uriel for clairvoyance and healing, seventeenth century. Image courtesy of the Wellcome Collection, London.

cariell has a fair appearance and wears a garland crown. Crystal shew-stones were used widely by Elizabethan and Renaissance magicians, the most famous being Dr. John Dee. See also *BOOK OF OBERON*, JOHN DEE.

Aseliel: An infernal king named in the *Ars Theurgia*. Aseliel rules in the direction south by east in the greater hierarchy of the east as overseen by the emperor Carnesiel. In his conjurations, Aseliel is also given the title of prince. He has ten chief spirits who serve him during the day and another twenty who serve during the hours of the night. According to the *Ars Theurgia*, this demon and all of his servants manifest in forms that are very beautiful to behold. They behave in a very loving and courteous manner to those who interact with them. Aseliel also appears in Trithemius's *Steganographia*, where he holds similar ranks and associations. See also *ARS THEURGIA*, CARNESIEL.

Asflas: A servant of the demon-king Albunalich, who rules in the north over the element of earth. Asflas is a hard-working demon who is described as being both even-tempered and patient. According to the Driscoll edition of the *Sworn Book*, Asflas jealously guards the treasures of the earth, but he will bestow gold and gems upon those who have gained his favor. He has a fondness for certain incenses and perfumes, and he is more likely to manifest if these are burned in his name. He tells the future, imparting knowledge of things to come, and he is also versed in events from the past. He has the power to manipulate the emotions, inspiring rancor even between friends. He is also a greedy guardian of the treasures of the earth, and if someone he does not like goes seeking these treasures, he will wear them down and frustrate their goals. See also ALBUNALICH, ALFLAS, *SWORN BOOK*.

Asimiel: A demon in the service of Camuel, the infernal prince of the southeast. Asimiel's name and seal appear in the *Ars Theurgia*, where he is said to belong to the hours of the night. Despite his association with the nighttime, Asimiel manifests during the day. He holds the rank of duke and has one hundred lesser spirits to serve him. Asiriel is also named in the *Steganographia* of Johannes Trithemius. He has the same rank and affiliations in this work. See also *ARS THEURGIA*, CAMUEL.

Asmadiel: An infernal duke in the hierarchy of the demon Macariel. As a demon of rank, Asmadiel commands four hundred minor spirits of his own.

According to the *Ars Theurgia*, he most often appears as a many-headed dragon, although he actually has command over a diversity of forms. Unlike many of the spirits named in the *Ars Theurgia*, Asmadiel is tied to no particular hour but may manifest at any time, day or night. See also *ARS THEURGIA*, MACARIEL.

Asmaiel: A demon ranked as chief duke in the hierarchy of Armadiel, king of the northeast. According to the *Ars Theurgia*, Asmaiel commands a total of eighty-four lesser spirits. If the day is divided into fifteen equal portions, Asmaiel's time falls in the ninth portion. He will refuse to appear during any other time of the day. See also ARMADIEL, *ARS THEURGIA*.

Asmiel: A demon connected with the hours of the day, Asmiel serves the infernal king Symiel. Reputed to possess a good and obedient nature, Asmiel holds the position of duke and rules over sixty lesser spirits. His name and seal appear in the *Ars Theurgia*, where he is identified with the direction north. Asmiel also appears as one of a number of demons listed in Mathers's translation of the *Sacred Magic of Abramelin the Mage*. Here Asmiel is said to be a servant of the four demonic princes of the cardinal directions: Oriens, Paimon, Ariton, and Amaimon. As such, he can be summoned and controlled in the name of his superiors. See also AMAIMON, ARITON, *ARS THEURGIA*, MATHERS, ORIENS, PAIMON, SYMIEL.

Asmoday: A variant spelling for the demon Asmodeus that has, in several texts, come to be viewed as a separate and distinct entity. In Dr. Rudd's early-seventeenth-century work, *A Treatise on Angel Magic*, Asmoday (spelled *Asmodai*) is curiously described as a demon who "hath one Idea called Muriel incorporated into two figures Geomantic, called Populus by day and Via by night."[38] Nothing further is offered to help make sense of this enigmatic statement. In addition to this curious declaration, Dr. Rudd's work describes Asmodai as a spirit connected with the moon.

Asmoday is also identified as one of the seventy-two Goetic demons. According to the *Goetia*, he is a king with seventy-two legions of spirits beneath him. When he manifests, he comes riding a dragon. His form is monstrous, having three heads, a serpent's tail, and webbed feet. He has the head of a bull, a ram, and a man, and he vomits fire. He tries to deceive people about his true nature, often giving the name *Sidonay* instead of Asmoday. Those dealing with him are cautioned to press him until he acknowledges his true name. As a Goetic demon, Asmoday can make people invisible and disclose the whereabouts of hidden treasure. Additionally, he teaches arithmetic, astronomy, geometry, and handicrafts. He also has the power to bestow an enchanted item known as the Ring of Virtues. In Wierus's *Pseudomonarchia Daemonum*, Asmoday is mentioned in connection with Solomon's Brazen Vessel. Here, he is described as the third in rank of the seventy-two infernal kings shut up in that vessel by the biblical Patriarch. According to the *Goetia of Dr. Rudd*, he is an infernal king serving under Amaimon, the demonic ruler of the east. In this text, his name is spelled *Asmodai*, and he is said to be constrained in the name of the angel Vasariah.

According to the *Book of Oberon*, a magickal text from Elizabethan England, Asmoday is one of twelve primary ministers to Amaimon, the reigning king of the south. In this text, Asmoday teaches music, arithmetic, astronomy, and ge-

---

38. Adam McLean, *A Treatise on Angel Magic*, p. 51.

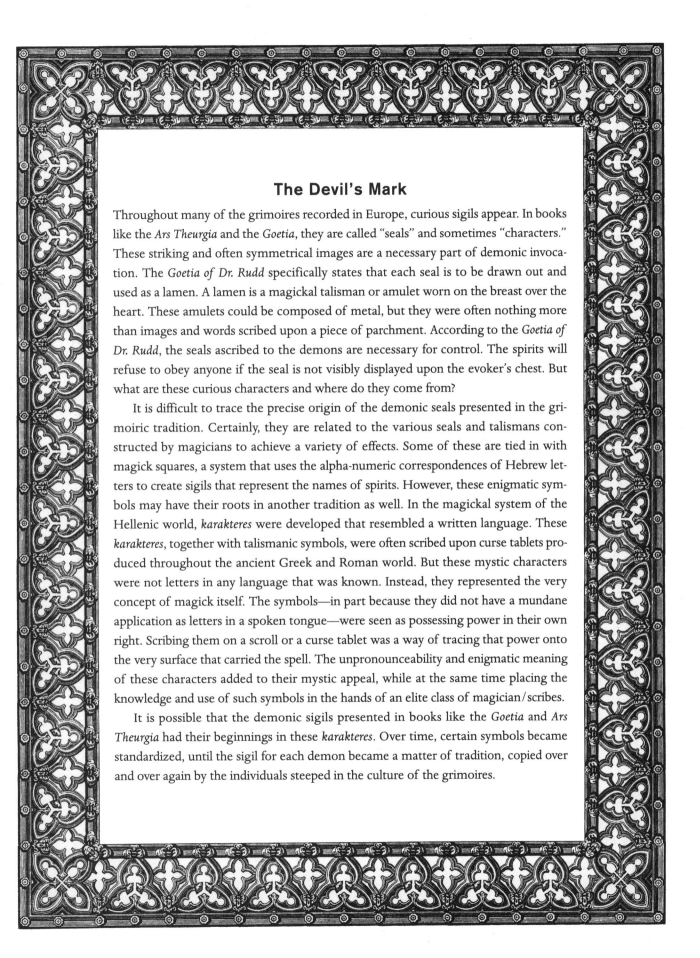

The Devil's Mark

Throughout many of the grimoires recorded in Europe, curious sigils appear. In books like the *Ars Theurgia* and the *Goetia*, they are called "seals" and sometimes "characters." These striking and often symmetrical images are a necessary part of demonic invocation. The *Goetia of Dr. Rudd* specifically states that each seal is to be drawn out and used as a lamen. A lamen is a magickal talisman or amulet worn on the breast over the heart. These amulets could be composed of metal, but they were often nothing more than images and words scribed upon a piece of parchment. According to the *Goetia of Dr. Rudd*, the seals ascribed to the demons are necessary for control. The spirits will refuse to obey anyone if the seal is not visibly displayed upon the evoker's chest. But what are these curious characters and where do they come from?

It is difficult to trace the precise origin of the demonic seals presented in the grimoiric tradition. Certainly, they are related to the various seals and talismans constructed by magicians to achieve a variety of effects. Some of these are tied in with magick squares, a system that uses the alpha-numeric correspondences of Hebrew letters to create sigils that represent the names of spirits. However, these enigmatic symbols may have their roots in another tradition as well. In the magickal system of the Hellenic world, *karakteres* were developed that resembled a written language. These *karakteres*, together with talismanic symbols, were often scribed upon curse tablets produced throughout the ancient Greek and Roman world. But these mystic characters were not letters in any language that was known. Instead, they represented the very concept of magick itself. The symbols—in part because they did not have a mundane application as letters in a spoken tongue—were seen as possessing power in their own right. Scribing them on a scroll or a curse tablet was a way of tracing that power onto the very surface that carried the spell. The unpronounceability and enigmatic meaning of these characters added to their mystic appeal, while at the same time placing the knowledge and use of such symbols in the hands of an elite class of magician/scribes.

It is possible that the demonic sigils presented in books like the *Goetia* and *Ars Theurgia* had their beginnings in these *karakteres*. Over time, certain symbols became standardized, until the sigil for each demon became a matter of tradition, copied over and over again by the individuals steeped in the culture of the grimoires.

ometry. He also has the power to bestow invisibility and reveal the location of hidden treasure. His appearance is chimerical: he has the tail of a serpent, donkey's feet, and three heads (that of a donkey, a bull, and a ram). When he speaks, fire erupts from his mouth(s). In the French *Livre des esperitz*, he can grant those who summon him a full year during which they will have all the things they desire. See also AMAIMON, ASMODEUS, *BOOK OF OBERON, LIVRE DES ESPERITZ*, RUDD, SIDONAY, SOLOMON, WIERUS.

Asmodeus: Described as "the king of the demons," Asmodeus appears in the *Book of Tobit* (sometimes also known as the Book of Tobias). According to this story, the demon Asmodeus fell in love with the beautiful Sarah, daughter of Raguel. Asmodeus wanted Sarah for himself, and he refused to allow her to be married to any human man. Subsequently, each time that Sarah was married, the demon came to the marriage bed and took the life of her new husband. Seven men fell to the predations of this jealous demon, until Tobias, the eponymous author of the book, received a visit from the angel Raphael, who instructed him on how to handle the demonic paramour. Tobias married Sarah and drove the demon away. Asmodeus reportedly fled to the furthest reaches of Egypt, where he was then bound by the angel Raphael. In the *Testament of Solomon*, Asmodeus also plays a significant role. Here, the demon is called up by King Solomon, who demands to know its names and functions. This version of Asmodeus claims to have been put in charge of the destruction of fidelity, either by separating man and wife through calamities or by causing husbands to be led astray. He is also said to attack the beauty of virgins, causing them to waste away. In a passage that echoes the *Book of Tobit*, Asmodeus admits that the angel Raphael holds power over him. He could also be put to flight by burning the gall of a certain fish.

Further in the *Testament of Solomon*, Asmodeus claims to have been "born an angel's seed by a daughter of man,"[39] a statement that connects him firmly with the tradition of the Watcher Angels. The statement is also reflected in the portion of the Jewish Haggadah concerned with the life of Noah. Here, Asmodeus is said to have been born of the union of the fallen angel Shamdon and the lustful maiden Naamah. He was reputedly bound by King Solomon with iron, a metal that was often presented as an anathema to demons. Curiously, in the faerie lore of the British Isles, iron is also a metal that can harm or drive away the fey.

The *Grimoire of Armadel* mentions Asmodeus in conjunction with Leviathan, claiming that these two demons can teach about the malice of other devils. However, that text cautions against summoning these two beings, citing the fact that they lie. Francis Barrett's *The Magus* depicts an image of Asmodeus, associating him with the sin of wrath. Asmodeus is mentioned in Arthur Edward Waite's 1910 *Book of Black Magic and Pacts*, where he is listed as the superintendent of Hell's casinos. This demonic hierarchy stems from the writings of the nineteenth-century demonologist Charles Berbiguier.

Rendered *Asmodée* in the Mathers translation of the *Sacred Magic of Abramelin the Mage*, this demon is identified as one of eight sub-princes ruling over all the other demons. According to this text, Asmodeus has the power to produce food, typically in the form of vast, impressive banquets. He can learn the secrets of any person. He also has the power to transmute metals and transmogrify people and animals, changing their shapes at will.

---

39. Conybeare, *Testament of Solomon*, p. 25.

He also appears as the thirty-second demon of the *Goetia* under the name *Asmoday*. In the grimoire known as the *Janua Magica Reserata*, or *Keys to the Gateway of Magic*, Asmodeus appears in a nine-tiered hierarchy of evil spirits intended to echo the nine orders of angels. According to this text, Asmodeus presides over the *Ultores Scelorum*, or "Revengers of Evil." This is the fourth order of demons in the hierarchy, over which he reigns as prince. Variations of this demon's name include Asmoday, Ashmedai, Asmodée, and Asmodai. See also ASMODAY, BERBIGUIER, *GOETIA*, *JANUA MAGICA RESERATA*, LEVIATHAN, MATHERS, SOLOMON, WAITE.

Asmoo: A demon named in the Elizabethan grimoire known as the *Book of Oberon*. His name is also spelled *Asmo* in the same text. He appears in a list of seven infernal senators who are called upon to control other, lesser spirits. Asmoo, whose name is likely a variation on the more familiar *Asmoday*, is said to serve Tantavalerion, a being identified as the supreme ruler of all spirits. See also ASMODAY, BOELL, *BOOK OF OBERON*, DANALL, ORYMELL, PASCARY, SALARICA, TANTAVALERION, TYGRA.

Asorega: A demon connected with the *Sacred Magic of Abramelin the Mage*. He is a servitor of the four infernal princes of the cardinal directions: Oriens, Paimon, Ariton, and Amaimon. Asorega is named in two of the surviving manuscripts of the *Abramelin* material: the manuscript kept at the Wolfenbüttel library and the edition published in Cologne by Peter Hammer. In Mathers's translation, Asorega's name is given as *Astrega*. See also AMAIMON, ARITON, MATHERS, ORIENS, PAIMON.

Asoriel: A mighty duke ruled by the demon Cabariel. Asoriel appears with fifty attending spirits. He is one of a number of demons associated with the points of the compass as defined in the *Ars Theurgia*. Both Asoriel and his immediate superior serve in the hierarchy of the west, underneath the demon-king Amenadiel. See also AMENADIEL, *ARS THEURGIA*, CABARIEL.

Aspar: In the *Ars Theurgia*, Aspar is named as a chief duke of the night serving the demon-king Malgaras. He has twenty lesser spirits at his command and he will only appear to mortals during the hours of darkness. He is connected with the west. See also *ARS THEURGIA*, MALGARAS.

Asperim: According to Mathers, the name of this demon is derived from the Latin word *aspera*, meaning "perilous" or "dangerous." The meaning of the name is perhaps a subtle warning regarding the demon's true nature. Asperim is one of many demons who serve in the hierarchy of the four demonic princes of the cardinal directions. He is summoned as part of the extensive Holy Guardian Angel rite detailed in the *Sacred Magic of Abramelin the Mage*. See also AMAIMON, ARITON, MATHERS, ORIENS, PAIMON.

Asphiel: A chief president said to serve the prince Aseliel during the hours of the night. Asphiel's name and seal appear in the *Ars Theurgia*. According to this text, he rules over thirty principal spirits and twenty ministering servants. He is part of the hierarchy of the east due to his allegiance to Aseliel. See also *ARS THEURGIA*, ASELIEL.

Asphor: A demon said to hold the rank of chief duke in the court of the infernal prince Dorochiel. He is tied to the hours of the day and will only manifest between noon and dusk. According to the *Ars Theurgia*, he commands no fewer than four hundred lesser spirits. His direction is west. See also *ARS THEURGIA*, DOROCHIEL.

Aspiel: A servant of the infernal king Malgaras. Aspiel appears in the *Ars Theurgia*, where he is said to hold the rank of chief duke. He governs thirty lesser spirits and will only deign to appear during the hours of the night. He is affiliated with the court of the west. Aspiel also appears in this same work in the capacity of a duke serving beneath the demon Asyriel. Here, Aspiel is said to serve during the hours of the night, with ten lesser spirits to minister to his needs. Through Asyriel, this version of Aspiel is allied with the south. See also *ARS THEURGIA*, ASYRIEL, MALGARAS.

Assaba: One of several infernal dukes in service to the demon-king Gediel. According to the *Ars Theurgia*, Assaba has a total of twenty lesser spirits under his command. He is affiliated with the hours of the day and the direction of the south. See also *ARS THEURGIA*, GEDIEL.

Assaibi: A demon who serves beneath the infernal king Maymon, associated with both the planet Saturn and the direction north. Assaibi appears in Peterson's translation of the *Sworn Book of Honorius*. As a Saturnine spirit, Assaibi reputedly can inspire the emotions of sadness, anger, and hatred. Assaibi answers to the angels Bohel, Cafziel, Michrathon, and Satquiel. There is a strong likelihood that this demon and the demon *Assalbi* are one in the same— but for a scribal error somewhere along the way. See also ASSALBI, MAYMON, *SWORN BOOK*.

Assalbi: A minister of the infernal king Albunalich who rules the element of earth from the direction of the north. As a creature of earth, Assalbi holds sway over all the things buried in it, but especially gold and precious stones. He is said to have the power to wear down and utterly frustrate anyone seeking buried treasure. He greedily guards the treasures of the earth but will bestow them upon those he favors. He is an oracular spirit, imparting knowledge of the future as well as the past. He can incite disagreements between people, causing anger among friends and bringing them to violence. Compare to *Assaibi* in the Driscoll edition of the *Sworn Book*. See also ALBUNALICH, ASSAIBI, *SWORN BOOK*.

The demon Astaroth, from Collin de Plancy's *Dictionnaire Infernal*. From the archives of *Dark Realms Magazine*.

Assuel: A demon with the title of duke in the court of the infernal king Maseriel. Assuel is affiliated with the hours of the day and, through his service to Maseriel, is also connected with the direction of the south. According to the *Ars Theurgia*, he has thirty lesser spirits under his command. See also *ARS THEURGIA*, MASERIEL.

Astael: A demon tied to the hours of the day whose name and sigil appear in the *Ars Theurgia*. Astael appears in connection with the demon Raysiel, an infernal king of the north. Astael himself holds the rank of duke and has fifty lesser spirits at his command. See also *ARS THEURGIA*, RAYSIEL.

Astaroth: One of the seventy-two demons named in the *Goetia*. His name appears in Wierus's *Pseudomonarchia Daemonum*, where he is said to hold the rank of duke with command over forty legions of lesser spirits. When he appears, he takes the shape of an obscene and loathsome angel. He rides an infernal dragon and carries a viper in his right hand. In de Plancy's 1863 edition of the *Dictionnaire Infernal*, he is depicted as a naked man with angel's wings riding a dragon. In Francis Barrett's *The Magus*, Astaroth is listed as the prince of the demonic order of accusers and inquisitors. The only major difference between Astaroth's descriptions in de Plancy's work and those in *The Magus* is that the demon rides a wolf or a dog, not a dragon. Astaroth is said to teach the liberal sciences and, like many of the Goetic spirits, he will also discourse on matters of the past, present, and future, as well as the secrets of occult knowledge. Astaroth can confer heavenly knowledge as well: he is said to speak freely about the creator of spirits, the fall of the spirits, and the various sins they committed that inspired their fall. Wierus's *Pseudomonarchia* also says that Astaroth has horribly fetid breath. For this reason, the magician is warned to keep his distance from the demon and to hold a magickal ring of silver against his face to protect himself from any injury.

Astaroth appears in the *Book of Oberon*, an Elizabethan manual of ceremonial magick. Here, Astaroth is one of a dozen principal spirits serving beneath Amaimon, king of the south. When he manifests, he arrives riding an infernal dragon. In one hand he carries a serpent with a venomous sting. The *Book of Oberon* describes him as a horrible spirit who should not be allowed near those who summon him. For those who dare to work with him, he is said to give true answers when asked about any events from the past, present, or future. He also teaches the seven liberal arts.

Astaroth's name is given as *Elestor* in the Lansdowne text known as the *True Keys of Solomon*. Here, he is said to govern all the spirits in the Americas. In the *Goetia of Dr. Rudd*, he is said to be constrained with the name of the angel Reiajel. In the *Sacred Magic of Abramelin the Mage*, Astaroth is one of eight sub-princes who rule over all other demons. He has the power to discover mines and transmute metals. He can reveal the location of treasure—so long as it is not magickally guarded. He has impressive powers of destruction, causing tempests and demolishing buildings. He can also transform men and animals.

This demon has his origins in the Bible, where, in the Book of Judges and in the first Book of Samuel, he is referred to as "the Ashtaroth" and is mentioned in connection with "the Baals," other foreign gods forbidden to the Israelites. Many later readers took both of these words to be proper names. However, in the time of the ancient Israelites, the Baals and the Ashtaroths were general terms for deities. Baals were the male deities, while the Ashtaroths denoted the female deities. As this would imply, in the process of becoming a demon, Astaroth underwent a gender switch somewhere along the way.

The term *Astaroth* is derived from the name of the Semitic goddess Astarte, a goddess who appears in Ugaritic, Phoenician, and Akkadian sources. She is a cognate of the Babylonian goddess Ishtar. Because she is connected with forbidden things in the Bible, namely with religions that were viewed as false and heretical by the ancient Israelites, Astarte cum Astaroth was demonized along with a host of other foreign deities. She, now a he, has remained a demon ever since—at least as far as most of Western civilization is concerned.

Perhaps because Astarte was such a widely revered goddess in her day, the demon Astaroth is typically depicted as holding significant rank among the hordes of Hell. In a dubious document produced as evidence against the parish priest Urbain Grandier, who was accused of practicing witchcraft and diabolism in seventeenth-century France, Astaroth was one of several well-known demons whose name appears as a signature witnessing Grandier's pact with Satan. In the *Grand Grimoire*, Astaroth is listed as the Grand Duke of Hell. In Berbiguier's infernal hierarchy, Astaroth is one of the Ministers of Hell and is listed as the Grand Treasurer. According to the spurious *Grimoire of Pope Honorius*, Astaroth is the demon of Wednesday. Variations on this demon's name include Ashtaroth, Ashteroth, Ashtoreth, Astareth, and Astarot. As prince of the *Criminatores*, he presides over the eighth order of evil spirits in an infernal hierarchy described in the *Janua Magica Reserata*. According to this text, his Greek name is Diabolos. See also AMAIMON, BARRETT, BERBIGUIER, *BOOK OF OBERON*, DE PLANCY, *GOETIA, GRAND GRIMOIRE, JANUA MAGICA RESERATA*, RUDD, SCOT, WIERUS.

Astib: A duke of the infernal king Barmiel. Astib is said to serve his master during the hours of the night. This demon is named in the *Ars Theurgia*. Through his affiliation with Barmiel, Astib is connected with the direction south. Although he holds the rank of duke, this demon has no servants or ministering spirits of his own. See also *ARS THEURGIA*, BAAL, BARMIEL.

Astolit: A demon connected with the *Sacred Magic of Abramelin the Mage*. According to this text, Asto-

lit is ruled by the demon Paimon, one of the four infernal princes of the cardinal directions. See also MATHERS, PAIMON.

Astor: A servant of the demon Asyriel. Astor is a chief duke with forty servants of his own to carry out his commands. According to the *Ars Theurgia*, he is tied to the hours of the day and will only manifest during this time. Through Asyriel, Astor is connected with the hierarchy of the south. See also *ARS THEURGIA*, ASYRIEL.

Asturel: In his translation of the *Sacred Magic of Abramelin the Mage*, Mathers suggests that this demon's name comes from a Hebrew word meaning "bearing authority." Asturel is one of many demons who serve beneath Oriens, Paimon, Ariton, and Amaimon, the four demonic princes of the cardinal directions. See also AMAIMON, ARITON, MATHERS, ORIENS, PAIMON.

Asuriel: A duke of the infernal prince Usiel who serves his master by night. Asuriel has twenty ministering spirits at his command, and according to the *Ars Theurgia*, he has the power to hide treasure from thieves through the use of charms and enchantments. He can also reveal items hidden through these same means. Through his association with Usiel, he is tied to the court of the west. See also *ARS THEURGIA*, USIEL.

Asyriel: A mighty king named in the *Ars Theurgia*. Asyriel is the third spirit in rank serving beneath the demon Caspiel, infernal Emperor of the South. Asyriel himself rules from the southwestern point of the compass. He has a total of forty demonic dukes under his command. Twenty of these serve him by day and the other twenty serve during the hours of the night. According to the *Ars Theurgia*, Asyriel and his demonic court are all good-natured beings, quick to obey those with

The seal of Asyriel, a demon from the *Ars Theurgia*. Based on the design in the Henson edition of the *Lemegeton*. By M. Belanger.

the knowledge to command them. See also *ARS THEURGIA*, CASPIEL.

Ataf: An evil angel named in the *Sword of Moses*. The magician is supposed to invoke this being, along with several others, in order to separate a man from his wife. In addition to striking the magician's enemy so that his family is sundered, these angels are also said to preside over a variety of disorders, including pain, inflammation, and dropsy, a condition associated with heart disease. See also GASTER, *SWORD OF MOSES*.

Athesiel: A demon who is bound to appear only once per day in the eleventh portion of time when the hours of the day are divided into fifteen equal parts. Serving beneath the wandering prince Icosiel, Athesiel holds the rank of duke and has dominion over two thousand two hundred lesser spirits. According to the *Ars Theurgia*, he and his fellow dukes under Icosiel have a fondness for pri-

vate homes and are most likely to be found in such locations. See also *ARS THEURGIA*, ICOSIEL.

Atloton: A servitor of the four princes of the cardinal directions: Oriens, Ariton, Amaimon, and Paimon. Atloton is named in the *Sacred Magic of Abramelin* material. See also AMAIMON, ARITON, MATHERS, ORIENS, PAIMON.

Atniel: One of twelve infernal dukes said to serve the demon-king Maseriel during the hours of the day. In the *Ars Theurgia*, Atniel is said to rule over thirty lesser spirits of his own. He is associated with the hours of the day and with the southern point of the compass. See also *ARS THEURGIA*, MASERIEL.

Atranrbiabil: A demon associated with the element of fire. He serves in the hierarchy of the infernal king Jamaz, who holds sway over that element. As a demon of fire, Atranrbiabil is reportedly hot-headed, with a quick and energetic nature and a complexion like flame. He has power over death and decay. He can kill with a word, and raise an army of one thousand soldiers—presumably from the grave. If something has decayed, he can reverse the effects, restoring it to its original state. He can also prevent decay entirely. Atranrbiabil appears in Daniel Driscoll's 1977 edition of the *Sworn Book*, where it is said that he can be enticed to make an appearance if an individual burns the proper perfumes. No clear pronunciation of this demon's rather complicated name is provided by the text. See also JAMAZ, *SWORN BOOK*.

Atraurbiabilis: A servant of the demon Iammax, infernal king of the spirits of the planet Mars. Atraurbiabilis appears in the Peterson translation of the *Sworn Book of Honorius*. According to this text, Atraurbiabilis has the power to sow destruction, murder, and warfare. When he manifests, he is small and lean with a color that resembles live coals. This demon is one of five under the rule of Iammax who are described as being subject to the east wind in addition to their affiliation with the south. The angels Samahel, Satihel, Ylurahihel, and Amabiel hold sway over this demon. Compare to *Atranrbiabil*, named in the Driscoll translation of the *Sworn Book*. See also ATRANRBIABIL, IAMMAX, *SWORN BOOK*.

Atrax: In the extra-biblical text known as the *Testament of Solomon*, Atrax is named as the sixteenth demon of thirty-six spirits associated with the decans of the zodiac. All of these demons are composite horrors, possessing the bodies of men but the heads of animals. They are also demons of affliction and disease. In the case of Atrax, he delights in tormenting humanity with fevers. He can be driven away by invoking the name of the Throne of God. These details appear in the Conybeare translation of the work. In a later and more accurate translation working from a more complete collection of source materials, McCown gives this demon's name as *Katrax*. Instead of the "Throne of the Most High," the Greek god Zeus is named as the "angel" with power to dispel him. See also SOLOMON.

Atriel: One of the demons in service to the infernal king Maseriel. Atriel is named in the *Ars Theurgia*, where he is given the title of duke. He has command over thirty ministering spirits. He is tied to the hours of the night and serves his master only during this time. As part of the court of the demon Maseriel, Atriel is affiliated with the direction of the south. See also *ARS THEURGIA*, MASERIEL.

Audameoth: The demon of the twenty-second decan of the zodiac. Audameoth's name appears in the McCown translation of the *Testament of Solomon*, where he is given the title *Rhyx*, or "king." His name is absent entirely from earlier translations of this seminal work, primarily because McCown had the opportunity to work from a more complete collection of texts. Audameoth is said to cause heart pain. By saying the name of the angel Raiouoth, you can send him away. See also SOLOMON.

Auel: In the *Liber de Angelis*, this angel is invoked in a spell to achieve control over demons. The spell itself calls for a wax figure and the blood of both a black rooster and a white dove. Although it is unclear from the wording of the spell whether or not Auel is a fallen angel, he is invoked along with the demon Baal. If Auel still counts himself among the heavenly hierarchy, one wonders why he keeps such company. See also BAAL, *LIBER DE ANGELIS*.

Auras: A demon who appears in the form of a wild donkey. He is a carrier of corpses, moving them to wherever his summoner wishes. According to the *Book of Oberon*, he will give answer to all questions asked of him. He serves in the court of Egin, king of the north, where he is one of twelve chief ministers. See also *BOOK OF OBERON*, EGIN.

Autothith: The thirty-fourth demon associated with the thirty-six decans of the zodiac, Autothith appears in the pseudepigraphal *Testament of Solomon*. In that text, Autothith proclaims himself a demon of strife. He has the power to cause fighting and grudges between people. He can be driven away by invoking the power of the Alpha and Omega. In the McCown translation, these are instead Alpha and Beta. Although the McCown translation is generally viewed as the more accurate of the two, this difference seems strange. The name of the demon alters only slightly. In McCown, he is called Rhyx Authoth. *Rhyx* is a title meaning "king." See also SOLOMON.

Avnas: One of the seventy-two demons of the *Goetia*. His name is also spelled *Amy*. Avnas is a great president of Hell with thirty-six legions of lesser spirits at his command. According to Wierus's *Pseudomonarchia Daemonum*, he is partly of the Order of Angels and partly of the Order of Powers. He reveals treasures that have been hidden under the guardianship of other spirits. He also provides familiars and teaches both astrology and the liberal sciences. When he first manifests, he appears as a burning flame, but he can also put on a human form when commanded. This demon is also named in Scot's *Discoverie of Witchcraft* and the *Goetia of Dr. Rudd*. In this latter text, his name is rendered *Auns*, and he is said to be constrained by the angel Jejalel. See also *GOETIA*, RUDD, SCOT, WIERUS.

Axiôphêth: A vicious demon of disease that afflicts victims with consumption and hemorrhage. He is sometimes also known simply as Phêth, an abbreviated version of his full name. Axiôphêth appears in the extra-biblical *Testament of Solomon*, and is listed as the twenty-seventh demon associated with the thirty-six decans of the zodiac. All of these demons are said to appear with the heads of beasts and the bodies of men, and all of them torment humanity with some manner of ailment. Like his infernal brethren, Axiôphêth can be put to flight by uttering a sacred name. Normally, this is the name of an angel that holds sway over the demon. In a few cases, it is one of the Hebrew names of God. In Axiôphêth's case, however, the name that has power over him is given as "the elev-enth aeon." The true meaning of this phrase has been lost to the years. In the McCown translation of the *Testament of Solomon*, which varies slightly due to improved source material, this demon afflicts people with diarrhea and hemorrhoids. His name is presented as Rhyx Axesbuth, where *Rhyx* is a title meaning "king." He is put to flight using the power of his own name, rather than the obscure eleventh aeon. See also SOLOMON.

Axosiel: Commanding one thousand eight hundred and forty legions, Axosiel is one of twelve chief dukes who serve the infernal prince Soleviel. According to the *Ars Theurgia*, Axosiel is free to appear at any hour, day or night, and he only serves his demonic master every other year. See also *ARS THEURGIA*, SOLEVIEL.

Ayal: A name of the night-demon Lilith, transliterated from the original Hebrew. This name of Lilith appears in connection with Hebrew textual amulets intended for protection. Ayal appears in T. Schrire's 1966 publication *Hebrew Magic Amulets*. See also LILITH.

Aycolaytoum: In the fifteenth-century magickal text known as the *Liber de Angelis*, Aycolaytoum is a demon connected with the powers of the planet Jupiter. He serves beneath the infernal king Marastac, and he can be called upon to bend the will of a woman so that she will love the magician unfailingly. The name of this demon may be a corruption or even a play upon the word *acolyte*. It has its origins in the Greek term *akólouthos*, which means "follower" or "attendant." In the context of this spell, "follower" may be intended, as the demon has the power to make a "follower" of the intended victim of the spell. See also *LIBER DE ANGELIS*, MARASTAC.

Aym: A great and powerful duke said to rule over a total of twenty-six legions of infernal spirits. He is one of the seventy-two Goetic demons. According to Wierus's *Pseudomonarchia Daemonum*, he has three heads: that of a serpent, a man, and a cat. He comes riding a viper, and he carries a flaming brand in one hand. Aym is said to make people witty and to answer truthfully about private matters. With his flaming brand, he is said also to burn cities and towers. He is alternately known as *Harborym*. In Scot's *Discoverie of Witchcraft*, this secondary name is spelled *Harborim*. In the *Goetia*, his name is spelled *Aim*, and his human face is described as having two stars upon its head. The *Goetia of Dr. Rudd* says that he can be constrained in the name of the angel Melahel. See also *GOETIA*, RUDD, SCOT, WIERUS.

Ayylalu: In the 1977 Driscoll edition of the *Sworn Book of Honourius*, Ayylalu is named as one of the ministers of the demon-king Harthan. He is associated with the element water and the direction west. He has a jealous nature is also witty and agreeable. He has the power to provide strength and resolve and to help others avenge wrongs done to them. In addition, he can move things from place to place and provide darkness when needed, possibly to aid in thieving. When he manifests, his body is mottled in complexion and amply fleshed. See also HARTHAN, *SWORN BOOK*.

Azael: One of four evil angels said to guard the cardinal directions, Azael is named in the Faustian text *Magiae Naturalis et Innatural*, published in Passau in 1505. In this text, Azael is associated with the element of water. Henry Cornelius Agrippa was likely referring to this text when he mentioned Azael in connection with the demons of the cardinal directions. He gives Azael as an alternate name

used by "the Hebrew Doctors"[40] for Paimon, king of the west. Occultist S. L. MacGregor Mathers repeats this same information in his edition of the *Sacred Magic of Abramelin the Mage*. See also AGRIPPA, MATHERS, PAIMON.

Azathi: One of several demons named in the *Munich Handbook*. Azathi assists the magician in matters of divination. He is called upon in a spell that uses a young and virginal boy as an intermediary for the spirits. See also *MUNICH HANDBOOK*.

Azazel: In Leviticus 16, Azazel is named in connection with the scapegoat as part of the Jewish ritual that became Yom Kippur (the Day of Atonement). In these passages, two goats are selected and lots are cast to determine which goat is for Yahweh and which is for Azazel. The goat for Yahweh is sacrificed and its blood is used to purify the innermost portions of the temple. The goat for Azazel is kept alive, and after the sins of the people are confessed over it, the animal is driven into the desert to meet what is presumed will be a dismal fate.

Although these passages in Leviticus do not elaborate on who or what Azazel is, his location in the wastes of the desert draws a clear line to one of the chiefs of the Watcher Angels named in the *Book of Enoch*. Here, Azazel, sometimes under the variations Asael and Azael, is bound hand and foot in the desert as punishment for his role in leading the Sons of Heaven astray. The *Book of Enoch* contains two parallel stories explaining the corruption of the Watchers. In the first, Shemyaza leads his people astray through the sin of lust. In the second, Azazel is blamed for the dissemination of forbidden knowledge. Specifically, he teaches the

---

40. Agrippa's *Three Books of Occult Philosophy*, Tyson edition, p. 533.

crafting of weapons of war. Both threads of the story lead to Heavenly retribution: the destruction of the Watchers' children, their imprisonment in the desert, and, ultimately, the Flood. So begins a rich history of wickedness and rebellion associated with this figure. Together with his compatriot Shemyaza, sometimes named Shemhazai, Azazel features throughout Jewish folklore. In the *Chronicles of Jerahmeel*, Azazel appears with the angel Azah (likely an abbreviated form of Shemyaza), where the two are sentenced to be suspended forever between Heaven and Earth for their role in bringing wickedness to the mortal plane. Azazel, however, escapes and remains on earth, unrepentant. As an evil angel bent on leading others astray, he is named in the Haggadah, in Ginsburg's *Legends of the Jews*, and in the *Midrash of Shemhazai and Aza'el*. He appears also in Islamic lore and is mentioned by name in the Qu'ran in connection with the fallen angels Harut and Marut. He is sometimes also identified by Muslims as the so-called "peacock angel" of the Yezidi people, a much-maligned faith group with connections to the ethnic Kurds. The Yezidi are often erroneously typified as Devil worshippers as a result. Azazel, under the spelling *Azazil*, is sometimes given as the holy name of the Islamic Satan, Ibliss, before he fell. Azazel's connection to the peacock angel likely ties back to his depiction in the *Book of Enoch*. In addition to teaching the crafting of weapons and armor, Azazel also shared the secrets of making cosmetics, jewelry, and dyes. The wearing of many-colored clothes is frequently decried as a sign of wickedness throughout Old Testament material, sometimes explicitly because of Azazel's own colorful predilections.

In his 1921 publication *Immortality and the Unseen World*, the Reverend W. O. E. Oesterley argues convincingly that Azazel is an intentionally corrupted rendition of a Hebrew name meaning "strength of God." Henry Cornelius Agrippa gives Azazel as the Hebrew version of the demon Amaimon, king of the south. This attribution may be derived from *Magiae Naturalis et Innatural*, a text associated with the Faust tradition and published in Passau in 1505. In this work, Azazel is assigned to the element of air. Mathers repeats Agrippa's information in his *Sacred Magic of Abramelin the Mage*. See also AGRIPPA, AMAIMON, SHEMYAZA, WATCHER ANGELS.

Azemo: One of several demons said to serve Camuel, the infernal prince of the southeast. Azemo is named in the *Ars Theurgia*, where he is said to belong to the hours of the night. Despite this nocturnal affiliation, Azemo nevertheless manifests during the day. He is a mighty duke of Hell and ten ministering spirits serve beneath him. See also *ARS THEURGIA*, CAMUEL.

Aziabelis: Also named *Aziabel* in the *Sixth and Seventh Books of Moses*, this demon is said to appear in the form of a man wearing a large crown of pearls. One of the Seven Great Princes of Spirits, Aziabelis governs the spirits of the water and of mountains. When summoned, he is often amiably disposed toward the magician, and he can command the spirits under his dominion to yield up their treasures.

Aziel: According to the *Sixth and Seventh Books of Moses*, this spirit is one of seven great infernal princes. He is said to appear in the form of a wild ox. He is an excellent treasure-hunter, revealing valuables that have been secreted away both in earth and sea.

Azimel: One of several infernal dukes named in the court of the demon-king Maseriel. Azimel's name and seal appear in the *Ars Theurgia*, where he is said to rule over thirty lesser spirits of his own. He is affiliated with the hours of the day and the southern point of the compass. See also *ARS THEURGIA*, MASERIEL.

Baaba: A demon named in the *Ars Theurgia*. Baaba appears in the court of Barmiel, the first and chief spirit of the south under the emperor Caspiel. Baaba holds the rank of duke and he is said to serve his infernal lord during the hours of the night. Despite his rank, Baaba has no servants or lesser spirits under his command. See also *ARS THEURGIA*, BARMIEL, CASPIEL.

Baal: The Canaanite word for "god" or "lord." When the Israelites entered Canaan, they encountered the cult of Baal. Baal-worship was widespread in this ancient land, and each place had its own particular Baal. The Baals were the male deities, while the female counterparts were the Ashtaroths or Astaroths. The religion of Baal was, for a time, a direct competitor with the religion of Yahweh, and this competition gave rise to the endless polemics raised by the Patriarchs against Baal throughout the Old Testament. The incident with the golden calf was likely the result of Baal worship, and in several places through-out the Old Testament, the children of Israel are directly forbidden from making sacrifices to "the Baals." The ideological struggle presented in the Old Testament between the worship of Baal and the worship of Yahweh paved the way for Baal to become demonized in later Abrahamic culture. His title, "Prince Baal," is mocked in 2 Kings 1:2, 3, and 16, where the name is rendered "Baal-zebub," or "Lord of the Flies." This name, as Beelzebub, eventually became equated with one of the major devils of Hell. Another Baal, "Baal-peor," appears in Numbers 25:3 and Deuteronomy 4:3, eventually giving rise to the demon "Belphegor." Baal and its plural form, "Baalim" can also be found echoed again and again in the infernal literature as one of the great demons of Hell. Bael, an alternate form of Baal, has even developed into a completely separate deity. In the Elizabethan *Book of Oberon*, his name is rendered *Baall*, and he is one of the twelve highest-ranking servitors of Oriens, king of the east. In this text, Baall can compel the love of

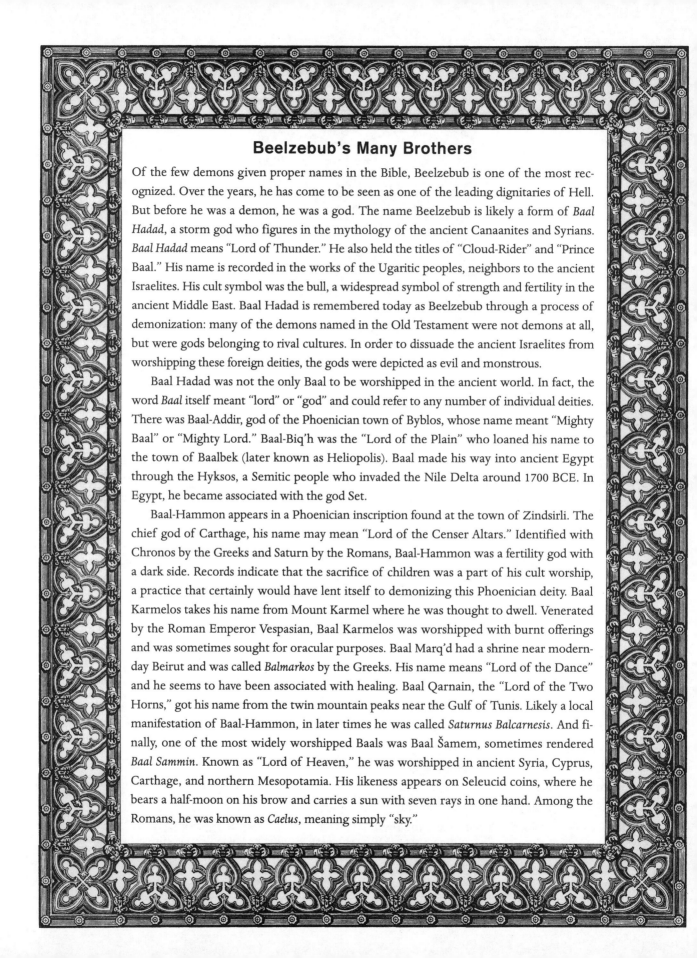

Beelzebub's Many Brothers

Of the few demons given proper names in the Bible, Beelzebub is one of the most recognized. Over the years, he has come to be seen as one of the leading dignitaries of Hell. But before he was a demon, he was a god. The name Beelzebub is likely a form of *Baal Hadad*, a storm god who figures in the mythology of the ancient Canaanites and Syrians. *Baal Hadad* means "Lord of Thunder." He also held the titles of "Cloud-Rider" and "Prince Baal." His name is recorded in the works of the Ugaritic peoples, neighbors to the ancient Israelites. His cult symbol was the bull, a widespread symbol of strength and fertility in the ancient Middle East. Baal Hadad is remembered today as Beelzebub through a process of demonization: many of the demons named in the Old Testament were not demons at all, but were gods belonging to rival cultures. In order to dissuade the ancient Israelites from worshipping these foreign deities, the gods were depicted as evil and monstrous.

Baal Hadad was not the only Baal to be worshipped in the ancient world. In fact, the word *Baal* itself meant "lord" or "god" and could refer to any number of individual deities. There was Baal-Addir, god of the Phoenician town of Byblos, whose name meant "Mighty Baal" or "Mighty Lord." Baal-Biq'h was the "Lord of the Plain" who loaned his name to the town of Baalbek (later known as Heliopolis). Baal made his way into ancient Egypt through the Hyksos, a Semitic people who invaded the Nile Delta around 1700 BCE. In Egypt, he became associated with the god Set.

Baal-Hammon appears in a Phoenician inscription found at the town of Zindsirli. The chief god of Carthage, his name may mean "Lord of the Censer Altars." Identified with Chronos by the Greeks and Saturn by the Romans, Baal-Hammon was a fertility god with a dark side. Records indicate that the sacrifice of children was a part of his cult worship, a practice that certainly would have lent itself to demonizing this Phoenician deity. Baal Karmelos takes his name from Mount Karmel where he was thought to dwell. Venerated by the Roman Emperor Vespasian, Baal Karmelos was worshipped with burnt offerings and was sometimes sought for oracular purposes. Baal Marq'd had a shrine near modern-day Beirut and was called *Balmarkos* by the Greeks. His name means "Lord of the Dance" and he seems to have been associated with healing. Baal Qarnain, the "Lord of the Two Horns," got his name from the twin mountain peaks near the Gulf of Tunis. Likely a local manifestation of Baal-Hammon, in later times he was called *Saturnus Balcarnesis*. And finally, one of the most widely worshipped Baals was Baal Šamem, sometimes rendered *Baal Sammin*. Known as "Lord of Heaven," he was worshipped in ancient Syria, Cyprus, Carthage, and northern Mesopotamia. His likeness appears on Seleucid coins, where he bears a half-moon on his brow and carries a sun with seven rays in one hand. Among the Romans, he was known as *Caelus*, meaning simply "sky."

either men or women. He also has the power to make people invisible. When he appears, he wears the form of a king and he speaks in a hoarse, raspy voice. See also ASTAROTH, BAEL, BALAAM, BEELZEBUB, BELPHEGOR, *BOOK OF OBERON*, ORIENS.

Baalberith: A demon named as Hell's Minister of Treaties in Berbiguier's nineteenth-century work *Les Farfadets*. In addition to his appearance in *Les Farfadets*, Baalberith's name also appears at the bottom of a document produced in the seventeenth-century trial of Urbain Grandier. The document, of dubious origin, is supposedly a pact signed by Grandier with Satan and a number of other high-profile devils in witness. Grandier was accused of witchcraft and diabolism in Loudun, France, and this little document was one of the things that sent him to the stake. Baalberith appears as "scriptor," and as far as this document is concerned, he seems to function in the role of scribe or secretary for Satan's pacts. Interestingly, Baalberith's name may clearly define this particular job description. *Baal* meant "lord" in several ancient Semitic languages, and was typically used as a title of an order of Canaanite gods, all duly objected to by the monotheistic Israelites and generally decried as demons. *Berith* is Hebrew for "covenant." It refers to the sacred covenants established between the Lord God and his chosen people, and it is used as one of the names of God. Here, perverted into the name of a demon, it seems to suggest that Baalberith is the "Lord of Covenants," which, in demonic lingo, would make him the Lord of Pacts. Notably, Berith appears as a demon in the *Goetia* and elsewhere in the grimoiric literature. See also BERBIGUIER, BERITH.

Baasan: An infernal king who serves alongside Belial in the court of Paimon, ruler of the spirits of the west. He has the power to bestow invisibility. His name appears in the Elizabethan grimoire known as the *Book of Oberon*. See also BELIAL, *BOOK OF OBERON*.

Bachiel: A demon in the court of the south. According to the *Ars Theurgia*, Bachiel is a servant of the demon-king Maseriel. He holds the title of duke and has thirty lesser spirits at his command. He is a night-demon, serving his infernal master only during the hours of darkness. See also *ARS THEURGIA*, MASERIEL.

Baciar: A demon from the *Ars Theurgia* governed by Raysiel, the infernal king of the north. Baciar appears during the hours of the day, and it is during these hours that he serves his king Raysiel. He holds the rank of duke and has fifty lesser spirits beneath him. See also *ARS THEURGIA*, RAYSIEL.

Badad: According to Mathers, the name of this demon is from Hebrew, and it means "the Solitary One." Badad serves in the hierarchy beneath Oriens, Paimon, Ariton, and Amaimon, the four demonic princes of the cardinal directions. He is summoned during one of the many days devoted to the Holy Guardian Angel rite, as outlined in the *Sacred Magic of Abramelin the Mage*. See also AMAIMON, ARITON, MATHERS, ORIENS, PAIMON.

Badalam: A demon named in the *Munich Handbook*. He is called upon in a spell intended to bind and compel a woman to love someone. Badalam is described as an infernal lord, and he is presented as having the power to command a series of subordinate demons to harry and afflict the target. Satan is named as one of the demons connected to him, although strangely he is presented as being in a subordinate position to Badalam. See also *MUNICH HANDBOOK*, SATAN.

Bael: A variation on the spelling of the demon Baal, which has come to represent a demon in its own right. He is named as the very first demon in the *Goetia*. In the early-seventeenth-century work *A Treatise on Angel Magic*, scholar Thomas Rudd connects Bael with the power of the east. According to Wierus's *Pseudomonarchia Daemonum*, Bael (spelled both *Baell* and *Baëll* in this work) is the first king of the power of the east. Baell is said to speak with a hoarse voice. When he manifests, he takes a form with three heads: the head of a man, a cat, and a toad. He has sixty-six legions of spirits under his command and he can be charged to make men invisible. In the *Goetia of Dr. Rudd*, Vehujah is the name of the angel said to have power over him. In the *Welsh Book of Incantations*, he is said to have diverse shapes, sometimes taking all of his forms at once. His seal is to be worn as a lamen on the breast of those daring enough to call upon him.

The demon Bael, from the 1863 edition of Collin de Plancy's *Dictionnaire Infernal*. From the archives of *Dark Realms Magazine*.

See also BAAL, *BOOK OF INCANTATIONS*, *GOETIA*, RUDD, WIERUS.

Bafamal: One of several demons named in the hierarchy of the infernal ruler Astaroth. Bafamal appears in Mathers's edition of the *Sacred Magic of Abramelin the Mage*. See also ASTAROTH, MATHERS.

Bahal: A demon said to serve his master Astaroth exclusively. Bahal appears in the Mathers translation of the *Sacred Magic of Abramelin the Mage* in connection with the Holy Guardian Angel working. See also ASTAROTH, MATHERS.

Bakaron: A demon named in connection with the Holy Guardian Angel working central to the *Sacred Magic of Abramelin the Mage*. Bakaron is said to serve the infernal lord Asmodeus. In his 1898 translation of this material, occultist Mathers suggests that the name of this demon comes from a Hebrew term meaning "first born." In his version, the name of this demon is spelled *Bacaron*. See also ASMODEUS, MATHERS.

Balaken: According to occultist S. L. Mathers, the name of this demon is connected to a word meaning "ravagers." Balaken is a servitor of the infernal prince Oriens. Through Oriens, Balaken is associated with the east. Both Oriens and Balaken are named in the *Sacred Magic of Abramelin the Mage*. Variations of this demon's name include *Balachan* and *Balachem*. See also MATHERS, ORIENS.

Balalos: A demon in service to Oriens, Paimon, Ariton, and Amaimon, the four infernal kings of the cardinal directions. Balalos appears in the *Sacred Magic of Abramelin the Mage*. In his 1898 translation of this work, occultist S. L. MacGregor Mathers suggests that the name of this demon may be derived from a Greek root meaning "to throw." See also AMAIMON, ARITON, MATHERS, ORIENS, PAIMON.

Balam: A demon of the Order of Dominions, Balam is the fifty-first demon of the *Goetia*. Balam also appears in Wierus's *Pseudomonarchia Daemonum*, where he is described as a great and terrible king. He has forty legions at his command and he has the power to make people invisible. When he manifests, he appears with three heads: that of a bull, a man, and a ram. He rides upon a bear and speaks with a hoarse voice. His eyes appear to burn like flames; instead of legs, he has the tail of a serpent. In the Welsh *Book of Incantations*, he governs thirty-six legions and can make anyone go invisible at will. He is reputed to answer truly to any questions put to him. According to Scot's *Discoverie of Witchcraft*, he carries a hawk upon his fist. In the *Goetia of Dr. Rudd*, he is said to be constrained by the angel Hahasiah. See also *BOOK OF INCANTATIONS*, *GOETIA*, RUDD, SCOT, WIERUS.

Balanchus: A demon who is summoned into one's bedchamber so he may be questioned. His name appears in a sixteenth-century spell recorded in the *Book of Oberon*. In this spell, the demon is summoned with incense of aloeswood (also known as jinko or agar), together with a short incantation, but this can only be done on a Wednesday in the hour of Mercury. If successful, Balanchus will appear as a bearded man and answer whatever questions one asks. The spell appears in the final folio of the grimoire known as the *Book of Oberon*. Although Balanchus is called upon specifically while his summoner is in bed, there is no suggestion of a sexual element, so Balanchus is probably not an incubus. See also *BOOK OF OBERON*.

Balath: A demon of illness and disease, he strikes down the healthy and can steal a person's wits. He also has powers of transportation, magickally carrying people from one place to another. He is cunning in the sciences and can earn fame and esteem for the one who conjures him. His name appears in the *Book of Oberon*, where he is listed among the twelve principal servitors of Paimon, king of the west. When summoned, Balath appears misshapen and speaks with a hoarse and rasping voice. See also *BOOK OF OBERON*, PAIMON.

Balfori: A servant of the arch-demon Beelzebub. Balfori appears in the *Sacred Magic of Abramelin the Mage*. In certain versions of this text, his name is spelled *Baalsori*. See also BEELZEBUB, MATHERS.

Balidcoh: A demon connected with the element of earth. He is described as both hard-working and patient with an even temper. He has an appearance that is both bright and beautiful, and he is one of the guardians of the treasures of the earth. He serves as a minister to the infernal king Albunalich, and he can give gifts of gold and precious stones to those who have gained his favor. For others, he guards these treasures jealously and will utterly frustrate their attempts to uncover the riches of the earth. According to Daniel Driscoll's 1977 edition of the *Sworn Book*, he is also an oracular spirit, having the ability to reveal things from the future as well as the past. He can bring rain, and he can also incite rancor and violence between men. See also ALBUNALICH, *SWORN BOOK*.

Balidet: In Dr. Rudd's early-seventeenth-century work *A Treatise on Angel Magic*, Balidet is described as a minister of king Maymon, one of the ruling spirits of the west. See also MAYMON, RUDD.

Balsur: A demon who commands an impressive total of three thousand eight hundred and eighty lesser spirits. Balsur holds the rank of duke, and according to the *Ars Theurgia*, he is one of several hundred dukes in service to the demon Amenadiel, infernal Emperor of the West. See also AMENADIEL, *ARS THEURGIA*.

Baoxes: A mighty duke in the hierarchy of the north who commands thousands of lesser spirits. Baoxes serves the demon-king Baruchas, at least according to the *Ars Theurgia*. Baoxes will only appear during hours and minutes that fall into the ninth portion of the day, assuming the day has been divided into fifteen equal portions. See also *ARS THEURGIA*, BARUCHAS.

Baphomet: A demon commonly depicted as a goat-headed being, often hermaphroditic, sometimes with wings. Baphomet made his (or her) entrance into the annals of demonology through transcripts of the trials of the Knights Templar. For a variety of reasons, most of them monetary, this knightly order came under suspicion in Europe, and the entire group was ultimately arrested and tried—with many of the knights being put to death. Among the charges brought against the Templars was the assertion that they had abandoned their Christian faith, instead worshiping a curious idol given the name *Baphomet*. Material that has survived from French troubadours active in the twelfth and thirteenth centuries suggests that the name *Bafomet* was originally a corruption of the name Muhammad which at the time was commonly rendered *Mahomet*. If this is true, then the figure of Baphomet may have come up in relation to the Templars as an implication that they had turned to the faith of their enemies, the Muslims. In the confessions extracted under torture from members of the Knights Templar, Baphomet is variously described as a figure with three heads, a cat, and a severed head. Because these descriptions were given under duress, there is no way

Baphomet, the Sabbatic Goat. From a pen drawing in the nineteenth-century French occult work *La Magie Noire*.

to know whether or not Baphomet had any real connections with the activities and beliefs of the Knights Templar—although it should be noted that no reference to this being appears in either the *Templar Rule* or in any other documents related to the Templars. The mystery of the figure lived on, however, and Baphomet resurfaced in the nineteenth century as a demonic idol associated with the occult. In 1854, occultist Eliphas Lévi included an image of Baphomet in his book *Rituals of High Magic*, describing the demon as the "Sabbatic Goat." The image used by Lévi strongly resembles depictions of the Devil that appear on early Tarot cards. It has become the *de facto* image associated with this being.

Baraquiel: A Watcher Angel named in the *Book of Enoch*. He is listed as one of the "chiefs of tens" and thus had command over a small troop of these fallen angels. When the Watchers left Heaven to come to earth, they allegedly brought with them forbidden secrets. Baraquiel is said to have taught the art of astrology to his human charges. Elsewhere in the text, his name is spelled *Baraqel*. See also WATCHER ANGELS.

Barbais: A spirit of the wilds who can teach the languages of birds and beasts. He also has the power to undo witchcraft. He manifests in the form of an archer from the wilds. (We might more readily describe him as a ranger.) He is one of twelve principal servitors of Oriens, king over the east. Not to be confused with Barbas, also of Oriens's court. His name may be a variation on *Barabares*, also described in the *Book of Oberon*. See also BARBARES, BARBAS, *BOOK OF OBERON*, ORIENS.

Barbares: A demon named in the *Book of Oberon* who appears in two separate entries (fifty-one and fifty-three). In both he is associated with archers and beasts. In the first entry he is said to take the form of a woodsman or archer. In the second entry he also appears as an archer but is half-man and half-beast, like the traditional representation of the zodiac sign Sagittarius. He holds influence over many rulers and can reveal innumerable hidden treasures. In addition, he can confer the power to understand the speech of birds and beasts. He is said to be accompanied by four minstrels bearing four trumpets of gold, silver, ivory, and brass. The *Book of Oberon*, the Elizabethan grimoire in which he appears, identifies his rank as both lord and viscount. Depending on which entry you source, twenty-six or twenty-nine legions of lesser spirits serve under him. An alternate version of his name is given as Barbates. Compare this name and powers to the Goetic demon *Barbatos*, identified in the *Pseudomonarchia Daemonum*, Scot's *Discoverie*

of Witchcraft, and Mathers's *Lesser Key of Solomon*. He also has much in common with the demon Barbais, also named in the *Book of Oberon*, and one may actually represent an alternate spelling of the other's name. Note that *barbaros* is Greek, meaning "strange" or "foreign," and gave rise to the word *barbarian*. See also BARBAIS, BARBATOS, *BOOK OF OBERON*.

Barbarus: In the fifteenth-century grimoire known as the *Munich Handbook*, Barbarus is described as holding the title of both count and duke. When summoned, he appears heralded by war trumpets. According to the text, this demon has the power to reveal the location of any treasure not protected by magick. As a demon of rank within the hierarchy of Hell, he has thirty-six legions of devils under his command. Note the similarity between this name and the more widely recognized Goetic demon, Barbatos. See also BARBATOS, *MUNICH HANDBOOK*.

Barbaryes: A martial demon, Barbaryes appears in the form of a soldier armed with a spear and carrying a banner. He strikes enemies blind, sapping their strength and deafening their ears. He can sway others into friendship. Named in the *Book of Oberon*, a grimoire dating to Elizabethan England, he is identified as a prince with fifty legions to serve him. See also *BOOK OF OBERON*.

Barbas: Barbas appears in the *Livre des esperitz*, a sixteenth-century French grimoire. He is also a well-positioned demon in the court of the east in the Elizabethan *Book of Oberon*. In that text, Barbas is one of a dozen other spirits serving King Oriens at the highest and most influential rank. His name is alternately given as Corbas. When he manifests, he takes the shape of a man. He holds the rank of chief. Among his powers, he can change people into beasts. There are several demons in the *Book of Oberon* who share very similar names, and at least some of these may represent alternate spellings of the same demon, including Barbais and Barbares. See also BARBAIS, BARBARES, *BOOK OF OBERON*, ORIENS.

Barbatos: One of the seventy-two demons listed in the *Goetia*. He also appears in the *Pseudomonarchia Daemonum* of Johannes Wierus and the *Discoverie of Witchcraft* by Reginald Scot. In these texts, he is identified as both a count and an earl. In Dr. Rudd's *Treatise on Angel Magic*, his rank is listed as duke. In most of these texts, he is said to rule over thirty legions of lesser spirits. The *Goetia of Dr. Rudd* gives this number as three hundred. When he manifests, Barbatos is reputed to appear with a grand retinue that includes troops and companies of infernal spirits, along with four kings. He can teach all manner of inhuman languages, from the barking of dogs to the songs of birds and the lowing of cattle. He can also detect treasure that has been hidden with enchantments. He was originally of the angelic Order of Virtues. He appears when the sun is in Sagittarius and he can be constrained by the angel Cahetel. He is also named in the Welsh grimoire known as the *Book of Incantations*. In this text, he is again a duke who governs thirty legions. See also *BOOK OF INCANTATIONS*, *GOETIA*, RUDD, SCOT, WIERUS.

Barbil: A demon said to serve the infernal king Barmiel. Through Barmiel, he is affiliated with the south. According to the *Ars Theurgia*, Barbil holds the rank of duke and has twenty lesser spirits under his command. He is said to serve his lord and master during the hours of the day. See also *ARS THEURGIA*, BARMIEL.

Barbis: A night-demon in the court of king Barmiel. Barbis is named in the *Ars Theurgia*, where he is said to hold the rank of duke. He has twenty ministering spirits at his command. He is connected with the south. See also *ARS THEURGIA*, BARMIEL.

Barbuel: According to the *Sixth and Seventh Books of Moses*, this demon appears in the form of a wild hog. He is a master of all arts and all hidden things, and he further has the ability to produce treasure for the magician. He is included in the *Sixth and Seventh Books of Moses* as one of the Seven Great Princes of Spirits. There is some evidence in this text that Barbuel is related to the Goetic demon Marbas. In the *Sixth and Seventh Books of Moses*, the name of Marbas is rendered Marbuel, only one letter off from Barbuel. See also MARBAS.

Barchan: In the fifteenth-century magickal manual known as *Liber de Angelis*, Barchan is the main demon who oversees the construction of the Ring of the Sun. This astrological talisman, once properly crafted, enables the magician to summon a black horse whenever there is need. Further, the ring can be used to bind the tongues of one's enemies. Use of the ring requires a number of animal sacrifices, and the magician is cautioned to wear this ring whenever any of these sacrifices are carried out. See also *LIBER DE ANGELIS*.

Barchiel: A demon tied to wetlands and watery locales. He is said to possess a good and courteous nature, and he has one thousand three hundred and twenty lesser spirits to attend him. Barchiel himself serves Hydriel, a so-called wandering duke who moves from place to place with his retinue. According to the *Ars Theurgia*, Barchiel manifests in the form of a serpent with a virgin's head. Elsewhere in the *Ars Theurgia*, this demon is described

Forbidden Tomes

Can books be inherently magickal or even cursed? This is a concept that we have been exposed to in both fiction and film. Perhaps the most infamous of these fictional tomes is the dreaded *Necronomicon*, a book so heinous and corrupt that to read its words is to court madness. The *Necronomicon* is of course a fictional work that stemmed from the imagination of early-twentieth-century horror author H. P. Lovecraft. Lovecraft invented the legend of the *Necronomicon* to make his spine-tingling tales seem to have a grain of truth—a technique called *supernatural realism*, which he felt heightened the fear factor of the stories.

Although the *Necronomicon* is a fictitious work, Lovecraft erected the foundation of his mythic tome on a very real history. The grimoires of medieval and Renaissance Europe served as inspirations for the *Necronomicon*, and in the past, people believed very firmly that these books had a dark power all their own. The art of writing was a fundamental part of the grimoiric tradition, and the significance placed upon both the written and spoken word stretches all the way back to the ancient world. There was a process to copying these books of magick, and the books themselves were often viewed as being charged with power. A late medieval text known as the *Book of Consecrations* contains instructions on how to reconsecrate a tome of magick in order to recharge the power of its spells.

The authors and copyists of these books were not the only ones to view them with inherent power. Clergy and Inquisitors often typified the grimoires as haunted objects which, once consecrated to the black arts, served as gateways to the infernal realm. Thus, figures like the fifteenth-century Florentine archbishop Antoninus, who famously burned any magickal books that he came across, held the opinion that the books themselves attracted the demons named within their pages. The grimoires were not only seen as beacons that invited demonic forces, but in at least a few instances, they were also treated as living entities in their own rights. In *Forbidden Rites*, Professor Richard Kieckhefer describes a book of magick that was actually put on trial in Dijon, France. On the sixth of August, 1463, the book in question was carefully examined in the presence of numerous local authorities. Once it was found guilty of being an infernal tome, the book was executed by committing it to the flames.

as a companion to the infernal duke Larmol. Both Barchiel and Larmol are tied to the wandering prince Menadiel. This version of Barchiel is bound to appear in the second hour of the day immediately following Larmol. Larmol is bound to the first hour. See also *ARS THEURGIA*, HYDRIEL, LARMOL, MENADIEL.

Barfas: A demon connected to the hours of the day. He holds the rank of chief duke and oversees twenty lesser spirits. Barfas is named in the *Ars Theurgia*, where he is said to serve in the court of the demon-king Malgaras. Through Malgaras, he is connected with the west. See also *ARS THEURGIA*, MALGARAS.

Barfos: In the *Ars Theurgia*, Barfos is a demon in the court of Usiel. Through Usiel, he is affiliated with the west. Barfos holds the rank of duke and commands forty lesser spirits of his own. He has the power to hide treasure through magick and enchantments, keeping it safe from prying eyes and from potential thieves. He is also reputed to be able to break the obscuring enchantments of others, revealing things that have been hidden. He serves his infernal master during the hours of the night. See also *ARS THEURGIA*, USIEL.

Bariet: A servitor of the demon Gediel. Bariet serves his infernal king during the hours of the day. His name and seal both appear in the *Ars Theurgia*. Through Gediel, Bariet is allied with the southern point of the compass. He holds the rank of duke and has twenty ministering spirits to attend his needs. See also *ARS THEURGIA*, GEDIEL.

Barkan: King over the spirits of the sun, at least according to the Elizabethan *Book of Oberon*. Barkan appears with his helpers Bybell, Mylalu, and Buesaba. They are all tall and thick-bodied, with gold-tinted skin. They move like the glittering of

the sky. Barkan carries a scepter and wears garments of yellow or gold, as befits his solar correspondence. He has the power to grant honors and noble titles, to break down hostilities between people, to cause or cure illness, and to procure all shining things—gold, jewels, and other fine treasure. If people suddenly break out into a sweat, it may mean King Barkan is near. See also *BOOK OF OBERON*, BUESABA, BYBELL, MYLALU.

Barmiel: The first and chief spirit named in the hierarchy of Caspiel, the infernal Emperor of the South. Barmiel appears in the *Ars Theurgia*, where he is said to rule over a total of thirty demonic dukes. Ten of these dukes serve him by day while the other twenty serve during the hours of the night. According to the *Ars Theurgia*, Barmiel is an essentially good-natured demon, inclined to obey those with the knowledge to command him. The name of this demon can also be found in the *Steganographia* of Trithemius, written around 1499. See also *ARS THEURGIA*, CASPIEL.

The seal of the demon Barmiel. He is a principal spirit of the south in the *Ars Theurgia*. Based on the design in the Henson *Lemegeton*. By M. Belanger.

Baron: A great prince who appears in a man's shape. According to the *Book of Oberon*, his office is to acquire treasure, up to six thousand pounds. He is conjured with circle, scepter, and two types of swords. A textual talisman required to control him is particularly grisly. It must be written on the skin of a fetal dog and inscribed in the blood of a lapwing. His name has several variations in the *Book of Oberon*: Baaran, Bareth, and Baryth. This last one suggests that he may have some connection to the Goetic demon Berith. See also BERITH, *BOOK OF OBERON*.

Baros: A night-demon in the court of the infernal king Maseriel. Through Maseriel, he is affiliated with the south. Baros holds the title of duke and has thirty lesser spirits beneath him. His name and seal appear in the *Ars Theurgia*. See also *ARS THEURGIA*, MASERIEL.

Barrett, Francis: The author of *The Magus, or Celestial Intelligencer*. Little is known about Barrett beyond what can be gleaned from this book. Barrett was likely born in the 1770s or 1780s. *The Magus* was published in 1801, and an advertisement in the front indicates that Barrett ran a school of occult studies from his home in London, at 99 Norton Street in the Marylebone area. Although the book bears Barrett's name as the author, it is more of a compilation of preexisting magickal texts. The book cribs from a variety of sources, including selections from Cornelius Agrippa's *Three Books of Occult Philosophy* and Peter de Abano's *Heptameron* (as translated by Robert Turner in 1655). Occult scholar Joseph Peterson views Barrett as a plagiarist who simply stole and reprinted other people's material, presenting it as his own. Considering that Barrett was running a school for magick, there is a slight possibility that *The Magus* was developed as a textbook and, as such, was intended to be an instructive compilation of

work that had come before. However, Barrett does little within the scope of *The Magus* to expand upon the concepts of natural and celestial magick as they had been put forth by his predecessors. See also AGRIPPA.

Barsafael: A demon of migraines, Barsafael can be put to flight by invoking the name of the angel Gabriel. This demon, along with several others attributed with the power to bring illness and disease to humans, appears in the pseudepigraphal *Testament of Solomon*. His name is also spelled Barsafel. See also SOLOMON.

Barsu: A demon holding the rank of duke in the hierarchy of the infernal prince Usiel, Barsu is said to reveal treasure. He can be called upon to conceal treasure as well, protecting it from both theft and discovery. He has command over thirty lesser spirits. The name and seal of this demon of appear in the *Ars Theurgia*. He owes fealty to the court of the west. See also *ARS THEURGIA*, USIEL.

Barsy: A demon called upon in archery so people do not miss their mark. Appropriately, he manifests in the guise of an archer. He is also reputed to help start wars. His name appears in the Elizabethan grimoire known as the *Book of Oberon*, where he is described as a great ruler and a captain with thirty legions under him. See also *BOOK OF OBERON*.

Bartax: Called upon to discover treasure, this demon assumes the guise of an elderly man. In the *Book of Oberon*, he is said to hold the position of a ruler with four legions beneath him. See also *BOOK OF OBERON*.

Barthas: A great prince who manifests in a beautiful form. He answers what is asked of him and reveals hidden things. He also changes people's faces at whim and teaches astronomy perfectly. According to the sixteenth-century French grimoire

Livre des esperitz, Barthas rules thirty-six legions of demons. See also *LIVRE DES ESPERITZ*.

Barton: This demon appears as a great bear with a dragon's tail. He is named in the Elizabethan grimoire known as the *Book of Oberon*, where it is said he will teach the lore of herbs and stones. He also has the power to transport people magickally over long distances. In the infernal hierarchies, he holds the rank of duke, with thirty legions of lesser devils in his retinue. See also *BOOK OF OBERON*.

Bartyn: A demon named in the Elizabethan grimoire known as the *Book of Oberon*. Bartyn is said to assume the form of a bear. In this form he will teach those who summon him the secret properties of stones and herbs. He is also reputed to transport people, although the text is unclear about whether he does so through an act of teleportation or simply by allowing his summoners to ride around on his back. Described as a strong duke, Bartyn is said to have twenty legions of spirits serving him. See also *BOOK OF OBERON*.

Baruch: One of the many demons named in the *Ars Theugia*. Baruch is not to be confused with the infernal king Baruchas named in the same text. Baruch is described as a companion demon. He follows his partner Chamor in all things. As Chamor manifests in the fifth hour of the day, Baruch manifests in the sixth hour. He serves the wandering prince Menadiel. See also *ARS THEURGIA*, BARUCHAS, CHAMOR, MENADIEL.

Baruchas: A demon found in the *Ars Theurgia* who is said to rule as a king over the direction east by north. Baruchas is fourth in line under Demoriel, the infernal Emperor of the North. Baruchas has a number of demonic servitors beneath him. They all hold the rank of duke and have scores of lesser spirits attending them. Interestingly, the word *Ba-ruch* is found in the Bible. According to the Book of Jeremiah, the prophet Jeremiah had a scribe by the name of Baruch. There is also an apocryphal text named after this scribe. The *Book of Baruch* is not recognized as gospel by any churches except those among eastern Christianity, such as the Greek Orthodox Church. Despite the similarities between the name of this demon and the biblical scribe, there is no indication of a direct connection between the two. Later in the *Ars Theurgia*, the name of this demon is spelled *Barachus*. King Baruchas is also named in Johannes Trithemius's *Steganographia*. See also *ARS THEURGIA*, DEMORIEL.

Baruel: In his 1898 translation of the *Sacred Magic of Abramelin the Mage*, Mathers renders this demon's name as meaning "nourishment from God." Baruel is said to serve the demon Magoth. In the Mathers edition is this demon said to also serve Kore. See also KORE, MAGOTH, MATHERS.

Baruth: In the *Munich Handbook*, Baruth is one of several demons named in a spell for divination. He is connected with the art of scrying. His name is likely a variation of the demon Baruch. See also BARUCH, *MUNICH HANDBOOK*.

Basiel: A chief duke in the court of Malgaras. His fealty to Malgaras ties him to the west. Basiel has only ten lesser spirits at his command. He is named in the *Ars Theurgia*, where it is said that he serves his demonic master by night, only manifesting in the hours between dusk and dawn. See also *ARS THEURGIA*, MALGARAS.

Bason: One of the twelve principal ministers in the court of the west under King Paimon. This three-headed demon rides a wild bear and carries a goshawk on his wrist. Of his three heads, one is a raven's, one is a dog's, and one is a man's. When he speaks, he vomits fire. He is said to answer all questions and have the power to grant invisibility. His name appears in the *Book of Oberon*, an Elizabethan grimoire. See also BOOK OF OBERON, PAIMON.

Batariel: One of the fallen angels named in the *Book of Enoch*. These angels, called *Watchers, Irin,* or *Grigori,* arranged themselves in groups of ten, with each group having its own chief. Batariel is described as one of these "chiefs of tens." He helped to lead the Watchers to their fall. See also WATCHER ANGELS.

Bathin: The eighteenth demon named in the *Goetia,* Bathin appears in a number of texts, including Rudd's *Treatise on Angel Magic,* Scot's *Discoverie of Witchcraft,* and Wierus's *Psueodmonarchia Daemonum.* Scot gives an alternate name of *Mathim* for this demon. Scot's source material, the *Pseudomonarchia Daemonum,* presents slightly different spellings of both of these names. According to the *Pseudomonarchia,* the name of this demon is *Bathym,* and the alternate name is *Marthim.* Both texts agree that this demon is a great and strong duke ruling over thirty legions of infernal spirits. He is said to appear as a very strong man with a serpent's tail. He comes riding a pale horse, much like the specter of Death in the biblical Book of Revelation. He has the power to transport people suddenly from place to place. In addition, he understands the virtues of herbs and precious stones, and will presumably impart this knowledge to those that call him up. He rules over a total of thirty legions of infernal spirits. According to the *Goetia of Dr. Rudd,* the angel Caliel has the power to command and constrain this demon. See also *GOETIA,* RUDD, SCOT, WIERUS.

Batternis: According the Mathers translation of the *Sacred Magic of Abramelin the Mage,* the name of this demon is based on a word meaning "to use vain repetitions" and thus can be taken to mean "the Babbler." Batternis serves the infernal lord Magoth. In other versions of the *Abramelin* material, his name is rendered *Batirmiss* and *Batrinas.* See also MAGOTH, MATHERS.

Batthan: According to the Peterson translation of the *Sworn Book of Honorius,* Batthan is the king of the spirits of the sun. Batthan and his court are bright demons. Their skins are golden in color and they behave with all gentleness. Batthan has the power to make people wealthy, powerful, and well-loved. He can also magickally maintain a person's health. The angels Raphael, Cashael, Dardyhel, and Hanrathaphael have power over this demon. See also *SWORN BOOK.*

Baxhathau: A servant of the demon Batthan. Baxhathau is one of the demons connected with the sun. The angels Raphael, Cashael, Dardyhel, and Hanrathaphael rule him and all spirits of the sun. According to the Peterson translation of the *Sworn Book of Honorius,* this demon has the power to make people healthy, wealthy, powerful, and well-loved. Baxhathau is one of four demons from the hierarchy of the sun said also to be subject to the north wind. See also BATTHAN, *SWORN BOOK.*

Baysul: A demon in service to the infernal king Abdalaa. Baysul is mentioned by name in the fifteenth-century magickal manual known as the *Liber de Angelis,* where he is invoked as part of a spell to compel a woman's love. See also ABDALAA, *LIBER DE ANGELIS.*

Baytivakh: A transliterated Hebrew name attributed to the night-demon Lilith. A large number of Hebrew textual amulets remain that were intended to protect women and children against Lilith's attacks. According to T. Schrire's 1966 book *Hebrew*

Magic Amulets, Baytivakh is one of the many Lilith-names that can be found on these amulets. See also LILITH.

Bealphares: In Dr. Rudd's early-seventeenth-century work, *A Treatise on Angel Magic*, this demon makes an appearance as a great king or prince of the air. His name also appears in Scot's *Discoverie of Witchcraft*. In this text, Bealphares appears in a summoning spell. The spirit is called up and dismissed again in order to practice conjuration. He appears in the *Book of Oberon* under the spelling *Beallphares*. Here, he is an efficient and reliable demon who serves in the court of Oriens, king of the east. He is described as an excellent carrier, fetching treasure as well as lost or stolen items. See also *BOOK OF OBERON*, ORIENS, RUDD, SCOT.

Beball: A king of the infernal realms who is mentioned in connection with the demon Paimon in Wierus's *Pseudomonarchia Daemonum*. According to this text, Beball is an attendant of the demon Paimon, even though he himself holds the rank of king. If a sacrifice is made to Paimon, Beball typically appears alongside his partner Abalam as part of Paimon's retinue. In the *Goetia*, these demons go by the names *Labal* and *Abali*. See also ABALAM, PAIMON, WIERUS.

Bechar: A demon named in the *True Keys of Solomon*. Bechar is said to serve beneath chief Sirachi, who himself serves directly beneath Lucifer. Given his powers, Bechar could easily be called the demon of Forteana. He is said to govern rains of blood, toads, and other phenomenon in addition to having the power to cause more natural meteorological events. See also SIRACHI, LUCIFER.

Bechaud: A demon named in Peterson's *Grimorium Verum*. He is supposed to be conjured only on Fridays. He serves under Syrach, a duke of Hell, and is the third demon in that duke's retinue. When summoned by the magician, Bechaud can be commanded to exercise power over storms of all sorts, raising hail, lightning, and strong winds. He even has power over toads, and can presumably make these rain from the sky as well. See also SYRACH.

Béchet: The demon ruling Friday. Béchet appears in the *Grimoire of Pope Honorius*. He is likely a variation on the demons Bechar and Bechaud from the related *Grimorium Verum* and *True Keys of Solomon*. See also BECHAR, BECHAUD, *GRIMORIUM VERUM*, *TRUE KEYS*.

Bedary: A duke in the hierarchy of the infernal Emperor of the East, Carnesiel. Bedary's seal, integral for summoning this demon, appears in the second book of the *Lesser Key of Solomon*, known as the *Ars Theurgia*. See also *ARS THEURGIA*, CARNESIEL.

Beelzebub: The name of this demon first appears in the Bible in 2 Kings, where he is described as being the false god worshipped by the Philistine people at the city of Ekron. Rabbinical texts interpreted the name to mean Lord of the Dunghill, and hence, Lord of the Flies. Baal-zebub, as it appears in the Bible, probably means "Prince Baal," but *zebub* is close enough in sound to *zebal*, meaning "to make dung," that it allowed the name to be twisted by those ancients opposed to the worship of this Middle Eastern deity. While Beelzebub is certainly viewed as a false god in the Old Testament, it is not until the New Testament that he becomes styled as the very chief of demons. The passage in Matthew 12:24 describes Beelzebub as the Prince of Demons, and this cinches Beelzebub's place in the infernal hierarchy for years to come.

In the Mathers edition of the *Grimoire of Armadel*, Beelzebub, under the name *Belzebut*, is said to join together with Lucifer and Astaroth to teach the summoner about the rebellion and fall of the angels. In the *Sacred Magic of Abramelin the Mage*, Beelzebub is said to have the power to transform men into animals and animals into men. He is a sower of discord and helps to cast curses and cause harm. He is named as one of the eight sub-princes who rule over all the other demons. In the 1863 edition of Collin de Plancy's *Dictionnaire Infernal*, the demon Beelzebub is depicted directly as an infernal fly with a skull-and-crossbones motif on its wings. In the *Grand Grimoire*, Beelzebub, spelled *Belzebuth*, is listed as the Prince of Hell. In an 1821 work by Frenchman Charles Berbiguier, Beelzebub supplants Satan as the ruler of Hell. He is given the very colorful title of Supreme Chief of the Infernal Empire and the Founder of the Order of the Fly. In the *True Keys of Solomon*, Beelzebub is said to rule all the spirits of the Americas together with the demon Astaroth.

Beelzebub also appears in the *Testament of Solomon* under the name *Beelzeboul*. Here, he claims primacy among the demons because he is not the child of an angel but an angel himself. He further claims to have been the First Angel of the First Heaven before his fall, a statement that ties him to both Shemyaza and Azazel in the Watcher tradition and Lucifer in more standard views of demonology. As a result of his supposed angelic status, Beelzeboul claims to answer only to one of the names of God. Several texts spell his name *Belzebuth*. Beelzebub appears in a hierarchy of evil spirits outlined in the grimoire known as the *Janua Magica Reserata*, or *Keys to the Gateway of Magic*. Here he is a prince ruling over the *Pseudothei*, or False Gods. They are the first of nine orders of demons. See also ASTAROTH, AZAZEL, BAAL, BELZEBUTH, BEELZEBOUL, BERBIGUIER, DE PLANCY, *GRAND GRIMOIRE*, LUCIFER, MATHERS, SHEMYAZA, SOLOMON.

Behemoth: This great beast, described in detail in chapter 40 of the Book of Job, is a terrible power that walks the land. Described as an herbivore that eats grass "as an ox," Behemoth is nevertheless a fearsome, deadly beast. The creature has bones like iron and brass, with a tail so powerful that it sweeps with the strength of a cedar. He resides near brooks and fens, and supposedly no snare can entrap him. In later stories, he is depicted as struggling against the great Leviathan, a sea creature equally fierce and powerful. The Behemoth is said to gore the Leviathan with his great horns as the Leviathan leaps from the sea to attack. In the end, God slays both of these horrific beasts with his mighty sword. There are parallels between Behemoth and a creature of Babylonian myth, Bahamut. Both represent implacable primordial forces. Many of the traditional biblical depictions of the Behemoth seem to closely mirror Mithraic images that show the god

In the Mithraic Mysteries, the great beast can only be slain by its maker. The same is said of the biblical Behemoth. From the *Encyclopedia of Occultism* by Lewis Spence, courtesy of Dover Publications.

Mithras slaying an ox. It is likely that the idea of the Behemoth was at least partly inspired by the Bull of Heaven, a mythic creature tied to the goddess Ishtar that plays a significant role in the *Epic of Gilgamesh*. In Berbiguier's infernal hierarchy (often misattributed to Johannes Wierus) Behemoth is given a relatively low rank in the demonic hierarchy. He holds the position of Grand Cup Bearer, like some infernal Ganymede. See also LEVIATHAN.

Belamith: According to the *Clavicula Salomonis*, Belamith has the power to confer invisibility to those who summon him. He is conjured as part of an invisibility spell overseen by Almiras, a demon described as the Master of Invisibility. The same invisibility spell, and thus the same set of demons, also appears in the Mathers translation of the *Sacred Magic of Abramelin the Mage*. See also ALMIRAS, *CLAVICULA SALOMONIS*, MATHERS.

Belbel: A demon said to attack the hearts and minds of men, distorting them. He is one of the demons associated with the thirty-six decans of the zodiac in the *Testament of Solomon*. According to that text, written approximately around the last few centuries before the Common Era, Belbel can be driven off by invoking the name of the angel Araêl. In the same text, this angel also holds sway over the demon Sphandôr. According to a later translation by McCown, which was drawn from a more complete collection of source texts, the angel who has power over Belbel is actually named Kerael. See also SOLOMON, SPHANDÔR.

Beleth: A mighty and terrible king who rides a pale horse, like Death in the Book of Revelation. He is named in the Welsh grimoire known as the *Book of Incantations*, where he is said to belong to the Order of Powers. The sound of trumpets and other musical instruments marks his presence. He is not an easy spirit to deal with, and the *Book of Incantations* cautions those summoning him to have a hazel stick and a silver ring prepared ahead of time to help compel Beleth to obedience. His main office concerns love between men and women, which he can inspire. He rules either eighty-five or fifty-five legions. The handwritten text is unclear. See also *BOOK OF INCANTATIONS*.

Belferith: Identified specifically as a *demon malignus*, or "malignant demon," in the *Munich Handbook*, Belferith's name appears in connection with a curse. When the magician seeks to strike an enemy by robbing them of their senses, this demon, along with several others, must be summoned and set upon the target in order to accomplish the task. See also *MUNICH HANDBOOK*.

Belial: Sometimes also rendered *Beliaal* or *Beliar*, this name is derived from a Hebrew term most often translated as meaning "worthless" or "without value." Belial appears numerous times in the Old Testament of the Bible, especially in the King James Version. Here, the word is almost always used in conjunction with a class of people, such as "sons of Belial" and "daughters of Belial." In more modern translations of the Bible, including the New King James Version, the name Belial is frequently omitted from these passages and translated directly into "wickedness" or "perversion." In 2 Corinthians 6:15, Belial is depicted in direct opposition to Christ, and this passage is read by many to indicate that *Belial* is another name for Satan.

Because of the way this name is treated in the Old Testament material, there is some debate about whether Belial was intended as a proper name at all. Few modern biblical translators currently approach it as a proper name. However, Belial nevertheless enjoys quite a reputation in several books connected with the biblical tradition. Chief among these is the *Testaments of the Twelve Patriarchs*. Numbered among the apocryphal ("hidden") scriptures connected with the Old Testament, the *Testaments of the Twelve Patriarchs* supposedly contain the final words and commands of the twelve sons of Jacob, father of the nation of Israel. In these books, Belial, styled *Beliar* by the Hellenized Jewish author of the *Testaments*, is directly depicted as God's adversary. Like the more familiar Satan, Beliar is a tempter, and when the children of Israel stray from the path of righteousness, they play into his hands. In another apocryphal text, the *Ascension of Isaiah*, Belial, named *Beliar* and *Matanbuchus*, is depicted as the angel of lawlessness and true ruler of the earthly world.

Belial appears also in a famous text of the Dead Sea Scrolls designated 1QM, known as the "War of the Sons of Light and the Sons of Darkness." Here, Belial is described as the "angel of hostility." His dominion is darkness, and he exists to bring wickedness and guilt to the sons of man. In the cosmic war depicted in this document, Belial is the leader of the Sons of Darkness, and all of the angels under him are angels of destruction. Belial appears in another fragment from Qumran known as the *Testament of Amram*. Here he is similarly depicted as the head of the armies of the Sons of Darkness, working in direct opposition against Michael, who heads the armies of the Sons of Light. In this text, Belial is described as having a dark and frightful countenance, with a "visage like a viper."[41] His titles include the King of Evil and the Prince of Darkness.

In the *Goetia*, Belial appears as the sixty-eighth Goetic demon. He is attributed with the rank of king among the demons, and he is said to have been created second only after Lucifer. When summoned, he grants offices and other distinctions to his supplicants, and he also brings favor to the magician from both friends and foes. He is said to speak with a comely voice and to appear in the form of not one, but two beautiful angels standing in a chariot of fire. The description of two angels is almost certainly an error transmitted by this text, as all other grimoires dealing with Belial describe only one angel in connection with his appearance. According to the *Book of Incantations*, Belial was created next after Lucifer and belongs to the same angelic order. He appears in the form of a beautiful angel sitting in a chariot of fire. He gives excellent familiars and governs eighty or fifty legions. In the *Book of Oberon*, his name is spelled *Beliall* and he is identified as one of the twelve principal spirits ministering to Paimon, king of the west. According to this text, he appears as a sweet-voiced angel who rides a chair of fire (possibly an error originally intended to read "chariot"). His powers in this text are also concerned with fame and favor. He is also named in Dr. Rudd's *Treatise on Angel Magic*.

In a traditional hierarchy by demonologist Charles Berbiguier, Belial is listed as Hell's ambassador to Turkey. Belial also enjoyed widespread popularity in fifteenth-century Europe through a widely circulated morality tale recorded in the *Buche de Belial* by Jacobus de Teramos. This depicts Belial as an active tempter of humanity, and the tradition of the *Buche de Belial* may have helped to inspire the Faust legend. In Mathers's translation of the *Sacred Magic of Abramelin the Mage*, Belial is identified as one of the four principal spirits overseeing all the others. In this, he is ranked alongside Satan, Leviathan, and Lucifer.

---

41. Jean-Yves Lacoste, *Encyclopedia of Christian Theology*, p. 66.

In Wierus's *Pseudomonarchia Daemonum*, the name of the demon is given as *Beliall*. Together with Bileth and Asmoday, he is listed as one of three top-ranking demons in a collection of seventy-two infernal kings imprisoned by King Solomon in a vessel of brass. In this text, he is described as the father and seducer of all the other angels that fell. He is an extremely deceitful spirit, and he will only tell the truth if compelled under the threat of divine names. When he manifests, the *Pseudomonarchia* says that he takes the form of a single beautiful angel in a fiery chariot. Later in the same passage, he is said to also take the form of an exorcist in the bonds of spirits. He rules over a total of eighty legions, some from the Order of Virtues and some from the Order of Angels. He provides excellent familiars. According to the *Goetia of Dr. Rudd*, Belial is constrained by the angel Habujah. This text also states that Belial belongs to the same angelic order as Lucifer. In a hierarchy of evil spirits recorded in the *Janua Magica Reserata*, Belial is named as the Prince of the Third Order. This order is known as the *Vasa Iniquitatus*, or "Vessels of Iniquity." See also ASMODAY, BERBIGUIER, BILETH, *BOOK OF INCANTATIONS*, *BOOK OF OBERON*, *GOETIA*, *JANUA MAGICA RESERATA*, LEVIATHAN, LUCIFER, MATANBUCHAS, PAIMON, RUDD, WIERUS.

Bell: Another name for the demon Beelzebub, this spelling appears in the Elizabethan grimoire known as the *Book of Oberon*. According to that text, he is one of three primary devils who oversee all the other infernal spirits. His is said to give gold and silver, teach all sciences, and provide demonic servants. Bell, whose name is also given as Bellsabube and Bellzebub in the text, is described as the prince of devils who was of the Order of Cherubim prior to his fall. Millions of devils or wicked spirits minister to him. Curiously, the *Book of Oberon* says that he was worshipped as the God Charon before the time of Solomon. Charon, of course, was the demi-divine ferryman of the underworld in Greek myth. The *Book of Oberon* warns that he is known to slay conjurors who call him up incorrectly. See also BEELZEBUB, *BOOK OF OBERON*.

Belphegor: Mentioned as "Baal-peor" in Numbers 25:3 and Deuteronomy 4:3, Belphegor started life as a Moabite god. In the continuing struggle among the early biblical Patriarchs to keep their religion pure, he was demonized so that the children of Israel would not turn away from their monotheistic worship of Yahweh. According to Waite's presentation of the *Grand Grimoire*, Belphegor is Hell's duly appointed ambassador to France. This colorful attribution stems from the French demonologist Charles Berbiguier. See also BAAL, BERBIGUIER, WAITE.

In the *Goetia of Dr. Rudd*, the seal of the demon Belial differs slightly from other versions of the *Goetia*. From a talisman by M. Belanger.

Necromancy and the Black Arts

In Professor Richard Kieckhefer's work *Forbidden Rites*, the fifteenth-century *Munich Handbook* is described as a necromancer's manual. For modern readers, this might seem a little confusing, as the contents of the *Munich Handbook* have very little to do with raising the dead. In modern magick, the term *necromancy* has come to indicate a method of magick that harnesses the dead—usually in body as well as soul. It's derived from the Greek roots *necro*, meaning "dead," and *mantia*, meaning "magic" or "divination." Taken literally, necromancy is a method of divination that makes use of the dead, although it tends to have much darker connotations than simple methods of spirit communication. Necromancy conjures images of people hanging out in graveyards and digging up corpses in the middle of the night, resurrecting them as shambling hordes.

Some of that dark reputation may actually be a holdover from the Middle Ages, but not because necromancy and grave-robbing were always thought to go hand in hand. In medieval Europe, necromancy was widely used as another term for demonic magick. Books from the fourteenth and fifteenth centuries indicate that the word *necromancy* was often used interchangeably with the term *nigromancy* (sometimes also spelled *nygromancy*). Nigromancy was a catch-all term for the black arts. Writing in the first half of the fifteenth century, scholar Johannes Hartlieb identifies *nigromancia* as one of the seven forbidden arts. In his *Book of All Forbidden Arts*, a treatise written between the years 1456 and 1464, he typifies it as "the worst of all, because it proceeds with sacrifices and services that must be rendered to the devils."* Here, nigromancy is clearly tied to demons and not the dead, and yet in the 1496 printing of the book *Dives and Pauper*, nigromancy is defined as witchcraft done by dead bodies. This shows the blurry lines between these two terms. Just as a practitioner of nigromancy might be seen as someone who harnessed the bodies of the dead for their nefarious work, so, too, could a necromancer be seen as someone who called up and compelled demons to affect their magick. This is the definition of necromancer at work in the *Munich Handbook*, where many of the spirits conjured in the text are specifically defined as demons.

---

* Richard Kieckhefer, *Forbidden Rites*, p. 33.

Belsay: A chief duke ruled by Raysiel, an infernal king of the north. Belsay is a demon of the night, reputedly ill-tempered and stubborn. He only manifests during the hours of the night. His name and sigil appear in the *Ars Theurgia*, where he is said to command twenty infernal spirits. See also *ARS THEURGIA*, RAYSIEL.

Belzebuth: Variant spelling of Beelzebub that appears in the seventeenth-century Venetian grimoire *Secrets of Solomon*. In that text, Belzebuth is one of three prime rulers of Hell, along with Lucifer and Elestor. He holds the rank of prince, one step beneath Lucifer's position of emperor. The *Secrets of Solomon*, like several texts that came after it, assigns demonic overlords by continent. Thus, Belzebuth oversees all demonic affairs in Africa. In the *Secrets of Solomon*, Belzebuth is said to appear in the form of a fly, but also sometimes takes the shape of a monstrous calf with human feet. In this form, he howls like a wolf and vomits flame when angered. Identified as an "earthly" (as opposed to "airy," or ethereal) demon, he is powerful enough to take physical form. This variant spelling of his name also appears in the *Livre des esperitz*, a French grimoire from the sixteenth century. See also BEELZEBUB, ELESTOR, *LIVRE DES ESPERITZ*, LUCIFER, *SECRETS OF SOLOMON*.

Benodiel: A demon accorded the title of duke. He has three hundred and ninety lesser spirits at his command, and he serves in the retinue of the infernal prince Menadiel in the hierarchy of the west. Benodiel is bound only to appear during the seventh planetary hour of the day. According to the *Ars Theurgia*, he is immediately followed by Nedriel, who appears in the eighth hour. See also *ARS THEURGIA*, MENADIEL, NEDRIEL.

Benoham: According to the *Ars Theurgia* contained in the Henson edition of the *Lesser Key of Solomon*, Benoham is a duke in the hierarchy of the east. He serves the infernal emperor Carnesiel and can be summoned in his name. See also *ARS THEURGIA*, CARNESIEL.

Berbiguier, Charles: A Frenchman who lived between 1765 and 1851, Berbiguier believed himself to be plagued by a host of demons whom he referred to as *farfadets* ("goblins"). His full name was Alexis-Vincent-Charles Berbiguier and he lived near Terre-Neuve du Thyme. He claimed not only to have been repeatedly victimized by these demons (among other things, they were responsible for the death of his pet squirrel, Coco), but he also allegedly carried out extensive correspondence with them, both sending and receiving letters from the various emissaries of Hell. Berbiguier wrote and illustrated his three-volume autobiography and published it between the years of 1818 and 1821, for the benefit of others who might learn how to battle with demons through his own experiences. He titled the massive, rambling work *Les Farfadets, ou tous les démons ne sont pas de l'autre monde* (Goblins, or Not All Demons Are from the Other World).

In this work, he offers extensive information on the court of Hell, describing Satan as a deposed prince, with Beelzebub ruling in his place. Rhotomago, the demon who served as Berbiguier's personal tormentor, supposedly answered directly to Beelzebub. The hellish hierarchy gets even more colorful—apparently patterning his concept of the infernal court off of the court of Louis XIV, Berbiguier goes on to define roles for various demons found in no other existing demonic hierarchy. This includes a Gentleman of the Bedchamber, a Lord of the Casinos, and even a Grand Pantler of Hell!

The word *pantler*, for the record, comes from the French word for bread, *pain*, and is totally unrelated to pants. In the court of Europeans kings, the pantler was the master of the pantry.

Berbiguier's work was known by Collin de Plancy, the eminent demonographer responsible for the extensive *Dictionnaire Infernal*. De Plancy disparagingly referred to Berbiguier as the "Don Quixote of demons," but nevertheless included Berbiguier's material on demons in his dictionary. Several occult scholars, including A. E. Waite, drew upon Berbiguier's material via de Plancy, frequently mistaking the original source of the hierarchy. Waite, for example, attributed much of Berbiguier's work to Johannes Wierus. See also BEELZEBUB, DE PLANCY, RHOTOMAGO, WAITE, WIERUS.

Berith: The twenty-eighth demon of the *Goetia*. According to both Wierus's *Pseudomonarchia Daemonum* and Scot's *Discoverie of Witchcraft*, Berith is known by three different names. Some know him as *Beal*, a possible variation of Bael and/or Baal. Among necromancers, he is said to be called Bolfri (Scot renders this name *Bolfry*). Finally, his name among Jews is said to be Berith (which Scot renders *Berithi*). *Berith* is, in fact, a Hebrew word, but it is not connected with anything infernal. In the Hebrew language, *berith* means "covenant," and it is used most often to refer to the covenant between God and his chosen people. How exactly this word made its way into demonology as the name of a demon is something of a puzzle, although considering the vast number of Hebrew names—specifically names of God—co-opted by predominantly Christian medieval magicians for their invocations, this corruption of *Berith* should not exactly be surprising.

In both the *Pseudomonarchia Daemonum* and Scot's *Discoverie of Witchcraft*, Berith is said to appear in the form of a red soldier. His clothes and horse are also red in color. These details very firmly establish Berith as a martial demon, as the planet Mars was believed to be tied to soldiers, warfare, and the color red. Curiously, his powers do not seem to include anything particularly connected with Mars. He is said to turn all metals into gold and to confer dignities. He speaks on the occult as well as all things concerning the past, present, and future. In this, he is said to speak truthfully, but later in the same passage, he is specifically described as a liar. This may be a warning to indicate that he will lie freely unless otherwise compelled by the magician. He is ranked as a great and terrible duke with twenty-six legions of spirits beneath him. The *Goetia of Dr. Rudd* gives his alternate names as *Beale* and *Bolfry*. He is said to be governed by the angel Seechiah. In the *Munich Handbook*, Berith is a guardian of the east called upon to provide a cloak of invisibility. In the *Book of Oberon*, he is described as one of twelve principal demons serving the king of the south, Amaimon. His preferred appearance is that of a knight with two red crowns and a red horse, reaffirming his planetary connections with Mars. In the *Livre des esperitz*, his name is spelled *Berteth*. His powers similarly encompass alchemical transformation and societal influence. See also AMAIMON, BAAL, BAEL, *BOOK OF OBERON*, *GOETIA*, *LIVRE DES ESPERITZ*, RUDD, SCOT, WIERUS.

Beschard: A demon under Duke Syrach named in the seventeenth-century Venetian grimoire *Clavicula Salomonis de Secretis*, or *Secrets of Solomon*. Beschard is a count reputed to command the weather. He can summon hail, lightning, hoarfrost, and even supernatural phenomena, such as rains of toads, stones, or blood. He can also be called upon to still stormy skies. See also *SECRETS OF SOLOMON*, SYRACH.

Betasiel: According to the *Ars Theurgia*, Betasiel is a chief duke under the command of Raysiel, a demon-king of the north. Betasiel serves his master during the hours of the day and he will only appear to mortals during those same hours. He has fifty lesser spirits to serve him. See also *ARS THEURGIA*, RAYSIEL.

Betel: In the *Grimoire of Armadel* as translated by occultist S. L. MacGregor Mathers, Betel is described as a docile spirit. It is best to summon him outside, preferably in a forest or a secluded garden. He is said to teach the wisdom of Adam and to reveal both the virtues of the Creator and the laws that govern those virtues. Like many of the demons in the *Grimoire of Armadel*, Betel seems to have access to a good deal of heavenly wisdom despite his infernal status. See also MATHERS.

Betor: A demon said to reveal the names and offices of the Angels of Darkness. Betor is named in Mathers's edition of the *Grimoire of Armadel*, where it is said that he can also assist in acquiring an angel of darkness as a familiar. See also MATHERS.

Bialot: One of several demons said to serve the arch-fiends Astaroth and Asmodeus. Bialot appears in the Mathers translation of the *Sacred Magic of Abramelin the Mage*. See also ASTAROTH, ASMODEUS, MATHERS.

Bianakith: According to the *Testament of Solomon*, Bianakith is the thirty-sixth demon connected with the thirty-six decans of the zodiac. Possessing the body of a man and the head of a beast, Bianakith is a particularly nasty demon of disease. He can torment his victims by making their bodies waste away. He can cause their flesh to rot, decaying even while they still live. As with many of the demons

mentioned in the *Testament of Solomon*, Bianakith has a weakness for holy or magickal names. To drive this demon from a home, three names must be written upon the front door of the afflicted house. Those names are Mêltô, Ardu, and Anaath. These are presumably names of angels. In a later translation of the *Testament of Solomon*, this demon appears under the name Rhyx Mianeth. *Rhyx* is a title meaning "king." See also SOLOMON.

Bidiel: A demon described as a wandering prince of the air in the *Ars Theurgia*. Bidiel is the last spirit to be named as such in that text. He is said to have twenty dukes under his command. In addition to these, he has another two hundred inferior dukes and many more minor spirits beneath him. He is reputed to be a good and even-tempered spirit. He manifests in a human form, very beautiful to behold. Under the spelling of *Bydiel*, the name of this demon can also be found in Trithemius's *Steganographia*. See also *ARS THEURGIA*, TRITHEMIUS.

Bifrons: A demon attributed with the power to move the bodies of the dead from one place to another, Bifrons is named in Scot's *Discoverie of Witchcraft* and Wierus's *Pseudomonarchia Daemonum*, as well as the *Book of Incantations*. He is said first to take the form of a monster, but he can also appear as a man. He teaches astrology, geometry, and other arts and sciences, as well as the virtues of precious stones and woods. He also empties coffins and lights corpse candles on graves. Although neither the *Pseudomonarchia Daemonum* nor Scot's *Discoverie of Witchcraft* credit him with a specific rank, he is nevertheless said to rule over a total of twenty-six legions of spirits. In both the *Goetia* and the *Book of Incantations*, Bifrons is accorded the rank of earl. According to these texts, he only has six legions of spirits beneath him. The *Goetia of Dr. Rudd* claims that the angel Ariel (possibly spelled *Ariet*) has the power to constrain him. See also *BOOK OF INCANTATIONS, GOETIA,* RUDD, SCOT, WIERUS.

The Witch of Endor calls Samuel up from the dead for King Saul. Demons crowd the background. Engraving by J. Taylor in the style of S. Rosa, 1813. Image courtesy of the Wellcome Collection, London.

Bileth: A great and terrible king of Hell with eighty-five legions of spirits at his command. He is said to belong to the angelic Order of Dominions, and to maintain hope that he will someday return to the seventh throne of Heaven. Wierus's *Pseudomonarchia Daemonum* renders his name *Byleth*. According to both this text and Scot's *Discoverie of Witchcraft*, this demon can embroil people in foolish and misguided love, but he can be tricky to command. When first summoned, he puts on a furious appearance to deceive the magician. His appearance is heralded by trumpets and all man-

ner of music, and Bileth himself manifests astride a pale horse. The summoner is cautioned not to be intimidated by Bileth's initial manifestation, but instead to keep a hazel rod in one hand and force the demon to manifest more amiably in a special triangle constructed outside of the summoning circle. If space does not allow for the construction of such a triangle, both the *Pseudomonarchia Daemonum* and Scot suggest placing a bowl of wine outside the circle to entice this spirit. There is some danger in dealing with Bileth, and the magician is further cautioned to wear a silver ring on the middle finger of the left hand and to keep this pressed close against the face as a method of protection. This method of protection is said to be used when summoning the demon Amaimon as well. There is apparently some pay-off that makes all this trouble involving Bileth worth the effort. In addition to procuring the love of others, Bileth is said to become a fast friend and obedient helper once he has been properly summoned and had his prideful ego appeased.

Further in the *Pseudomonarchia Daemonum*, Bileth is credited with being connected to the first necromancer. According to this portion of the text, Noah's son Cham founded the dark art of necromancy, and the first demon he called up was Bileth. He subsequently founded an art in the demon's name, and this art is decried as a wicked abomination by the author of Wierus's source text. In the *Pseudomonarchia Daemonum*, the name is spelled alternately as *Byleth* and *Beleth*. Bileth is also named in connection with the legend of Solomon's Brazen Vessel. He is said to have been the chief of the seventy-two infernal kings shut up in this vessel by the biblical Patriarch. Under the name *Beleth*, he appears as the thirteenth spirit in the *Goetia*. In the *Goetia of Dr. Rudd*, he is said to be

Secret Libraries of the Learned

Writing in the thirteenth century, scholar Richard of Fourniville compiled a *biblionomia*—that is, a careful and detailed catalogue of the books in his library. He possessed almost two hundred and sixty manuscripts, which was an amazing number in his day, when each book was still lettered, illuminated, and bound by hand. Although Richard of Fourniville marked with precision even the table of contents of those books that contained more than one treatise, he nevertheless left a full thirty-six manuscripts unremarked and unnamed. He cites these as his secret books, and it is the opinion of Robert Mathiesen, a modern scholar of magickal texts writing in the book *Conjuring Spirits*, that the unnamed tomes in the *Biblionomia* were magickal grimoires. Johannes Trithemius, writing in 1485, engaged in a similar omission when compiling his *De Scriptoribus Ecclesiasticis*. He left off all of the books in his library that could be considered magickal texts. This is perhaps unsurprising, considering that in those days many books were forbidden by the church and simply owning them could carry a stiff penalty. The downside to this cautious self-censorship is that scholars today now have no way of knowing the titles of many of the earliest magickal grimoires—nor how widespread their readership really was.

Trithemius was unusually helpful to modern historians of grimoiric magick in that he compiled a second list of books, the *Antipalus Maleficiorum*. This compilation, rather than omitting forbidden texts, specifically describes all of his books on the magickal arts. The list includes titles, publication dates when known, and a brief commentary on each individual work. As leader of the Benedictine abbey of Sponheim, perhaps Trithemius felt his position would allow him to skate by the jaundiced eyes of Church Inquisitors. Even so, he is careful to decry the evil of many of the books on his list, deriding their contents as silly or blasphemous—all of this despite the fact that he himself penned a book involving demonic magick at the end of the fifteenth century, known as the *Steganographia*. This book contains an extensive list of spirits that appears later in the *Ars Theurgia*.

constrained by the angel Jezalel. In the *Liber de Angelis*, this demon, under the name *Bilet*, is said to be a king of Hell. He oversees a number of demons dedicated to suffering and disease. In the *Book of Oberon*, Bileth is one of the twelve principal spirits serving Amaimon, king of the south. That text states that he turns people invisible and possesses the power to bless or curse items.

He also appears in several spells recorded in the *Munich Handbook*. He is found in the *Sworn Book of Honorius* as a minister of the demon-king Harthan. In Driscoll's edition of this work, Bileth is associated with the element water. In the Peterson translation of this work, he is instead connected with the spirits of the moon. Other variations of his name include *Beleth*, *Byleth*, and *Bilet*. See also AMAIMON, *BOOK OF OBERON*, *GOETIA*, HARTHAN, *LIBER DE ANGELIS*, *MUNICH HANDBOOK*, RUDD, SCOT, *SWORN BOOK*, WIERUS.

Bilgall: A demon described in the Elizabethan book of magic known as the *Book of Oberon*. Bilgall is said to appear as an ox with a man's head. In a later illustration in the same text, the head is shown bearded; the ox has the tail of a serpent. Bilgall is conjured through the use of a crystal shewstone, a scrying device used most famously by the Elizabethan magician Dr. John Dee. When summoned, Bilgall arrives vomiting flame from her mouth. And, yes, you read that correctly. The female pronoun may be an error in the manuscript, but there is no sure guarantee. Gender, as much as appearance, is a malleable attribute for demons. Lucifer is invoked as Bilgall's superior, as are the demons Portisan, Fortisan, and Alingon. See also ALINGON, *BOOK OF OBERON*, FORTISAN, JOHN DEE, LUCIFER, PORTISAN.

Bilico: The name of this demon means "the Lord of Manifestations," at least according to occultist S. L. MacGregor Mathers. In his translation of the *Sacred Magic of Abramelin the Mage*, Mathers lists Bilico among the demons ruled by the infernal lord Beelzebub. Another version of this name is *Bilek*. See also BEELZEBUB, MATHERS.

Bilifares: The "Lord of Division," according to Mathers in his 1898 translation of the *Sacred Magic of Abramelin the Mage*. This demon answers to Beelzebub, acting as one of that greater demon's many servitors. An alternate spelling of the name is *Belifares*. The name of this demon may be a derivative of Bealphares, a demon mentioned in Scot's *Discoverie of Witchcraft*. See also BEALPHARES, BEELZEBUB, MATHERS, SCOT.

Bilifor: Mathers parses this demon's name as "lord of glory" in his edition of the *Sacred Magic of Abramelin the Mage*. In this text, Bilifor is said to be ruled by the greater demon Beelzebub. Other versions of the *Abramelin* material spell the name *Bilifot*. See also BEELZEBUB, MATHERS.

Biriel: A demon governed by both Asmodeus and Magoth. In his translation of the *Sacred Magic of Abramelin the Mage*, Mathers suggest that this demon's name means "stronghold of God." While the list of demonic servitors attributed to Asmodeus and Magoth appears in one other version of the *Abramelin* material, this particular demon name is unique to the Mathers edition. See also ASMODEUS, MAGOTH, MATHERS.

Bitur: A great marquis who assumes the guise of a handsome young man. He can command the love of women and the respect of powerful men. In addition, he can lay waste to castles, cities, and towns. His name appears in the *Livre des esperitz*, a sixteenth-century French grimoire. Thirty-six legions of lesser spirits serve in his retinue. See also *LIVRE DES ESPERITZ*.

Boab: According to the *Book of Oberon*, this demon holds the rank of prelate, making Boab one of the few demons with a title that is traditionally tied to religious rather than secular authority. He has a startling appearance: kitted out like a soldier, he comes riding a black horse. He has a head like a lion and eyes that shine like fire. He speaks with a hoarse voice and has teeth like an ox, blunt and huge. His main power is to enable his summoner to understand the barking of dogs. He can also transpose gold and silver, moving those riches from place to place (presumably using this power to enrich those who summon him). Like many demons in the *Book of Oberon*, he also has knowledge of hidden things. He has an alternate name of Boall (not to be confused with Boell) and is said to command forty-four legions of lesser spirits. See also BOELL, *BOOK OF OBERON*.

Bobêl: Named as the thirteenth demon among the thirty-six connected with the decans of the zodiac, Bobêl appears in the Conybeare translation of the *Testament of Solomon*. According to that version of the text, he is constrained by the angel Adonaêl. In McCown's later translation, however, his name is Phobothel and the power that controls him is none other than Adonai. McCown, notably, was working from a more complete selection of surviving manuscripts. In both versions, Bobêl (aka Phobothel) is a demon of disease. He loosens the tendons, causing weakness. See also SOLOMON.

Boell: Probably a variation on *Bael*, Boell appears as one of seven demonic senators said to serve the supreme emperor Tantavalerion. This demonic ruler and his immediate subordinates are called upon to keep other spirits in line in a spell appearing in the Elizabethan grimoire known as the *Book of Oberon*. See also ASMOO, *BOOK OF OBERON*, DANALL, ORYMELL, PASCARY, SALARICA, TANTAVALERION, TYGRA.

Bofar: A chief president said to serve the greater demon Aseliel. According to the *Ars Theurgia*, Bofar is tied to the hours of the night and the hierarchy of the east. He rules over thirty principal spirits. In addition, he has another twenty ministering spirits to serve him. When he manifests, he assumes a beautiful and courtly form. See also *ARS THEURGIA*, ASELIEL.

Bolferth: A messenger loyal to Paimon, king of the west. His name appears in the *Book of Oberon*, a grimoire from Elizabethan England. See also *BOOK OF OBERON*.

Bonoham: A ruler of the fiery regions. Bonoham is described as a great duke in the hierarchy of Hell. His name appears in Dr. Rudd's *Treatise on Angel Magic*. See also RUDD.

Bonyel: In the *Ars Theurgia*, Bonyel is a chief duke beneath the demon-king Symiel. As a spirit of rank, Bonyel has ninety lesser spirits to attend him. He will only appear during the hours of the day and is known for his good and obedient nature. He is allied with the court of the north. See also *ARS THEURGIA*, SYMIEL.

Book of Enoch: Sometimes referred to as *1 Enoch*, or the *Ethiopic Enoch*. The *Book of Enoch* was supposedly written by the biblical Patriarch Enoch, allegedly born to the seventh generation of Adam and believed to have become the first prophet and scribe. Enoch is one of the rare biblical figures said to have been bodily assumed into Heaven. Long thought to be a Christian text, the *Book of Enoch* was actually written some time before the Christian era. Multiple copies of this text appear among the Dead Sea Scrolls, dating it to at least the first through third centuries BCE.

Lost to Western scholars for nearly thirteen hundred years, the *Book of Enoch* contains the most complete account of the Watcher Angels, heavenly beings said to have walked out of Heaven in order to take wives among the daughters of men. This part of the Watcher Angel story is referenced obliquely in Genesis 6:1–4, but it remains a fragment that is never fully resolved within the biblical text. The children of the Watcher Angels are widely known as the *Nephilim*, human-angel hybrids reputed to be bloodthirsty, ambitious, and cruel. Their angelic fathers, who also sinned by teaching forbidden knowledge of magickal arts to humanity, were eventually punished for mixing the seed of angels with the children of the earth. Bound hand and foot in the desert, the leaders of the Watcher Angels, called *Shemyaza* and *Azazel*, were forced to witness the destruction of their earthly empire as their descendants were set against one another in battle. The survivors were drowned in the Flood.

The *Book of Enoch* was originally recognized as official Scripture, but it was cut from the Bible around 300 CE. It was so aggressively suppressed by later Church fathers that it was eventually lost to European Christendom, only to be discovered again in an Ethiopian monastery by adventurer James Bruce in the eighteenth century. Nevertheless, multiple references to the Watcher Angels and their story remained woven throughout the demonology of the Middle Ages and Renaissance.

The *Testament of Solomon* makes allusions to the concept of the human-angel union presented in the *Book of Enoch*, although it does not directly reference the text itself. According to this book, many demons haunting the earth are the ill-begotten progeny of the Watchers. This may have given rise to a persistent yet anecdotal belief in the Middle Ages that many demons were the spirits of the slaughtered sons of the Watcher Angels, condemned never to take flesh again but also unable to ever leave the mortal plane. This belief is also present in Ludovico Sinistrari's seventeenth-century work *Demoniality*, in which women visited by incubus demons are said to bear children with qualities suspiciously close to those described as belonging to the Nephilim in the *Book of Enoch*. See also SOLOMON, WATCHER ANGELS.

Book of Incantations: Working title of a manuscript in the collection of the National Library of Wales with the designation NLW MS 11117B. This is a cunning-man's personal manual of spells, spirits, and medicine dating to the early portion of the 1800s. It was written and maintained by John Harries of Pantcoy, Cwrtycadno, Carmarthenshire, astrologer and medical practitioner. Harries was baptized on April 10, 1785 (no birth date seems to survive for him) and he died in the year 1839, passing his tomes and his practice to his son. The Harries family was famous in the country as surgeons, astrologers, and medical practitioners. They were especially well known for their skills at divination, spirit invocation, and counteracting witchcraft. Although their communities sought out their expertise, they nevertheless suffered widespread condemnation from the religious mainstream, like most cunning-men and cunning-women of the time. This book is handwritten and supplemented with many illustrations, sigils, and astrological signs. It has been rebound and is likely no longer in the same order as when John Harries worked from it. Currently it opens with fifteen pages devoted to Harries's version of the *Goetia*, with notes and sigils for all the spirits. See also *GOETIA*.

Book of Jubilees: Likely written in the second century BCE, the *Book of Jubilees* is a history of the biblical world from Creation to the time of Moses.

Sigil of the demon Baal as recorded in John Harries's *Book of Incantations*. Early 19th century. Image by Catherine Rogers.

First written in Hebrew, an Ethiopian text is the only complete version to survive to the present day. The *Book of Jubilees* is concerned with calendar reform, and, accordingly, it arranges the history of the world into forty-nine-year periods known as jubilees. It contains, among other details, the names of the daughters of Adam and Eve, a suggested three-hundred-and-sixty-four-day solar calendar, and the story of a demonic entity known as Mastema. Although the *Book of Jubilees* does not appear directly in the Bible, biblical scholar R. H. Charles maintained that portions of this text were incorporated into the Greek version of the Jewish *Septuagint*. See also MASTEMA.

Book of Oberon: A manuscript stored at the Folger Shakespeare Library in Washington, DC, under the title *Book of Magic, with Instructions for Invoking Spirits, etc.* The actual title of the book has been lost, assuming it ever had one. It has been transcribed and published by the team of Daniel Harms, Joseph H. Peterson, and James R. Clark as the *Book of Oberon*. The manuscript itself shows the penmanship of several authors, and sections of the text have been separated and rearranged over the years. Although the precise date of its creation is uncertain, the first date recorded in the work is 1577. While not unique among grimoires, the *Book of Oberon* stands out because its conjurations are not concerned merely with angels and demons: as its name implies, the grimoire contains spells for conjuring faeries as well. The most interesting of these is a spirit identified as both a fallen angel and the king of the faeries, *Oberion* (also spelled *Oberyon* several times in the text). Oberion is more familiar under the spelling of *Oberon* through the play *A Midsummer Night's Dream* by William Shakespeare. Notably, the grimoire was produced in England at the same time that Shakespeare was writing his plays, making it highly likely that they were influenced by similar sources. The *Book of Oberon* contains numerous sigils, illustrations, and diagrams, in addition to a wealth of names and descriptions of a wide variety of spirits. Many of the demons familiar from the *Goetia* make an appearance, along with a sizable number of spirits whose names appear to be unique to the manuscript. The spellings in certain sections are particularly erratic, which may account for some of the apparently unique names. See also OBERION, *GOETIA*.

Book of Tobit: A late Jewish work that never officially became a part of the Jewish canon. Nevertheless, the *Book of Tobit* (sometimes also known as the *Book of Tobias*) is included in the Christian *Apocrypha*—books associated with the biblical tradition that are often appended to the Bible itself. The *Book of Tobit* contains a tale about the demon Asmodeus, and how Tobit, through prayer and the intercession of the angel Raphael, saved his future wife Sarah from the predations of this demon. It is the main book in which Raphael is named as an angel of the Lord. See also ASMODEUS.

Borasy: A chief duke said to serve beneath the demon Malgaras. According to the *Ars Theurgia*, Borasy is attended by thirty lesser spirits of his own. He is tied to the hours of daylight and will not appear at night. As a demon in service to Malgaras, Borasy is connected with the western point of the compass. See also *ARS THEURGIA*, MALGARAS.

Borob: A servant of the infernal lord Beelzebub, and one of several such servants whose name is a palindrome. Borob appears in the *Sacred Magic of Abramelin the Mage*, and in the magickal tradition of this and other works, palindromes—words that can be read the same way forward or backward—were seen as inherently magickal. Interestingly, in the *Abramelin* material, a great many of Beelzebub's demonic servants have palindromes for names. See also BEELZEBUB, MATHERS.

Bos: A demon connected with matters of divination, Bos appears in the fifteenth-century magickal text known as the *Munich Handbook*. He is part of a spell intended to enchant a surface for scrying. See also *MUNICH HANDBOOK*.

Bothothêl: The thirteenth spirit of the thirty-six demons associated with the decans of the zodiac, as described in the *Testament of Solomon*. Bothothêl is a demon of affliction who attacks mortals by giving them the jitters and weakening their nerves. To protect someone from the predations of this demon, one must invoke the name of the angel Adonaêl. See also SOLOMON.

Botis: The seventeenth spirit in the *Goetia*. In Wierus's *Pseudomonarchia Daemonum*, Botis is listed as both an earl and a president. He is said to have sixty legions of lesser spirits at his command. He manifests first in the shape of the worst sort of viper, but he can be commanded to take the form of a man. His human shape still retains aspects of his infernal nature, showing great teeth and having two horns. He also comes carrying a sword. He can reconcile friends and foes as well as answer questions about the past, present, and future. Scot gives his name alternately as *Otis* and describes his original appearance as an ugly viper. The *Goetia of Dr. Rudd* describes Botis as a "prince under an earl," further adding that the angel Loviah has the power to constrain him. See also *GOETIA*, RUDD, SCOTT, WIERUS.

Bramsiel: A great duke who serves the wandering prince Bidiel. Bramsiel and his fellow dukes each command a total of two thousand and four hundred ministering spirits. According to the *Ars Theurgia*, he assumes a pleasing human form when he manifests. See also *ARS THEURGIA*, BIDIEL.

Brufiel: A demon whose name and seal both appear in the *Ars Theurgia*. Here he is said to serve the infernal prince Macariel. Brufiel holds the rank of duke and has a total of four hundred lesser spirits at his command. He is said to be able to assume a variety of shapes, but he has a preference for appearing as a dragon with many heads. Each of the heads is that of a virgin, comely and sweet. He is tied to no specific hour but may manifest at any time during the day or night. See also *ARS THEURGIA*, MACARIEL.

Brufor: A demon who teaches about demonkind, at least according to the Mathers edition of the *Grimoire of Armadel*. This text says that Brufor willingly reveals the hierarchy of Hell, along with the names and titles of all of the demons to any that deal with him. He can grant the power to bind infernal spirits and to drive them away. He also supposedly teaches others how to force demons to explain their favorite ways of ensnaring mortals. In these functions, he bears striking similarities to the demon Ornias from the *Testament of Solomon*, although no connection between their names appears in either text. Despite the fact that Brufor seems to function more or less as Hell's stool pigeon, the *Grimoire of Armadel* cautions against summoning him. See also MATHERS, ORNIAS, SOLOMON.

Brulefer: In Peterson's edition of the *Grimorium Verum*, this demon is said to have the power to inflame the love of persons of the opposite sex. He is also reputed to teach astronomy. Under the spelling *Bruselfer*, he appears in the Wellcome Library's 1709 version of the *Clavicle of Solomon*, a text related to the *Secrets of Solomon*. In that manuscript, he serves Hael and Sergulaf, ministers of the Duke Resbiroth. See also HAEL, RESBIROTH, *CLAVICLE OF SOLOMON*, *GRIMORIUM VERUM*, SERGULAF.

Bryman: Also given the name of *Myniciorom*, this demon appears in the Elizabethan grimoire known as the *Book of Oberon*. When summoned, Bryman appears as a glib little goose. With very pleasant speech, he will happily give a discourse on the hidden properties of everything from flowers, to metals, to woods, fish, birds, beasts, waters, herbs, and stones. Although his appearance may be disarming, this demon also has a dark side. He can cause people to fall into a coma and die, although he requires a sacrifice if he is expected to use this power on command. He holds the rank of earl and has a total of thirty legions of lesser spirits serving beneath him. See also *BOOK OF OBERON*.

Brymiel: A demon whose name and seal appear in the *Ars Theurgia* in connection with the court of the wandering prince Uriel. Brymiel holds the rank of duke and has a total of six hundred and fifty lesser spirits at his command. He prefers to assume the shape of a human-headed serpent, which is perhaps appropriate given that he is de-

scribed as having a dishonest and wholly evil nature. See also *ARS THEURGIA*, URIEL.

Bubana: A demon in the hierarchy of Astaroth and Asmodeus. Bubana is named in the Mathers translation of the *Sacred Magic of Abramelin the Mage*. Mathers presents this demon's name as meaning "emptiness." See also ASTAROTH, ASMODEUS, MATHERS.

Bucafas: A servant of Carnesiel, the infernal Emperor of the East. According to the *Ars Theurgia*, Bucafas holds the title of duke. See also *ARS THEURGIA*, CARNESIEL.

Bucal: A grand duke who assumes the guise of an angel. He can make great waters and abysses appear in the air when they are not really there. A total of twenty-eight legions of lesser spirits form his retinue. Named in the *Livre des esperitz*, he answers truly when demanded. See also *LIVRE DES ESPERITZ*.

Bucon: A demon of strife and discord, Bucon provokes people to hatred and jealousy. He appears in the 1709 version of the *Clavicle of Solomon* kept at Britain's Wellcome Library. According to that text, he serves beneath Hael and Sergulaf, both of whom serve in the court of Duke Resbiroth. See also HAEL, RESBIROTH, *CLAVICLE OF SOLOMON*, SERGULAF.

Budar: A night-demon willing to appear only during the hours of darkness. Budar serves the infernal king Asyriel and thus is allied with the court of the south. His name and seal appear in the *Ars Theurgia*. According to this text, he has a total of ten lesser spirits at his command. See also *ARS THEURGIA*, ASYRIEL.

Budarim: One of several demons who serve in the hierarchy of Caspiel, the infernal Emperor of the South. Budarim holds the title of duke, and he is reputed to be stubborn and churlish in nature. He commands a total of two thousand two hundred and sixty lesser spirits. Budarim appears in the *Ars Theurgia*. In Rudd's *Treatise on Angel Magic*, this demon appears under the name *Budarym*. Here, he is a spirit invoked together with Larmol, a duke in the court of Emperor Caspiel. Both Larmol and Budarym appear in Rudd's work in connection with the magickal table of Mercury. See also *ARS THEURGIA*, CASPIEL, LARMOL.

Budiel: A demon named in the *Ars Theurgia* from Henson's translation of the complete *Lemegeton*. Budiel serves in the hierarchy of the east. His immediate superior is the infernal prince Camuel, who rules in the southeast. Budiel himself is a duke, and he commands ten ministering spirits of his own. He is a demon of the daylight hours, but he manifests during the hours of the night. See also *ARS THEURGIA*, CAMUEL.

Buer: The tenth demon named in the *Goetia*. According to Wierus's *Pseudomonarchia Daemonum*, this demon holds the rank of president and oversees fifty legions of lesser spirits. He is reputed to give the best familiars—helper spirits often thought to take the form of small animals, such as cats or toads. Furthermore, he teaches a wide variety of disciplines, from moral and natural philosophy to logic. He also teaches the virtues of herbs and can heal disease. There is an omission in the text, where Buer is said to appear in a specific sign, but no sign is given. This omission is filled in with the *Goetia of Dr. Rudd*. Here, Buer is said to appear when the sun is in Sagittarius. He is constrained by the angel Aladiah. The *Book of Incantations* affirms his connection to Sagittarius. He also appears in Scot's *Discoverie of Witchcraft*. See also *BOOK OF INCANTATIONS*, *GOETIA*, RUDD, SCOTT, WIERUS.

Buesaba: A demon who can appear as a man or woman, tall and gold-skinned, wearing robes of brilliant yellow. He is one of three helpers who serve the demon-king Barkan, ruler of the spirits of the Sun. Buesaba has power to grant noble titles, such as duke or earl, and he can further help people win the respect and support of their peers. He resolves conflicts and hostilities and also procures wealth. He is named in the *Book of Oberon* along with two other aides to King Barkan, Bybell and Mylalu. See also BARKAN, *BOOK OF OBERON*, BYBELL, MYLALU.

Bufiel: A demon of the night ruled by the wandering duke Buriel. Bufiel assumes the monstrous form of a massive serpent with a human head whenever he appears. He so despises the light that he will only appear during the hours of darkness. He holds sway over eight hundred and eighty lesser spirits. His name and his seal appear in the *Ars Theurgia*. According to this text, Bufiel and his compatriots are so malevolent that they are despised by all other spirits. See also *ARS THEURGIA*, BURIEL.

Bugan: A demon with vast alchemical powers, Bugan can transmute any metal or change water into wine or even oil. He holds the rank of king and has thirty-four legions of lesser spirits to minister to him. His name appears in the *Livre des esperitz*, where it is said he also makes people wise. See also *LIVRE DES ESPERITZ*.

Bulfas: A grand prince who sows discord and war. According to the sixteenth-century French grimoire *Livre des esperitz*, he must be strongly constrained if he is to do what is asked of him. Thirty-six legions are under him. See also *LIVRE DES ESPERITZ*.

Buk: According to the Mathers translation of the *Sacred Magic of Abramelin the Mage*, Buk is one of a number of demons in service to the arch-fiends Asmodeus and Astaroth. According to this text, the name of this demon supposedly means "perplexity." See also ASTAROTH, ASMODEUS, MATHERS.

Buldumêch: This demon is named as the eighteenth of thirty-six infernal spirits associated with the decans of the zodiac. He appears in the *Testament of Solomon*, where he is said to attack husbands and wives, dividing them with anger and causing their tempers to flare against one another. When Buldumêch is present in a home, he can be made to flee by invoking the names of three of the biblical Patriarchs: Abraham, Isaac, and Jacob. In a later, more accurate translation of the source material, the beings with power over this demon are simply called the *Eight Fathers*. The demon's name is different as well: *Modebel*. See also SOLOMON.

Bulls: This curiously named demon appears in the night-bound hierarchy of the infernal prince Dorochiel. Given the style of most angel names (fallen or otherwise), this demon may have originally been *Buells*. According to the *Ars Theurgia*, where his name appears, Bulls will only manifest at a specific hour in the first half of the night. Through Dorochiel, he owes fealty to the court of the west. Granted the rank of chief duke, he has forty lesser spirits under him. See also *ARS THEURGIA*, DOROCHIEL.

Bune: The twenty-sixth demon named in the *Goetia*, Bune is a great and strong duke said to rule a total of thirty infernal legions. In Wierus's *Pseudomonarchia Daemonum*, Bune is said to appear as a dragon with three heads. The third head is that of a man. He has power over the dead and can make them change their place. He can also cause demons to congregate on the sepulchers of the dead. He is said to speak with a divine voice and can make those that summon him rich, eloquent, and wise. He has many of the same powers in Scot's *Discoverie of Witchcraft*. In the *Goetia of Dr. Rudd*, the name of this demon is given as *Bim*. According to this text, he can be constrained by the angel Haajah. In the French *Livre des esperitz*, he holds the rank of duke and commands thirty-five legions. See also *GOETIA*, *LIVRE DES ESPERITZ*, RUDD, SCOTT, WIERUS.

Buniet: A demon associated with the direction of the south. Buniet's name and seal appear in the Henson translation of the *Ars Theurgia*. According to this text, he is in service to the infernal king Asyriel, who rules in the southwest. Buniet holds the rank of chief duke and has forty lesser spirits under his command. He is tied to the hours of the day and will only manifest during this time. See also *ARS THEURGIA*, ASYRIEL.

Burasen: One of several demons whose names appear in the *Sacred Magic of Abramelin the Mage*. According to this text, Burasen is a servant of the infernal king Amaimon. Mathers suggests that the name is derived from Hebrew roots. The reading he offers is strange and complex: he takes this name to mean "destroyers by stifling, smoky breath." In the 1725 Peter Hammer edition of the *Abramelin* material, the name of this demon is rendered *Bumaham*. It appears with the same spelling in the version kept at the Dresden library as well. See also AMAIMON, MATHERS.

Burfa: One of several night-demons who serve in the court of prince Usiel. He is associated with the west. Burfa's name appears in the *Ars Theurgia*, where it is said that he rules over forty ministering spirits. He has the power to reveal or conceal treasure. He can also break enchantments. See also *ARS THEURGIA*, USIEL.

Buriel: A so-called "wandering duke" whose name and seal appear in the *Ars Theurgia*. According to this work, Buriel and his entire retinue are despised by all of the other spirits. They are unremittingly evil and they can only be called upon at night because they flee the light of day. Buriel is reputed to appear in a truly monstrous form: a human-headed serpent that speaks with a man's rough voice. He is tied to no particular direction of the compass but instead wanders with his retinue wherever he will. Buriel also appears in Johannes Trithemius's *Steganographia*. See also *ARS THEURGIA*, TRITHEMIUS.

Buriol: A demon ruled by the infernal king Amaimon. Buriol's name appears in the *Sacred Magic of Abramelin the Mage*. According to the Mathers translation, the name of this demon means "the devouring fire of God." The name is also spelled *Bariol*. See also AMAIMON, MATHERS.

Burisiel: One of twelve dukes serving the demon Demoriel, whose names and seals are specifically given in the seventeenth-century magickal text known as the *Ars Theurgia*. Through his affiliation with Demoriel, Burisiel is connected with the direction north. He is further connected with the fourth set of two planetary hours of the day. These are derived by dividing the day up into twelve equal portions of time, known as *planetary hours*. The exact length of these hours differs depending on the amount of daylight at any given time during the year. Burisiel is bound to appear only during his designated hours. As a demon of rank, he oversees a total of one thousand one hundred and forty ministering spirits. See also *ARS THEURGIA*, DEMORIEL.

Buriul: In the Mathers translation of the *Sacred Magic of Abramelin the Mage*, Buriul is one of a number of demonic servitors said to operate under the direction of both Asmodeus and Astaroth. As such, he can be summoned and compelled with the names of his superiors. According to Mathers, the name of this demon can be taken to mean "in terror and trembling." See also ASTAROTH, ASMODEUS, MATHERS.

Busiel: In the *Ars Theurgia*, Busiel's name appears in conjunction with the infernal prince Dorochiel and thus the hierarchy of the west. Here, he serves in the capacity of chief duke, with four hundred lesser spirits beneath him. He is said to appear during the second half of the day, in the hours between noon and dusk. See also *ARS THEURGIA*, DOROCHIEL.

Busin: A demon with necromantic powers, Busin can magickally transport dead bodies. In addition, he can compel one of the many spirits under his command to animate a corpse. While possessed, the dead body will be able to speak and do everything a living person might, with the exception of consuming food. Busin's name appears in the Elizabethan grimoire known as the *Book of Oberon*, where he is listed as one of twelve principal ministers under Amaimon, king of the south. That text describes his appearance as that of a fair woman who speaks with a hoarse voice. Compare to the Goetic demon *Bune*. See also AMAIMON, *BOOK OF OBERON*, BUNE.

Butarab: One of several demons said to serve the arch-fiend Magoth in the *Sacred Magic of Abramelin the Mage*. According to the Mathers translation, Butarab is also a servant of Kore. In other versions of the *Abramelin* material, this demon's name is spelled variously as *Butharuth* and *Butharath*. See also KORE, MAGOTH, MATHERS.

Bybell: A demon who causes those nearby to break out in a sweat. Bybell is one of the helpers of King Barkan, who rules the spirits of the sun. He appears as a tall and thick-limbed being with gold-tinted skin. He can manifest as any gender and may also take the form of a lion or rooster. His office is to ameliorate people and break down hostilities. He can also cause or cure disease. He is named in the *Book of Oberon* along with Mylalu and Buesaba, additional helpers in King Barkan's court. See also BARKAN, *BOOK OF OBERON*, BUESABA, MYLALU.

Byleth: A demon in the court of the Moon, Byleth is one of four helpers working with King Harkam. His name appears in the *Book of Oberon*, where he is said to have the power to give silver, to make horses swift, to reveal secrets, and to transport objects. If he takes human form, he can appear as either a king armed with arrows or a huntress. Rainstorms break out around him. See also ACUTEBA, *BOOK OF OBERON*, BYLETHOR, HARKAM, MYLU.

Bylethor: One of four spirits serving King Harkam as helpers. Bylethor is a spirit of the Moon and thus appears wearing green or silvery garments. His skin is the color of a dark cloud and he has tusks like a boar. He has powers of transportation and can magickally move objects from place to place. He can also increase the speed of horses. He knows all the secret and hidden things from the past, present, and future and can procure silver. A rainstorm breaks out wherever he manifests. He is named in the *Book of Oberon*, a grimoire from Elizabethan England. See also ACUTEBA, *BOOK OF OBERON*, BYLETH, HARKAM, MYLU.

Caap: In the French *Livre des esperitz*, Caap is a great prince who appears in the shape of a knight. He gives true responses to all demanded of him. He brings gold and silver wherever one wishes. He governs twenty legions. His name may be a variation of the Goetic demon *Gaap*. See also *LIVRE DES ESPERITZ*, GAAP.

Cabariel: A mighty prince ruling in the west by north. Cabariel ranks fourth under the demon Amenadiel, Emperor of the West. Cabariel himself commands fifty chief dukes by day and another fifty during the hours of the night. He prefers to appear in remote and isolated locations, such as hidden groves or wooded islands. Possessing an airy nature that does not allow him to manifest clearly to the naked eye, Cabariel can best be seen in a stone crystal or scrying glass—at least according to the *Ars Theurgia*. Cabariel also appears in Trithemius's *Steganographia*. See also AMENADIEL, *ARS THEURGIA*, TRITHEMIUS.

Cabarim: A duke in the hierarchy of the demon Demoriel. According to the *Ars Theurgia*, Demoriel is the infernal Emperor of the North, and thus Cabarim is also affiliated with the north. Cabarim is a duke with dominion over one thousand one hundred and forty lesser spirits of his own. He will only manifest during the second two planetary hours of the day. See also *ARS THEURGIA*, DEMORIEL.

Caberyon: A demon named in the *Book of Oberon*. He holds the rank of minister and is listed second among the four advisors to King Oberion. Oberion occupies an interesting place between fallen angel and faerie, as the *Book of Oberon* identifies him as both. There is a possibility that all of the demons in Oberion's court fit in the same category, including Caberyon. See also *BOOK OF OBERON*, OBERION.

Cabiel: One of several demons who serve the infernal king Malgaras during hours of the day. In the *Ars Theurgia*, he is said to hold the rank of chief duke with thirty subordinate spirits to serve him. He is affiliated with the west. See also *ARS THEURGIA*, MALGARAS.

Cabron: A demon named in the *Ars Theurgia*. Cabron is said to serve the infernal prince Dorochiel. He himself holds the rank of chief duke and has a total of four hundred lesser spirits at his command. Tied to the hours of the day, he will only manifest between noon and dusk. His connection with Dorochiel places him in the hierarchy of the west. See also *ARS THEURGIA*, DOROCHIEL.

Cadriel: A chief duke in the hierarchy of Dorochiel, infernal prince of the west by the north. The *Ars Theurgia* describes Cadriel as a night-demon who serves his master in the hours between midnight and dawn. He allegedly oversees no fewer than four hundred subordinate spirits. See also *ARS THEURGIA*, DOROCHIEL.

Cagyne: One of twelve principal ministers to Paimon, king of the west, Cagyne is named in the *Book of Oberon*. That text gives the alternate name of *Cogin*. This demon appears in the form of a pale horse and has power over the dead. He is said to be able to bring any soul to speak before his summoner, provided that soul is not under the control of any heavenly or infernal power. This proviso suggests Cagyne's power is over souls in Limbo, a between-state used historically by the Church as a repository for souls that belong neither to Heaven nor to Hell. See also *BOOK OF OBERON*, PAIMON.

Caim: One of the seventy-two demons associated with the *Goetia*, Caim was reputedly a member of the Order of Angels before his fall. According to Scot's *Discoverie of Witchcraft*, he holds the title of president and has a total of thirty legions of spirits under his command. He is said to manifest first in the form of a thrush, but he can also assume a human form. When he takes the form of a man, he appears carrying a sharp sword in his hand. He is said to give his answers in burning ashes. Among his powers, he is said to make people able to understand the inhuman languages of birds, dogs, and cattle. He can even gift a mortal with the ability to comprehend the meaning in the sounds of rivers, oceans, and streams. He is best at answering questions concerning the future. In Wierus's *Pseudomonarchia Daemonum*, his name is spelled *Caym*. According to Collin de Plancy, Martin Luther, the founder of the Protestant Reformation, claimed to have had an encounter with this demon. In the *Goetia of Dr. Rudd*, his name is spelled *Camio*. Here, he is said to bow to the power of the angel Nanael. See also DE PLANCY, *GOETIA*, RUDD, SCOTT, WIERUS.

Calach: A servant of the demon Ariton named in the *Sacred Magic of Abramelin the Mage*. In the Mathers translation of this work, his name is rendered *Galak*. Accordingly, Mathers relates the name to a Greek root meaning "milky." See also ARITON, MATHERS.

Caleos: A mendacious demon, he must be carefully constrained or else he will mislead any who interact with him. When manifesting, he takes the form of a knight astride a crocodile. He wears two crowns upon his head. His principal office is to grant fame and esteem. He also has knowledge of treasure. His name appears in the Elizabethan grimoire known as the *Book of Oberon*, where he is described among twelve principal servants of Paimon, king of the west. See also *BOOK OF OBERON*, PAIMON.

Calim: A demon in the hierarchy of the east, Calim serves the infernal prince Camuel. According to the *Ars Theurgia*, Calim is a duke and he rules over a hundred ministering spirits. He is tied to the hours of the night but appears by day. See also *ARS THEURGIA*, CAMUEL.

Minions of the Devil

Throughout the Middle Ages, people in Europe believed that the Devil and his minions were a very real presence in the world. Not only did these demons seduce and torment humanity, but they also recruited certain mortals to their side, gifting them with unholy powers. The fear of witchcraft held the people of Europe in such an awful grip that they lashed out against their neighbors, torturing thousands of people to death on suspicion of practicing the black arts. These witch hunts were a dark period of European history that lasted roughly from the fourteenth through the seventeenth centuries. Called the *Witchcraze* by some scholars, such as Anne Llewellyn Barstow and Jeffrey Burton Russell, this terminology reflects the hysterical nature of the witchcraft fears of the time.

The vast majority of people accused of practicing witchcraft were marginalized individuals and second-class citizens. An alarming number of women were accused, and while they were not the only people tortured and killed for practicing witchcraft during this time, the popularized image of a witch was that of a woman—usually decrepit and old.

Central to the notion of European witchcraft during this time was the Witches' Sabbat. This was a gathering—often described as an orgy—that took place in the woods. Witches were thought to fly there, either by leaving their bodies or by riding through the sky in sieves or on brooms. At the Sabbat, witches were said to dance naked in the woods, feasting on foul foods and sometimes sacrificing children. They were thought to plot against their neighbors at this wild gathering, dreaming up the harm they would do in the coming months. And of course, they met with the Devil—often in the form of a tall man with soot-black skin or in the form of a great black goat.

Perhaps unsurprisingly, nearly all of the confessions of witches that described things like flying to the Witches' Sabbat or sacrificing children to the Devil were acquired under extreme torture. The few accounts that were volunteered often came from individuals that even some inquisitors had to admit were simply mad. Fear of the Devil and, more than that, fear of one's neighbor, inspired a truly dark period in European history, the impact of which we are still working to understand.

Woodcut of the Devil from seventeenth-century England. The Devil was often said to appear as a tall man with coal-black skin. Courtesy of Dover Publications.

Calvamia: A demon who serves beneath the king of the northeast, Armadiel. Calvamia is a mighty duke, waited upon by eighty-four lesser spirits. His name and seal both appear in the *Ars Theurgia*. Many of the demons described in this text are also tied to certain times of the day. In the case of Calvamia, if the day is divided into fifteen equal portions, Calvamia's portion is the fourth. He is bound to appear only during these hours. See also ARMADIEL, *ARS THEURGIA*.

Cam: A great president who appears in the form of a thrush but after a while puts on the shape of a man. He carries in his hand a sharp sword and seems to tread on burning ashes. According to the *Book of Incantations*, he is a good disputer. His office is to give understanding of the many languages of the natural world: birds, dogs, cattle, and even the voice of waters. He gives true answers of things to come. Prior to his fall, he belonged to the Order of Angels. Thirty legions serve him. See also *BOOK OF INCANTATIONS*.

Camal: A demon ruled by Astaroth. Camal's name appears in the Mathers translation of the *Sacred Magic of Abramelin the Mage*. According to Mathers, this demon's name means "to desire God." See also ASTAROTH, MATHERS.

Camarion: A servitor of the demon Beelzebub whose name appears in the *Sacred Magic of Abramelin the Mage*. Several manuscript versions of this work exist, and the fifteenth-century French manuscript sourced by Mathers for his translation of the work contains a variant of this demon's name. In that version, it is spelled *Lamarion*, a difference almost certainly due to scribal error. See also BEELZEBUB, MATHERS.

Cambra: A demon in the court of Amaimon, king of the south. Cambra appears as a swan and has power over birds. According to the *Book of Oberon*, Cambra can make any bird tame, providing it as a pet. He also has knowledge of the virtues of herbs and stones, and can teach these when asked. See also AMAIMON, *BOOK OF OBERON*.

Cambores: A servant of the demon Sarabocres. According to the Peterson edition of the *Sworn Book of Honorius*, Cambores is connected with the planet Venus. As such, he has the power to incite love and lust as well as laughter. When he manifests, he is said to have a middling form with skin whiter than snow. Cambores is one of four demons in Sarabocres's court ruled by the east and west winds. See also SARABOCRES, *SWORN BOOK*.

Cambriet: A demon named in the *Ars Theurgia* who is tied to specific hours and minutes of the day. He can only appear during the eighth portion of the day, when the day has been measured out into fifteen portions of time. Holding the rank of duke, Cambriet has two thousand two hundred lesser spirits beneath him. He is a servant of the demon-king Icosiel. He is, for some reason, especially attracted to houses and will most often manifest there. See also *ARS THEURGIA*, ICOSIEL.

Camel: Ruled by Demoriel, the infernal Emperor of the North, Camel is named in the *Ars Theurgia*. In this text, he is said to have one thousand one hundred and forty spirits at his command. If the day is divided into twelve sections consisting of two hours each, Camel is connected with the seventh set of two planetary hours. The name of this demon may have originally been intended to be *Camiel*, a name that appears several times in the hierarchies of other demonic lords in the *Ars Theurgia*. See also *ARS THEURGIA*, DEMORIEL.

Camiel: The name of this demon appears frequently in the *Ars Theurgia*. Each time, it seems as if a separate and distinct demon is implied, as Camiel has very different qualities depending on where his name appears. He shows up as a demon in the court of prince Hydriel. Here, he appears in the form of a great serpent with the head of a beautiful woman. This version of Camiel is said to be drawn to wet locations like swamps. He (or possibly she) is reputed to have a total of one thousand three hundred and twenty ministers to attend his needs. Camiel also appears under the command of the demon Amenadiel, the Great Emperor of the West. Here, Camiel is said to hold the rank of duke, ruling over a total of three thousand eight hundred and eighty lesser spirits of his own. Camiel is named again in the court of the wandering duke Bursiel. In this manifestation, Camiel is reputed to be a being of great malevolence. He fears the light of the day and will

only manifest at night. Camiel and his fellow spirits under Bursiel are hated by all of the other spirits due to their roguish and evil natures. This version of Camiel is similar in appearance to the one who serves Hydriel. When he manifests, he appears as a terrible serpent with a human head. He commands a total of eight hundred and eighty ministering spirits. He also appears as one of several dukes serving beneath the demon Malgaras. Here, Camiel belongs to the hours of the day and commands thirty lesser ministering spirits. See also AMENADIEL, *ARS THEURGIA*, BURSIEL, HYDRIEL, MALGARAS.

Camodiel: A duke in the hierarchy of Emoniel, a wandering prince whose retinue is described in the *Ars Theurgia*. Camodiel is described as possessing a basically good nature, and he prefers to manifest in wooded areas. When he appears, he is likely to be accompanied by at least some of his one thousand three hundred and twenty attending spirits. See also *ARS THEURGIA*, EMONIEL.

Camonix: According to the *Sacred Magic of Abramelin the Mage*, Camonix is a demon who exclusively serves the infernal ruler Astaroth. His name may be related to a Greek word pertaining to battle. See also ASTAROTH, MATHERS.

Camory: A stubborn and churlish spirit who serves the Emperor of the South, Caspiel. Camory holds the rank of duke and is one of twelve infernal dukes who attend upon Caspiel directly. He himself has a total of two thousand two hundred and sixty lesser spirits at his command. Camory is described as an aerial spirit, meaning that his nature has more in common with air than with earth or flesh. Because of this, the *Ars Theurgia* recommends making him appear in a scrying crystal or specially prepared glass vessel so he can be seen with the naked eye. See also *ARS THEURGIA*, CASPIEL.

Camoy: A particularly malignant spirit who can be called up as part of a curse. This demon and his brethren have the power to strike people senseless, and in the *Munich Handbook* there is a spell that shows the magician how to set these nasty little devils upon one's enemies. See also *MUNICH HANDBOOK*.

Demons descend in the form of locusts to plague the unworthy. 16th century Bible illustration of Revelation 9: 1–11. Woodcut. Artist unknown. Image courtesy of the Wellcome Collection, London.

Camuel: Although he sometimes appears as an angel, in the *Ars Theurgia* Camuel is listed as the third spirit in rank beneath the infernal king Carnesiel, Emperor of the East. In this text, Camuel is said to rule the direction of the southeast, with ten infernal dukes to carry out his commands. In Dr. Rudd's *Treatise on Angel Magic*, Camuel is again identified as a demon. Here he is described as the "Chief King of the East," apparently replacing Carnesiel entirely in this role. Camuel is also named in the *Steganographia* of Johannes Trithemius, a work dating to the end of the 1400s. See also *ARS THEURGIA*, CARNESIEL.

Camyel: A demon named in the *Ars Theurgia*, Camyel serves the infernal prince Camuel. He is allied with the court of the east. Awarded the rank of duke, he holds sway over a total of one hundred ministering spirits. He is tied to the hours of the day but manifests during the night. He appears wearing a beautiful form that speaks courteously to all seeking discourse with him. See also *ARS THEURGIA*, CAMUEL.

Canibores: A demon devoted to lust, passion, and earthly delights, Canibores appears in Driscoll's translation of the *Sworn Book*. A president of the order who serves the demon-king Sarabocres, Canibores cannot be conjured visibly himself. Instead, he must be reached through his three ministers, Tracatat, Nassar, and Naassa. According to the *Sworn Book*, Canibores has a malleable nature and his body shines like a brilliant star. He can incite lust and passion between all people. He is also said to possess the power to produce "boundless enjoyment" in the opposite sex. See also NAASSA, NASSAR, SARABOCRES, *SWORN BOOK*, TRACATAT.

Canilel: A demon said to serve the infernal king Barmiel, the first and chief spirit of the south. Canilel's name and seal both appear in seventeenth-century magickal text known as the *Ars Theurgia*. According to this text, Canilel holds the rank of duke. He has twenty lesser spirits who serve him, and he is connected with the hours of the night. See also *ARS THEURGIA*, BARMIEL.

Capriel: In the *Ars Theurgia*, Capriel appears in the hierarchy of the demon Carnesiel, infernal Emperor of the East. Holding the rank of duke, Capriel can be summoned and compelled in the name of his emperor. See also *ARS THEURGIA*, CARNESIEL.

Caraham: One of several demons in the *Sacred Magic of Abramelin the Mage* whose name is a matter of some dispute. In the fifteenth-century French manuscript sourced by Mathers, the name of this demon is given as *Came*. In the 1720 version kept at the Dresden library, the name is *Carah*, while the version at the Wolfenbüttel library in Germany gives the name as *Larach*. Since the original fourteenth-century source of the *Abramelin* material has been lost to time, there is no way to know which spelling is correct. All versions agree, however, that this demon answers to Paimon, one of four infernal princes of the cardinal directions. See also MATHERS, PAIMON.

Carasch: A demon ruled by the arch-fiends Astaroth and Asmodeus. Carasch is named in the 1898 Mathers translation of the *Sacred Magic of Abramelin the Mage*. Mathers attempts a rough etymology of this name, suggesting it comes from a Hebrew root and can be taken to mean "the Voracious One." See also ASTAROTH, ASMODEUS, MATHERS.

Carasiba: A demon who is bound to only appear during a very specific time of the day. The *Ars Theurgia* contains the formula for calculating this time. According to this book, the day must be divided into fifteen equal portions. Of the hours and minutes that fall into each of these, Carasiba will only manifest himself during the twelfth section of the day. He is a mighty duke who serves the demon-king Armadiel and is thus connected with the hierarchy of the north. Eighty-four lesser spirits serve beneath the demon Carasiba. See also ARMADIEL, *ARS THEURGIA*.

Carba: In the *Ars Theurgia*, Carba is ranked as a chief duke with forty lesser spirits under his command. He himself serves in the hierarchy of the demon-prince Dorochiel. He is tied to the hours of the day and will only manifest to mortals before noon. His direction is west. See also *ARS THEURGIA*, DOROCHIEL.

Cardiel: An infernal knight who commands a total of two thousand lesser spirits. Cardiel's name and seal appear in the *Ars Theurgia*, where he is said to serve the greater demon Pirichiel. See also *ARS THEURGIA*, PIRICHIEL.

Carga: A chief duke in the court of the demon-king Asyriel. Carga commands forty lesser spirits of his own. In the *Ars Theurgia*, Carga is reputed to manifest only during the daylight hours. He is associated with the south. See also *ARS THEURGIA*, ASYRIEL.

Cariel: A demon named in the *Ars Theurgia*. According to this text, Cariel is in service to the infernal prince Camuel, a ruler in the hierarchy of the east. Cariel himself is a duke, and he oversees a total of ten ministering spirits. He belongs to the hours of the day, but he is best conjured at night. See also *ARS THEURGIA*, CAMUEL.

Carifas: A demon in the retinue of the Emperor Amenadiel. In the Henson translation of the *Ars Theurgia*, Carifas is connected with the direction west. He holds the rank of duke and commands a total of three thousand eight hundred and eighty lesser spirits. He is one of hundreds of dukes who serve his infernal master, but one of only twelve that are specifically named in this seventeenth-century text. See also AMENADIEL, *ARS THEURGIA*.

Carmas: A demon who serves King Iammas, ruler of the spirits of Mars. Carmas appears wearing red garments to indicate his affiliation with the planetary powers of Mars. A particularly violent demon, he causes battles, death, and murder. He also lights fires. In his human guise, he has antlers and claws and he's preceded by thunder and lightning. He is named in the Elizabethan grimoire known as the *Book of Oberon*, where he is said to serve with three other martial demons. See also *BOOK OF OBERON*, IAMMAS, ITAMALL, PALFRAME, PALFRAMEN.

Carmehal: A servant of the infernal king Iammax, ruler of the spirits of Mars. Carmehal appears in the Joseph Peterson translation of the *Sworn Book of Honorius*. This demon is one of five under the rule of Iammax who are described as being subject to the east wind. As a spirit of Mars, Carmehal stirs up murder, warfare, and bloodshed. His form is dry and lean, with skin the color of embers. The angels Samahel, Satihel, Ylurahihel, and Amabiel are said to have power over him. Compare to the demon Carnical in the Driscoll translation of the *Sworn Book*. See also CARNICAL, IAMMAX, *SWORN BOOK*.

Carmelyon: The third advisor in the court of Oberion, Carmelyon may tread the line between demon and fey. His superior, Oberion, certainly does. Appearing in the eponymous *Book of Oberon*, he is identified as both the king of the faeries and a former angel of the light. Given that Carmelyon serves as one of his top four ministers, there is a high chance he occupies a similarly mixed state of being. See also *BOOK OF OBERON*, OBERION.

Carmerin: A demon lord with command over thirty legions, his name appears in the magickal text known as the *Book of Oberon*. In that same book, *Cayenam* is given as his alternate name. (It is not uncommon for alternate spellings to be collected in these entries.) This demon enjoys spying on women and is best summoned by those aspiring to be Peeping Toms. As with several other demons who possess the power to sexually coerce women, he manifests as a woman himself. In this form he comes riding a camel and wearing a double crown. Compare his appearance and powers to Gemyem and Gemon, both from the same text. See also *BOOK OF OBERON*, GEMON, GEMYEM.

Carmola: A great prince who can grant understanding of the speech of birds. He makes people invisible and can also entrap thieves and murderers. According to the sixteenth-century French grimoire *Livre des esperitz*, he gives truthful answers to any question demanded of him and oversees twenty-six legions of spirits. See also *LIVRE DES ESPERITZ*.

Carmox: A demon connected with the planet Mars. According to the Peterson translation of the *Sworn Book of Honorius*, Carmox serves the infernal king Iammax. Carmox has the power to incite anger and bloodshed, driving people to murder and war. He is likely a variation of the demon Carnax. See also CARNAX, IAMMAX, *SWORN BOOK*.

When summoned, many demons first appeared in inhuman form. Many of these shapes were monstrous, but others appeared as angels, many-winged and limned with fire. Illustration by Kirsten Brown.

Carnax: In the Driscoll edition of the *Sworn Book of Honourius*, Carnax is a minister of the demon-king Jamaz. Through Jamaz, he is connected with the element fire and thus Carnax has a complexion like flame. He is energetic, quick, and strong with a temperament best described as hot and impetuous. He has the power to cause death, but he can also stave off decay. Additionally, he can restore that which has decayed to its original state. He has familiars in the form of soldiers, and he can also raise an army of one thousand soldiers for whatever use is deemed fit. He is likely a variation upon the demon Carmox. See also CARMOX, JAMAZ, *SWORN BOOK*.

Carnesiel: In the *Ars Theurgia*, one book of the larger *Lesser Key of Solomon*, Carnesiel is named as the Chief Emperor of the East. He is served by one thousand great dukes and one hundred lesser dukes as well as a host of other ministering spirits. When conjured with his seal, he appears both by day and by night. Part of an extensive list of spirits associated with the points of the compass, Carnesiel sits at the head of the hierarchy of spirits associated with the east. All of the spirits beneath him can be summoned and compelled in his name. Carnesiel also appears in Trithemius's *Steganographia*. See also *ARS THEURGIA*, TRITHEMIUS.

Carnical: According to the 1977 Driscoll translation of the *Sworn Book*, Carnical is a demon in service to Jamaz, the infernal king of fire. As a demon tied to this element, Carnical has a complexion that resembles flame. He is also said to possess a nature that is hot and hasty as well as energetic and quick. He has power over the process of decay, and can reverse its effects or stave it off entirely. He can cause death with but a word and raise an army of one thousand soldiers, possibly from the grave. Compare Carnical to the demon Carmehal in the Peterson edition of the *Sworn Book*. See also CARMEHAL, JAMAZ, *SWORN BOOK*.

Carnor: A demon in the hierarchy of Caspiel, infernal Emperor of the South. According to the *Ars Theurgia*, Carnor holds the title of duke. He is one of twelve dukes serving Caspiel whose names and seals are specifically presented in this seventeenth-century work on the summoning and compelling of spirits. Allegedly, Carnor oversees two thousand two hundred and sixty lesser spirits. See also *ARS THEURGIA*, CASPIEL.

Caromos: According to the *Sacred Magic of Abramelin the Mage*, Caromos is a demonic servitor of prince Ariton. In the Mathers translation of this work, the name Caromos is thought to mean "joy," from a Greek root. In other versions of the *Abramelin* material, this demon's name is spelled *Calamosy*. See also ARITON, MATHERS.

Caron: A demon governed by the infernal king Malgaras. Caron is a chief duke of the night with thirty lesser spirits under him. His name appears in the *Ars Theurgia*. Through Malgaras, he is tied to the court of the west. Caron also appears as a servant of the demon Ariton in the *Sacred Magic of Abramelin the Mage*. Caron is very likely a variant of the name *Charon*, the Greek ferryman said to convey the dead across the river Styx and into Hades. Because of his associations with the underworld, Charon was often demonized. See also ARITON, *ARS THEURGIA*, MALGARAS, MATHERS.

Carpiel: A demon from the *Ars Theurgia* said to serve the infernal king Barmiel. Through his association with Barmiel, Carpiel is connected with the south. He holds the rank of duke and rules over twenty ministering spirits. He is one of ten demonic dukes who serve Barmiel during the hours of the day. It is sometimes tempting to relate the names of demons to the words that they resemble, but there is no indication that Carpiel bears any

Scribal Mission Impossible

Your mission: make an accurate copy of a text that has no punctuation, virtually no spaces between words, and letters that are not always standard. On top of this, try tackling this near-impossible task in low-light conditions while using inks and pigments that could very well kill you if ingested or handled improperly. Sound impossible? Year after year throughout the Middle Ages, this was exactly what European scribes did. Before the advent of the printing press, books were copied, illustrated, and bound by hand, and each individual volume became a singular work of art. But it was no easy task to copy these precious tomes accurately. Each time period and often each region had its own particular script, and although this was generally standardized, each scribe had his or her own particular hand, with the vagaries that always accompany hand-crafted work. Additionally, scribes would sometimes use shorthand, especially if they were running out of room on a line, and if you did not clearly understand their notations, you generally had to guess about their meaning when making a copy of that section for yourself. The *sigla*, or shorthand, of some manuscripts are so unique that certain historians can date a manuscript based on the nature of its abbreviations alone!*

On top of all of these factors, almost all of these manuscripts were written in Latin, at best a second language for most scribes. While all of the above circumstances are true for books that were formally produced during the Middle Ages, even more trying circumstances often surrounded the copying of grimoires. Forbidden books that had to be hidden and passed around on the sly, all of the early grimoires were copied by hand. As with the material contained in the *Sacred Magic of Abramelin the Mage*, at some point there was an original, but the copy that an individual magician found himself working from may have been several times removed from that original. This separation, as well as the manner in which the texts were reproduced, opened the grimoiric tradition to a host of errors—most of them simple issues of copying. A vast number of demon names, as well as talismans and sigils (a term taken from the word for scribal abbreviation), have almost certainly come down to the modern day rife with inaccuracies. In some cases, entire names of demons were inadvertently created when one scribe along the line of descent copied a letter incorrectly. Since the original versions of nearly all the grimoires have been lost to time, it's important to keep in mind that some of those really garbled-sounding demon names may, in fact, be medieval typos.

---

* Stephen R. Reimer, *Manuscript Studies: Medieval and Early Modern*.

resemblance to a fish. See also *ARS THEURGIA*, BARMIEL.

Carsiel: In the *Ars Theurgia*, Carsiel is named as one of a dozen chief dukes in service to the demon-prince Dorochiel. Associated with the hours of the day, Carsiel commands a total of forty ministering spirits. Through Dorochiel, he is affiliated with the hierarchy of the west. See also *ARS THEURGIA*, DOROCHIEL.

Cartael: A demon whose name and seal appear in the book known as the *Ars Theurgia*. Cartael is said to serve in the hierarchy of the north, and his immediate superior is the demon-king Baruchas. Cartael himself holds the rank of duke and commands thousands of lesser spirits. He will only appear during hours and minutes that fall in the fourteenth portion of the day, when the day has been divided into fifteen parts. See also *ARS THEURGIA*, BARUCHAS.

Casael: A demon whose name may be a variant of Carsiel. This spelling of the name appears in the *Ars Theurgia* in conjunction with the infernal prince Dorochiel. Casael is said to serve in the capacity of chief duke, with four hundred lesser spirits beneath him. He is tied to the hours of the second half of the day, manifesting between noon and dusk. His direction is west. See also *ARS THEURGIA*, CARSIEL, DOROCHIEL.

Casbriel: An evil demon of the night who so hates the light that he refuses to manifest during the hours of the day. Casbriel serves the demon Buriel, who is described in the *Ars Theurgia* as a "wandering duke," which is to say that, among the spirits associated with the points of the compass, Buriel and his company change their location and move however they please. Casbriel is such a roguish and malevolent spirit that he and his compatriots are despised by all other spirits. Within his own hierarchy, he is popular enough that he commands eight hundred and eighty lesser spirits. When he manifests, Casbriel assumes a monstrous form. He appears as a massive serpent with a human head. See also *ARS THEURGIA*, BURIEL.

Casiet: One of several demons said to serve in the court of the west beneath the infernal king Malgaras. Casiet holds the rank of chief duke and commands thirty ministering spirits. According to the *Ars Theurgia*, he is tied to the hours of the day and will only manifest during these hours. The name of this demon may have been generated through scribal error, as it is one letter off from the more common name *Casiel*. See also *ARS THEURGIA*, CARSIEL, MALGARAS.

Cason: According to the fifteenth-century grimoire known as the *Munich Handbook*, this grand duke of Hell commands no fewer than forty-five legions of devils. When summoned, he appears as a courtly seneschal, and he grants the magician any dignities he may wish. The demon can discourse on matters concerning the past, present, or future, and he can bring favor to the magician from friend or foe alike. The name of this demon may be a variation on *Curson*, an alias given in Scot's *Discoverie of Witchcraft* for the Goetic demon Purson. See also *MUNICH HANDBOOK*, PURSON, SCOT.

Caspiel: A great and chief emperor named in the *Ars Theurgia*. Caspiel is one of a number of demons associated with the points of the compass. His dominion is the south. He has a vast array of demons who serve under him, including two hundred great dukes and four hundred lesser dukes. The dukes who serve beneath him are described as stubborn and churlish. Caspiel has an airy nature.

Consequently, if he manifests, it is often through images in a glass or in a specially prepared shewstone. In Dr. Rudd's *Treatise on Angel Magic*, Caspiel is also identified as the chief demon ruling over the south. He also appears in the *Steganographia* of Johannes Trithemius. See also ARS THEURGIA, TRITHEMIUS.

Castumi: A demon of invisibility, Castumi appears as part of an invisibility spell outlined in the *Clavicula Salomonis*. According to this text, Castumi serves Almiras, the demonic Master of Invisibility. Castumi can also be found associated with invisibility spells in Mathers's translation of the *Sacred Magic of Abramelin the Mage*. See also ALMIRAS, *CLAVICULA SALOMONIS*, MATHERS.

Caudes: A servant of the demon Batthan. Caudes appears in the Peterson translation of the *Sworn Book of Honorius*. Here, he is said to be connected with the sun. He has the power to bring power and riches to any mortal. He can also confer good health and the favor of friends. Caudes is governed by the angels Raphael, Cashael, Dardyhel, and Hanrathaphael. He is one of four demons in the hierarchy of the sun that are also said to be subject to the north wind. See also BATTHAN, *SWORN BOOK*.

Cavayr: A demon in the service of King Baruchas. As such, he is part of the court of the north. Cavayr holds the rank of duke and oversees thousands of lesser spirits. He is bound to appear during a very specific time frame. In the work known as the *Ars Theurgia*, the following formula is given to calculate when Cavayr may manifest during the day: divide the day into fifteen portions of time. Cavayr belongs to the fourth portion. See also *ARS THEURGIA*, BARUCHAS.

Cayros: One of a number of demons named in the *Ars Theurgia* as chief dukes who serve the infernal prince Dorochiel. Cayros is a night-demon, bound to serve his master in the hours between midnight and dawn. He is tied to the hierarchy of the west. As a demon of rank, he has four hundred ministering spirits to carry out his wishes. See also *ARS THEURGIA*, DOROCHIEL.

Cazul: According to the *Ars Theurgia*, Cazul is an evil-natured and deceptive demon associated with the night. He serves directly beneath the demon Cabariel, the ruling prince of the direction west by north. For those daring enough to summon him, Cazul typically appears only at night with an

A scribe copying pages from a manuscript. From an illuminated booklet on the scribe's art by Jackie Williams.

entourage of fifty lesser spirits to minister to his needs. See also *ARS THEURGIA*, CABARIEL.

Cerbere: A great marquis who gives perfect understanding in all sciences and makes people great in both honor and wealth. Nineteen legions serve him. He appears in the *Livre des esperitz*, a sixteenth-century French grimoire. His name is almost certainly derived from *Cerebus*, the three-headed hound who guarded the gates of Hades in Greek myth. Cerebus's name, incidentally, translates to *Spot*. See also *LIVRE DES ESPERITZ*.

Chabri: One of ten chief dukes attributed to the court of the wandering prince Uriel. According to the *Ars Theurgia*, Chabri has six hundred and fifty companions and servants to attend him. He is reputed to have an evil nature and to be stubborn, disobedient, and false in all his dealings. When he manifests, he assumes the form of a monstrous serpent with a human head. See also *ARS THEURGIA*, URIEL.

Chamor: A demon named in the *Ars Theurgia*. Chamor is one of six chief dukes in the court of Menadiel, a wandering prince of the air. He has three hundred and ninety lesser spirits to serve him. In addition, he has a specific companion in the demon Baruch. Where Chamor will manifest only during the fifth hour of the day, Baruch always follows after him, appearing in the sixth planetary hour. His name is also spelled *Clamor*. See also *ARS THEURGIA*, BARUCH, MENADIEL.

Chamoriel: One of the twelve dukes who follow the demon Hydriel, a wandering prince of the air. Chamoriel commands a total of one thousand three hundred and twenty lesser spirits. He is named in the *Ars Theurgia*, a text that also contains the seal that summons and compels him. Although Chamoriel is a spirit of the air, he is nevertheless drawn to moist and watery locations, preferring to manifest in wetlands and swamps. When he appears, Chamoriel behaves in a polite and courteous manner which may seem at odds with his appearance: Chamoriel's manifest form is that of a serpent with a human head. See also *ARS THEURGIA*, HYDRIEL.

Chamos: According to the demonic hierarchy of Charles Berbiguier, Chamos serves in Hell's royal household. In Berbiguier's early-nineteenth-century work, *Les Farfadets*, Chamos is listed as the Lord High Chamberlain and a Knight of the Fly. Occultist A. E. Waite presents Chamos in the same capacity in his treatment of the *Grand Grimoire* in his *Book of Black Magic and Pacts*. Chamos is almost certainly a variation of *Chemosh*, an ancient Moabite god named in the Bible. In the Bible, Chemosh is variously known as "the destroyer," "the subduer," and "the abomination of Moab." As was the case with nearly all foreign gods, the early Israelites didn't like Chemosh much, hence his transformation from god to demon. See also BERBIGUIER, *GRAND GRIMOIRE*, WAITE.

Chanael: A demon of the day ruled by the infernal king Raysiel. Chanael holds the title of chief duke and has an unspecified number of attendants who exist to carry out his commands. Chanael's name appears in the *Ars Theurgia*. Through Raysiel, Chanael owes allegiance to the court of the north. See also *ARS THEURGIA*, RAYSIEL.

Chansi: One of thirty dukes said to serve the infernal king Barmiel. According to the *Ars Theurgia*, Barmiel is the first and chief spirit of the south. Through his allegiance to this demon, Chansi is also connected with the south. As a demon of rank, Chansi oversees twenty ministering spirits of his own. He serves his king during the hours of the day. See also *ARS THEURGIA*, BARMIEL.

Charas: A demon in service to Aseliel, a prince in the hierarchy of the east. According to the *Ars Theurgia*, Charas belongs to the hours of the day. He holds the rank of chief president and has thirty principal spirits and twenty ministering spirits under his command. See also *ARS THEURGIA*, ASELIEL.

Chariel: A duke of the demon Hydriel. Chariel has one thousand three hundred and twenty lesser spirits under his command. This demon is said to have a great love for damp and moist places, and he is most likely to manifest in places like swamps. He assumes the form of a massive serpent with a human head, and while this semblance can be frightening, the *Ars Theurgia* assures readers that Chariel is a good and courteous spirit. See also *ARS THEURGIA*, HYDRIEL.

Chariet: One of twelve main dukes who serves in the hierarchy of the demon Caspiel, Emperor of the South. Chariet is said to be a stubborn spirit with a churlish disposition. He holds dominion over two thousand two hundred and sixty lesser spirits. He can be summoned and compelled in the name of his emperor, or he can be controlled through the use of his name and his seal. The seal can be found in the *Ars Theurgia*, the second book of the *Lesser Key of Solomon*. See also *ARS THEURGIA*, CASPIEL.

Charnos: One of several demons said to serve the infernal prince Aseliel during the hours of the night. In the *Ars Theurgia*, Charnos is described as a chief president connected with the east through his allegiance to Aseliel. He is said to rule over thirty principal spirits, with another twenty min-istering servants at his command. See also *ARS THEURGIA*, ASELIEL.

Charoblel: A demon known to manifest in a human form that is beautiful and pleasing to the eye. Charoblel serves the infernal prince Bidiel is one of his ten great dukes. He oversees a retinue of two thousand four hundred lesser spirits of his own. The name and seal of this demon appear in the *Ars Theurgia*. See also *ARS THEURGIA*, BIDIEL.

Charoel: An infernal duke attended by four hundred ministering spirits. Charoel appears in the hierarchy of the demon Macariel, described as a wandering prince in the *Ars Theurgia*. Charoel and his compatriots are free to appear in any hour of the day or night. He has command over diverse forms but often prefers to appear as a many-headed dragon. He also appears as one of twelve chief dukes said to serve the demon Soleviel, another wandering prince of the air. This version of Charoel only serves his demonic master every other year. One thousand eight hundred and forty ministering spirits exist to carry out his commands. See also *ARS THEURGIA*, MACARIEL, SOLEVIEL.

Charsiel: A demon named in the *Ars Theurgia*. Charsiel serves in the hierarchy of Menadiel, a so-called wandering prince of the air who moves from place to place with his massive retinue. Charsiel himself oversees a total of three hundred and ninety lesser spirits. He is also bound to the demon Curasin, who functions as his companion. Where Charsiel goes, Curasin follows after. Accordingly, Charsiel may only appear during the ninth hour of the day, and Curasin appears only in the tenth. See also *ARS THEURGIA*, CURASIN, MENADIEL.

Chasor: One of twelve infernal dukes said to serve the demon-king Maseriel during the hours of the day. Chasor is named in the *Ars Theurgia*, where he is said to rule over thirty lesser spirits of his own. Through his service to Maseriel, Chasor is connected with the south. See also *ARS THEURGIA*, MASERIEL.

Chatas: In the *Liber de Angelis*, Chatas is named as one of the demons in service to the infernal ruler Barchan. Chatas is summoned as part of the spell for crafting a Ring of the Sun. This potent astrological talisman requires the blood of a white bird during its construction. Once finished, it can be used to bind the tongues of enemies or to summon a great black horse to claim as one's steed. Several of the spells connected with this talisman require animal sacrifice, and the magician is cautioned to wear this ring whenever he carries out these sacrifices. See also BARCHAN, *LIBER DE ANGELIS*.

Chaudas: A demon named in the Peterson translation of the *Sworn Book of Honorius*. Chaudas is a minister of Batthan, the king of the spirits of the sun. He is tied to the region of the east and has the ability to bring people riches and worldly power. In addition to this, he can make people healthy and well loved. His manifest form is large and bright with skin the color of the sun. The angels Raphael, Cashael, Dardyhel, and Hanrathaphael have power over him. See also BATTHAN, *SWORN BOOK*.

Chemosh: In 1 Kings, Solomon is said to have built a sanctuary to Chemosh on the Mount of Olives. This biblical monarch, hailed in his younger years for his faith and wisdom, is credited with later introducing the Israelites to the worship of this foreign god. Chemosh was a deity in the pantheon of the Moabites, a neighboring people with whom the early Israelites had contact. Chemosh's name is often given as meaning "the destroyer" or "the subduer." He was possibly a god of war. This notion is supported by the fact that Mesha, a hero of the Moabites, attributed his victories over the Israelites to the god Chemosh. De Plancy and Berbiguier render this name as *Chamos*. See also BERBIGUIER, CHAMOS, DE PLANCY.

Cherasa: Affiliated with the planetary sphere of Saturn. With a long, slender body, wickedly beaked mouth, and translucent black skin, this demon has a monstrous appearance. Like many demons, he can assume other shapes, including that of a pig, a horned owl, a dragon, or an old woman leaning on canes. His office is to inspire hatred and murder, tempt people with evil thoughts, and sow chaos and discord. He is associated with the color black and the metal lead. Named in the *Book of Oberon*, he is said to serve alongside four other similarly monstrous spirits in the court of King Maymon. See also ALBEWE, ALDEE, *BOOK OF OBERON*, ETHEYE, MALYKE, MAYMON.

Cheros: This demon is named as the minister of Almiras, Master of Invisibility. In Mathers's translation of the *Clavicula Salomonis*, both Cheros and his superior Almiras are conjured up to lend their powers to an invisibility spell. This demon also appears in the Mathers translation of the *Sacred Magic of Abramelin the Mage* in association with an invisibility spell. See also ALMIRAS, *CLAVICULA SALOMONIS*, MATHERS.

Chomiell: A demon said only to manifest in the twelfth set of two planetary hours of the day. Chomiell's name and seal appear in the *Ars Theurgia*. Here he is said to serve Demoriel, the infernal Emperor of the North. Through his service to Demoriel, Chomiell is also affiliated with the north. He is a mighty duke with dominion over one thousand one hundred and forty lesser spirits. This demon also appears in Rudd's *Treatise on Angel Magic* with the spelling *Chomiel*. See also *ARS THEURGIA*, DE-MORIEL.

Chremoas: In the *Ars Theurgia*, Chremoas is one of ten great dukes who serve the infernal prince Bidiel. Chremoas oversees no fewer than two thousand and four hundred inferior spirits. When he manifests, he is reputed to take a human shape that is beautiful and pleasant to look upon. See also *ARS THEURGIA*, BIDIEL.

Chronicles of Jerahmeel: An extensive collection of Jewish history and folklore edited and translated by Hebrew scholar Dr. Moses Gaster. This massive work was published in 1899 under the title *The Chronicles of Jerahmeel or, the Hebrew Bible Historiale*. The original compiler of the *Chronicles* gives his name as Eleasar ben Asher the Levite. According to Gaster, Eleasar lived in the fourteenth century and was not the original compiler of the work. That distinction Gaster gives to the enigmatic figure of Jerahmeel, referenced within portions of the book—hence his choice in titles. While some of the material in the *Chronicles* is as recent as the Crusades, the majority of the work deals with much older time periods, going back as far as the lives of biblical figures like Noah and Moses. The *Chronicles* are of particular interest to this work because they contain Hebrew and Aramaic variations on early books of the Bible, expanding on figures like Samael, Lilith, and the Watcher Angels. The Jewish legends surrounding these figures bled into the Christian tradition, and many concepts established in material like the *Chronicles* can be found in the depictions of these figures in both grimoiric magick and in Christian demonology. See also GASTER, LILITH, SAMAEL, WATCHER ANGELS.

Chrubas: A demon who serves in the hierarchy of the north. He holds the rank of duke, and his

The mournful King Hades guards the gate to Hell. To his left are the three-headed hound Cerebus and a figure that may be Proserpine. From an engraving by T. Stothard, 1792. Image courtesy of the Wellcome Collection, London.

immediate superior is the demon-king Symiel, who rules in the north by east. According to the *Ars Theurgia*, Chrubas has a total of one hundred lesser spirits beneath him. These minister to their duke and carry out his commands. See also *ARS THEURGIA*, SYMIEL.

Chuba: According to the *Ars Theurgia*, Chuba is a demon who serves the infernal king Baruchas. Holding the rank of duke, Chuba oversees thousands of lesser spirits. He will manifest himself in a scrying glass or crystal but only during very specific hours and minutes of the day. If the day is divided into fifteen equal parts, then Chuba belongs to the twelfth portion of time. Through king Baruchas, Chuba is allied with the hierarchy of the north. See also *ARS THEURGIA*, BARUCHAS.

Churibal: A demon in the court of Demoriel, Emperor of the North. According to the *Ars Theurgia*, Churibal is a duke with one thousand one hundred and forty ministering spirits at his command. If the day is divided into twelve sections of two hours each, Churibal is said to appear only during the tenth set of two planetary hours. See also *ARS THEURGIA*, DEMORIEL.

Chuschi: In his translation of the *Sacred Magic of Abramelin the Mage*, Mathers suggests that this demon's name is derived from a Hebrew word meaning "silent." As the Silent One, Chuschi is summoned as part of the elaborate Holy Guardian Angel rite. He serves beneath all four of the demonic princes who oversee the cardinal directions: Oriens, Paimon, Ariton, and Amaimon. See also AMAIMON, ARITON, MATHERS, ORIENS, PAIMON.

Cimeries: In Wierus's *Pseudomonarchia Daemonum*, Cimeries is said to be associated with parts of Africa. According to that text, this demon holds the rank of marquis. He rules over twenty legions of lesser spirits. He teaches grammar, logic, and rhetoric, and also has the power to reveal hidden things. In Scot's *Discoverie of Witchcraft*, he is said to transform men into soldiers. His name also appears among the seventy-two demons of the *Goetia*, where it is sometimes rendered *Cimeies*. In the *Goetia of Dr. Rudd*, he is said to be governed by the angel Marakel. According to the Welsh *Book of Incantations*, he assumes the guise of a soldier riding a stalwart horse and he can make a man appear to be a soldier in his own likeness. In that text, his name is spelled *Cimerjes*. See also *BOOK OF INCANTATIONS*, *GOETIA*, RUDD, SCOTT, WIERUS.

Cirecas: A night-demon named in the Henson translation of the *Ars Theurgia*. According to this text, Cirecas is associated with the court of the south. His direct master is the demon-king Gediel, who ranks as the second spirit beneath the infernal Emperor of the South, Caspiel. Cirecas himself holds the rank of duke and has dominion over twenty lesser spirits of his own. See also *ARS THEURGIA*, GEDIEL.

Citgara: A servant of the demon Camuel. Through his allegiance to Camuel, Citgara is tied to the court of the east. In the *Ars Theurgia*, Citgara is said to hold the rank of duke and to have one hundred lesser spirits at his command. He is tied to the hours of the day but he is called forth by night. See also *ARS THEURGIA*, CAMUEL.

Claniel: One of twelve chief dukes who serve the wandering prince Macariel in the *Ars Theurgia*. Claniel can appear in any hour of the day or night and has four hundred lesser spirits to attend him. Although he can allegedly appear in a variety of forms, Claniel prefers to assume the shape of a many-headed dragon. See also *ARS THEURGIA*, MACARIEL.

Claunech: Named in Peterson's *Grimorium Verum*, Claunech is ranked first in the hierarchy of demons serving under Duke Syrach. He is reputed to be greatly loved by Lucifer, and thus he has a great many powers, mostly concerning wealth. For the magician who works amicably with him, Claunech will reveal the location of hidden treasure and can also swiftly bring great riches to his master. In the Venetian *Secrets of Solomon*, his name is spelled *Claunth*. See also *GRIMORIUM VERUM*, LUCIFER, *SECRETS OF SOLOMON*, SYRACH.

Clavicula Salomonis: Also known as the *Key of Solomon* or the *Clavicle of Solomon the King*. It is not to be confused with the *Lesser Key of Solomon*, also known as the *Lemegeton*. The *Clavicle of Solomon* is mainly comprised of planetary correspondences, a variety of spells, and a series of talismanic images or pentacles associated with the seven celestial spheres. Multiple versions of the work exist. Many of these can be found in the Sloane and Harley collections

Ends in -*el*

If you pay close attention to a number of names in this text, you'll find that there is a traditional convention to the spelling of most angel names. Nearly all angel names end in either *-iel* or *-ael*. The Semitic root *el* means "Lord" or "God," and in the case of angels, it is usually read as meaning "of God." Thus, the name of the angel Raphael is taken to mean "healing of God," as the root *raph* means "to heal." This is generally interpreted as a demonstration of that angel's devotion to the Creator. However, the name could also be taken to mean "god of healing"—a reading suggestive of the possibility that all the angels were once members of an ancient pantheon predating Jewish monotheism.

Many demons began life as angels, and quite a few of them still retain their angelic-sounding names despite their fallen status. This of course raises problems with clearly discerning the fallen from the unfallen, as their names can be virtually identical. Even the magickal grimoires that endeavor to describe methods for calling up demons to make use of their skills acknowledge that these infernal be-

ings are roguish and deceitful by nature and, unless properly bound and compelled, will seek to mislead people. The seventeenth-century scholar Dr. Thomas Rudd devised a solution: he outlined an extensive question-and-answer session intended to trick demons into revealing their infernal natures. It begins with getting the spirit's name and ends by asking the spirit to agree that all the fallen have been justly condemned. The idea here is that a fallen angel will balk at this statement, and reveal itself by trying to argue the point.

Lucifer's minions crowd the skies of Hell, indistinguishable from the Heavenly Hosts. From Doré's illustrations of Milton's *Paradise Lost*.

at the British Museum, including Harley 3981 and Sloane 3091. These date to around the eighteenth century, but the origins of this work are older by far. Trithemius makes note of a copy of the *Clavicula Salomonis* in his list of necromantic books. This list, included in his *Antipalus Maleficiorum*, was compiled in the early 1500s. As a result, we know that at least some version of the *Key of Solomon* was written prior to 1500. The most widely read translation of the *Key of Solomon* was produced by occultist S. L. MacGregor Mathers in 1889. Mathers sources seven manuscripts for his translation, including Harley MS 3981, Sloane MSS 1307 and 3091, King's MS 288, and two manuscripts from the Lansdowne collection, numbered 1202 and 1203. These were not necessarily the oldest nor were they the most accurate manuscripts, but Mathers's work is still widely referenced by modern students of the occult.

Not all manuscripts bearing the title *Clavicles of Solomon* are derived from the same work. Among these is the British Museum's Lansdowne MS 1203, entitled *Les Véritables Clavicules de Salomon*. It likely dates to the mid-eighteenth century and, aside from some pentacles included near the end, it is very different in content from the *Clavicles* sourced by Mathers. See also LEMEGETON, MATHERS.

Clavis Inferni: Published as the *Grimoire of St. Cyprian* by occult researchers Stephen Skinner and David Rankine, this is a transcription of the manuscript stored as Wellcome MS 2000 in London's Wellcome Library. It is credited to M: L: Cypriani, likely a reference to Saint Cyprian of Antioch, who lived during the third and fourth centuries of the Common Era. Before his conversion, Saint Cyprian had a widespread reputation as a powerful magician, and as a result, many grimoires were credited to him, particularly in Scandinavia. A Cyprian tradition is also extant in Spanish and Portuguese books of magick, but this text is distinct from those. The provenance of this particular Cyprian grimoire is currently uncertain, aside from being broadly Western European. The manuscript, written on vellum and comprising a slim twenty-one pages, is dated "MCCCCCCLLXVII," possibly intended to read "1717." Rankine and Skinner suggest a date of 1757. It is the opinion of the library that the script places the creation of the book closer to the latter half of that century. (It was not uncommon for decades and even centuries to be subtracted from the actual publication date of grimoires, and so the error is probably intentional.) The grimoire's full title is *Clavis Inferni sive magia alba et nigra approbata Metratona*, or *The Key of Hell with White and Black Magic Proven by Metatron*.[42] It is concerned primarily with the demon-kings of the four directions (in this case, Maymon, Egyn, Urieus, and Paymon), and it provides numerous elaborate color illustrations of the spirits, their sigils, and the figures necessary for safe summoning. The text is in Latin, with Greek and Hebrew, all of it obscured through a simple code that alters the position of words in each sentence.

Cleraca: Mathers suggests that the name of this demon means "the clerk." Cleraca is said to serve the demon-kings Amaimon and Ariton. This spelling of the demon's name appears in the 1898 Mathers translation of the *Sacred Magic of Abramelin the Mage*. In other versions of the *Abramelin* material, the name is spelled variously as *Kloracha* and *Klorecha*. See also AMAIMON, ARITON, MATHERS.

---

42. The term *proven* in this case means "tested" and is used to validate the efficacy of the magic. The use of the term can be found as far back as the collection of spells known as the *Egyptian Book of the Dead*. See R. O. Faulkner, *The Ancient Egyptian Book of the Dead*.

Clisthert: This demon, named in Peterson's *Grimorium Verum*, is the eighth demon who serves beneath Duke Syrach. At the command of the magician, he will change night to day or day to night, instantly. See also *GRIMORIUM VERUM*, SYRACH.

Clyssan: A mighty duke ruled by the demon-prince Cabariel. Clyssan is one of a hundred such dukes. Fifty serve by day and fifty serve by night. Clyssan holds his office by day, preferring to manifest during the daylight hours. He is reputed to be good-natured and obedient and has fifty lesser spirits who serve beneath him. Through Cabariel, he is associated with the direction west. Clyssan and his compatriots appear in the second book of the *Lesser Key of Solomon*, known as the *Ars Theurgia*. See also *ARS THEURGIA*, CABARIEL.

Coap: A grand prince with power over women. He treats them as chattel and can make them go anywhere. He can even change their appearance to something exotic, if such is preferred. He oversees twenty-seven legions of lesser spirits. His name appears in the *Livre des esperitz*, a sixteenth-century French grimoire. His name is a variation of the Goetic demon *Gaap*, sometimes also spelled *Goap*. See also GAAP, *LIVRE DES ESPERITZ*.

Cobel: The name of this demon appears twice in the fifteenth-century French manuscript sourced by Mathers for his translation of the *Sacred Magic of Abramelin the Mage*. The name is given as both *Cobel* and *Sobel*. *Abramelin* scholar Georg Dehn has suggested that Mathers's source material was inherently flawed, and this certainly seems to be the case with this demon. In all other surviving versions of the *Abramelin* text, the name is spelled *Lobel*. Regardless of spelling, this demon is said to serve the infernal ruler Magoth. See also MAGOTH, MATHERS.

A magician conjures a woman from his mirror. A disturbing number of spells were aimed at coercing women into having sex. Soft ground etching by F. Rops. 19th century. Image courtesy of the Wellcome Collection, London.

Cobusiel: A demon who serves in the court of Soleviel, a wandering prince of the air described in the *Ars Theurgia*. Cobusiel holds the rank of duke and oversees one thousand eight hundred and forty lesser spirits. He switches year by year with another duke in Soleviel's court, only serving his infernal master one year out of every two. See also *ARS THEURGIA*, SOLEVIEL.

Codriel: One of twelve dukes in the court of the demon Amenadiel whose names and seals appear in the *Ars Theurgia*. Through his service to Amenadiel, Codriel is connected with the west. He holds the rank of duke and is said to govern no fewer than three thousand eight hundred and eighty lesser spirits. See also AMENADIEL, *ARS THEURGIA*.

Coelen: One of many demons named in the *Sacred Magic of Abramelin the Mage*, Coelen is summoned as a part of the extensive Holy Guardian Angel rite. Mathers suggests that the name of this demon is related to the Latin word for "heaven," and may mean "from the heavens." Given his identification as a demon who serves the four infernal princes of the cardinal directions, this would seem to suggest that Coelen was originally an angel who later fell. See also MATHERS.

Coliel: A demon governed by the infernal king Gediel. Coliel serves his master by day and has twenty servants to help him carry out his duties. He holds the rank of duke and, through his service to Gediel, is associated with the hierarchy of the south that is established within the *Ars Theurgia*. See also *ARS THEURGIA*, GEDIEL.

Colvam: Mathers takes this demon's name to mean "shame." In the Mathers translation of the *Sacred Magic of Abramelin the Mage*, Colvam is said to serve under the joint leadership of Magoth and Kore. Variations on his name include *Kobhan* and *Kofan*. See also KORE, MAGOTH, MATHERS.

Coolor: A demon named in the *Book of Oberon*. According to this text, he holds the rank of prince, with thirteen legions of lesser spirits that serve him. His main power is to find hidden treasure. When summoned, he appears as a winged child riding a two-headed dragon. His wings are like those of a goshawk, making him identical in appearance, if not in name, to the fiftieth demon of the *Pseudomonarchia Daemonum*, Volac. See also *BOOK OF OBERON*, VOLAC.

Corcaron: A demon in service to the infernal rulers Asmodeus and Astaroth. Corcaron appears in the Mathers translation of the *Sacred Magic of Abramelin the Mage*. See also ASMODEUS, ASTAROTH, MATHERS.

Corilon: A demon ruled by the infernal prince Beelzebub. Corilon is named in the *Sacred Magic of Abramelin the Mage* as translated by occultist S. L. MacGregor Mathers. See also BEELZEBUB, MATHERS.

Cormes: A demon with the power to help reveal the identity of thieves. Cormes is one of several such demons invoked in a spell that appears in the fifteenth-century *Munich Handbook*. He is also associated with scrying and divination. See also *MUNICH HANDBOOK*.

Cornyx: A demon with power over birds. His name appears in the *Book of Oberon*, where he is alleged to gather birds all in one place and snatch them, presumably to then give them to his summoner. Described as a captain, he is served by seven legions of lesser spirits. See also *BOOK OF OBERON*.

Corocon: In the *Sacred Magic of Abramelin the Mage*, Corocon is a demon said to serve the arch-fiend Magoth. In the fifteenth-century French manuscript sourced by Mathers for his translation of this work, the name of the demon is spelled *Corodon*, and he is said also to serve the infernal ruler Kore. See also KORE, MAGOTH, MATHERS.

Corsone: A demon whose preferred form is that of a lion-faced man. He is crowned with a diadem and carries a viper. According to the *Book of Oberon*, where this version of his name appears, he has an earthly body, which means he is powerful enough to fully manifest as a physical being. Although the text does not clearly position Corsone in any demonic court, his "earthly" body may indicate an affiliation with the element of earth, thus placing him beneath the king of the north. The only power attributed to him in the *Book of Oberon* is the ability to reveal buried treasure. Corsone holds the rank of either count or earl (the text gives both) and holds power over six legions of lesser spirits. His name is very similar to one of the Goetic demons first encountered in Wierus's *Pseudomonarchia Daemonum*, Curson. See also *BOOK OF OBERON*, CURSON, WIERUS.

Crowley, Aleister: An author, poet, mountaineer, and possible spy, Crowley was one of the most controversial figures associated with magick and the occult to have lived in the twentieth century. Born Edward Alexander Crowley in Warwickshire, England, in 1875, he eventually changed his name to Aleister, the Gaelic form of Alexander. The child of a preacher, Crowley took an interest in the occult starting in December 1896. He sought membership in the Hermetic Order of the Golden Dawn, where he studied alongside the Irish poet William Butler Yeats and occultist A. E. Waite. Crowley grew close with S. L. Mac-Gregor Mathers, one of the founding members of the Golden Dawn. Eventually, however, he and Mathers had a bitter falling-out, and Crowley decided to found his own magickal system. He got involved with a German-based group known as the Ordo Templi Orientis and ultimately founded his own tradition, known as Thelema. He also founded an order, known as the A. A., which is generally said to stand for the *Argenteum Astrum*, or Silver Star.

Crowley was a brilliant but quirky individual, and he had a marked penchant for sensationalistic behavior. He styled himself the Great Beast, identifying with the number 666. Quite a few wild stories circulated about his beliefs and practices. Rather than dispel any of the rumors, the flamboyant Crowley frequently chose to feed them. As a result, his is most widely remembered as a hedonist, drug addict, promiscuous bisexual, and practitioner of the black arts. He had a marked fascination with the demons of the *Goetia* and claimed to have successfully summoned several of them. Whether or not hallucinogenic drugs were involved in the invocations of these beings is a matter of some conjecture. Crowley died in 1947. His most influential works include *Magick in Theory and Practice* and *The Book of the Law*. He is also responsible for establishing the convention of spelling *magick* with a *k*, to differentiate between the occult art and sleight-of-hand. See also *GOETIA*, MATHERS.

Cruchan: A demon in the hierarchy of the wandering prince Bidiel. Cruchan has a pleasing appearance, assuming a beautiful human shape whenever he manifests to mortals. According to the *Ars Theurgia*, he has two thousand and four hundred servants to carry out his commands. He is described as a "great duke." See also *ARS THEURGIA*, BIDIEL.

Cruhiet: A demon ruled by the wandering prince Emoniel. Cruhiet holds the rank of duke and has one thousand three hundred and twenty lesser spirits at his command. According to the *Ars Theurgia*, Cruhiet and his companions all have a fondness for wooded settings and are able to manifest equally as well during the day as during the night. See also *ARS THEURGIA*, EMONIEL.

Cubi: One of several chief dukes who serve the demon Malgaras. The *Ars Theurgia* numbers thirty lesser spirits beneath him. According to this text, Cubi is bound to manifest only during the hours of the night. His direction is west. See also *ARS THEURGIA*, MALGARAS.

Cubiel: A demon tied to the hours of the day whose name appears in the *Ars Theurgia*. Cubiel serves the infernal prince Aseliel, who belongs to the hierarchy of the east. Ranked as a chief president, Cubiel has thirty principal spirits and twenty ministering spirits at his command. His manifest form is both courtly and beautiful. See also *ARS THEURGIA*, ASELIEL.

Cugiel: A demon who serves the infernal prince Cabariel and is thus allied to the court of the west. Cugiel holds the rank of chief duke, and he is one of fifty such dukes said to serve Cabariel during the hours of the night. According to the *Ars Theurgia*, he is of an evil nature and will be reluctant to obey those who deal with him. Cugiel prefers tricks and deception to obedience and niceties. See also *ARS THEURGIA*, CABARIEL.

Culmar: A demon of the night who possesses a particularly evil and obstinate nature. Culmar appears in the *Ars Theurgia*, where he is ascribed the rank of chief duke. In this capacity, he serves beneath the demon Raysiel, an infernal king of the north. Culmar only appears at night, and he has forty lesser spirits at his command. He can be summoned and compelled through the combined use of his name and his sigil. See also *ARS THEURGIA*, RAYSIEL.

Cumariel: A duke of the demon Icosiel, Cumariel is said to have two thousand two hundred lesser spirits to attend him. According to the *Ars Theurgia*, he has a fondness for houses and is drawn to manifesting in people's homes. He is bound to the hours and minutes of the day and is only able to appear during the twelfth portion of the day, when the day has been divided into fifteen measurements of time. As his lord Icosiel is a wandering duke, Cumariel is not affiliated with any particular direction. Elsewhere in the *Ars Theurgia*, Cumariel appears in the infernal hierarchy of the east where he is said to hold the rank of duke. Here he serves directly beneath Carnesiel, the demonic Emperor of the East. See also *ARS THEURGIA*, CARNESIEL, ICOSIEL.

Cuphal: A duke governed by prince Cabariel. Through his infernal master, Cuphal is connected with the hierarchy of the west. His name appears in the *Ars Theurgia*. See also *ARS THEURGIA*, CABARIEL.

Cupriel: A demon of the night bound never to appear during the hours of the day, Cupriel hates the light and flees from it. Cupriel serves the demon Buriel, who is described as a "wandering duke" in the seventeenth-century work known as the *Ars Theurgia*. Cupriel and his superior are spirits of the air that wander the points of the compass, never remaining in one place for very long. According to the *Ars Theurgia*, Cupriel is a truly vile and evil being. He and all of the others who serve Buriel are despised by the other spirits, although there are still eight hundred and eighty lesser spirits willing to serve beneath him. When Cupriel appears to mortals, he takes the form of a monstrous serpent with a human head. Although the head of this serpent is that of a beautiful woman, he nevertheless speaks with the rough voice of a man. See also *ARS THEURGIA*, BURIEL.

Cuprisiel: A knight who serves in the retinue of Pirichiel, a wandering prince of the air. According to the *Ars Theurgia*, Cuprisiel and his fellow knights each have two thousand ministering spirits beneath them. See also *ARS THEURGIA*, PIRICHIEL.

Curasin: A lesser duke ruled by the so-called chief duke Charsiel. Charsiel is bound only to appear in the ninth hour of the day. As Curasin follows his superior in all things, he will only manifest in the tenth hour of the day. In the *Ars Theurgia*, both Curasin and Charsiel belong to the court of the wandering prince Menadiel. See also *ARS THEURGIA*, CHARSIEL, MENADIEL.

Curiel: A demon of the night, known for his stubborn manner. Curiel is ruled by the infernal king Symiel and is thus connected to the court of the north. Holding the rank of chief duke, Curiel has a total of forty lesser spirits to attend to his needs. He appears in the *Ars Theurgia*. Elsewhere in this book, Curiel is named as a night-demon in the hierarchy of prince Aseliel. Here Curiel holds the rank of chief president and presides over thirty principal spirits and twenty lesser spirits. Through his association with Aseliel, Curiel is tied to the east. See also *ARS THEURGIA*, ASELIEL, SYMIEL.

Cursas: A demon of the night loyal to the infernal prince Dorochiel. Cursas is named in the *Ars Theurgia*, where it is said that he commands forty lesser spirits. He holds the rank of chief duke and will only manifest in the first half of the night, between dusk and midnight. Through Dorochiel, he owes fealty to the court of the west. See also *ARS THEURGIA*, DOROCHIEL.

Curson: A grand king of Hell who appears as a man with a lion's face, Curson manifests astride a horse, heralded by trumpets. He wears a crown and clutches a serpent in one hand. According to the fifteenth-century grimoire known as the *Munich Handbook*, he has the power to provide the magician with familiar spirits. He can reveal the whereabouts of treasure, and he can foil any lock that safeguards such treasure. When commanded, he can assume a body like that of a man or like that of a spirit of the air. He can answer questions about the past, present, or future. Unlike a great many demons, Curson is also well-versed in divine matters, and he can answer questions about the nature of God as well as the creation of the world, engaging the magician in profound theological discourse. He has twenty-two legions of devils under his command. In Scot's *Discoverie of Witchcraft*, Curson is given as an alias of the Goetic demon Purson. In Rudd's *Treatise on Angel Magic*, he appears under the name *Corson*. See also *GOETIA*, PURSON, RUDD, SCOT.

Curtnas: A demon who appears in the form of a monstrous serpent with a woman's head. His name, as well as the seal that is used to summon and command him, both appear in the *Ars Theurgia*. He is allegedly a member of the court of the wandering prince Uriel, where he holds the rank of duke. He has a total of six hundred and fifty lesser spirits with additional infernal companions to carry out his commands. Curtnas is anything but a nice spirit. The *Ars Theurgia* describes him as evil and dishonest in all of his dealings. See also *ARS THEURGIA*, URIEL.

Cusiel: A demon in the court of the infernal king Asyriel. Through Asyriel, Cusiel is associated with the court of the south as described in the *Ars Theurgia*. Cusiel holds the title of duke and has twenty lesser spirits at his command. He is associated with the hours of the day and serves his master only during this time. See also *ARS THEURGIA*, ASYRIEL.

Cusriet: A chief duke in the court of the south, Cusriet appears in the *Ars Theurgia*, where he is said to serve the infernal king Asyriel. According to this text, he is tied to the hours of the night and only serves his infernal master during this time. He has forty lesser spirits to serve him. See also *ARS THEURGIA*, ASYRIEL.

The Four Archangels

Demonology as we know it has its roots in the civilizations of the Fertile Crescent. The world of the ancient Sumerians was crawling with spirits—both beneficent and hostile—and the Sumerians bequeathed this demonic legacy to their cultural inheritors, the empires of Babylon, Assyria, and Akkad. As most people know, the ancient Israelites were a syncretic people, meaning they tended to borrow ideas from other religions and slowly integrate them into their own. During the period of the Babylonian Captivity (605–536 BCE), the Israelites were exposed to the rather elaborate demonology of Mesopotamia. When they eventually left Babylon, they took a rich tradition of demons and angels with them. Lilith hails from the mythos of Babylon, where she started life as a spirit haunting a tree mentioned briefly in the *Epic of Gilgamesh*.

The three archangels directly named in the Bible may also have come from the Babylonian tradition. Michael and Gabriel are both named directly in the Canonical Bible. Raphael is named in the *Book of Tobit*, which in some traditions is collected in the Apocrypha and may not appear in every tradition's version of the Bible. The fourth archangel is never clearly identified in the canonical biblical books—a fact that has led to a number of different names being supplied for this fourth scion of Heaven. Uriel is the name most widely encountered, but Ariel and Oriel appear frequently as well.

The Babylonian origin of the archangels is certainly the opinion put forth in the Talmud by Rabbi Shimon ben Lakish, a rather colorful Jewish scholar who lived in the third century of the Common Era. Reputed to be a huge and immensely strong man, ben Lakish was one of the foremost authorities on the Jewish Law, and his theory of the Babylonian genesis of what we now know to be three of the four archangels is still held by many modern scholars.

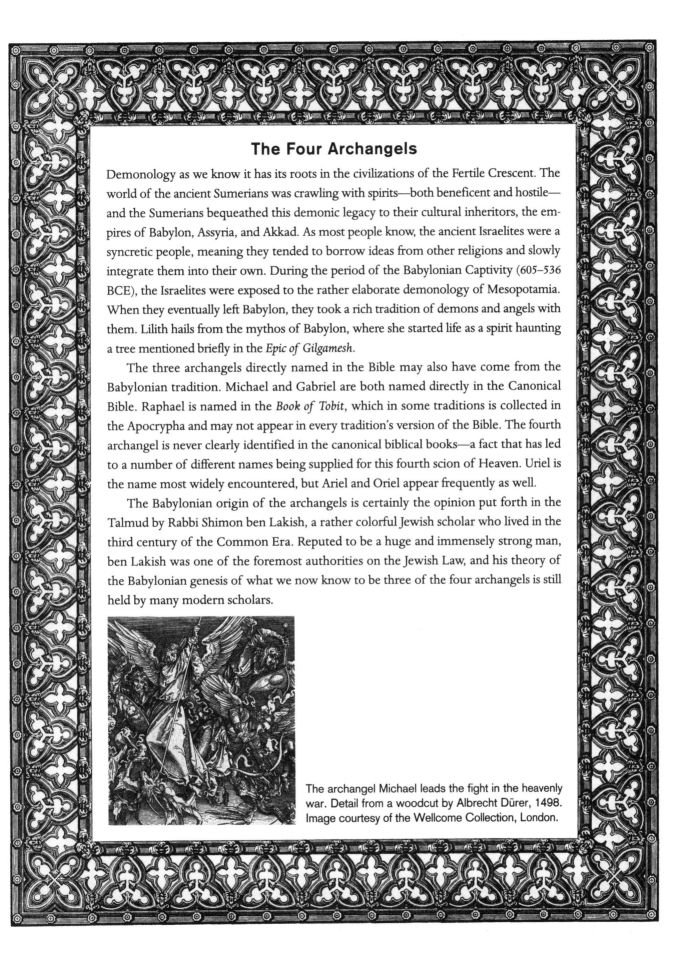

The archangel Michael leads the fight in the heavenly war. Detail from a woodcut by Albrecht Dürer, 1498. Image courtesy of the Wellcome Collection, London.

Cusyne: One of a number of demons who serve in the infernal hierarchy of prince Dorochiel. Thus, he is part of the court of the west. Cusyne is tied to the hours of the night, manifesting only at a specific time between dusk and midnight. According to the *Ars Theurgia*, he is a chief duke and oversees the governance of forty lesser spirits. See also *ARS THEURGIA*, DOROCHIEL.

Cutroy: A squire spirit with impressive powers of illusion. Cutroy is named in the *Munich Handbook*, where he is said to be able to help conjure an entire, well-fortified castle out of thin air. According to the text, Cutroy will only perform this feat outside in a remote location, far from prying eyes. An offering of milk and honey makes this demon more tractable to a mortal's will. See also *MUNICH HANDBOOK*.

Cynassa: A minister of the demon Sarabocres. According to Driscoll's edition of the *Sworn Book*, Cynassa has a nature like quicksilver, shining and malleable. When he manifests, his body is moderate in stature and colored like a shining star. He has the power to incite love and lust between mortals, significantly increasing a person's sense of pleasure. In addition to inspiring voluptuous passion, Cynassa also has the power to provide luxurious items such as costly perfumes and rich fabrics. In the Peterson translation of the *Sworn Book*, Cynassa also appears as a minister of Sarabocres. He is connected to the planet Venus, and the angels Hanahel, Raquyel, and Salguyel are said to have power over him. See also SARABOCRES, *SWORN BOOK*.

Daberinos: A demon connected with the eleventh set of two planetary hours of the day. According to the *Ars Theurgia*, Daberinos is bound to manifest only during a limited period of time each day. When the day is divided up into twelve sets of two hours each, this demon may appear during the eleventh set of two planetary hours. He is a duke in service to the infernal emperor Demoriel, who rules in the north. Daberinos himself holds dominion over one thousand one hundred and forty lesser spirits of his own, and these exist to carry out his bidding. See also *ARS THEURGIA*, DEMORIEL.

Dabuel: According to the *Sacred Magic of Abramelin the Mage*, Dabuel is a demon with the power to confer invisibility. His demonic superior is Almiras, who bears the title Master of Invisibility. Dabuel also answers to the demon Cheros, who serves Almiras as his minister. The same invisibility spell, and thus the same set of demons, also appears in the Mathers translation of the *Clavicula Salomonis*. See also ALMIRAS, CHEROS, MATHERS.

Dagiel: A demon listed in the *Ars Theurgia* as working within the hierarchy of the north. He specifically serves the demon-king Symiel and holds the rank of chief duke. Dagiel has command over one hundred lesser spirits that minister to him. He is tied to the hours of the day and will not manifest at night. See also *ARS THEURGIA*, SYMIEL.

Daglas: Spelled variously *Daglos* and *Daglus*, the name of this demon appears in the *Sacred Magic of Abramelin the Mage*. According to the 1898 Mathers translation, Daglas serves the infernal rulers Magoth and Kore. In all other surviving editions of this work, Daglas serves Magoth alone. See also KORE, MAGOTH, MATHERS.

Dagon: A Canaanite deity worshipped by the Philistine people described in the Bible. There has been a persistent rumor that Dagon was depicted with the upper body of a man and the lower body of a fish. The reality of this depiction is currently a matter of some debate. A fishy nature may not seem in keeping with the offices of this ancient god, who was a deity of fertility and grain, not fishmongering. The Semitic root of his name, *dag*, means "cereal" or "corn." The father of the great god Baal, Dagon was eventually supplanted by this more popular deity in his role of fertility god. As with so many of the gods competing with the religion of Yahweh in the early days of the ancient Israelites, Dagon found his way into the rolls of demonic beings, although he doesn't seem to hold a great deal of rank. In Berbiguier's infernal hierarchy, Dagon is the Grand Pantler of the Royal Household of Hell. A pantler is an old court position that amounts to keeper of the pantry. As bizarre as Berbiguier's demonic hierarchy is, it was repeated in both de Plancy's *Dictionnaire Infernal* and A. E. Waite's *Book of Black Magic and Pacts*. See also BAAL, BERBIGUIER, DE PLANCY, WAITE.

Daguler: One of a number of demonic servitors under the command of the arch-fiends Astaroth and Asmodeus. Daguler is named in the Mathers translation of the *Sacred Magic of Abramelin the Mage*. In other versions of this work, the name of this demon is given variously as *Dagulez* and *Paguldez*. See also ASTAROTH, ASMODEUS, MATHERS.

Dalep: In his translation of the *Sacred Magic of Abramelin the Mage*, occultist S. L. MacGregor Mathers relates this demon's name to a Hebrew root meaning "liquid putrefaction." Dalep is said to serve the infernal king Amaimon, listed as one of the rulers of the four cardinal directions. See also AMAIMON, MATHERS.

Daléte: A spirit named in the *Grimoire of Armadel* as translated by Mathers. Daléte reputedly grants

visions to those who seek him out. The text also asserts that this demon can reveal the secrets of the mystical formation of the first man, Adam. See also MATHERS.

Dam: A great count who appears in a beautiful shape, although this beauty is deceiving. He holds power over life and death and can make people languish or die. He can force women to dance totally naked or despoil themselves. He knows all their secrets. He also carries treasure, bringing gold and silver or any other valuable one might want. Twenty-five legions of lesser spirits work at his command. This vile being is named in the sixteenth-century French grimoire known as the *Livre des esperitz*. See also *LIVRE DES ESPERITZ*.

Damariell: An infernal knight ruled by the wandering prince Pirichiel. According to the *Ars Theurgia*, Damariell has two thousand lesser spirits who serve beneath him. Because he follows the lead of Pirichiel, Damariell has no fixed direction and moves from place to place. See also *ARS THEURGIA*, PIRICHIEL.

Danael: One of several chief dukes named in the hierarchy of the demon-prince Dorochiel. Danael commands four hundred lesser spirits. His name and seal appear in the *Ars Theurgia*. He is affiliated with the court of the west. Danael also appears in the *Book of Enoch*. Here, he is named as one of the "chiefs of tens" among the Watcher Angels. These lieutenants of the fallen angels followed their chiefs Shemyaza and Azazel in an illicit exodus from Heaven. See also *ARS THEURGIA*, AZAZEL, SHEMYAZA, WATCHER ANGELS.

Danall: One of seven infernal senators who serve the emperor Tantavalerion. Danall and his fellows are called upon to compel other spirits to answer their summons, as well as to prevent them from causing any harm or mischief. His name appears in the *Book of Oberon*, a grimoire from Elizabethan England. See also ASMOO, BOELL, *BOOK OF OBERON*, ORYMELL, PASCARY, SALARICA, TANTAVALERION, TYGRA.

Daniel: In the *Ars Theurgia*, Daniel is named as one of ten ministering spirits who serve Camuel. He has ten ministering spirits of his own and belongs to the hours of the day. Despite his association with the daylight hours, Daniel is called forth by night. He is tied to the court of the east. See also *ARS THEURGIA*, CAMUEL.

Dantalion: A great and mighty duke, Dantalion is said to rule over thirty-six legions of lesser spirits. He is named as the seventy-first demon of the *Goetia*. According to this text, he knows the thoughts of all men and women and can thus declare the innermost secrets of any individual. He can also use an illusory power to create an image of any person from anywhere in the world. This image will be accurate in all respects, regardless of how far away this person may be. When he manifests, he is said to have the body of a man holding a book in his right hand. He has many faces, however, and these faces belong to both men and women of various sorts. In addition to his other powers, he can cause love and teach all arts and sciences. According to the *Goetia of Dr. Rudd*, the angel Hajajel has the power to constrain him. In this text, his name is rendered *Dantaylion*. He also appears in the Welsh *Book of Incantations*. See also *BOOK OF INCANTATIONS*, *GOETIA*, RUDD.

Darascon: In the Mathers translation of the *Sacred Magic of Abramelin the Mage*, Darascon is one of a host of demons who serve beneath the four infernal princes of the cardinal directions: Oriens, Paimon, Ariton, and Amaimon. As with most sub-servient demons, Darascon can be summoned and compelled in the name of his superiors. See also AMAIMON, ARITON, MATHERS, ORIENS, PAIMON.

Darborl: A chief duke in the night-bound hierarchy of the demon-prince Dorochiel. Darborl is named in the *Ars Theurgia*, in which it is said that he holds the rank of chief duke. Forty ministering spirits attend him. Through Dorochiel, he owes allegiance to the west. He will only manifest at a specific time between dusk and midnight. See also *ARS THEURGIA*, DOROCHIEL.

Darek: According to the 1898 publication of the *Sacred Magic of Abramelin the Mage* as translated by Mathers, Darek is one of the demons serving beneath the infernal ruler Astaroth. The name of this demon differs in other versions of the *Abramelin* material, appearing variously as *Barak* and *Barook*. These spellings may indicate that the name was originally derived from the Hebrew name *Baruch*, meaning "blessed." See also ASTAROTH, MATHERS.

Darial: A demon of hatred, and one of two demons in the service of the infernal king Zombar. Darial is named in the *Liber de Angelis*, where he appears as part of a spell to sow discord among men. If the magician should fashion an image of lead and invoke Darial and his brethren by name, that image will become imbued with their discordant power. Buried beneath a road near any human habitations, the charm will begin to divide all of the people who pass by it, filling them with hatred and causing them to fall upon one another like wild dogs. See also *LIBER DE ANGELIS*, ZOMBAR.

Dariel: An angel, presumably fallen, who is invoked together with the demon Baal in the *Liber de Angelis*. The spell in question claims to give the aspiring magician power over demons. It requires the blood of a black rooster as well as that of a white dove. A wax figure is also involved. See also BAAL, *LIBER DE ANGELIS*.

Darokin: The name of this demon may be derived from a Chaldean word meaning "paths" or "ways." Darokin appears in the Mathers translation of the *Sacred Magic of Abramelin the Mage*, where he is said to serve beneath the arch-fiends Astaroth and Asmodeus. In other surviving manuscripts of the *Abramelin* work, this demon's name is spelled *Darachim*. See also ASTAROTH, ASMODEUS, MATHERS.

De Plancy, Collin: A French writer who lived between 1793 and 1887. He belonged to the movement of freethinkers and was influenced by the writings of Voltaire. De Plancy is best known as an occultist and a demonologist. His most widely recognized work is the *Dictionnaire Infernal*, or *Infernal Dictionary*, first published in 1818. Later editions of the work were released in 1822 and 1863. He is the author of nearly forty other books, mainly on legends, folklore, and history. Entries in his *Dictionnaire Infernal* indicate that he was familiar with the work of his fellow countryman Charles Berbiguier. See also BERBIGUIER.

Debam: A demon whose name may mean "strength." Debam appears in a list of demonic servitors who are jointly ruled by Magoth and Kore. This joint leadership is unique to the Mathers edition of the *Sacred Magic of Abramelin the Mage*. In all other versions of this book, Debam serves only Magoth. See also KORE, MAGOTH, MATHERS.

Decarabia: The sixty-ninth demon of the *Goetia*. This demon has a most unusual appearance: he is said to manifest in the form of a star. In both Wierus's *Pseudomonarchia Daemonum*, Scot's *Discoverie*

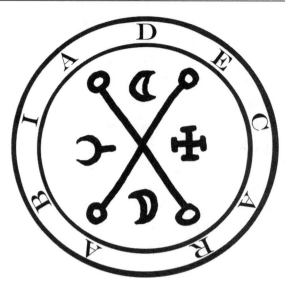

The seal of the demon Decarabia stands out among the other sigils in the *Goetia*. It is suggestive of phases of the moon. From a talisman by M. Belanger.

of Witchcraft, and the *Book of Incantations*, the text does not include the word *star*, but a star-like symbol is taken to represent the demon's form. The *Goetia of Dr. Rudd* goes one step further, stating that the demon appears as a star inside of a pentagram and includes the image of that star in its text. Fortunately, this peculiar form is only temporary, and the demon is able to assume a human form after his initial manifestation.

The primary power of this demon involves birds. He is said to be able to make any and all types of birds manifest before his master. They will drink and sing and otherwise behave as if tame for as long as their presence is desired. He also has knowledge of herbs and precious stones and can impart this when requested. Scot's *Discoverie of Witchcraft* fails to attribute a title to this demon, although it states that he commands thirty legions. The *Pseudomonarchia Daemonum* identifies Decarabia as a king and an earl. In the *Goetia of Dr. Rudd*, he is given the title of marquis. This text also says

It's All Greek

Our modern word *demon* comes originally from a Greek word, often transliterated *daimon* or *daemon*. Many books of the New Testament in the Bible were composed by Semitic-speaking people writing in Greek. When they needed a word for an unclean spirit, such as the demons believed to possess the Gerasene man in Luke 8 and Mark 5, they used the Greek word *daimon* to designate these creatures. The problem with such usage, at least as far as the Greeks were concerned, is that the word *daimon* does not categorically indicate an evil or unclean spirit. To the ancient Greeks, *daimones* were spirits that existed somewhere above humanity yet below the gods. According to the *The New Schaff-Herzog Encyclopedia of Religious Knowledge*, the word *daimones* was sometimes even used as a synonym for *theos*, or god! Although *daimones* were often fickle toward humanity, they were not perceived as being evil through and through. Followers of the philosopher Plato believed in the existence of two types of daimones: *eudaimones* and *kakodaimones*. Of these, the *eudaimones* were essentially good, and they often served in the role of a genius or guiding spirit. In this capacity, they would instruct and guide people and help them maintain a healthy, balanced state between body and soul. The *kakodaimones* were bad demons. More chaotic than evil, they sought to encourage imbalance between body and soul.*

The belief in both good demons and bad demons in ancient Greece left many thinkers in the European Renaissance with some troubling philosophical questions. A fundamental part of Renaissance thought involved a rediscovery and reaffirmation of the values of Classical teachings. The works of Greek thinkers like Plato, Aristotle, and Socrates were all held in high regard. At the same time, Europe was aggressively Christian, and these ancient Greek thinkers were unredeemed Pagans, every last one. Their beliefs about demons were seen as especially distasteful—at least to the majority of individuals associated with the European Renaissance. Some Renaissance scholars were actually fascinated by the notion of good and bad demons, and particularly the Greek idea of the individual *genius* that could guide and instruct an avid seeker. Although the notion of a genius spirit was suspiciously close to the European idea of the witches' familiar, at least a few writers in the Renaissance dabbled in demonic magick with the express desire of attracting one of these benevolent demons.

---

* Noel L. Brann, *The Debate Over the Origin of the Genius During the Italian Renaissance*, p. 195.

that the angel Roehel has the power to constrain him. An alternate version of his name is *Carabia*. See also *BOOK OF INCANTATIONS*, *GOETIA*, *RUDD*, *SCOT*, *WIERUS*.

Decariel: In the *Ars Theurgia*, Decariel is described as a mighty duke. He serves in the hierarchy of the north under the demon-king Baruchas. As a demon of rank, Decariel has thousands of lesser spirits that minister to him and carry out his commands. He will only appear during the hours and minutes that fall in the fifteenth portion of the day, when the day has been divided into fifteen equal sections of time. See also *ARS THEURGIA*, *BARUCHAS*.

Deccal: Translated by Mathers as "the Fearful One," this demon's name may also be related to the Latin word for "ten." Deccal appears in the *Sacred Magic of Abramelin the Mage*, where he is named as part of the extensive hierarchy of the four demonic princes of the cardinal directions: Oriens, Paimon, Ariton, and Amaimon. See also *AMAIMON*, *ARITON*, *MATHERS*, *ORIENS*, *PAIMON*.

Dee, Dr. John: A well-traveled scholar who famously served as the court astrologer of Queen Elizabeth I, Dr. John Dee (1527–1608) was a scientist, mathematician, alchemist, astrologer, cryptographer, and possibly a spymaster. In occult circles, he is best known for inventing the Enochian system of magick (distinct from the *Book of Enoch*). This system involves work with entities believed to be angels. Dee "discovered" Enochian magick with the help of Edward Kelley, a dubious individual who worked as his scryer. Kelley would sit long nights gazing into a convex piece of crystal known as a "shew-stone." According to Dee's own account, this shew-stone was given to him in November 1582 by the angel Uriel as a reward for his prayers and dedication to the mystic arts.

Dee was an avid reader, and he had an extensive collection of occult books and grimoires. Several of these manuscripts can now be found in the collection of esoteric works in the library at the British Museum. Although he was supported by the crown for a good portion of his life, Dee's work nevertheless gained him a great deal of notoriety and censure. When Queen Mary came to the throne in 1553, he was accused of attempting to kill the new sovereign through magickal means. He was imprisoned at Hampton Court and while he gained his liberty soon afterward, few people forgot the accusation. In 1604, he submitted a petition to James I asking for protection against the rumors and tales surrounding his work. Dee's work with Kelley and the Enochian spirits was presented in Méric Casaubon's 1659 book, *A True and Faithful Relation of What Passed Between Dr. John Dee and Some Spirits*.

Deilas: A night-demon in the court of the infernal king Malgaras. According to the *Ars Theurgia*, in addition to serving Malgaras, Deilas oversees twenty subordinate spirits. He is tied to the west. See also *ARS THEURGIA*, *MALGARAS*.

Demediel: An infernal knight in the retinue of the demon Pirichiel, a wandering prince of the air. In the *Ars Theurgia*, Demediel and his fellow knights are said to carry out Pirichiel's wishes. Demediel himself has a total of two thousand ministering spirits to assist him in his duties. See also *ARS THEURGIA*, *PIRICHIEL*.

Demor: A demon of illusion described in the *Munich Handbook*. According to this text, he is best called in a remote and secret location. He can be enticed with an offering of milk and honey. As a so-called "squire spirit," he has power to conjure an entire, realistic castle from thin air. The text also gives his name as *Denior*. See also *MUNICH HANDBOOK*.

Demoriel: One of four demons named in the *Ars Theurgia* in connection with the cardinal directions. According to this text, Demoriel is the primary Emperor of the North, and he rules in this point of the compass with a retinue of four hundred great dukes and six hundred lesser dukes. Demoriel can be called any time in the day or night. Those that would conjure him are advised to retire to a private and out-of-the-way place so that their experiments with his manifestation will remain undisturbed. He is said to possess an airy nature, and thus he is best viewed by the naked human eye through the medium of a crystal stone or scrying glass. Demoriel also appears in the *Steganographia* of Johannes Trithemius, a work that likely influenced the *Ars Theurgia*. See also ARS THEURGIA, TRITHEMIUS.

Demon Princes: A book compiled from material found in several versions across the manuscripts designated Sloane MS 3824, Sloane MS 3821, and Rawlinson D. 1363, all kept in the collection of the British Library. Of these, Rawlinson is the most recent and is clearly copied from a previous source. Two of the texts were bought by Sir Hans Sloane (1660–1753) in late 1739 or early 1740 from the collection of Sir Joseph Jekyll (1663–1738). As such, they represent a part of what the transcribers describe as the "English aristocratic angel magic tradition."[43] The dates on the manuscripts themselves vary, though broadly they can be traced to the 1600s. The *Demon Princes* is transcribed, compiled, and reprinted in *The Keys to the Gateway of Magic* by the team of Stephen Skinner and David Rankine, where it appears alongside several other

sourceworks, including the *Janua Magica Reserata*, the *Nine Hierarchies*, and the *Nine Celestial Keys*. The *Demon Princes* is a short work concerned primarily with the four kings of the cardinal directions (called *princes* in this text) and the various spirits serving as their ministers. The majority of names are similar if not identical to those recorded in sources like the *Book of Oberon*. Most differences, when they occur, appear to be an issue of spelling or transcription.

Derisor: A trickster demon specializing in the magick of mockery and deceit. He can be called upon to assist with illusions and spells that obscure things and make them seem invisible. Derisor appears in the *Sacred Magic of Abramelin the Mage* as well as in the Mathers translation of the *Clavicula Salomonis*. See also CLAVICULA SALOMONIS, MATHERS.

Destatur: A prevaricator who specializes in spells that mislead the senses, Destatur appears in the Mathers translations of the *Sacred Magic of Abramelin the Mage* and the *Clavicula Salomonis*. He is said to be especially useful in casting illusions and spells of invisibility. See also CLAVICULA SALOMONIS, MATHERS.

Deydo: A demon from the Elizabethan text known as the *Book of Oberon*, whose name is also given as *Deyoo*. Deydo is said to have the power to make trees grow and bloom out of season. He can further be used as an instructor, teaching languages, mathematics, and sciences. Holding the rank of earl, a full 414 legions serve beneath him. When summoned, he assumes the disarming figure of a child. See also BOOK OF OBERON.

Dictionnaire Infernal: A French work whose title translates as *Infernal Dictionary*. Written by demonographer Collin de Plancy, this book was

---

43. Stephen Skinner and David Rankine. *The Keys to the Gateway of Magic: Summoning the Solomonic Archangels and Demon Princes*, p. 35.

first published in Paris in 1818. It rapidly became one of the most widely recognized authorities on the subject of demonology in its day. It was subsequently reprinted numerous times throughout the nineteenth century. An extensive, revised edition was released in 1863 with a new introduction by de Plancy. This edition included a number of images produced by artist Louis Breton and then engraved for reproduction by M. Jarrault.

The work has received some criticism over the years, in part because de Plancy included a great deal of anecdotal material on demons and possession. For example, de Plancy is responsible for integrating the infernal hierarchy of Charles Berbiguier into the popular canon of demonology, even though de Plancy himself felt that Berbiguier was at best an unreliable source. Some of the most recent complaints about de Plancy's scholarship involve his criteria for what defined a demon. Many of his demons are deities taken from non-Christian religions, including the faith of the Hindus. See also BERBIGUIER.

Dimirag: In his 1898 translation of the *Sacred Magic of Abramelin the Mage*, Mathers takes this demon's name to mean "compulsion." Unfortunately, his reading is based upon a flawed spelling of the name, which appears differently in other versions of the *Abramelin* material. Elsewhere, the name is *Garinirag*. Notably, this is a palindrome—a word that can be read the same way backward as well as forward. Palindromes were used extensively as magickal words, especially in the early Greek and Roman magick that influenced some aspects of the grimoiric tradition. As a result, it's highly likely that the longer name is correct. However his name is spelled, the *Abramelin* material agrees that this

Image of a witch summoning a demon. Taken from Sebastian Munster's *Cosmographia Universalis*, 1544. Courtesy of Dover Publications.

demon serves the arch-fiend Beelzebub. See also BEELZEBUB, MATHERS.

Dimurgos: A servant of the infernal rulers Astaroth and Asmodeus, Dimurgos is named in the Mathers translation of the *Sacred Magic of Abramelin the Mage*. The name of this demon may be derived from the Greek term *demiurge*, meaning a public worker or craftsman. In Gnosticism, the Demiurge was the flawed and evil creator of the material world. He is sometimes associated with Samael. See also ASTAROTH, ASMODEUS, MATHERS, SAMAEL.

Diopos: According to Mathers, the name of this demon is derived from a Greek word meaning "overseer." Diopos appears in the Mathers translation of the *Sacred Magic of Abramelin the Mage*. He is said to serve beneath the arch-fiends Asmodeus and Magoth. See also ASMODEUS, MAGOTH, MATHERS.

Dioron: A servitor of the arch-fiends Astaroth and Asmodeus. Dioron appears in the Mathers translation of the *Sacred Magic of Abramelin the Mage.* In this text, Mathers suggests that the name of this demon is related to the Greek word for "delay." In other editions of the *Abramelin* work, the name is given as *Dosom.* See also ASMODEUS, ASTAROTH, MATHERS.

Diralisin: A demon whose name may mean "ridge of a rock," Diralisin appears in a list of demons who serve the infernal lord Beelzebub. He appears in the Mathers translation of the *Sacred Magic of Abramelin the Mage.* In other versions of this material, the name is spelled *Diralisen.* See also BEELZEBUB, MATHERS.

Discobermath: According to the Munich Handbook, this demon is one of several who hold sway over the cardinal directions. Discobermath is invoked in the course of a spell aimed at obtaining information about a theft. See also *MUNICH HANDBOOK.*

Discoverie of Witchcraft: Englishman Reginald Scot self-published this book in 1584 as a refutation of the witchcraft panic that gripped most of Europe in his day. A large portion of the book is concerned not with magick but with prestidigitation and other sleight-of-hand tricks used by jugglers and other individuals in order to give the appearance of magickal acts. Scot's main purpose was to debunk the Witchcraze in general, and he took specific aim at the wildly fanatical *Malleus Maleficarum,* or "Hammer of Witches," written by Catholic Inquisitors Kramer and Sprenger. Scot does address issues of the magician's art in his book, copying a number of magickal texts in part

or whole. One significant resource drawn upon by Scot was the *Pseudomonarchia Daemonum,* a list of demons compiled by scholar Johannes Wierus in 1563 and appended to his larger work, *De Praestigiis Daemonum.* Another source is a manuscript on magick published in 1570 by an author who gave only the initials "T. R." Scot's book was highly influential, but not exactly for the reasons for which it was intended. An anonymous author expanded Scot's book in 1665, and this individual was far less skeptical about magick and witchcraft than Scot himself. As a result, his book became more a source for magick and witchcraft than an argument against the existence of these arts. A particularly popular section involves a nearly word-for-word reprint of an English translation of Wierus's *Pseudomonarchia Daemonum.* Occult scholar Joseph Peterson suggests Scot's book may have influenced later editions of the *Lemegeton,* specifically the first book commonly known as the *Goetia.* See also *GOETIA, LEMEGETON,* SCOT, WIERUS.

Dison: According to the Mathers translation of the *Sacred Magic of Abramelin the Mage,* the name of this demon means "divided." Dison is said to serve under Paimon, one of the four infernal princes of the cardinal directions. In other versions of the *Abramelin* material, the name of this demon is spelled *Ichdison.* See also MATHERS, PAIMON.

Distolas: A great marquis who appears in a pleasing shape. He brings precious stones and can supply a magickal horse who can travel up to three hundred leagues in an hour. Twenty lesser spirits serve in his retinue. His name appears in the *Livre des esperitz,* where it may be a variation on *Stolas,* from the *Pseudomonarchia Daemonum.* See also *LIVRE DES ESPERITZ, PSEUDOMONARCHIA DAEMONUM, STOLAS.*

Diusion: A great king who assumes the guise of a handsome man. He answers whatever questions are put to him and will reveal the location of treasures buried in the earth. He holds sway over twenty-four legions. His name can be found in the *Livre des esperitz*, a sixteenth-century grimoire from France, where it is likely a variation of the name *Gusion*. See also GUSION, *LIVRE DES ESPERITZ*.

Diviel: Named in the *Ars Theurgia*, Diviel is said to serve in the hierarchy of the infernal prince Dorochiel. He holds the rank of chief duke and commands a total of four hundred ministering spirits. He is bound to appear only between noon and dusk each day. His direction is west. See also *ARS THEURGIA*, DOROCHIEL.

Dobiel: A night-demon in service to prince Camuel. Dobiel is named in the *Ars Theurgia*. Here, he is ranked as a duke, and he commands a total of one hundred ministering spirits. Through his allegiance to Camuel, he is tied to the court of the east. See also *ARS THEURGIA*, CAMUEL.

Dodiel: In the court of the demon-king Malgaras, Dodiel serves as a chief duke of the day. He owes fealty to the west. According to the *Ars Theurgia*, thirty attending spirits minister to his wishes. See also *ARS THEURGIA*, MALGARAS.

Dominus Penarum: This demon, known as the Lord of Torments, appears in the *Liber de Angelis* as part of a love spell. It may seem strange to conjure a creature with such a forbidding name in an attempt to gain love, but there is nothing sweet or nice about this particular spell. Serving beneath the infernal king Marastac, Dominus Penarum is connected with Jovian energy, and thereby power and control. The demon is called upon to completely break the will of the desired woman so that she will be bound to the magician and have

no choice whatsoever but to come to him and submit. In this context, his name makes sense, for many such binding spells call for the victim to be tormented until such time as she relents to the compulsion. As the Lord of Torments, this demon would be well suited to make the target's life a living hell. See also *LIBER DE ANGELIS*, MARASTAC.

Doodall: Used as an intermediary to gather other spirits together, this demon's name appears in the *Book of Oberon*. In that text, he is described as a mighty soldier holding the rank of knight, with command over six legions. He is most often used to consult with other spirits about calamities or ill luck that has befallen the person who summoned him. Through this discourse, Doodall discovers possible remedies for previous problems as well as methods for staving off future ones. See also *BOOK OF OBERON*.

Doolas: A great prince with power over twenty legions of lesser spirits, Doolas appears in the Elizabethan grimoire known as the *Book of Oberon*. He provides household spirits and can also summon serpents. Like many demons, he has knowledge of hidden treasure and the spirits that guard it. When summoned, he takes the form of a child with angel's wings who rides upon a two-headed dragon. See also *BOOK OF OBERON*.

Dorak: A demon ruled by Beelzebub. He appears in the Mathers translation of the *Sacred Magic of Abramelin the Mage*. In this work, Mathers suggests that the name of this demon is derived from a Hebrew term meaning "proceeding" or "walking forward." Dorak only appears in the fifteenth-century French manuscript sourced by Mathers. See also BEELZEBUB, MATHERS.

Doriel: A duke in service to the demon Demoriel. Doriel is one of only twelve such dukes whose

Detail of an illustration depicting Dr. John Dee and his associate Edward Kelley in the act of summoning the dead. Courtesy of Dover Publications.

as *Dorothiel* in Johannes Trithemius's *Steganographia*. See also AMENADIEL, *ARS THEURGIA*.

Drabos: A demon said to assume the form of a monstrous serpent with a human head. The head is invariably that of a young woman—a detail that only adds to the monstrosity. Drabos serves in the hierarchy of the wandering prince Uriel as defined in the *Ars Theurgia*. He has a total of six hundred and fifty companions and servants beneath him. He is said to be false and disobedient, possessing an overall evil nature. See also *ARS THEURGIA*, URIEL.

Dragon: An appropriately named demon in the court of the wandering prince Uriel. In the *Ars Theurgia*, Dragon is defined as a spirit possessing a stubborn, evil, and dishonest nature. He holds the rank of duke and has six hundred and fifty lesser spirits under his command. He takes the form of a massive serpent with a human head. See also *ARS THEURGIA*, URIEL.

Dramas: One of several demons said to serve beneath Astaroth and Asmodeus. Dramas appears in the Mathers translation of the *Sacred Magic of Abramelin the Mage*. His name is likely related to the Greek root of "drama." See also ASTAROTH, ASMODEUS, MATHERS.

Dramiel: In the *Ars Theurgia*, Dramiel is named as one of the twelve dukes who serve the demon Emoniel. Through his association with Emoniel, Dramiel has a preference for manifesting in woodland settings. He is not bound to any specific hours of the day but can manifest during the day as well as the night. He is said to have a total of one thousand three hundred and twenty ministering spirits at his command. See also *ARS THEURGIA*, EMONIEL.

Drap: A grand duke who speaks with a low, deep voice. He strikes people blind and deaf when commanded. In the *Livre des esperitz*, in which he

names and seals are given in the *Ars Theurgia*. According to this text, Doriel commands one thousand one hundred and forty lesser spirits of his own. He is tied to the fifth pair of two planetary hours of the day and will only manifest to mortals during this time. He is tied to the court of the north. See also *ARS THEURGIA*, DEMORIEL.

Dorochiel: In the *Ars Theurgia*, Dorochiel is ranked as the second spirit under Amenadiel, the Emperor of the West. Dorochiel rules as a mighty prince over the dominion of west by north. He has forty chief dukes to serve him by day and another forty who serve him by night. A unique sigil exists that summons and binds this potent demon. This intricate geometric pattern appears in the *Ars Theurgia* along with Dorochiel's name. This name is given appears, he is said to have command over either four or twenty-four legions of lesser spirits. An error in the text makes the exact number unclear. See also *LIVRE DES ESPERITZ*.

Draplos: One of ten infernal dukes named in the hierarchy of the demon Uriel. According to the *Ars Theurgia*, Draplos has dominion over a total of six hundred and fifty minor spirits. When he manifests, he assumes the shape of a serpent with a maiden's face. He is unpleasant to deal with, for he is both evil-natured and dishonest. See also *ARS THEURGIA*, URIEL.

Drasiel: A demon in command of a total of three hundred and ninety lesser spirits. He serves in the court of Menadiel, a wandering prince in the *Ars Theurgia*. Drasiel will only to appear in the third planetary hour of the day. He has a companion demon named Amasiel. Amasiel follows Drasiel in all things, appearing in the hour following Drasiel's. See also AMASIEL, *ARS THEURGIA*, MENADIEL.

Drewchall: A demon of warfare who helps to conquer fortresses by making those guarding them fall asleep. He is named in the *Book of Oberon* and is said to appear as a great hart with horns. In addition to making watchmen fall asleep, Drewchall can also provide the illusion of a great army, presumably to intimidate one's enemies into surrendering. The *Book of Oberon* lists his rank as prince or king, with no clarification as to which is definitive. Thirty-six legions of lesser demons serve him. See also *BOOK OF OBERON*.

Drisoph: A servant of the demon Amaimon. Drisoph is named in the *Sacred Magic of Abramelin the Mage*, where he is said to serve the demon-king Amaimon. In the 1898 Mathers translation of this work, the name of the demon is spelled *Dresop*. Mathers relates it to a Hebrew root meaning "tremulous attackers." The name may actually have more in common with the Greek root *sophia*, meaning "wisdom." In Gnostic beliefs, *Pistis Sophia* was the female aspect of God and represented divine wisdom. In a selfish act of creation, she brought forth the evil Demiurge. See also AMAIMON, MATHERS.

Drohas: A minister of the demon Zobha, a great president of the subterranean realms. In Driscoll's edition of the *Sworn Book of Honourius*, Drohas knows what treasures are buried in the earth and can provide gold and silver in great abundance. He has power over earthly affairs, conferring great honors and dignities. Drohas is also said to have a destructive streak. He can bring down buildings and other structures, presumably through the manipulation of earthquakes. In the Peterson translation of the *Sworn Book*, Drohas is a demon connected to the west and southwest winds who serves under Habaa, king of the spirits of the planet Mercury. As a demon tied to the planet Mercury, this version of Drohas is largely a teaching spirit, revealing secret knowledge and providing useful familiars. See also HABAA, *SWORN BOOK*, ZOBHA.

Drsmiel: A fallen angel who governs spells of infidelity and strife in marriages. Drsmiel is named in the *Sword of Moses*. Here he is part of a spell directed at harming an enemy. He can be invoked to help separate a man from his wife. He is also said to preside over a variety of maladies, including sharp pains, inflammations, and dropsy, or excessive swelling. See also GASTER, *SWORD OF MOSES*.

Drubiel: According to the *Ars Theurgia*, Drubiel is a demon who serves the wandering duke Bursiel. He

Even the angels that faithfully served the Heavenly Hosts could be formidable and aggressive beings. From *Doré's Bible Illustrations*.

is a deeply malevolent spirit, and he hates the light and everything it represents. When he manifests, it is only in the dark hours of the night. He assumes the form of a monstrous snake that has a human head. Drubiel and his fellows are so evil that they are hated by all other spirits. Within his own hierarchy he holds dominion over eight hundred and eighty lesser spirits. See also *ARS THEURGIA*, BURSIEL.

Drusiel: A demon who serves the wandering duke Bursiel. Drusiel appears to mortals in the form of a monstrous serpent bearing a human head. The head of this serpent appears to be that of a beauti-

ful woman, but when he speaks, Drusiel still speaks with a deep and gravelly masculine voice. He is a demon tied to the hours of the night, and he will never appear during the day for he despises the light. He commands eight hundred and eighty lesser spirits. According to the *Ars Theurgia*, Drusiel and his ilk are hated and feared by all other spirits, owing to their evil natures. A second instance of this demon's name appears in the *Ars Theurgia*. Here, he is named as an infernal duke who holds dominion over no fewer than four hundred subordinate spirits. This version of Drusiel serves the wandering prince Macariel, and will appear in any hour of the day or night. According to the *Ars Theurgia*, he prefers take the form of a many-headed dragon when he manifests, although he is actually capable of assuming a variety of forms. See also *ARS THEURGIA*, BURSIEL, MACARIEL.

Dubarus: A demon of the day who serves the infernal king Raysiel. Dubarus and Raysiel are both a part of the hierarchy of the north. In the *Ars Theurgia*, Dubarus is described as a chief duke, and he has fifty lesser spirits that carry out his commands. He has an airy nature, which means that he is not easily perceived without the aid of a shewstone. A glass vessel can also be provided to help him to appear. See also *ARS THEURGIA*, RAYSIEL.

Dubiel: A deceptive and malevolent demon of the night named in the *Ars Theurgia*. Dubiel is a mighty duke in service to the infernal prince Cabariel. Dubiel is said to have fifty lesser spirits under his command. All of these infernal minions share his evil nature and exist primarily to carry out his will. See also *ARS THEURGIA*, CABARIEL.

Dubilon: One of twelve infernal dukes from the hierarchy of Demoriel whose names and seals appear in the *Ars Theurgia*. Demoriel is the infernal Emperor of the North, and through his service, Dubilon is also affiliated with that direction. He is further tied to a specific window of time each day. If the day is divided into twelve sets of two hours each, Dubilon is connected to the eighth set of these planetary hours and is said to manifest only during this time. See also *ARS THEURGIA*, DEMORIEL.

Ducay: A great marquis who can bring worldly influence and the love of women. He can grant the ability to comprehend all languages and can transport people instantly from place to place. He is named in the French grimoire known as the *Livre des esperitz*, where he is assigned a retinue of twenty-five legions. See also *LIVRE DES ESPER-ITZ*.

Dulid: A demon governed by Magoth and Kore. Dulid appears in the Mathers translation of the *Sacred Magic of Abramelin the Mage*. In other versions of this text, the name is spelled *Duellid*. See also KORE, MAGOTH, MATHERS.

Dusiriel: A demon who serves as one of twelve dukes to the infernal prince Hydriel. Hydriel and all of his courts are connected to watery places, and accordingly Dusiriel prefers to appear in swamps and other moist locales. In keeping with his predilection for wet places, Dusiriel assumes the form of a naga when he appears. This fabled being has the body of a serpent surmounted by the head of a beautiful woman. Although his appearance is monstrous, Dusiriel is reputed to be a basically good being, and he behaves in a civil and courteous manner. He commands a sizable host of lesser spirits—his ministers number one thousand three hundred and twenty. His name and seal appear in the *Ars Theurgia*. In this text, Dusiriel's immediate superior, Hydriel, is said to have no fixed point on the compass. Instead, he wanders from place to place with his retinue. See also *ARS THEURGIA*, HYDRIEL.

Dydones: One of several demons named in the *Munich Handbook*. Dydones holds power in matters of scrying and divination. He appears in a spell of justice intended to help obtain information concerning any theft. See also *MUNICH HANDBOOK*.

Dyelagoo: A demon with shapeshifting powers, he can alter a person's appearance or turn them invisible at will. His name appears in the Elizabethan magickal text known as the *Book of Oberon*, where he is ranked as a great prince with twenty legions of lesser spirits beneath him. When summoned, he is reputed to appear as a beautiful angel, and the text describes him as a trustworthy spirit to work with. Like many of the spirits in the *Book of Oberon*, he is said to reveal the location of hidden treasure. He can also be called upon to compel the love of women and to garner the favor of both friends and enemies. See also *BOOK OF OBERON*.

Dyrus: A demon whose name is invoked in a spell intended to reveal the identity of a thief. Dyrus appears in the *Munich Handbook*, where he is associated with the arts of scrying and divination. See also *MUNICH HANDBOOK*.

Earos: A demon affiliated with the southern point of the compass. In the *Ars Theurgia*, Earos is said to serve in the court of the infernal king Maseriel. Here he holds the title of duke and holds sway over a total of thirty lesser spirits. He is affiliated with the night, and he serves his master only during the hours of darkness. See also *ARS THEURGIA*, MASERIEL.

Earviel: A demon named in the court of the infernal king Maseriel. In Henson's translation of the *Ars Theurgia*, Earviel is accorded the title of duke, and he is said to have no fewer than thirty lesser spirits to serve him. He is associated with the south and will only manifest during the hours of the day. See also *ARS THEURGIA*, MASERIEL.

Ebal: Described as a *spiritus infernalis*, or "infernal spirit," this demon appears by name in the fifteenth-century magickal manual known as the *Munich Handbook*. Ebal is invoked as part of a love spell. He has power over lust and passion, and he can cause a woman to become so obsessed that she will know no peace until she has given in to her desires.

Ebaron: A demon attributed to the rule of Paimon, one of four infernal princes of the cardinal directions. Ebaron appears in the *Sacred Magic of Abramelin the Mage*. See also MATHERS, PAIMON.

Ebeyeth: A demon who appears as only a crowned head. The *Book of Oberon* describes him as a king and great ruler. He has eighty legions that serve him, and he teaches which spirits make the best familiars. See also *BOOK OF OBERON*.

Ebra: A demon reputedly useful for chasing off other spirits. According to the *Ars Theurgia*, Ebra is particularly good at clearing haunted houses and driving away other spirits of darkness. This usefulness comes at a price, however. Ebra himself is an evil and deceitful spirit, and he should never be trusted with secret matters. He holds the rank of duke and serves the demon-king Pamersiel, the first and chief spirit of the east beneath the emperor Carnesiel. See also *ARS THEURGIA*, CARNESIEL, PAMERSIEL.

Ebuzoba: According to the *Liber de Angelis*, this demon has the power to incite passion and lust. He is a subordinate of the infernal king Abdalaa, and he is called forth to compel a woman's love. See also ABDALAA, *LIBER DE ANGELIS*.

Edriel: A mighty duke in service to the demon Emoniel. Edriel is reputed to be able to manifest during the day as well as the night, and he has a fondness for woodland settings. His name, as well as the seal used to summon and command him, both appear in the *Ars Theurgia*. One thousand three hundred and twenty lesser spirits exist to do his bidding. See also *ARS THEURGIA*, EMONIEL.

Egyn, who reigns as king over all the spirits of the north, as depicted in the eighteenth-century grimoire *Clavis Inferni*. He is drawn with his sigil and what appears to be a bear. Image courtesy of the Wellcome Collection, London.

Efiel: A demon of the day said only to manifest in the hours between dawn and noon. Efiel holds the rank of chief duke in the court of the demon-king Dorochiel. Through Dorochiel, he owes allegiance to the court of the west. According to the *Ars Theurgia*, Efiel has forty infernal minions of his own. See also *ARS THEURGIA*, DOROCHIEL.

Efrigis: A demon whose name may mean "the quiverer," at least according to the Mathers translation of the *Sacred Magic of Abramelin the Mage*. In the *Abramelin* work, Efrigis is identified as a demonic servant of the infernal king Amaimon. There may be a relation between this name and the Arabic word *efreet*, which refers to a type of Jinn, or otherworldly spirit typically associated with the element of fire. See also AMAIMON, MATHERS.

Egakireh: Also spelled *Egachir*, this demon is said to serve the infernal ruler Magoth. His name appears in the *Sacred Magic of Abramelin the Mage*. According to the Mathers translation of this work, Egakireh is also ruled by the demon Kore. See also KORE, MAGOTH, MATHERS.

Egin: Sometimes spelled Egyn or Aegyn, he is one of the great kings called in the four quarters. According to several grimoires, including the Elizabethan *Book of Oberon*, he rules over all the spirits of the north. The *Clavis Inferni* spells his name Egyn and places him under the control of the angel Uriel. In this text, he is also associated with the element of earth. His animal is a bear.

A full twelve thousand legions of lesser spirits serve in Egin's retinue. His powers are many, as befits his station. He can teach medicine, singing, the *ars notoria*, nigromancy, and a technique called *memorativia*. This is almost certainly a reference to the *signacula memorativa*, Hebraic mnemonic signs used in Qabbalah for communicating with angels. In addition, Egin has the power to speak of diverse parts of the world, to reveal gems, precious metals, water, and all other hidden things in the earth. He can expound on the natural sciences and also on the nature of the created world. He further has knowledge of the Pit. He has influence over worldly powers and can bestow titles. He consecrates books (presumably the ones used by conjurors and magicians), and he can help people win at games. When he manifests, he wears the form of a man and his face is very clear (or possibly bright). Flames issue from his mouth and he has two tusks protruding from his cheeks. He wears a crown of precious stones and has a long, sharp nose with sharper nostrils. He rides a dragon and bears on his right side two shining serpents, a detail that may hearken back to the burning seraphim referenced in the Bible. His name appears in numerous grimoires, as he and the other three kings of the cardinal directions are integral to the ceremony followed for summoning all of the spirits beneath them. In the sixteenth-century French grimoire *Livre des esperitz*, his name is given as *Equi*. In Scot's *Discoverie of Witchcraft*, the king of the north is identified not as Egin but as the demon Zimimar. See also *BOOK OF OBERON, CLAVIS INFERNI, LIVRE DES ESPERITZ*, SCOT, ZIMIMAR.

Ekalike: One of over three hundred demons named in the *Sacred Magic of Abramelin the Mage*. In the Mathers translation of this work, Ekalike's name is related to a possible Greek root meaning "at rest" or "quiet." Ekalike is a demon who serves the four infernal princes of the cardinal directions: Oriens, Paimon, Ariton, and Amaimon. See also AMAIMON, ARITON, MATHERS, ORIENS, PAIMON.

Ekdulon: The "Despoiler." The name of this demon appears in the *Sacred Magic of Abramelin the Mage*. According to this text, he is loyal to the four princes of the cardinal directions: Oriens, Paimon, Ariton, and Amaimon. See also AMAIMON, ARITON, MATHERS, ORIENS, PAIMON.

Ekorok: According to nineteenth-century occultist S. L. MacGregor Mathers, the name of this demon is derived from Hebrew and means "thy barrenness." Ekorok appears in the *Sacred Magic of Abramelin the Mage*. He is a servant of the infernal prince Ariton. See also ARITON, MATHERS.

Eladeb: A demon connected with the planet Mercury. In the Peterson translation of the *Sworn Book*, Eladeb is named as a minister of the demon-king Habaa. According to this text, Eladeb is governed by Michael, Mihel, and Sarapiel. These are angels who hold sway over the power of Mercury. As a Mercurial spirit, Eladeb is a master of secret knowledge. He can also provide familiar spirits. When he manifests, he is said to have a form that resembles clear glass or the whitest flame of a fire. See also HABAA, *SWORN BOOK*.

Grotesques like this image by artist Joseph Vargo were often included as architectural elements in medieval churches to remind the faithful of the horrors of Hell.

Elafon: According to Mathers, the name of this demon is derived from a Greek word meaning "stag." Elafon appears in the Mathers translation of the *Sacred Magic of Abramelin the Mage*, where he is said to serve two of the infernal kings of the cardinal directions, Amaimon and Ariton. See also AMAIMON, ARITON, MATHERS.

Elantiel: A demon under chief Sirachi, Elantiel is named in the *True Keys of Solomon*. According to this text, he has dominion over riches. He is alternately known as *Chaunta*. See also SIRACHI, *TRUE KEYS*.

Elaton: A demonic servant of the infernal kings Amaimon and Ariton, Elaton appears in the Mathers translation of the *Sacred Magic of Abramelin the Mage*. Based on this spelling, Mathers suggests that the name is related to the Latin root for *elation*. In the version of the *Abramelin* material kept at the Wolfenbüttel library in Germany, the name of this demon is rendered *Yeyatron*. In the Peter Hammer edition, the name instead appears as *Yriatron*. See also AMAIMON, ARITON, MATHERS.

Elburion: In the *Testament of Solomon*, Elburion claims to be falsely worshipped as a god. Associated with the seven stars of the Pleiades, this demon claims that his worshippers once burned lights in his name. According to the text, Elburion is not his true name, but unfortunately the demon's true name is not revealed within the *Testament*. See also SOLOMON.

Elcar: A demon tied to the hours of the day that nevertheless manifests at night, Elcar serves the infernal prince Camuel and thus is associated with the direction of the east. In the *Ars Theurgia*, Elcar is said to hold the rank of duke and to oversee a total of ten lesser spirits. See also *ARS THEURGIA*, CAMUEL.

Elelogap: Also known by the name *Elcogap*, this demon appears in the Peterson translation of the *Grimorium Verum*. According to this text, he has the power to influence any travel occurring by sea. A variation of this name can be found in the *Secrets of Solomon*, which likely influenced the *Grimorium Verum*. Here, the demon is addressed as Elelogaphatel, and he is called upon in a spell to bring rain. He serves beneath Duke Agaleraptarkimath. See also AGALERAPTARKIMATH, *SECRETS OF SOLOMON*, *GRIMORIUM VERUM*.

Elerion: A name meaning "the laugher" or "the mocker." Elerion appears in the Mathers translation of the *Sacred Magic of Abramelin the Mage*, where he is said to serve the infernal king Ariton. In other versions of the *Abramelin* text, his name is spelled *Elamyr*. See also ARITON, MATHERS.

Elestor: An infernal duke named in the seventeenth-century Venetian grimoire *Secrets of Solomon*. In that text, Elestor is identified as the Count of Hell, one of the three highest-ranking infernal powers. Lucifer is his emperor and Belzebuth (a variant of Beelzebub) is his prince. Elestor is perceived as an incredibly violent demon, and the text includes many warnings about interacting with him. Of particular danger is the knotted belt he wears around his belly. When angered, he uses this as a lash to punish his subordinates, striking so many blows that he is notorious for killing people. The *Secrets of Solomon* assigns each of the three primary demonic rulers specific continents over which they hold the greatest sway. For Elestor, his place(s) of power are North and South America. His sigil strongly resembles a Native war-club. In the *Grimorium Verum*, which contains a similar hierarchy of infernal powers, Elestor is replaced with Astaroth. See also ASTOROTH, BELZEBUTH, *GRIMORIUM VERUM*, LUCIFER, *SECRETS OF SOLOMON*.

Eligor: The fifteenth demon of the *Goetia*. Eligor appears in both the *Pseudomonarchia Daemonum*

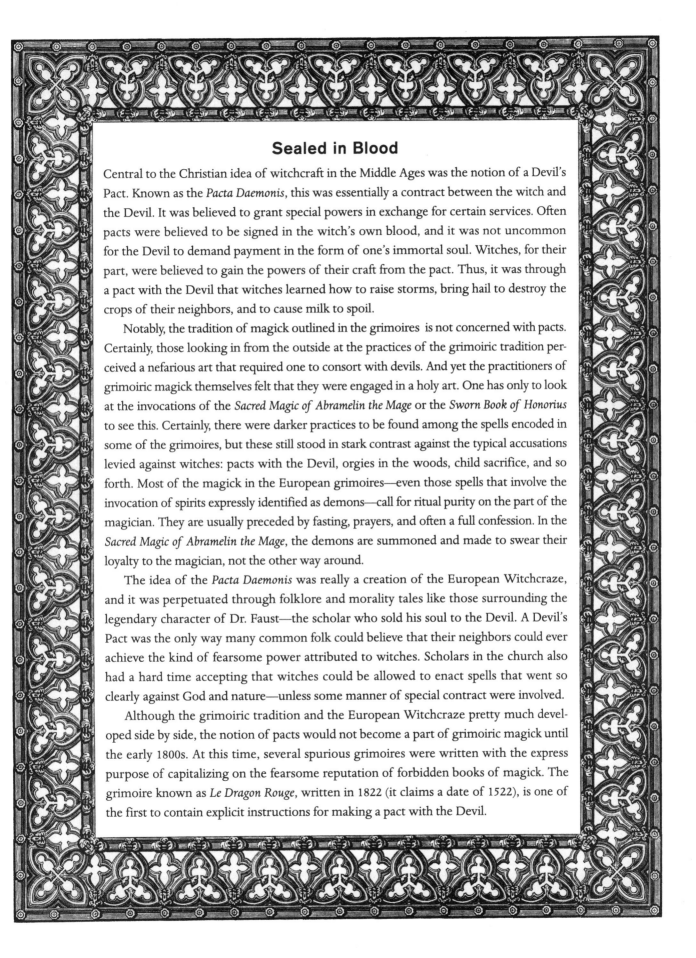

Sealed in Blood

Central to the Christian idea of witchcraft in the Middle Ages was the notion of a Devil's Pact. Known as the *Pacta Daemonis*, this was essentially a contract between the witch and the Devil. It was believed to grant special powers in exchange for certain services. Often pacts were believed to be signed in the witch's own blood, and it was not uncommon for the Devil to demand payment in the form of one's immortal soul. Witches, for their part, were believed to gain the powers of their craft from the pact. Thus, it was through a pact with the Devil that witches learned how to raise storms, bring hail to destroy the crops of their neighbors, and to cause milk to spoil.

Notably, the tradition of magick outlined in the grimoires is not concerned with pacts. Certainly, those looking in from the outside at the practices of the grimoiric tradition perceived a nefarious art that required one to consort with devils. And yet the practitioners of grimoiric magick themselves felt that they were engaged in a holy art. One has only to look at the invocations of the *Sacred Magic of Abramelin the Mage* or the *Sworn Book of Honorius* to see this. Certainly, there were darker practices to be found among the spells encoded in some of the grimoires, but these still stood in stark contrast against the typical accusations levied against witches: pacts with the Devil, orgies in the woods, child sacrifice, and so forth. Most of the magick in the European grimoires—even those spells that involve the invocation of spirits expressly identified as demons—call for ritual purity on the part of the magician. They are usually preceded by fasting, prayers, and often a full confession. In the *Sacred Magic of Abramelin the Mage*, the demons are summoned and made to swear their loyalty to the magician, not the other way around.

The idea of the *Pacta Daemonis* was really a creation of the European Witchcraze, and it was perpetuated through folklore and morality tales like those surrounding the legendary character of Dr. Faust—the scholar who sold his soul to the Devil. A Devil's Pact was the only way many common folk could believe that their neighbors could ever achieve the kind of fearsome power attributed to witches. Scholars in the church also had a hard time accepting that witches could be allowed to enact spells that went so clearly against God and nature—unless some manner of special contract were involved.

Although the grimoiric tradition and the European Witchcraze pretty much developed side by side, the notion of pacts would not become a part of grimoiric magick until the early 1800s. At this time, several spurious grimoires were written with the express purpose of capitalizing on the fearsome reputation of forbidden books of magick. The grimoire known as *Le Dragon Rouge*, written in 1822 (it claims a date of 1522), is one of the first to contain explicit instructions for making a pact with the Devil.

of Johannes Wierus and Scot's *Discoverie of Witch-craft*. Eligor is described as a great duke with sixty legions of spirits who serve him. He takes the form of a handsome knight carrying a lance, ensign, and scepter. He can see the future and answer questions concerning martial matters, foretelling the outcome of duels. In addition to this, he can also help to procure the favor of lords and knights. An alternate version of his name is given as *Abigor*. In the *Goetia of Dr. Rudd*, his name is spelled *Eligos*. He is said specifically to cause the love of lords and great persons. The angel Haziel has power to constrain him. See also *GOETIA*, RUDD, SCOT, WIERUS.

Elimi: A demon who allegedly tormented and possessed a number of nuns at a convent in Loudun, France. Elimi's name appears on the supposed pact of Urbain Grandier. This seventeenth-century priest was accused of conspiring with the demons to corrupt the nuns, a crime for which he was burned at the stake.

Elitel: According to the *Ars Theurgia*, Elitel is a mighty duke in service to the infernal prince Cabariel. Elitel is one of fifty demonic dukes who serve Cabariel during the day. Another fifty serve by night. As a demon of some significant rank, Elitel has fifty lesser spirits that tend to his needs and carry out his orders. His name and sigil appear in a list of demons associated with the points of the compass. See also *ARS THEURGIA*, CABARIEL.

Ellet: A demon named in the *Ars Theurgia* from Henson's translation of the complete *Lemegeton*. Ellet is one of twelve infernal dukes said to serve the demon-king Maseriel during the hours of the night. As a demon of rank, Ellet has command over thirty lesser spirits of his own. He is affiliated with the southern point of the compass. See also *ARS THEURGIA*, MASERIEL.

Elmis: This demon's name appears in an extensive list outlined in Mathers's translation of the *Sacred Magic of Abramelin the Mage*. Elmis is said to serve Oriens, Paimon, Ariton, and Amaimon, the four demonic princes of the cardinal directions. According to Mathers, the name of this demon is derived from a Coptic word that means "flying." See also AMAIMON, ARITON, MATHERS, ORIENS, PAIMON.

Elonim: A servant of the demon Ariton. His name is absent from the Mathers translation of the *Sacred Magic of Abramelin the Mage*, but Elonim appears in the version of this work kept at the Wolfenbüttel library in Germany. In the Peter Hammer edition published in Cologne, the name of this demon is rendered *Ekorim*. See also ARITON, MATHERS.

Elpinon: A servant of Beelzebub, this demon is called up as a part of the Holy Guardian Angel rite as described in the *Sacred Magic of Abramelin the Mage*. In the 1898 Mathers translation, drawn from a fifteenth-century French manuscript, this name is spelled *Elponen*. See also BEELZEBUB, MATHERS.

Elzegan: In Mathers's translation of the *Sacred Magic of Abramelin the Mage*, this demon's name is given as meaning "he turns aside." This name may be meant to imply that Elzegan turns people away from the righteous path by leading them astray. Elzegan's name appears alongside a vast array of other demons, all of whom are said to serve beneath Oriens, Paimon, Ariton, and Amaimon, the four infernal princes of the cardinal directions. See also AMAIMON, ARITON, MATHERS, ORIENS, PAIMON.

Emlon: Also called *Maltrans*. A messenger of the south who serves directly beneath King Amaimon. Emlon is a king in his own right and appears along

Witches making a pact with the Devil. From the *Compendium Maleficarum* by Francesco Maria Guazzo, 1608. Courtesy of Dover Publications.

with his fellow messengers, Ocarbydatonn and Madyconn, when Amaimon is summoned. His name appears in the *Book of Oberon*. Elsewhere in the manuscript, his compatriots are named Femell, Alphasis, and Rodabell. See also ALPHASIS, AMAIMON, *BOOK OF OBERON*, FEMELL, MADYCONN, OCARBYDATONN, RODABELL.

Emogeni: A divinatory demon, Emogeni is summoned to assist in the discovery of a theft. He is invoked in a spell that appears in the *Munich Handbook*. The second half of his name may be related to the Greek root for "genius," often used to denote a class of guiding spirits. See also *MUNICH HANDBOOK*.

Emoniel: The fifth spirit described by the *Ars Theurgia* as a wandering prince. Emoniel rules over one hundred princes and chief dukes with another twenty lesser dukes to do his bidding. In addition to the princes and dukes, Emoniel also has scores of lesser spirits to minister to his needs. Emoniel and his followers are reputed to inhabit mostly forests in wooded areas. Although he has a tie to natural woodland settings, Emoniel is neverthe-

less an airy spirit, which is to say that his substance is more subtle than physical and he is unlikely to appear visibly without the aid of a crystal stone. The name of this demon can also be found in Trithemius's *Steganographia*. See also *ARS THEURGIA*, TRITHEMIUS.

Emphastison: In his translation of the *Sacred Magic of Abramelin the Mage*, Mathers suggests that the name of this demon is derived from a Greek word meaning "image" or "representation." As such, Emphastison may have some connection to poppets or other images, often constructed of wax, and used to represent the living target of a curse or spell. Emphastison is listed among the many demons who serve beneath the four demonic princes who guard the cardinal directions: Oriens, Paimon, Ariton, and Amaimon. See also AMAIMON, ARITON, MATHERS, ORIENS, PAIMON.

Emuel: According to the *Ars Theurgia*, Emuel is a demon with four hundred lesser spirits at his command. He holds the rank of chief duke and serves the demon-prince Dorochiel in the second half of the day, between noon and dusk. He is associated with the western point of the compass. See also *ARS THEURGIA*, DOROCHIEL.

Enaia: The "Afflicted One." Enaia appears in the Mathers translation of the *Sacred Magic of Abramelin the Mage*, where he is said to serve the four demonic princes of the cardinal directions. As a subordinate of Oriens, Paimon, Ariton, and Amaimon, Enaia shares in their powers and, when summoned, can assist the magician by summoning spirits; answering questions about the past, present, and future; or even enabling the magician to fly. See also AMAIMON, ARITON, MATHERS, ORIENS, PAIMON.

Enarkalê: A demon of invisibility and illusion, Enarkalê appears in Peterson's edition of the *Grimorium Verum*. He is called upon as part of a spell. See also *GRIMORIUM VERUM*.

Enei: A demon said to serve beneath Asmodeus in the *Sacred Magic of Abramelin the Mage*. In the fifteenth-century French manuscript sourced by Mathers, the name of this demon is spelled *Onei*. See also ASMODEUS, MATHERS.

Enenuth: In the extra-biblical *Testament of Solomon*, Enenuth is named as a demon of the thirty-six decans of the zodiac. He is a demon of affliction, and he can torment the living by visiting them with suffering and disease. Enenuth's specialty seems to be connected with the complaints of old age, for he is said to have the power to weaken the teeth so they grow loose and fall out. He also has the power to addle the mind and to change the heart—a possible reference to senile dementia. As fearsome as this demonic entity may be, he can be driven away by uttering a single name: Allazoôl. In McCown's translation of the *Testament*, Enenuth's name is spelled *Enautha* and he is given the title of *Rhyx*, meaning "king." The name that controls him is that of the angel Kalazael. See also SOLOMON.

Enêpsigos: A demon connected with the moon, according to the *Testament of Solomon*. Enêpsigos is one of several demons in the *Testament of Solomon* that are said to specifically be female in form. She has a triple form, which Solomon ultimately binds with a triple chain. The triplicity assigned to this demon, as well as her association with the moon, seems to connect her to ancient forms of the Triple Goddess, often connected with witchcraft. This connection seems to be supported by the assertion that Enêpsigos can be invoked to accomplish the magickal act of drawing down the moon. This was an ancient power attributed to witches and used to explain lunar eclipses. Witches were once believed to gather in caverns by night and literally pull the moon down from its heavenly sphere, binding it underground for their own ends. Enêpsigos is said to be bound by the name of the angel Rathanael. See also SOLOMON.

Eniuri: A demon said to serve the arch-fiend Asmodeus. Eniuri is one of several demons named in the *Sacred Magic of Abramelin the Mage* whose name varies greatly between different versions of this text. The 1720 manuscript in the Dresden library gives this name as *Jemuri*. The manuscript maintained at the Wolfenbüttel library renders the name *Iemuri*. Finally, the 1725 edition published by Peter Hammer gives the spelling *Ieniuri*. No original has survived for these copies to be compared against. See also ASMODEUS, MATHERS.

Ennoniel: The first of twelve dukes listed as the chief servants of the wandering prince Emoniel. According to the *Ars Theurgia*, Ennoniel has a basically good nature, and he can appear during the day as well as the night. He is drawn to wooded areas and is most likely to manifest in these locations. As a demon of rank, Ennoniel commands a total of one thousand three hundred and twenty lesser spirits. See also *ARS THEURGIA*, EMONIEL.

Ephippas: A demon who appears in the extra-biblical *Testament of Solomon*. In that text, King Solomon first hears reports of Ephippas because the demon has assumed the form of an ill wind. In that form, he has harried a distant country, killing all in his path. King Solomon has the demon shut up into a flask and brought to him. Through the power of a special ring given to him by the Lord God, Solomon then questions the demon about his nature. Because of the power of the ring, Ephippas has no choice but to comply. He reveals that he can blight and wither trees, destroying entire mountains with his hellish wind. He can reveal treasure—from silver to gold to precious gems. In addition to all of this, he can command a mighty pillar of air capable of moving even the heaviest objects. When Ephippas reveals this last detail about his power, King Solomon realizes exactly what he should do with this infernal creature. Invoking his power over demons, King Solomon commands Ephippas to aid in the construction of his temple. In obedience to Solomon's command, Ephippas then lifts a massive stone rejected by the builders because it was too heavy for them to work with. With his pillar of wind, Ephippas moves this stone easily, and it becomes the cornerstone of the temple—at least according to the *Testament of Solomon*. Later in the *Testament of Solomon*, Ephippas helped King Solomon imprison Beelzebub's child Abezithibod, a demon who once haunted the waters of the Red Sea. See also ABEZITHIBOD, BEELZEBUB, SOLOMON.

Eramael: A demon named in the *True Keys of Solomon*, Eramael is said to serve as one of four principal spirits under the direction of Satanachi, a chief of the demon Lucifer. See also LUCIFER, SATANACHIA, *TRUE KEYS*.

Erekia: According to S. L. MacGregor Mathers, the name of this demon means "the sunderer." Erekia appears in the *Sacred Magic of Abramelin the Mage*, where he is said to serve the infernal king Amaimon. Other spellings include *Erkeya* and *Erkaya*. See also AMAIMON, MATHERS.

Erenutes: A demon whose name appears in the Mathers translation of the *Sacred Magic of Abramelin the Mage*. He is one of a number of spirits who serve in the hierarchy of the four demonic princes of the cardinal directions: Oriens, Paimon, Ariton,

and Amaimon. See also AMAIMON, ARITON, MATHERS, ORIENS, PAIMON.

Ergonion: One of Beelzebub's many demonic servitors, this name is listed in the *Sacred Magic of Abramelin the Mage*. In his 1898 translation of this work, occultist S. L. MacGregor Mathers gives this demon's name as *Ergamen*. See also BEELZEBUB, MATHERS.

Espoel: According to the *Ars Theurgia*, Espoel is a demon with the title of duke. He serves the infernal king Maseriel during the hours of the day and has thirty lesser spirits under his leadership. He is affiliated with the south. See also *ARS THEURGIA*, MASERIEL.

Etaliz: According to the Mathers translation of the *Sacred Magic of Abramelin the Mage*, the name of this demon is related to a Hebrew word meaning "to furrow" or "to plow." Etaliz is one of a number of demons who serve both Astaroth and Asmodeus. See also ASTAROTH, ASMODEUS, MATHERS.

Ethan: A name given as that of a demonic servitor of the arch-demons Asmodeus and Astaroth in the Mathers translation of the *Sacred Magic of Abramelin the Mage*. See also ASTAROTH, ASMODEUS, MATHERS.

Ethanim: A curious name that Mathers presents as meaning either an ass or a furnace in his translation of the *Sacred Magic of Abramelin the Mage*. Ethanim is said to serve the demonic princes of the four directions: Oriens, Paimon, Ariton, and Amaimon. See also AMAIMON, ARITON, MATHERS, ORIENS, PAIMON.

Etheye: A demon belonging to the planetary sphere of Saturn. He serves King Maymon, along with his fellow ministers Cherasa, Etheye, Aldee, Malyke, and Albewe. Etheye may appear as a pig or horned owl or something entirely monstrous. If compelled to take human form, he can take the guise of an old man or old woman. Both will wear black robes and carry either canes or a sickle. His office is to spread chaos, hatred, and discord, inciting mutilation and murder. He appears in the *Book of Oberon*, an English grimoire written during the time of Shakespeare. See also ALBEWE, ALDEE, *BOOK OF OBERON*, CHERASA, ETH-EYE, MALYKE, MAYMON.

Ethiel: A night-demon in the hierarchy of the infernal prince Usiel, Ethiel commands ten lesser spirits of his own. His name and seal appear in the *Ars Theurgia*. In this text, Ethiel is said to have some of the most puissant powers of illusion when it comes to hiding away precious objects or revealing the location of treasure hidden by magickal means. He is tied to the west. See also *ARS THEURGIA*, USIEL.

Etimiel: A demon connected with the hours of the day, Etimiel holds the title of duke. He serves the demon Cabariel, who rules in the west by north. Etimiel has fifty ministering spirits beneath him and the seal to summon and compel him appears in the *Ars Theurgia*. See also *ARS THEURGIA*, CABARIEL.

Euronymous: According to demonologist Charles Berbiguier, Euronymous is the Prince of Death. He holds a respectable rank within the hierarchy of Hell envisioned by this curious Frenchman. Among his distinctions, Euronymous has been awarded the Grand Cross of Beelzebub's Order of the Fly. Euronymous went from Berbiguier's book *Les Farfadets* to Collin de Plancy's *Dictionnaire Infernal*, thus establishing his name within the canon of demonology. Euronymous is almost certainly a misspelling of the Greek name *Eurynomos*. Eurynomos appeared in the great painting of the Assembly Room at Delphi, executed by the fifth-century BCE Greek artist Polygnotos. In Henry Beauchamp Walters's *Art of the Greeks*, Eurynomos is described as a "demon of savage aspect"[44] who overlooks the shades of Hades on the reedy shores of the River Acheron. Later in the same text, Eurynomos is said to devour the flesh of the dead in Hades. He is represented as having bluish-black skin reminiscent of a bluebottle fly. See also BERBIGUIER, DE PLANCY.

Exteron: In his 1898 translation of the *Sacred Magic of Abramelin the Mage*, occultist S. L. MacGregor Mathers gives this demon's name as meaning "foreign" or "distant." Exteron is a demonic servitor in the hierarchy beneath Astaroth and Asmodeus. See also ASTAROTH, ASMODEUS, MATHERS.

Ezequiel: One of several fallen angels named in the *Book of Enoch*, Ezequiel was one of the Watcher Angels entrusted with secret knowledge of the heavens. In addition to lusting after human women, he sinned by teaching this forbidden knowledge to humanity. Ezequiel shared the knowledge of the clouds, including how to divine omens and portents through patterns seen in the sky. See also WATCHER ANGELS.

---

44. Henry Beauchamp Walters, *The Art of the Greeks*, p. 149.

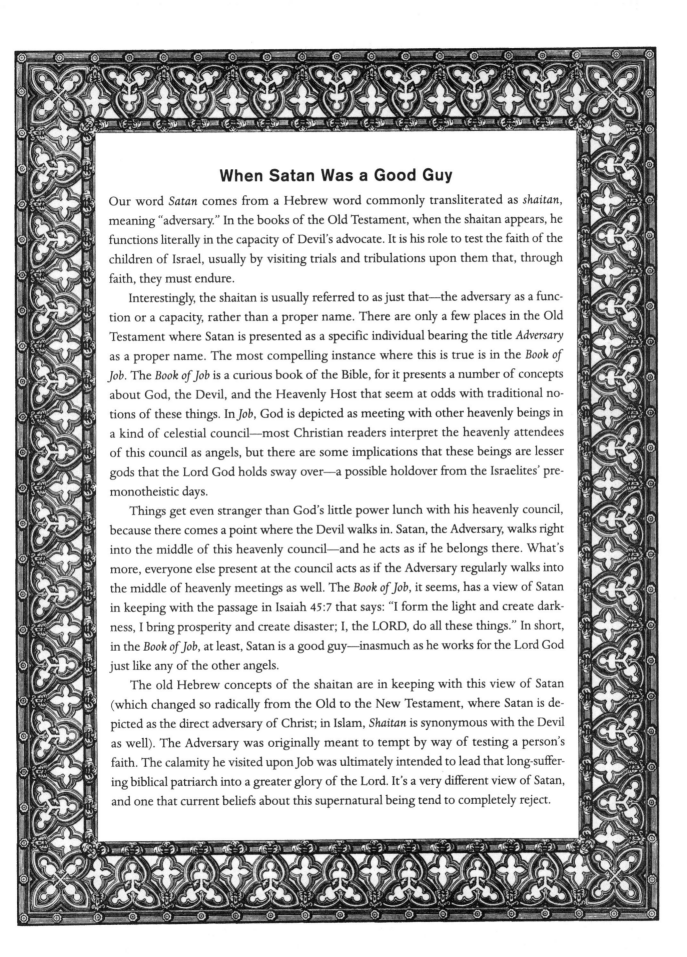

When Satan Was a Good Guy

Our word *Satan* comes from a Hebrew word commonly transliterated as *shaitan*, meaning "adversary." In the books of the Old Testament, when the shaitan appears, he functions literally in the capacity of Devil's advocate. It is his role to test the faith of the children of Israel, usually by visiting trials and tribulations upon them that, through faith, they must endure.

Interestingly, the shaitan is usually referred to as just that—the adversary as a function or a capacity, rather than a proper name. There are only a few places in the Old Testament where Satan is presented as a specific individual bearing the title *Adversary* as a proper name. The most compelling instance where this is true is in the *Book of Job*. The *Book of Job* is a curious book of the Bible, for it presents a number of concepts about God, the Devil, and the Heavenly Host that seem at odds with traditional notions of these things. In *Job*, God is depicted as meeting with other heavenly beings in a kind of celestial council—most Christian readers interpret the heavenly attendees of this council as angels, but there are some implications that these beings are lesser gods that the Lord God holds sway over—a possible holdover from the Israelites' pre-monotheistic days.

Things get even stranger than God's little power lunch with his heavenly council, because there comes a point where the Devil walks in. Satan, the Adversary, walks right into the middle of this heavenly council—and he acts as if he belongs there. What's more, everyone else present at the council acts as if the Adversary regularly walks into the middle of heavenly meetings as well. The *Book of Job*, it seems, has a view of Satan in keeping with the passage in Isaiah 45:7 that says: "I form the light and create darkness, I bring prosperity and create disaster; I, the LORD, do all these things." In short, in the *Book of Job*, at least, Satan is a good guy—inasmuch as he works for the Lord God just like any of the other angels.

The old Hebrew concepts of the shaitan are in keeping with this view of Satan (which changed so radically from the Old to the New Testament, where Satan is depicted as the direct adversary of Christ; in Islam, *Shaitan* is synonymous with the Devil as well). The Adversary was originally meant to tempt by way of testing a person's faith. The calamity he visited upon Job was ultimately intended to lead that long-suffering biblical patriarch into a greater glory of the Lord. It's a very different view of Satan, and one that current beliefs about this supernatural being tend to completely reject.

Fabar: A demon of divination, Fabar is named in the *Munich Handbook*, where he is called upon to help transform a human fingernail (still attached) into a scrying mirror. He can help the viewer perceive all manner of secret and hidden things. See also *MUNICH HANDBOOK*.

Fabariel: A demon of the day who serves the infernal prince Usiel in the court of the west. Fabariel commands thirty ministering spirits and he holds the rank of duke. In the *Ars Theurgia*, Fabariel is named as one of the most skilled demons for revealing hidden treasure. He is also said to have the power to hide precious objects through the use of charms and enchantments. See also *ARS THEURGIA*, USIEL.

Fabath: A demon summoned to obtain information to help bring a thief to justice. His name appears in the fortieth spell of the *Munich Handbook*. He is connected with the arts of scrying and divination. See also *MUNICH HANDBOOK*.

Fabiel: A servant of the infernal prince Dorochiel. Fabiel appears in the *Ars Theurgia*, where he is said to hold the rank of chief duke and serve in the hierarchy of the west. He is tied to the hours of the day, preferring to be conjured before noon. Forty ministering spirits attend him. See also *ARS THEURGIA*, DOROCHIEL.

Faccas: This demon makes an appearance in the fifteenth-century magickal text known as the *Liber de Angelis*. He is one of two demons said to serve the infernal king Zombar. Faccas is a demon of hatred and discord. He is mentioned as part of a spell that involves a lead image that, once enchanted, should be buried in a place where many people pass by. The influence of the demon will cause people to fall upon one another in bitter arguments and fights. See also *LIBER DE ANGELIS*, ZOMBAR.

Fagani: In the 1898 Mathers translation of the *Sacred Magic of Abramelin the Mage*, the name of this demon is given to mean "devourers." Fagani is said to serve the infernal ruler Astaroth, and to do so exclusively. See also ASTAROTH, MATHERS.

Falcas: Another name for the demon Lewteffar, described in the *Book of Oberon*. See also *BOOK OF OBERON*, LEWTEFFAR.

Faseua: An infernal spirit of the night, Faseua holds the title of duke in the hierarchy of the demon-king Asyriel. His name and seal appear in the Henson translation of the *Ars Theurgia*. According to this text, he has ten servants beneath him. He is affiliated with the direction of the south. See also *ARS THEURGIA*, ASYRIEL.

Faturab: This curious name appears in all surviving versions of the *Sacred Magic of Abramelin the Mage*. Faturab is said to serve the demon Magoth. In his presentation of the *Abramelin* material, occultist S. L. MacGregor Mathers also ranks Kore as a demon in command of Faturab. See also KORE, MAGOTH, MATHERS.

Febat: According to the *Munich Handbook*, Febat should be called upon by those seeking the power of divination. He may be related to Fabath, a demon called upon in a similar spell that appears in the same manuscript. See also FABATH, *MUNICH HANDBOOK*.

Fegot: A demon named in the *True Keys of Solomon*. He is one of several servants of chief Sirachi, an agent of Lucifer. Fegot is a demon of illusion, and he can make nightmarish monsters and chimeras appear to be real. See also LUCIFER, SIRACHI, *TRUE KEYS*.

Felsmes: This demon is summoned to charm a human fingernail so that it will show images. The spell to achieve this method of divination appears in the fifteenth-century magickal text known as the *Munich Handbook*. The fingernail should still be attached to a living person who then must use the nail's surface as a scrying mirror to perform acts of divination. See also *MUNICH HANDBOOK*.

Femell: A demon invoked whenever the four kings of the cardinal directions are called upon in ceremony. He functions as a messenger and appears with Alphasis, Emlon, and Rodabell. Femell appears in the *Book of Oberon*, a grimoire from Elizabethan England. He must be constrained before Baall is called up. Two variants of his name are given in the *Book of Oberon*: Bellferit and Bellfarto. These names also appear in the *Demon Princes*, where they are spelled Belferit and Belfarto. This text identifies the demon as a messenger of Oriens, king of the east. See also ALPHASIS, *BOOK OF OBERON*, EMLON, *DEMON PRINCES*, RODABELL.

Femor: Reputed to be a stubborn and cantankerous demon, Femor appears in the second book of the *Lesser Key of Solomon*, known as the *Ars Theurgia*. He is one of twelve dukes said to serve the infernal Emperor of the South, Caspiel. As a demon of rank, Femor commands two thousand two hundred and sixty lesser spirits. See also *ARS THEURGIA*, CASPIEL.

Feremin: A demon named in the *Munich Handbook*. He is said to appear riding a horse. He is called up to help create a magickal bridle. This enchanted item is said to summon an infernal steed that will carry its owner swiftly to any location desired. Feremin is described as a spirit that waits upon sinners. See also *MUNICH HANDBOOK*.

Fersebus: A demon said to serve the arch-fiend Magoth. In the 1898 Mathers translation of the *Sacred Magic of Abramelin the Mage*, Fersebus is also said to serve Kore, who is implied to be a demon. Fersebus is likely an alternate spelling of this demon's name, as all other surviving versions of the *Abramelin* material render this name *Fernebus*. See also KORE, MAGOTH, MATHERS.

Fersone: A demon with the rank of king named in the *Book of Oberon*. He appears as a man with the face of a lion. Forty heralds and minstrels play before him to announce his coming. He knows past, present, and future, reveals hidden treasure, and has seventy-two legions under him. The *Book of Oberon* says that this demon desires sacrifice of those who call him, and the cost is high: not satisfied with mere incense or even the blood of an animal, Fersone demands the offering of a brazen (i.e., shameless) maid. The text does not elaborate on what the demon will do to her if offered to him. See also *BOOK OF OBERON*.

Fessan: A knowledgeable demon, he is well learned in astronomy and arithmetic. He appears like a flame and speaks with a soft, rasping voice. In the *Book of Oberon*, which records his name, he is said to be one of twelve chief servants of the demon-king of the north, Egin. See also *BOOK OF OBERON*, EGIN.

Fewrayn: A demon who teaches languages, Fewrayn is named in the Elizabethan grimoire known as the *Book of Oberon*. Said to appear meekly with the countenance of a woman, he holds the rank of governor or marquis (the text gives both). This demon can bestow the ability to speak and understand foreign languages. He can be called upon in love magic, where he specifically targets women. He is said to have only nine legions of lesser spirits serving under him. Despite his feminine appearance, male pronouns are used throughout this demon's entry, suggesting that his gender is more complicated than a human binary. See also *BOOK OF OBERON*.

Finaxos: A servitor of the demons Astaroth and Asmodeus, Finaxos's name appears in the Mathers translation of the *Sacred Magic of Abramelin the Mage*. In other versions of the *Abramelin* material, the name of this demon is rendered *Tinakos*. See also ASTAROTH, ASMODEUS, MATHERS.

Finibet: This demon is called upon to lend infernal aid in a process of divination. According to the *Munich Handbook*, he has the power to charm the reflective surface of a human fingernail so that it will reveal images concerning the identity of a thief. See also *MUNICH HANDBOOK*.

Firiel: A demon associated with the region of the west. Firiel is named in the fifteenth-century grimoire known as the *Munich Handbook*. In this text, he is one of four demons called up to provide an enchanted cloak. This infernal item reputedly has the power to render anyone who wears it invisible. The demons must be called up on a Wednesday in a remote location during the first hour of the day in a waxing moon. Use of the cloak does not come without its risks, however. According to the text, unless proper precautions are taken, Firiel and his compatriots will kill anyone who uses the cloak after a period of a week and three days. See also *MUNICH HANDBOOK*.

Flauros: In Wierus's *Pseudomonarchia Daemonum*, Flauros is said to appear in the form of a powerful leopard. He can also assume a human form, but when he does, his demonic nature shows through in his horrible face and burning eyes. He is said to hold the rank of duke with twenty legions of lesser spirits to carry out his commands. He can be a liar and a deceiver, although he can also be forced to destroy a person's enemies, striking them down with fire. If care is taken to make him answer truthfully, he can speak of the past, present, and future, as well as divinity, Creation, and the Fall. According to Scot's *Discoverie of Witchcraft*, he can also be commanded to protect someone from temptations. Flauros also appears in the *Goetia*. In the *Goetia of Dr. Rudd*, he is said to govern

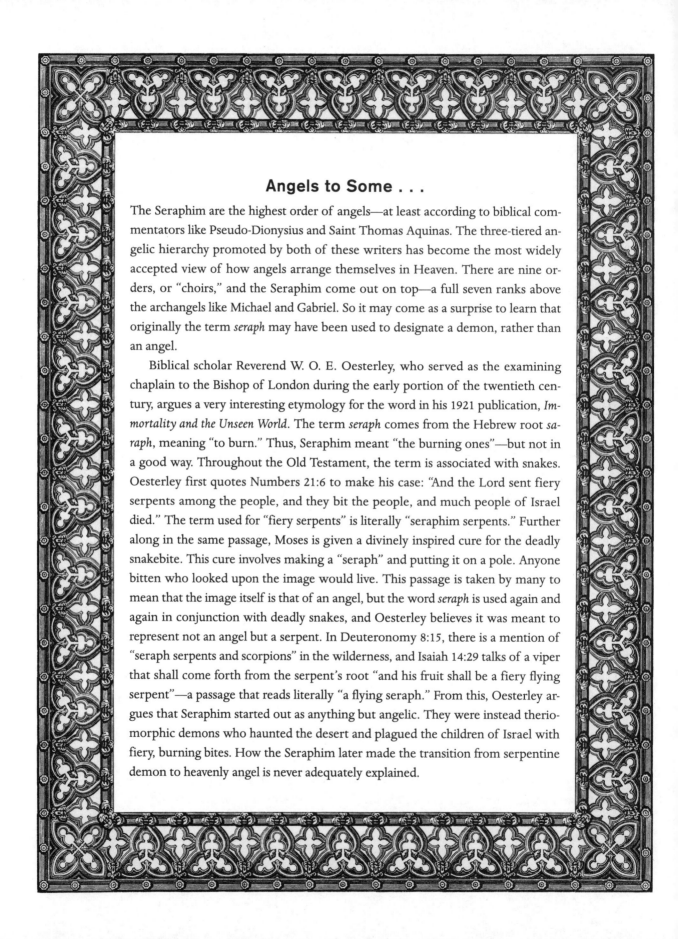

Angels to Some . . .

The Seraphim are the highest order of angels—at least according to biblical commentators like Pseudo-Dionysius and Saint Thomas Aquinas. The three-tiered angelic hierarchy promoted by both of these writers has become the most widely accepted view of how angels arrange themselves in Heaven. There are nine orders, or "choirs," and the Seraphim come out on top—a full seven ranks above the archangels like Michael and Gabriel. So it may come as a surprise to learn that originally the term *seraph* may have been used to designate a demon, rather than an angel.

Biblical scholar Reverend W. O. E. Oesterley, who served as the examining chaplain to the Bishop of London during the early portion of the twentieth century, argues a very interesting etymology for the word in his 1921 publication, *Immortality and the Unseen World*. The term *seraph* comes from the Hebrew root *saraph*, meaning "to burn." Thus, Seraphim meant "the burning ones"—but not in a good way. Throughout the Old Testament, the term is associated with snakes. Oesterley first quotes Numbers 21:6 to make his case: "And the Lord sent fiery serpents among the people, and they bit the people, and much people of Israel died." The term used for "fiery serpents" is literally "seraphim serpents." Further along in the same passage, Moses is given a divinely inspired cure for the deadly snakebite. This cure involves making a "seraph" and putting it on a pole. Anyone bitten who looked upon the image would live. This passage is taken by many to mean that the image itself is that of an angel, but the word *seraph* is used again and again in conjunction with deadly snakes, and Oesterley believes it was meant to represent not an angel but a serpent. In Deuteronomy 8:15, there is a mention of "seraph serpents and scorpions" in the wilderness, and Isaiah 14:29 talks of a viper that shall come forth from the serpent's root "and his fruit shall be a fiery flying serpent"—a passage that reads literally "a flying seraph." From this, Oesterley argues that Seraphim started out as anything but angelic. They were instead theriomorphic demons who haunted the desert and plagued the children of Israel with fiery, burning bites. How the Seraphim later made the transition from serpentine demon to heavenly angel is never adequately explained.

either three or thirty-six legions of spirits. This text also renders his name as *Haures*. Elsewhere, it is *Hauros*. The angel Mehiel is said to have power to constrain this demon. See also *GOETIA*, RUDD, SCOT, WIERUS.

Flavos: A demon called upon to destroy one's enemies. In the French *Book of Spirits (Livre des esperitz)*, he is identified as a great duke who gives true answers to what is asked of him. Twenty legions serve in his entourage. Compare to the Goetic demon Flauros. See also FLAUROS, *LIVRE DES ESPERITZ*.

Flaxon: This name means "to rend asunder," at least according to occultist S. L. MacGregor Mathers. Flaxon appears in the *Sacred Magic of Abramelin the Mage*, where he is listed among the demons who serve the infernal prince Ariton. In the versions of the *Abramelin* material kept in the German libraries at Wolfenbüttel and Dresden, the name of this demon is spelled *Filaxon*. See also ARITON, MATHERS.

Fleurèty: A demon who appears in both the *Grimorium Verum* and the *Grand Grimoire*, Fleurèty is listed as a lieutenant-general in the hierarchy of Hell. Bearing some qualities in common with brownies and other beings from faerie lore, Fleurèty is attributed with the power to accomplish any task set to him overnight. Should it be requested, he is also empowered to bring a rain of hail down upon any desired location. Beneath him are many mighty spirits, including the Goetic demons Bathin, Purson, and Eligos (Eligor). See also BATHIN, ELIGOR, *GRAND GRIMOIRE*, *GRIMORIUM VERUM*, PURSON.

Focalor: The forty-first demon of the *Goetia*. According to Wierus's *Pseudomonarchia Daemonum*, Focalor has power over the winds and seas. He can overturn ships of war and drown people in the wa-

ters. Although he has the power to kill, he can be commanded to leave people unharmed and he is said to willingly consent to this request. In Scot's *Discoverie of Witchcraft*, he is one of the demons said to retain hope for returning to Heaven. He is a great duke with three legions of spirits under him. When he manifests, he takes the form of a man with gryphon's wings. He is named as the forty-first spirit of the *Goetia*. According to the *Goetia of Dr. Rudd*, he is constrained in the name of the angel Hahahel. Here, his name is given as Forcalor. In the *Book of Incantations*, his name is given as Focator. Here he is a mighty duke with command over thirty-one legions. His office is to kill. See also *BOOK OF INCANTATIONS*, *GOETIA*, RUDD, SCOT, WIERUS.

Foliath: One of several demons named in the *Munich Handbook*, Foliath is part of an operation that requires the use of a young boy, preferably a virgin. The magician invokes the names over the child and then uses the boy as an intermediary between himself and the infernal spirits. This method of divination bears a striking resemblance to similar rites recorded in Hellenic Egyptian papyri from the third century of the Common Era, particularly those recorded in the *Leyden Papyrus*. See also *MUNICH HANDBOOK*.

Foras: The thirty-first demon of the *Goetia*. In Scot's *Discoverie of Witchcraft*, Foras is described as a great president. He has a total of twenty-nine legions of spirits at his command. He is sometimes known as *Forcas*. In Wierus's *Pseudomonarchia Daemonum*, his name is spelled *Forras*. He reportedly grants wit, eloquence, and longevity to those willing to deal with him. He also has the power to make people invisible. He is a teaching demon, with knowledge of logic and ethics, as well as the magickal properties of herbs and precious stones.

A variation on the seal of Foras that appears in the *Goetia of Dr. Rudd.* Ink on parchment by M. Belanger.

Finally, he can recover lost items and reveal hidden treasure. When he manifests, he takes the shape of a strong and powerfully built man. According to the *Goetia of Dr. Rudd*, he is constrained by the angel Lectabal. See also *GOETIA*, RUDD, SCOT, WIERUS.

Forcas: In the *Livre des esperitz*, a sixteenth-century French grimoire, Forcas is a prince with thirty legions. In the *Book of Oberon*, a grimoire from Elizabethan England, he is recorded under the name *Forcase*. Here, he is a great prince who can reveal treasure and restore sight to the blind. He is served by ten legions, and when he manifests, he takes the form of a "great man"—possibly a reference to the biblical "mighty men" (*Gibburim*) or giants. Compare to the Goetic demon Foras. See also *BOOK OF OBERON*, FORAS, *LIVRE DES ESPERITZ*.

Forfason: A servant of the demon Ariton. Forfason is connected with the *Sacred Magic of Abramelin the Mage*, although his name is absent from the Mathers translation of this work. He appears in the Peter Hammer edition as well as the version kept at the Dresden library. In the manuscript kept at the Wolfenbüttel library in Germany, the name is spelled *Forfaron*. See also ARITON, MATHERS.

Forman: In the *Book of Oberon*, Forman is king over all the spirits who fall under the planetary sphere of Jupiter. He is said to appear as a man of medium stature, with reddish or yellowish-brown skin. He speaks with a soothing voice, although he jitters when moving. He has other forms as well and may appear as a man riding a stag, a girl crowned with laurels, a robed man with a miter, or even a peacock. His garments are azure blue and he may carry an unsheathed sword. He has the power to settle quarrels, calm enemies, and make people jovial. He can also clear a person of condemnation and bestow the love of women. He is served by the spirits Gewthren and Gewthem. Compare to Formione. See also *BOOK OF OBERON*, FORMIONE, GEWTHEM, GEWTHREN.

Formecones: Named in the *Book of Oberon*, Formecones is a teaching demon reputed to possess marvelous cunning in astronomy and science. He knows the virtues of herbs and stones and all manner of wisdom. In addition to teaching the properties of stones, he will also fetch precious gems for his master. When summoned, he first appears as a bull, although he can be persuaded to take human form. He holds the rank of prince, with thirty-six legions to serve him. See also *BOOK OF OBERON*.

Formione: The king of the spirits of Jupiter. Formione is a demon named in Joseph Peterson's translation of the *Sworn Book of Honorius*. According to this text, he is overseen by the angels Satquiel, Raphael, Pahamcocihel, and Asassaiel. He has the power to bring love and joy to people, bestowing a variety of positive emotions. He can also help people to earn favor with others. He is connected to the east and the south. See also *SWORN BOOK*.

Forneus: The thirtieth demon named in the *Goetia*. According to Wierus's *Pseudomonarchia Daemonum*, Forneus is a great marquis with twenty-nine legions of spirits to serve him. Some of these infernal minions belong to the Order of Angels and others belong to the Order of Thrones. In appearance, he resembles a sea monster. He can be called upon to teach languages and to make people wonderfully skilled in rhetoric. He can also cause the love of friends and foes alike and secure fame. According to the *Goetia of Dr. Rudd*, he is constrained by the angel Omael. In this text, his name is spelled *Forners*. See also GOETIA, RUDD, SCOT, WIERUS.

Fornnouc: A mighty king who rules in the east over the element of air. He is described as being full of life but capricious by nature. According to the Driscoll edition of the *Sworn Book*, Fornnouc is a healer-spirit. He is attributed with the ability to heal weakness and to prevent the onset of any infirmity. For those who earn his regard, Fornnouc will also consent to be an inspiring tutor. In the fourteenth century, when the *Sworn Book* was most likely penned, the element of air was associated with the human intellect and reason. Accordingly, any demonic tutor hailing from this element would prove highly learned. See also *SWORN BOOK*.

Forteson: A demon who serves Magoth and Kore, at least according to Mathers's presentation of the *Sacred Magic of Abramelin the Mage*. Other versions identify Forteson as a servitor of Magoth alone. Mathers suggests that the name is derived from a Greek word meaning "burdened." This name is alternately spelled *Fortesion* in the Wolfenbüttel library version of the *Abramelin* material. In the *Book of Oberon*, he is named Fortisan and serves under Lucifer. In that text, Fortisan is named along with his companions Alingon and Portisan in a spell in-tended to summon the demon Bilgall. See also ALINGON, BILGALL, *BOOK OF OBERON*, KORE, LUCIFER, MAGOTH, MATHERS, PORTISAN.

Frasmiel: A demon who commands six hundred and fifty lesser spirits. In the *Ars Theurgia*, Frasmiel serves the wandering prince Uriel in the capacity of duke. Frasmiel and his fellow dukes are all infamous for their stubborn and evil natures. They are dishonest and misleading in all of their dealings. When he manifests, Frasmiel takes the form of a monstrous serpent with a human head. See also *ARS THEURGIA*, URIEL.

Frastiel: A servant of chief Sirachi, Frastiel is named in the *True Keys of Solomon*, where he reputedly has power over life and death. He can bring anyone back from the dead. Alternately, he can also cause any mortal to die. He is sometimes known by the name *Frulhel*. See also SIRACHI, *TRUE KEYS*.

Friblex: A demon who, according to the *Book of Oberon*, holds the ranks of both duke and marquis. In appearance, he is like an angel and his temperament is described as both meek and true. According to the text, he has six legions to serve him. No specific powers are listed, although he is said to be mighty. Within the same entry, his name is also spelled *Friplex*. See also *BOOK OF OBERON*.

Frimoth: A demon of passion and lust who can either incite or squelch desire. He can also make women miscarry. According to the *True Keys of Solomon*, Frimoth serves the demon Sirachi. He also appears in the Peterson translation of the *Grimorium Verum*. Here he is a servant of the infernal Duke Syrach, standing in the fourth rank of that hierarchy. He retains many of the same powers, having particular influence over the passions and pleasures of women. His name is also used during the construction of the magick wand. In the

Secrets of Solomon, his name is spelled *Frimodth*. Here, he also stokes passions, but he can inflame a person literally: he is called upon in a spell to help warm a person in the cold. See also *SECRETS OF SOLOMON*, SIRACHI, SYRACH, *TRUE KEYS*.

Fritath: In the *Munich Handbook*, this demon is named in conjunction with the four cardinal directions. He is one of several demons who must be invoked prior to enacting a divinatory spell. See also *MUNICH HANDBOOK*.

Frulthiel: One of eighteen demons serving under Duke Syrach in the *Secrets of Solomon*. Frulthiel holds power over the living and the dead. He can call up any person from any era and cause them to answer questions. He can also resuscitate a corpse long enough for it to speak. See also *SECRETS OF SOLOMON*, SYRACH.

Fruthmerl: A demon with a fine palate and unparalleled skills in designing menus at dinner parties. Named in the seventeenth-century Venetian grimoire *Secrets of Solomon*, Fruthmerl is said to conjure lavish feasts. No culinary masterpiece is beyond his reach, as he is able to bring fine wines and delicacies to the table, as well as sumptuous fruits, plump hares, savory thrushes, and stuffed partridges. He is one of eighteen high-ranking ministers who serve Duke Syrach. See also *SECRETS OF SOLOMON*, SYRACH.

Ftheruthi: A demon holding the rank of duke who serves in the court of Prince Belzebuth. Together with Agaleraptarkimath, Ftheruthi is alleged to be one of the foremost powers in Belzebuth's retinue. His name appears in the *Secrets of Solomon*, a seventeenth-century grimoire confiscated during the Venetian Inquisition. See also AGALERAPTARKIMATH, BELZEBUTH, *SECRETS OF SOLOMON*.

Fureas: A tutelary demon named in the Welsh *Book of Incantations*, he appears as a cruel man with a long and sharp weapon. He rides a pale horse. His office is to teach philosophy, astrology, rhetoric, and logic. He has under his command twenty legions. His name is probably a variant of *Furcas*. See also *BOOK OF INCANTATIONS*, FURCAS.

Furcas: A demon said to appear in the form of a cruel man with grizzled hair and a long beard. He rides a pale horse and carries a sharp spear. Furcas is named in both Wierus's *Pseudomonarchia Daemonum* and Scot's *Discoverie of Witchcraft*. He also appears as the fiftieth demon in the *Goetia*. He is credited with the rank of knight and is said to command twenty legions. Despite his intimidating appearance, Furcas is primarily a teaching demon. He is said to instruct people in philosophy, rhetoric, astronomy, and logic. He also teaches the occult arts of chiromancy (palm reading) and pyromancy (divination by fire). Furcas is the only one of the seventy-two Goetic demons credited with the rank of knight. David Rankine and Stephen Skinner, the editors of the *Goetia of Dr. Rudd*, suggest that this is the result of a misinterpretation of a Latin word in the *Pseudomonarchia Daemonum*'s description of this demon. They feel that the term *miles*, which means "soldier," was intended to be associated with the demon's appearance, not his rank. They attribute a rank of duke to Furcas instead. According to the *Goetia of Dr. Rudd*, he can be constrained in the name of the angel Daniel. See also *GOETIA*, RUDD, SCOT, WIERUS.

Furfur: This curiously named demon has an equally curious shape. According to Wierus's *Pseudomonarchia Daemonum*, he takes the form of a deer with a tale of flame. He holds the rank of earl and oversees twenty-six legions of spirits. He is the thirty-fourth demon named in the *Goetia*. Furfur

Painted Black

From the *schwarze Pudel* of the Faust myth to the classic witch's familiar of a black cat, demons and blackness go hand in hand in the European tradition. When this blackness is ascribed to an animal, like the goat of the Witches' Sabbat, the color seems innocuous enough. Nefarious deeds are done under the cover of darkness, so the connection seems founded on reasonable metaphor. But then we must consider that the Devil did not always appear in the form of a goat. Tales of the dark man at the crossroads abound, and there is no avoiding the implication once we view illustrations like those of the demon-kings in the *Clavis Inferni* (see page 158).

Throughout European iconography, in both witchcraft and the grimoiric tradition, demons are depicted as Black men. We can make some feeble arguments explaining this. Black is the color of Saturn, and many chthonic entities are associated with that sphere. As we see in texts like the *Book of Oberon*, the physical appearance of many spirits is influenced by their ruling planet, so those associated with the Moon are white and milky, spirits of Mars are red like fire (and can even bear that color in their name, as in the case of *Rubeus Pugnator*), etc. But there is a racial element as well, one that cannot be avoided when we fully turn our attention to these demons' depictions.

The images from the *Clavis Inferni* make it very clear that these demons are not merely black because of an association with the underworld. They are dressed in garments that are recognizably African and Arabian in origin. Their identity as Black men is unavoidable, and this frequent presentation has left us a troubling legacy where Black bodies are seen as evil, seen as threatening, seen as Other. These stereotypes, firmly seeded in the European imagination from the Middle Ages onward, are things that haunt us still. And they need to be acknowledged and, with effort, deconstructed.

We cannot erase this past, but we must learn from it.

A woodcut by Hans Burgkmair featuring the Four Horsemen of the Apocalypse. From a German copy of the New Testament printed by Silvan Othmar in 1523.

is a deceitful demon, and he will lie in all things unless otherwise compelled through the use of magick or divine names. He can assume a human form if asked to do so, and when he does, he is said to speak with a hoarse voice. His powers are many and varied. He can inspire love between a man and woman, and he can answer on matters occult as well as divine. In addition, he is credited with the ability to cause thunder, lightning, and tremors. In the *Goetia of Dr. Rudd*, he does not create tremors but wild gusts of wind, making him very clearly a demon associated with storms. This text also claims that the angel Lehahiah has the power to compel and constrain him. Furfur also appears in Scot's *Discoverie of Witchcraft*. In the Welsh *Book of Incantations*, he is a great and mighty earl with command over twenty-five legions. He brings love between man and wife and causes violent storms, probably not at the same time. In the French *Livre des esperitz*, he holds the rank of count and appears in the form of an angel. See also *BOOK OF INCANTATIONS*, *GOETIA*, *LIVRE DES ESPERITZ*, RUDD, SCOT, WIERUS.

Fursiel: A subordinate to the demon Raysiel. Through allegiance to his master, Fursiel serves in the hierarchy associated with the north. He holds the rank of chief duke and has fifty lesser spirits to serve him. According to the *Ars Theurgia*, he is only active during the day. See also *ARS THEURGIA*, RAYSIEL.

Furtiel: According to the *Ars Theurgia*, Furtiel is an evil and roguish demon who serves the wandering duke Buriel. Furtiel commands eight hundred and eighty lesser spirits who follow and attend him. He is tied to the hours of the night and he hates the day. He will flee from the light and only manifest in darkness. When he does manifest, he assumes the form of a monstrous human-headed serpent. He is such a malevolent being that all other spirits, save those in his own hierarchy, despise him. See also *ARS THEURGIA*, BURIEL.

Futiel: A night-demon said to have a total of four hundred ministering spirits at his command. Futiel is named as a chief duke in the *Ars Theurgia*, where it is said that he serves the infernal prince Dorochiel from midnight to dawn each night. His region is the west. See also *ARS THEURGIA*, DOROCHIEL.

Fyrus: A demon named in the fifteenth-century text known as the *Munich Handbook*. Fyrus is connected with matters of justice and divination. In particular, he can help reveal the identity of a thief. See also *MUNICH HANDBOOK*.

Gaap: A demon named in both the *Pseudomonarchia Daemonum* of Johannes Wierus and Scot's *Discoverie of Witchcraft*. Gaap is also one of the traditional seventy-two demons of the *Goetia*. He is described as both a president and a prince, although there is evidence in the *Goetia of Dr. Rudd* that suggests his real title should be king. He has a total of sixty-six legions under his command. In Heaven, he reputedly belonged to the angelic Order of Powers, sometimes also called the Order of Potestates. He is said to appear in a sign in the meridian, but the exact sign is left unspecified in the *Pseudomonarchia*. In the *Goetia*, he is said to appear when the sun is in certain southern signs (it doesn't say which signs). When he assumes human form, he appears as a doctor, and he is said to be an excellent "doctor" of women, causing them to burn with love for men. Gaap is also credited with being as mighty a demon as the infernal king Bileth, and he acts as a guide to the four principal kings. In addition to his ability to make women lust after men, he is credited with a number of powers. He is said to steal familiar spirits from other conjurors. He teaches philosophy and the liberal sciences, and he answers on matters concerning the past, present, and future. He can also inspire love and hatred among people, and he has the power to transport individuals from one country to another. He can make people invisible and can also strike people senseless. Finally, he has the power to consecrate things under the dominion of the infernal king Amaimon, although the precise utility of this power is unclear. Alternate versions of his name include *Tap* and *Goap*. In the *Goetia of Dr. Rudd*, Gaap is said to belong to Amaimon, thus allying him with the court of the east. He can be constrained by the angel Jehujah. In the Binsfeld hierarchy of demons connected to the Seven Deadly Sins, Gaap is equated with Satan. He is also named in the Welsh *Book of Incantations*, where it affirms that he appears when the sun is in one of the southern signs. He holds the rank of prince and governs sixty-six legions. Later in the same manuscript, his rank is given as president. He teaches philosophy and science, transports people from place to place, and can cause love or hatred. See also AMAIMON, BILETH, *BOOK OF INCANTATIONS*, *GOETIA*, RUDD, SATAN, SCOT, WIERUS.

Gabio: One of several demons whose names appear in the *Ars Theurgia* in connection with the infernal king Barmiel. Gabio is said to serve Barmiel during the hours of the night. He holds the rank of duke but has no servants or ministering spirits of his own. Through his service to Barmiel, Gabio is associated with the south. See also *ARS THEURGIA*, BARMIEL.

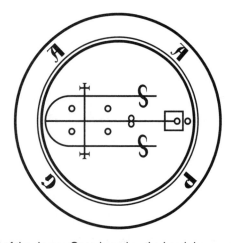

Seal of the demon Gaap based on the hand-drawn version in John Harries's *Book of Incantations*. This early ninteenth-century Welsh grimoire has several unique variations on the traditional sigils. Image by Catherine Rogers.

Gadriel: A fallen angel mentioned in the *Book of Enoch*, Gadriel allegedly taught humanity all the blows of death. Like the fallen angel Azazel, he is said to have taught humanity how to craft weapons and armor. In addition to all of this, he is directly credited as being the angel that led Eve astray. See also AZAZEL, WATCHER ANGELS.

Gaeneron: A duke with twenty-seven legions under his command, Gaeneron appears as a beautiful woman riding a camel. According to the fifteenth-century grimoire known as the *Munich Handbook*, this demon is especially gifted at procuring the love of beautiful women. He can also reveal hidden treasure and respond to any questions concerning the past, the present, or the future. Compare this demon's description and powers to Gemory, one of the traditional seventy-two demons of the *Goetia*. See also GEMORY, *GOETIA*, *MUNICH HANDBOOK*.

Gagalin: According to the Mathers translation of the *Sacred Magic of Abramelin the Mage*, this demon serves the infernal kings Amaimon and Ariton. Mathers attempts to relate the name of this demon to the word *ganglion*, although the connection is rather dubious. In another version of the *Abramelin* material kept at the Wolfenbüttel library in Germany, this demon's name is presented as *Gagolchon*. See also AMAIMON, ARITON, MATHERS.

Gagalos: A demon named in Mathers's presentation of the *Sacred Magic of Abramelin the Mage*. He is said to serve the arch-demons Asmodeus and Astaroth. Mathers suggests that the name Gagalos may come from a Greek word meaning "tumor." See also ASTAROTH, ASMODEUS, MATHERS.

Gagison: A servant of the demon Oriens, according to the *Sacred Magic of Abramelin the Mage*. In his translation of this work, occultist Mathers suggests that this demon's name is derived from a Hebrew term meaning "spread out flat." See also MATHERS, ORIENS.

Gahathus: A demon named in the Peterson edition of the *Sworn Book of Honorius*. According to this text, Gahathus is a servant of the infernal king Batthan. He is tied to the sphere of the sun, and,

The Demons of the Four Directions

The idea that the four quarters or four cardinal directions are watched over by specific otherworldly beings is an old one. In the Christian tradition, four archangels are often thought to oversee one of each of the four directions, and the four authors of the Gospels were often equated with the four winds as well as the four quarters. Perhaps as an antinomian response to this tradition, there was also a widespread belief in medieval and Renaissance Europe that certain demons held sway over the cardinal directions. This belief is reflected in the grimoires, where many of the demons are assigned an affiliation to the hierarchy of a particular direction. These directional correspondences are especially important to the demons of the *Ars Theurgia*, all of whom are associated with specific points along the compass. Although the notion that certain demons rule over particular directions is a common one in the grimoiric tradition, no source seems to agree on exactly which demons are in charge of which directions. There are so many different demons said to be the "first and supreme" ruler of a particular cardinal point that it can be fairly mind-boggling to keep them all straight. Here are just a few of the lists compiled from the magickal texts sourced within this book:

Source	East	West	North	South
Abramelin	Oriens	Paimon	Ariton	Amaimon
Agrippa	Urieus	Paymon	Egin	Amaimon
Ars Theurgia	Carnesiel	Amenadiel	Demoriel	Caspiel
Clavis Infernis	Oriens	Paimon	Egin	Amaimon
Dr. Rudd	Amaimon	Gaap	Zinamar	Corson
Oberon	Oriens	Paymon	Egyn	Amaimon
Sworn Book*	Fornnouc	Harthan	Albunalith	Jamaz

* Driscoll edition. In the Peterson edition of the *Sworn Book*, the demonic rulers are associated with the seven planetary spheres rather than the four cardinal directions.

as such, he has power to confer wealth, fame, and worldly favor. When he manifests, his body appears bright with golden skin. This demon is one of four who serve in the hierarchy of the sun that are said to also be subject to the north wind. See also BATTHAN, *SWORN BOOK*.

Galand: A demon named in the seventeenth-century grimoire *Secrets of Solomon*. A powerful servitor in the court of Duke Syrach, Galand is a demon of affliction. He can visit venereal disease and crabs upon his victims, though he can also be called upon to cure these ailments. He appears in a spell designed to bring death to an enemy. A variant of his name is given as *Galant*. In the *True Keys of Solomon*, he is said to be a servant of chief Sirachi. See also *SECRETS OF SOLOMON*, SIRACHI, SYRACH, *TRUE KEYS*.

Gallath: A demon tied to the art of divination. He is named in the fifteenth-century *Munich Handbook* in connection with a scrying spell. He is called upon to help reveal the identity of a thief and bring justice for their victim. See also *MUNICH HANDBOOK*.

Galtim: A duke of Hell whose name may also be spelled *Galtym*. He appears in the *Munich Handbook*, along with a number of other demons called upon to help work a series of spells. See also *MUNICH HANDBOOK*.

Gamasu: A demon in the hierarchy of Usiel, Gamasu is said to excel at both revealing and concealing hidden treasure. He is also skilled at illusions and enchantments. The *Ars Theurgia* gives his rank as duke, further saying that he has thirty lesser spirits to serve him. He will only manifest during the hours of the day. He serves in the region of the west. See also *ARS THEURGIA*, USIEL.

Gamigin: The fourth spirit named among the demons of the *Goetia*. According to Scot's *Discoverie of Witchcraft*, Gamigin is a great marquis ruling over thirty legions of lesser spirits. He first manifests in the form of a little horse, but he can change this shape to assume the form of a man. Gamigin's main power is a form of necromancy. He is reputed to be able to call upon the souls of those drowned in the sea as well as any souls confined to purgatory and cause them to appear in "airy" or non-physical bodies. He can further force them to submit to interrogation, answering any questions put to them. His name is given as *Gamygyn* by Wierus in his *Pseudomonarchia Daemonum*. In the *Goetia of Dr. Rudd*, the demon's initial form is said to be that of both a little horse and an ass. He is constrained by the angel Elemiah. In the *Book of Incantations*, he is also a marquis who appears in the form of a little horse or donkey. He teaches liberal sciences and gives an account of the souls who die in sin. See also *BOOK OF INCANTATIONS*, *GOETIA*, RUDD, SCOT, WIERUS.

Gamor: Also spelled *Gaymor*. A demon of knowledge and instruction who takes the form of a flaming spark. Gamor teaches astronomy as well as all the other sciences. In addition, he can help his summoner to gain favor among rich and influential people. He can also reveal the location of hidden treasure and describe the spirits that guard over it. His name appears in the Elizabethan grimoire known as the *Book of Oberon*, where he is one of the twelve principal demons serving under Amaimon, king of the south. See also AMAIMON, *BOOK OF OBERON*.

Gana: An infernal spirit connected with justice and divination. He is named in the *Munich Handbook*. In this text he helps to reveal the person or persons responsible for a theft by showing their images to a scryer. See also *MUNICH HANDBOOK*.

Garadiel: A demon named in the second book of the *Lesser Key of Solomon*, known widely as the *Ars Theurgia*. In this work, Garadiel is described as a prince of the air who wanders with his massive retinue of attendant spirits, never remaining in one place for very long. Garadiel, together with the thousands of lesser spirits who wait on him, are described as having indifferent natures—neither good nor bad but more properly disposed to good than to evil. See also *ARS THEURGIA*.

Gariel: A night-demon in service to the infernal prince Dorochiel. Gariel is one of several demons accorded the rank of chief duke in Dorochiel's western hierarchy. According to the *Ars Theurgia*, Gariel is responsible for the governance of four hundred lesser spirits. He will only manifest in a specific hour in the second half of the night. See also *ARS THEURGIA*, DOROCHIEL.

Garsone: A demon named in the *Book of Oberon*. In the margins of that Elizabethan grimoire, he is noted as a "good and true spirit." Like many demons named in the *Book of Oberon*, he knows the location of hidden treasure and will reveal it to those who know how to summon him. Additionally, he can reveal divine secrets about the creation of the world—knowledge that heavily implies that he bore personal witness to the event before his fall. When he manifests, he assumes the guise of an ordinary man. Seven legions of lesser spirits serve under his command. See also *BOOK OF OBERON*.

Gartiraf: According to the *Liber de Angelis*, Gartiraf is a demon whose specialty is disease. He is invoked as part of a spell intended to curse an enemy. At the magician's whim, this demon, along with his fellows, will fly forth and inflict every kind of suffering upon a target. In addition to disease, he can cause fever, trembling, and weakness in the limbs. Gartiraf answers to Bilet, an infernal king also invoked in the course of this spell. Bilet is a variation on the Goetic demon Bileth. See also BILETH, *LIBER DE ANGELIS*.

Gasarons: Named in the *Sacred Magic of Abramelin the Mage*, Gasarons is said to serve the demon Oriens. Other versions of the *Abramelin* material present this demon's name as *Gezeron*. See also ORIENS, MATHERS.

Gaster, Dr. Moses: A noted scholar of Hebrew who lived from 1856 until 1939. Born in Romania, he received his PhD in Leipzig in 1878 and then went on to study at the Jewish Seminary in Breslau. Political troubles in Romania brought him to England in 1885, where he established himself within the Spanish and Portuguese Congregation in London. In 1887, he was appointed *hakham* of this congregation, an honorific that acknowledged his scholarship. He produced a number of books on Jewish folklore and beliefs. Many of these were translations of rare or unusual works, such as the *Sword of Moses* and the *Chronicles of Jerahmeel*. Although a good portion of his collection of manuscripts was damaged during World War II, Gaster managed to salvage an impressive amount of material, including codices and scrolls in Hebrew on topics ranging from astronomy to liturgy. The Moses Gaster collection now resides at the University of Manchester, in England. See also *SWORD OF MOSES, CHRONICLES OF JERAHMEEL*.

Gasyaxe: A demon with a wide range of talents, Gasyaxe appears in the Elizabethan grimoire known as the *Book of Oberon*. He is described there as a great ruler who teaches how to capture spirits, helping to determine the strengths and talents of each. He also aids in determining whether or not a spirit will be inclined to answer questions truthfully. Gasyaxe himself can be used in a necromantic ritual where he is summoned into the head of a dead man. (The text does not specify whether the entire corpse is required or just the head.) When summoned thusly through a corpse, Gasyaxe will use the dead person's voice to teach magic, necromancy, and other sciences. When not forced to inhabit someone else's discarded flesh, the demon takes the shape of a hare. He is said to have sixteen legions of lesser spirits serving beneath him. Geenex, another demon described in the same section of the *Book of Oberon*, shares almost all of Gasyaxe's qualities, to the point that Geenex may simply be an alternate name for the same demon. See also *BOOK OF OBERON*, GEENEX.

Gazon: A great duke who tells of things from past, present, and future. He grants honors and helps people to rise in society, making everyone love and respect them. Identified in the *Livre des esperitz*, his name translates in French to *grass* or *turf*, although the similarity is probably accidental. See also *LIVRE DES ESPERITZ*.

Gebath: A demon named in the *Munich Handbook*. According to this text, Gebath is associated with matters of divination and scrying. The name of this demon is likely appropriated from the Hebrew language. In the Talmud, Gebath is a frontier town mentioned several times in connection with the Antipatris. According to the *Jewish Encyclopedia*, it may be connected with the city of Gabbatha. A number of demonic names used in magickal grimoires are borrowed directly from Hebrew or represent corrupted words from this language. See also *MUNICH HANDBOOK*.

Gediel: According to the *Ars Theurgia*, Gediel is the second spirit under the demon Caspiel, infernal Emperor of the South. Gediel himself rules as a king by the south and west. He has twenty chief spirits who serve him by day and another twenty who serve at night. He has a fairly benign temperament as demons go. The *Ars Theurgia* describes him as loving, courteous, and eager to work with those who call upon him. Gediel also appears in a list of demons from Johannes Trithemius's *Steganographia*, written around 1499. See also *ARS THEURGIA*, CASPIEL.

Geenex: A demon who instructs in the making of an enchanted glass to reveal the location of lost or stolen items. Geenex also teaches how to capture spirits and how to make them tell the truth. In addition, he teaches those who summon him how to craft magic rings that compel answers from certain spirits. His name appears in the *Book of Oberon*, where he is said to hold the rank of knight, with twenty legions under his command. He can appear in the form of a valiant military captain but more often takes the form of a hare. Like the demon Gasyaxe, also named in the *Book of Oberon*, Geenex can be summoned into a dead man's head to ask him questions. Given the similarities in both their appearance and powers, Geenex and Gasyaxe may be two different names for the same demon. See also *BOOK OF OBERON*, GASYAXE.

Geloma: A demon named in the *Sacred Magic of Abramelin the Mage*, Geloma's name appears in an extensive list of demons identified as servants of the infernal princes of the four cardinal directions: Oriens, Paimon, Ariton, and Amaimon. In 1898, occultist S. L. MacGregor Mathers attempted a translation of this work from a fifteenth-century French manuscript, and he suggests that Geloma's name may be derived from a Hebrew word meaning "wound together." See also AMAIMON, ARITON, MATHERS, ORIENS, PAIMON.

Gemer: A great king who teaches the virtue of herbs and all sciences. He cures the sick and can afflict healthy people with illness. Forty legions of spirits serve him. He is named in the *Livre des esperitz,* a sixteenth-century French grimoire. He may have connections with the Goetic demon Gomory. See also GEMORY, *LIVRE DES ESPERITZ.*

Gemitias: A demon thought to grant clairvoyance, under the proper circumstances. In the fifteenth-century *Munich Handbook,* he is conjured forth to aid the magician in divinatory arts. The magician invokes the demon with the aid of a young boy, and the child serves as a mediator between the demons and the magus. See also *MUNICH HANDBOOK.*

Gemmos: A demon who appears riding a red horse, Gemmos was a member of the Order of Archangels before his fall. When summoned, he appears as a knight, speaking with a strong and powerful voice. He reveals information about stolen objects and teaches physics and logic, but his greatest value rests with his knowledge of alchemy. He can teach those who summon him how to turn all metals into the purest gold. He confers the coveted philosopher's stone and is also a good physician. His name appears in the Elizabethan grimoire known as the *Book of Oberon,* where he is identified as a strong lord with twenty-seven legions beneath him. See also *BOOK OF OBERON.*

Gemon: A demon described as a valiant captain. His name appears in the *Book of Oberon,* a grimoire from Elizabethan England. According to this tome, Gemon finds hidden treasure and will truthfully answer questions about anything tied to the past, present, or future. When he manifests, he takes the form of a fair woman. She wears a crown and rides a camel. Several other demons named in the *Book of Oberon* manifest with a near-identical appearance, including Gemyem and Carmerin. Notably, Paimon, king of the west, also traditionally assumes a feminine form and rides a camel. Given the ease with which *C* and *G* names can be confused in transcription of these old manuscripts, combined with the fact that several demons have multiple variations on their names, it is possible that several of these named in the *Book of Oberon* are not distinct demons but rather versions of the same being. It is equally possible that they all share a similar manifestation because they all operate from within the court of the king of the west, although this affiliation is not overtly stated in the text. Either way, the powers and appearance of this cluster of demons should be compared to those of a more familiar Goetic entity, *Gemory,* named in several versions of the *Clavicle of Solomon,* as well as the *Pseudomonarchia Daemonum.* See also *BOOK OF OBERON,* CARMERIN, GEMYEM, GEMORY, PAIMON, *PSEUDOMONARCHIA DAEMONUM, CLAVICLE OF SOLOMON.*

Gemory: The fifty-sixth demon of the *Goetia.* Gemory is a strong and mighty duke in charge of twenty-six legions of lesser spirits. Spelled *Gomory* in Wierus's *Pseudomonarchia Daemonum,* this demon is said to answer truthfully on matters concerning the past, present, and future as well as the whereabouts of hidden treasure. Scot's *Discoverie of Witchcraft* attributes Gemory with the ability to procure the love of women—especially that of young maids. Although Gemory is described using a male pronoun, he is nevertheless said to assume the appearance of a fair woman. In this form, he wears a ducal crown about his waist and rides upon a camel. In the *Goetia of Dr. Rudd*, his name is spelled *Gremory*. According to this text, the angel Poiel has power over this demon. In the Welsh *Book of Incantations*, he also appears in the guise of a beautiful woman, but here it is a duchess's girdle that is worn round the waist. His (or her) office is to procure the love of women, young and old. See also *BOOK OF INCANTATIONS*, *GOETIA*, RUDD, SCOT, WIERUS.

Throughout grimoiric literature, demons were equated with "spirits of the air" due to their ethereal and mutable bodies. Illustration by Kirsten Brown.

Gemyem: According to the Elizabethan *Book of Oberon*, this demon manifests as a fair woman riding a camel. She wears the crown of a duchess, which is befitting of this demon's rank of duke (although later in the same entry, the demon is said to be a prince). Gemyem's powers include clairsentience and the discovery of hidden treasure. Gemyem also holds sway over love and lust, helping those who summon him (or her) to compel the attentions of women, particularly maidens. Curiously, Gemyem is also said to know "in which places do appear half women."[45] This statement raises some interesting questions about Elizabethan concepts of gender. Compare this demon's description to *Gemory* and the name to *Gamigin*, both demons traditionally included among the seventy-two demons of the *Goetia*. See also *BOOK OF OBERON*, GAMIGIN, GEMORY

Geremitturum: This demon with the tongue-twisting name appears in the *Munich Handbook* in connection with a spell for outing a thief. He assists with matters of divination. See also *MUNICH HANDBOOK*.

Gerevil: Working from a fifteenth-century French manuscript, occultist Mathers identifies this demon as one of several serving beneath the four demonic princes of the cardinal directions: Oriens, Paimon, Ariton, and Amaimon. According to Mathers, Gerevil's name is derived from a Hebrew word meaning "divining lot." See also AMAIMON, ARITON, MATHERS, ORIENS, PAIMON.

Geriel: A demon from the *Ars Theurgia* who holds the rank of duke and commands a total of two thousand two hundred and sixty lesser spirits, Geriel is one of twelve dukes in service to the demon-king Caspiel. Through Caspiel, Geriel is part of the hierarchy connected with cardinal south. Further along in the *Ars Theurgia*, Geriel appears as a

45. Daniel Harms, James R. Clark, and Joseph H. Peterson, *The Book of Oberon*, p. 201.

duke in the hierarchy of the north. Here he serves the demon-king Baruchas and commands thousands of ministering spirits. This version of Geriel is bound only to manifest himself during the hours and minutes that fall into the tenth portion of the day, when the day has been divided into fifteen equal parts. See also *ARS THEURGIA*, BARUCHAS, CASPIEL.

Gesegas: A demon whose name appears in the several manuscript versions of the *Sacred Magic of Abramelin the Mage*, Gesegas serves under the four infernal princes of the cardinal directions: Oriens, Paimon, Ariton, and Amaimon. In the Mathers translation of this work, the name of this demon is given as *Gosegas*. Mathers suggests that his name means "trembling." See also AMAIMON, ARITON, MATHERS, ORIENS, PAIMON.

Gewthem: A demon in the court of Forman, king of the planetary spirits of Jupiter. Gewthem serves alongside his fellow Gewthren. Both are pleasing spirits who speak in soothing tones, although their movements are jittery. Gewthem can cure or cause illness, attract the love of women, soothe conflicts, or remove condemnation. He is named in the *Book of Oberon*. Compare his name and office to *Guth*, another spirit associated with a Jovian hierarchy. See also *BOOK OF OBERON*, FORMAN, GEWTHREN, GUTH.

Gewthren: A spirit of Jupiter who serves King Forman. Gewthren is a mild spirit with soothing speech. He eases conflict, making even enemies feel convivial. He has the power to cure or cause illness and he can also attract the love of women. He appears in the *Book of Oberon*, named alongside Gewthem, his fellow minister. Compare his name and office to *Guthryn*. See also *BOOK OF OBERON*, GEWTHEM, GUTHRYN.

Geyll: A great earl named in the *Book of Oberon*, Geyll is summoned to bring wealth and fame. His preferred form is that of an elephant, although he can be compelled to take the shape of a man. He also holds sway over wild beasts and can summon these at will, giving them over to the control of his master. When he speaks, it is with a hoarse voice. Fifty legions of lesser spirits are at his command. See also *BOOK OF OBERON*.

Gilarion: A demonic servitor of the infernal lord Asmodeus, Gilarion appears in the fifteenth-century French manuscript sourced by Mathers for his translation of the *Sacred Magic of Abramelin the Mage*. The name of this demon is also spelled *Gillamon*. See also ASMODEUS, MATHERS.

Gimela: A demon whose name was likely derived from the Hebrew letter "gimel." According to the Mathers translation of the *Grimoire of Armadel*, Gimela enables swift travel. He can cause a mortal to move up to one hundred leagues in an hour, and if that's not quick enough, he can also whisk people away, transporting them instantly from one place to another. As with many spirits named in the *Grimoire of Armadel*, Gimela also speaks on biblical mysteries. Thus, he is reputed to reveal the form of the serpent that tempted Eve, and he can further confer the mysteries of that serpent to those who seek such forbidden power. See also MATHERS.

Ginar: A demon named as part of the Holy Guardian Angel working in the *Sacred Magic of Abramelin the Mage*, Ginar is said to serve the infernal ruler Astaroth. In all other surviving versions, this name is spelled *Giriar*. See also ASTAROTH, MATHERS.

Glasya Labolas: One of seventy-two demons traditionally associated with the *Goetia*, Glasya Labolas has several variants of his name. These variations include *Glacia Labolas* and *Glasya-la Bolas*, among others. In Wierus's *Pseudomonarchia Daemonum*, he is said to also be known by the names *Caacrinolaas* and *Caassimolar*, just to add to the confusion. This demon is reputed to hold the rank of president and he is said to govern thirty-six legions of lesser spirits. When he manifests, he appears as a dog with gryphon's wings. He is said to have the power to turn people invisible. He also teaches knowledge of the arts and can explain all present and future occurrences. Although many of the abilities attributed to this demon seem relatively benign, he is nevertheless also described as a captain of all manslayers. The *Goetia* included in the *Lemegeton* says that he has the power to teach all arts in an instant. It further ascribes to him the power to incite slaughter and bloodshed. In the *Goetia of Dr. Rudd*, he is said to be governed by the angel Nathhajah. See also *GOETIA*, RUDD, SCOT, WIERUS.

Glesi: In his presentation of the *Sacred Magic of Abramelin the Mage*, Mathers relates this name to a Hebrew root describing the horrible glistening of an insect. In this work, Glesi appears as one of several demonic servitors under the command of the infernal king Amaimon. The name of this demon is also spelled *Glysy*. See also AMAIMON, MATHERS.

Glithrel: A demon of illusion in service to Duke Syrach. Glithrel conjures many marvels, making spectators think day is night or night is day. His name appears in the seventeenth-century grimoire *Clavicula Salomonis de Secretis*. See also *SECRETS OF SOLOMON*, SYRACH.

Glitia: According to the *True Keys of Solomon*, this demon can make sumptuous banquets and fine wines appear out of thin air. He is one of several demons of illusion in service to chief Sirachi. See also SIRACHI, *TRUE KEYS*.

Globa: This infernal duke appears in the form of an ordinary man. He is a demon of lust and fertility, forcing women to submit sexually and causing them to be barren in case conception would prove inconvenient to those assaulting them. His name appears in the *Book of Oberon*, where it is said twenty legions of spirits serve him. See also *BOOK OF OBERON*.

Gloolas: Identified in the *Book of Oberon* as a great king or prince with command over twenty legions of spirits. When he appears, he takes the form of a dog with wings. Like many of the demons named in the *Book of Oberon*, he is attributed with near-omniscience, knowing all things from the past, present, and future. He can also turn someone invisible. Additionally, he can report on the activities of both friends and enemies. Compare his name and appearance to *Glasya Labolas*, the eighteenth spirit described in the *Pseudomonarchia Daemonum*. See also *BOOK OF OBERON*, GLASYA LABOLAS, WIERUS.

Godiel: In the *Ars Theurgia*, Godiel is described as an infernal duke in the hierarchy of the demon-king Amenadiel. He is tied to the region of the west. Godiel's immediate superior is the demon Cabariel, a mighty prince ruling in the west by north. Godiel is one of a hundred dukes who serve Cabariel, half by day and half by night. This demon's office is tied to the day, and hence he will only appear during the hours of daylight. He is reputed to be an obedient creature with a generally good temperament. Elsewhere in the *Ars Theurgia*, Godiel appears as one of several demons who serve the infernal prince Usiel during the hours of the night. Here Godiel is listed as a duke with

The Skin of a Virgin Kid

Many of the manuscripts from the grimoiric tradition describe spells and instruct their readers to write these spells on the skin of a virgin kid. Some modern readers have taken this to imply animal sacrifice, but it actually had more to do with the scribe's art. So what did early writers mean exactly when they spoke of virgin parchment?

During the Middle Ages in Europe, the favored writing material was parchment, made from the skin of animals. Skins of varying qualities and cost were available, and the common form of parchment became specifically defined as being made from the skins of young sheep, goats, or other non-bovine animals. A finer quality of parchment called *vellum* was also introduced, made primarily from the skin of calves, and occasionally from lamb or rabbit. The finest quality of parchment was called *uterine vellum*, made exclusively out of the skin of stillborn, aborted, or newly born calves. It was highly desired for its smooth surface and purity of white color, making it extremely expensive and thus rarely used for manuscript production. Color was also important, and parchment guilds would strive to create a skin of the whitest color possible. Yellowed skins were undesirable and considered to be of lesser quality. To achieve the whitest parchment, the animal chosen should also have a white coat. Because of the cost, parchment was carefully used and often reused. A spell requiring the "virgin skin of a kid" was requiring a brand-new, unused sheet of goat parchment.

—*Jackie Williams, traditional scribe*

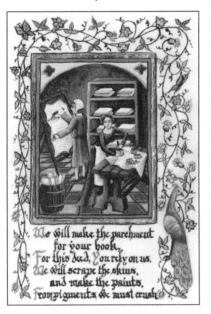

Medieval scribes preparing skins for books. From an illuminated booklet on the scribe's art by Jackie Williams.

forty lesser spirits beneath him. He is a revealer of secrets, helping mortals to discover hidden treasure. His magick can be used in the reverse, hiding treasures away from prying eyes and potential thieves. See also AMENADIEL, *ARS THEURGIA*, CABARIEL, USIEL.

Goetia: The first book of the grimoire known as the *Lemegeton*, or the *Lesser Key of Solomon*. Although the earliest known copy of the *Lemegeton* dates to 1641, occult scholar David Rankine suggests that the *Goetia* itself is at least 350 to 400 years older. The *Goetia* features a series of seventy-two demons together with their seals. The seals, sometimes known as sigils, are geometric symbols of uncertain origin that are integral to the process of summoning and binding the demons. Although many books from the grimoiric tradition will waffle on the nature of the spirits they purport to conjure, presenting some demons as essentially good beings, the demons of the *Goetia* are specifically identified as evil spirits. Notably, the Solomonic manuscript of seventeenth-century scholar Thomas Rudd presents this book under the alternate title, *Liber Malorum Spirituum*—the *Book of Evil Spirits*. The *Goetia* is probably the most widely known of the five books of the *Lesser Key of Solomon*, owing to the fact that a partial translation of this work was undertaken by occultists S. L. MacGregor Mathers and Aleister Crowley in the early part of the twentieth century. This translation was never fully completed, and the single book of the *Goetia* was published in 1904 as the *Lesser Key of Solomon*.

The *Goetia of Dr. Rudd* features a full list of the traditional seventy-two demons with slight variations on their names and seals. Part of the Harley collection of manuscripts that tie back to the seventeenth-century scholar Thomas Rudd, occultists Stephen Skinner and David Rankine are of the opinion that Rudd's work represents an earlier and more accurate version of the *Goetia* than is currently contained in any of the extant editions of the *Lemegeton*. Notably, the *Goetia of Dr. Rudd* also includes the names and seals of the seventy-two angels of the Shemhamphorash. These are paired with the Goetic demons and are to be summoned along with the demons in order to help control and compel the infernal spirits. Many versions of the *Goetia* include the word *Shemhamphorash* without any elaboration upon what this means. The *Goetia of Dr. Rudd* seems to confirm the long-held suspicion that these seventy-two angel names are integral to the conjurations of the *Goetia*.

There is some debate as to the exact age of the material contained within the *Goetia*. Although a conceptual line of descent can be traced back to the *Testament of Solomon* from the first few centuries of the Common Era, the *Testament* and the *Goetia* have virtually no demon names in common, with the possible exception of the Solomonic demon Ornias, who may appear as Orias in the *Goetia*. The *Lemegeton* itself is typically dated to the seventeenth century, but textual evidence demonstrates that the demons of the *Goetia* are older by at least a hundred years. The names of these evil spirits appear in Wierus's *Pseudomonarchia Daemonum*, a catalogue of demons appended to his 1563 work, *De Praestigiis Daemonum*. Wierus himself took his list from an older work, whose title he gives as *Liber Officiorum Spirituum*. The French *Livre des esperitz* appears also to draw upon this source. If this is the same *"de officio spirituum"* referenced in Trithemius's catalogue of necromantic books in his *Antipalus Maleficiorum*, then the work dates at least to the start of the 1500s and likely a good deal before that. Grimoiric scholar Joseph Peterson points out that the Sloane manuscript version of the *Goetia* contains names and omissions that appear in Reginald Scot's 1584 translation of the *Pseudomonarchia*, published in his larger work, the *Discoverie of Witchcraft*. Because of this, Peterson suggests that this edition of the *Goetia* was written after Scot's work and probably used it as a source. Although this helps to establish a tentative date for the Sloane manuscripts in the collection at the British Museum, it does not establish a date for the source of the Goetic tradition itself. Considering that versions of the Goetic demons also appear in the fifteenth-century necromancer's manual known as the *Munich Handbook*, it is safe to say that the Goetic tradition is quite old. The word *Goetia* itself is from an ancient Greek root, *goeteia*, meaning "witchcraft" or "sorcery." This word itself may originate from the root *goês*, meaning "to groan, to bewail." This latter word may connect it obliquely to necromancy and the souls of the dead. During the Renaissance, the Goetic arts were often associated with black magick, in contrast to theurgy, viewed as white magick. See also CROWLEY, *LEMEGETON*, MATHERS, RUDD, SCOT, SHEM-HAMPHORASH, TRITHEMIUS, WIERUS.

Gog: A biblical name that occurs in conjunction with *Magog*. Gog first appears in Ezekiel 38 and 39, where the Son of Man is urged to "set thy face against Gog and the land of Magog." Revelation 20:7 contains the following reference: "Satan shall be loosed out of his prison and shall go forth and seduce the nations which are over the four quarters of the earth, Gog and Magog: And shall gather them together to battle . . ." Although Gog and Magog are referenced multiple times in the *Book of Ezekiel*, it is hard to discern what the terms are intended to mean. Gog is clearly a leader of some sort, set against the children of Israel. Magog seems to be the land over which this leader reigns, but whether this is intended as a literal or metaphoric country is unclear from the text. In Revelation, the names are taken to represent foes of the church. From these passages, a lively tradition has sprung up, wherein both Gog and Magog are seen as individual entities, typically depicted as giants. The names have certainly made their way into the demonology of the grimoires, although they are often rendered *Guth* and *Maguth* or *Magot*. See also MAGOG, MAGOTH.

Goleg: One of several demonic servitors of Astaroth and Asmodeus named in the 1898 Mathers translation of the *Sacred Magic of Abramelin the Mage*. In another version of the *Abramelin* manuscript kept at the Wolfenbüttel library, the name of this demon is spelled *Golog*. Goleg also appears among the demonic servitors ascribed to the arch-fiend Asmodeus, although he appears in this capacity in all the *Abramelin* manuscripts *except* the one sourced by Mathers. Notably, as with a number of the demon names recorded in the *Abramelin* material, Golog is a palindrome. See also ASTAROTH, ASMODEUS, MATHERS.

Golen: "Cavern-dweller." According to the Mathers translation of the *Sacred Magic of Abramelin the Mage* Golen serves the arch-fiend Astaroth. In other versions of the *Abramelin* material, his name is given as *Golog*, a demon name that also appears in the hierarchy ruled by both Astaroth and Asmodeus. See also ASTAROTH, ASMODEUS.

Gomeh: A demon specializing in tricks and illusions, Gomeh is said to offer assistance with spells that involve the deceit of the senses. This demon appears in both the *Sacred Magic of Abramelin the Mage* and the *Clavicula Salomonis*, Mathers translations. See also *CLAVICULA SALOMONIS*, MATHERS.

Gonogin: One of several demons said to serve the infernal ruler Astaroth exclusively. Gonogin's name appears in the Mathers translation of the *Sacred Magic of Abramelin the Mage*. In the version of the *Abramelin* material kept at the Wolfenbüttel library, this demon's name is spelled *Gomogin*. The version kept in the Dresden library offers the curious variation *Gomoynu*. See also ASTAROTH, MATHERS.

Goorox: A demon with great knowledge of astronomy and the liberal sciences who also can teach the virtues of herbs and precious stones. His name appears in the Elizabethan grimoire known as the *Book of Oberon*, where he is identified as an earl with thirty legions of spirits beneath him. When summoned, he first manifests as a bull but can be coerced into taking the form of a man. See also *BOOK OF OBERON*.

Gordonsor: One of the twelve principal spirits in the court of Paimon, king of the west. He appears as a good angel with a dark face. Named in the *Book of Oberon*, he is said to be both truthful and efficient. He will swiftly and mightily accomplish all errands given to him. See also *BOOK OF OBERON*, PAIMON.

Gorilon: In his translation of the *Sacred Magic of Abramelin the Mage*, occultist S. L. MacGregor Mathers gives the meaning of this demon's name as "cleaving asunder." Gorilon is said to serve beneath the four demonic princes who guard the cardinal directions: Oriens, Paimon, Ariton, and Amaimon. Although Mathers suggests that this demon's name is derived from a Coptic word, the exact etymology of the name remains uncertain. See also AMAIMON, ARITON, MATHERS, ORIENS, PAIMON.

Gorsay: A great duke who can make people good at their work, their duties, and their words. He catches murderers and thieves and can bring these to wherever he is commanded. He can also bring pain and suffering to one's enemies. Fifteen legions of lesser spirits look to him as their master. He is named in the *Livre des esperitz*, a sixteenth-century French grimoire. See also *LIVRE DES ESPERITZ*.

Gorsyar: When summoned, Gorsyar comes riding a bear. He wears a crown upon his head, as befits his rank of king. He carries a viper and has a face like a lion. With only six legions of spirits to serve him, he oversees fewer demons than most kings. His powers include finding lost and hidden things, particularly treasure. He knows the answers to secret questions and is a revelator of knowledge. See also *BOOK OF OBERON*.

Gotifan: Mathers takes this demon's name to mean "crushing" or "overturning" in his presentation of the *Sacred Magic of Abramelin the Mage*. Gotifan is said to serve the arch-demon Beelzebub, and both are invoked as a part of the Holy Guardian Angel rite central to the *Abramelin* work. In other versions of this text, the name is spelled *Iotifar*. See also BEELZEBUB, MATHERS.

Goyle: A demon with the power to make people charming and charismatic, although the exact words of the text state that Goyle "makes men gorgeous and gay." This quote appears in the *Book of Oberon*, a grimoire written in England during the Elizabethan age when *gay* still meant "joyous." Named as one of twelve high-ranking ministers to the demon-king of the north, Egin, Goyle is said to appear as a lion rampant. See also *BOOK OF OBERON*, EGIN.

Gramon: In the *Sacred Magic of Abramelin the Mage*, Gramon is said to serve the infernal lord Beelzebub. Both are invoked as part of the Holy Guardian Angel ritual that is the culmination of the *Abramelin* work. See also BEELZEBUB, MATHERS.

Grand Grimoire: Reputedly one of the darkest books of magick available to the aspiring magician. Occultist Arthur Edward Waite, writing in his *Book of Black Magic and Pacts*, presents the *Grand Grimoire* as an atrocious tome, and he omits portions of the book from his own translation of the work in an attempt to protect misguided practitioners from attempting some of its nastier spells. The *Grand Grimoire* claims to reveal a system of black magick intended to teach an aspiring magician how to summon demons. It stands out among grimoires in that it also presents a method of forging a pact with infernal powers. It includes the names of superior demons, their sigils, and their place in the demonic hierarchy. A French edition of this book, dating to 1845, claims to derive from an older text, published in 1522. This older edition was supposedly written in Italian by one Antonio Venitiana del Rabina. Although this name translates roughly to Anthony of Venice the Rabbi, the book further claims to have originally been published in Rome, an oblique attempt at connecting it to other supposedly diabolical texts produced by members of the Roman Church. In all likelihood, the publication date as well as the identity of the author are fabrications intended to trump up both the antiquity and importance of the work. It is not impossible that the material contained within this grimoire dates only to the early part of the nineteenth century, when a fascination with black magick and diabolical pacts was on the rise. Notably, the *Grand Grimoire* bears much in common with another nineteenth-century French grimoire, *Le Dragon Rouge*. There is so much cognate material between these two texts, in fact, that it is highly likely that they are merely different

Illustration of a book of spirits from Francis Barrett's 1801 work, *The Magus*. From a collection by Grillot de Givry, courtesy of Dover Publications.

versions of the same spurious work. See also *LE DRAGON ROUGE*, WAITE.

Grasemin: An infernal servitor of the demon-kings Amaimon and Ariton, Grasemin appears in the Mathers translation of the *Sacred Magic of Abramelin the Mage*. An alternate spelling of the demon of this demon is *Irasomin*. The discrepancy may be due to scribal error. See also AMAIMON, ARITON, MATHERS.

Gremiel: A demon whose name and seal both appear in the *Ars Theurgia*, Gremiel belongs to the hierarchy of Macariel, a wandering prince of the air. He has a total of four hundred lesser spirits at his command, and he is free to appear in any hour of the day or night. When Gremiel makes his appearance, he has the power to assume a variety of shapes but prefers that of a many-headed dragon. See also *ARS THEURGIA*, MARACRIEL.

Gressil: A demon of impurity, uncleanness, and nastiness. His special adversary is Saint Bernard.

Gressil appears in the *Admirable History* of Sebastien Michaelis. His name and adversary are reportedly revealed by the demon Berith. See also BERITH.

Grimoire of Armadel: The earliest recorded mention of this book can be found in a bibliography of occult works compiled by Gabriel Naude in 1625. It was supposedly written by Armadel, a mythic figure associated with a number of books of magick. In the seventeenth century, several unrelated texts were produced under this name. Notably, the name is suspiciously similar to the titles of two other well-established magickal works. One is the *Arbatel of Magic*, a work dating to 1575. The other is the *Almadel*, a text attributed to King Solomon and generally included in the *Lemegeton*. There is a possibility that the *Grimoire of Armadel* is a spurious text, produced expressly to capitalize upon the name-recognition established by the other two books. Whether or not it is a legitimate book of magick remains a matter of debate. Either way, a French version (MS 88) called the *Liber Armadel* is kept at the Bibliothèque de l'Arsenal (Library of the Arsenal) in Paris, and this was translated by S. L. MacGregor Mathers in the early 1900s. Most of the information contained within the book is concerned with angels, but it contains the names of a few infernal spirits as well. An unrelated text calling itself *The True Keys of Solomon the King by Armadel* (*Les Vrais Clavicules du Roi Salomon par Armadel*) appears at the end of Lansdowne manuscript 1202, kept at the British Museum. The first two parts of this manuscript were used by Mathers for his translation of the *Clavicula Salomonis*, or *Key of Solomon*. He omitted this third book on the grounds that the *Key of Solomon* is reputed to be comprised of only two books and the *Armadel* material bore much in common with the *Grimorium Verum*. In fact, occultist Joseph Peterson includes a translation of this French text at the end of his 2007 edition of the *Grimorium Verum*. See also *CLAVICULA SALOMONIS, GRIMORIUM VERUM, LEMEGETON,* MATHERS.

Grimoire of Pope Honorius: This book is a strange amalgam of Catholic ritual and material culled from grimoires such as the *Clavicula Salomonis* and the *Grimorium Verum*. It has been decried by both nineteenth-century scholar Eliphas Lévi and occultist A. E. Waite as one of the most wicked and diabolical of all books on the black arts. Most versions of this work date to the seventeenth and eighteenth centuries. The book is almost certainly a spurious fabrication of intentionally black magick intended to capitalize upon the reputation of the thirteenth-century grimoire *The Sworn Book of Honorius*.

The *Grimoire of Pope Honorius* claims to have been penned by Pope Honorius, and this was likely intended to be Pope Honorius I. He served as pontiff from 625 to 638. Forty years after his death, an anathema was issued against him by the Third Council of Constantinople, and he was cast posthumously from the church. Despite the unpopularity of some of his opinions, there is no indication that Honorius I ever practiced any form of the dark arts.

Throughout the sixteenth and seventeenth centuries, however, there were persistent fears among the populace that certain members of the clergy dabbled in necromancy and black magick. Interestingly enough, Benedict XIII (Pedro de Luna, who is considered an Antipope by the Catholic Church) was accused of necromancy by the Council of Pisa in 1409. This Benedict XIII (distinct from Pietro Francesco Orsini, who, in 1724, also took the title of Pope Benedict XIII) held his office from 1395 to 1417. He stood in opposition to Boniface IX, Innocent VII, and Gregory XII during a period of controversial leadership of the Roman Church. After a thorough search of his chambers, a rare tome of necromancy was allegedly discovered. This had been secreted away beneath the pontiff's bed. The allegations against Benedict XIII may have been enough to establish a legend concerning papal involvement in the diabolical arts to make the existence of a whole book on black magick written by a pope more credible to readers. See also *CLAVICULA SALOMONIS, GRIMORIUM VERUM, SWORN BOOK,* WAITE.

Grimorium Verum: A book of black magick that includes an extensive list of demons. The name translates to the "True Grimoire." The *Grimorium Verum* makes a point of including invocations for several of the most hated and feared demons in Christendom, including Lucifer, Astaroth, and Beelzebub. Both French and Italian editions of this book exist. The Italian version claims the title *La Clavicola del Re Salomone,* connecting it with the *Clavicula Salomonis* at least in name, if not in content. There are Italian editions published in 1880 and 1868. The French edition, published in 1817, lists an original publication date of 1517. This version of the book claims to have been written first in the ancient city of Memphis by Alibeck the Egyptian. Notably, Alibeck the Egyptian is also the name given on versions of the *Red Dragon Grimoire,* although in the case of this book, he is said to have published in Cairo. As no references to the *Grimorium Verum* predate the nineteenth century, it is highly likely that the French edition subtracted three hundred years from the true publication date in the interest of making the book seem more legitimate and ancient. The *Grimorium Verum,* the *Grand Grimoire,* and *Le Dragon*

Rouge are all likely products of an early-nineteenth-century demand for grimoire-like tomes devoted to expressly black magick. These texts are not completely spurious, however. The Venetian grimoire known as the *Secrets of Solomon,* written in the seventeenth century and seized by the Inquisition, almost certainly served as one of their primary sources of inspiration. See also ASTAROTH, BEELZEBUB, *CLAVICULA SALOMONIS,* GRAND GRIMOIRE, *LE DRAGON ROUGE,* LUCIFER, *SECRETS OF SOLOMON.*

Gromenis: A servant of the demon Astaroth, Gromenis is named in the Mathers translation of the *Sacred Magic of Abramelin the Mage.* In another version of the *Abramelin* material kept at the Wolfenbüttel library, this demon's name is rendered *Iromenis.* See also ASTAROTH, MATHERS.

Guagamon: The name of a demon who appears in the Mathers translation of the *Sacred Magic of Abramelin the Mage.* According to this text, Guagamon serves the greater demons Astaroth and Asmodeus. The name of this demon is rendered *Yragamon* in other versions of the *Abramelin* material. See also ASTAROTH, ASMODEUS, MATHERS.

Gudiel: According to the *Ars Theurgia,* the demon Gudiel is tied to the second half of the day, in the hours between noon and dusk. He serves in the hierarchy of the infernal prince Dorochiel and is thus connected with the region of the west. He has four hundred lesser spirits to minister to him. He holds the rank of chief duke and is said to be both good-natured and obedient. See also *ARS THEURGIA,* DOROCHIEL.

Gugonix: A demon reputed to serve both Astaroth and Asmodeus, Gugonix is named in Mathers's edition of the *Sacred Magic of Abramelin the Mage,* where it eludes even that diligent occultist's attempts at etymological unraveling. In the Peter Hammer edition of the *Abramelin* material, the name of this demon is spelled *Gagonir*. See also ASTAROTH, ASMODEUS, MATHERS.

Guland: According to Peterson's translation of the *Grimorium Verum*, this demon holds power over disease. At the whim of the magician, he can cause any ailment in any living being. Conjured only on Saturday, Guland serves as the fourteenth demon beneath Duke Syrach. See also *GRIMORIUM VERUM*, SYRACH.

Gusoin: The eleventh demon named in the *Goetia*, Gusoin is described as a great and strong duke with forty legions of lesser spirits at his command. Like many demons, he is said to answer questions about the past, present, and future. Additionally, he can reconcile friends and distribute dignities. According to Scot's *Discoverie of Witchcraft*, he appears in the form of a Xenophilus. A lot of ink has been spilled over what exactly a Xenophilus looks like, as no descriptions of such an animal survive from the ancient world. However, it is possible that a Xenophilus is not intended to be an animal, but a proper name. In particular, Xenophilus was a Pythagorean philosopher and musician mentioned in volume two of Pliny's *Natural History*.[46] This fellow was said to have lived in perfect health until the age of one hundred and five, an impressive feat in the world of the ancient Greeks. The use of this name may be intended to imply that Gusoin appears as an elderly sage, which would be appropriate, considering that most of the Goetic demons were sought for their knowledge and wisdom. Another notable figure to bear the name Xenophilus was a Greek officer in command at the citadel at

Susa who eventually defected to Antigonus.[47] Of course, spelling may also be important in understanding exactly what was meant regarding this demon's form. In Wierus's *Pseudomonarchia Daemonum*, Gusoin, spelled *Gusoyn*, is said to appear *in forma zenophali*. Zenophilus is still a proper name, but in this spelling, it may refer to a Roman proconsul active in Christian Africa between 320 and 330 CE.[48] His name appears in the letters of Athanasius and also the *Gesta apud Zenophilum*. This is part of a Roman dossier recording an investigation undertaken in 320 CE by Zenophilus and others to determine which Christians among the Numidian community had surrendered their copies of the scriptures to the state as part of a Roman effort to curtail the spread of Christianity. If this Zenophilus is intended, then the anti-Christian sentiments associated with his name lend Gusoin a far more nefarious air. In the *Goetia of Dr. Rudd*, he is said to answer to the angel Laviah. The editors of this text suggest that Xenophilus may be read as a Greek word, *xenophalloi*. This gives the term a very different connotation. The *Book of Incantations*, a Welsh cunning-man's grimoire from the early nineteenth century, explicitly states that Xenophiles was a historic figure reputed to live for 150 years without illness, neatly settling the debate. See also *BOOK OF INCANTATIONS*, *GOETIA*, RUDD, SCOT, WIERUS.

Guth: A minister of Formione, the king of the spirits of Jupiter named in Joseph Peterson's translation of the *Sworn Book*. This demon is described as being subject to the north winds. As a spirit of Jupiter, Guth can inspire positive emotions such as love and joy among mortals. He can also bring

---

46. Pliny, *Natural History*, vol. 2, p. 207.

47. William Smith, *Dictionary of Greek and Roman Antiquities*, vol. 3, p. 1297.

48. T. D. Barnes, "Proconsuls of Africa, 337–92," *Phoenix*, pp. 144–153.

Graven Images and Colossal Forms

In the Bible, especially in the Old Testament, a word that is consistently translated as *demon* is the Hebrew term *shedim*. Appearing only in its plural form, shedim often refers to the false gods of other cultures. This was especially true of those that demanded human sacrifice, as in Deuteronomy 32:17. The word is likely derived from the Akkadian word *shedu*, which refers to a type of guardian spirit common to the mythology of Babylon and Akkad. The shedu were typically represented as immense hybrid creatures, combining aspects of bulls, lions, serpents, and men. They often bore wings to indicate their otherworldly nature. These spirits could be beneficent or malevolent, depending upon the situation and their disposition at the time. The shedu were almost always named in conjunction with another variety of spirit, the *lamassu*, and in fact, the two can be used interchangeably. In his *Immortality and the Unseen World*, Reverend Oesterley describes the lamassu as the "colossal forms." They were often used to guard doorways and entrances. For common houses, a tablet containing a graven image of a shedu was typically buried beneath the threshold. For cities and palaces, colossal statues flanked the entrances, and several examples of these can be found in museums today. Many of these gate guardians take the form of winged bulls, often with bearded, human faces. Stories of or direct exposure to these ancient statues

may have served as the inspiration for similarly described demons, such as Bilgall from the *Book of Oberon*. The descriptions of several other demons may also have been influenced by knowledge of pagan statues from the ancient world. The Goetic demon Marbas (as well as a number of other demons across the grimoiric tradition) is traditionally described as a lion-headed man who carries a serpent in his hand. The *leiocephalus* was a popular icon from the cult of Mithras. He was depicted as a winged man with a lion's head whose body was twined in the coils of a great serpent.

The *leiocephalus* (literally, "lion-headed") was a popular cult figure among followers of Mithras. Art by Catherine Rogers.

worldly favors to people. He is governed by the angels Satquiel, Raphael, Pahamcocihel, and Asassaiel. His name may be derived from the biblical Gog. See also FORMIONE, GOG, *SWORN BOOK*.

Guthac: A trickster demon who should be conjured in spells involving mockery and deceit, Guthac appears in the *Sacred Magic of Abramelin the Mage*. He can assist the magician with illusions and invisibility. He appears in the same capacity in the Mathers translation of the *Clavicula Salomonis*. See also MATHERS.

Guthor: A demon of trickery, deceit, and illusion. He is named in the Mathers translation of the *Clavicula Salomonis* as well as the *Sacred Magic of Abramelin the Mage*. Guthor can be called upon to help turn a person invisible. See also MATHERS.

Guthryn: A demon said to have the power to bestow favors and worldly status. According to the Peterson edition of the *Sworn Book of Honorius*, he is a minister of Formione, the king of the spirits of Jupiter. Here he is described as being subject to the north winds. In addition to his ability to make someone more favorable in the eyes of others, he can also inspire positive emotions, such as love and gladness. Compare to the demon *Gutthyn* in the Driscoll translation of the same text. See also FORMIONE, GUTTHYN, *SWORN BOOK*.

Gutly: A minister of the infernal king Fornnouc, and thus allied with the element of air. Gutly is a lively spirit, both agile and active. However, Driscoll's translation of the *Sworn Book* also describes him as a capricious spirit. He will function as a tutor for those who gain his favor, and being a demon from the element of air, he is knowledgeable in all rational and learned sciences. Gutly and his fellows in the court of king Fornnouc are also

healers. They can prevent infirmities and cure existing weaknesses. Compare to the demon Guth, minister of Formione. See also FORMIONE, FORNNOUC, GUTH, *SWORN BOOK*.

Gutthyn: A demon named in Driscoll's edition of the *Sworn Book*, Gutthyn is the third minister beneath the infernal king Fornnouc. Gutthyn is allied with the element of air, and therefore he oversees matters connected with the mind and intelligence. He will serve as a demonic tutor for those who have gained his favor. He cures infirmities and weaknesses, but only when he is approached with the appropriate gift. He is said to be a lively spirit, both active and agile (presumably in mind as well as body). It is warned, however, that he is also capricious. See also FORNNOUC, *SWORN BOOK*.

Guziel: In the *Sword of Moses*, this being, described as an evil angel, is invoked as part of a curse. Guziel is called upon to bring ruin upon an enemy, binding mind, mouth, throat, and tongue. With his wits addled, unable to speak in his own defense, the target of this spell is further doomed when the wicked angel works with three of his brethren to plant poison in his belly. See also GASTER, *SWORD OF MOSES*.

Gyell: According to the *Book of Oberon*, Gyell is a demon of uncertain rank who may be either a count or an earl. He commands seven legions and appears in the guise of an elephant. See also *BOOK OF OBERON*.

Gyton: According to the fifteenth-century magickal text known as the *Munich Handbook*, Gyton is one of the demons who must be conjured forth in order to turn a human fingernail into a scrying device. See also *MUNICH HANDBOOK*.

Haagenti: One of seventy-two demons named in the *Goetia*. Haagenti also appears in Wierus's *Pseudomonarchia Daemonum* and Scot's *Discoverie of Witchcraft*. He is said to be an alchemical demon, with the power to transform base metals into gold. He can also change water into wine and wine into water. The rank he holds is president, and he commands thirty-three legions of spirits. His manifest form is that of a bull with gryphon's wings. He can also assume the form of a man. In the *Goetia of Dr. Rudd*, he is said to be controlled in the name of the angel Mihael. The Welsh *Book of Incantations* describes him as a president who governs thirty-three legions. His main power is transmutation. See also *BOOK OF INCANTATIONS*, *GOETIA*, RUDD, SCOT, WIERUS.

Habaa: The king of the spirits of the planet Mercury. As a Mercurial spirit, Habaa has the power to give answers about the past, present, and future. He can also reveal the secrets of spirits as well as all mortals. According to the Peterson's translation of the *Sworn Book of Honorius*, when he manifests, he takes a mutable body with skin that shimmers like glass. The angels Michael, Mihel, and Sarapiel have power over him and all the spirits of Mercury. See also *SWORN BOOK*.

Habhi: In the *Sacred Magic of Abramelin the Mage*, Mathers identifies Habhi as one of the demons who serves the demons Oriens, Amaimon, Ariton, and Paimon. He defines the demon's name as meaning "hidden." See also AMAIMON, ARITON, MATHERS, ORIENS, PAIMON.

Habnthala: A minister of the demon Harthan, king of the element of water. According to Driscoll's edition of the *Sworn Book*, when he manifests he appears with a mottled complexion and with a body that is large and amply fleshed. He has a witty and an agreeable nature, and is also observant as well as somewhat jealous. He can be called upon to invisibly move things from place to place,

Mercury with his winged caduceus. The spirits of each celestial sphere were typically assigned attributes in keeping with their ruling planet. Engraving by N. Dorigny, 1695. Image courtesy of the Wellcome Collection, London.

provide darkness, and avenge wrongs. He can also help others to achieve strength in resolution. See also HARTHAN, *SWORN BOOK*.

Hacamuli: In his presentation of the *Sacred Magic of Abramelin the Mage*, Mathers suggests that this demon's name is derived from a Hebrew root meaning "withering" or "fading." Hacamuli is a servant of the demonic lord Beelzebub, and he is summoned as a part of the Holy Guardian Angel rite central to the *Abramelin* material. In other versions of this text, his name is spelled *Hayamen*. See also BEELZEBUB, MATHERS.

Hacel: This demon reportedly teaches languages and letters. In the *True Keys of Solomon*, Hacel is said to also teach how to discover the meaning of hidden and secret letters. This may be an oblique reference to the practice of steganographia established by Trithemius in the fifteenth century. See also *TRUE KEYS*.

Hachamel: A demonic servitor of Paimon, named in the *Sacred Magic of Abramelin the Mage*. In the manuscript used by occultist S. L. Mathers for his translation of this work, the name of this demon is given instead as *Achaniel*. Mathers takes the name to mean "truth of God." Both Hachamel and Achaniel resemble angel names, although clearly this particular angel is no longer associated with the Heavenly Hosts. Hachamel is reasonably close to *Hochmiel*, the angel credited with having transmitted the material of the *Sworn Book of Honorius*. His name is derived from the Hebrew word *hochmah* (or *chokmah*), meaning "wisdom." Given the Jewish character of the *Abramelin* material, this root may have been intended for Hachamel as well. *See* also MATHERS, PAIMON.

Hael: In the *Grimorium Verum*, Hael is ranked as the first spirit serving beneath the demon Nebiros. He holds great power over language, and, when summoned, he can cause the magician to speak any language whatsoever. In addition to speech, he can instruct the magician in the art of writing many and diverse letters. As with many demons with access to the mysteries of the spirit world, Hael can also reveal details about hidden things. Together with the demon Seruglath, Hael commands several demons of his own. According to the *Secrets of Solomon*, he is one of two high-ranking demons serving under the infernal duke Resbiroth. In addition to teaching all letters and writing, he enables people to understand even the most difficult ciphers—a particularly useful ability for a Renaissance magician when many books of magick were written in code. His fellow minister is Sergulaf, and together they oversee an additional eight powerful demons. See also *GRIMORIUM VERUM*, NEBIROS, RESBIROTH, *SECRETS OF SOLOMON*, SERGULAF, SERUGLATH.

Borrowed Jewish Mysticism

A great deal of the grimoiric tradition from the Middle Ages and Renaissance was influenced by the magickal traditions of Jews. Demons and angels both play a significant role in a Jewish system known as the Qabbalah, and while the Qabbalah is part of a mystical system, many of its concepts were also believed to have a more direct application in magickal workings. Much of Qabbalistic magick revolves around something called the Tree of Life. This is a kind of mystic ladder that represents a map of reality. It has ten steps or points, known as the *Sephiroth*. Each of these steps along the ladder is seen as a different emanation of divinity into the mortal realm. In Qabbalistic magick, a trained individual seeks to ascend the ladder of the Tree of Life through rigorous practices that involve fasting, meditation, and ceremony. Encounters with demons and angels are an integral part of this mystical journey, with a vision of the Throne of God being the ultimate goal. Sacred names of divinity written in Hebrew play a role in the process, as do the Hebrew names of angels and demons encountered along the way. Christian seekers in medieval Europe had a limited understanding of the Qabbalistic system—but they knew enough to attribute to it great power. Subsequently,

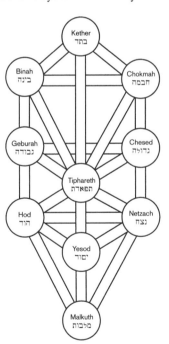

the grimoires of Europe—many penned by Christian practitioners of magick—borrowed heavily from this system, adopting Hebrew names of God as well as concepts like the significance of letters, words, and numbers. The most influential text is the *Sepher Yetzirah*, penned in the early centuries of the Common Era. This Hebrew treatise lays the foundation for the Qabbalah. Many of the names and concepts taken from Jewish mysticism are badly garbled once they make it into the grimoires, and yet these essentially Jewish elements can be found throughout the Christian magick of medieval and Renaissance Europe. It is important to note that appropriated concepts like the Shemhamphorash and the Tetragrammaton were not used with Jewish consultation or consent, and anti-Semitic sentiment is clear in certain elements, such as the demonization of the word *Berith*.

Hagion: A demon whose name may mean "sacred" or "holy." Mathers, in his translation of the *Sacred Magic of Abramelin the Mage*, related the name to the Greek word *hagios*. This interpretation seems sound, right up until one compares the spelling of Hagion's name in Mathers's source with the other surviving versions of the *Abramelin* material. In other versions, this demon's name is spelled variously as *Nagar* and *Nagan*. As the original text has been lost and all surviving versions are merely copies, there is no way of knowing which version is correct. Hagion, alias Nagan, is said to serve under the joint rule of the demons Magoth and Kore. See also KORE, MAGOTH, MATHERS.

Hagog: A demon connected with the Holy Guardian Angel rite from the *Sacred Magic of Abramelin the Mage*. Hagog is said to serve the greater demon Magoth. In the versions of *Abramelin* kept at the Dresden and Wolfenbüttel libraries in Germany, this name is also spelled *Hagoch*. See also MAGOTH, MATHERS.

Haibalidech: A demon named in the Joseph H. Peterson translation of the *Sworn Book of Honorius*. Haibalidech is said to serve the demon-king Maymon, who, in this text, governs the direction north and the planet Saturn. Haibalidech answers to the angels Bohel, Cafziel, Michrathon, and Satquiel, who rule over the planet Saturn. He has the power to call up storms of snow and ice. He can also incite negative feelings like anger, sorrow, and hatred. See also MAYMON, *SWORN BOOK*.

Hali: A demon tied to the element of earth, Hali serves the infernal king Albunalich. His hierarchy is described in the 1977 Driscoll translation of the *Sworn Book*. According to this book, Hali holds the rank of minister. He appears in a form that is large and amply fleshed with a bright and beautiful complexion. He is said to have charge over gold and precious stones. These he guards greedily, but will share them with those who have gained his favor. Others he will wear down and utterly frustrate if they seek the treasures of the earth. He has the ability to inspire bad feelings between people, inciting rancor and even bringing them to blows. In addition to this, he can also impart knowledge of both the past and the future, and he can call temperate rains. See also ALBUNALICH, *SWORN BOOK*.

Haligax: One of several demons said to serve the infernal rulers Asmodeus and Astaroth. Haligax is named in the Mathers translation of the *Sacred Magic of Abramelin the Mage*. In other versions of the *Abramelin* material, the name is presented as *Haynax*. See also ASTAROTH, ASMODEUS, *SWORN BOOK*.

Halphas: The thirty-eighth demon of the *Goetia*. Halphas is a martial demon said to manifest as a stork with a hoarse voice. According to Scot's *Discoverie of Witchcraft*, he is best known for his ability to build up the weapons and munitions of a town. If asked for reinforcements, he has the power to send warriors to any place appointed to him. Among the minions of Hell, he holds the rank of earl and commands a total of twenty-six legions of spirits. He is also listed in Wierus's *Pseudomonarchia Daemonum*. In the *Goetia of Dr. Rudd*, he appears not as a stork but as a stock dove. Here, his name is given as *Malthas*. He is said to be constrained by the angel Haamiah. In the Welsh grimoire known as the *Book of Incantations*, he appears also as a stock-dove. His office is to build towers and furnish ammunition. See also *BOOK OF INCANTATIONS*, *GOETIA*, RUDD, SCOT, WIERUS.

Hamas: An infernal spirit of the night in service to the demon-king Asyriel. Asyriel is the third spirit in rank beneath Caspiel, the infernal Emperor of the South, at least according to the *Ars Theurgia*. Thus, Hamas is also connected with the direction of the south. He is said to serve only during the hours of the night. Holding the title of duke, he has ten lesser spirits to carry out his commands. See also *ARS THEURGIA*, ASYRIEL, CASPIEL.

Hamorphiel: A demon named in the *Ars Theurgia*. Hamorphiel is a duke of Pamersiel, the first and chief spirit of the east under emperor Carnesiel. Hamorphiel is said to possess an evil nature, and he should never be trusted with secret matters, as he is given to deceit. Due to his inherently aggressive nature, he is said to be useful in driving away other spirits of darkness, especially those that haunt houses. See also *ARS THEURGIA*, PAMERSIEL.

Hanan: This demon's natural appearance is that of a living flame, although he can take human form when such is demanded of him. A great prince named in the *Book of Oberon*, he holds sway over eight legions of lesser spirits and is said to bring favor to any who summon him. When hidden treasure is protected by spirits, he can describe how many spirit guardians there are, their types, and how to deal with them. He is also reputedly gifted at astronomy. See also *BOOK OF OBERON*.

Haniel: A spirit that appears in several texts both as a fallen angel and a heavenly being. In the Mathers translation of the *Grimoire of Armadel*, Haniel is said to have power over alchemy and can teach the transformation of all precious stones. He will also provide as many jewels as one might wish. This text further says that Haniel should be invoked on a Friday at daybreak. See also MATHERS.

Hanni: In the fifteenth-century grimoire known as the *Munich Handbook*, this president of Hell commands thirty legions of devils. When summoned, he appears in the form of pure and living fire. However, he can be compelled to take a less dangerous human form, should the magician so command. A puissant spirit, Hanni can cause princes and magnates to smile favorably upon the magician. He also teaches astronomy and the liberal arts, as well as granting familiars. Finally, he has the power not only to reveal treasure, but he is capable of revealing the location of treasure guarded by other spirits. Presumably, he can also assist the magician in liberating this treasure from its otherworldly guardians. Although their names are quite different, compare Hanni's appearance and powers to the Goetic demon known as Avnas or Amy. See also AVNAS, *SWORN BOOK*.

Hanyey: A demon connected to the planetary sphere of Mercury. He can open locks, appease judges, give victory in battle, and unbind spirits. According to the *Book of Oberon*, he serves the demon-king Saba and appears as an armed soldier, very attractive, who speaks with a pleasing voice. See also ALVEDIO, *BOOK OF OBERON*, SABA, YRON.

Harchase: With twenty-six legions under him, this demon named in the *Book of Oberon* is said to reveal all places that contain hidden treasure. He can also bestow invisibility. He holds the rank of king and appears as a ferocious bear. See also *BOOK OF OBERON*.

Harex: A demon connected with the element of air, Harex serves in the court of the infernal king Fornnouc, as described in the Driscoll translation of the *Sworn Book*. According to this text, as a demon of the element of air, Harex is active and lively in nature. He is also capricious, although he makes an excellent tutor for those seeking to learn the secrets of the arts and sciences from a demon. If he is given the proper offerings, he will also function as a healer, preventing infirmities and curing weaknesses. He can be convinced to appear if the proper perfumes are burned in his name. See also FORNNOUC, *SWORN BOOK*.

Haril: A demon mentioned in the Mathers translation of the *Sacred Magic of Abramelin the Mage*, Haril is listed among a vast number of other demons said to serve the four infernal princes of the cardinal directions: Oriens, Paimon, Ariton, and Amaimon. In attempting to identify the origin of Haril's name, Mathers suggests that it is related to a Hebrew root meaning "thorny." See also AMAIMON, ARITON, MATHERS, ORIENS, PAIMON.

Hariston: A demon with power over fire. Hariston can enable a person to walk through flames safely and without harm. He serves beneath the demons Hael and Sergulaf in the court of Duke Resbiroth, all named in the *Secrets of Solomon*, a seventeenth-century grimoire confiscated by the Inquisition in Venice. See also HAEL, RESBIROTH, *SECRETS OF SOLOMON*, SERGULAF.

Haristum: A demon from the *Grimorium Verum*, Haristum serves beneath the demons Hael and his partner Sergulath. He has power over living flame and can teach a person the secret to walking through fire safely and without harm. As the *Grimorium Verum* was most likely derived from the *Secrets of Solomon*, his name is probably a variation on Hariston. See also *GRIMORIUM VERUM*, HAEL, HARISTON, SERGULATH.

Harith: A servant of Formione, the king of the spirits of Jupiter named in Joseph Peterson's translation of the *Sworn Book*. He can confer favors upon people and promote positive emotions such as gladness and joy. Harith is described as being connected to the east, presumably the eastern winds. See also FORMIONE, *SWORN BOOK*.

Harkam: In the *Book of Oberon*, Harkam is king of the spirits of the Moon. He moves like a mighty storm at sea and has skin the color of a dark and brooding cloud. His eyes are watery, his head bald, and his teeth are tusked like a boar. Wherever he appears, a huge rainstorm breaks out. He has the power of silver and secrets, bestowing riches or revealing the most deeply guarded things. He can also transport objects or bewitch horses so they have the speed of the wind. He can take the form of a man or a woman, a cow, doe, or goose. When he is a woman, he appears as a huntress. When he is a man, he takes the guise of a king armed with arrows. He has four helpers: Bylethor, Mylu, Byleth, and Acuteba. See also ACUTEBA, *BOOK OF OBERON*, BYLETH, BYLETHOR, MYLU.

Harombrub: "Exalted in Greatness." According to S. L. MacGregor Mathers, this name comes from a Hebrew root. This demon appears in the *Sacred Magic of Abramelin the Mage*, where he is said to serve the infernal prince Ariton. The name is alternately rendered *Horasul* in the seventeenth-century Peter Hammer edition of the *Abramelin* work. See also ARITON, MATHERS.

Harpax: A demon associated with the thirty-six decans of the zodiac. According to the *Testament of Solomon*, he has the power to afflict his victims with insomnia. He can be abjured through the use of the name *Kokphnêdismos*. In the later McCown translation of the *Testament*, this name is split into two, Kok and Phedismos. Harpax is accorded the title of *Rhyx*, or "king," and his name is spelled *Hapax*. See also SOLOMON.

Harthan: A demon whose name appears in the Driscoll translation of the *Sworn Book*. He is described as the king of the element of water, and therefore he is also associated with the direction west. According to the text, when he manifests he has a large and ample body with a mottled complexion. He has a witty and agreeable nature. He is also observant and prone to jealousy. He can bestow strength and resolve to those who require it. He avenges wrongs and provides darkness when needed—presumably to help someone hide something. Along the same vein, he is also capable of moving things from place to place. In Peterson's translation of the same material, Harthan is named as the king of the spirits of the Moon. In this text, he is said to have the power to change people's thoughts and help with journeys. See also *SWORN BOOK*.

Hauges: A demon from Mathers's translation of the *Sacred Magic of Abramelin the Mage*, Hauges is said to serve the demon-kings Amaimon and Ariton. Mathers tentatively connects the name of this demon with a Greek word meaning "brilliance." A variation on the spelling of this demon's name is *Harog*. See also AMAIMON, ARITON, MATHERS.

Hauros: Also *Hauvos*. In the *Book of Incantations*, a cunning-man's grimoire from nineteenth-century Wales, Hauros is a great duke who appears at first like a mighty leopard. In his human form, he has fiery eyes and a terrible countenance. If commanded to appear within a triangle drawn upon the floor, he will answer truthfully, but if these precautions are not taken, he will lie about all things. He will gladly talk of divinity, of the creation of the world, and of the fall of spirits, including

himself. He destroys and burns all your enemies if commanded. Once you have begun working with Hauros, he will jealously guard you from the temptations of other spirits or entities. Thirty-six legions of lesser spirits serve him. See also *BOOK OF INCANTATIONS*.

Hebethel: A demon in the hierarchy of king Harthan, who rules the element of water. Hebethel can provide darkness and move things from place to place. He assists in the avenging of wrongs and helps others to achieve strength and resolve. His manifest form tends to be corpulent with a mottled appearance. By nature, he is described as being both witty and agreeable, but also somewhat jealous. According to Driscoll's edition of the *Sworn Book*, he can be summoned with the aid of the appropriate perfumes. In Peterson's translation of the *Sworn Book*, Hebethel remains connected to the demon Harthan, but here Harthan is identified as the king of the spirits of the Moon. See also HARTHAN, *SWORN BOOK*.

Hegergibet: A demon who guards the cardinal directions. He is paired with the demon Sathan in the *Munich Handbook*. *Sathan* is a variation on Satan. The two infernal powers are invoked in association with the north. See also *MUNICH HANDBOOK*.

Hekesha: A name attributed to the demon Lilith. Demons of the Lilith-type were thought to attack people at night, particularly going after infants in their cribs. As a form of Lilith, Hekesha is tied to night and darkness. Her name is one of many that once were scribed upon special amulets to protect against her attacks. This name is recorded in a 1966 collection by author T. Schrire entitled *Hebrew Magic Amulets*. See also LILITH.

Heme: According to the *Ars Theurgia*, Heme is a demon in the court of the infernal prince Usiel. He serves during the hours of the day, and he holds the rank of duke. Forty ministering spirits serve him. Heme has the power to either obscure or reveal treasure. This name may be derived from the medical term *heme*, used to describe the iron-rich pigment in blood. See also *ARS THEURGIA*, USIEL.

Hemis: In his 1898 translation of the *Sacred Magic of Abramelin the Mage*, Mathers reads this name as being directly related to the Greek word *hemi*, meaning "half." This demon appears in a list of infernal servitors of the arch-fiend Magoth. He is also said to serve Kore, but this name only appears as a leader of the demonic hierarchy in the version of the *Abramelin* material from which Mathers was working. In the other extant versions of the *Sacred Magic*, the name of this demon appears as *Somis*. See also KORE, MAGOTH, MATHERS.

Hemostophilé: This curious name appears in the Mathers translation of the *Grimoire of Armadel*. It is very probably a corruption of the traditional name *Mephistopheles*, although the prefix *hemo-* would seem to also link this demon's name with blood. According to the text, Hemostophilé can show how to conjure devils and can help people to acquire infernal servants. He is a demon of deception that can change a person's shape as well as that person's passions. Perhaps because of his mastery of illusion, the text warns against summoning this demon. See also MATHERS, MEPHISTOPHELES.

Hepath: In the *Clavicula Salomonis de Secretis*, or *Secrets of Solomon*, Hepath is named among eighteen powerful servitors of the demonic Duke Syrach. A demon of teleportation and manifestation, He-path has the power to cause people to appear at will, from armies to emperors to lost loved ones. Whether these are people he is transporting from physical locations or beings he calls back from the grave is unclear. See also *SECRETS OF SOLOMON*, SYRACH.

Hephesimireth: In the *Testament of Solomon*, Hephesimireth is named as one of thirty-six demons associated with the decans of the zodiac. A demon of disease, he can torment his victims by visiting upon them a lingering illness. To drive this demon away, one has only to invoke the names of the Seraphim and Cherubim. In the Conybeare translation of this text, Hephesimireth is associated with the thirty-first decan of the zodiac. In a later translation by McCown, widely accepted as more accurate, he appears as the demon of the thirtieth decan of the zodiac. His name changes as well, adding the title of *Rhyx*, or king, and spelling it *Physikoreth*. See also SOLOMON.

Hepoth: A demon of illusion named in the *True Keys of Solomon*, Hepoth reputedly has the power to cause any man, woman, or child from any distant region to seem to appear across that distance. According to the grimoire where his name appears, Hepoth is a servant of chief Sirachi, who himself is a servant of Lucifer. See also LUCIFER, SIRACHI, *TRUE KEYS*.

Heptameron: This work, traditionally attributed to Peter de Abano, was published nearly two hundred years after his death in 1316 CE. For this reason, many scholars dispute the claim that Abano authored the text. Occult scholar Joseph Peterson suggests that the earliest version of this text was produced in Venice in 1496. A part of the rich grimoiric tradition of the Renaissance, the *Heptameron* served as a main resource for Agrippa in his

Sacrificial Victims

Throughout the Middle Ages, there were persistent beliefs that demons sought children as sacrifices to the Devil. Early biblical demons, such as Moloch, certainly set the stage for a belief in child sacrifice, but the beliefs may also have been perpetuated by a certain style of divinatory magick popular from Hellenic Egyptian times onward. Traditional spells involving bowl and lamp divinations called for a young, virgin boy to participate in the magick—not as a sacrifice, but as a spirit medium. The fear and sensationalism surrounding the magickal arts, however, allowed essentially harmless practices like this to inspire a variety of superstitious tales. One such tale recorded by Nicholas Remy involved the demon Abrahel. Remy worked as procurer-general of the duchy of Lorraine during the sixteenth century. According to Remy, the manipulative demon Abrahel first appeared to a young goatherd in a form that resembled a girl from his village. The goatherd, whose name is only given as Pierron, was from the village of Dalhem, located between the Moselle and Saar rivers. The demon seduced Pierron and, after she had won his affections, she then demanded that Pierron sacrifice his only son to prove his devotion. Pierron naturally had reservations about this, but the demon assured the naive young goatherd that the boy would be fine as long as he followed her orders. With a heavy heart, Pierron acquiesced to the demands of the demon. Once the boy was dead,

Child promised by his parents to the Devil. From Geoffrey Landry's *Ritter vom Turn*, printed in 1493 by Michael Furter.

Abrahel reportedly brought the child back to life. Pierron decided that he had gotten the bad end of the deal only after his son's behavior and personality changed radically following this infernal death and resurrection. At this point, Pierron finally sought help from the local clergy to rid himself of the demon. Reportedly, his son died again about a year later. Remy's account is quoted by theologian and historian Dom Augustin Calmet, in the 1746 work *The Phantom World*.

Three Books of Occult Philosophy. The *Heptameron* also has some details in common with grimoires such as the *Sworn Book of Honorius*. For example, one of the "angels" said to reign on Friday in the *Heptameron* is called Sarabotes. This name is suspiciously close to the *Sworn Book's* demon, Sarabocres. Although some of its names seem to be identified as demons elsewhere, the *Heptameron* very specifically identifies all of the spirits presented in the text as angels and not of the fallen variety. Many of its spirits are ascribed positions in one of the seven heavens. The schema of seven heavens was originally derived from Jewish sources and later adapted to the seven planetary spheres. Although the *Heptameron* is a tremendously influential magickal text, because the spirits contained within are expressly identified as angels, none of their names have been included in this book—even though variations of some of those supposedly angelic names appear in the *Sworn Book* as demons. See also AGRIPPA, *SWORN BOOK*.

Heramael: This demon, named in Peterson's *Grimorium Verum*, is apparently a walking marvel of medicine. One of four great spirits serving the demon Satanachia, Heramael teaches how to cure diseases. He is able to instruct the magician on the nature of all plants and herbs, revealing their habitats, their powers, and the best times at which to gather them. He can then teach precisely how these are to be prepared in order to produce the most potent and miraculous cures. The *Secrets of Solomon* offers *Heramuel* as an alternate spelling of his name. See also *SECRETS OF SOLOMON*, SATANACHI, SATANACHIA, *GRIMORIUM VERUM*.

Heresiel: A mighty duke who has two thousand two hundred lesser spirits under his command. Heresiel himself owes fealty to the demon Icosiel, the sixth wandering prince of the air described in the *Ars Theurgia*. Heresiel and his fellow dukes all are reportedly drawn to private homes, where they are allowed to manifest during specific times of the day. In the case of the demon Heresiel, the hours and minutes of his appearance fall in the fourteenth portion of time if the day is divided into fifteen equal parts. See also *ARS THEURGIA*, ICOSIEL.

Herg: In his presentation of the *Sacred Magic of Abramelin the Mage*, Mathers suggests that the name of this demon comes from a Hebrew root meaning "to slay." Herg belongs to a hierarchy of demons who are believed to serve only the archfiend Astaroth. In the 1720 version of the *Abramelin* material kept in the Dresden library, the name of this demon is presented as *Hirich*. See also ASTAROTH, MATHERS.

Hergotis: The name of this demon may be derived from a Greek root meaning "laborer." Hergotis appears in the *Sacred Magic of Abramelin the Mage*, where he is said to serve the infernal king Amaimon. In the versions of the *Abramelin* material kept at the libraries in Dresden and Wolfenbüttel in Germany, the name is spelled *Cargosik*. See also AMAIMON, MATHERS.

Hermiala: In the Mathers translation of the *Sacred Magic of Abramelin the Mage*, Hermiala serves the demons Astaroth and Asmodeus. In another version of the *Abramelin* material kept at the Wolfenbüttel library in Germany, the name of this demon is spelled *Ermihala*. See also ASTAROTH, ASMODEUS, MATHERS.

Hermon: One of ten infernal dukes who serve in the hierarchy of the wandering prince Uriel. Hermon, despite his rather mundane-sounding name, typically manifests in the form of a serpent with a human head. He is unrepentantly evil and anyone interacting with him should take care, as he has a reputation for being dishonest in all of his dealings. His name and the seal that can compel him both appear in the *Ars Theurgia*. According to the same text, he has six hundred and fifty lesser spirits who serve beneath him. See also *ARS THEURGIA*, URIEL.

Hethatia: In the Mathers translation of the *Grimoire of Armadel*, this demon is said to teach the science and wisdom of Moses as well as the secrets of the Egyptian Magi. He is reputed to have the power to grant perfect happiness and to teach how to strike fear into the hearts of men. See also MATHERS.

Hiepacth: Listed as the eleventh demon under Duke Syrach in Peterson's *Grimorium Verum*, Hiepacth has the ability to whisk any person away and cause them to appear instantly before the magician. See also *GRIMORIUM VERUM*, SYRACH.

Hifarion: The name of this demon appears in connection with the Holy Guardian Angel working in the Mathers translation of the *Sacred Magic of Abramelin the Mage*. Mathers suggests that the name means "little horse." Hifarion is supposedly a servant of the demon Asmodeus, but this name only appears in the fifteenth-century French manuscript of the *Abramelin* material sourced by Mathers. See also ASMODEUS, MATHERS.

Himacth: A demon named in the *True Keys of Solomon*. According to this text, Himacth serves as one of three chief spirits beneath the arch-fiend Belzébut, a variation of Beelzebub. See also BEELZEBUB, *TRUE KEYS*.

Hinbra: According to the *Book of Oberon*, Hinbra speaks in such a quiet voice that it is nearly impossible to hear him. Perhaps appropriately, he tells secrets. He can also acquire friendships and earn fame for the person who summons him. Despite his tiny voice, he manifests as a giant. Hinbra, along with eleven others, serves at the will of Egin, king of the north, and is among that demon's highest-ranking ministers. See also *BOOK OF OBERON*, EGIN.

Hipogon: A demon named in the *Sacred Magic of Abramelin the Mage*, Hipogon is said to serve the demon Magoth. His name is likely related to the Greek term *hipo*, meaning "below" or "under." In the fifteenth-century French manuscript sourced by Mathers, this name is spelled *Hepogon*. In this version of the *Abramelin* material, which tends to vary from all the rest, this demon is said also to serve the infernal ruler Kore. See also KORE, MAGOTH, MATHERS.

Hipolos: A servitor of the arch-fiend Astaroth, Hipolos appears in the Mathers translation of the *Sacred Magic of Abramelin the Mage*. In both the version of the *Abramelin* kept in the Dresden library and the one at the Wolfenbüttel library, the name of this demon is spelled *Hipolepos*. The word may actually be derived from the Greek roots *hipo*, meaning "below," and *lepis*, meaning "scale." In the modern day, *hypolepis* is a word used to designate a genus of fern. See also ASTAROTH, MATHERS.

Hissain: In the *Ars Theurgia*, Hissain is named as one of several infernal dukes who serve the demon-prince Usiel during the hours of the day. He is affiliated with the court of the west. A revealer of hidden things, Hissain can also prevent the theft and discovery of treasure through the use of enchantments. Thirty lesser spirits exist to carry out his commands. See also *ARS THEURGIA*, USIEL.

Holastri: Mathers takes the name of this demon to mean "to surround," seeing it as having been derived originally from a Coptic term. In the Mathers translation of the *Sacred Magic of Abramelin the Mage*, Holastri appears among a list of demons said to serve the arch-fiend Beelzebub. See also BEELZEBUB, MATHERS.

Holba: A servant of Asmodeus. In his translation of the *Sacred Magic of Abramelin the Mage*, Mathers connects the name of this demon to a word meaning "fat," parsing it as "the Obese One." In other versions of the text, this demon's name is spelled *Hyla*. See also ASMODEUS, MATHERS.

Hooab: A demon of lust, with specific powers over women. He is called upon to bespell women into having sex, and may even change their appearance so they may not be recognized as they do so. When called, he appears as a black bird, although he can also assume human form. The *Book of Oberon*, in which he is named, gives his title as both prince and governor, saying that a total of twenty-six legions of lesser spirits serve him. See also *BOOK OF OBERON*.

Horanar: In the Mathers translation of the *Sacred Magic of Abramelin the Mage*, Horanar appears as one of several demons who serve Astaroth and Asmodeus. Mathers was working from a fifteenth-century French manuscript kept at the Bibliothèque de l'Arsenal in Paris. Other surviving manuscripts of the *Abramelin* material give this demon's name as *Horamar*. See also ASTAROTH, ASMODEUS, MATHERS.

Hosen: A demon who ranks beneath the four infernal kings of the cardinal directions, serving Oriens, Paimon, Ariton, and Amaimon equally. Hosen appears in the *Sacred Magic of Abramelin the Mage*, and Mathers suggests that his name means "vigorous" or "powerful." See also AMAIMON, ARITON, MATHERS, ORIENS, PAIMON.

Hudac: A prevaricator and illusionist, Hudac appears in the Mathers translation of the *Clavicula Salomonis*. He is called upon in spells concerning trickery and deceit. He can also assist the magician in spells of invisibility. The Mathers edition of the *Sacred Magic of Abramelin the Mage* also contains a reference to this demon. Here, he is again associated with trickery, illusion, and deceit. See also MATHERS.

Huictugaras: This demon, named in Peterson's *Grimorium Verum*, possesses power over sleep. He can curse someone with insomnia or cause them to be overcome by an irresistible somnolence. He is the eighteenth and final being serving under Duke Syrach. See also *GRIMORIUM VERUM*, SYRACH.

Humet: Also rendered *Humots*. A sort of infernal librarian, this demon can be commanded to instantly bring whatever books a person desires. His name appears in Peterson's *Grimorium Verum*. He is the twelfth-ranking demon under the leadership of Duke Syrach. Humet also appears in the *True Keys of Solomon*. In this text, he retains his association with books. In the *Secrets of Solomon*, a seventeenth-century grimoire that likely gave rise to the *Grimorium Verum*, this demon's name is spelled *Humeth*. See also *GRIMORIUM VERUM*, *SECRETS OF SOLOMON*, SYRACH.

Hurchetmigaroth: A demon with power over guards and watch-keepers. He can help them to remain vigilant or he can cause them to fall asleep— a convenient trick if you want to murder prisoners and make it look like a suicide. He is a subordinate of the infernal duke Syrach, named in the seventeenth-century Venetian grimoire *Secrets of Solomon*. See also *GRIMORIUM VERUM*, SYRACH.

Hursiel: In the *Ars Theurgia*, Hursiel is said to hold the rank of knight. He serves beneath the demon

Pirichiel, a wandering prince of the air. Hursiel has a total of two thousand lesser spirits at his beck and call. See also *ARS THEURGIA*, PIRICHIEL.

Hutgin: In his imaginative three-volume work *Les Farfadets*, French writer Charles Berbiguier identifies this demon as Hell's ambassador to Italy. Although Berbiguier was more deluded than informed on the topic of demonology, encyclopedist Collin de Plancy nevertheless reproduced his colorful demonic hierarchy in his classic *Dictionnaire Infernal*. See also BERBIGUIER, DE PLANCY.

Hyachonaababur: A servant of the demon Iammax, infernal king of the spirits of the planet Mars. According to the Peterson translation of the *Sworn Book of Honorius*, he is connected to the region of the south. His appearance is dry and lean, and he has power to incite destruction and warfare. This demon is one of five under the rule of Iammax who are described as being subject to the east wind. See also IAMMAX, *SWORN BOOK*.

Hycandas: A subordinate of King Barchan, Hycandas is connected with the sun. This demon is called upon to assist in the creation of a potent magickal talisman known as the Ring of the Sun. The first step involves finding a wild bird of any species, so long as it is white. The sacrifice of this animal begins the process of creating the talisman. The ring is used for bindings as well as to summon a black steed whenever and wherever the magician chooses. The whole operation for the creation and use of this talisman appears in the fifteenth-century magickal text *Liber de Angelis*. See also BARCHAN, *LIBER DE ANGELIS*.

Hydriel: A wandering prince of the air who moves with his retinue through the various points of the compass. He rules over one hundred great dukes and two hundred lesser dukes, with countless minor spirits attending him as well. Hydriel, as his name would seem to imply, has a great love for waters and moist locales, such as bogs and swamps. He is predisposed to manifest in such locations. When he appears, Hydriel resembles a naga, bearing the head of a maiden but the body of a snake. According to the *Ars Theurgia*, the seventeenth-century magickal text that contains Hydriel's name and seal, he is a very courteous demon primarily disposed toward good. Hydriel is also named in the *Steganographia* of Johannes Trithemius. See also *ARS THEURGIA*, TRITHEMIUS.

Hyiciquiron: A minister of the demon-king Abas, who rules the subterranean realms below the earth. Named in Driscoll's edition of the *Sworn Book*, Hyiciquiron is said to know the location of all manner of precious metals. If properly appeased, he will provide both silver and gold directly from the bowels of the earth. He is described as possessing a rapacious nature, and he can pull down buildings and other structures with but a whim—a probable reference to earthquakes. See also ABAS, *SWORN BOOK*.

Hyyci: A minister of the demon Habaa, king of the spirits of the planet Mercury. According to the Peterson translation of the *Sworn Book*, Hyyci reveals the secrets kept by both mortals and spirits. He can also answer questions concerning the past, present, and future. His sphere is governed by the angels Michael, Mihel, and Sarapiel. See also HABAA, *SWORN BOOK*.

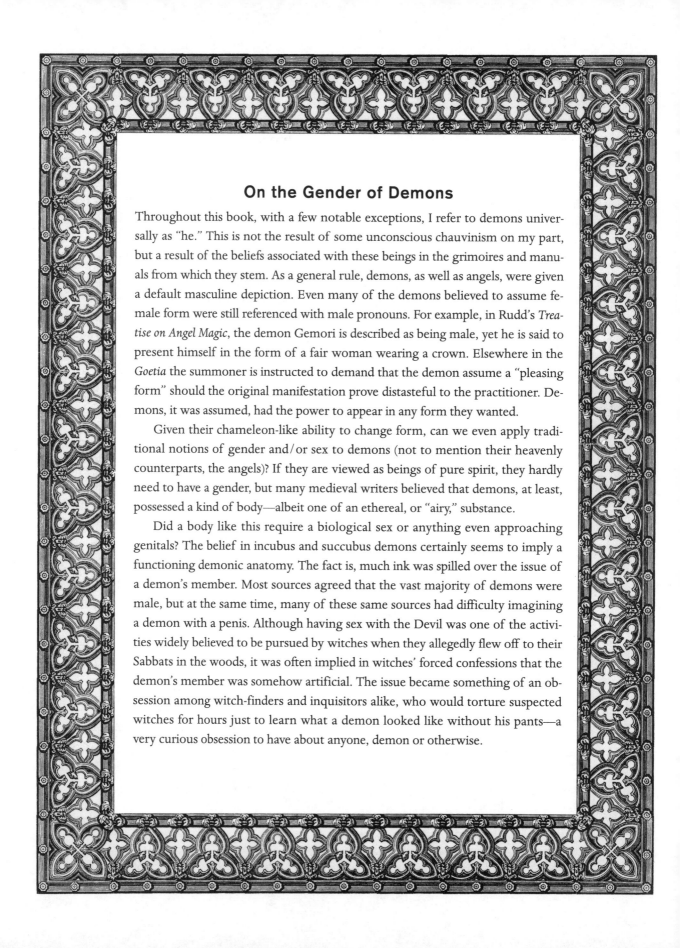

On the Gender of Demons

Throughout this book, with a few notable exceptions, I refer to demons universally as "he." This is not the result of some unconscious chauvinism on my part, but a result of the beliefs associated with these beings in the grimoires and manuals from which they stem. As a general rule, demons, as well as angels, were given a default masculine depiction. Even many of the demons believed to assume female form were still referenced with male pronouns. For example, in Rudd's *Treatise on Angel Magic*, the demon Gemori is described as being male, yet he is said to present himself in the form of a fair woman wearing a crown. Elsewhere in the *Goetia* the summoner is instructed to demand that the demon assume a "pleasing form" should the original manifestation prove distasteful to the practitioner. Demons, it was assumed, had the power to appear in any form they wanted.

Given their chameleon-like ability to change form, can we even apply traditional notions of gender and/or sex to demons (not to mention their heavenly counterparts, the angels)? If they are viewed as beings of pure spirit, they hardly need to have a gender, but many medieval writers believed that demons, at least, possessed a kind of body—albeit one of an ethereal, or "airy," substance.

Did a body like this require a biological sex or anything even approaching genitals? The belief in incubus and succubus demons certainly seems to imply a functioning demonic anatomy. The fact is, much ink was spilled over the issue of a demon's member. Most sources agreed that the vast majority of demons were male, but at the same time, many of these same sources had difficulty imagining a demon with a penis. Although having sex with the Devil was one of the activities widely believed to be pursued by witches when they allegedly flew off to their Sabbats in the woods, it was often implied in witches' forced confessions that the demon's member was somehow artificial. The issue became something of an obsession among witch-finders and inquisitors alike, who would torture suspected witches for hours just to learn what a demon looked like without his pants—a very curious obsession to have about anyone, demon or otherwise.

Some believed that incubi and succubi could change not only their appearance but also their gender. Image by Kirsten Brown.

Iabiel: According to the *Sword of Moses*, Iabiel is an evil angel who can be called upon in operations involving the black arts. He is crucial to a spell intended to strike at an enemy by separating him from his wife. He is also said to have the power to inflict sharp pain, inflammation, and dropsy, a condition often brought about by a bad heart. See also GASTER, *SWORD OF MOSES*.

Iachadiel: In Mathers's translation of the *Clavicula Salomonis*, this name is connected with the amulet known as the Fifth Pentacle of the Moon. Iachadiel is described as an angel, but he is said to serve destruction and loss. He is also invoked to accomplish spells of necromancy. His status as a fallen angel seems fixed by the remark that he can also be called upon by the names *Abdon* and *Dalé*. Although the origin and meaning of the name *Dalé* is somewhat unclear, Abdon is likely a corruption of the name *Abaddon*. As noted elsewhere, Abaddon is widely known as the Angel of the Abyss. See also ABADDON, MATHERS.

Ialchal: A bright and gentle demon connected to the sphere of the sun. Ialchal appears in the Peterson edition of the *Sworn Book of Honorius*, where he is said to serve as a minister of Batthan, the king of the spirits of the sun. Ialchal can bring love, favor, and riches to mortals. He can also keep people healthy. The angels Raphael, Cashael, Dardyhel, and Hanrathaphael hold power over him. See also BATTHAN, *SWORN BOOK*.

Iamai: One of the demonic servants of the infernal lord Beelzebub, Iamai is named in the *Sacred Magic of Abramelin the Mage*. Interestingly, the name of this demon is a palindrome: It reads the same backward and forward. This particular type of wordplay was a significant part of the magickal tradition represented by works like that of *Abramelin*. Words like the name of this demon were often seen as magickal in their own right because of their structure. See also BEELZEBUB, MATHERS.

Iammas: A demon who appears as an armed king riding a wolf. He has deer antlers and griffin claws, and he bellows like a raging bull. He rules the spirits of Mars and wears the red garments of that station. Thunder and lightning precede his arrival. He sows discord and inspires murder. He has the power to kill and to catch things on fire. He revels in battle and can provide two thousand soldiers to fight for one's cause. He appears in the *Book of Oberon*, where it is said he is served by four ministers. His name is likely a variation on *Iammax*, also a king of Mars. See also *BOOK OF OBERON*, CARMAS, IAMMAX, ITAMALL, PALFRAME, PALFRAMEN.

Iammax: The king of the spirits of the Mars, Iammax influences murder and warfare as well as death and the destruction of all earthly things. He is said to be governed by the angels Samahel, Satihel, Ylurahihel, and Amabiel. He appears in the Peterson translation of the *Sworn Book of Honorius*. He is affiliated with the region of the south. See also *SWORN BOOK*.

Iarabal: An infernal spirit of the sun, Iarabal serves the demon-king Batthan, and he is one of four in that hierarchy said also to be subject to the north wind. According to the Peterson translation of the *Sworn Book of Honorius*, Iarabal has the power to bestow love, wealth, and good health upon people. He can also grant a person worldly favor and status. He answers to the angels Raphael, Cashael, Dardyhel, and Hanrathaphael, who govern the sphere of the sun. See also BATTHAN, *SWORN BOOK*.

Iaresin: A demon in service to the infernal princes of the four directions: Oriens, Paimon, Ariton, and Amaimon. Iaresin appears in S. L. MacGregor Mathers's translation of the *Sacred Magic of Abramelin the Mage*. Mathers suggests that this demon's name is derived from a Hebrew word meaning "possessing." See also AMAIMON, ARITON, MATHERS, ORIENS, PAIMON.

Iat: This demon can be summoned to assist the magician in any spells involving trickery or deceit. He is a master of lies and illusion, and he appears in a list of several similar demons in the *Sacred Magic of Abramelin the Mage*. He appears in the same capacity in the *Clavicula Salomonis*. See also MATHERS.

Iax: This name appears in the *Testament of Solomon* in connection with the demon Roêlêd. Roêlêd is a demon of disease associated with the thirty-six decans of the zodiac, and the name *Iax* is invoked to put this demon to flight. Although not directly stated in the text, Iax appears to be an alternate name for the demon Roêlêd. See also ROÊLÊD, SOLOMON.

Ichthion: A demon who appears in the pseudepigraphal *Testament of Solomon*, Ichthion is one of thirty-six demons associated with the decans of the zodiac. He is said to appear with the head of a beast and the body of a man, and he causes muscle cramps and spasms. If he is feeling especially vicious, he can also completely paralyze the muscles of his victims. This demon of disease and suffering can be driven away with the name *Adonaêth*. This name is very likely a variant of *Adonai*, one of the Hebrew names of God. His name is also spelled *Ichthnon*. See also SOLOMON.

Icosiel: In the *Ars Theurgia*, Icosiel is described as the sixth wandering prince of the air. He is reputed to possess a good and compliant nature, and he has a total of one hundred dukes at his command. In addition to the dukes, he has three hundred companions and a multitude of other spirits to wait upon him and carry out his wishes. Icosiel and his court are attracted to houses and homesteads, and thus are most likely to manifest in private residences. The name of this demon can also be found in Trithemius's *Steganographia*. See also *ARS THEURGIA*, TRITHEMIUS.

Ieropaêl: According to the *Testament of Solomon*, Ieropaêl is a demon of disease associated with the thirty-six decans of the zodiac. In appearance, he is a composite monster, with the body of a man and the head of a beast. He torments humanity by afflicting people with convulsions and epilepsy. Ieropaêl can be driven off by invoking three names: *Indarizê, Sabunê*, and *Denôê*. In a later, more accurate translation by McCown, there are only two, rendered *Iouda* and *Zizabou*. The demon's name appears as *Ieropa*. See also SOLOMON.

Iesse: A demon who manifests if the proper perfumes are burned in his name, Iesse serves in the court of the infernal king of the air, Fornnouc. According to the Driscoll edition of the *Sworn Book*, Iesse can cure weakness and infirmity, and he also makes an inspiring tutor for those who gain his favor. Although he has a quick and agile mind, he is a capricious demon, prone to rapid changes in mood. In Peterson's translation of the *Sworn Book*, Iesse appears in the court of Formione, the king of the spirits of Jupiter. As a Jovian spirit, he governs positive emotions and worldly favors. In this text, he is also described as being connected to the east, presumably the eastern winds. See also FORMIONE, FORNNOUC, *SWORN BOOK*.

Igarak: A demon whose name appears in the extensive list of infernal servants to the four demonic princes of the cardinal directions found in Mathers's translation of the *Sacred Magic of Abramelin the Mage*. In attempting to offer a possible origin of this demon's name, Mathers wanders far afield, suggesting that Igarak is actually derived from a Celtic word, *carac*, meaning "terrible." In other versions of the *Abramelin* material, this demon's name is spelled *Igarag*, and it may have originally been a palindrome. See also AMAIMON, ARITON, MATHERS, ORIENS, PAIMON.

Igilon: Mentioned in Mathers's translation of the *Sacred Magic of Abramelin the Mage*, Igilon is a demon who serves under Paimon, Ariton, Oriens, and Amaimon, the four infernal princes of the cardinal directions. See also AMAIMON, ARITON, MATHERS, ORIENS, PAIMON.

Igis: According to the Mathers translation of the *Sacred Magic of Abramelin the Mage*, Igis is one of a number of demons governed by the demonic princes of the four cardinal directions: Oriens, Paimon, Ariton, and Amaimon. Mathers was working from a fifteenth-century French manuscript of the Abramelin material. In other surviving versions of this work, the name of this demon is given as *Sigis*. See also AMAIMON, ARITON, MATHERS, ORIENS, PAIMON.

Ikon: One of several demons ruled by Beelzebub in the *Sacred Magic of Abramelin the Mage*. Ikon's name is likely derived from the Greek word for "image." The manuscript sourced by Mathers for his translation is the only *Abramelin* work that renders this name *Ikonok*. See also BEELZEBUB, MATHERS.

Ilagas: A demon under the rule of Oriens, Paimon, Ariton, and Amaimon, the four infernal princes of the cardinal directions. This version of the demon's name only appears in the Mathers translation of the *Sacred Magic of Abramelin the Mage*. In the version of the *Abramelin* material kept at the Wolfenbüttel library in Germany, the name of this demon is given as *Isagas*. See also AMAIMON, ARITON, MATHERS, ORIENS, PAIMON.

Ilarax: "The Cheerful One." Ilarax appears in a list of demons said to serve the infernal ruler Magoth. In the Mathers edition of the *Sacred Magic of Abramelin the Mage*, Ilarax is jointly ruled by Magoth and Kore. Another spelling of this name is *Ilerak*. See also KORE, MAGOTH, MATHERS.

The Devil's Work

During the Middle Ages, the Devil seemed to be everywhere in Europe. If one credits the Witchcraze, Satan himself spent a great deal of time touring the countryside and seducing hapless old women into flying off with him to have wild orgies in the woods. Through a liberal application of torture, witch-finders would pull colorful, elaborate, and wholly incredible confessions from suspected witches, and many of these detailed the varied and devious ways in which the Devil and his many demons sought to corrupt and obtain human souls.

According to some folklore, however, demons weren't always a nuisance to humanity. Occasionally, the Devil, or one of his cohorts, could be put to productive use. Grillot de Givry, in his lavishly illustrated collection *Witchcraft, Magic and Alchemy*, recounts a number of tales that attribute feats of great industry to demonic beings. A variety of bridges and other building projects were supposedly constructed with the help of the Devil, including sacred structures such as chapels and cathedrals. His traditional payment? Old Nick would request the soul of the first living being to make use of his work. Wily villagers would apparently take the Devil's help, but then find a way to trick him out of the agreed-upon price. This gave rise to the tale of the Wolf's Door at the cathedral in Aachen, Germany, where a wolf was supposedly driven into the new cathedral upon its inauguration, so that this wild beast could fall prey to the Devil in place of some righteous soul. A similar folk belief is recorded in the stained glass at the old church in Saint-Cado, France. Here, the Devil reportedly finished construction on a local bridge. Accordingly, he requested the soul of the first living being to walk across as payment for his efforts. Saint Cado showed up the day that the bridge was finished with a cat from the village. The terrified feline crossed the bridge first, thus cheating the Devil of his due.

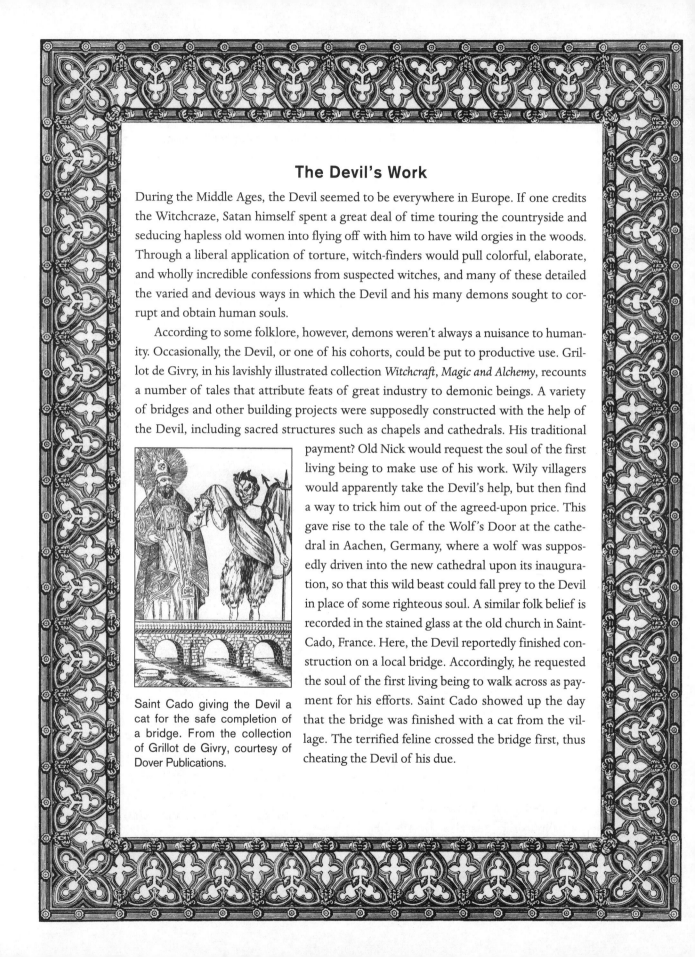

Saint Cado giving the Devil a cat for the safe completion of a bridge. From the collection of Grillot de Givry, courtesy of Dover Publications.

Ileson: A demon said to serve the infernal ruler Astaroth. He is named in the Mathers translation of the *Sacred Magic of Abramelin the Mage*. In all other versions of this work, this demon's name is spelled *Iloson*. See also ASTAROTH, MATHERS.

Illirikim: A demon under the governance of the infernal ruler Amaimon, Illirikim is named in the *Sacred Magic of Abramelin the Mage*. In the Mathers translation of this work, his name is said to mean "they who shriek with a long and drawn-out cry." See also AMAIMON, MATHERS.

Imink: A demon said to serve beneath Oriens, Paimon, Ariton, and Amaimon, the four infernal princes of the cardinal directions. Imink appears in the *Sacred Magic of Abramelin the Mage*, translated by S. L. MacGregor Mathers from a fifteenth-century French manuscript. Although the etymology of this demon's name is dubious, Mathers suggests that Imink's name may mean "devourer." See also AMAIMON, ARITON, MATHERS, ORIENS, PAIMON.

Inachiel: An infernal duke serving the demon Soleviel, a mighty and potent prince who wanders the air with his retinue. One thousand eight hundred and forty lesser spirits carry out Inachiel's will. He is one of twelve chief dukes who answer to Soleviel, and he serves his master every other year. According to the *Ars Theurgia*, he is not bound by any specific time to appear but may manifest during the hours of either the day or the night. See also *ARS THEURGIA*, SOLEVIEL.

Innyhal: An infernal spirit of Mars. He serves as a minister to the demon Iammax, the king of the spirits of Mars. According to the Peterson edition of the *Sworn Book of Honorius*, Innyhal wields power over death, destruction, warfare, and slaughter. This cheery fellow is one of five under the rule of Iam-

max described as subject to the east wind. The angels Samahel, Satihel, Ylurahihel, and Amabiel, who govern the sphere of Mars, hold power over this demon. See also IAMMAX, *SWORN BOOK*.

Inokos: One of several demons said to serve the infernal kings Asmodeus and Magoth. The manuscript translated by Mathers is only one of two versions of the *Sacred Magic of Abramelin the Mage* to contain either the name of this demon or its hierarchy. In the other, a 1608 manuscript originally in cipher, kept at the Wolfenbüttel library in Germany, the name of the demon is spelled *Unochos*. See also ASMODEUS, MAGOTH, MATHERS.

Iogion: According to nineteenth-century occultist S. L. MacGregor Mathers, the name of this demon is connected with a Greek root meaning "the noise of battle." Mathers got this demon's name from an extensive list of demons in the *Sacred Magic of Abramelin the Mage*. According to the *Abramelin* material, Iogion is one of a vast array of demons who serve beneath the four demonic princes of the cardinal directions: Oriens, Paimon, Ariton, and Amaimon. See also AMAIMON, ARITON, MATHERS, ORIENS, PAIMON.

Ipakol: A demon whose name may be derived from a Hebrew root meaning "breathing forth," Ipakol appears in S. L. MacGregor Mathers's translation of the *Sacred Magic of Abramelin the Mage*. According to this text, Ipakol is governed by the demons Oriens, Paimon, Ariton, and Amaimon, the four infernal princes of the cardinal directions. See also AMAIMON, ARITON, MATHERS, ORIENS, PAIMON.

Iparkas: According to Mathers, the name of this demon is derived from a word meaning "commander of cavalry." In the *Sacred Magic of Abramelin the Mage*, Iparkas serves the four princes of the

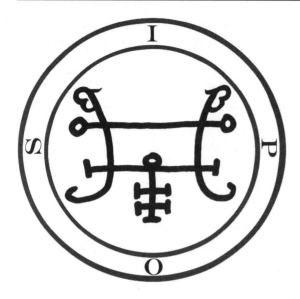

The seal of the demon Ipos varies little between different versions of the *Goetia*. Ink on parchment by M. Belanger.

cardinal directions: Oriens, Paimon, Ariton, and Amaimon, and thus he shares their power to confer knowledge, familiars, and visions to the magician who boldly summons him. See also AMAIMON, ARITON, MATHERS, ORIENS, PAIMON.

Ipos: The twenty-second demon named in the *Goetia*, Ipos is a great earl and prince. The *Pseudomonarchia Daemonum* gives the name of this demon as *Ipes*, with an additional variation of *Ayporos*. In both Wierus's *Pseudomonarchia* and Scot's *Discoverie of Witchcraft*, this demon is reputed to know the past and future. He also possesses the power to make men audacious and witty. Ipos manifests in the curious form of an angel with a lion's head, goose's feet, and the tail of a hare. Scot describes him as "more obscure and filthy than a lion."[49] He commands thirty-six legions. In the *Goetia of Dr. Rudd*, he is said to be constrained with the name of the angel Jajael. See also *GOETIA*, RUDD, SCOT, WIERUS.

---

49. Reginald Scot, *The Discoverie of Witchcraft*, p. 219.

Irix: A name that possibly means "hawk" or "falcon," at least according to occultist S. L. MacGregor Mathers. In his 1898 translation of the *Sacred Magic of Abramelin the Mage*, Irix is said to serve under the joint leadership of the demons Magoth and Kore. In other versions of the *Abramelin* material, the name of this demon is spelled *Hyris*. See also KORE, MAGOTH, MATHERS.

Irmasial: A demon named in the *True Keys of Solomon*. According to this text, Irmasial is one of four principal spirits under the direction of chief Satanachi, and an agent of Lucifer. Under the variant spelling *Irmasliel*, this demon appears in the seventeenth-century Venetian grimoire *Secrets of Solomon*. In this text, Irmasliel governs both alchemy and chemistry. He can teach the transmutation of metals and he also knows the secret to making something called "projection powder." Irmasliel, whose name is alternately given as *Trmael* in this text, is one of four high-ranking demons in the court of Duke Satanachi. See also LUCIFER, *SECRETS OF SOLOMON*, SATANACHI, *TRUE KEYS*.

Irmenos: A name that occultist S. L. MacGregor Mathers relates to a Greek root meaning "the expounder." Irmenos is named in the *Sacred Magic of Abramelin the Mage*. In this text, he is said to serve the infernal king Ariton, one of the rulers of the four cardinal directions. See also ARITON, MATHERS.

Irminon: Working from a fifteenth-century French manuscript on the *Sacred Magic of Abramelin the Mage*, occultist Mathers lists this demon among the many servants of Oriens, Paimon, Ariton, and Amaimon, the four infernal princes of the cardinal directions. According to Mathers, Irminon's name is derived from a Greek word meaning "support-

Biblical Species of Demons

The ancient Israelites believed in a vast and colorful array of demons. Some of them, like Ashteroth, were once worshipped as Semitic gods, but they were eventually demoted to demonic status after the conversion to monotheism. Others, like the Lilin (sometimes rendered *Lilim*), were adopted from the traditions of other countries that the Israelites came into contact with. The Lilin originated in Sumer and Babylon, but they ultimately evolved into uniquely Jewish monsters. The Lilin are associated with Lilith, the Jewish night-demon par excellence. Often depicted as the first wife of Adam, Lilith was greatly feared for her supposed attacks on women in childbirth. She was also blamed for crib-death, and a wide variety of Hebrew talismans were constructed in an attempt to protect infants from her attacks. In the Jewish tradition, she is associated with the night because her name bears strong similarities to the word for night, *layelah*. However, she is more properly a demon of tempests, since the Sumerian root of her name, *lil*, means "storm."

In addition to the Lilin, there are several references to the Shedim in both the Old Testament and the Jewish Midrash (official commentary on the Hebrew Bible). The Shedim can refer to a general species of demons, although the name is sometimes translated "the violent ones." Like the Lilin, the Shedim almost certainly came to the ancient Israelites through the people of Babylon. In Babylonian mythology, the Shedu are spirits—some good, some bad—often referenced in conjunction with the *Lamassu*, or "colossal forms." The *Ruchin*, another class of Jewish demons, were probably demons of the storm. Their name is derived from the Hebrew word *ruach*, or "wind." The Lilin, the Ruchin, and the Shedim could all be lumped together under the general category of the *Mazzikin*, a collective term translated as "harmful spirits." The Mazzikin have been popularized in recent years by author Neil Gaiman, who turned this plural species of demon into a compelling single demoness, *Mazikeen*, whose face is whole and beautiful on one side and rotten and corrupted on the other. Mazikeen appears in the fictional work *The Sandman* and in a spin-off series about the fallen angel Lucifer.

Popular Hebrew amulet to protect mother and child from Lilit during childbirth. Medieval period. Image courtesy of the Wellcome Collection, London.

ing." See also AMAIMON, ARITON, MATHERS, ORIENS, PAIMON.

Iromes: A demon governed by the infernal lord Beelzebub, Iromes appears in several versions of the *Sacred Magic of Abramelin the Mage*. In the Mathers edition of this work, the name of this demon is rendered *Tromes*. Accordingly, Mathers takes it to mean "trauma." He is likely wrong. See also BEELZEBUB, MATHERS.

Irroron: According to nineteenth-century occultist S. L. MacGregor Mathers, the name of this demon may be derived from a Latin root meaning "sprinkling with dew." Mathers records the name of Irroron in an extensive list of demonic servants who function beneath the four infernal princes of the cardinal directions: Oriens, Paimon, Ariton, and Amaimon. All of these demons, as well as a vast array of other infernal entities, are named in the *Sacred Magic of Abramelin the Mage*. See also AMAIMON, ARITON, MATHERS, ORIENS, PAIMON.

Ischigas: A servant of the arch-demon Astaroth, Ischigas appears in the Mathers translation of the *Sacred Magic of Abramelin the Mage*. In another version of the *Abramelin* material kept at the Wolfenbüttel library in Germany, this demon's name is given as *Ychigas*. See also ASTAROTH, MATHERS.

Ischiron: "The Mighty One." Ischiron, with the variant spelling *Ysquiron*, is said to serve the infernal ruler Magoth. He appears in the *Sacred Magic of Abramelin the Mage*. In the Mathers translation of this material, Ischiron is said also to be ruled by Kore. See also KORE, MAGOTH, MATHERS.

Isekel: In the Mathers edition of the *Sacred Magic of Abramelin the Mage*, Isekel is a demon who acts as a servant to the four infernal princes of the cardinal directions: Oriens, Paimon, Ariton,

and Amaimon. See also AMAIMON, ARITON, MATHERS, ORIENS, PAIMON.

Isiamon: A demon whose name may come from a Hebrew root meaning "desolation." In the Mathers translation of the *Sacred Magic of Abramelin the Mage*, Isiamon is said to serve the infernal ruler Astaroth. Another version of this demon's name is spelled *Asianon*. See also ASTAROTH, MATHERS.

Isigi: According to occultist Mathers, the name of this demon means "to err." In the *Sacred Magic of Abramelin the Mage*, Isigi is said to serve the archfiends Astaroth and Asmodeus. All other surviving manuscripts of the *Abramelin* working give this demon's name as *Igigi*. See also ASTAROTH, ASMODEUS, MATHERS.

Itamall: A demon of death and destruction, Itamall serves King Iammas, ruler of the spirits of Mars. Itamall can appear as a shield maiden or as an armed king riding a wolf. He wears garments of red to show his allegiance to the planet of battle, and his skin has a similar tone. He has the power to catch things on fire, to kill people, and to incite fighting and murder. He appears along with three fellow ministers in the *Book of Oberon*, an Elizabethan grimoire. See also *BOOK OF OBERON*, CARMAS, IAMMAS, PALFRAME, PALFRAMEN.

Itrasbiel: A demon used to clear other spirits out of haunted houses. Itrasbiel is named in the *Ars Theurgia*, where he is said to serve Pamersiel as a duke in the hierarchy of the east. Itrasbiel is an evil and deceitful spirit: arrogant, aggressive, and hard to control. Nevertheless, the *Ars Theurgia* maintains that he can be useful when pitted against other spirits of darkness to drive them away. See also *ARS THEURGIA*, PAMERSIEL.

The seal of Itrasbiel, a demon from the *Ars Theurgia* used to chase other spirits away. Artwork by M. Belanger.

Itules: One of several demons named in the *Ars Theurgia* in connection with Pamersiel, the first and chief spirit of the east under the infernal emperor Carnesiel. Itules is an ill-tempered spirit, said to be lofty and stubborn as well as evil and deceitful. He holds the rank of duke and can be used to drive spirits out of haunted houses—assuming one wishes to fight fire with fire. See also *ARS THEURGIA*, CARNESIEL, PAMERSIEL.

Iudal: In the extra-biblical *Testament of Solomon*, Iudal is described as a demon of affliction and disease. He plagues humanity with deafness and ailments that attack the hearing. If someone wishes to overcome this demon, they have only to invoke the name of the angel that governs him, Uruel. See also SOLOMON.

Jamaz: In the Driscoll edition of the *Sworn Book*, Jamaz is identified as the infernal king of the element of fire. As a fire demon, Jamaz is said to be hot-headed and impulsive. He is also energetic and strong, and he can be generous to those he favors. His complexion is like fire, and he wields power over death and decay. Consequently, he can either restore that which has already decayed or he can prevent decay in an item or object. He can cause death with but a word, and he can also raise an army of one thousand soldiers. Driscoll suggests that Jamaz accomplishes this by raising these soldiers from the grave. On top of all of this, he can give familiars. In keeping with his martial qualities, his familiars have a tendency to have the likeness of soldiers. See also *SWORN BOOK.*

Jambex: The *Book of Oberon* identifies this demon as a captain, a marquis, and a great governor with command over twenty-five legions of spirits. He is called upon in love magic where he consecrates a specially prepared waxen image. This image is purported to cause any man or woman exposed to it to fall in love with the person it was fashioned for. Jambex prefers to appear as a woman with a pleasant voice. In this form, he is especially gifted at compelling the love of men. Despite appearances, the text uses male pronouns throughout, suggesting that gender, sex, and appearance are quite malleable when it comes to demons. See also *BOOK OF OBERON.*

Janiel: A mighty duke in the hierarchy of the north. According to the *Ars Theurgia*, Janiel has thousands of ministering spirits in his retinue. He answers to the infernal king Baruchas, and will only manifest during the seventh portion of the day, when the day is divided into fifteen sections of time. See also *ARS THEURGIA*, BARUCHAS.

Janua Magica Reserata: A text drawn primarily from a manuscript designated Sloane MS 3825, where it appears along with the *Nine Celestial Keys* and the *Tenth Key*, appended in a different hand. The Latin title translates to *Keys to the Gateway of*

Magic. In the British Library system, the document is simply entitled *Treatise on Magic*. Handwritten, this grimoire was likely produced in the early seventeenth century. It is believed to have been owned at some point in its history by Elias Ashmole (1617–1692), an English politician known to have practiced astrology and alchemy. The book is mainly concerned with angel magic, although it also presents a hierarchy of nine orders of demons that stand as a direct infernal reflection of the nine orders of angels. The book discusses the ranks of spirits and the importance of correspondences and chain of command, and enumerates the various types of spirits that can be summoned and controlled, including infernal, celestial, and terrestrial beings. The hierarchy of infernal princes outlined in the nine orders has later echoes in Francis Barrett's early nineteenth-century work *The Magus*, demonstrating a line of descent. See also BARRETT.

Jasziel: A demon described in the *Ars Theurgia*, Jasziel holds the rank of duke and serves in the north-bound hierarchy of the demon-king Armadiel. Eighty-four lesser spirits serve beneath him. He is bound to appear only during a very specific time of the day. The *Ars Theurgia* gives the following formula for calculating that time: divide the day into fifteen equal portions. Whatever hours and minutes fall in the tenth of these portions of time will be Jasziel's. The demon will only appear during this time. See also ARMADIEL, *ARS THEURGIA*.

Jequon: A name sometimes also rendered *Yequon*. He is a fallen angel mentioned in the *Book of Enoch*. Jequon appears in *1 Enoch* 68:4, where he is identified as the angel who first led all the others astray. In earlier portions of the *Book of Enoch*, the angels Shemyaza and Azazel carry this blame. See also AZAZEL, SHEMYAZA, WATCHER ANGELS.

Jomjael: A fallen angel named in the *Book of Enoch*, Jomjael was one of the Watchers, or *Grigori*, and he was charged with looking after humanity. Instead, he fell in love with mortals and left Heaven to take a human wife. He is counted among the "chiefs of tens," lieutenants of the Watcher Angels trusted to lead the rest. His immediate superiors were the angels Shemyaza and Azazel. See also AZAZEL, SHEMYAZA, WATCHER ANGELS.

Joorex: The name of this demon, when enclosed in a ring and worn on the forefinger, will enable the wearer to win at all games. Joorex appears in the Elizabethan *Book of Oberon*, where he is said to appear in the form of a hart. When he speaks, it is in a small voice, very difficult to hear. In addition to helping those who summon him win at games of chance, this demon has knowledge of astronomy and also teaches how to craft musical instruments. Although the text does not give a specific rank, Joorex is said to rule over nine legions of lesser spirits. See also *BOOK OF OBERON*.

Jubutzis: A demon named in the fifteenth-century *Munich Handbook*, Jubutzis is invoked in a spell of divination to help reveal the identity of a thief. See also *MUNICH HANDBOOK*.

Kabada: A servant of the arch-fiend Beelzebub. Kabada and his brethren appear in the *Sacred Magic of Abramelin the Mage*. See also BEELZEBUB, MATHERS.

Kabersa: The name of this demon may be derived from a Hebrew term meaning "wide measure." Kabersa appears in the Mathers edition of the *Sacred Magic of Abramelin the Mage*. In this text, he is identified as a servant of the infernal prince Paimon, one of the rulers of the cardinal directions. Other versions of the *Abramelin* material present this demon's name as *Kalgosa*. See also MATHERS, PAIMON.

Kadolon: According to the Mathers translation of the *Sacred Magic of Abramelin the Mage*, Kadolon is a demon who acts as a servant to the four infernal princes of the cardinal directions: Oriens, Paimon, Ariton, and Amaimon. See also AMAIMON, ARITON, MATHERS, ORIENS, PAIMON.

Kafles: A demon governed by Paimon, one of the four infernal princes of the cardinal directions named in the *Sacred Magic of Abramelin the Mage*. In his 1898 translation of this work, occultist S. L. Mathers gives the name of this demon as *Roffles*, taking this to come from a Hebrew term that means "the lion trembling." See also MATHERS, PAIMON.

Kairoxanondalon: Identified as the fifth demon among thirty-six spirits connected with the decans of the zodiac. His name appears instead as *Iudal* in the Conybeare translation of the *Testament of Solomon*, but McCown, working later with a better collection of source texts, corrects this. Kairoxanondalon is said to obstruct the ears, causing deafness. His name may mean "torch." Ourouel is given as the name of the angel who constrains him. See also SOLOMON.

Kaitar: A demon who may inhabit mountains or other lofty locales. Kaitar's name is probably derived from a Hebrew term meaning "crown" or "summit." Kaitar appears in the Mathers edition of the *Sacred Magic of Abramelin the Mage*, where he is said to serve the demons Magoth and Kore. In other versions of this text, the name of this demon is rendered variously as *Caytar* or *Cayfar*. See also KORE, MAGOTH, MATHERS.

Kamusil: One of several demons said to serve both Magoth and Kore. According to the Mathers translation of the *Sacred Magic of Abramelin the Mage*, the name of this demon may mean "rising" or "elevation." See also KORE, MAGOTH, MATHERS.

Karelesa: A demonic servant of Beelzebub whose name appears in the *Sacred Magic of Abramelin the Mage*. In the Mathers presentation of this work, the name is rendered *Carelena*. See also BEELZEBUB, MATHERS.

Karmal: According to the *Liber de Angelis*, this demon is connected with the planet Mars. As a result, he is also connected to all things involving soldiers and war. He is the subordinate of the infernal king known only as *Rubeus Pugnator*, and he is summoned to assist with the creation of the potent Ring of Mars. Properly conjured, Karmal lends his destructive power to the ring so that the magician may use the talisman to bring ruin to all enemies. See also *LIBER DE ANGELIS*, RUBEUS PUGNATOR.

Kasdeja: A fallen angel named in the *Book of Enoch*, Kasdeja was one of the Watcher Angels charged to oversee the well-being of mankind. When he broke his trust with Heaven, he is said to have revealed some of the most controversial forbidden knowledge to humanity. First and foremost, Kasdeja taught methods of abortion, described as the "smitings of the infant in the womb." He also taught the smitings of spirits and demons, spells for "the smitings of the soul" by

snakebite, and even spells for sunstroke.[50] See also WATCHER ANGELS.

Katanikotaêl: In the *Testament of Solomon*, Katanikotaêl is the eleventh demon belonging to a group of thirty-six demons of affliction and disease associated with the decans of the zodiac. Katanikotaêl is a particularly spiteful being, causing strife and unrest at home and making tempers flare. He also makes the residents of a home feel uneasy. While most of the zodiac demons described in the *Testament of Solomon* have a specific angel that can be called upon to drive them away, Katanikotaêl instead must be driven from a home using specially

The angel of death called to slay all the firstborn of Egypt. From the Gustav Doré illustrated Bible.

50. R. H. Charles, *The Book of Enoch the Prophet*, p. 65.

prepared holy water. The "cure" for his presence calls for seven laurel leaves that are scribed with holy names. These laurel leaves are then washed in water. Sprinkling this water around the house is reputed to cause the demon to depart. See also SOLOMON.

Kataron: According to occultist Mathers, the meaning of this demon's name may come from a Greek term meaning "to cast down." Kataron serves the infernal ruler Astaroth and is invoked as a part of the Holy Guardian Angel rite. This serves as the central working of the *Sacred Magic of Abramelin the Mage*. See also ASTAROTH, MATHERS.

Katini: This demon serves in the hierarchy overseen by Oriens, Paimon, Ariton, and Amaimon, the four demonic princes of the cardinal directions. According to the *Sacred Magic of Abramelin the Mage*, he is one of many lesser demons summoned as a part of the extensive Holy Guardian Angel rite. See also AMAIMON, ARITON, MATHERS, ORIENS, PAIMON.

Katolin: In the *Abramelin* material, this demon is ruled by Magoth. In Mathers's translation of the *Sacred Magic of Abramelin the Mage*, Katolin is also a servant of Kore. The version of the *Abramelin* material kept at the Wolfenbüttel library in Germany gives this name as *Nasolico*. The version at the Dresden library is spelled *Natolico*. No original survives for comparison. See also KORE, MAGOTH, MATHERS.

Kawteeah: One of a number of names attributed to the night-demon Lilith. Lilith, by all of her names, was believed to walk abroad at night, preying upon infants and children. She was also thought to attack women in childbirth. In Jewish lore, Lilith-demons were connected with night, darkness, and death. This Hebrew name, translit-

erated into English, appears in author T. Schrire's 1966 work, *Hebrew Magic Amulets*. It is one of the many names of Lilith scribed upon ancient talismans believed to protect women and newborns from the demon's attacks. See also LILITH.

Kayne: A thieving demon who takes the form of a raven to fly forth and steal treasures from the houses of kings. According to the *Book of Oberon*, the Elizabethan grimoire where he appears, Kayne holds the rank of duke and oversees a total of twenty subordinate legions. He does not always have to be a raven; he can be compelled to appear in human form. See also *BOOK OF OBERON*.

Kele: A demonic servitor of Asmodeus and Magoth, at least according to the Mathers edition of the *Sacred Magic of Abramelin the Mage*. Mathers suggests that this demon's name means "to consume." A variant of this name appears in only one other version of the *Abramelin* material. In this manuscript, kept at the Wolfenbüttel library, the demon's name appears as *Kela*. See also ASMODEUS, MAGOTH, MATHERS.

Kelen: "The Swift One." Kelen and a host of other demonic entities are all named in the *Sacred Magic of Abramelin the Mage*. His infernal masters are Oriens, Paimon, Ariton, and Amaimon, the four demonic princes of the cardinal directions. See also AMAIMON, ARITON, MATHERS, ORIENS, PAIMON.

Kemal: According to occultist S. L. MacGregor Mathers, the name of this demon means "desire of God." Clearly, Kemal suffered a fall somewhere along the way, because in the *Sacred Magic of Abramelin the Mage*, he is listed among the demonic servants of Beelzebub. See also BEELZEBUB, MATHERS.

The angel Raphael shows Tobias how to foil the demon Asmodeus by burning the gall of a fish. Engraving by S. F. Ravenet (1767) after a painting by Eustache Le Sueur. Wellcome Collection, London.

Keriel: A duke of the demon Barmiel named in the *Ars Theurgia*. Through his association with Barmiel, Keriel is connected with the hierarchy of the south. He serves his infernal master during the hours of the day and has twenty lesser spirits at his command. See also *ARS THEURGIA*, BARMIEL.

Keryth: A demon called upon to answer questions about lost items or objects hidden in the earth. Those who wish to summon him are instructed to work in the first quarter of the night and inscribe a specific figure in the courtyard of their homes. After writing their question on a slip of paper and leaving this in the center of the figure, they are to go to bed. According to the *Book of Oberon*, Keryth will write the reply on the paper by morning. See also *BOOK OF OBERON*.

Keteb: A demon named in Psalms 91:6 alongside the demon of midday—who apparently does not warrant a proper name. According to Reverend W. O. E. Oesterley in his authoritative work of 1921, *Immortality and the Unseen World*, the name *Keteb* is from a Hebrew root. In modern versions of the Bible, the word is often translated as "plague." In this, Keteb can be connected to a number of Sumerian and Babylonian demons of disease. In the rabbinical commentary on the Psalms known as the *Midrash Tehillim*, Keteb is described as being a poisonous demon covered with both scales and hair. He purportedly has only one good eye in his face, as the other is inexplicably located in the middle of his heart. He is a demon of twilight, achieving his greatest power neither in full darkness nor in full light but in the midpoints between. He is supposedly most active from the seventeenth of July through the ninth of August.

Khailaw: According to occultist T. Schrire's publication *Hebrew Magic Amulets*, Khailaw is one of the many names of the demon Lilith. In Jewish lore, Lilith is a night-demon with a penchant for attacking infants and pregnant women. She was particularly feared by women in childbirth, and any complications from childbirth were often attributed to her. In the past, amulets were inscribed with these names and used to protect people from the Lilith-demon attacks. See also LILITH.

Khavaw Reshvunaw: A transliterated name of Lilith, taken from a treatise on Hebrew magickal amulets. This name translates roughly to "the First Eve." In the Talmud and in later rabbinical lore, Lilith was believed to be the first wife of Adam. When she defied both Adam and God, she was cast from the Garden and Adam was given a more docile wife, Eve. Wandering far from the Garden, Lilith was believed to have given birth to demons. She retained a long-standing jealousy and hatred of women, and in Jewish lore she is credited as causing trouble in childbirth as well as crib death. A large number of textual amulets survive that were intended to protect against Lilith's attacks. These textual amulets often feature various names of Lilith, each of which was believed to hold some power over the demon.

The Five Accursed Nations

Mathers' translation of the *Clavicula Salomonis*, or *Key of Solomon the King*, contains a curious appendix that purports to be an ancient fragment of the *Key of Solomon* originally translated by Eliphas Lévi. This fragment describes, among other things, ten different orders of heavenly beings associated with each of the ten Sephiroth of the Tree of Life and the ten different orders of demons who oppose them. Within this section of the fragment, there is a further reference to the "five accursed nations." These are five nations that Joshua was to destroy in the Old Testament, and the text interprets them as representing five distinct orders, or "nations," of demons. The list has been reproduced in a variety of books on demons, and it remains a compelling, if somewhat mysterious, roll call of evil beings. According to this fragmentary text the five accursed nations include:

1. The Amalekites, known as the Aggressors
2. The Geburim (aka Gibborim) known as the Violent Ones
3. The Raphaim (sometimes spelled Rephaim) called the Cowards
4. The Nephilim, known as the Voluptuous Ones
5. The Anakim, called "the Anarchists" in the text

In keeping with the Qabbalistic nature of this text, each of the Five Accursed Nations are said to be vanquished by a different Hebrew letter from the Tetragrammaton, the ineffable name of God. Thus, *Yod* vanquishes the Anarchists. The first letter *He* vanquishes the Violent Ones. The Cowards are overcome by *Vau*, which the text associates with the sword of Michael the archangel. The Nephilim are vanquished by the second *He*, and the Aggressors are overcome by the *Schin*, a letter that does not directly appear in the Tetragrammaton but is described as "the Fire of the Lord and the equilibrating Law of Justice."[*]

---

[*] S. L. MacGregor Mathers, *Clavicula Salomonis*, p. 124.

This name, along with a number of others, appears in the 1966 publication *Hebrew Magic Amulets* by T. Schrire. See also LILITH.

Khil: A demon who commands the tremors of the earth, Khil can be called upon to cause an earthquake anywhere in the world. Named in Peterson's *Grimorium Verum*, he serves as the sixth demon under the infernal duke Syrach. Compare his name and powers to the demon *Khleim* from the *True Keys of Solomon*. See also GRIMORIUM VERUM, KHLEIM, SYRACH, *TRUE KEYS*.

Kiligil: In the *Sacred Magic of Abramelin the Mage*, Kiligil is named as a demon who serves beneath the arch-fiend Magoth. In the fifteenth-century French manuscript sourced by Mathers for his own translation of this book, Kiligil is also ruled by Kore. See also KORE, MAGOTH, MATHERS.

Kilik: A demon whose name Mathers supposes is from Hebrew, meaning "wrinkled with age," Kilik is named in the *Sacred Magic of Abramelin the Mage*, where he is reputedly governed by the four infernal princes of the cardinal directions: Oriens, Paimon, Ariton, and Amaimon. As such, he can be summoned and compelled in the names of his superiors. See also AMAIMON, ARITON, MATHERS, ORIENS, PAIMON.

Kilikim: A servant of the demon Amaimon whose name appears in the *Sacred Magic of Abramelin the Mage*. In the Mathers translation of this work, the name is spelled *Illirikim*. Mathers takes this name to mean "shriekers." See also AMAIMON, MATHERS.

Kipokis: A demon said to serve the infernal lord Beelzebub, Kipokis appears in the *Sacred Magic of Abramelin the Mage*. An alternate spelling of this demon's name is *Ipokys*. See also BEELZEBUB, MATHERS.

Kirik: A demon governed by Astaroth and Asmodeus. He is named in the Mathers translation of the *Sacred Magic of Abramelin the Mage*. See also ASTAROTH, ASMODEUS, MATHERS.

Kleim: A demon of earthquakes, Kleim is named in the *True Keys of Solomon*, where he is said to serve Sirachi, the immediate chief of Lucifer. Kleim has power over towns and houses, presumably because he can inspire earth tremors to threaten these things. An alternate version of his name is given as *Klic*. See also KHIL, LUCIFER, SIRACHI, *TRUE KEYS*.

Demons dancing with their mortal servants. A woodcut from Guazzo's *Compendium Maleficarum*, courtesy of Dover Publications.

Klepoth: A demon of illusion named in the *True Keys of Solomon*. According to this text, Klepoth can conjure illusory music that seems entirely real. He can also make a person feel as if they are spinning and dancing even when they are merely standing still. He serves chief Sirachi, who himself serves directly beneath Lucifer. Klepoth also appears in Peterson's edition of the *Grimorium Verum*. Here, he is called upon in the ritual preparation of the magician's staff. In addition, he is credited with the power to let the magician see all manner of dances. Klepoth serves as the fifth demon under the infernal duke Syrach. In the *Secrets of Solomon*, he will whisper the contents of your opponents' hands helpfully into your ear to help you cheat at cards. In addition to helping people win at cards, Klepoth materializes hecklers out of thin air to jeer, or an elegant entourage dressed in rich garments of silk to impress and entertain. The name of this demon is curiously close to *Qlippoth*, a term unique to Qabbalism. Although opinions vary, the Qlippoth of the Qabbalah are generally perceived as emanations of the Dark Tree of Life. See also *GRIMORIUM VERUM*, LUCIFER, *SECRETS OF SOLOMON*, SIRACHI, SYRACH, *TRUE KEYS*.

Klio: A demon of destruction who can be called upon to shake houses or tumble entire cities with earthquakes. Klio serves in the court of the infernal duke Syrach, himself a subordinate to Lucifer. His name appears in the seventeenth-century text known as the *Secrets of Solomon*, a grimoire of infernal magick confiscated by the Venetian Inquisition. Although there is no indication of a connection in the text, Klio's name is strikingly similar to that of Clio, the Greek muse of history. See also LUCIFER, *SECRETS OF SOLOMON*, SYRACH.

Klothod: A demon whose name means "battle," at least according to the *Testament of Solomon*. Klothod is one of a group of seven female demons called up and bound by King Solomon in this extra-biblical text dating to the last few centuries before the Common Era. Klothod and her sisters are almost certainly personifications of the Pleiades, a star cluster that is frequently represented by seven sisters in world mythology. As a demon, Klothod is reputed to cause discord and fighting among men. Her sisters are no better, as they are called Deception, Strife, Jealousy, Power, Error, and "the

Worst." Solomon is said to have put all seven of them to work building the foundations of his great temple. See also SOLOMON.

Kobal: Ranked among the Masters of Revels in Berbiguier's infernal hierarchy, Kobal reputedly serves as Stage Manager in Hell. This colorful vision of the hierarchy of Hell appears in Berbiguier's three-volume autobiography, *Les Farfadets*. Kobal's name is almost certainly derived from the Greek word *kobaloi*. This term designated a class of mischievous spirits, from which we get the modern word *kobold*. Kobal is also mentioned in Waite's translation of the *Grand Grimoire*. See also BERBIGUIER, *GRAND GRIMOIRE*, WAITE.

Kokobiel: An angel connected to the stars, Kokobiel is one of the fallen Watcher Angels named in the *Book of Enoch*. According to this text, Kokobiel was entrusted with sacred knowledge regarding the constellations. When he left Heaven, he taught these secrets to humanity even though this knowledge was forbidden. His name is sometimes rendered *Kochbiel* or *Koshbiel*. See also WATCHER ANGELS.

Kolofe: According to Mathers in his presentation of the *Sacred Magic of Abramelin the Mage*, the name of this demon comes from a Greek word meaning "summit" or "the height of achievement." Kolofe serves the demon-king Astaroth. See also ASTAROTH, MATHERS.

Kore: In the Mathers edition of the *Sacred Magic of Abramelin the Mage*, Kore is identified as one of the principal spirits ruling a number of lesser demons. In this text, Kore is most often paired with the demon Magoth, another one of the eight infernal sub-princes thought to serve directly beneath the fiends Satan, Lucifer, Leviathan, and Belial. The joint hierarchy of Magoth and Kore is unique to the Mathers version of the *Abramelin* material. In all

The goddesses Demeter and Persephone (Kore) accompany an initiate into the Eleusinian Mysteries. From the *Encyclopedia of Occultism* by Lewis Spence, courtesy of Dover Publications.

other versions, this collection of demons is said to be ruled over by Magoth alone.

Kore is another name for the Greek goddess Persephone, consort of Hades. Hades was the Greek lord of the Underworld, and Persephone was his unwilling bride. Because of their associations with the Underworld, these ancient deities were sometimes integrated into the demonology of the Middle Ages and Renaissance. Notably, Charles Berbiguier identifies Persephone as a queen of Hell, and her status as an infernal ruler is repeated in Collin de Plancy's *Dictionnaire Infernal*. Of course, to the ancient Greeks there was nothing infernal about this goddess. Connected with the rites of the Eleusinian Mysteries, she was a powerful and respected deity in the ancient world. The Roman version of this goddess was married to Pluto. See also BELIAL, LEVIATHAN, LUCIFER, MAGOTH, MATHERS, PLUTO, SATAN.

Kumeatêl: A demon of illness and disease, Kumeatêl afflicts his victims with fits of shivering and torpor. He is the fourteenth of thirty-six demons associated with the decans of the zodiac. His name appears in the extra-biblical *Testament of Solomon*. Kumeatêl is governed by the angel Zôrôel. Invoking this angel's name will cause Kumeatêl to flee. In a later, more accurate translation of this work, his name is instead rendered as *Leroel*. He causes chills, shivering, and sore throat. The names Iax and Solomon cause him to flee. See also SOLOMON.

Kunos Paston: In the *Testament of Solomon*, this demon appears to King Solomon in the shape of a horse with the hind parts of a fish. This strange composite beast is tied to the watery depths. He wrecks ships in order to steal the gold and silver inside. Although people sometimes drown in these shipwrecks, this demon is not interested in their deaths, preferring instead to cast these victims out of his watery domain. On a less dangerous note, he also causes sea sickness. He is said to be able to appear as a man or as waves upon the ocean. He is so tied to his element that he will die without water. He can be bound in the name of the angel Iameth. See also SOLOMON.

Kurtaêl: This is one of several demons of disease listed in the extra-biblical *Testament of Solomon*. Kurtaêl is attributed with the power to cause intestinal cramps and other complaints, and he uses these ailments to torment humanity. If Kurtaêl is attacking someone, he can be put to flight by invoking the name of the angel Iaôth, who has power over him. In a later translation of the same text, this demon's name is given as *Kourtael*. The same angel holds power over him. See also SOLOMON.

St. Catherine of Sienna battles a demon. Woodcut in the Wellcome Collection, London.

Kwphin: From the *Book of Oberon*. Kwphin is a spirit identified as the brother of Lambricon, from the court of the north. He is presumably a demon (as Lambricon is identified as such) and alleged to have been killed by Saint Katherine. If the text means *Catherine of Siena*, that saint famously had several run-ins with demons. However, there is no specific record of *Kwphin* in her hagiography. See also BOOK OF OBERON, LAMBRICON.

Labisi: A servant of the demon Amaimon named in the *Sacred Magic of Abramelin the Mage*. In the Peter Hammer edition and the version kept at the Dresden library, this name is spelled *Lapisi*. See also AMAIMON, MATHERS.

Laboneton: A name given as meaning "to grasp" or "to seize" by Mathers in his version of the *Sacred Magic of Abramelin the Mage*. Laboneton is said to serve under the dual leadership of the demons Magoth and Kore. See also KORE, MAGOTH, MATHERS.

Laboux: A demon governed by Asmodeus and Astaroth, at least according to the Mathers translation of the *Sacred Magic of Abramelin the Mage*. See also ASTAROTH, ASMODEUS, MATHERS.

Ladiel: A recalcitrant demon who appears during the hours of the night. Ladiel is reputed to possess an evil and misleading nature, preferring to use trickery and deceit when dealing with people. He holds the rank of duke and has fifty ministering spirits beneath him to attend to his needs. He serves in the hierarchy of the west, and his immediate superior is the infernal prince Cabariel. Ladiel's name and sigil both appear in the *Ars Theurgia*. See also *ARS THEURGIA*, CABARIEL.

Laftalium: In the fifteenth-century magickal manual known as the *Liber de Angelis*, Laftalium appears in a spell to bring harm to one's enemies. A demon of disease who serves beneath the infernal king Bileth, Laftalium will rain suffering down upon a target when conjured forth. He afflicts the limbs so they weaken and tremble, and he scorches the body all over with terrible fever. There is no cure for these symptoms. Only the magician can counter the spell. See also BILETH, *LIBER DE ANGELIS*.

Lagan: A great king and president. According to the *Book of Incantations*, he appears in the form of a bull with griffin wings. He has powers of transmutation, changing all metals to gold. He can turn water into wine and wine into blood, a trick that may be a mockery of the Catholic rite of transubstantiation. He belongs to the Order of Dominion and governs thirty-three legions. See also *BOOK OF INCANTATIONS*.

Lagasuf: A demon from the Mathers translation of the *Sacred Magic of Abramelin the Mage*, Lagasuf is governed by the four infernal princes of the cardinal directions: Oriens, Paimon, Amaimon, and Ariton. According to Mathers, who attempted a rough etymology of each of the demon names mentioned in the *Abramelin* material, Lagasuf's name is derived from a Hebrew root meaning "the Pale One." See also AMAIMON, ARITON, MATHERS, ORIENS, PAIMON.

Laginx: A demon whose name appears in the Mathers translation of the *Sacred Magic of Abramelin the Mage*. He is said to serve beneath both Astaroth and Asmodeus. In another version of the *Abramelin* material kept at the Wolfenbüttel library in Germany, the name of this demon is written *Lagiros*. See also ASTAROTH, ASMODEUS, MATHERS.

Lamael: A demon governed by Amenadiel, the infernal Emperor of the West. Lamael is named in Henson's translation of the *Ars Theurgia*, where he is said to hold the rank of duke. He has three thousand eight hundred and eighty ministering spirits at his command. See also AMENADIEL, *ARS THEURGIA*.

Lamalon: According to the Mathers translation of the *Sacred Magic of Abramelin the Mage*, the name of this demon comes from a Hebrew term that means "turning aside." Lamalon is a servant of the greater demon Beelzebub, and both are summoned as a part of the Holy Guardian Angel working that serves as the main focus of the *Abramelin* material. See also BEELZEBUB, MATHERS.

Lamas: A chief duke under the rule of the demonic king Raysiel. According to the *Ars Theurgia*, both Lamas and Raysiel are connected with the north. Reputed to be stubborn and ill-natured, Lamas rules over a total of twenty lesser spirits who exist to carry out his commands. The name of this demon is particularly close in spelling to *Lammas*, a traditional Pagan holiday celebrated on the first of August. This celebration has its origins in a medieval harvest festival celebrated in the British Isles. Despite the similarities in spelling, there is no clear line of connection between the demon Lamas and the festival of Lammas. See also *ARS THEURGIA*, RAYSIEL.

Lambricon: Or *Lambracaron*. He is called in conjunction with Egin, the king of the north. Lambricon appears in the *Book of Oberon*, which gives *Lambracaron* as an alternate version of his name. His brother Kwphin was allegedly killed by Saint Katherine, and he's still not over it. See also *BOOK OF OBERON*, EGIN.

Lameniel: A demon who takes the form of a human-headed serpent, Lameniel is one of twelve dukes who serve the mighty Hydriel. Lameniel's name and sigil, both used in summoning and binding him, appear in the *Ars Theurgia*. According to this text, Lameniel and his fellow dukes are all spirits of the air that wander from point to point along the compass. Despite his airy nature, Lameniel is nevertheless attracted to places that are wet and moist, preferring to manifest in wetlands, bogs, and swamps. When he appears, he takes the form of a great serpent with a woman's head. Although monstrous in appearance, Lameniel is reputed to possess a benevolent temperament, comporting himself in a polite and civilized manner. He is attended by over a thousand ministering spirits who carry out his wishes and see to his needs. Elsewhere in the *Ars Theurgia*, Lameniel appears as one of ten great dukes who serve the infernal prince Bidiel, a spirit of the air who wanders with no fixed place. This version of Lameniel is said to have no fewer than two thousand and four hundred lesser spirits to carry out his wishes. When he manifests, he appears in the shape of a beautiful human. See also *ARS THEURGIA*, BIDIEL, HYDRIEL.

Lamolon: In the *Sacred Magic of Abramelin the Mage*, Lamolon is said to serve beneath the infernal lord Beelzebub. Lamolon's name appears in close proximity with that of another demon, Amolon. Given the similarities between these two names, there is a chance that they are not separate and distinct devils at all, but the result of a scribal error that eventually transformed one name into two. See also AMOLON, BEELZEBUB, MATHERS.

Laphor: One of a number of demons associated with the points of the compass. Laphor holds the rank of duke and serves beneath Carnesiel, the infernal Emperor of the East. He is described as having a very "airy" nature, and when summoned he should be made to appear in a scrying glass so that his form is visible to the naked eye—at least according to the *Ars Theurgia*, where this demon's name appears. See also *ARS THEURGIA*, CARNESIEL.

Larael: A demon who serves as one of several chief dukes in the hierarchy of Symiel, king of the north by east. Larael is a demon who manifests only during the day. According to the *Ars Theurgia*, he is attended by a total of sixty ministering spirits. See also *ARS THEURGIA*, SYMIEL.

Larfos: A demon governed by the infernal prince Dorochiel. He serves in the court of the west in the capacity of chief duke. Larfos is connected with the second half of the day, manifesting only at a specific hour between noon and dusk. According to the *Ars Theurgia*, Larfos has four hundred lesser spirits in his retinue. See also *ARS THEURGIA*, DOROCHIEL.

Lariel: A servant of the demon-king Armadiel. Both Lariel and his superior demon are tied to the hierarchy of the north, as outlined in the seventeenth-century work known as the *Ars Theurgia*. According to this text, Lariel has a total of eighty-four lesser spirits to attend his needs. If the day is divided into fifteen portions of time, Lariel's time is the third of these portions. He is bound only to appear during those hours. See also ARMADIEL, *ARS THEURGIA*.

Larmol: In Rudd's *Treatise on Angel Magic*, Larmol is identified as one of twelve dukes who wait upon Caspiel, the Emperor of the South. Larmol appears in connection with the magickal diagram tied to the planet Mercury. This is one of seven Tables of Enoch presented by Rudd in his work. In the *Ars Theurgia*, Larmol is one of six chief dukes who serve the wandering prince Menadiel. Here he has three hundred and ninety servants to attend him. According to this text, he will manifest himself in the first hour of the day. He has a companion demon who also serves prince Menadiel. This companion, Barchiel by name, is tied to the hour immediately following Larmol's and will only manifest in that time. See also *ARS THEURGIA*, BARCHIEL, CASPIEL, MENADIEL, RUDD.

Larmot: One of twelve mighty dukes who serve the demon Caspiel, the infernal Emperor of the South. Larmot and his demonic brethren are reputed to possess very difficult natures. According to the *Ars Theurgia*, they are churlish and stubborn spirits. Larmot is also a so-called "spirit of the air," which is to say that his essential nature is more subtle than physical. When he manifests, he may be difficult for mortals to see without the aid of a scrying crystal or shew-stone. He has no fewer than two thousand two hundred and sixty lesser spirits who serve beneath him. This name may well be a variation on the demon *Larmol* found in Rudd's *Treatise on Angel Magic*. See also *ARS THEURGIA*, CASPIEL, RUDD.

Larphiel: One of fifteen dukes under the rule of the demon Icosiel, a wandering prince of the air. Larphiel prefers to appear in houses, but he is bound to only manifest during specific hours and minutes each day. The *Ars Theurgia* contains the formula for calculating his appearance: if the day is divided into fifteen equal parts, Larphiel's time is defined by the sixth portion of time. He will only appear during this time each day. When he manifests, he is typically accompanied by at least some of the two thousand two hundred lesser spirits who attend him. See also *ARS THEURGIA*, ICOSIEL.

Las Pharon: In the seventeenth-century magickal text known as the *Ars Theurgia*, Las Pharon is named as one of several infernal dukes in the service of the demon-prince Usiel. Las Pharon is tied to the region of the west and the hours of the night. He only manifests during the dark hours each day. He allegedly has the power to reveal the location of treasures hidden through charms and enchantments. He can also hide precious objects through similar means. He has only ten ministering spirits at his command. See also *ARS THEURGIA*, USIEL.

Lassal: A demon named in the *Liber de Angelis*. He is tied to the moon and its powers. He appears in a compulsion spell intended to rob a person of their will. See also *LIBER DE ANGELIS*.

Launé: This demon is described as a deceiver who will do everything possible to entrap those fool-ish enough to summon him. His name appears in Mathers's translation of the *Grimoire of Armadel*, where he is said to be the keeper of terrible mysteries. He can reputedly reveal secrets about the nature and habitation of demons, and he can also reveal the secret names of the minions of Hell. This is especially useful for those demons who underwent a significant name change as a result of their fall. See also MATHERS.

Lautrayth: In the *Munich Handbook*, Lautrayth is described as a spirit that waits upon sinners. He is called upon in a spell for obtaining an infernal steed. According to the text, when Lautrayth is called up, he comes riding a great horse. He will enchant a bridle for the one who summons him. This item will then summon a demon in the form of a horse that will provide transportation anywhere. See also *MUNICH HANDBOOK*.

Laycon: A demon named in a spell for creating books. According to the *Book of Oberon*, Laycon and several other scribal demons can speedily produce books on topics such as alchemy, nigromancy, conjuration, and the sciences. From the text of the spell, the demons seem to work overnight, leaving the finished books for their summoner in the morning. A variation of his name is given as *Lasys*. See also *BOOK OF OBERON*.

Lazaba: In the *Ars Theurgia*, Lazaba is listed among the chief dukes of the demon Raysiel, who serve this infernal king of the north during the hours of the night. As a night-demon, Lazaba appears only during the hours between sundown and sun-up. He has forty ministering spirits to attend to his needs. He is described as having an evil and obstinate nature, but he can be compelled to behave by someone who possesses both his name and his seal. See also *ARS THEURGIA*, RAYSIEL.

Demons Summoned in the Name of God

Summoning demons in the name of God may seem counterintuitive to some modern readers, but it made perfect sense in the mind of the medieval magickal practitioner. Medieval Europe was all about hierarchy. In both secular and religious society, everyone had their place in the pecking order. The legions of spirits were typically portrayed as aping human hierarchies, so all the spirits were seen as having a strict pecking order of their own. Just as a squire had to answer to his knight and a serf had to answer to the lord who owned his land, every demon (and angel) had someone up the chain they had to answer to. In order to compel and control one of these spirits, it was often enough to know the name of that spirit's superior and compel his obedience in that name.

Of course, in medieval and Renaissance Europe, there was no greater authority than the authority of God, and so most invocations went straight to the heart of the matter, compelling spirits from both Heaven and Hell in the name of the Creator. A variety of names and titles for the Almighty existed as part of the grimoiric tradition, and these were often scribed around the summoning circle while also being uttered out loud in lengthy orations. Among these, the Tetragrammaton—considered to be the most holy name of God—is the most common to appear. Other names of God used in demonic invocation in the Middle Ages and Renaissance Europe include *Adonai*, *Sabaoth*, *Elohim*, and *El Shaddai*. All of these are Jewish names for God that appear in the Old Testament. Modern exorcists operate in the shadow of this same tradition when they seek to compel demons and unclean spirits in the name of Jesus Christ.

The Seal of God as depicted in the Driscoll edition of the *Sworn Book of Honorius*. According to the text, this symbol is essential for compelling summoned spirits.

Leban: A great giant who carries people wherever they wish to go. Identified in the Elizabethan grimoire known as the *Book of Oberon*, Leban is described as a knight and a mighty soldier. Forty legions of lesser spirits serve him. In addition to carrying people, this obliging demon will also port around hills, castles, riches, and even whole mountains, placing these wherever his master commands. See also *BOOK OF OBERON*.

Lecher: While *lecher* is normally a word used for a despicably lascivious person, this demon has nothing to do with lust or sex magick. Instead, Lecher is summoned to help you make friends. He also has vast knowledge of scientific secrets. He appears as a knight with a red lion's face, and he speaks as if he's very sad. He serves in the court of the west under Paimon, where he is one of twelve high-ranking ministers. His name appears in the Elizabethan grimoire known as the *Book of Oberon*. See also *BOOK OF OBERON*, PAIMON.

Legion: In the New Testament, both Mark and Luke tell of a Gerasene man possessed by devils. The man seeks out Jesus in the hopes of being cured, and Jesus drives the demons out into a herd of swine. Before Jesus exorcises the spirit, he demands to know its name. The correct name of a demon was thought to be integral to exorcising or binding that spirit from Sumerian times onward. According to the text, the demon responds, "My name is legion, for we are many."[51] Given the time period and location of this incident, the name *legion* most likely referred to a Roman legion. A typical Roman legion numbered approximately six thousand well-armed men, and these infantry units of the Roman Empire were universally feared throughout the Mediterranean world. This

Christ casts out demons. Illustration of Epistel. Ephes. V. v. 1 from a German Bible, 1700s. Image courtesy of the Wellcome Collection, London.

biblical passage may be the reason why many grimoires portray demons as ruling over legions of lesser spirits. In his *Discoverie of Witchcraft*, Scot states that an infernal legion is comprised of 6666 spirits. See also SCOT.

Lemegeton: Known also as the *Lesser Key of Solomon*, this treatise instructs the reader in the fine art of summoning and compelling spirits. It is intricately tied to the belief, common throughout medieval Europe, that the biblical King Solomon was given power over demons and subsequently used this power to enslave a number of infernal beings to help complete the work of his great temple. Most of the current copies of this book date to the seventeenth century and are drawn from translations of a pair of manuscripts known as Sloane 3825 and Sloane 2731. These are held in a collection at the British Museum. The tradition from which the *Lemegeton* stems, however, is much older than the Sloane manuscripts. Many of the spirits that appear in this work can also be found in other manuscripts, such as the *Pseudomonarchia Daemonum*, compiled by Johannes Wierus in 1563, and the *Munich Handbook*, a fifteenth-century nec-

---

51. Mark 5:9.

romancer's handbook translated in recent years by scholar Richard Kieckhefer.

The *Lemegeton* is traditionally composed of five books: the *Goetia*, the *Ars Theurgia*, the *Pauline Art*, the *Almadel*, and the *Ars Notoria*. The *Goetia*, sometimes known as the *Theurgia-Goetia*, deals with spirits that are expressly identified as evil. The *Ars Theurgia* purports to deal with "good" demons, all of which are tied to specific directions along the points of the compass. The *Pauline Art* is concerned with the names of angels connected with the hours of the night and the day, as well as the angels of the zodiac. The *Almadel* concerns itself with the invocation of angels connected with the four quarters. The *Ars Notoria*, or *Notary Art of Solomon*, is a curious book of images and orations presented as having the ability to magickally enhance wisdom, memory, and communication skills. This is not a unique work but a style of book that was popular in the Middle Ages and Renaissance. Occultist Mitch Henson, who produced a translation of the *Lemegeton* in 1999, suggests that the *Ars Notoria* was not originally a part of the *Lesser Key* but was appended by James Turner in his 1657 edition.

As this probably suggests, the *Lemegeton* that has come down to us is not a book that was written from cover to cover by the same individual, but a compilation of a series of related manuscripts. Furthermore, not all of the books of the *Lemegeton* were composed at the same time. The *Almadel* dates internally to 1641, while the similarities between the Goetic demons and those in the *Pseudomonarchia* suggest that the *Goetia* is older by at least a hundred years. The pseudepigraphal *Testament of Solomon*, likely composed in the first few centuries of the Christian era, is certainly the inspiration, if not the source, for much of the material contained within the *Lemegeton*. If a direct line of descent connecting these books exists, however, it has been lost through the ages. See also *ARS THEURGIA, GOETIA, MUNICH HANDBOOK, WIERUS*.

Lemel: One of several demonic servitors said to fall under the command of Astaroth and Asmodeus. Lemel's name appears in the Mathers translation of the *Sacred Magic of Abramelin the Mage*, where he is made to swear allegiance to the magician as a part of the Holy Guardian Angel working. At least three other versions of the *Abramelin* material exist, and they contain variations on the spelling of many of these demon names. Both the manuscript kept at the Dresden library and the Peter Hammer edition published in Cologne give the name of this demon as *Leniel*. See also ASTAROTH, ASMODEUS, MATHERS.

Lemodac: A demon who serves Macariel, a wandering prince of the air. Lemodac is said to assume the form of a dragon with many heads, although according to the *Ars Theurgia*, he has the power to transform into a variety of shapes. He has four hundred lesser spirits at his command and is tied to no particular hour of the day or the night. Consequently, Lemodac may manifest whenever he pleases. He holds the infernal rank of duke. See also *ARS THEURGIA*, MACARIEL.

Leonard: According to Collin de Plancy's *Dictionnaire Infernal*, Leonard is the Grand Master of Sabbats and the Inspector General of sorcery, witchcraft, and the black arts. He can take many forms, but generally prefers to take on a humanoid form with goat-like qualities. He is said to have three horns and flaming eyes. He is also reputed to have a face on his rear end. He presents this to be kissed at the Sabbats. Leonard is listed in Waite's presentation of the *Grand Grimoire*, attributed incorrectly to sixteenth-century scholar Johannes

Wierus. Leonard is ranked within the top tier of this hierarchy, alongside such distinguished beings as Satan and Beelzebub. He is also accorded the rank of Knight of the Order of the Fly, a distinction allegedly established by Beelzebub. Leonard's connection with the Witches' Sabbat arises from the medieval belief that the Devil often presided over these wild nighttime orgies in the form of a goat. See also BEELZEBUB, BERBIGUIER, DE PLANCY, SATAN, WIERUS.

Lepaca: In his translation of the *Sacred Magic of Abramelin the Mage*, occultist S. L. MacGregor Mathers suggests that the name of this demon means the "opener" or "discloser." Lepaca is said to serve under the command of the infernal ruler Astaroth. A variant spelling of this name is *Lepacha*. See also ASTAROTH, MATHERS.

Leraie: The fourteenth demon of the *Goetia*. The name of this demon appears in many forms, depending on the source consulted. In Wierus's *Pseudomonarchia Daemonum*, his name is given as *Loray*. The same text suggests that he is sometimes also known as *Oray*. In Scot's *Discoverie of Witchcraft*, the name of this demon is spelled *Leraie*, which is curious, considering Scot was merely translating Wierus's *Pseudomonarchia*. In the *Goetia of Dr. Rudd*, the name is given as *Leraic*, while elsewhere in manuscripts attributed to Dr. Rudd (including the *Treatise on Angel Magic)*, it is spelled variously *Leraje* and *Leraye* and *Leraiel*. By the time it gets to Steve Savedow's *Goetic Evocation*, the name is spelled *Leriakhe*. Despite the confusion on the spelling of his name, almost all sources agree that this demon appears in the form of an archer, complete with a bow and a quiver full of arrows. He is a martial demon with the power to putrefy all wounds made by arrows. He is also said to instigate battles. He holds the rank of marquis and has

a regiment of thirty legions at his command. In the *Goetia of Dr. Rudd*, he is called *Leraic*, and he is constrained by the angel Mebahel. See also GOETIA, RUDD, SCOT, WIERUS.

Les Farfadets: The three-volume autobiography of Charles Berbiguier, a Frenchman who claimed to have been locked in a desperate struggle with the forces of Hell ever since having his cards read by a disreputable fortuneteller. Published between 1820 and 1822, this work details Berbiguier's struggles with his personal demon Rhotomago, said to serve directly beneath the arch-fiend Beelzebub. Berbiguier includes his own illustrations in the work and likely funded the publication himself. Berbiguier made a number of curious claims in his autobiography. He asserted that he maintained detailed correspondence with the various princes and dignitaries of Hell, exchanging very real, physical letters with these beings. He suspected a number of living persons to be in league with these beings and described these individuals in terms of hellish ambassadors on earth. Several of these were doctors or other functionaries that Berbiguier had run afoul of in his ongoing pursuit to prove that he was afflicted with demonic influence. Berbiguier was almost certainly delusional and mentally ill, but at least a few of his ideas about demons—including an extensive hierarchy that includes a Grand Pantler of Hell—found their way into more serious works on demonology. Notably, demonographer Collin de Plancy included Berbiguier's infernal hierarchy in his 1822 edition of his *Dictionnaire Infernal*. Although de Plancy credited Berbiguier and his work *Les Farfadets* as the source of this information, when occultist A. E. Waite reprinted this hierarchy in his presentation of the *Grand Grimoire*, he mistakenly attributed it to the sixteenth-century scholar Johannes Wierus, author of the

"The Scourge of the Goblins," Berbiguier's self-portrait from his book *Les Farfadets*. Image courtesy of Dover Publications.

Pseudomonarchia Daemonum. Waite's translation of the *Grand Grimoire* appears in his 1910 work *The Book of Black Magic and Pacts*, and can be found in a stand-alone edition reprinted by editor Darcy Kuntz. Because of Waite's citation, Berbiguier's infernal hierarchy has survived long after his life and works have been all but forgotten. See also BEELZEBUB, DE PLANCY, *GRAND GRIMOIRE*, RHOTOMAGO, WAITE, WIERUS.

Leviathan: His name means "twisted" or "coiled" in the Hebrew language. He is mentioned five times in the Bible. Oddly, Psalm 104 implies that God made Leviathan to "sport with." A description of this massive beast, given in chapter 41 of the *Book of Job*, suggests that it is a sea creature. Later Jewish myths directly identify Leviathan as a sea monster, a terrible being capable of devouring one whale a day. There is a legend tracing back to Rashi, a rabbi from eleventh-century France, who explains that God created both a male and a female leviathan, but killed the female shortly thereafter because, were these creatures to procreate, mankind could not stand against them. A further story in the Talmud suggests that on the Day of Judgment, God will slay the leviathan, using its meat to prepare a feast for the righteous and using its hide to create the tent wherein this feast will be laid out. In many stories, Leviathan is pitted against the great beast Behemoth. In the trial of Urbain Grandier, a pact was produced, which was purported to be Grandier's contract with Satan for his immortal soul. Grandier, a Jesuit-trained priest, was burned at the stake in 1634 in the French town of Loudun, after having allegedly orchestrated the possession of a number of nuns under his care. Leviathan was one of several distinguished devils who supposedly signed his name to Grandier's pact. Leviathan is also mentioned in the *Sixth and Seventh Books of Moses*, in connection with a spell. There is a high likelihood that Leviathan is a holdover from early Babylonian influences and is in fact a Jewish version of the Babylonian and Sumerian monster Tiamat, also connected with water. In Mathers's translation of the *Sacred Magic of Abramelin the Mage*, Leviathan is identified as one of the four principal spirits, ranked alongside

Kiss my . . . er, Goat?

People were obsessed with witches in the Middle Ages. Everyone was afraid that their neighbor might be a witch, and this fear exploded so completely out of proportion that men, women, and even children were accused, tried, and executed for witchcraft. Witchcraft was a confusing subject for common people, especially given the many powers attributed to the witch. So authors like Ambrosian monk Francesco Maria Guazzo put together books like the *Compendium Maleficarum*, explaining exactly what witches did and why. Of course, Guazzo's book, as well as the more famous *Malleus Maleficarum* ("Hammer of Witches"), contained a great deal of odd notions—almost none of which were actually practiced by anyone save for the witches dreamed up in the lurid imaginations of the authors. Perhaps one of the most bizarre traditions attributed by these books to witches was the Devil's Kiss.

Known as the *osculum infame*, or the shameful kiss, this was supposedly the traditional greeting of the witch. If the various treatises written on witches at the time are to be believed, witches would come from far and wide to attend the Witches' Sabbat. At this event, which amounted to a wild, naked party in the woods (usually with some child sacrifice thrown in for kicks), witches would meet with their lord and master, Satan. Satan apparently liked getting a little kiss from his minions to show that they cared, but since he was Satan, he didn't want just any kiss. The *osculum infame* was a kiss planted directly on the Devil's hindparts. When the Devil didn't show up looking like a human being, often this shameful kiss was supposed to be applied to the ass-end of a goat. A few confessions of witches—inevitably derived through torture—as-

sert that the kiss might also be applied to the backside of a cat. Authors like Guazzo and his contemporaries Heinrich Kramer and Jacob Sprenger, the Catholic Inquisitors who wrote the *Malleus Maleficarum*, were obviously very concerned about the dangers of witchcraft. Reading their works through the lens of time, however, it is tempting to worry more about the authors themselves.

Depiction of the *osculum infame*, or "shameful kiss," supposedly bestowed by witches upon the Devil's hindquarters. From Guazzo's *Compendium Maleficarum*, courtesy of Dover Publications.

Lucifer, Satan, and Belial. See also BEHEMOTH, BELIAL, LUCIFER, SATAN.

Lewteffar: This demon's name may be a play on the more familiar *Lucifer*. Lewteffar appears in the Elizabethan grimoire known as the *Book of Oberon*, where he is described as a prince reigning over twenty legions. With the head of a devil and the tail of a viper, his appearance is bizarre enough, but he is also crowned with a rainbow. He has fiery, stinking breath and his chest is an open wound. Additionally, he has hands like a bear and feet like those of a mole. A third eye peers from his forehead and all his eyes are starry. He will not cross running water. The text warns that he is a liar and grows very desperate when pressed. Among his powers is the ability to inflict madness and discord. He is also extremely learned and can teach all aspects of necromancy, astronomy, astrology, geomancy, and the liberal sciences. He provides riches in addition to worldly influence, and he can also make women fall in love. For all of this, he requires sacrifice and will only appear during the seventh hour of the day. He is given two alternate names: Falcas and Abarak. *Abarak* is apparently a secret name, for the text says that even when pressed, he will not admit to it. Compare this secret name to *Abraxas*, a divine being associated with the Gnostics. See also *BOOK OF OBERON*, FALCAS, LUCIFER.

Liber de Angelis: The *Liber de Angelis* is a book of spells and spirits that was kept in the collection of Osbern Bokenham, an English Augustinian friar who lived in the first half of the 1400s. Although the *Liber de Angelis* is sometimes mistakenly attributed to him, it was not written by him. The book was not even transcribed by Bokenham; it simply existed in his collection of books. The book was probably produced between 1441 and 1445, and there is evidence that it was compiled from various sources rather than copied directly from a previously existing manuscript. Although the work is pseudonymously attributed to an individual named Messayaac (a transcription of the Hebrew word for *Messiah*), little is known of its true author or authors. The book is kept at Cambridge University under the designation MS Dd. xi. 45, and it was presented to the public through the *Magic in History* series published by Penn State Press.

Liber Officiorum Spirituum: A book sourced by Johannes Wierus for his *Pseudomonarchia Daemonum*. Its title translates to the *Book of the Offices of the Spirits*. This compilation of demon names was appended to Wierus's larger work *De Praestigiis Daemonum*, published in 1653. Neither the author nor the exact date of publication are known for the *Liber Officiorum Spirituum*, but considering its inclusion in Wierus's work, it is safe to say that it predates the 1650s. Occult scholar Joseph Peterson points out that there are redactions and variations in the names of the demons as they appear in Wierus's work, and this suggests that the *Liber Officiorum Spirituum* was part of a fairly old tradition even when Wierus was sourcing it. A copy of this book likely appears in Trithemius's catalogue of occult works under the title *De Officio Spirituum*. This places its publication to some time prior to 1508, when Trithemius's catalogue was compiled. It is entirely possible that Wierus learned of the book through Trithemius, who had served as the mentor of Wierus's own mentor in the occult arts, Henry Cornelius Agrippa. Trithemius describes the book as an execrable and totally diabolical work. It also appears to be the source of the French *Livre des esperitz*. See also AGRIPPA, TRITHEMIUS, WIERUS, *LIVRE DES ESPERITZ*.

Liblel: A demon under the dominion of Malgaras, infernal king of the west. Liblel appears in the *Ars Theurgia*, where he is said to rule over thirty lesser spirits. He holds the rank of chief duke and serves during the hours of the night. See also *ARS THEURGIA*, MALGARAS.

Licanen: A demon in the *Sacred Magic of Abramelin the Mage*. He is said to work as a servitor of the greater demon Beelzebub. This spelling of the demon's name appears in the 1898 Mathers translation. In other versions of the work, the name is given as *Eralicarison*. See also BEELZEBUB, MATHERS.

Ligilos: One of the demons said to serve the infernal king Ariton, Ligilos is named in the *Sacred Magic of Abramelin the Mage*, but he appears only in the copies of this work that are kept in the German libraries at Wolfenbüttel and Dresden. See also ARITON, MATHERS.

Lilith: A demon with a long and colorful history who is currently depicted as the night-demon *par excellence*. Lilith can be traced back to the mythology of the Babylonians and Sumerians, where she appears most recognizably as the *Ardat Lili*, a maiden ghost that preys upon men in their sleep. Supposedly, this being died without first tasting the pleasures of sex, and henceforth she yearns for what she could not have. Her amorous embraces were considered fatal, however, and so this night-dwelling being was greatly feared. Although the *Ardat Lili* was often thought to haunt the night, Lilith's connection to night was most likely established by the similarity of her name with that of the Hebrew word for "night," *laileh* or *layla*. Lilith's name did not originate in Hebrew, however, and so this connection is somewhat misleading. Her name is more properly derived from the Su-

merian word *lil*, meaning "storm." In this respect, she fits in neatly with traditional Sumerian demonology, where many demons were associated with destructive forces such as storms, earthquakes, and disease.

In her earliest days, Lilith was not a singular being. Rather, the *lilin* or *lilitu* were a class of demons believed to haunt the deserts and wastelands. Perhaps because of this, Lilith is often associated with owls and other wild beasts. In Isaiah 34:14 (King James Version), the name *Lilith* is translated directly as "screech owl." Her connection with birds may trace back to one of her first appearances in written language. One of the first known references to Lilith in literature appears in the *Epic of Gilgamesh*. Here, she appears as a demon who inhabits the Huluppa-Tree along with a dragon and something called the Zu-bird. When the Sumerian hero Gilgamesh slays the dragon that has curled up around the foot of the tree, Lilith is said to tear her house down and flee into the wilderness. This ancient passage may very well have established many of Lilith's traditional associations, from birds to dragons to her abode in the wild spaces of the world.

In later years, Lilith became central to Jewish demonology. In the Talmudic Erebim (18b), it is said that while Adam was under the curse (before the birth of Seth), he sired demons—both *shedim* and *lilin*. *Lilin* is a plural form of Lilith. There is a similar passage in the Nidda (16b).[52] This was during the time immediately following the death of Abel and the banishment of Cain. For one hundred and thirty years, Adam would not lie with his wife, Eve. Lilith came to him instead and bore all manner of demons by his seed. Later rabbinical

---

52. Moncure Daniel Conway, *Demonology and Devil-Lore,* vol. 2, p. 92.

This figure from a Sumerian bas-relief is frequently identified as Lilith. In one Jewish myth, after uttering the *Shemhamphorash*, Lilith grew wings and flew from Eden. Courtesy of Dover Publications.

sources identified her as the first wife of Adam, cast from the Garden because she would not submit completely to his rule. Here, again, she fled into the wilderness, where many traditions say she became the mother of demons after coupling with fallen angels like Lucifer and Samael. Jewish folklore, in works like the Haggadah and the *Chroni-*

cles of Jerahmeel, often presents her as the consort of these fallen angels.

Certainly, Lilith was a being greatly feared by Jews, as numerous protective amulets have survived designed to keep her evils at bay. She was said to have a particular fondness for attacking infants and mothers in childbirth, and the profusion of Lilith talismans intended to protect these two classes of people certainly attest to this belief. Like her predecessor, the *Ardat Lili*, Lilith was also thought to attack men, seducing them and luring them to their deaths. Although the development of the Christian traditions of Lilith remains hazy, she is eventually depicted as the consort of Lucifer or Satan. Although she does not appear by name in the *Testament of Solomon*, it is worth noting that several of the female demons described demonstrate very Lilith-like qualities. Given the profusion of names attributed to this being, it is not beyond the realm of possibility that each of these are simply variations of Lilith appearing under different names.

Like many of the demons with roots in Jewish folklore, Lilith still managed to make her way into the predominantly Christian grimoiric tradition of medieval and Renaissance Europe. The *Munich Handbook* is representative of these works. In this fifteenth-century German book, Lilith features in a spell for enchanting a mirror. Appropriately enough, this item is called the "Mirror of Lilith." Her name in this work is rendered variously *Lylet* and *Bylet*, a detail that may demonstrate an association between Lilith and the demon Bileth, named throughout the grimoiric material. See also BILETH, LUCIFER, *MUNICH HANDBOOK*, SAMAEL, SATAN.

Lirion: A servant of the four demonic princes of the cardinal directions, Lirion can be summoned and compelled in the name of his superiors: Oriens, Paimon, Ariton, and Amaimon. Lirion's name appears in an extensive list of demons recorded in Mathers's translation of the *Sacred Magic of Abramelin the Mage*. Mathers suggests that the demon's name comes from a Greek word meaning "lily." See also AMAIMON, ARITON, MATHERS, ORIENS, PAIMON.

Lirochi: Possibly derived from a Hebrew term meaning "in tenderness," the name of this demon appears in Mathers's translation of the *Sacred Magic of Abramelin the Mage*. Here, Lirochi appears among the demonic servitors of the arch-fiend Beelzebub. The version of the *Abramelin* material kept at the Wolfenbüttel library in Germany records this name as *Liroki*. See also BEELZEBUB, MATHERS.

Livre des esperitz: Catalogued as Cambridge, Trinity College, ms. O.8.29, fos 179–182vo, this is the oldest known treatise of demonic magick to survive in the French language. Dated to the end of the fifteenth or beginning of the sixteenth century, it is slightly older than the influential *Pseudomonarchia Daemonum*. The two texts clearly share the same root source, as they have numerous names in common. There is enough divergence to demonstrate that one is not merely a translation of the other. Of the two, the *Livre des esperitz* appears to be more complete, particularly in its opening, where Satan, Lucifer, and Beelzebub are directly named as the prime rulers of all the infernal spirits. As such, the French text provides greater insight into the uppermost hierarchies, details that Wierus intentionally left out so his work could not be used for summoning. Currently the only available version of the *Livre des esperitz* is a French transcription by Jean-Patrice Boudet, published in the spring 2003 edition of the academic journal *Mediévales*. See also AMAIMON, BEELZEBUB, EGYN, LUCIFER, ORIENS, PAIMON, *PSEUDOMONARCHIA DAEMONUM*, SATAN.

Locater: Another demon named in connection with the *Sacred Magic of Abramelin the Mage* whose name varies depending on the source material. In the fifteenth-century French manuscript sourced by Mathers, the name is *Locater*. In the Peter Hammer edition, it appears as *Lochaty*. In the versions kept at the Wolfenbüttel and Dresden libraries, the name is presented as *Lachatyl*. As all of these texts are distant copies of an original dating to the fourteenth century, there is no way to know for certain which is correct. All texts agree, however, that this demon functions as a servant of the infernal ruler Magoth. Mathers's text asserts that he also serves Kore, who is normally seen as a Greek goddess. See also KORE, MAGOTH, MATHERS.

Lodiel: A chief duke in the court of the infernal prince Dorochiel, Lodiel is said to manifest only in a specific hour between midnight and dawn. According to the *Ars Theurgia*, this night-demon oversees a total of four hundred ministering spirits that carry out his commands. He is tied to the region of the west. See also *ARS THEURGIA*, DOROCHIEL.

Lomiol: One of a number of demons governed by Oriens, Paimon, Ariton, and Amaimon. Lomiol appears in an extensive list of demons in the *Sacred Magic of Abramelin the Mage*. See also AMAIMON, ARITON, MATHERS, ORIENS, PAIMON.

Lomor: According to the *Ars Theurgia*, Lomor serves the demon Dorochiel. He functions in the capacity of chief duke and he is tied to the hours of the day. He is one of a number of demons who serve under Dorochiel in the court of the west. He oversees the governance of four hundred lesser spirits of his own. See also *ARS THEURGIA*, DOROCHIEL.

Loriol: A demon whose name is thought to relate to a Hebrew word meaning "unto horror." Loriol is said to serve the arch-demons Astaroth and Asmodeus. His name can be found in the *Sacred Magic of Abramelin the Mage*. See also ASTAROTH, ASMODEUS, MATHERS.

Losimon: According to Mathers's translation of the *Sacred Magic of Abramelin the Mage*, Losimon is one of a number of demons who serve beneath the four infernal princes of the cardinal directions. As such, he can be summoned and compelled in the name of his superiors: Oriens, Paimon, Ariton, and Amaimon. See also AMAIMON, ARITON, MATHERS, ORIENS, PAIMON.

Luciel: A demon who appears as a serpent with a woman's head, Luciel is one of twelve dukes who serve the greater demon Hydriel. Luciel and his fellow dukes are described in the *Ars Theurgia*, where they are said to possess courteous and benevolent natures, despite their monstrous appearance. Luciel has a great love for damp places like swamps or bogs and has one thousand three hundred and twenty ministering spirits to carry out his commands. See also *ARS THEURGIA*, HYDRIEL.

Lucifer: Lucifer has come to be one of the most recognizable names for the Devil. He is depicted variously as Satan, the Serpent in Genesis, and the Dragon in Revelation. The name *Lucifer* itself is derived from a passage in Isaiah 14:12, translated in the King James Version of the Bible to read: *How art thou fallen from heaven, O Lucifer, son of the morning! how art thou cut down to the ground, which didst weaken the nations!* The word translated here as Lucifer is the Hebrew *helal*, meaning "morning star." The word *Lucifer* itself comes from the

Latin Vulgate version of the Bible. In Latin, *lucifer* means "light-bearer." At the time that the Latin Vulgate version of the Bible was being translated, the word *lucifer* referred specifically to the planet Venus in its capacity as the morning star. Saint Jerome, the translator of this passage, was not in error when he parsed the Hebrew *helal* for the Latin *lucifer*, as both words refer directly to an astrological phenomenon, not an individual. Later readings of the passage, however, interpreted *Lucifer* as a proper name. Notably, most modern biblical scholars assert that this passage in Isaiah referenced not the fall of an angel, but the fall of the king of Babylon. A few lines earlier, in Isaiah 14:4, the portion of the text that includes the reference to the fallen morning star is introduced as an extensive taunt to be taken up against the king of Babylon. Despite this, early Church fathers took Isaiah 14:12 as a direct reference to Satan, connecting it with Luke 10:18, where Jesus declares, "I saw Satan fall like lightning from heaven." The only real connection between these two passages, at least linguistically, is the reference to a fall. Saint Paul helps enable the association between Satan and the Light-Bearer with his passage in 2 Corinthians 11:14 that says, ". . . even Satan disguises himself as an angel of light." Through these three passages, plus the story in Revelation where the Devil is cast out of Heaven, a rich mythic history about Lucifer has evolved.

This mythos is based more on material written *about* the Bible than upon the biblical passages themselves, but this has done nothing to dampen its allure. According to this mythic history, Lucifer was once the foremost angel in Heaven, second only to God himself. He was known as the Light-Bearer and the Morning Star, and he was the most beautiful of all the angels in the Heavenly Host.

His sin, however, was pride, and eventually this led him to rebel against his creator. There was a war in Heaven, and Michael the Archangel led the troops of the Lord against the rebels. Lucifer was vanquished, and cast out of Heaven. Following the story recorded in Revelation, a third of the angels fell with him. Drawing upon material from the lost *Book of Enoch* as well as further material from the *Book of Revelation*, Lucifer was then cast into the Abyss. Here he was bound until the final Judgment, but his war with Heaven was far from over. From his new place in Hell, Lucifer is believed to lash out at the mortal world, seeking to torture and torment humanity, with the ultimate goal of acquiring human souls in order to keep them from God. In this ongoing war with Heaven and humanity, Lucifer bears much in common with the figure of Belial. This demon appears in certain fragments of the Dead Sea Scrolls. In the mythology of the Essenes, Belial was deeply embroiled in a war between the Sons of Darkness and the Sons of Light. In the Qumran fragment known as the *Visions of Amram*, Belial is given the title "Prince of Darkness," a title often later accorded to Lucifer. According to the *Visions of Amram*, Belial leads the forces of darkness against the angel Michael, who heads the armies of the Light. Another name given to this "Prince of Darkness" in these texts is *Malchiresha*. Although the manuscripts at Qumran were lost for many centuries, the influence of the Essene eschatology is clear in the lingering mythos that surrounds Lucifer.

Interestingly, among certain sects of Gnostic Christians, Lucifer was not seen as evil at all, but instead was depicted as the first-born son of God who sought to save humanity with the gift of knowledge. In Mathers's translation of the *Sacred Magic of Abramelin the Mage*, Lucifer is identified as

Lucifer contemplates the serpent. From a nineteenth-century edition of Milton's *Paradise Lost*, illustrated by Gustav Doré.

one of the four principal spirits, ranked alongside Leviathan, Satan, and Belial. He is invoked several times in the *Munich Handbook*. In the *True Keys of Solomon*, Lucifer is one of three demons said to command all others. In this text, Lucifer rules over all the demons who inhabit Europe and Asia. In later legends focusing on the demon Lilith, Lucifer is often presented as her unholy consort.

The seventeenth-century Venetian grimoire *Clavicula Salomonis de Secretis (Secrets of Solomon)* confirms Lucifer as Emperor of Hell, who has charge of all spirits in Europe and Asia. In this text, when Lucifer manifests, he takes the form of a beautiful boy whose eyes flash red when he's angered. His name and sigil are used in a spell to bring snow. An "earthly" demon, he is not limited to mere visions but can also take physical form. In the French *Livre des esperitz*, Lucifer governs the west, directly overseeing King Paimon. His name appears in the *Book of Oberon* under several variant spellings, including *Lucipher* and *Lucypher*. In that grimoire, he is called the father of all devils, but it is not possible to summon Lucifer himself, as he is bound in the depths of Hell. Rather, his name is invoked to keep all the other demons in line. In this, the *Book of Oberon* compares him to Tantavalerion. See also BELIAL, LEVIATHAN, LILITH, MALCHIRESHA, *MUNICH HANDBOOK*, SATAN, TANTAVALERION, *TRUE KEYS*.

Lucifuge Rofocale: One of six superior spirits named in the *Grand Grimoire*, a text attributed to Antonio Venitiana del Rabina. Lucifuge Rofocale is named as the Prime Minister of Hell, and he is depicted in illustrations within this text as a bandy-legged demon with goat's hooves, wearing what appears to be a jester's cap. He stands by a fire and grips a bag of gold in one hand and a hoop of some sort in the other. He is said to hold dominion over three of the traditional demons from the *Goetia*—namely, Bael, Agares, and Marbas. Supposedly, he has been entrusted by Lucifer himself with control over all the wealth and treasure of the earth. Additionally, Lucifuge Rofocale, at least within the context of the *Grand Grimoire*, appears to act as Lucifer's go-between. This seems appropriate, given his stated position of Prime Minister. When calling upon Lucifer, who sits at the very top of the demonic hierarchy depicted in Venitiana's work, the magician addresses Lucifuge to forge the pact. Lucifuge is probably derived from the Latin word *lucifugus*, meaning "light-fleeing." See also AGARES, BAEL, *GOETIA*, *GRAND GRIMOIRE*, LUCIFER, MARBAS.

Lucubar: A great duke who makes people subtle of wit and full of great ingenuity. He can transmute lead into gold or pewter into purest silver. The *Livre des esperitz*, in which he appears, assigns him no legions of subordinates, although this may simply be an oversight on the part of the scribe. See also *LIVRE DES ESPERITZ*.

Luesaf: A demon governed by the infernal ruler Magoth. In the Mathers translation of the *Sacred Magic of Abramelin the Mage*, Luesaf is said also to serve Kore, another name for the Greek consort of Hades, Persephone. In the other versions of the *Abramelin* material that exist, the name of this demon is spelled *Mesaf*. See also KORE, MAGOTH, MATHERS.

Lundo: A name associated with the *Sacred Magic of Abramelin the Mage*, Lundo appears only in the version of that work translated by occultist S. L. MacGregor Mathers. The demon is reputedly subservient to the infernal rulers Asmodeus and Magoth. See also ASMODEUS, MAGOTH, MATHERS.

Luziel: One of twelve infernal dukes said to serve the demon Amenadiel, Emperor of the West. Luziel's name appears in the *Ars Theurgia*, traditionally included as the second book in the grimoire known as the *Lemegeton*. Luziel commands an impressive number of lesser spirits, having no fewer than three thousand eight hundred and eighty beneath him. See also AMENADIEL, *ARS THEURGIA*.

Lwnael: A demon with a particularly unpronounceable name, Lwnael appears in the *Ars Theurgia*, where he is said to serve in the hierarchy of the north beneath the infernal king Baruchas. Lwnael himself holds the title of duke and has thousands of lesser spirits at his command. He is bound only to manifest during the hours and minutes that fall in the thirteenth portion of time when the day is divided into fifteen equal portions. See also *ARS THEURGIA*, BARUCHAS.

Lytay: According to the *Munich Handbook*, this demon of illusion can help to conjure a whole castle out of thin air. This is reputed not only to be a visible illusion but one that deceives all of the senses. Lytay can only be called upon to achieve this impressive task in a remote and secluded location. The text says that he should be summoned with an offering of milk and honey on the tenth night of the moon. His name is also spelled *Lytoy*. See also *MUNICH HANDBOOK*.

Lytim: One of the many alternate names of the demon Lilith. This version of her name appears in conjunction with a spell known as the "Mirror of Lilith." Detailed in the fifteenth-century magickal text known as the *Munich Handbook*, the "Mirror of Lilith" uses the invocation of demons, including Lilith herself, to charm a glass so it may be used as a scrying mirror. See also LILITH, *MUNICH HANDBOOK*.

Lyut: A demon serving in the hierarchy of Harthan, an infernal king of the element of water. Lyut is also affiliated with the region of the west. This demon's name appears in the Driscoll edition of the *Sworn Book*, a fourteenth-century text that deals with the summoning of both angels and demons. According to this text, when Lyut manifests, he has a mottled complexion with a large and ample body. By nature, he is witty and agreeable but also somewhat jealous. He can help others avenge wrongs. He is capable of moving things from place to place and providing a cover of darkness. He is said to be one of several spirits that can be summoned with the aid of special perfumes. See also HARTHAN, *SWORN BOOK*.

Mabakiel: A name thought to be related to words for "weeping" and "lamentation," Mabakiel is defined in the *Sacred Magic of Abramelin the Mage* as translated by occultist S. L. MacGregor Mathers. According to this text, Mabakiel is governed by the infernal rulers Asmodeus and Magoth. See also AS-MODEUS, MAGOTH, MATHERS.

Macariel: The ninth spirit in the order of the so-called wandering princes from the *Ars Theurgia*. Macariel is said to appear in diverse forms but most commonly assumes the form of a dragon with multiple heads. Each of these heads has the comely face of a woman. He is attended by dukes and many inferior spirits, of which his twelve chief dukes are named in the text. Despite his often monstrous appearance, he is described as possessing a basically good nature. In another portion of the same text, Macariel appears again. Here he is described as a mighty duke who serves the prince Icosiel. He has two thousand two hundred lesser spirits to serve him. This version of Macariel de-

lights in houses and often manifests in private homes. Macariel is also named in the *Steganographia* of Johannes Trithemius, a work dating to the end of the 1400s. See also *ARS THEURGIA*, ICOSIEL.

Maccathiel: The name of this demon is thought to mean "the retribution of God." As such, he is a fallen angel in charge of vengeance. Maccathiel is named in Moncure Daniel Conway's two-volume work, *Demonology and Devil-Lore*, published in 1881. Conway includes Maccathiel—along with Samael, Azazel, and Azael—as four demons who personify elemental forces of the universe. See also AZAEL, AZAZEL, SAMAEL.

Machin: A great duke who appears in the guise of a powerful man, Machin teaches the virtues of herbs and gems. He is named in the sixteenth-century French grimoire *Livre des esperitz*, where it is said he can also transport people instantly from place to place. He has thirty-seven legions of ministering spirits beneath him. His name is likely an alternate form of *Bathin*. See also BATHIN, *LIVRE DES ESPERITZ*.

Madail: In his 1898 translation of the *Sacred Magic of Abramelin the Mage*, Mathers lists this demon among those commanded by Magoth and Kore. He suggests that Madail's name means "to draw out from" or "to consume." See also KORE, MAGOTH, MATHERS.

Mador: Named in the *Ars Theurgia*, Mador is a duke serving the demon-prince Cabariel in the hierarchy of the west. Associated with night, he is known to be a deceiver who misleads those who work with him. As a demon of some rank, he oversees fifty lesser spirits, all of which are as false and misleading as he is. Further in the same manuscript, he appears again as a servant of the demon Demoriel, Emperor of the North. Here, Mador is a duke with one thousand one hundred and forty lesser spirits at his command. He is far more agreeable in this incarnation. See also *ARS THEURGIA*, CABARIEL, DEMORIEL.

Madriel: According to the *Ars Theurgia*, Madriel is a demon with the title of duke. He is governed by the infernal king Pamersiel, who is the first and chief spirit of the east beneath Emperor Carnesiel. Madriel and his fellow dukes are foul and ill-tempered spirits. They are lofty and arrogant, thoroughly evil, and given to deceit. Despite this, the *Ars Theurgia* suggests that they can be useful in driving off other spirits of darkness. Madriel and his fellows are especially useful in chasing away any spirits that haunt houses. See also *ARS THEURGIA*, CARNESIEL, PAMERSIEL.

Madyconn: A demonic king who serves the great king Amaimon, ruler of all spirits of the south. When Amaimon is summoned, Madyconn appears as herald, along with Emlon and Ocarbydatonn.

This hierarchy appears in the *Book of Oberon*. See also AMAIMON, *BOOK OF OBERON*, EMLON, OCARBYDATONN.

Mafalac: The name of this demon may come from a Hebrew term meaning "a fragment." In the Mathers translation of the *Sacred Magic of Abramelin the Mage*, Mafalac is reputed to be ruled by the demon Oriens, one of the four infernal princes of the cardinal directions. See also MATHERS, ORIENS.

Mafayr: A demon whose name and seal appear in the *Ars Theurgia*, Mafayr is a duke who serves beneath Armadiel, an infernal king who rules in the northeast. Mafayr is tied to the hours and minutes that fall into the fourteenth portion of time if the day is divided into fifteen equal parts. He will not manifest himself beyond this very specific time. When he appears, he is attended by eighty-four ministering spirits who serve to carry out his wishes. See also ARMADIEL, *ARS THEURGIA*.

Mafrus: One of a thousand chief dukes ruled by the demon-king Symiel during the hours of the night, Mafrus is described as being stubborn and reluctant to appear to mortals, even when summoned—at least according to the *Ars Theurgia*. He holds sway over seventy ministering spirits of his own. He serves in the region of the north. See also *ARS THEURGIA*, SYMIEL.

Magael: One of twelve chief dukes who serve the infernal king Dorochiel in the hours of the day. Through his allegiance to Dorochiel, he is affiliated with the west. Magael has forty servants and will only appear in daylight hours before noon. His name, as well as the seal that summons him and binds him, appears in the seventeenth-century text known as the *Ars Theurgia*. See also *ARS THEURGIA*, DOROCHIEL.

Webbed, cloven, or clawed feet, horns, and other physical aberrations were often attributed to demons as outward expressions of their corrupt natures. Image: Tomb of the Demon Queen, 2015, by Joseph Vargo.

Magalast: According to the *Sacred Magic of Abramelin the Mage*, this demon is ruled by Beelzebub. Occultist S. L. MacGregor Mathers suggests that his name may mean "greatly" or "hugely." See also BEELZEBUB, MATHERS.

Mageyne: This demon shows up in the form of a hedgehog. Possibly intended to be called upon as a familiar spirit, Mageyne is said to make an excellent companion. According to the *Book of Oberon*, he is a domestic demon of hearth and home and will assist his summoner with husbandry and other work around the homestead. Although he is not attributed any specific rank, he is said to have twenty legions of lesser spirits at his beck and call. Mageyne's appearance, coupled with his domestic duties, makes it tempting to identify him as a demonized member of the faerie courts, possibly a pixie or a brownie—a type of fey rather famous for doing chores around the farm. To a casual reader, this confusion of fey and demon might seem strange, but even a few hundred years ago, the dividing lines between different classes of supernatural beings were not as concrete as they are perceived to be now. The *Book of Oberon* in particular is noteworthy for openly blurring the line between faeries and demons. The text includes, among other things, an extensive ritual for summoning and constraining the "demon" Oberion, who is also identified within the text as the king of the faeries. See also BOOK OF OBERON.

Maggid: Given as *Maggias* in the 1720 Dresden library version of the *Sacred Magic of Abramelin the Mage*, the Mathers translation of this work related the name of this demon with a Greek term meaning "precious things." Maggid is one of several demons said to serve the arch-fiend Asmodeus. See also ASMODEUS, MATHERS.

Magiros: A demon ruled by Asmodeus and Magoth. Another variant of his name is *Magyros*. The name is of this demon may be related to the word *magus*, meaning "mage" or "sorcerer." Magiros appears in the *Sacred Magic of Abramelin the Mage*. See also ASMODEUS, MAGOTH, MATHERS.

Magni: This name may possibly be derived from the Latin word *magnus*, meaning "great." Magni appears in the *Ars Theurgia* and is listed among the many chief dukes who serve the infernal prince Usiel. According to this text, Magni is a revealer of hidden things, and he can also hide away treasure, enchanting it so it may not be discovered or stolen. He serves his infernal master during the hours of the day and has forty lesser spirits to carry out his commands. He serves in the region of the west. See also *ARS THEURGIA*, USIEL.

Magog: A biblical place-name that typically occurs in conjunction with *Gog*. Magog is first referenced in Ezekiel 38 and 39, where the Son of Man is urged to "set thy face against Gog and the land of Magog." Revelation 20:7 contains the following reference: "Satan shall be loosed out of his prison and shall go forth and seduce the nations which are over the four quarters of the earth, Gog and Magog: And shall gather them together to battle . . ." Neither Ezekiel nor Revelation are very clear as to whether Gog and Magog are intended to represent a literal ruler and his lands or something more figurative. The only thing that is obvious from the biblical passages is that Gog and Magog are opposed to the children of Israel. Later, in the *Book of Revelation*, this is taken to mean that they stand in opposition to the Church. Over time, both Gog and Magog have developed into individual demon names. They are typically depicted as giants.

The names have made their way into the demonology of the grimoires, although they are often rendered *Guth* and *Maguth* or *Magoth*. According to the Mathers translation of the *Sacred Magic of Abramelin the Mage*, Magog is one of the demonic servitors of the arch-fiends Asmodeus and Magoth (who is, himself, merely a variation on the name *Magog*). Interestingly, the list of demons under Asmodeus and Magoth appears only in the fifteenth-century French manuscript that served as Mathers's source and one other version of the *Abramelin* material kept at the Wolfenbüttel library in Germany.

Magog, under the guise of *Maguth*, also appears in the *Sworn Book of Honorius*. In the Joseph Peterson translation of this work, Maguth is a minister of Formione, king of the spirits of Jupiter. Here, he has the power to inspire positive emotions such as love, gladness, and joy. He can also help people to gain status in the eyes of others. When this version of the demon manifests, he takes on a body the color of the heavens. He is also connected with Thursdays and the north wind. Another variation on this name is *Magot*. See also ASMODEUS, FORMIONE, GOG, GUTH, MAGOTH, MATHERS, *SWORN BOOK*.

Magoth: A demon identified in the *Sacred Magic of Abramelin the Mage* as one of eight infernal sub-princes ruling beneath the four principal spirits Lucifer, Leviathan, Satan, and Belial. Occultist S. L. MacGregor Mathers relates this demon's name to the French word *magot*, often used in fairy tales to denote an evil elf or dwarf. Mathers also relates it to the word *magus*, meaning "wizard" or "magician." According to the *Abramelin* material, Magoth has the power to hinder operations of magick and necromancy. He can bring books and produce lavish banquets of food. He also has the ability to cause comedies, operas, and dances to appear for the amusement of those who call him. Through his powers of illusion, the demon can also transform someone's appearance. Magoth oversees a vast number of spirits, and each of these can perform acts of magick similar to those described in this demon's sphere. In some versions of the *Abramelin* material, the demon's name is spelled *Maguth*. Magoth is a version of the biblical *Magog*. See also BELIAL, LEVIATHAN, LUCIFER, MAGOG, MATHERS, SATAN.

Mahazael: According to the Mathers edition of the *Sacred Magic of Abramelin the Mage*, this demon's

Eight Demonic Princes of the *Magus*

In 1801, an aspiring occultist by the name of Francis Barrett published a book on demons, hermetic magick, and occult philosophy entitled *The Magus: Or the Celestial Intelligencer*. A compilation of several sources on magick, *The Magus* is probably most memorable for its information on summoning demons. Like many authors on the subject of demonology, Barrett offers his own take on the demonic hierarchy, naming eight demonic princes and attributing to them power over some evil concept or group of people:

* Mammon: seducers
* Asmodai: vile revenges
* Satan: witches and warlocks
* Pithius: liars and liar spirits
* Belial: fraud and injustice
* Merihem: pestilence and spirits that cause pestilence
* Abaddon: war, evil against good
* Astaroth: inquisitors and accusers

Barrett's list is an incomplete echo of a nine-tiered demonic hierarchy appearing in the seventeenth-century grimoire known as *Janua Magica Reserata*.

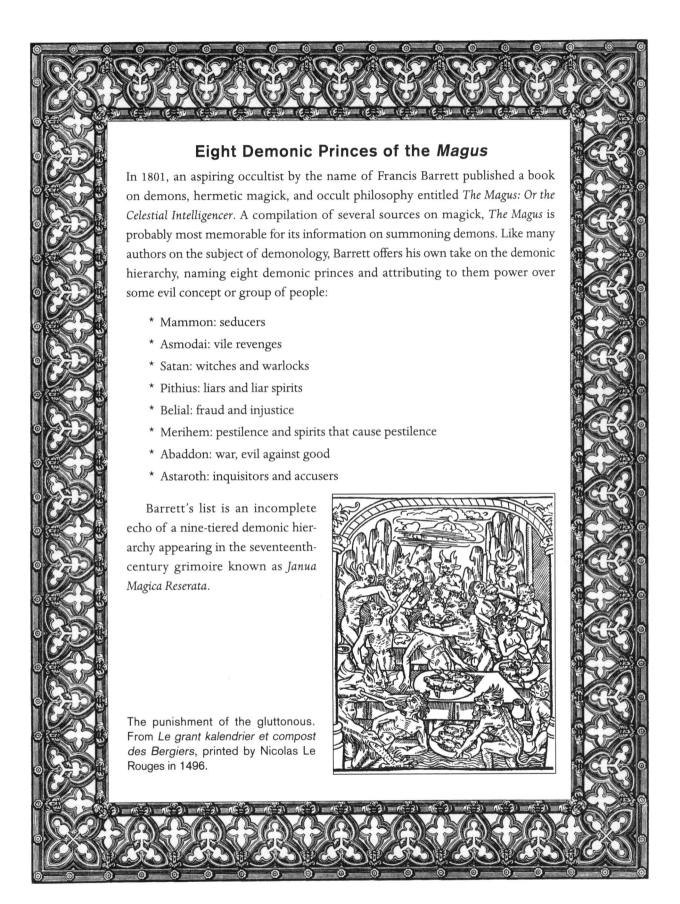

The punishment of the gluttonous. From *Le grant kalendrier et compost des Bergiers*, printed by Nicolas Le Rouges in 1496.

name means "the Devourer." In his *Three Books of Occult Philosophy*, Henry Cornelius Agrippa identifies Mahazael as the Hebrew equivalent of the demon *Egin*, or Ariton, king of the north. Mathers was likely drawing upon Agrippa's work when he presented Mahazael as an alternate name for this demon in his commentary on the *Abramelin* material. In Godwin's *Cabalistic Encyclopedia*, Mahazael is listed as a demonic prince presiding over the element of earth. Mahazael also appears as a ruler of this element in the 1505 *Faustbuch, Magiae Naturalis et Innatural*. See also AGRIPPA, ARITON, MATHERS.

Mahue: One of twelve infernal dukes in the court of Maseriel said to serve that demon during the hours of the day. Mahue's name and seal appear in the *Ars Theurgia*, where he rules over thirty lesser spirits of his own. He is affiliated with the direction of the south. See also *ARS THEURGIA*, MASERIEL.

Maisadul: A demon connected with the *Sacred Magic of Abramelin the Mage*, whose name is spelled variously *Masadul* and *Mahadul*, depending on the source material. Maisadul is said to serve the demon Magoth. In the fifteenth-century French manuscript sourced by Mathers, he is also ruled by Kore. See also KORE, MAGOTH, MATHERS.

Maitor: A demon named in the *Clavicula Salomonis*, Maitor is a demon of trickery and illusion, and he is called upon in a spell to render a person invisible. He is governed by the demon Almiras and his minister Cheros. Maitor appears in the *Sacred Magic of Abramelin the Mage*, also in connection with an invisibility spell. See also ALMIRAS, CHEROS, *CLAVICULA SALOMONIS*, MATHERS.

Makalos: Occultist S. L. MacGregor Mathers gives the meaning of this demon's name as "wasted" or "gaunt." Makalos appears in the Mathers translation of the *Sacred Magic of Abramelin the Mage*. A servant of the greater demon Magoth, this demon's name varies greatly between the different surviving texts of the *Abramelin* material. The 1608 version kept at the Wolfenbüttel library renders the name *Mokaschef*. The Peter Hammer edition offers *Cheikaseph*. And the version kept at the Dresden library splits it into two names, *Mei* and *Kaseph*. All of these are copies of a lost original, so there is no telling which spelling is correct. See also MAGOTH, MATHERS.

Malchiresha: Also spelled *Malchiresa* or *Melchireša*. Malchiresha is a demon whose name appears in several of the Dead Sea Scrolls and may have influenced modern perceptions of the Prince of Darkness. Often presented as the equivalent of or an alternate name for the demons Belial and Lucifer, Malchiresha is said to control all the darkness filling the world. He most famously appears in the *Visions of Amram*, a text in the Dead Sea Scrolls that survived in six variously fragmented copies (4Q543–548). In Amram's vision, Malchiresha presents himself as one of two angels competing for Amram's soul. One, an angel of light, rules over the Sons of Light, a vast army in conflict with the darkness in the world. This angel is typically identified as Michael. Malchiresha, in contrast, rules over the Sons of Darkness, the army to which the light is opposed. According to Amram, Malchiresha holds the title "Prince of Darkness," an epithet frequently reserved for only Satan himself. Malchiresha appears with a dark face and slitted or hooded eyes reminiscent of those of a serpent. The text further states that he wears colorful clothes. To modern readers, this may seem an innocuous detail, but it suggests a connection between Malchiresha and the fallen angel Azazel. There is a rabbinic warning against being seduced by the vivid garb associated with the angel Azazel. Notably, in Enoch 1, Azazel also corrupts humanity by teaching the arts of cosmetics and jewelry-making. In the Yazidi faith of the ethnic Kurds, Azazel appears as the "Peacock Angel," likely another reference to his brilliant attire. Malchiresha may also have some connection to the Angel of Death as portrayed in the Testament of Abraham. See also AZAZEL, BELIAL, LUCIFER, SATAN.

Malcranis: Also spelled *Malcranus*. His name may mean "bad head" or "headache." Notably, it was not uncommon for demons' names to echo the diseases they caused. Identified in the *Book of Oberon*, Malcranis is called upon, along with two others, to procure treasure—specifically 100,000 pounds of gold and silver in lawful coinage. If he fails in this task or chooses to disobey, he is threatened with having his image tossed into a fire along with foul-smelling substances, including cat shit. See also *BOOK OF OBERON*, RASINET, SYLQUAM.

Malgaras: In the *Ars Theurgia*, Malgaras appears as the first spirit in rank beneath the infernal Emperor of the West, Amenadiel. Malgaras is said to rule with thirty dukes who serve him by day and another thirty who serve him by night. He is described as being both courteous and obedient. His name is sometimes rendered *Maigaras*. Malgaras is also named in the *Steganographia* of Johannes Trithemius, a work dating to approximately 1499. See also AMENADIEL, *ARS THEURGIA*.

Malgron: A demon of the daylight hours known for his good and obedient nature, Malgron is ruled by infernal king Symiel. He is one of only ten demons ranked as dukes in service to Symiel during the day. According to the *Ars Theurgia*, Malgron has twenty ministering spirits beneath him.

He serves in the region of the north. See also *ARS THEURGIA*, SYMIEL.

Malguel: A demon with the title of duke in the court of the infernal king Asyriel. Malguel is associated with the hours of the day and the direction of the south. According to the *Ars Theurgia*, he has twenty lesser spirits at his command. See also *ARS THEURGIA*, ASYRIEL.

Malphas: The thirty-ninth spirit named in the *Goetia*. Malphas is a demon connected with the builder's craft. He is said to erect houses and high towers upon command. He quickly brings artificers together, and he can also strike out at the towers and edifices of an enemy, tearing these down. He is said to give good familiars. When he manifests, he first takes the form of a crow. When he puts on a human shape, he nevertheless retains the rasping voice of this bird. According to both the *Pseudomonarchia Daemonum* of Wierus and Scot's *Discoverie of Witchcraft*, he holds the rank of president and rules over forty legions. He is further said to willingly accept sacrifices but to deceive all those who make sacrifices unto him. The *Goetia of Dr. Rudd* has a slightly different entry on this demon. The spelling of his name remains the same, but instead of destroying the towers of enemies, he is said to have the power to destroy an enemy's thoughts, desires, and works. This text further states that Malphas can be constrained in the name of the angel Rehael. The Welsh *Book of Incantations* identifies him as both a builder of towers and a destroyer of minds. In that text, he is assigned the rank of president and governs 110 legions. The Welsh text warns against making any offerings to this demon: if he is given any kind of sacrifice, he will become deceptive. See also *BOOK OF INCANTATIONS*, *GOETIA*, RUDD, SCOT, WIERUS.

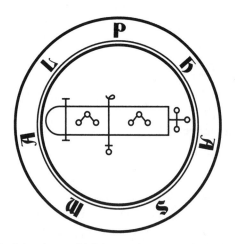

Sigil of the demon Malphas as it appears in the Welsh *Book of Incantations*. This same demon appears in a variety of other grimoires under various permutations of his name. Image by Catherine Rogers.

Malpharas: A grand lord who builds towers, castles, bridges, abbeys, and convents. He can also transport buildings from place to place. He appears in the French *Book of Spirits* (*Livre des esperitz*), where he is said to be an obedient and courteous helper. He commands a total of thirty legions. Under the name *Mallapas*, he appears in the Elizabethan *Book of Oberon*, where he is identified as one of the twelve demons who serve in the court of Amaimon, king of the south. Both of these names are almost certainly variations of the demon *Malphas*. See also *BOOK OF INCANTATIONS, BOOK OF OBERON, LIVRE DES ESPERITZ, MALPHAS*.

Malutens: The "Deceiver." In the *Sacred Magic of Abramelin the Mage*, Malutens is one of a number of demons who serve the four infernal princes of the cardinal directions. As such, he shares in the power of his demonic masters: Oriens, Paimon, Ariton, and Amaimon. When summoned, the magician can compel him to grant some of these powers, providing familiars, summoning armed men for protection, and even raising the dead. See also AMAIMON, ARITON, MATHERS, ORIENS, PAIMON.

Malyke: A wicked demon who serves as minister to King Maymon, ruler of Saturn. Malyke has a monstrous appearance, with a beaked mouth, too many faces, and dark, translucent skin. If compelled to take a more human appearance, he will wear the guise of an old man or woman. His color is black and his metal is lead. He sows chaos and discord, inspiring evil thoughts and driving people to murder and mutilation. He can be found in the *Book of Oberon*, a grimoire from Elizabethan England. See also ALBEWE, ALDEE, *BOOK OF OBERON*, CHERASA, ETHEYE, MAYMON.

Mammon: Originally an Aramaic word meaning "riches," Mammon is personified in the New Testament by Matthew and Luke. Both Luke 16:13 and Mark 6:24 teach that "you cannot serve God and mammon." At this point, Mammon was not yet clearly identified as a demon among the ranks of Hell. However, the Christian bishop, Gregory of Nyssa, writing in the fourth century of the Common Era, identified Mammon with Beelzebub. By the Middle Ages, Mammon had become personified as a demon of avarice and greed. He is listed as a demon in Francis Barrett's 1801 edition of *The Magus*, where he is described as being the prince of the demonic order of "tempters and ensnarers."[53] In Collin de Plancy's extensive 1863 edition of the *Dictionnaire Infernal*, Mammon is depicted as a wizened old miser hoarding his gold. In A. E. Waite's presentation of the *Grand Grimoire*, Mammon is listed as Hell's ambassador to England. Although Waite attributes this hierarchy to the sixteenth-century scholar Johannes Wierus, it

---

53. Francis Barrett, *The Magus* (Weiser edition), p. 47.

actually stems from the works of nineteenth-century demonologist Charles Berbiguier. In a more legitimate hierarchy, Mammon is named prince of the ninth order of evil spirits, otherwise known as the Ensnarers. This nine-tier hierarchy appears in the grimoire known as the *Janua Magica Reserata*. See also BARRETT, BEELZEBUB, BERBIGUIER, DE PLANCY, *JANUA MAGICA RESERATA*, WAITE, WIERUS.

Manasa: Named in the *Book of Oberon*, he is one of two ministers in the court of King Sarabotres, who rules the planetary sphere of Venus. He may appear as a young woman with flowing green and white garments or as a girl, completely nude. He also has associations with camels. Manasa has power over emotions and can make people feel love and peace and an urge for extravagance. He can arrange marriages and sweetly make men long for women. See also *BOOK OF OBERON*, NASAR, SARABOTRES.

Maniel: One of twelve chief dukes said to serve the demon Dorochiel. According to the *Ars Theurgia*, Maniel has forty ministering spirits at his command. He is said to be tied to the hours of the day, preferring to appear before noon. In his allegiance to Dorochiel, he is associated with the western point of the compass. See also *ARS THEURGIA*, DOROCHIEL.

Mansi: One of ten demons governed by the infernal king Barmiel, Mansi is part of the hierarchy of the south, and he serves his infernal master during the hours of the day. His name appears in the *Ars Theurgia*, where it is said that he has twenty lesser spirits at his command. See also *ARS THEURGIA*, BARMIEL.

Mantan: Another demonic name that appears in connection with the *Sacred Magic of Abramelin the Mage* that nevertheless appears quite differently from one version of the text to another. In the version of the *Abramelin* material kept at the Wolfenbüttel library in Germany, the name is spelled *Matatam*. Yet in the version found at the library of Dresden, the name is *Pialata*. As none of these are the original *Abramelin* text, there is no way of knowing which spelling is correct. All texts agree, however, that this demon is a follower of the archfiend Magoth. See also MAGOTH, MATHERS.

Mantiens: This name is likely derived from *manteia*, a Greek word referencing any practice of divination. As such, the demon's name can be taken to mean "the Diviner." Mantiens appears in the *Sacred Magic of Abramelin the Mage* as one of several demons serving beneath the four infernal princes of the cardinal directions. He is summoned as part of the main *Abramelic* operation, an elaborate and time-consuming spell designed to put the magician in contact with a tutelary force known as the Holy Guardian Angel. See also AMAIMON, ARITON, MATHERS, ORIENS, PAIMON.

Marae: One of several night-demons who serve in the court of the infernal prince Usiel. Marae has twenty lesser spirits at his command, and he has the power to reveal hidden treasure. He can also use charms and enchantments to secret away precious things, thus preventing them from being stolen. The name and seal of this demon both appear in the *Ars Theurgia*. He serves in the region of the west. The name of this demon may be derived from the Old Norse *mara*, a root connected with our modern word *nightmare*. The *mara* was a night-demon thought to attack people in their sleep. She was often said to sit or lie upon their chests, pressing them down or stealing their breath. She bears some connections to the incubus and succubus myths of the Middle Ages and Renaissance. See also *ARS THEURGIA*, USIEL.

Marag: A demon said to serve under the dual leadership of Magoth and Kore in the *Sacred Magic of Abramelin the Mage*. In the 1725 edition of this work published by Peter Hammer in Cologne, the name of this demon is spelled *Charag*. See also KORE, MAGOTH, MATHERS.

Maraloch: According to the *Munich Handbook*, this demon possesses knowledge of every subject a person can ever learn. His academic expertise is called upon in a spell aimed at improving a person's intellect. According to the text, when properly summoned he will appear in dreams, spending the whole night imparting all that he knows. See also *MUNICH HANDBOOK*.

Maralock: This name appears in the first spell of the *Munich Handbook*, a fifteenth-century magickal text devoted to operations of necromancy and spirit-summoning. Summoned together with "Sathan," the demon Maralock has the power to reveal great knowledge to the magician, particularly in the realm of the liberal arts. See also *MUNICH HANDBOOK*.

Maranton: One of several demons said to serve the infernal prince Ariton in the *Sacred Magic of Abramelin the Mage*. In his translation of this work, occultist S. L. Mathers relates Maranton's name to a Greek root meaning "quenched" or "extinguished." In the Peter Hammer edition of this work, the name of this demon is spelled *Charonton*. See also ARITON, MATHERS.

Maraos: A demonic servitor of the infernal king Amaimon, Maraos appears in the *Sacred Magic of Abramelin the Mage*. The exact spelling of this demon's name is a matter of some dispute. In the version of the *Abramelin* material kept at the Dresden library, the name is spelled *Meraos*. In the Peter Hammer edition, it is rendered *Eheraos*. And in the 1898 Mathers translation, the name is given as *Mames*. See also AMAIMON, MATHERS.

Maras: According to the *Ars Theurgia*, Maras is one of twelve great dukes who serve beneath the demon-king Caspiel, Emperor of the South. Maras and his fellow dukes are reputed to be cantankerous and stubborn, although proper use of their names and their seals will nevertheless allow a skilled individual to compel them to behave. Maras oversees two thousand two hundred and sixty ministering spirits that attend to his needs. Later in the *Ars Theurgia*, Maras is named among the demons subject to the infernal prince Maseriel. Here, Maras is a duke serving by night with thirty ministering spirits. The name of this demon may be related to the mara, a vicious night-demon thought to prey upon people in their sleep. See also *ARS THEURGIA*, CASPIEL, MASERIEL.

Marastac: This demon holds the rank of king in the hierarchy of Hell, at least according to the *Liber de Angelis*. He has beneath him two subordinates, Aycolaytoum and a demon known only as *Dominus Penarum*, or "Lord of Torments." Marastac and his associates are connected with the planet Jupiter. They are summoned as part of a spell designed to compel the love of a woman by binding her to the will of the magician. See also AYCOLAYTOUM, DOMINUS PENARUM, *LIBER DE ANGELIS*.

Marbas: The fifth spirit named in the *Goetia*, Marbas is ranked as a president with command over thirty-six legions. In Wierus's *Pseudomonarchia Daemonum*, he is said to appear as a mighty lion, but he can take the form of a man when commanded. He speaks of all secrets and hidden things. He can cause and cure disease. He teaches both the mechanical arts and handicrafts and confers wisdom in general. He can also change men into other shapes. His name is alternately given as *Barbas*. He appears in Scot's *Discoverie of Witchcraft*, the Welsh *Book of Incantations,* and the *Goetia of Dr. Rudd*. According to Dr. Rudd, Marbas falls under the power of the angel Mahasiah. See also *BOOK OF INCANTATIONS, GOETIA*, RUDD, SCOT, WIERUS.

Marbuel: According to the *Sixth and Seventh Books of Moses*, Marbuel is one of the Seven Great Princes of Spirits. When summoned, he appears in the form of a great, old lion. He is a finder of secret things and can bestow honors upon the magician. He is also able to deliver treasures from both water and land to the summoner. Given Marbuel's leonine form, together with his office as a revealer of secrets, it is tempting to relate this being with the Goetic demon known as Marbas. There is a pattern of three circles connected by radiating lines in Marbuel's seal that distantly echoes the traditional Goetic sigil of Marbas. This lends credence to a connection between these two beings. See also MARBAS.

Marchosias: The thirty-fifth demon of the *Goetia*, Marchosias is said to appear as a cruel she-wolf with the wings of a gryphon. One of the traditional seventy-two Goetic demons, Marchosias is attributed with the rank of marquis in Scot's *Discoverie of Witchcraft*. Here, he is said to rule over thirty legions of lesser spirits. He can take a man's form, and when he does so, he is a powerful fighter. He answers truthfully all questions put to him and he will faithfully carry out any business requested. Marchosias is one of several Goetic demons said to entertain hopes of returning to the seventh throne of Heaven. Wierus's *Pseudomonarchia Daemonum* spells his name *Marchocias*. According to the *Goetia of Dr. Rudd*, he is constrained by the angel Chavakiah. In the *Book of Incantations*, he is a strong fighter who belonged to the Order of Dominions before his fall. According to this Welsh grimoire, Marchosias told his chief master Solomon that, after twelve hundred years, he had hopes to return to the seventh throne of Heaven. See also *BOOK OF INCANTATIONS, GOETIA*, RUDD, SCOT, WIERUS.

Marderô: A demon of disease who has the power to afflict his victims with terrible fever. He is one of thirty-six demons associated with the decans of the zodiac whose names are listed in the *Testament of Solomon*. In the Conybeare translation of this material, he is tied to the twentieth decan. In the later McCown translation, it is the nineteenth. As McCown was working from a more complete collection of manuscripts, his translation is generally accepted as the most accurate. In both, Marderô is a fearsome entity, appearing with the body of a man and the head of a beast. According to Conybeare, he can be driven off by invoking the names *Sphênêr* and *Rafael*. In McCown's text, it is the demon's own name that controls him. See also SOLOMON.

Marguns: A demon in the hierarchy of the south, as outlined in the *Ars Theurgia*. Marguns is a duke of the infernal king Barmiel, whom he faithfully serves during the hours of the night. As a demon of some rank, he has twenty servants of his own to carry out his commands. See also *ARS THEURGIA*, BARMIEL.

Marianu: A night-demon who serves in the hierarchy of the north, at least according to the *Ars Theurgia*. Marianu is a mighty duke who commands one hundred lesser spirits. His immediate superior is the demon Symiel, who rules as a king in the north by east. Marianu is reputedly stubborn by nature and is reluctant to appear to mortals, even when commanded. When he is willing to make an appearance, he will only manifest during the hours of the night. See also *ARS THEURGIA*, SYMIEL.

Mariel: A demon belonging to the hours of the day, Mariel is named in the *Ars Theurgia*, where he is listed as a chief president in the hierarchy of the demon Aseliel. Mariel commands thirty principal spirits and twenty ministering servants. His manifest form is courtly, courteous, and beautiful to behold. Through Aseliel, he is connected with the east. See also *ARS THEURGIA*, ASELIEL.

Maroth: A chief duke of the demon Asyriel. Maroth appears in the *Ars Theurgia*, where he is said to have forty lesser spirits at his command. He is associated with the night and with the direction of the south. See also *ARS THEURGIA*, ASYRIEL.

Aside from some flourishes, the seal of the demon Marchosias remains the same in various editions of the *Goetia*. Ink on parchment by M. Belanger.

Marshiones: A demon purported to magickally transport people from country to country. He holds the rank of duke, with thirty legions beneath him. When he manifests, he appears as a powerful man with the tail of a serpent. According to the *Book of Oberon*, he is also an expert in the lore and properties of stones and herbs. His name bears striking similarities with the Medieval title *marchioness*, although no direct connection to this word is evidenced in the text. Compare him also to the Goetic demon *Marchosias*. See also *BOOK OF OBERON*, MARCHOSIAS.

Mathias: A demon who manifests in the form of a bear with flames erupting from his mouth. He is named in the Elizabethan grimoire known as the *Book of Oberon*. According to that text, he is a demon of travel, carrying people from country to country. He holds the rank of lord and has thirty-six legions under him. See also *BOOK OF OBERON*.

Martinet: According to French writer Charles Berbiguier, Martinet is Hell's duly appointed ambassador to Switzerland. He also appears in this capacity in A. E. Waite's presentation of the *Grand Grimoire*. At least a few of Berbiguier's hellish ambassadors were based off of real, living people he had encountered in his daily life. Martinet may be the last name of one of Berbiguier's supposed demons in disguise. See also BERBIGUIER, *GRAND GRIMOIRE*, WAITE.

Masaub: A demon in the court of Magoth. In his 1898 translation of the *Sacred Magic of Abramelin the Mage*, Mathers also lists this demon as a servant of Kore. Mathers tries to relate Masaub's name to a Hebrew word meaning "circuit." In the other Abramelin texts, the name is rendered *Masadul*. See also KORE, MAGOTH, MATHERS.

Maseriel: In the *Ars Theurgia*, Maseriel is named as the fourth spirit in rank beneath Caspiel, the infernal Emperor of the South. According to this text, he holds dominion over the west by south and his

Dr. Faust and the Devil

Dr. Faust made a deal with the Devil. This decadent scholar-turned-wizard is the focus of several famous literary works, including Goethe's *Faust*, completed in the early 1800s, and Christopher Marlowe's Elizabethan play *The Tragical Historie of Doctor Faustus*. Both Goethe and Marlowe drew their inspiration for the life and times of this curious figure from a publication entitled *Historia von Doctor Johann Fausten*. This chapbook was published by Johann Spies in Frankfurt in 1587. It was a collection of stories featuring Dr. Faust, and it became the first *Faustbuch*—a book exclusively devoted to Faust's infernal experiments. *Faustbücher* (Faust books) became extremely popular reading in the latter years of the sixteenth century. Many of the books were presented as Christian morality tales, recounting the escapades of Faust while including religious commentary and admonitions. All of the Faustbücher dealt with demonic magick and the summoning of spirits—at least in the context of the nefarious deeds perpetrated by Dr. Faust. At least one of these books, entitled *Magia Naturalis et Naturalis*, actually addresses the art of magick itself. In *The Fortunes of Faust*, scholar Elizabeth M. Butler makes an impressive case for how the Faust legend was inspired by real practitioners of the magickal arts and, through its extensive portrayal in popular culture, in turn influenced the practice of ceremonial magick.

Most people assume that Faust was a figure of legend, a character created to express some of the anxieties experienced by a largely Christian society struggling to cope with delusional fears of a witchcraft conspiracy on one side and the very real magick of Renaissance occultists such as Henry Cornelius Agrippa on the other. But according to Agrippa's own student Johannes Wierus, the legend of Dr. Faust was based on a real man. In his work, *De Praestigiis Daemonum*, Wierus identifies Johann Faust as an individual born in the little town of Kundling (Knittlingen) in the late fifteenth century or early part of the sixteenth century. He allegedly studied magick in Krakow, where, Wierus notes, "in olden days it was taught openly."[*] From the descriptions given by Wierus, Faust's magick was part chemistry and part chicanery, and he was not above using it to swindle people. After his death, an unknown biographer sought to explain Faust's abilities by alleging that Faust had made a deal with the Devil. The rest, as they say, is history.

---

[*] Johannes Wierus, *De Praestigiis Daemonum*, p. 52.

title is king. He has many lesser spirits beneath him, and the chief of these are twelve dukes who attend him during the day. Another twelve stand in attendance during the hours of the night. Maseriel is reputed to be a tractable and good-natured spirit, as are all the spirits who serve beneath him. The name of this demon can also be found in the *Steganographia* of Johannes Trithemius. See also *ARS THEURGIA*, CASPIEL.

Mashel: A demon in the hierarchy of the infernal king Gediel. According to the *Ars Theurgia*, he holds the rank of duke. Affiliated with the direction south, Mashel has command over a total of twenty lesser spirits. He serves his infernal master during the hours of the day and is most inclined to manifest during this time. See also *ARS THEURGIA*, GEDIEL.

Mastema: The chief of evil spirits as described in the *Book of Jubilees*. In this book, when God drives the evil spirits from the world, Mastema begs the Creator to allow himself and at least a portion of spirits to stay in order to commit their works against humanity. Mastema may have some connection with the demon *Malchiresha*, recorded in the Dead Sea Scrolls. See also MALCHIRESHA.

Mastuet: A demon tied to no particular hour of the day, Mastuet may manifest whenever he pleases. He is part of the retinue of the infernal prince Macariel, described in the *Ars Theurgia*. Mastuet commands a total of four hundred lesser spirits, and he often appears in the form of a many-headed dragon. See also *ARS THEURGIA*, MACARIEL.

Matanbuchus: An alternate name for the demon Belial given in chapter 2, verse 4, of the apocryphal *Ascension of Isaiah*. Here, Belial, named Beliar, is presented as the angel of lawlessness. He is also described as the true ruler of the world. See also BELIAL.

Mathers, Samuel Liddell MacGregor: One of the founding members of the Hermetic Order of the Golden Dawn, a magickal society founded in London in 1888. Mathers was a complex and colorful individual who lived from 1854 to 1918. He was mentored by Dr. Anna Kingsford, an early women's rights activist whose views on vegetarianism and the humane treatment of animals had a profound impact upon Mathers. In addition to his interests in magick and the occult, Mathers had a striking facility for languages. One of his most significant legacies in the field of the occult involves his many translations of early grimoires and Qabbalistic source works. From his many translations, it seems as if Mathers had at least some familiarity with Hebrew, Latin, French, Celtic, Coptic, and Greek. Many of these languages seem to have been self-taught, and although his accuracy and scholarship have been called into question by various detractors (such as his former student Aleister Crowley), most of Mathers's translations continue to be used and republished today. His works include translations of the *Grimoire of Armadel*, *The Sacred Magic of Abramelin the Mage*, and the *Clavicula Salomonis*, or *Key of Solomon the King*. He is also responsible for the translation of the *Goetia* later published by Aleister Crowley. See also *CLAVICULA SALOMONIS*, CROWLEY.

Maxayn: This demon has a ferocious appearance, taking the form of a fire-breathing bear with a serpent's tail. One of twelve high-ranking demons in service to Oriens, king of the east, Maxayn is named in the *Book of Oberon*. He has powers of transportation, swiftly conveying people from region to region. He is also knowledgeable in the virtues of herbs, stones, and trees. See also *BOOK OF OBERON*, ORIENS.

Maylalu: A demon of fiery lust, Maylalu appears in the fifteenth-century *Liber de Angelis*, where he is summoned, along with his demonic king Abdalaa, to compel a woman's love. See also ABDALAA, *LIBER DE ANGELIS*.

Maymon: King of the spirits of Saturn. He appears in the Peterson translation of the *Sworn Book of Honorius*. Here, he is associated with the direction north. When he manifests, he reputedly takes a body that is both slender and pale. He can bring about the emotions of sadness, anger, and hatred. He also has the power to create snow and ice. Maymon answers to the angels Bohel, Cafziel, Michrathon, and Satquiel, who jointly rule the sphere of Saturn. His name may be a truncated form of *Amaimon*. The *Book of Oberon* also names him as king over the spirits of Saturn. In that text, he possesses a very different appearance: a monstrous guise with faces on each knee and another at the back of his head. He is long and slender, with black, translucent skin, and the ground goes white, like snow or lead, when he appears. If compelled to take human form, he will appear as an old man with black robes and a sickle. He rides a fierce dragon. He oversees murder, mutilation, hatred, and chaos. He inspires evil thoughts and gives lead like some poisonous Krampus. Five demons, each as vile and monstrous as himself, serve as his ministers. See also ALBEWE, ALDEE, AMAIMON, *BOOK OF OBERON*, CHERASA, ETHEYE, MALYKE, MAYMON, *SWORN BOOK*.

Mayrion: This demon is known as "the Black One Who Calls the Void," a title that makes him particularly suited for magick of the darkest sort. Mayrion appears in the *Liber de Angelis*, where he is named in a vicious spell of vengeance. When prop-

A witch recites a spell above a blazing cauldron. A young woman kneels before her. An arcane circle surrounds both of them. Mezzotint by J. Dixon, 1773. Image courtesy of the Wellcome Collection, London.

erly invoked, he has the power to utterly destroy a person's enemies. He is invoked using an image of lead or iron. He is connected with the planets Saturn and Mars. See also *LIBER DE ANGELIS*.

Maziel: A demon named in the *Ars Theurgia* who is said to serve the infernal prince Dorochiel. Maziel is one of a number of demons reputed to possess the rank of chief duke in Dorochiel's hierarchy. He is tied to the hours of the night and the region of the west. He is said to command no fewer than four hundred ministering spirits. See also *ARS THEURGIA*, DOROCHIEL.

Mebbesser: A servitor of the greater demon Asmodeus. According to occultist Mathers in his translation of the *Sacred Magic of Abramelin the*

Mage, the name of this demon means "flesh." In the 1720 version of the *Abramelin* material kept in the Dresden library, this demon's name is spelled *Mephasser*. See also ASMODEUS, MATHERS.

Meclu: One of several demons said to serve Demoriel, the infernal Emperor of the North. Meclu's name and seal appear in the *Ars Theurgia*, where he is said to rule over one thousand one hundred and forty lesser spirits of his own. He holds the rank of duke and, in addition to his connection with the direction north, he is also connected with the ninth set of two planetary hours of the day. He is said to only manifest to mortals during this time. See also *ARS THEURGIA*, DEMORIEL.

Megalak: According to Mathers in his 1898 translation of the *Sacred Magic of Abramelin the Mage*, the name of this demon comes from a Hebrew term meaning "cutting off." He is said to serve the infernal rulers Magoth and Kore, although Kore's status as a demon is questionable. In the edition of *Abramelin* published in Cologne by Peter Hammer, this name is rendered *Magalech*. See also KORE, MAGOTH, MATHERS.

Megalogim: One of several demons said to serve the infernal prince Ariton in the *Sacred Magic of Abramelin the Mage*. Occultist Mathers parses this name as meaning "in great things," from a Greek root. The name is alternately spelled *Megalosin*. See also ARITON, MATHERS.

Meklboc: One of the more unusual demon names, Meklboc appears in the Mathers edition of the *Sacred Magic of Abramelin the Mage*. Here he is said to serve beneath the infernal rulers Magoth and Kore. Mathers suggests that the name of this demon means "dog-like." In other versions of the *Abramelin* material, the name is spelled *Mechebber*. See also KORE, MAGOTH, MATHERS.

Melamud: A demon ruled by Oriens, Paimon, Amaimon, and Ariton, the four demonic princes of the cardinal directions. In the *Sacred Magic of Abramelin the Mage*, Melamud is one of over three hundred demons whose names must be scribed as part of the second day of the Holy Guardian Angel working. According to Mathers, Melamud's name may derive from a Hebrew word meaning "stimulus" or "exertion." See also AMAIMON, ARITON, MATHERS, ORIENS, PAIMON.

Melas: A demon in the court of the infernal prince Aseliel, who rules the direction south by east. Through his allegiance with Aseliel, Melas is a part of the demonic hierarchy of the east, as outlined in the *Ars Theurgia*. According to this text, Melas has thirty principal spirits at his command with another twenty ministering spirits to serve him. He holds the rank of chief president. See also *ARS THEURGIA*, ASELIEL.

Melcha: A demon ranked as a chief duke, with fifty lesser spirits under him. Melcha himself serves the demon-king Raysiel. Raysiel is one of the infernal kings of the north, as described in the *Ars Theurgia*. The operation for summoning Melcha and his associates is best carried out in a remote location or in a secret room of the house where no bystanders are likely to interfere. Melcha is reputedly tied to the hours of the day and thus will only make an appearance between dawn and dusk. See also *ARS THEURGIA*, RAYSIEL.

Melchom: A duke who commands thousands of lesser spirits, Melchom serves the mighty king Baruchas in the north. This spirit will not manifest to mortals outside of a very specific time frame. The *Ars Theurgia*, a book on spirits associated with the points of the compass, contains the formula for determining when Melchom will appear. According to the text, you must divide the day into fifteen parts. Melchom will manifest only during the third section of time.

In a curious demonic hierarchy often misattributed to Johannes Wierus, Melchom is described as the paymaster of the royal household in Hell. The hierarchy stems from the early-nineteenth-century works of the self-described demonologist Charles Berbiguier. The name *Melchom* itself is a corruption of *Moloch*. A scribal error in 1 Kings 11:7 transforms the name "Moloch" to "Milcom," and it is highly likely that the name of this demon derives directly from that biblical reference. See also *ARS THEURGIA*, BARUCHAS, BERBIGUIER, MILCOM, MOLOCH, WIERUS.

Melemil: A demon called upon to provide an enchanted cloak. According to the *Munich Handbook*, this infernal item has the power to make anyone who wears it completely invisible. Melemil is one of the demonic guardians of the four directions called upon to provide this marvelous object. He is invoked in the direction of the south. The spell calls for Melemil and his compatriots to be called upon in a remote location during the first hour of the night on a Wednesday during the waxing of the moon. See also *MUNICH HANDBOOK*.

Melhaer: In the *Sacred Magic of Abramelin the Mage*, Melhaer appears among the ranks of demons who serve Oriens, Paimon, Ariton, and Amaimon, the four demonic princes of the cardinal directions. His name may mean "separation from purity." See also AMAIMON, ARITON, MATHERS, ORIENS, PAIMON.

Meliel: In the *Ars Theurgia*, Meliel is one of the chief dukes ruled by the infernal king Malgaras. Meliel serves in the court of the west. Preferring to manifest only during the hours of daylight, Meliel is said to command an entourage of thirty ministering spirits. See also *ARS THEURGIA*, MALGARAS.

Melna: A demon whose name may mean "abider." According to the Mathers translation of the *Sacred Magic of Abramelin the Mage*, Melna is ruled by the four infernal princes of the cardinal directions. As a servant of Oriens, Paimon, Ariton, and Amaimon, he can be summoned in their name and called upon to use any of their powers. See also AMAIMON, ARITON, MATHERS, ORIENS, PAIMON.

Memnolik: Given as *Menolik* in the 1898 Mathers translation of the *Sacred Magic of Abramelin the Mage*, this demon is said to serve the infernal prince Paimon. See also MATHERS, PAIMON.

Menadiel: The eighth so-called wandering prince listed in the *Ars Theurgia*. Like many demons of significant rank, Menadiel is said to have a host of other spirits loyal to him. The court of Menadiel consists of twenty infernal dukes, one hundred companions, and a vast number of other demonic servants. All are reputed to be obedient and civil, possessing basically good natures—or at least as good as anything classified as a demon can be. Menadiel is also named in a list of demons from Johannes Trithemius's *Steganographia*, written around 1499. See also *ARS THEURGIA*, TRITHEMIUS.

Menador: One of hundreds of demons said to serve the infernal Emperor of the North, Demoriel. According to the *Ars Theurgia*, Menador holds the rank of duke, and he is one of twelve such dukes whose names and seals are specifically provided within the text. Also according to this text, Menador has command over one thousand one hundred and forty lesser spirits of his own. He is connected with the third set of two planetary hours of the day and the region of the north. See also *ARS THEURGIA*, DEMORIEL.

Menail: One of eighteen of the highest-ranking demons in the court of Duke Syrach. Menail appears in the *Secrets of Solomon*, a seventeenth-century grimoire seized by the Inquisition of Venice. According to that text, Menail is a demon of thieves and thievery with the power to make people invisible when they enter a house. He also appears in the *True Keys of Solomon*, where he serves Chief Sirachi, an agent of Lucifer. See also LUCIFER, *SECRETS OF SOLOMON*, SIRACHI, SYRACH, *TRUE KEYS*.

Menariel: In the *Ars Theurgia*, Menariel is named as an infernal knight who serves the wandering prince Pirichiel. Two thousand lesser spirits answer to him. See also *ARS THEURGIA*, PIRICHIEL.

Mephistopheles: In the *Sixth and Seventh Books of Moses*, this demon is identified as one of Seven Great Princes of Spirits. Variations upon his name appear within the text, alternating between *Mephistopilis* and *Mephistophiles*. According to this text, the demon appears in the form of a youth when summoned, and he appears promptly and with an eagerness to serve. He offers the magician help in any and all of the skilled arts, and he further provides familiars. Like most of the other Seven Great Princes named in this work, he is also reputed to retrieve treasure from earth and sea, according to the whim of the operator.

Under the spelling *Mephostophiles*, this demon also appears in the *History of Doctor Johann Faust*, published in Frankfurt in 1587, which was the first *Faustbuch* (see also the "Dr. Faust and the Devil" sidebar). This book collected a series of popu-

Detail from the title page of the 1631 chapbook of Christopher Marlowe's play *The Tragical Historie of Doctor Faustus*. Faustus summons the demon Mephistopheles.

lar tales about an ambitious scholar who sold his soul to the Devil. The Faust legends are arguably where the name of this demon originates. Although the origin of Mephistopheles may lie with the *Faustbücher* (Faust books), the meaning of the demon's name remains a matter of some debate. Georg Rudolf Widmann, who published a Faustbuch in 1599, suggests a Persian origin for the name, although this has never been substantiated. Some scholars are eager to equate the latter half of Mephistopheles's name with the Greek words *theophiles* or *theopilos*, meaning, roughly, "lover of God." Unfortunately, this leaves the meaning of *mephis* completely unaccounted for. As a result, a Greek origin of the name also remains unsubstantiated. Owing to the popularity of the *Faustbücher* in the sixteenth and seventeenth centuries, the inclusion of Mephistopheles in the *Sixth and Seventh Books of Moses* may well point to the fact that the purported magickal book was influenced by the Faust tradition and not the other way around.

Merach: One of twelve chief dukes governed by the infernal prince Dorochiel. He serves in the court of the west. According to the *Ars Theurgia*, he commands a total of forty ministering spirits and will only appear in the daylight hours before noon. See also *ARS THEURGIA*, DOROCHIEL.

Meras: A demon in the service of Camuel, the infernal prince of the southeast. According to the *Ars Theurgia*, Meras is a duke and he has one hundred ministering spirits to attend him. He is said to belong to the hours of the night, but he appears instead during the hours of the day. See also *ARS THEURGIA*, CAMUEL.

Merasiel: One of the great dukes ruled by the wandering prince Bidiel. Merasiel oversees a vast retinue of no fewer than two thousand and four hundred lesser spirits. He manifests in a human shape and, according to the *Ars Theurgia*, he is always beautiful and pleasing to the eye. See also *ARS THEURGIA*, BIDIEL.

Merfide: A demon of transportation, Merfide has the power to instantly teleport people to any desired location. According to the Peterson edition of the *Grimorium Verum*, Merfide is the seventh demon in the hierarchy serving Duke Syrach. This name is also rendered *Merfilde*, depending upon which version of the *Grimorium Verum* one references. See also *GRIMORIUM VERUM*, SYRACH.

Merfiel: One of eighteen powerful demons in service to Duke Syrach, a subordinate of Lucifer named in the *Secrets of Solomon*. According to this text, Merfiel's main office involves transportation. He is able to whisk people away instantly to whatever place they wish. His powers of teleportation are not limited to people but can also include objects, making him exceptionally useful for acquiring rare, costly, or hard-to-find items. His name eventually becomes *Merfide* in the *Grimorium Verum*, a text derived from the *Secrets of Solomon*.

See also *GRIMORIUM VERUM*, MERFIDE, *SECRETS OF SOLOMON*, SYRACH.

Merihem: In Francis Barrett's 1801 publication *The Magus*, Merihem is listed as one of eight demonic princes who hold sway over a variety of evil concepts and classes of beings. As a demonic prince ranked at the top of the infernal hierarchy, Merihem oversees pestilence and spirits that cause pestilence. See also BARRETT.

Meririm: A prince of the air named in Francis Barrett's *The Magus*. According to the text, Meririm is a boiling spirit connected with the regions of the south. Occultist Barrett connects him to the four angels in the *Book of Revelation* who visit destruction upon the earth. In the grimoire known as *Janua Magica Reserata*, Meririm is also named as a prince of aerial powers. In this text, there is an order of demons in an infernal hierarchy that also includes the Revengers of Evil and the Spirits of Lies. The *Aeriae Potestates* stand at the sixth of nine orders in this hierarchy. See also BARRETT, *JANUA MAGICA RESERATA*.

Mermo: In the *Sacred Magic of Abramelin the Mage*, Mermo is named as one of several demons who serve the infernal princes of the cardinal directions. Mathers suggests that the name is connected with the ocean and may mean "across the water." However, the name of this demon may also be a variation of *Mormo*, a title associated with the Greek goddess Hecate, later taken up as a patron of witches. The name Mormo was made famous by Hippolytus in a passage from his third-century-CE work *Philosphumena*. Here Hecate is addressed as "Gorgo, Mormo, thousand-faced Moon." There is some debate as to the origin and meaning of the name Mormo, although the most common explanation is that it is tied to a Greek ogress who was a devourer of children. No solid evidence supports this assertion, however, and the name remains a mysterious title accorded to Hecate in her ancient rites. See also MATHERS.

Merosiel: A night-demon governed by the wandering duke Buriel. Merosiel despises the light of day and will only manifest when it is dark out. According to the *Ars Theurgia*, he is a roguish spirit, possessed of a wholly evil nature. Merosiel and all of the other demons who serve beneath Buriel are hated and reviled by all of the other spirits. When Merosiel appears, he takes the form of a human-headed serpent. Although the head of this serpent is that of a beautiful young girl, Merosiel nevertheless speaks with a rough male voice. As a demon awarded the title of duke, Merosiel has eight hundred and eighty lesser spirits at his command. See also *ARS THEURGIA*, BURIEL.

Meroth: A demon who serves the infernal prince Dorochiel in the capacity of a chief duke. The *Ars Theurgia* links him to the demonic court of the west. He is said to rule over four hundred lesser spirits, all of whom are willing to carry out his commands. Allegedly, he is tied to the hours of the second half of the night, serving his infernal master between midnight and dawn. See also *ARS THEURGIA*, DOROCHIEL.

Mertiel: A demon of transportation who can send a person to any location in an instant. He is also known by the name *Inertiel*. This demon appears in the *True Keys of Solomon*, where he is said to serve chief Sirachi, an agent of Lucifer. See also LUCIFER, SIRACHI, *TRUE KEYS*.

Metafel: A demon who serves beneath the four infernal princes of the cardinal directions: Oriens, Paimon, Ariton, and Amaimon. Metafel appears in the Mathers edition of the *Sacred Magic of Abra-melin the Mage*. See also AMAIMON, ARITON, MATHERS, ORIENS, PAIMON.

Metathiax: According to the *Testament of Solomon*, Metathiax is a demon of disease that causes the veins to ache. One of thirty-six demons associated with the decans of the zodiac, Metathiax can be driven away with the name of the angel Adônaêl, who holds power over him. See also SOLOMON.

Mextyura: A demon ruled over by Maymon, king of the spirits of Saturn. In the Joseph H. Peterson translation of the *Sworn Book of Honorius*, Mextyura is said to have power to inspire hatred, anger, and sorrow. He can call down storms of snow and ice. He is associated with the region of the north but is also subordinate to the southwest wind. How exactly this demon is related to two distinctly different directions remains unclear within the text. Compare this name with *Zynextur*, a demon said to serve Albunalich, demon-king of the earth, in the Driscoll translation of the *Sworn Book*. See also ALBUNALICH, MAYMON, *SWORN BOOK*, ZYNEXTUR.

Milalu: A demon who can change the thoughts and wills of others. He can also influence journeys and bring rain. Milalu is a minister of the demon Harthan, king of the spirits of the moon. He appears in the Peterson translation of the *Sworn Book of Honorius*. According to this text, he serves in the region of the west. When he manifest, his body resembles a dim and milky crystal or a dark cloud. See also HARTHAN, *SWORN BOOK*.

Milau: Ruled by the demon-king Harthan, Milau serves in the region of the west. He is connected with the sphere of the moon and thus has the power to cause rain, influence journeys, and change a person's thoughts. Milau appears in the Peterson edition of the *Sworn Book of Honorius*.

Ancient Exorcisms

The ancient Sumerians had a demon for practically every ailment, and in Sumerian rituals of exorcism, the name of the demon possessing the afflicted individual was believed to be instrumental in driving that demon away. Often, the name was not known, and so Sumerian exorcisms frequently included a litany of demonic names, working on the theory that if all of the demons who could possibly be responsible for the possession were named, at least one of those names would hit its mark.

In addition to utilizing the power of names, Sumerian exorcisms frequently made use of an animal substitute for the possessed individual. Through ritual and incantations, the essence of the demon was transferred from the possessed human into this animal sacrifice. Goats or pigs were commonly used as the sacrificial animals in these ancient exorcisms. The demon was bound to the animal with the power of its name—and with a little help from the gods whose names were also invoked to control and compel the demon. With the demon thus trapped in this substitute flesh, the animal was then destroyed, an act that was thought to drive the demon from the earthly plane.

Consider this Babylonian spell quoted by Reginald Campbell Thompson:

Give the pig in his stead,
And give the flesh as his flesh,
The blood as his blood,
And let him [the demon] take it;
Its heart set upon the man's heart.
Give as his heart
And let the demon take it.

Animal sacrifices were not always used. Sometimes an object was crafted as the ritual substitute instead. Waxen images were popular, and once the demon had been driven into this substitute form, the figure of wax was typically placed in or near a fire and allowed to melt. As the figure melted, so too was the power of the demon believed to melt away.

---

* Thompson, *Devils and Evil Spirits of Babylonia*, p. xxxiii.

According to this text, he is also affiliated with the west wind. See also HARTHAN, *SWORN BOOK*.

Milion: "The destroyer of the day," at least according to occultist S. L. MacGregor Mathers. This demon is reputedly a servant of prince Ariton, one of four rulers of the cardinal directions named in the *Sacred Magic of Abramelin the Mage*. In other versions of the *Abramelin* material, this demon's name is rendered *Nilion*. See also ARITON, MATHERS.

Mimosa: In his 1898 translation of the *Sacred Magic of Abramelin the Mage*, Mathers suggests that the name of this demon means "imitator," from the same root as *mimic*. Mimosa is said to serve under the joint leadership of the demons Magoth and Kore. See also KORE, MAGOTH, MATHERS.

Minal: A demon with the power to raise an army of one thousand soldiers, Minal appears in the Driscoll translation of the *Sworn Book*, where he is identified as a minister of the demon Jamaz, infernal king of the element of fire. As a creature of fire, Minal manifests with a complexion that resembles living flame. By nature, he is hot and impetuous, but he also possesses great strength and generosity. He can cause death instantly, but he can also prevent and completely reverse the effects of decay. See also JAMAZ, *SWORN BOOK*.

Minosum: For those individuals with a yen for gambling, Minosum can be summoned to assist in games of chance, allowing a mortal to win whenever desired. In Peterson's *Grimorium Verum*, Minosum is listed as serving in the seventh rank beneath the demons Hael and Sergulath. Under the name *Minotous*, he appears along with his sigil in the Wellcome Library's 1709 version of the *Clavicle of Solomon*. According to that text, an alternate version of his name is *Minoson*. See also *GRIMORIUM VERUM*, HAEL, RESBIROTH, *CLAVICLE OF SOLOMON*, SERGULAF, SERGULATH.

Misiel: A chief duke of the day said to serve in the court of the demon-king Malgaras. Misiel appears in the *Ars Theurgia*, where his name is also presented as *Masiel*. Twenty minor spirits exit to carry out his commands. His region is the west. See also *ARS THEURGIA*, MALGARAS.

Misroch: In A. E. Waite's version of the *Grand Grimoire*, Misroch is identified as the Grand Steward of the Royal Household of Hell. Although Waite's *Book of Black Magic and Pacts* cites this title as originating from the work of the sixteenth-century scholar Johannes Wierus, the designation is not quite that old. Misroch and his infernal hierarchy actually stem from *Les Farfadets*, the early-nineteenth-century work by self-styled demonologist Charles Berbiguier. See also BERBIGUIER, *GRAND GRIMOIRE*, WAITE, WIERUS.

Mistalas: This demon appears as a night raven and is knowledgeable in witchcraft and necromancy. He can be called upon to teach the same, as well as to pass along knowledge of the virtues of stones, trees, and herbs. Named in the *Book of Oberon*, Mistalas is one of twelve principal servants of the demon-king of the west, Paimon. See also *BOOK OF OBERON*, PAIMON.

Mithiomo: A demon called upon to assist in the art of scrying. Mithiomo is named in the *Munich Handbook*, where he is said to assist in the discovery of thieves. See also *MUNICH HANDBOOK*.

Mitruteeah: One of a number of Hebrew names believed to belong to the night-demon Lilith. In Jewish lore, Lilith was believed to be the first wife of Adam, cast out of the Garden for refusing to submit. She then wandered the wilderness, becoming the mother of demons. She jealously

Death stroking a raven. Ravens, as birds that fed on corpses, were often associated with spirits and demons. Process print by Walter Appleton Clark, ninteenth century. Image courtesy of the Wellcome Collection, London.

preyed upon mothers in childbed and newly born babes, and a wide variety of talismans were constructed in order to protect against her attacks. It was believed that scribing Lilith's names upon these talismans would ward her away. Author T. Schrire, in his 1966 work *Hebrew Magic Amulets*, presents a number of these traditional names. See also LILITH.

Molael: A servant of the demon Symiel, who rules in the north by east, Molael is a demon with an obdurate nature. He appears only at night, and even then he is often reluctant to make himself visible to others. According to the *Ars Theurgia*, he holds the rank of chief duke and has ten lesser spirits in his entourage. He is connected with the north. See also *ARS THEURGIA*, SYMIEL.

Molbet: According to the *Munich Handbook*, this demon holds the rank of prince in the hierarchy of Hell. He is summoned forth in a spell concerned with revealing the identity of a thief. He is also connected in general with the art of divination and can help to charm a human fingernail into showing all manner of images should the magician desire. See also *MUNICH HANDBOOK*.

Molin: A demon whose name appears in Mathers's edition of the *Sacred Magic of Abramelin the Mage*, translated from an anonymous French manuscript of the same work. Molin is one of a large number of demons said to serve the four infernal princes of the cardinal directions: Oriens, Paimon, Ariton, and Amaimon. Mathers suggests that Molin's name means "abiding in a place." See also AMAIMON, ARITON, MATHERS, ORIENS, PAIMON.

Moloch: Originally a Canaanite deity, Moloch became famously demonized in the Bible through a passage in 2 Kings 23:10. This passage describes how children were consecrated to Moloch and cast into flames as a sacrifice. According to demonographer Manfred Lurker, the name *Moloch* itself may be derived from a Punic root *MLK*, meaning "offering" or "sacrifice." From this, he suggests that Moloch may not have originally been a proper name, and was instead a formal term for this kind of sacrifice. Regardless of its roots, the name *Moloch*, through its association with child sacrifice, was rapidly adopted into demonology. According to a demonic hierarchy found in Waite's treatment of the *Grand Grimoire*, Moloch holds the title of

"Prince of the Land of Tears." Like several other demons in this hierarchy, Moloch is also associated with Beelzebub's knightly Order of the Fly. He is said to have been awarded the Grand Cross of the Order of the Fly. Although A. E. Waite credits the origin of these titles to Wierus in his 1910 publication *The Book of Black Magic and Pacts*, the real source is *Les Farfadets* by Charles Berbiguier. Interestingly, Berbiguier includes two versions of the biblical demon Moloch in his hierarchy: the demon *Melchom* is mentioned along with Moloch. *Moloch* is a Greek transcription of the Hebrew *Molech*, and in other parts of the Bible it is variously rendered *Melchom* and *Milcom*. See also BEELZEBUB, BERBIGUIER, *GRAND GRIMOIRE*, MELCHOM, MILCOM, WAITE, WIERUS.

Moloy: According to the *Munich Handbook*, this demon is a squire spirit with an affinity for castles, soldiers, and fortifications. He is also a demon of illusion. He is called upon to help conjure an illusory castle from thin air. This operation is to only be undertaken in a remote location on the tenth night of the moon. See also *MUNICH HANDBOOK*.

Momel: One of a number of demons in the nightbound hierarchy of prince Dorochiel. According to the *Ars Theurgia*, Momel will only manifest in a specific hour in the first half of the night. He has a total of forty ministering spirits to attend him and he holds the rank of chief duke. He serves in the west. See also *ARS THEURGIA*, DOROCHIEL.

Monael: A demon under the rule of the infernal king Baruchas, Monael holds the rank of duke and commands thousands of lesser spirits. His name and seal appear in the *Ars Theurgia*. According to this work, Monael will only appear during very specific times of the day. If the day is divided into fifteen equal portions of time, then Monael will only manifest himself during the hours and minutes that fall into the eleventh portion. He serves in the region of the north. See also *ARS THEURGIA*, BARUCHAS.

Moracha: A demon in command of one thousand eight hundred and forty lesser spirits, Moracha is free to manifest during any hour, day or night. According to the *Ars Theurgia*, he is one of twelve chief dukes beneath the wandering prince Soleviel. Half serve in one year and half in the next, thus sharing the workload from year to year. See also *ARS THEURGIA*, SOLEVIEL.

Morael: A demon in service to the infernal king Raysiel, Morael is a demon of the night, only appearing during the hours when darkness holds power over the land. His rank beneath Raysiel is given as chief duke, and he has a total of twenty lesser spirits that minister to him. Morael's name and seal both appear in the *Ars Theurgia*. Under Raysiel, he owes fealty to the court of the north. See also *ARS THEURGIA*, RAYSIEL.

Morail: A demon of invisibility and illusion. According to Peterson's translation of the *Grimorium Verum*, Morail is the sixteenth demon serving beneath Duke Syrach. See also *GRIMORIUM VERUM*, SYRACH.

Morax: The twenty-first demon of the *Goetia*. According to Wierus's *Pseudomonarchia Daemonum*, Morax first manifests in the form of a bull. When he puts on human shape, he teaches astronomy and the liberal sciences as well as the virtues of herbs and precious stones. He also provides familiar spirits that are both wise and good-natured. He holds the titles earl and president, and he oversees thirty-six infernal legions. He is sometimes known by the name *Foraii*. In the *Goetia of Dr. Rudd*, his name is given as *Marax*. Here, he is said to govern only three legions of lesser spirits. The angel Nelchael constrains him. See also *GOETIA*, RUDD, SCOT, WIERUS.

Morcaza: A demon in the court of the infernal king Barmiel, the first and chief spirit of the south. Morcaza and his fellows are named in the *Ars Theurgia*, where he is said to manifest only at night. Although he holds the rank of duke, he has no spirits or ministers under his command. See also *ARS THEURGIA*, BARMIEL.

Morel: In the *Sacred Magic of Abramelin the Mage*, Morel is one of a multitude of demons who serve Oriens, Paimon, Ariton, and Amaimon, the demonic princes of the four cardinal directions. According to Mathers, his name means "the rebellious one." See also AMAIMON, ARITON, MATHERS, ORIENS, PAIMON.

Moriel: A servant of the demon Camuel. According to the *Ars Theurgia*, Moriel is a duke, but he has no ministering spirits of his own. He belongs to the night but must be called during the day. He is tied to the hierarchy of the east, and when he manifests, he assumes a form that is beautiful to behold. He speaks courteously with those willing to converse with him. See also *ARS THEURGIA*, CAMUEL.

Morilen: "The Babbler," Morilen appears in the Mathers translation of the *Sacred Magic of Abramelin the Mage*. He is governed by Oriens, Paimon, Ariton, and Amaimon, the four demonic princes of the cardinal directions. See also AMAIMON, ARITON, MATHERS, ORIENS, PAIMON.

Morlas: A demon of the night ruled by the infernal prince Cabariel. Morlas possesses a dark and deceptive nature. A mighty duke, he oversees fifty lesser spirits that tend to him and carry out his will. Morlas is tied to the court of the west. The seal that compels him appears in the *Ars Theurgia*, the second book of the *Lesser Key of Solomon*. See also *ARS THEURGIA*, CABARIEL.

Mortoliel: A duke who serves the demon Hydriel. Mortoliel is drawn to wet or watery locales. According to the *Ars Theurgia*, he is very courteous in nature and possesses a good temperament. When he manifests, he takes the form of a serpent with a virgin's head. He is a creature of the air, wandering from place to place in the retinue of his prince, and he has a total of one thousand three hundred and twenty lesser spirits to attend him. See also *ARS THEURGIA*, HYDRIEL.

Mosacus: A demon with a rather piebald appearance. Mosacus has ass's ears, a dragon's tail, goose feet, a mole's hands, and an elephant's nose. Additional faces can be found at every joint and in his nethers. Two eyes peer out of his belly and he carries a crook and a scepter. If this guise is a bit too startling, Mosacus can be commanded to take the form of a seven-year-old boy with red hair. In the *Book of Oberon*, his conjuring circle is drawn using a palm blessed on Palm Sunday. When Mosacus is commanded to depart, the name *Effinnelion* is also invoked, although it is not clear from the text whether this is the name of a spirit superior to Mosacus or an alternate name of Mosacus himself. This spirit also appears in the manuscript designated as *e Musaeo 173* in the Bodleian Library and published by Daniel Harms under the title *Of Angels, Demons & Spirits*. Here, Mosacus is described only in his boy form. The text gives good reason to conjure him: he is said to accomplish more work in a day than a mortal might do in seven years. See also *BOOK OF OBERON*.

Moschel: When he manifests, this demon may appear to flit and flutter about the conjuration space;

The Devil as a composite beast with extra faces. Detail of an engraving after Buonamico di Martino called *Buffalmacco*. Fifteenth century. Image courtesy of the Wellcome Collection, London.

Mathers gives his name as meaning "to move oneself about." Moschel is a servant of the four demonic princes who oversee the cardinal directions: Oriens, Paimon, Ariton, and Amaimon. He appears in the *Sacred Magic of Abramelin the Mage* and is summoned on the third day of the Holy Guardian Angel working. See also AMAIMON, ARITON, MATHERS, ORIENS, PAIMON.

Motmyo: A demon who aids with the art of divination. He is called upon as part of a spell to gain information through psychic means in the fifteenth-century *Munich Handbook*. See also MUNICH HANDBOOK.

Moyle: A great lion with griffin's wings, Moyle appears in the Elizabethan *Book of Oberon*. Holding the rank of marquis, he commands thirteen legions and has the power to give victory over one's enemies. He can make someone an instant expert in feats of arms and can bestow the favor of great men. In addition to this, Moyle himself is very well educated and can make those who summon him witty and learned in the sciences. See also *BOOK OF OBERON*.

Mudiret: One of ten great dukes under the rule of the wandering prince Bidiel, Mudiret is an essentially good spirit and his appearance reflects this: when he manifests, he assumes the form of a radiantly beautiful human. He has command over two thousand and four hundred inferior spirits. His name, as well as the seal that commands and binds him, appear in the *Ars Theurgia*. See also *ARS THEURGIA*, BIDIEL.

Mulach: According to the *Sacred Magic of Abramelin the Mage*, this demon serves beneath all four infernal princes of the cardinal directions. Mathers believes that his name is a variation on *Moloch*, a Moabite deity who later evolved into one of the more fearsome denizens of Hell. Moloch's demonic transformation should not come as a surprise, since he was reputedly worshipped through the sacrifice of infants. The Mulach of *Abramelin* may also have another origin, as his name bears a strong resemblance to the Arabic word *malak*. This term is often translated as "angel." See also AMAIMON, ARITON, MOLOCH, ORIENS, PAIMON.

Mullin: A demon named in A. E. Waite's presentation of the *Grand Grimoire* from his 1910 publication *The Book of Black Magic and Pacts*. Mullin appears in a colorful hierarchy of Hell, where he is named as the First Gentleman of the Bedchamber in Hell's Royal Household. Waite cites the sixteenth-century scholar Wierus as the source of this hierarchy, but it really stems from the work of the early-nineteenth-century demonologist Charles Berbiguier. It can also be found repeated from Berbiguier's work in the *Dictionnaire Infer-*

nal of Collin de Plancy. See also BERBIGUIER, *GRAND GRIMOIRE*, WAITE.

Munefiel: Holding sway over a total of two thousand two hundred minor spirits, this infernal duke is said to serve the wandering prince Icosiel. According to the *Ars Theurgia*, Munefiel has a preference for lingering around homes and private residences. Perhaps fortunately, he can only manifest during a specific time each day. If the day is divided into fifteen equal parts, Munefiel belongs to the hours and minutes falling in the thirteenth of those fifteen sections of time. See also *ARS THEURGIA*, ICOSIEL.

Munich Handbook: A fifteenth-century Latin manuscript kept at the Bavarian State Library in Munich, filed under the designation CML 849. Because the first folio of the manuscript has been lost over time, there is no way to know the name of the author or the original title (if any) of the book. Its exact date of publication is also unknown. The book is a miscellany of magick with spells devoted mainly to illusion, divination, and compulsion. The author makes no effort to hide the fact that many of these spells are enacted with the help of spirits specifically classed as demons. Several of the demons described within the text are variations on names traditionally included among the seventy-two demons of the *Goetia*. The *Munich Handbook* probably would have gone unremarked in the Munich library without the efforts of Professor Richard Kieckhefer, who published a full edition of the Latin text along with commentary and analysis in his 1997 book, *Forbidden Rites*.

Murahe: A mighty duke who serves the demon-king Symiel, Murahe is waited upon by a total of thirty ministering spirits. A demon ruled by the hours of the night, he is stubborn and often un-

willing to appear to mortals. According to the *Ars Theurgia*, he serves in the court of the north. See also *ARS THEURGIA*, SYMIEL.

Murmur: The fifty-fourth demon named in the *Goetia*. Scot's *Discoverie of Witchcraft* identifies this demon as both a duke and an earl. He is said to appear in the shape of a soldier riding a gryphon. As befitting his rank, he wears a ducal crown upon his head. He has command over thirty legions of lesser spirits, and when he manifests, two of his ministers go before him, sounding trumpets. Wierus's *Pseudomonarchia Daemonum* says that he once belonged partly to the heavenly Order of Thrones and partly to the Order of Angels. The Welsh *Book of Incantations* agrees. Murmur teaches philosophy and has the power to call the souls of the departed, making them appear and answer any questions put to them. In the *Goetia of Dr. Rudd*, his name is given as *Murmus*. He is said to be constrained in the name of the angel Nithael. See also

Murmur appears in the *Goetia of Dr. Rudd* under the name "Murmus." This is his seal in that text. Ink on parchment by M. Belanger.

BOOK OF INCANTATIONS, *GOETIA*, RUDD, SCOT, WIERUS.

Mursiel: A demon governed by the wandering prince Soleviel. Mursiel is free to manifest at any hour of the day or the night, and he serves his master only one year out of every two. His name and seal appear in the *Ars Theurgia*, where it is said that he has 1,840 minor spirits beneath him. See also *ARS THEURGIA*, SOLEVIEL.

Muryell: A demon named in the *Book of Oberon*, Muryell appears as a white lion. Serving in the court of the demon-king in the north, Egin, Muryell is one of twelve high-ranking ministers. His principal power is to make people fall in love. In addition, as with many demons in the *Book of Oberon*, he can reveal the location of hidden treasure. See also *BOOK OF OBERON*, EGIN.

Musiniel: A demon with a fondness for the woods, Musiniel holds the title of duke and as such he commands a total of one thousand three hundred and twenty lesser spirits. His immediate superior is the wandering prince known as Emoniel. According to the *Ars Theurgia*, Musiniel has no particular preference for the hours of the day over the hours of the night. With the name and seal described in that work, he can be made to manifest at any time. See also *ARS THEURGIA*, EMONIEL.

Musiriel: A demon in the service of Amenadiel, the infernal Emperor of the West, Musiriel holds the rank of duke and has command over three thousand eight hundred and eighty lesser spirits. His name and seal both appear in Mitch Henson's translation of the *Ars Theurgia*. See also AMENADIEL, *ARS THEURGIA*.

Musisin: A demon skilled in political matters, Musisin can exercise influence over the lords and leaders of the world. Furthermore, he can gather information from all republics and countries. In Peterson's *Grimorium Verum*, he is ranked as the second demon under the infernal duke Syrach. See also *GRIMORIUM VERUM*, SYRACH.

Musor: According to the *Ars Theurgia*, Musor is a chief duke ruled by the infernal king Symiel. Through Symiel, Musor serves in the court of the north. Musor commands one hundred and ten lesser spirits, and he only appears during the hours of the day. His name and seal appear in the *Ars Theurgia*, the second book of the *Lesser Key of Solomon*. See also *ARS THEURGIA*, SYMIEL.

Musuziel: A demon with a strong predilection for damp and watery locations such as wetlands and swamps. As is appropriate for a being drawn to such wet locales, Musuziel appears in the form of a naga, having the body of a serpent but the head of a beautiful young woman. Although he typically manifests in a monstrous form, Musuziel is nevertheless a good-natured spirit with a polite and courteous manner. He serves the demon Hydriel, described as a wandering duke in the *Ars Theurgia*. According to that text, Musuziel himself oversees a host of lesser spirits numbering one thousand three hundred and twenty. See also *ARS THEURGIA*, HYDRIEL.

Muziel: A demon governed by the infernal prince Dorochiel. Tied to the hours of the night, Muziel is said to serve his master each night between midnight and dawn. He holds the title of chief duke and commands four hundred lesser spirits of his own. His region is the west. Note the similarity between this demon's name and that of *Maziel*, who serves in the same hierarchy and is attached to the same period of time each night. The names and sigils of both of these demons appear in the

Detail from an anti-Catholic engraving depicting torture by demons in Hell. The selling of indulgences is criticized as one is forced to swallow gold. Image courtesy of the Wellcome Collection, London.

seventeenth-century *Ars Theurgia*. See also *ARS THEURGIA*, DOROCHIEL.

Mylalu: A messenger in the court of the Sun, Mylalu serves King Barkan. This demon's planetary affiliation means that he appears as a tall and thick-limbed person (man or woman), with gold-tinted skin and yellow, shining robes. He has the power to make friends out of enemies, to confer honors and dignities, to grant public office, and to procure gold, jewels, and all glittering things. He also has control over illness and disease, curing or causing afflictions. He is named in the *Book of Oberon* along with his fellows, Buesaba and Bybell. When nearby, he causes people to break out in an uncontrollable sweat. See also BARKAN, *BOOK OF OBERON*, BUESABA, BYBELL.

Mylu: A phlegmatic demon who serves King Harkam in the court of the Moon. If Mylu takes human shape, he is tall, with a bald head and a soft body. His skin is the color of a storm cloud. He has the power to give silver, to transport objects, to increase the speed of horses, and to reveal secrets from the past, present, and future. He is named in the *Book of Oberon*, where he is said to serve beside three other helpers to the Moon king. See also ACUTEBA, *BOOK OF OBERON*, BYLETH, BYLETHOR, HARKAM.

Myrezyn: A duke who serves beneath the mighty demon Carnesiel, Emperor of the East. Myrezyn's name appears in a list of demons associated with the points of the compass in the *Ars Theurgia*, the second book of the *Lesser Key of Solomon*. Myrezyn and his compatriots are described as having very "airy" natures, and thus they will appear most clearly if they are summoned into a vessel of glass or shew-stone. See also *ARS THEURGIA*, CARNESIEL.

Naadob: In the Peterson translation of the *Sworn Book of Honorius*, Naadob is said to have the power to make people feel love, gladness, and joy. He can also make a person more favorable. He is ruled by Formione, the king of the spirits of Jupiter. When he manifests, he assumes a body the color of the heavens or of a pure, clear crystal. He is governed by the angels Satquiel, Raphael, Pahamcocihel, and Asassaiel, who rule the sphere of Jupiter. See also FORMIONE, *SWORN BOOK*.

Naasa: A servant of the demon Sarabocres, king of the planet Venus. According to the Peterson edition of the *Sworn Book of Honorius*, Naasa answers to the angels Hanahel, Raquyel, and Salguyel, who rule the sphere of Venus. He has power over lust and desire, invoking pleasure in mortals. His manifest appearance is beautiful and pleasant, with a face as white as snow. This demon is also said to be one of four in Sarabocres's court ruled by the east and west winds. Compare to the demon Naassa

from the Driscoll translation of the *Sworn Book*. See also NAASSA, SARABOCRES, *SWORN BOOK*.

Naassa: A demon ruled by the infernal president Canibores, Naassa holds the rank of minister and is one of three such demons reputed to appear and speak for their master. Canibores himself cannot be conjured into visible appearance. In the Driscoll edition of the *Sworn Book*, Naassa is said to cause men to fall in love with women, and women to fall in love with men. He can incite lust and passion, as well as inspiring boundless enjoyment in those who pursue physical pleasure. A demon firmly devoted to earthly delights, Naassa not only holds sway over lust and passion, but he can also cause luxurious items—such as rare perfumes and costly fabrics—to appear. When he manifests, he assumes a body of moderate stature with flesh that shines like a brilliant star. As is common among demons who serve within the same hierarchy, Naassa's name closely parallels that of his fellow minister under Canibores, Nassar. Also compare his name and manifest powers to those of the demon Naasa, from Peterson's *Sworn Book*. See also CANIBORES, NAASA, NASSAR, *SWORN BOOK*.

Nabam: A demon invoked on Saturdays, Nabam appears in the *Grimorium Verum* as translated by occult scholar Joseph H. Peterson. See also *GRIMORIUM VERUM*.

Naberius: The twenty-fourth demon of the *Goetia*. According to Scot, he is also known as *Cerberus*. Cerberus was the name of the three-headed hound in Greek myth said to guard the gates to Hades. Naberius has little to show from this possible canine association, as he is described as appearing in the form of a crow that speaks with a hoarse voice. Scot ranks this demon as a marquis with nineteen legions at his command. He is attributed with the power to make men amiable and cunning in rhetoric. Further, he is said to help strip people of dignities and status. In Wierus's *Pseudomonarchia Daemonum*, this demon's name is rendered *Naberus*. In the *Goetia of Dr. Rudd*, he is said to initially flit about the chamber in the shape of a crow when he appears. He is constrained by the angel Haiviah. See also *GOETIA*, RUDD, SCOT, WIERUS.

Nacheran: A servitor of the demon Magoth. The Mathers translation of the *Sacred Magic of Abramelin the Mage* also lists Nacheran as a servant of Kore. See also KORE, MAGOTH, MATHERS.

Nadriel: A demon named in the Henson translation of the *Ars Theurgia*, Nadriel serves in the court of Pamersiel, the first and chief spirit of the east. Nadriel holds the rank of duke, and like all of the dukes of the demon Pamersiel, he is said to be arrogant, stubborn, and thoroughly evil. Because he is given to deceit, he should never be trusted with secret matters. However, his aggressive na-

ture makes him useful for driving off other spirits, particularly those that haunt houses. See also *ARS THEURGIA*, PAMERSIEL.

Nadroc: A demon named in the *Ars Theurgia* from Henson's translation of the complete *Lemegeton*. Nadroc is one of twelve demons holding the rank of duke listed by name in the hierarchy of Amenadiel, the infernal Emperor of the West. Nadroc himself has three thousand eight hundred and eighty ministering spirits at his command. As with all of the demons named in the *Ars Theurgia*, he is said to possess an airy nature and is best seen through a crystal stone or scrying glass. See also AMENADIEL, *ARS THEURGIA*.

An example of the summoning circle from Scot's *Discoverie of Witchcraft*. The spirits are conjured outside of this circle while the magician sits safely within. Courtesy of Dover Publications.

Nadrusiel: Commanding one thousand eight hundred and forty lesser spirits, Nadrusiel is a chief duke governed by the infernal prince Soleviel. According to the *Ars Theurgia*, Nadrusiel serves his demonic master only one year of every two,

The Rise of the Decans

The *Testament of Solomon* features a series of demons assigned to the thirty-six decans of the zodiac. But what is a decan, and why is it significant to demonology? In modern Western astrology, there are twelve signs of the zodiac, and each of these signs can be broken down into three decans each. In this, the decans represent ten degrees of the ecliptic, which, being a circle, is 360 degrees. But this was not the original purpose of the decans. The decans were initially separate from the zodiac as we know it. Developed in Egypt during the First Intermediate Period (2181–2040 BCE), they were used to mark the hours of the night.

For a period of ten days, each decan hung in the sky as the last and brightest constellation before dawn. Their heliacal rising helped mark 360 out of the 365-day year. (The ancient Egyptians tossed in five feast days, called *epagomenal days*, to make up the difference.) Theresa Ainsworth explains, "As hour-markers, the star or constellation that made up each decan was seen as a lesser protective god, akin to a daimon."* These thirty-six daimons of the decans were depicted as animal-headed deities on numerous tombs, and by the time Hermeticism flourished in Egypt (circa 300 BCE), the decans had come to be more than timekeepers. They were also seen as holding power over disease.

In *Le Livre Sacré sur les Décans*, otherwise known as *The Sacred Book of Hermes to Asclepius*, these decanal daimons are described, along with their zodiac associations, the diseases they caused, and the talismans required to counter their effects. This hermetic text was written around the same time as the currently accepted date of the *Testament of Solomon*, and its influence is clear. Solomon's thirty-six demons are direct derivations of the ancient Egyptian daimons of the night.

---

* Theresa Ainsworth, "A Timeline of the Decans," p. 1.

switching off among his fellow dukes. See also *ARS THEURGIA*, SOLEVIEL.

Nagani: A servitor of the infernal king Ariton, Nagani appears in all known versions of the *Sacred Magic of Abramelin the Mage* with the exception of the manuscript translated by occultist S. L. MacGregor Mathers. See also ARITON, MATHERS.

Nagid: According to Mathers's translation of the *Sacred Magic of Abramelin the Mage*, this demon's name is derived from a Hebrew word meaning "leader." Nagid is one of a number of demons governed by the infernal princes of the cardinal directions: Oriens, Paimon, Ariton, and Amaimon. See also AMAIMON, ARITON, MATHERS, ORIENS, PAIMON.

Nahiel: A demon in the hierarchy of Dorochiel, an infernal ruler of the west. Nahiel's rank is listed in the *Ars Theurgia* as chief duke, and he is said to have forty ministering spirits beneath him. See also *ARS THEURGIA*, DOROCHIEL.

Najin: The 1898 translation of the *Sacred Magic of Abramelin the Mage*, produced by occultist S. L. MacGregor Mathers, suggests that the name of this demon may be derived from a Hebrew root meaning "propagating." Najin is one of a large host of demons ruled by the four infernal princes of the cardinal directions: Oriens, Paimon, Ariton, and Amaimon. Najin and his many other demonic cohorts are all mentioned as part of the working to achieve dialogue with the Holy Guardian Angel, a ritual central to the *Abramelin* material. See also AMAIMON, ARITON, MATHERS, ORIENS, PAIMON.

Nalael: According to the *Ars Theurgia*, Nalael is a duke in service to the demon Symiel, king of the north by east. Associated with the hours of the night, Nalael is attended by one hundred and thirty ministering spirits that carry out his will. He possesses an obstinate and ill-tempered nature and is reluctant to appear before mortals. See also *ARS THEURGIA*, SYMIEL.

Nambrot: A demon associated with Saturday in the *Grimoire of Pope Honorius*. In the same text, he is also named as the demon of Tuesday. In the Peterson translation of the *Grimorium Verum*, he appears under the name *Nambroth*. Here, he is also said to be associated with Tuesdays. See also *GRIMORIUM VERUM*.

Namiros: A servitor of the arch-fiend Beelzebub, Namiros is named in the *Sacred Magic of Abramelin the Mage*, in which he is called up and made to swear an oath as part of the Holy Guardian Angel working. See also BEELZEBUB, MATHERS.

Naôth: According to the pseudepigraphal *Testament of Solomon*, Naôth is the nineteenth of thirty-six demons associated with the decans of the zodiac. He is a demon of affliction and disease, attacking humanity by causing ailments of the knees and the neck. He appears in a monstrous form, possessing the body of a man and the head of a beast, and he is sometimes also known by the name *Nathath*. He can be driven away by calling upon the name *Phnunoboêol*. As *Rhyx Nathotho*, he is the twentieth demon in this list as translated later by McCown. Working from a more complete collection of source texts, McCown's translation is generally more accurate. In this version of the text, it is the angel Phounibiel who constrains him. See also SOLOMON.

Naras: A demon named in the *Ars Theurgia*. Naras is said to serve the demon-king Gediel. Holding the rank of duke, Naras is connected to the hours of the day and, through Gediel, he also has an affiliation with the southern point of the compass.

He has twenty lesser spirits to carry out his commands. See also *ARS THEURGIA*, GEDIEL.

Two men stand in a circle as they summon the Devil. Woodcut, 1720. Image courtesy of the Wellcome Collection, London.

Narsial: A chief duke who owes fealty to the infernal prince Dorochiel. In the *Ars Theurgia*, Narsial is said to be a demon of the night, serving his master in the hours between midnight and dawn. He has four hundred lesser spirits at his command. Through Dorochiel, he is connected with the region of the west. See also *ARS THEURGIA*, DOROCHIEL.

Nartniel: A duke in the hierarchy of the wandering prince Uriel, according to the *Ars Theurgia*. Nartniel is reputedly an evil, stubborn, and dishonest spirit. He appears in the form of a serpent with the head of a beautiful young woman. As a demon of rank, he has command over a total of six hundred and fifty companions and lesser spirits. See also *ARS THEURGIA*, URIEL.

Narzael: A stubborn and willful demon who is tied to the hours of the night. Narzael is one of a thousand demons holding the rank of chief duke who wait upon the infernal king Symiel during the nocturnal hours. Narzael himself holds power over a total of two hundred and ten lesser spirits.

Narzael is a part of a series of demons discussed in the Henson translation of the *Ars Theurgia*. He serves the court of the north. See also *ARS THEURGIA*, SYMIEL.

Nasar: A ministering spirit of King Sarabotres, the ruler of the planetary sphere of Venus. Nasar's color is green and he appears very handsome and agreeable. He may manifest as a naked girl or as a young woman dressed in beautiful garments of emerald and white. He has the power to influence feelings, encouraging love and harmonious interactions. He can also conjure all things that have movement, which is a rather broad category of items. He appears in the *Book of Oberon*, a grimoire written during the Elizabethan age in England. Compare to the demons *Naasar*, *Naassar*, and *Nassar*. See also *BOOK OF OBERON*, MANASA, SARABOTRES.

Nasiniet: A mighty duke with a total of one thousand three hundred and twenty ministering spirits to attend his needs. Nasiniet appears in the *Ars Theurgia* in a list of spirits who serve the infernal prince Emoniel. Nasiniet is said to have a fondness for forests and woods where he is able to manifest himself equally well during the hours of the day or the night. See also *ARS THEURGIA*, EMONIEL.

Nassar: One of three ministers who serve the demon Canibores, a powerful president of Hell. Daniel Driscoll's edition of the *Sworn Book of Honourius* tells us that Canibores cannot be conjured to visible appearance himself. Instead, he can be reached through his three ministers, each of whom possesses powers similar to their superior. Subsequently, when Nassar is summoned, he can create boundless enjoyment in the opposite sex and sow both love and lust between men and women. He has a nature that is as malleable as silver, and his body shines like a brilliant star. Nassar's name is conspicuously similar to that of one of his compatriots, Naassa. Such parallelism or pairing of names is common among demons who serve in the same infernal hierarchies. In the Peterson translation of the *Sworn Book*, Nassar is identified as one of two ministers of the demon Sarabocres. Here, he is connected with the planet Venus. As a Venusian spirit, many of his powers remain the same. In the *Ars Theurgia*, Nassar appears as a servant of the demon Armadiel, associated with the north. In this text, he is said to hold the title of duke. If the day is divided into fifteen sections, Nassar's time is the first portion of the day. He is attended by eighty-four ministering spirits. See also ARMADIEL, *ARS THEURGIA*, CANIBORES, NAASSA, SARABOCRES, *SWORN BOOK*.

Nastros: A demon of darkness who commands a total of eight hundred and eighty lesser spirits. Nastros appears in the *Ars Theurgia*, as translated by Mitch Henson. According to this work, Nastros serves the wandering duke Buriel, a prince of the air who moves from place to place along with his retinue. Nastros is an evil spirit who fears the light. When he manifests, it is only at night and he takes the form of a great serpent. This monstrous serpent bears a woman's head and speaks with a man's voice. Nastros and all the hierarchy of Buriel are so evil that they are hated and reviled by all other spirits. See also *ARS THEURGIA*, BURIEL.

Natales: A name derived from the Latin word for "nativity," Natales appears in the Mathers translation of the *Sacred Magic of Abramelin the Mage*. According to this text, he is a demon ruled by the archfiend Beelzebub. Another variant spelling of this name is *Natalis*. See also BEELZEBUB, MATHERS.

Nathes: A demonic prince listed in the *Munich Handbook*. He is conjured as part of a spell to obtain information concerning a theft. He helps with matters of divination. See also *MUNICH HANDBOOK*.

Nathriel: One of fifteen dukes governed by the infernal prince Icosiel. According to the *Ars Theurgia*, Nathriel commands a total of two thousand two hundred lesser spirits. He has a fondness for manifesting in people's houses, but he is bound only to appear during certain hours and minutes each day. If the day is divided into fifteen equal portions, the portion that belongs to Nathriel is the ninth. See also *ARS THEURGIA*, ICOSIEL.

Nebiros: A demon named in both the *Grimorium Verum* and the *Grand Grimoire*. He is a martial demon and is described as being Hell's field marshal. The *Grand Grimoire* also accords him the title of Inspector General of Hell's armies. Nebiros is credited with the ability to work evil upon whomsoever he wishes. He further possesses the secrets of the Hand of Glory, a grisly talisman much sought after by thieves. He knows the virtues of all vegetables, minerals, metals, and animals, and will reveal these to the magician bold enough to summon him forth. Additionally, he has the gift of prophecy, which he typically works through operations of necromancy. Beneath him are the Goetic demons Ipos, Glasya Labolas, and Naberius. The inclusion of Naberius among his ministers is curious, as Nebiros is almost certainly a variation on the name Naberius. See also GLASYA LABOLAS, *GRAND GRIMOIRE*, *GRIMORIUM VERUM*, IPOS, NABERIUS.

Nedriel: A roguish and malevolent demon who assumes the form of a human-headed serpent. Nedriel is a demon who loves night and darkness. He flees the light and refuses to manifest during the day. According to the *Ars Theurgia*, he serves beneath the wandering duke Buriel, and he commands a total of eight hundred and eighty lesser spirits of his own. Because of their vile and evil natures, Nedriel and all his ilk are hated and despised by other spirits. Elsewhere in the *Ars Theurgia*, this demon appears as one of several demonic companions, or "under dukes," named in connection with the court of the wandering prince Menadiel. In this hierarchy, Nedriel is said to follow the infernal duke Benodiel. As both are tied to specific hours of the day, Nedriel manifests in the eighth hour, following his master Benodiel, who manifests in the seventh. See also *ARS THEURGIA*, BENODIEL, BURIEL, MENADIEL.

Nemariel: A demon who holds the rank of knight. In this capacity, he works for the infernal prince Pirichiel, traveling from place to place and carrying out his will. Nemariel holds sway over a total of two thousand lesser spirits. His name appears in the Henson edition of the *Ars Theurgia*. See also *ARS THEURGIA*, PIRICHIEL.

Nenisem: In his 1898 translation of the *Sacred Magic of Abramelin the Mage*, Mathers includes Nenisem in a list of demons who serve Magoth and Kore. In the 1720 version of the *Abramelin* material kept in the Dresden library, the name of this demon appears as *Pasifen*. See also KORE, MAGOTH, MATHERS.

Neophon: A demon who appears in the form of a hound. He is named in the *Book of Oberon*, where he is identified as one of twelve high-ranking servitors to King Oriens, ruler of the spirits of the east. Neophon is a demon of prophecy and a revealer of secrets who also can grant favors and fame. If one has enemies, he can turn them into friends. All riches, dignities, and worship are his to grant. See also *BOOK OF OBERON*, ORIENS.

Nephthada: According to the *Testament of Solomon*, Nephthada is the twenty-third demon associated with the thirty-six decans of the zodiac. He is a demon of illness and disease, and he typically appears in a monstrous form with the head of a beast but the body of a man. Nephthada can be abjured by uttering the names *Iâthôth* and *Uruêl*. Sometimes, his name is also rendered *Nefthada*. In a later translation of this book, working from a more complete selection of source texts, the name of the twenty-third demon is *Rhyx Manthado*. *Rhyx* is a title meaning "king." He afflicts the kidneys and can be constrained by saying the names *Iaoth* and *Ouriel*. See also SOLOMON.

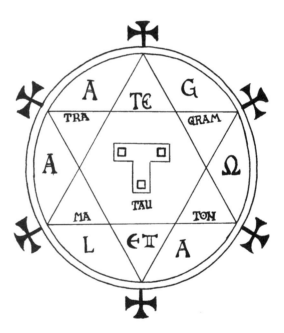

The Hexagram of Solomon. This symbol is found in several grimoires, including the *Lemegeton*. Art by Jackie Williams.

Nercamay: A demon who serves beneath all four princes of the cardinal directions, Nercamay appears in the *Sacred Magic of Abramelin the Mage*. Mathers suggests that his name arises from two Hebrew words meaning "boy" and "companion."

Nine Choirs of Heaven and Hell

By the Middle Ages, it was widely accepted that the Heavenly Hosts were comprised of nine distinct orders of angels. This celestial hierarchy was divided up into three tiers, or *spheres*, and these were ranked in order from those closest to the Throne of God to those closest to the physical realm. The most influential church scholar on this topic was Pseudo-Dionysius the Areopagite, who created his *Celestial Hierarchy* in the fourth or fifth century of the Common Era. Saint Thomas Aquinas also wrote on the angelic hierarchies in his *Summa Theologica*. Saint Gregory the Great additionally promoted the concept of the Nine Choirs in his works. Four of the orders of angels are drawn from Old Testament sources. These are the Angels, Archangels, Cherubim, and Seraphim. The remaining orders come from Paul's Letter to the Ephesians and his Letter to the Colossians.

Top Sphere: *Seraphim, Cherubim, Thrones*
Middle Sphere: *Dominions, Virtues, Powers*
Lower Sphere: *Principalities, Archangels, Angels*

In the Middle Ages and Renaissance, the Order of Dominions was sometimes also called the Order of Dominations. The Order of Powers was sometimes known as the Order of Potestates. Principalities and Powers were added as choirs in the angelic hierarchy at least in part because of a reference in Romans 8:38 that speaks of angels, principalities, and powers. Although the text does not clearly identify the principalities and powers as orders of angels, early church fathers, such as Pseudo-Dionysius, interpreted them as such.

As many demons were formerly angels before their fall, it made sense for medieval writers to assume that the demons would at least retain some vestiges of this ninefold hierarchy. Thus, works like the *Goetia* make note of which demons belonged to which orders before their fall. Sometimes, the orders of the demons are not presented in the past tense, suggesting that the hierarchy of Hell may simply be a dark reflection of the nine angelic orders. This would be in keeping with Qabbalistic notions which outline an angelic hierarchy based upon the ten Sephiroth of the Tree of Life. The system of the Qabbalah accounts for something called the Qlippoth. This is essentially a dark reflection of the Tree of Life, populated by demons who are viewed as husks or shells left over from an imperfect creation.

From there, it is not much of a stretch to suppose that Nercamay is something of a catamite. As a servant of the four cardinal princes, he shares all of their powers, and, if summoned, he can grant familiars to the magician or summon armed men for his protection. See also AMAIMON, ARITON, MATHERS, ORIENS, PAIMON.

Nergal: According to French demonologist Charles Berbiguier's three-volume work *Les Farfadets*, Nergal is a Minister of Hell and the Chief of the Secret Police. This title seems only fitting, considering that, in his earlier days, Nergal was a fierce warrior who later became the lord of the Underworld. In Assyro-Babylonian myth, Nergal ruled the land of dust and tears with his wife Ereshkigal, who was so nasty, she tortured and killed her own sister. Since one of Nergal's symbols was the sickle, he may have helped to influence later images of the Grim Reaper. Nergal is also described as Hell's Chief of Secret Police in A. E. Waite's *Book of Black Magic and Pacts* as well as Collin de Plancy's *Dictionnaire Infernal*. See also BERBIGUIER, DE PLANCY.

Neriel: A demon associated with the hours of the day who is nevertheless called forth by night. Neriel's name and seal appear in the *Ars Theurgia*, where he is said to serve Camuel, the infernal prince of the southeast. Neriel is ranked as a duke and he has ten ministering spirits at his command. See also *ARS THEURGIA*, CAMUEL.

Nesachnaadob: One of several demons who serve the infernal king Fornnouc. Nesachnaadob is said to appear when certain perfumes are burned in his name. He is a demon connected with the element of air and, accordingly, he has a nature that is both lively and capricious. He has an active and agile mind, and he will serve as an inspiring tutor for those who make the proper offering to him.

He also has the power to cure weaknesses and prevent further infirmities. He appears in Daniel Driscoll's 1977 edition of the *Sworn Book of Honourius*, a modern translation of a magickal text dating approximately to the fourteenth century. See also FORNNOUC, *SWORN BOOK*.

Nesaph: Ruled by the demon Formione, king of the spirits of Jupiter, Nesaph appears in the Peterson's translation of the *Sworn Book of Honorius*. In this text, he is said to grant favors to people. He also has the power to bring gladness, love, and joy. The angels Satquiel, Raphael, Pahamcocihel, and Asassaiel have the power to compel and constrain him. See also FORMIONE, *SWORN BOOK*.

Nessar: According to Driscoll's edition of the *Sworn Book*, Nessar is one of the ministers who serve the infernal king Sarabocres. Like his immediate superior, Nessar is a demon who possesses a shifting and malleable nature. In appearance, he is described as possessing a body of moderate stature colored like a brilliant star. His province is love, lust, and all earthly pleasures. He can bring gifts of rich and costly fabrics and perfumes, and he can inspire increased enjoyment during sex. See also SARABOCRES, *SWORN BOOK*.

Niagutly: A minister in the court of the demon-king Fornnouc, said to rule over the element of air. Niagutly can serve as a demonic tutor, teaching all rational arts and sciences. He has an agile mind, lively and active, but also fickle. He is additionally a healer, curing weakness and infirmity. His name appears in the Driscoll edition of the *Sworn Book*. See also FORNNOUC, *SWORN BOOK*.

Nilen: This demon's name is most likely derived from the Greek word for the River Nile. Nilen appears in the *Sacred Magic of Abramelin the Mage*, where he is said to be subject to the four princes of the cardinal directions: Oriens, Paimon, Ariton, and Amaimon. As such, he shares all of the powers that they can confer, from flight to visions to the raising of the dead. AMAIMON, ARITON, ORIENS, PAIMON.

Nilima: A name meaning "evil questioner," at least according to occultist S. L. MacGregor Mathers. In his translation of the *Sacred Magic of Abramelin the Mage*, Nilima is said to work as a servant of the demon-king Amaimon. He is summoned and bound through oaths during the Holy Guardian Angel working central to the *Abramelin* material. See also AMAIMON, MATHERS.

Nimalon: A servitor of the demons Astaroth and Asmodeus. In his translation of the *Sacred Magic of Abramelin the Mage*, Mathers strangely relates the name of this demon to the Hebrew word for circumcision. See also ASTAROTH, ASMODEUS, MATHERS.

Nimerix: A demon called upon in the course of the Holy Guardian Angel rite. Nimerix appears in the Mathers translation of the *Sacred Magic of Abramelin the Mage*, where he is said to have no master other than Astaroth. See also ASTAROTH, MATHERS.

Nimorup: One of several demon names that appear in the *Sacred Magic of Abramelin the Mage* that have radically different spelling from one version to the next. He appears as Nimorup on the Mathers translation. The version at the Wolfenbüttel library in Germany gives this name as *Mynymarup*, while the manuscript at the Dresden library renders it *Mynimorug*. All versions agree, however, that this demon is a servant of Beelzebub. See also BEELZEBUB, MATHERS.

Nodar: A night-demon who nevertheless appears during the hours of the day, Nodar is named in the *Ars Theurgia*. According to this text, he serves the infernal prince Camuel, ruler of the southeast. Nodar is a duke in this infernal hierarchy, and ten ministering spirits serve beneath him. See also *ARS THEURGIA*, CAMUEL.

Nogar: In the Mathers translation of the *Sacred Magic of Abramelin the Mage*, the name of this demon is related to a Hebrew word that means "flowing." Nogar is a part of the demonic hierarchy governed by all four infernal princes of the cardinal directions: Oriens, Paimon, Ariton, and Amaimon. See also AMAIMON, ARITON, MATHERS, ORIENS, PAIMON.

Nogen: A demon loyal to Oriens, Amaimon, Ariton, and Paimon. He is named in the Mathers translation of the *Sacred Magic of Abramelin the Mage*. *See also* AMAIMON, ARITON, MATHERS, ORIENS, PAIMON.

Noguiel: The third infernal duke said to serve the demon-king Maseriel during the hours of the night. Noguiel is named in the *Ars Theurgia*. According to this text, he has thirty lesser spirits that obey his command. In addition to his connection with the night, Noguiel is also affiliated with the south. See also *ARS THEURGIA*, MASERIEL.

Nominon: This infernal name is a bit redundant as it essentially means "name." Derived from a Latin root, this demon name appears in the *Sacred Magic of Abramelin the Mage*. Here, Nominon is said to serve the arch-demon Beelzebub. See also BEELZEBUB, MATHERS.

Noocar: This demon, with a name that did not age well, first appears in the Elizabethan manual of magic known as the *Book of Oberon*. He is a very obstreperous being and will refuse to tell the truth unless under duress. When he appears, he does so in the guise of an old man leaning on a staff. He

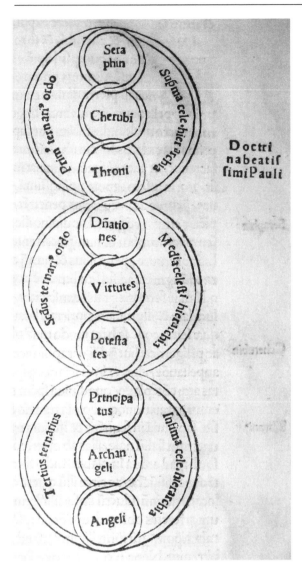

The nine orders of angels as defined by Pseudo-Dionysius. From a sixteenth-century edition of the *Celestial Hierarchy*.

has the tail of a viper but earthly feet. His hands are dirty and his voice is like that of a screech owl. He can reveal the locations of treasures that are kept under the powers of Saturn or Mercury. Of all the arts, he teaches necromancy best. He also has a great love for money, possibly as an offering. In rank, he is said to be a noble lord with com-

mand over twenty-seven legions. See also *BOOK OF OBERON*.

Notiser: A servant of the demon Ariton named in the Mathers translation of the *Sacred Magic of Abramelin the Mage*. Mathers suggests that the name comes from a Greek word meaning "to put to flight." The name is spelled variously *Notison* and *Notifer* in other versions of the *Abramelin* material. See also ARITON, MATHERS.

Nubar: This spirit, identified as a demon in the *Munich Handbook*, is conjured as part of a divination spell. The magician stands before a young boy, ideally a virgin, and invokes the demons so that they appear to the child. The demons then use the child as a mediator to reveal information to the magician. See also *MUNICH HANDBOOK*.

Nuditon: A demon whose name means "the naked one." He appears in the *Sacred Magic of Abramelin the Mage*. He is a servant of Oriens, Paimon, Ariton, and Amaimon, the four infernal rulers of the cardinal directions. See also AMAIMON, ARITON, MATHERS, ORIENS, PAIMON.

Nuthon: In Mathers's translation of the *Sacred Magic of Abramelin the Mage*, Nuthon is named as one of many demons who serve beneath Oriens, Paimon, Ariton, and Amaimon, the demonic princes of the four directions. In his attempt at tracing the etymology of the demon's name, Mathers suggests that Nuthon comes from a Greek word meaning "piercing." See also AMAIMON, ARITON, MATHERS, ORIENS, PAIMON.

Nybbas: Chief Mimic and one of the Masters of Revels, Nybbas appears in the Waite translation of the *Grand Grimoire* published in his 1910 work, *The Book of Black Magic and Pacts*. Waite credits sixteenth-century scholar Johannes Wierus with cooking up the curious hierarchy from which Nybbas is drawn, but the real culprit is the self-styled French demonologist Charles Berbiguier. Collin de Plancy sourced Berbiguier's work *Les Farfadets* for his extensive *Dictionnaire Infernal*, so Nybbas shows up here as well. De Plancy elaborates upon Nybbas's functions, describing him as a master of visions and dreams. He may be related to the ancient Samarian deity Nibhaz referenced in 2 Kings 17:31. See also BERBIGUIER, *GRAND GRIMOIRE*, WAITE, WIERUS.

Nymgarraman: Should an individual seek to cause great pain and suffering in another person, this demon will prove more than worthy of the task. One of the servants of the infernal king Bilet, Nymgarraman is named in the fifteenth-century *Liber de Angelis*. He is a demon of disease, and he has the power to inflict fever in a target, as well as a weakness and trembling in the limbs. He is called upon to curse an enemy, inflicting these symptoms as an act of vengeance. See also BILETH, *LIBER DE ANGELIS*.

Oaspeniel: One of twelve dukes governed by the wandering prince Emoniel. Both Oaspeniel's name and his demonic seal appear in the seventeenth-century magickal text known as the *Ars Theurgia*. He is said to have one thousand three hundred and twenty attending spirits beneath him. Unlike many spirits listed in this work, Oaspeniel has no great preference for any hour of the day or night but will manifest at any time. He does, however, have a predilection for wooded areas. See also *ARS THEURGIA*, EMONIEL.

Obagiro: A demon in service to the arch-fiend Magoth. Obagiro's name appears in connection with the Holy Guardian Angel working described in the *Sacred Magic of Abramelin the Mage*. In his 1898 translation of this work, occultist Samuel Mathers renders the name of this demon as *Abagiron*. See also MAGOTH, MATHERS.

Obedama: This demon appears in the *Sacred Magic of Abramelin the Mage*. Obedama is supposed to serve beneath all four of the demonic princes of the cardinal directions: Oriens, Paimon, Ariton, and Amaimon. In his reading of the name, Mathers suggests that *Obedama* may mean "hand maiden." See also AMAIMON, ARITON, MATHERS, ORIENS, PAIMON.

Oberion: Also spelled *Oberyon*. He is a principal spirit in the eponymous *Book of Oberon*. Although he is described as the King of the Faeries, the text also defines him as a being who once was an angel of light—making it pretty clear that, at least when the *Book of Oberon* was penned, no conflict was seen with a demon being both a faerie and a fallen angel. Oberion is said to appear as a great and mighty king with a crown on his head or as a three-year-old boy. Governed by both the sun and the moon, he is knowledgeable in the nature of herbs, stones, trees, and all metals and can reveal the location of hidden treasure. He can also fetch treasure out of the sea, carrying up to 1,000,000 £. (The text is unclear about whether that is intended to be an amount of currency or an actual weight.)

In addition to fetching treasure, he teaches medicine and has the power to confer invisibility. His name is likely more familiar to readers under the spelling *Oberon*, used by Shakespeare in his *Midsummer Night's Dream*. The *Book of Oberon* applies the same methods of summoning, compelling, and banishing faeries as it does for demons, and there is a real possibility that the people of the time saw little difference between these types of beings. Certainly, when Christianity came to the British Isles, the local faith—which included a rich belief in piskies, brownies, pookas, bogles, and other faerie folk—was forcibly suppressed. Efforts were made to demonize the faeries, as the Christian clergy of the time perceived as demonic all spirits that were not explicitly classed as angels. The faerie-faith of the Celtic peoples proved too strong, however, so legends evolved to ameliorate the faeries' position as neither wholly Christian nor wholly demonic in nature. Chief among these was the belief in the tithe to Hell, supposedly paid by the faeries every seven years so they could continue as free agents. Oberion does not appear exclusively in the *Book of Oberon*. The manuscript known as *e Musaeo 173* of the Bodleian Library also contains a spell for summoning this intriguingly liminal being. See also *BOOK OF OBERON*.

Obizuth: An exceptionally unsettling demon, Obizuth is said to appear as a woman without any limbs. According to the *Testament of Solomon*, Obizuth creeps around at night, visiting women in childbirth. She is said to strangle newborns. In addition to killing infants outright, she is also allegedly responsible for a variety of birth defects. She can blind babies and deafen them. She can also make them mute. She addles their senses and twists their bodies so that their limbs grow withered and unusable. In her abject hatred of newborns, Obizuth bears qualities in common with Jewish notions of the night-demon Lilith, although there is no indication in the *Testament of Solomon* that these two demons are one and the same. Beyond her limbless state, Obizuth is said to be very beautiful, with bright green eyes and long, flowing hair. Her hair appears to be tossed constantly as in a wind. According to the text, she is frustrated by the angel Afarôt, a form of the angel Raphael. Once Solomon gained control over her, he had her hung up by her hair over the entrance to the temple as a warning to all demonkind. See also LILITH, SOLOMON.

Obus: This demon makes a faithful familiar, and he will not suffer his master to be harmed by any other spirit. His name and description are recorded in the *Book of Incantations*, a cunning-man's grimoire from Wales. In that text, he is assigned the rank of prince. He governs twenty legions. His office is to discover things past, present, and future. He advances dignities and the favor of friends and foes. He wears the guise of a horse, and his name may actually be spelled *Oleus*. The *Book of Incantations* is a handwritten grimoire, and the penmanship makes this name difficult to decipher. See also BOOK OF INCANTATIONS.

Ocarbydatonn: A king in the court of the infernal ruler Amaimon. According to the Elizabethan grimoire known as the *Book of Oberon*, Ocarbydatonn appears with the demons Emlon and Madyconn to herald Amaimon when he is summoned. See also AMAIMON, *BOOK OF OBERON*, EMLON, MADYCONN.

Ocel: A wicked demon invoked as part of a retribution spell. According to the *Munich Handbook*, he attacks people's minds. He has the power to confuse them and addle their senses. See also *MU-NICH HANDBOOK*.

Oclachanos: According to the *Liber de Angelis*, Oclachanos is a demon of disease. He answers directly to Bilet, a king of the infernal realms, and he can be conjured to inflict disease upon an enemy. Oclachanos can inspire a vicious set of symptoms, including fever, trembling, and weakness in the limbs. See also BILETH, *LIBER DE ANGELIS*.

Odax: A servitor of the demon Magoth, named in the Mathers translation of the *Sacred Magic of Abramelin the Mage*. In all other versions of this work, the name is rendered *Odac*. See also MAGOTH, MATHERS.

Odiel: A demon named in the *Ars Theurgia*, Odiel appears in the hierarchy of the infernal prince Aseliel. Odiel holds the rank of chief president and has thirty principal spirits and another twenty ministering servants at his command. Odiel is tied to the court of the east and the hours of the night. See also *ARS THEURGIA*, ASELIEL.

Oemiel: A demon who serves beneath infernal king Armadiel in the hierarchy of the north. Oemiel's name and seal, as well as the best method for summoning and compelling him, appear in the *Ars Theurgia*. If the day is divided into fifteen parts, Oemiel's time is the final of these portions. He will not appear at any other point during the day. See ARMADIEL, *ARS THEURGIA*.

Ofsiel: One of a number of spirits who serve in the extensive hierarchy of the demon-prince Dorochiel. Ofsiel's name and seal appear in the *Ars Theurgia*, where he is said to hold the title of chief duke. He commands a total of forty lesser spirits. Tied to the hours of the night, Ofsiel will only appear during a specific hour between nightfall and

midnight. He serves in the region of the west. See also *ARS THEURGIA*, DOROCHIEL.

Ogilen: In the Mathers translation of the *Sacred Magic of Abramelin the Mage*, Ogilen is one of a number of demons who serve beneath Oriens, Paimon, Ariton, and Amaimon, the four infernal princes of the cardinal directions. Mathers suggests that this demon's name is derived from a Hebrew word originally meaning "wheel." See also AMAIMON, ARITON, MATHERS, ORIENS, PAIMON.

OGya: Named in the *Book of Oberon*, OGya (spelled exactly like that) is a demonic prince who appears as a horned viper with great teeth. He carries a sword in his hand, a fact that implies that only his head is perfectly snakelike. Although no specific powers are ascribed to him in the text, he is said to give true answers when questioned. A total of thirty-five legions of ministering spirits are at his command. Compare his description to that of the Goetic demon *Botis*. See also *BOOK OF OBERON*, BOTIS.

Okiri: A demon governed by the arch-fiend Astaroth, Okiri appears in the Mathers translation of the *Sacred Magic of Abramelin the Mage*. Mathers suggests that the demon's name may mean "to cause to sink" or "to fail." The name appears as *Okirgi* in another version of the *Abramelin* material kept at the Wolfenbüttel library in Germany. The 1720 version kept in the Dresden library gives the name as *Akrey*. The demon names in the *Abramelin* material tend to vary widely between different manuscripts. See also ASTAROTH, MATHERS.

Oliroomin: An infernal horseman whose name appears in the fifteenth-century *Munich Handbook*. Oliroomin is called upon to enchant a bridle. Once properly imbued with hellish power, this object is said to summon a demon in the form of a great, swift horse. This infernal mount will carry its owner to any location desired. See also *MUNICH HANDBOOK.*

Olisermon: A demon name that may mean "of short speech." Olisermon serves under the joint leadership of the demons Magoth and Kore. He appears in the *Sacred Magic of Abramelin the Mage.* His name is also spelled *Olosirmon.* See also KORE, MAGOTH, MATHERS.

Omages: According to occultist S. L. MacGregor Mathers, this demon's name is derived from the Greek term *magos,* meaning "mage." In the *Sacred Magic of Abramelin the Mage,* Omages is said to serve the arch-demons Astaroth and Asmodeus and is invoked as a part of the Holy Guardian Angel working focused on by the *Abramelin* material. In different manuscript versions of this work, the name of this demon is given as *Omagos,* lending credence to the Greek origin of this name. See also ASTAROTH, ASMODEUS, MATHERS.

Oman: A demon under the leadership of the arch-fiends Astaroth and Asmodeus, Oman is named in connection with the Holy Guardian Angel rite in the Mathers translation of the *Sacred Magic of Abramelin the Mage.* Mathers suggests that his name comes from a Chaldean word meaning "to cover" or "to obscure." See also ASTAROTH, ASMODEUS, MATHERS.

Ombalat: In the Mathers translation of the *Sacred Magic of Abramelin the Mage,* Ombalat is named in the hierarchy of demons who serve Astaroth. A variant spelling on this demon's name is *Ombalafa.* See also ASTAROTH, MATHERS.

Omet: One of several demons associated with the infernal lord Asmodeus in the *Sacred Magic of Abramelin the Mage.* This demon appears only in the Mathers translation of this work and is absent from all other versions of the *Abramelin* material. See also ASMODEUS, MATHERS.

Omich: A demon governed by Carnesiel, the infernal Emperor of the East. According to the *Ars Theurgia,* Omich holds the rank of duke. See also *ARS THEURGIA,* CARNESIEL.

Woodcut of a demon holding court. From the *Compendium Maleficarum* by Francesco Maria Guazzo, courtesy of Dover Publications.

Omiel: A demon named in the *Ars Theurgia,* Omiel appears in the hierarchy of the infernal prince Dorochiel. According to the text, Omiel is tied to the hours of the day and will only appear before noon. He holds the rank of chief duke and commands forty lesser spirits. Through Dorochiel, he is affiliated with the west. Omiel appears elsewhere in the *Ars Theurgia* as a chief duke in service to the demon Asyriel. Here, he is tied to the hours of the night and the court of the south. He still rules over only forty lesser spirits of his own. See also *ARS THEURGIA,* ASYRIEL, DOROCHIEL.

Omyel: A servant of the demon Camuel, an infernal prince connected with the court of the east.

According to the *Ars Theurgia*, Omyel has ten servants who attend him. He holds the rank of duke and belongs to the hours of the day. Despite his affiliation with the daylight hours, Omyel manifests only at night. See also *ARS THEURGIA*, CAMUEL.

Onaris: A demon connected with the arts of divination and scrying, Onaris appears in the *Munich Handbook*, where he is called upon to aid in visions. See also *MUNICH HANDBOOK*.

Onor: A demonic squire with powers of illusion. He is called upon in the *Munich Handbook* to conjure an illusory castle into being. The demon Onor will only perform this impressive task in a remote and secret location after a proper offering of milk and honey has been provided to him. He works on the tenth night of the moon. See also *MUNICH HANDBOOK*.

Onoskelis: A demon who is said to appear in the shape of a beautiful woman, fair of skin and very desirable. As such, Onoskelis is one of the few demons whose gender is clearly fixed as female. In the *Testament of Solomon*, Onoskelis is said to reside in a golden cave. She changes her abode often and can be found in caves, precipices, and ravines. She seduces men in order to kill them, and she claims to be worshipped as a goddess. Tied to the moon, she is subject to the angel Joel, whose name can be called upon to cause her to flee. Solomon puts Onoskelis to work weaving hemp for ropes. Many of her attributes seem to link this demon to Lilith, and she may be one of the many different aspects of this fearsome night-demon. See also LILITH, SOLOMON.

Oor: A demon reputed to possess the power to trick and deceive the senses. He is called upon in the *Munich Handbook* to create an elaborate illusion of a castle filled with servants, knights, and squires. According to the text, he can be cajoled with an offering of milk and honey. He is to be called up in a remote location on the tenth night of the moon. See also *MUNICH HANDBOOK*.

Opilm: One of several demonic servitors of the arch-fiends Astaroth and Asmodeus, Opilm is named in the Mathers translation of the *Sacred Magic of Abramelin the Mage*. Mathers suggests that his name may mean "eminence." In other versions of the *Abramelin* work, the name of this demon is given as *Opilon*. See also ASTAROTH, ASMODEUS, MATHERS.

Opun: A demon whose name appears only in the Mathers translation of the *Sacred Magic of Abramelin the Mage*. Opun supposedly serves beneath the demonic kings Asmodeus and Magoth. The name of this demon appears in none of the other surviving versions of the *Abramelin* material. See also ASMODEUS, MAGOTH, MATHERS.

Orariel: In the *Ars Theurgia*, Orariel is listed as an infernal duke governed by the demon-king Armadiel. Orariel is attended by eighty-four lesser spirits. He is tied to the hierarchy of the north, and he is bound also by time. If the day is divided into fifteen equal portions, Orariel is tied to the fifth portion of time. He will not manifest except during this specific time. See also ARMADIEL, *ARS THEURGIA*.

Oreoth: A particularly malevolent being described as a *demon malignus* in the *Munich Handbook*. He is invoked as part of a curse designed to strike one's enemies senseless. He binds people's minds and addles their senses. See also *MUNICH HANDBOOK*.

Orgosil: According to the Mathers translation of the *Sacred Magic of Abramelin the Mage*, the name of this demon means "tumultuous." Orgosil is one of several demons said to serve the arch-fiend Beelzebub. See also BEELZEBUB, MATHERS.

Orias: The fifty-ninth demon named in the *Goetia*. In Scot's *Discoverie of Witchcraft*, Orias is named as a great marquis with thirty legions under his command. He reportedly appears in the form of a lion with a serpent's tail. He comes riding a strong horse, and he carries two great, hissing serpents in his right hand. From this description, one can only assume that his leonine form has some anthropomorphic qualities. Perhaps appropriately, he is credited with the ability to transform people. He has perfect knowledge of astronomy, teaching the mansions of the planets. He also teaches the virtues of the stars. He is reputed to be able to confer dignities and inspire the favor of both friends and foes. His name appears in both Wierus's *Pseudomonarchia Daemonum* and the Welsh *Book of Incantations*. The name of this demon may stretch back to the *Testament of Solomon*, as it is only one letter off from *Ornias*, a demon who features strongly in that text. In the *Goetia of Dr. Rudd*, he is said to rule over only thirty legions of infernal spirits. This text names the angel Hazahel as the being set over the demon to constrain him. See also *BOOK OF INCANTATIONS, GOETIA,* ORNIAS, RUDD, SCOT, SOLOMON, WIERUS.

Oriel: A spirit whose name appears in several different places, variously described as a demon, an angel, and sometimes even an archangel (where the spelling of his name is interpreted as a variant of *Uriel*). In the second book of Trithemius's *Steganographia*, he appears as an angel. But Oriel also appears in the court of the demon Malgaras in the first book of the *Steganographia*. The spirits here are generally taken to be demons, and they are presented as such in the *Ars Theurgia*. According to this later text, Oriel serves Malgaras as a chief

duke of the day. He has thirty lesser spirits beneath him and he is tied to the court of the west. Elsewhere in the same text, Oriel is named as one of twelve dukes who serve the demon-king Caspiel, Emperor of the South. He is reputedly stubborn and difficult in nature and commands a total of two thousand two hundred and sixty lesser spirits. See also *ARS THEURGIA*, CASPIEL, MALGARAS, TRITHEMIUS, URIEL.

Seal of Oriel from the *Ars Theurgia*. Accorded heavenly rank elsewhere, in this text he is identified as a demon. Ink on parchment by M. Belanger.

Oriens: In the *Sacred Magic of Abramelin the Mage*, Oriens is one of four demons who preside over the cardinal directions. As the Latin root of his name suggests, Oriens is the infernal king of the east. Mathers equates him with the fallen angel Samael, further suggesting that a variation of his name is responsible for "Sir Uriens." According to Mathers, this was a title of the Devil popular in medieval times. According to the *Abramelin* material, Oriens is one of eight demonic sub-princes whose names are scribed upon paper on the second day of the

Holy Guardian Angel working. These demons are supposed to appear to the magician on the third day, at which time he must make them swear their loyalty to him—first on his wand and then on his book. The purpose of acquiring the loyalty of these demons is to have them lend their powers to magickal tasks. Oriens is attributed with the ability to provide wealth for the magician in the form of endless amounts of gold and silver. He can cause visions, and he can answer any questions about matters pertaining to the past, the present, or the future. He can give the magician the power to fly, and he is also excellent at providing familiar spirits. He can conjure servants for the magician, and he can bring the dead back to life. Oriens oversees a sizable number of other demons, all of whom share his powers and can lend these to the magician upon command. Oriens is a popular figure in the grimoiric tradition. His name appears in numerous works, including the *Sixth and Seventh Books of Moses*, the *Book of Oberon*, and the *Book of Incantations*. In the French *Livre des esperitz*, his name is spelled *Orient*. In Agrippa's *Three Books of Occult Philosophy*, Oriens appears under the spelling *Urieus*. Other variations include *Orience* and *Oraeus*. In the *Clavis Inferni*, his name appears as *Urieus*. He is associated with the element of fire and is depicted with a winged serpent biting its own tail. The angel Michael holds power over him. See also AGRIPPA, *BOOK OF OBERON, BOOK OF INCANTATIONS, CLAVIS INFERNI, LIVRE DES ESPERITZ*, MATHERS, SAMAEL, SCOT, RUDD.

Orinel: A demon who functions as a servant to the greater fiends Astaroth and Asmodeus, Orinel appears in the *Sacred Magic of Abramelin the Mage*. According to the 1898 Mathers translation of that work, his name means "ornament" or "tree of God." This would seem to suggest that

Orinel was once an angel, even though he is now classed among the unclean spirits of the *Abramelin* working. See also ASTAROTH, ASMODEUS, MATHERS.

Ormenu: A demon in the service of Pamersiel, the first and chief spirit under the Emperor of the East. Ormenu holds the rank of duke and is reportedly an unpleasant spirit to deal with, as he is arrogant, evil, and given to deceit. According to the *Ars Theurgia*, Ormenu and his fellows can be called upon to drive other spirits from haunted houses, should anyone be desperate enough to fight fire with fire in the realm of otherworldly beings. See also *ARS THEURGIA*, PAMERSIEL.

Ormion: In the *Sacred Magic of Abramelin the Mage*, Ormion is said to serve the demon-king Asmodeus. During the Holy Guardian Angel working central to this text, Ormion and a series of other demons are called up and forced to swear their allegiance to the summoner, thus increasing his power. See also ASMODEUS, MATHERS.

Ormonas: A servitor of the arch-fiend Magoth, Ormonas appears in the *Sacred Magic of Abramelin the Mage*. In the Mathers version of this work, the name is spelled *Horminos*. See also MAGOTH, MATHERS.

Ornias: The half-eater. This demon is pivotal to the *Testament of Solomon*. In this extra-biblical text, King Solomon is reputedly given the power to compel and control demons by the Lord God. Solomon prayed for this ability because a young laborer working on Solomon's temple was being victimized by a demon who ate half of his share of food every day. Ornias is that demon. He is the first demon who Solomon gains power over, and he subsequently leads Solomon to all the other demons named in this ancient text. Ornias is said

The Children of Smokeless Flame

In Jewish and Christian lore, King Solomon was the wisest of rulers, gifted by God with powers to control and bind demons. The part of his story involving demons is told outside of biblical canon, yet it is intricately intertwined with his mythic legacy. But what about Islam? Judaism and Christianity are not the only religions connected to the biblical tradition. Islam, founded by Muhammad in the seventh century of the Common Era, stems from the same sources and one of the figures—both religious and mythic—that it shares with Christianity and Judaism is King Solomon.

Muslims have rich lore revolving around Solomon, whose name in their tradition is typically rendered *Suleiman*. Suleiman (the Magnificent) is the same wise king, and he is similarly a powerful sorcerer possessing the ability to summon, bind, and compel supernatural beings. In Islam, however, the supernatural beings closely associated with Solomon aren't demons. They're *Jinn*.

Sometimes also spelled *Djinn*, these are a class of being created from smokeless fire (as opposed to Adam's clay). They exist side by side with humanity in a realm largely imperceptible to us. They are long-lived but ultimately mortal. They marry, they have children, they lead rich lives. In the English-speaking world, our most significant exposure to the idea of Jinn typically comes through *The Thousand and One Arabian Nights*. Lore of the Jinn is the source of our trope of the genie in a bottle, but for Muslims, they are so much more. Belief in Jinn is a fundamental and unavoidable aspect of Islam, because the Quran is in part addressed to them. The seventy-second chapter of the Quran is the *Sūrat al-Jinn*. It runs for twenty-eight verses and does not treat the Jinn merely as objectively real beings, but presents them as the one other species, in addition to humanity, capable of hearing the Prophet's words and being redeemed.

For this reason, belief in Jinn is canon to Muslims (although notably, it is not included among the six articles of Islamic faith). The Jinn are not the only supernatural beings that exist in the Muslim creation, of course. Islam has lore on angels and demons as well, but, significantly, the Muslim version of Satan is neither a demon nor a fallen angel. He is Ibliss, and he is a Jinn.

to appear as an incubus to women and as a succubus to men. An adept shapeshifter, he can also take the form of a lion. When he appeared to the young laborer, he was said to manifest in the form of a burning fire. Ornias is a demon of ambiguous intentions, as he also claims to strangle men who lust after noble virgins, demonstrating a protective, if violent, side. In his first interview with Solomon in the *Testament of Solomon*, Ornias states, "I am the offspring of the archangel Uriel, the power of God."[54] In this statement, Ornias links himself—as well as the Solomonic tradition—with the Watcher Angel myth that appears in the *Book of Enoch*. Possibly because of their blood relation, the name of the archangel Uriel is said to hold power over Ornias, and this name is used to command the demon to give up the names and whereabouts of his fellows. He may appear in later editions of the *Goetia* as the demon Orias, sometimes also rendered *Oriax*. See also ORIAS, SOLOMON, WATCHER ANGELS.

Orobas: The fifty-fifth demon of the *Goetia*, Orobas is named as a great prince with twenty legions under his command. He also appears in Scot's *Discoverie of Witchcraft* and Wierus's *Pseudomonarchia Daemonum*. As Goetic demons go, he is one of the nicer ones. It is said that he suffers no one to be tempted and, unlike so many demons, he makes no effort to deceive anyone. When he manifests, he takes the form of a horse, but after a while, he usually transforms into a man. He speaks of divine virtue and answers questions about God and Creation. He can also grant favors and dignities as well as make a person well-liked by both friends and foes. His name is likely derived from the Greek *ouroboros*, an image depicting a serpent that devours its own tail. It represents eternity. In the *Goetia of Dr. Rudd*, he has twenty-six legions of spirits under his command. According to this text, the angel Mebahiah has the power to compel and constrain him. In the *Book of Oberon*, an illustration attempts to depict his human form, which is monstrous. He has a horn like a rhino's protruding from the middle of his forehead, ass's ears, and a nose and tongue both as long and sharp as poignards. Among the promotions that he grants, the *Book of Oberon* states that he can make someone a *prelate*—an ecclesiastical title unusual for the office of a demon. In this text, he has only twelve legions of lesser spirits under his control. See also *BOOK OF OBERON*, *GOETIA*, RUDD, SCOT, WIERUS.

Oroia: A demon whose name appears in the Mathers translation of the *Sacred Magic of Abramelin the Mage*. Oroia is one of a vast array of demonic servants who work beneath Oriens, Paimon, Ariton, and Amaimon, the four infernal princes of the cardinal directions. The name of this demon only appears in one of the other known manuscripts of the *Abramelin* material, where it is given as *Oroya*. See also AMAIMON, ARITON, MATHERS, ORIENS, PAIMON.

Oropel: A demon named in the *Testament of Solomon*. Oropel is the fourth demon among those connected with the thirty-six decans of the zodiac. His name is absent from the Conybeare translation of this seminal work but is included in a later translation by McCown. McCown, notably, was working from a more complete collection of manuscripts. According to these texts, Oropel brings a sore throat. The angel Raphael holds power over him. See also SOLOMON.

---

54. Steven Ashe, *The Testament of Solomon*, p. 19.

Oropys: A demon with the power to craft books on virtually any subject overnight. He and several other bookish demons are invoked in a spell recorded in the *Book of Oberon*, a grimoire from Elizabethan England. There, Oropys, whose name is alternately given as *Arypys*, is said to be especially useful at making books on the topics of conjuration, alchemy, the magickal arts, and nigromancy (summoning demons and similar spirits). See also *BOOK OF OBERON*.

Orpemiel: In the Henson translation of the *Ars Theurgia*, Orpemiel is said to serve in the hierarchy of the east, directly beneath the infernal prince Camuel. In this text, Orpemiel is presented as a mighty duke with ten servants to attend his needs. He belongs to the hours of the day but appears during the hours of the night. When he manifests, he takes a form that is beautiful to behold. See also *ARS THEURGIA*, CAMUEL.

Orymell: Called upon to make other spirits obedient and docile, Orymell is named in the *Book of Oberon*. According to that text, he serves Tantavalerion, a demon identified as the supreme emperor of all spirits. Orymell is one of a group of seven demons holding the rank of senator. See also ASMOO, BOELL, *BOOK OF OBERON*, DANALL, PASCARY, SALARICA, TANTAVALERION, TYGRA.

Oryn: A chief duke governed by the demon-king Armadiel, Oryn has a total of eighty-four lesser spirits to do his bidding. He is part of the demonic hierarchy ultimately answerable to Demoriel, the infernal Emperor of the North. According to the *Ars Theurgia*, Oryn is tied to time as well as direction. To calculate the time for Oryn, divide the day into fifteen equal portions. The seventh of these sections of time marks the hours and minutes during which Oryn may manifest. See also ARMADIEL, *ARS THEURGIA*, DEMORIEL.

Ose: The fifty-seventh demon of the *Goetia*. Ose is demon of illusion said to often take the form of a leopard. He is not limited to this bestial shape and can also assume the shape of a man. He can drive people mad until they are overcome with delusions. He can also transform people into various forms. He is knowledgeable about the liberal sciences, and he is also privy to both divine and occult secrets. According to Scot's *Discoverie of Witchcraft*, he holds the rank of president and has some power over the passage of time. In Wierus's *Pseudomonarchia Daemonum*, his name is given as *Oze*. The *Goetia of Dr. Rudd* credits him with ruling over three legions. This same text gives the name *Nemamiah* as the angel set over this demon to control him. In the Welsh *Book of Incantations*, he transforms people and, more than that, makes it so the changed person does not wish to be anything but that new creature or thing. This text states that he rules thirty legions of spirits. In the *Book of Oberon*, his name can be found with the variant spelling of *Oze*. He is identified as one of the twelve principal ministers of Amaimon, king of the south. He appears again as *Oze* in the French *Livre des esperitz*. See also *BOOK OF INCANTATIONS, BOOK OF OBERON, GOETIA, LIVRE DES ESPERITZ*, RUDD, SCOT, WIERUS.

Ossidiel: A night-demon who holds the rank of duke, at least according to the *Ars Theurgia*. In that same text, Ossidiel is said to serve the infernal prince Usiel. He has forty lesser spirits under his command, and he excels at both revealing and concealing precious items. He serves in the court of the west. See also *ARS THEURGIA*, USIEL.

A Persian angel with a leopard's head and three sets of wings. Depictions of supernatural beings from other cultures helped to shape some of the forms attributed to demons. From an illuminated manuscript, 1750. Image courtesy of the Wellcome Collection, London.

Othey: When first summoned, Othey has a most remarkable appearance: he shows up looking like a tun of wine. If the prospect of a talking wine barrel seems off-putting, Othey can be compelled to take human form. In that shape, his eyes burn like fire. He is a demon of architecture, instantly building castles, towers, and whole towns. He is named in the *Book of Oberon*, where it is said that he serves as one of twelve principal demons in the court of Egin, king of the north. Note: No mention is made of the consequence of drinking Othey in his wine-barrel form, but it can't be good. See also *BOOK OF OBERON*, EGIN.

Othiet: A demon in the court of the south under prince Aseliel. Othiet's name and seal appear in the *Ars Theurgia*, where he is said to hold the rank of chief duke. He is connected with the hours of the night and will only manifest during this time. He holds dominion over thirty principal spirits and another twenty ministering servants. See also *ARS THEURGIA*, ASELIEL.

Otim: One of several chief dukes who serve in the hierarchy of the west beneath the demonic prince Cabariel. Otim has fifty lesser spirits who attend him. He is a demon of the night, appearing in the hours between dusk and dawn. He is very evil-natured and will attempt to trick and deceive anyone he comes into contact with. His name, as well as the seal that commands and binds him, both appear in the *Ars Theurgia*, the second book of a larger work known as the *Lesser Key of Solomon*. See also *ARS THEURGIA*, CABARIEL.

Otius: A great count in the hierarchy of Hell, Otius commands thirty-six legions of devils. According to the fifteenth-century grimoire known as the *Munich Handbook*, when summoned he appears to be human, except that he has three horns and exceptionally large teeth. He also comes bearing an extremely sharp sword. When asked, he can speak of all hidden things, revealing the secret nature of the past, present, or future. He is also able to sway the minds of men, causing friend and foe alike to look favorably upon those who summon him. Given this description of his appearance and powers, Otius may well be a variation on the Goetic demon Botis. See also BOTIS, *MUNICH HANDBOOK*.

Oylol: This demon is tied to the sphere of the moon. When he manifests, he assumes a body that is large and has the appearance of a whitish, dim crystal or a dark cloud. He is a servant of the demon-king Harthan, who rules over the spirits of the moon. Oylol is named in the Peterson translation of the *Sworn Book*, where he is said to help prepare for journeys and influence the minds of mortals. The angels Gabriel, Michael, Samyhel, and Atithael have power to compel and control him. See also HARTHAN, *SWORN BOOK*.

Ozia: A demon who appears as an old man riding an elephant. He is one of the twelve chief spirits serving in the court of the king of the north, Egin. Ozia has powers of transportation and invisibility and can also gain the favor of enemies. He is knowledgeable in all the arts and sciences. His name appears in the Elizabethan grimoire known as the *Book of Oberon*. See also *BOOK OF OBERON*, EGIN.

Pachel: A demon said to serve Astaroth and Asmodeus. Pachel appears in the Mathers translation of the *Sacred Magic of Abramelin the Mage*, where it is related to a Greek word meaning "thick" or "coarse." See also ASTAROTH, ASMODEUS, MATHERS.

Pachid: According to Mathers, the name of this demon is derived from a Hebrew word meaning "fear." Despite this potentially fearsome nature, Pachid is a relatively minor demon. He serves alongside many other demons of similar rank in the extensive hierarchy of the four infernal princes of the cardinal directions: Oriens, Paimon, Ariton, and Amaimon. All appear in the *Sacred Magic of Abramelin the Mage*. See also AMAIMON, ARITON, MATHERS, ORIENS, PAIMON.

Padiel: The second spirit in rank beneath Carnesiel, Emperor of the East, Padiel rules as the chief prince in the east by south. Named in the *Ars Theurgia*, Padiel holds sway over a massive retinue of spirits that consists of ten thousand ministers serving by day and another twenty thousand serving by night. According to the *Ars Theurgia*, Padiel and all the spirits in his retinue are essentially good by nature and can be trusted by those who choose to interact with them. Most of the demons of Padiel's rank named in this book have at least a dozen infernal dukes whose names and seals are also listed so that they can be called upon and compelled to action. Padiel, however, has none. The text indicates that none of his dukes possess any special powers save for those already conferred to them by Padiel himself. Padiel is also named in the *Steganographia* of Johannes Trithemius. See also *ARS THEURGIA*, CARNESIEL.

Pafesla: A demonic servant of the infernal kings Ariton and Amaimon, each connected to two of the cardinal directions. This spelling of the demon's name appears in the nineteenth-century translation of the *Sacred Magic of Abramelin the Mage* by occultist S. L. MacGregor Mathers. In the Peter Hammer edition, the name is given as *Pafessa*. See also AMAIMON, ARITON, MATHERS.

Pafiel: A night-demon who serves the infernal prince Dorochiel. Pafiel is tied to the second half of the night, manifesting only in a specific hour between midnight and dawn. According to the *Ars Theurgia*, he holds the rank of chief duke and has four hundred lesser spirits at his command. He is connected to the west. See also *ARS THEURGIA*, DOROCHIEL.

Paimon: Also spelled *Paymon*. A demon of the Order of Dominions, Paimon is believed to be one of four demons who preside over the cardinal directions. His domain is the west. In the *Goetia*, Paimon is listed as the ninth of seventy-two demons. According to this text, when Paimon is summoned, he is preceded by a host of spirits in the form of men playing trumpets, cymbals, and diverse other musical instruments. If this were not enough to herald his appearance, Paimon himself is said to manifest with a mighty roar of his booming voice. He comes astride a camel, and he appears as a man bearing a glorious crown upon his head. Wierus's *Pseudomonarchia Daemonum* further says that he has a very effeminate face, while de Plancy's *Dictionnaire Infernal* describes him as a man with a woman's face. All sources suggest that, of the various Goetic demons, Paimon has some of the strongest loyalties to Lucifer. Paimon's voice is unnaturally loud, and he will continue to speak at such an ear-splitting volume that the summoner will not be able to understand him, unless he commands the demon to alter his speech. When called up, Paimon can teach knowledge of the arts as well as the sciences. He can also reveal the true answers to such mysteries as the nature of the earth, the location of the Abyss, and the origin of the wind.

In addition to being a veritable font of knowledge, Paimon is credited with the ability to confer dignities. He provides familiar spirits and can be sent against enemies. He reportedly binds any that resist him in his own chains. His abode is said to be in the northwest, where he rules over no fewer than two hundred legions of spirits. Some of these are from the Order of Angels and some from the Order of Powers. Paimon himself is said to belong either to the Order of Dominions or the Order of Cherubim. He responds favorably to consecrations and libations. In his *Discoverie of Witchcraft*, Scot translates the Latin word for *libations* instead as *sacrifices*, lending a somewhat nefarious air to the operations involving Paimon.

In the Welsh grimoire known as the *Book of Incantations*, his name is spelled *Parmon*. This text also notes his obedience to Lucifer, which is given context in the French *Livre des esperitz*, where it is clear that Lucifer is his direct superior in the hierarchy of spirits. These texts agree that Paimon is so loud that he can be impossible to understand. As a solution, the *Book of Oberon* suggests tossing him a slip of paper upon which to write his messages. Many grimoires identify Paimon as a good source for familiar spirits, but the *Book of Incantations* openly states that he can bind humans to the magician's will as well, effecting a magickal enslavement. According to the *Book of Oberon*, he can additionally make all the fishes in the sea obedient.

Paimon sometimes manifests in the company of two lesser infernal kings. In the *Pseudomonarchia Daemonum*, these are named Beball and Abalam. In the *Goetia*, they are called Labal and Abali. The *Book of Incantations* calls these Babel and Abatano. When he manifests with these two kings, Paimon only brings along twenty-five legions of lesser spirits, at least according to the *Pseudomonarchia*. In this text, his name is spelled *Paymon*. Paimon also appears as the ninth demon named in the *Goetia of Dr. Rudd*. Here, he is accorded the rank of king and he is said to rule over only twenty-five legions of spirits. This text associates him with the Order of Powers. The angel Hasiel has the power to constrain him. In the *Clavis Inferni*, it is Raphael who has power over Paimon. In this text, the demonking is also associated with the element of water and an animal like a manticore.

Paimon also appears in the *Sacred Magic of Abramelin the Mage*. Here, he is one of the eight sub-princes who oversee all of the spirits summoned on the third day of the Holy Guardian Angel operation. He is attributed with the power to cause visions, raise the dead, give familiars, and summon spirits in diverse forms. He can further answer any questions about the past, present, or future, and he can make the magician fly. According to both Mathers and Agrippa, Paimon is equated with the fallen angel Azazel in rabbinical lore. See also ABALAM, ABALI, AGRIPPA, AZAZEL, BEBALL, *BOOK OF INCANTATIONS*, *BOOK OF OBERON*, DE PLANCY, *GOETIA*, LABAL, *LIVRE DES ESPERITZ*, LUCIFER, MATHERS, RUDD, SCOT, WIERUS.

Palas: In the Peterson translation of the *Sworn Book of Honorius*, Palas is a servant of the demon Habaa, king of the spirits of Mercury. In this text, Palas is tied the west and southwest, and he has the power to answer about the past, present, and future. He also helps to provide familiar spirits. He is further knowledgeable about secret thoughts and deeds, of both spirits and the living, and he will share these with any who know the proper way to call him up. The angels Michael, Mihel, and Sarapiel have power over him. Palas also appears in Driscoll's edition of the *Sworn Book*. In this

An elaborate depiction of the demon Paimon, king over all the spirits in the west. His sigil appears above his head. A manticore appears beside him. Detail from the eighteenth-century grimoire known as the *Clavis Inferni*. Image courtesy of the Wellcome Collection, London.

version of the text, Palas appears as one of three infernal ministers of the demon Zobha. Zobha cannot be conjured to visible appearance, and so Palas and his compatriots exist to carry out their master's will. According to Driscoll's version of the *Sworn Book*, Palas is a demon connected with the subterranean regions of the earth. He provides gold and silver in great abundance to those who know how to gain his favor. Palas can be a destructive demon, causing buildings and other structures to be torn down, probably by summoning earthquakes. Compare to *Pallas*, a title sometimes assumed by the Greek goddess Athena. See also HABAA, *SWORN BOOK*, ZOBHA.

Palframe: A martial demon named in the *Book of Oberon* who serves as an aid to King Iammas. Like other demons affiliated with the planetary sphere of Mars, he has ruddy skin and a bellowing voice and wears garments of red. He has antlers on his head and claws on his fingers and may appear either as an armed king riding a wolf or as a warrior-woman carrying a shield. He brings death and battle, igniting fires and the passions of people, who will fight at his command. There is a possibility that he is not a separate demon but simply the result of a typo carried forward through copied manuscripts, as one of his fellow ministers is named *Palframen*. See also *BOOK OF OBERON*, CARMAS, IAMMAS, ITAMALL, PALFRAMEN.

Palframen: A spirit of Mars in the court of King Iammas. He is identified as a separate entity from Palframe, despite the incredible similarity in their names. Palframen brings death and destruction, causing people to fight and murder one another. He can also strike people dead and catch things on fire. He has a ferocious appearance, with ruddy skin and blood-red robes. Antlered and clawed, he may assume the guise of an armed king or a woman bearing a shield. He is named in the *Book of Oberon*, a grimoire from Elizabethan England. See also *BOOK OF OBERON*, CARMAS, IAMMAS, ITAMALL, PALFRAME.

Pamelon: A demon described as a great ruler who oversees six legions of lesser spirits. He is named in the *Book of Oberon* and is said to manifest with a man's form. He can be called upon to tell of things hidden both in the water and in the earth, and he can help his summoner acquire those treasures. He is additionally good for coercing the love of maidens. This demon is so popular that he appears twice in the *Book of Oberon*, first as the sixty-fourth demon in a list of over eighty infernal spirits and then again as number seventy-four. In his second entry, the demon is said to appear in the form of a knight with ten, rather than six, legions under his control. An intermediary spirit, he has the power to compel other spirits to come from the four quarters of the world. *Paynelon* is given as

an alternate form of his name. See also *BOOK OF OBERON*.

Pamersiel: According to the *Ars Theurgia*, Pamersiel is the first and chief spirit of the east. He serves directly beneath the infernal emperor Carnesiel, who rules the eastern point of the compass. Pamersiel is a haughty and stubborn prince, and he oversees a court of one thousand spirits, all of whom share his less-than-desirable personality traits. Although they can be both difficult and dangerous to work with, Pamersiel and his followers are reputedly useful for driving off other spirits of darkness—especially those that have chosen to haunt houses. Pamersiel also appears as the first and chief spirit of the east in Trithemius's *Steganographia*, written around 1499. In Rudd's *Treatise on Angel Magic*, the Third Table of Enoch contains a symbol said to represent the name of the demon Pamersiel. This table is connected with the planet Venus. See also *ARS THEURGIA*, CARNESIEL, RUDD, TRITHEMIUS.

Pamiel: A demon in the service of Aseliel, a prince in the hierarchy of the east. Pamiel is named in the *Ars Theurgia*, where he is described as a chief president. He presides over thirty principal spirits and another twenty ministering spirits. He is bound to the hours of the day and manifests in a beautiful, courtly form. See also *ARS THEURGIA*, ASELIEL.

Pandiel: According to the *Ars Theurgia*, Pandiel is a chief duke under the rule of the mighty king Armadiel. Both Armadiel and Pandiel are part of the hierarchy of the north, which is overseen by the infernal emperor Demoriel. In addition to being tied to the direction of north, Pandiel is also bound to specific times of the day. If the day is divided into fifteen equal portions, this demon belongs to the eleventh portion. He will only manifest in

Even cast from Heaven, Satan retains much of his beautiful aspect. From an illustration by Gustav Doré.

the hours and minutes that fall into this section of time. When he appears, Pandiel is reputed to have eighty-four ministering spirits that carry out his wishes. Elsewhere in the same text, Pandiel is named as a duke who serves the demon Emoniel. He can appear with equal power either during the night or during the day. He is most likely to manifest in forests or wooded areas, and he has a total of one thousand three hundred and twenty lesser spirits at his command. See also ARMADIEL, *ARS THEURGIA*, DEMORIEL, EMONIEL.

Pandoli: A demon serving under the joint rule of Magoth and Kore, Pandoli appears in the *Sacred Magic of Abramelin the Mage*. As part of the Holy Guardian Angel ritual central to this work, Pandoli and a host of other demons are summoned and made to swear fealty to the magician. See also KORE, MAGOTH, MATHERS.

Pandor: An ill-natured demon of the night whose name appears in the *Ars Theurgia*, Pandor serves as a chief duke in the hierarchy of Cabariel, the infernal prince of the direction west by north. As a demon of rank, Pandor has fifty ministering spirits that attend him. He is a very difficult spirit, prone to both disobedience and deceit. His name may be derived from that of the mythic Greek figure Pandora. Pandora was credited with unleashing all manner of demons upon the earth as a result of her fatal flaw of curiosity. See also *ARS THEURGIA*, CABARIEL.

Paniel: A night-demon loyal to the infernal prince Dorochiel, Paniel is said to hold the rank of chief duke. He has forty lesser spirits at his command. According to the *Ars Theurgia*, where both his name and his sigil appear, Paniel will only manifest in a specific hour between dusk and midnight each night. Through Dorochiel, he owes fealty to the court of the west. See also *ARS THEURGIA*, DOROCHIEL.

Pantagnon: Named in a 1709 version of the *Clavicle of Solomon*, Pantagnon is said to have the power of invisibility. He can also win the favor of great leaders. A member of the court of Duke Resbiroth, Pantagnon serves directly beneath Sergulaf and Hael. See also HAEL, RESBIROTH, *CLAVICLE OF SOLOMON*, SERGULAF.

Panyte: A demon connected with the art of divination. His name appears in two different spells featured in the fifteenth-century grimoire known as the *Munich Handbook*. In both of these spells, Panyte is called upon to lend his powers to help with scrying. See also *MUNICH HANDBOOK*.

Parabiel: A chief duke serving beneath Armadiel in the hierarchy of the north. Parabiel has a total of eighty-five lesser spirits to do his bidding. If the day is divided into fifteen portions, Parabiel's time is the second of these. He will only appear during these hours. According to the *Ars Theurgia*, he is best called forth in a remote and secret location, using a crystal or glass to allow him to appear. See also ARMADIEL, *ARS THEURGIA*.

Parachmon: This demon's name appears in both the Dresden and Wolfenbüttel versions of the *Sacred Magic of Abramelin the Mage*. According to these texts, Parachmon is ruled by the greater demon Magoth. In the fifteenth-century French manuscript sourced for the Mathers translation of this work, the name of this demon is spelled *Paramor*, and he is said to also fall under the rulership of Kore. See also KORE, MAGOTH, MATHERS.

Paras: An ill-tempered night-demon in service to the infernal king Raysiel. Paras is described as a chief duke with forty lesser spirits beneath him. His name and seal appear in the *Ars Theurgia*, the second book of the *Lesser Key of Solomon*. According to this text, Paras serves in the hierarchy of spirits connected with the north. See also *ARS THEURGIA*, RAYSIEL.

Paraseh: This demon's name appears in an extensive list in the *Sacred Magic of Abramelin the Mage*. He is said to serve Oriens, Paimon, Ariton, and Amaimon—the four demonic princes in charge of the cardinal directions. Mathers, who published a translation of the *Sacred Magic of Abramelin the Mage* in 1898, suggests that the name of this demon is derived from a Chaldean word meaning "divided." See also AMAIMON, ARITON, MATHERS, ORIENS, PAIMON.

Parcas: A great prince who can make people cunning and wise in all the sciences. He appears in a beautiful form and commands thirty legions of lesser spirits. He knows the virtues of herbs and precious stones and can bring these upon command. He also brings gold and silver and any other treasures hidden in the earth. He can recover what is lost. With powers of transformation, he can make people invisible or he can make them old or young again. Thirty legions of spirits are under him. He is named in the *Livre des esperitz*, a sixteenth-century French grimoire. See also *LIVRE DES ESPERITZ*.

The demon Oriens, king of the east. Detail from an illustration in the *Clavis Inferni*. Image courtesy of the Wellcome Collection, London.

Pareht: One of a number of demons ruled by the four demonic princes of the cardinal directions. In the Mathers translations of the *Sacred Magic of Abramelin the Mage*, the name of this demon is said to be derived from a Hebrew word meaning "fruit." As a servant of Oriens, Paimon, Ariton, and Amaimon, he can be summoned and compelled in their names. See also AMAIMON, ARITON, MATHERS, ORIENS, PAIMON.

Parek: "The Savage One." According to occultist S. L. MacGregor Mathers, the name of this demon stems from a Hebrew root. Parek is named in the Mathers translation of the *Sacred Magic of Abramelin the Mage*. Here, he is said to serve beneath the four demonic princes of the cardinal directions: Oriens, Paimon, Ariton, and Amaimon. See also AMAIMON, ARITON, MATHERS, ORIENS, PAIMON.

Pariel: One of several demons said to serve the infernal prince Camuel in the *Ars Theurgia*. Through his service to Camuel, Pariel is tied to the direction of the east. He is also a demon of the day, but he appears at night. He holds the rank of duke and has a total of ten lesser spirits at his command. See also *ARS THEURGIA*, CAMUEL.

Paritesheha: Transliteration of a Hebrew name attributed to the night-demon Lilith. Lilith was believed to have many different names, and these were often scribed upon protective amulets. In Jewish lore, Lilith was thought to attack women in childbirth and kill newborns in their cribs. Each of Lilith's many names had power over her, and these amulets, typically written in Hebrew, were thought to keep her away. Author T. Schrire collected a number of these names in his 1966 publication *Hebrew Magic Amulets*. See also LILITH.

Parius: A lesser duke in the hierarchy of the infernal prince Cabariel. Parius is a demon of the day and therefore avoids appearing during the hours of the night. For those brave enough to summon him, the *Ars Theurgia* recommends conjuring Parius in a remote location in the hours between sun-up and sundown. He possesses an airy nature, which means that he can be difficult to see with the naked eye. Because of this, the *Ars Theurgia* further recommends that Parius, and all demons like him, be made to appear in a stone crystal or glass receptacle. Typically attended by fifty ministering spirits, this demon is reputed to have a good and obedient nature. He is affiliated with the direction of the west. See also *ARS THEURGIA*, CABARIEL.

Parmatus: The "shield bearer." According to the Mathers translation of the *Sacred Magic of Abramelin the Mage*, this demon serves beneath the four infernal princes of the cardinal directions: Paimon, Ariton, Oriens, and Amaimon. See also AMAIMON, ARITON, MATHERS, ORIENS, PAIMON.

Parsifiel: In the *Ars Theurgia*, Parsifiel appears in the hierarchy of the wandering prince Bidiel. He is said to assume a beautiful and pleasing human shape. Holding the rank of great duke, he commands a total of two thousand and four hundred lesser spirits. See also *ARS THEURGIA*, BIDIEL.

Partas: A demon named in the *Book of Oberon*. He is among twelve principal demons who serve the king of the south, Amaimon. When summoned, he can be made to take the shape of a man but will first appear as a wood bear. He has powers of invisibility and can restore sight to the blind. In addition, he teaches logic and the virtues of stones and herbs. Like many demons in the *Book of Oberon*, he can also reveal hidden treasure. See also AMAIMON, *BOOK OF OBERON*.

Parusur: A demon mentioned in Mathers's translation of the *Sacred Magic of Abramelin the Mage*. Parusur is governed by Oriens, Paimon, Ariton, and Amaimon, the four infernal princes of the cardinal directions. As a servitor of these demons, Parusur can be called upon and compelled in their names. See also AMAIMON, ARITON, MATHERS, ORIENS, PAIMON.

Pascary: Sometimes also spelled *Pastarie*, this demon holds the unusual rank of senator. He is named in the *Book of Oberon* along with six fellows in a spell to constrain and compel other spirits.

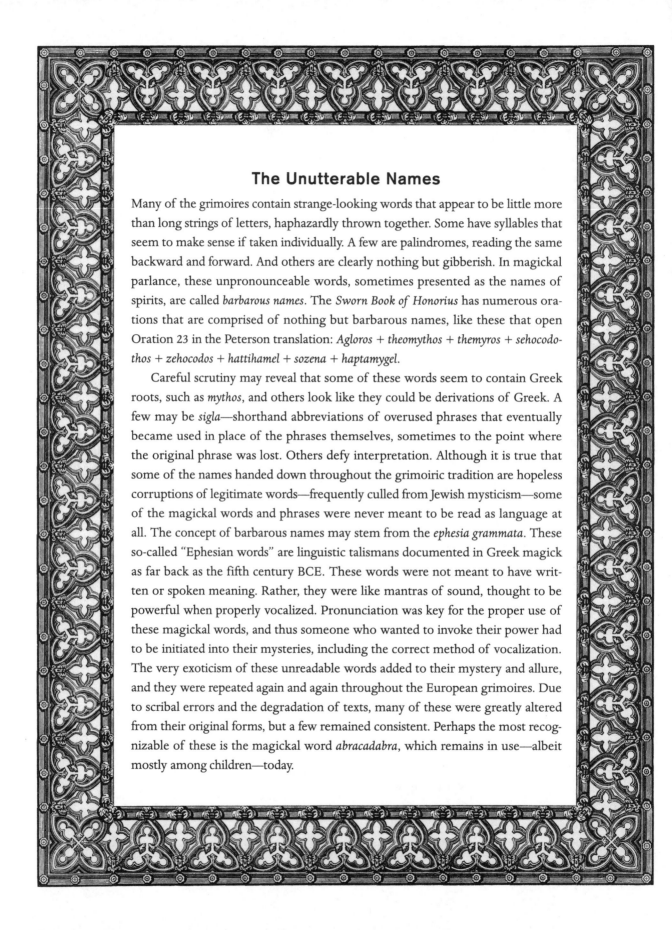

The Unutterable Names

Many of the grimoires contain strange-looking words that appear to be little more than long strings of letters, haphazardly thrown together. Some have syllables that seem to make sense if taken individually. A few are palindromes, reading the same backward and forward. And others are clearly nothing but gibberish. In magickal parlance, these unpronounceable words, sometimes presented as the names of spirits, are called *barbarous names*. The *Sworn Book of Honorius* has numerous orations that are comprised of nothing but barbarous names, like these that open Oration 23 in the Peterson translation: *Agloros + theomythos + themyros + sehocodothos + zehocodos + hattihamel + sozena + haptamygel.*

Careful scrutiny may reveal that some of these words seem to contain Greek roots, such as *mythos*, and others look like they could be derivations of Greek. A few may be *sigla*—shorthand abbreviations of overused phrases that eventually became used in place of the phrases themselves, sometimes to the point where the original phrase was lost. Others defy interpretation. Although it is true that some of the names handed down throughout the grimoiric tradition are hopeless corruptions of legitimate words—frequently culled from Jewish mysticism—some of the magickal words and phrases were never meant to be read as language at all. The concept of barbarous names may stem from the *ephesia grammata*. These so-called "Ephesian words" are linguistic talismans documented in Greek magick as far back as the fifth century BCE. These words were not meant to have written or spoken meaning. Rather, they were like mantras of sound, thought to be powerful when properly vocalized. Pronunciation was key for the proper use of these magickal words, and thus someone who wanted to invoke their power had to be initiated into their mysteries, including the correct method of vocalization. The very exoticism of these unreadable words added to their mystery and allure, and they were repeated again and again throughout the European grimoires. Due to scribal errors and the degradation of texts, many of these were greatly altered from their original forms, but a few remained consistent. Perhaps the most recognizable of these is the magickal word *abracadabra*, which remains in use—albeit mostly among children—today.

Pascary and his compatriots serve the supreme emperor Tantavalerion, a demon who wields ultimate authority over all spirits. No spirit will dare disobey or cause harm when Tantavalerion's name is invoked. See also ASMOO, BOELL, *BOOK OF OBERON*, DANALL, ORYMELL, SALARICA, TANTAVALERION, TYGRA.

Pasfran: A minister of Iammax, the king of the spirits of the planet Mars. Pasfran appears in the Joseph Peterson translation of the *Sworn Book of Honorius*. In this text, he is said to be governed by the angels Samahel, Satihel, Ylurahihel, and Amabiel, who rule over the sphere of Mars. Pasfran has the power to sow hate and anger among mortals, stirring up warfare and inciting murder. His region is the south, and when he manifests, his skin is fiery like burning embers. This demon also appears in the Driscoll translation of the *Sworn Book*, but there are differences between the two texts. In the Driscoll edition, Pasfran serves as a minister in the hierarchy of the infernal king Jamaz. He is a demon of the element fire and as a result has a hot-headed nature. He has power over death and decay. He can kill with a word, and he can completely reverse the effects of decay. According to Driscoll, he can also raise an army of one thousand soldiers from the dead. In addition to all of this, he is supposedly able to confer familiar spirits, and all of the familiars bestowed by him have the semblance of soldiers. See also IAMMAX, JAMAZ, *SWORN BOOK*.

Pathier: A demon in the court of prince Usiel, who rules in the hierarchy of the west. Pathier holds the title of duke and has twenty lesser spirits at his command. According to the *Ars Theurgia*, he is said to manifest only during the hours of the night. He has a special gift for revealing the location of hidden treasure. In addition, he can also obscure precious items, protecting them from thieves. See also *ARS THEURGIA*, USIEL.

Pathophas: A demon associated with the element of fire, Pathophas has the power to stave off decay, reversing its progress or stopping it completely. He can also kill with a word. According to the Driscoll translation of the *Sworn Book*, he will appear when enticed by the proper offering of incense and perfume. He serves in the court of the infernal king Jamaz, who rules over both the element of fire and the direction south. Pathophas is a hot and hasty demon with an energetic nature, and he has a complexion that resembles the fiery element of his hierarchy. He can raise an army of one thousand soldiers at a single command, and he provides familiar spirits in the form of soldiers. His name is likely a variation on that of the demon Proathophas. See also JAMAZ, PROATHOPHAS, *SWORN BOOK*.

Pathyn: A three-headed demon of destruction who can be commanded to burn down anything. He carries between his teeth a burning pin of iron, which is the source of his fire-starting abilities. His name appears in the *Book of Oberon*, where he is listed among the twelve principal ministers of Amaimon, the demon-king of the south. See also AMAIMON, *BOOK OF OBERON*.

Patid: The name of this demon may be taken from a Hebrew word meaning "topaz." In the Mathers translation of the *Sacred Magic of Abramelin the Mage*, Patid appears in the hierarchy of the four infernal rulers of the cardinal directions: Oriens, Paimon, Ariton, and Amaimon. He can be called and summoned in their names. See also AMAIMON, ARITON, MATHERS, ORIENS, PAIMON.

Patiel: A demon governed by the infernal king Maseriel. According to the *Ars Theurgia*, he serves his master during the hours of the day. He has dominion over thirty lesser spirits of his own and holds the title of duke. He is connected with the south. See also *ARS THEURGIA*, MASERIEL.

Peamde: A demon called upon to assist with divination in the *Munich Handbook*. He is tied to a spell of scrying that makes use of a young, virginal boy. The boy acts as an intermediary with the spirits summoned to inspire visions and reveal secret information. See also *MUNICH HANDBOOK*.

Pelariel: A servant of the demon Hydriel, wandering prince of the air. Pelariel holds the rank of duke and is attended by one thousand three hundred and twenty ministering spirits. A demon drawn to swamps and wetlands, Pelariel assumes the form of a snake with a woman's head when he chooses to appear. He is reputed to have a polite and courteous nature, and the method for summoning and compelling him appears in the magickal text known as the *Ars Theurgia*. See also *ARS THEURGIA*, HYDRIEL.

Pellipis: In his edition of the *Sacred Magic of Abramelin the Mage*, occultist S. L. Mathers interprets this demon's name as meaning "the Oppressor." Unfortunately, the name given for this demon in Mathers's source material is incorrect. In a more accurate version of the *Abramelin* text, the name of this demon is presented as *Sipillipis*. This name is a palindrome, reading the same forward and backward. This type of wordplay was a method of magick, and the resulting words were seen as powerful in their own right. Interestingly, Sipillipis is identified as a servant of Beelzebub. In the *Abramelin* material, Beelzebub has several other demonic servitors whose names are also palindromes. See also BEELZEBUB, MATHERS.

Pelusar: A demon said to hold the title of chief duke in the *Ars Theurgia*. In this text, Pelusar is said to serve in the hierarchy of the infernal prince Dorochiel. He governs a total of forty minor spirits of his own, and he is tied to the hours of the night, so that he may only manifest at a specific time between dusk and midnight. He is affiliated with the west. See also *ARS THEURGIA*, DOROCHIEL.

Penador: A demon who commands a vast host of lesser spirits numbering one thousand eight hundred and forty. Penador belongs to the court of the wandering prince Soleviel, where he serves every other year, switching off among his fellow dukes. In the *Ars Theurgia*, where the name of this demon appears, it is said that he has the freedom to appear at any hour of the day or night. See also *ARS THEURGIA*, SOLEVIEL.

Penemuê: A fallen angel named in the *Book of Enoch* who was apparently a scribe. In *1 Enoch* 68, he is said to have taught humanity the art of writing with pen and ink. Furthermore, he is said to have revealed all manner of forbidden wisdom, including knowledge of the bitter and the sweet. This is often taken to mean that he taught knowledge of herbs and possibly poisons. Penemuê was one of the leaders of the Watcher Angels. This order of angels was charged with looking after humanity. Instead, they left Heaven to take mortal wives. See also WATCHER ANGELS.

Pentagnony: A demon who can grant the favor of various earthly dignitaries, Pentagnony is listed in Peterson's *Grimorium Verum* as the fourth spirit serving beneath the demons Hael and Sergulath. He is also capable of making people invisible. See also *GRIMORIUM VERUM*, HAEL, SERGULATH.

Pereuch: In the *Sacred Magic of Abramelin the Mage*, this demon is summoned as a part of the Holy Guardian Angel working. He is ruled by Oriens, Amaimon, Ariton, and Paimon—the four infernal princes of the cardinal directions. Pereuch is one of several demonic entities that, although classed as unclean spirits, nevertheless seems to have an ambivalent relationship with the Divine. Mathers gives his name as meaning "given unto prayer." See also AMAIMON, ARITON, MATHERS, ORIENS, PAIMON.

Pestiferat: A demon invoked in connection with the cardinal directions. He appears in the fifteenth-century grimoire known only as the *Munich Handbook*. See also *MUNICH HANDBOOK*.

Peterson, Joseph H.: A writer best known for his definitive translations of occult works such as the *Grimorium Verum*, the *Sworn Book of Honorius*, and the *Arbatel of Magic*. Peterson has a degree in chemical engineering from the University of Minnesota, where he also studied languages and religions. In addition to his scientific interests, he has a long-standing interest in occult and esoteric texts. In 1995, he founded the websites avesta.org and esotericarchives.org. These sites rapidly became some of the most widely sourced archives of medieval and Renaissance texts on the Internet. Since their founding, Peterson has exhaustively digitalized and translated numerous rare and significant grimoires. In addition to offering translations of these works, Peterson also researches and attempts to unravel the often complicated relations of these texts, including their true authors, origins, and initial dates of publication. See also *GRIMORIUM VERUM, SWORN BOOK*.

Petunof: Mathers reads this name as meaning "exciting," in his translation of the *Sacred Magic of Abramelin the Mage*. He suggests that the name stems from a Coptic root. The spelling of this demon's name, and therefore its meaning, is somewhat disputed, however. In the version of the *Abramelin* material kept in the Dresden library, the name is presented as *Petariop*. In the Peter Hammer edition, the name is spelled *Petumos*. As none of these versions are the original text, there is no way to verify which spelling is correct. Petunof is said to serve under the dual leadership of the greater demons Magoth and Kore. See also KORE, MAGOTH, MATHERS.

Phalet: A demon named in the Mathers translation of the *Grimoire of Armadel*, Phalet is said to lead many lesser spirits that he can then grant to others as servants. He is also able to reveal all the mysteries of necromancy, including the magickal qualities of specific corpses and graves. See also MATHERS.

Phaniel: According to the *Ars Theurgia*, Phaniel is a servant of the greater demon Camuel. He holds the rank of duke and has ten lesser spirits to minister to his needs. He is a demon of the hours of the night, but he can be conjured by day. He is tied to the region of the east. See also *ARS THEURGIA*, CAMUEL.

Phanuel: In the *Ars Theurgia*, Phanuel appears among the list of twelve dukes who serve the wandering prince Emoniel. Emoniel and his followers are believed to have a fondness for woodland settings, and they can manifest during the hours of either day or night. As far as the *Ars Theurgia* is concerned, Phanuel holds dominion over one thousand three hundred and twenty lesser spirits. Phanuel also appears in the *Book of Enoch*, but here he is ranked as an archangel. In *1 Enoch* 40:9, Phanuel stands in Heaven alongside Michael and

Raphael. His name means "the face of God." He is one of several fallen angels whose names also appear in texts among the ranks of the Heavenly Hosts. See also *ARS THEURGIA*, EMONIEL.

Pharacte: A demon named in the *Munich Handbook*. He is associated with spells of divination that make use of a pure and innocent child as an intermediary with the spirits. See also *MUNICH HANDBOOK*.

Pharol: According to the *Ars Theurgia*, Pharol is a demon who holds the rank of duke. He serves in the hierarchy of the north beneath the infernal king Baruchas. Thousands of lesser spirits minister to him. When he manifests, it is only during a very specific time of the day. If the day is divided into fifteen portions of time, then the eighth portion belongs to Pharol. He will only appear during these hours and minutes each day. See also *ARS THEURGIA*, BARUCHAS.

Phoenix: The thirty-seventh demon of the *Goetia*. According to Scot's *Discoverie of Witchcraft*, this demon appears in the form of the mythical bird also known as a phoenix. He speaks in a child's voice but also sings sweetly like a bird. Upon his first appearance, Phoenix flies and flits around, sweetly singing, but his song is merely a distraction. Those who wish to constrain or compel this demon are cautioned to ignore his music and instead demand that he put on a human form. Once this has been done, the demon Phoenix will speak of science and poetry. He holds the rank of marquis and governs twenty legions of spirits. According to the *Goetia*, this demon can be made to compose poetry upon request. He also appears in the *Pseudomonarchia Daemonum* compiled by Johannes Wierus. He is *Fenix* in the French *Livre des esperitz*. In both the *Goetia of Dr. Rudd* and the Welsh *Book of Incantations*, his name is spelled *Phenix*. According to Rudd, he is constrained with the name of the angel Aniel. The name of this demon comes from the Greek legend of the phoenix, a mythic bird that lived for five hundred years. At the end of this time, it would set itself on fire and be reborn from the ashes. See also *BOOK OF INCANTATIONS*, *GOETIA*, RUDD, SCOT, WIERUS.

Phthenoth: A demon of affliction named as one of thirty-six demons of the decans of the zodiac. According to the *Testament of Solomon*, Phthenoth is able to cast the evil eye upon people. Although many of his infernal brethren can all be put to flight through the use of angel names or secret names of God, Phthenoth's power is also his Achilles' heel: he can be driven away simply through the use of images of the eye. McCown gives his name as *Rhyx Phtheneoth*. See also SOLOMON.

Pinen: A malignant spirit summoned to curse an enemy. Conjured as part of a spell appearing in the *Munich Handbook*, Pinen is credited with the power to strike a man senseless. He attacks the brain, addling the senses and causing delusions. See also *MUNICH HANDBOOK*.

Piniet: An evil-natured demon of the night, Piniet is one of fifty infernal dukes who serve the prince Cabariel from dusk until dawn. Piniet has another fifty lesser spirits beneath him, and all of these share his evil nature. According to the *Ars Theurgia*, Piniet is not only ill-tempered; he is also a liar. Through his master Cabariel, he is tied to the west. See also *ARS THEURGIA*, CABARIEL.

Pirichiel: According to the *Ars Theurgia*, Pirichiel is a wandering prince. He is tied to no specific direction but moves through the air wherever he will. Unlike many of the other demonic princes listed in the *Ars Theurgia*, Pirichiel has no dukes in his service. Instead, he rules over a number of infernal knights. These go out into the world and do his bidding. Under the spelling *Pyrichiel*, this demon can also be found in the *Steganographia* of Trithemius. See also *ARS THEURGIA*, TRITHEMIUS.

Demons were frequently depicted with animalistic qualities. Horns, possibly inspired by ancient deities like the Greek god Pan, were a favorite. Image by Joseph Vargo.

Pischiel: An infernal duke with two thousand and two hundred lesser spirits under his command. Pischiel is one of fifteen high-ranking spirits said to serve in the hierarchy of demon-prince Icosiel. Pischiel has a fondness for houses and is most likely to manifest in these locations. In addition, he is bound to specific hours of the day. The *Ars Theurgia* contains the formula for calculating the time during which Pischiel is allowed to manifest. If the day is divided into fifteen equal parts, Pischiel belongs to the hours and minutes that fall in the second part. See also *ARS THEURGIA*, ICOSIEL.

Pist: This demon appears within the spells of the *Munich Handbook*. According to the text, he is called upon to assist with the discovery of a theft. Through the art of divination, he can help to reveal the identity of the thief or thieves responsi-

ble so they may be brought to justice. In modern American slang, his name sounds much like how one might feel if they were the victim of a theft. See also *MUNICH HANDBOOK*.

Pithius: A demon whose name appears in a hierarchy compiled by Francis Barrett, author of *The Magus*. According to Barrett, Pithius is one of eight demonic princes given sway over a variety of evil concepts and classes of beings. As a demonic prince in the infernal hierarchy, Pithius holds sway over liars and liar spirits. The name of this demon might be derived from the Greek term *pythia*. The Pythia was the priestess of the Temple of Apollo on Mount Parnassus. She served as the mouthpiece of the famous oracle at Delphi. See also BARRETT.

Platien: Mathers suggests that this demon's name is derived from a Greek root meaning "flat" or "broad." In the *Sacred Magic of Abramelin the Mage*, Platien is one of many demons said to serve in the hierarchy beneath the four infernal princes of the cardinal directions: Oriens, Paimon, Ariton, and Amaimon. See also AMAIMON, ARITON, MATHERS, ORIENS, PAIMON.

Plegit: A demon ruled by Oriens, Paimon, Ariton, and Amaimon. Plegit's name appears in the Mathers translation of the *Sacred Magic of Abramelin the Mage*. In other versions of the *Abramelin* material, this demon's name is given as *Alogil*. See also AMAIMON, ARITON, MATHERS, ORIENS, PAIMON.

Plirok: A demon named in the 1898 translation of the *Sacred Magic of Abramelin the Mage* by occultist S. L. MacGregor Mathers, Plirok is listed as one of many demons who serve beneath the four infernal princes of the cardinal directions: Oriens, Paimon,

Ariton, and Amaimon. See also AMAIMON, ARITON, MATHERS, ORIENS, PAIMON.

Pluto: Originally the Roman version of Hades, god of the Underworld, Collin de Plancy's *Dictionnaire Infernal* ranks Pluto among the denizens of Hell. He is also described as the Prince of Fire. The hierarchy that features Pluto was later cited by Waite in his treatment of the *Grand Grimoire*. It stems from the works of French demonologist Charles Berbiguier. This same hierarchy also identifies Pluto's consort, Proserpine, as a demon. Proserpine is better known by her Greek name, Persephone. She was the goddess of the spring. She was also known as *Kore*. See also BERBIGUIER, DE PLANCY, KORE, PROSERPINE, WAITE.

Poculo: A demon who serves both Sergulaf and Hael and the court of Duke Resbiroth. Poculo, whose name is also given as *Proculo*, has powers over sleep. He can cause someone to fall into a profound slumber for a full twenty-four hours, although the text does not make it clear if this is intended as a blessing or a curse. This demon teaches about all aspects of sleep and presumably also dreams. His name appears in a version the *Secrets of Solomon* kept at the Wellcome Library in London. See also HAEL, RESBIROTH, *SECRETS OF SOLOMON*, SERGULAF.

Porax: A prince with nine legions serving beneath him, Porax appears as an angel with black skin. Named in the *Book of Oberon*, he is a demon of homesteads, with the power to build houses and to divide lands, woods, and waters. He plants fruit trees and sows seeds, teaching the virtue of the plants of the land. He also has the power to still waters. See also *BOOK OF OBERON*.

Portisan: One of three ministers in the court of Lucifer, at least according to the Elizabethan *Book of Oberon*. In that text, Portisan appears along with Fortisan and Alingon as messengers sent to compel the demon Bilgall to appear. See also ALINGON, BILGALL, *BOOK OF OBERON*, FORTISAN, LUCIFER.

Poter: A demon whose name is thought to mean "the Vessel," Poter appears in the Mathers translation of the *Sacred Magic of Abramelin the Mage*. He serves in the hierarchies of the four demonic princes who preside over the cardinal directions: Oriens, Paimon, Amaimon, and Ariton. See also AMAIMON, ARITON, MATHERS, ORIENS, PAIMON.

Potiel: A demon ruled by prince Usiel in the court of the west. The *Ars Theurgia* describes Potiel as a chief duke, with forty lesser spirits serving beneath him. He is connected with the hours of the day and is considered especially gifted at revealing hidden things or hiding valuables so they may not be stolen. See also *ARS THEURGIA*, USIEL.

Prasiel: One of twelve chief dukes ruled by the wandering prince Soleviel. Prasiel himself oversees a total of one thousand eight hundred and forty lesser spirits. According to the *Ars Theurgia*, he serves Soleviel only one year out of every two, sharing duties among the other dukes of Soleviel's court. See also *ARS THEURGIA*, SOLEVIEL.

Praxeel: The name and seal of this demon appear in the *Ars Theurgia*. He is one of twelve chief dukes in service to the demon Soleviel. Half of these serve one year and the other half serve in the next. According to this text, Praxeel is free to manifest during any hour of the day or night. He is in charge of one thousand eight hundred and forty subordinate spirits. See also *ARS THEURGIA*, SOLEVIEL.

Preches: A demonic servant of Asmodeus named in association with the Mathers translation of the *Sacred Magic of Abramelin the Mage*. In other versions of this work, the name of this demon is recorded variously as *Presfees* and *Brefsees*. See also ASMODEUS, MATHERS.

Proathophas: A servant of the demon Iammax, infernal king of Mars. Proathophas brings death, destruction, war, and bloodshed. His manifest form has red skin that glows like a burning coal. His region is the south. His name appears in the Joseph Peterson translation of the *Sworn Book of Honorius*, where he is also said to be subject to the angels Samahel, Satihel, Ylurahihel, and Amabiel. This demon is one of five under the rule of Iammax described as being subject to the east wind. Compare him to Pathophas, in the Driscoll translation of the *Sworn Book*. See also IAMMAX, PATHOPHAS.

Procell: The forty-ninth demon in the *Goetia*, where his name is spelled *Procel*. In Scot's *Discoverie of Witchcraft*, Procell is described as a great and strong duke with forty-eight legions under his command. He was once of the Order of Powers, and he appears in the form of an angel that speaks with a dark intensity. He can impart knowledge of geometry, the liberal arts, and the occult. He also has power over water, causing the sound of rushing water to manifest when there is no water nearby. He can also warm water up or disrupt the waters of healing baths at the command of his conjuror. In Wierus's *Pseudomonarchia Daemonum*, his name is spelled *Pucel*. Henson's edition of the *Lemegeton* renders this name *Perocel*. The *Goetia of Dr. Rudd* gives his name as *Crocell*. According to this text, he is frustrated by the angel Vehuel. According to the Welsh *Book of Incantations*, he gov-

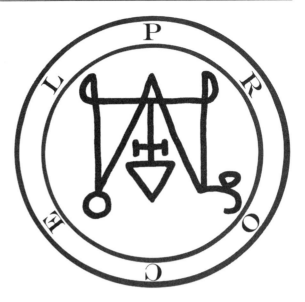

The design for the seal of the demon Procel that appears in the *Goetia of Dr. Rudd* varies greatly from other editions of the *Goetia*. From a talisman by M. Belanger.

erns only eighteen legions. See also *BOOK OF INCANTATIONS*, *GOETIA*, RUDD, SCOT, WIERUS.

Proculo: A demon of sleep, Proculo is reputed to be able to make anyone sleep for a period of twenty-four hours. Appearing in Peterson's *Grimorium Verum*, he is listed as the first spirit serving under Hael and Sergulath. This demon can further speak on all matters pertaining to sleep. He is also reputedly gifted with prophecy. See also *GRIMORIUM VERUM*, HAEL, POCULO, SERGULATH.

Progemon: In the *Munich Handbook*, Progemon is named in a spell designed to bring justice to thieves and restore stolen goods. He is called upon in acts of divination and scrying. See also *MUNICH HANDBOOK*.

Promakos: This demon's name may mean "a fighter on the front lines." He appears in the Mathers translation of the *Sacred Magic of Abramelin the Mage*. In this work, Promakos is said to serve beneath the demonic princes of the four directions: Oriens, Paimon, Ariton, and Amaimon. See also AMAIMON, ARITON, MATHERS, ORIENS, PAIMON.

Proserpine: A Roman goddess. She was the daughter of Ceres, goddess of the harvest, and the consort of Pluto, lord of the Underworld. She is the Roman version of Persephone, the Greek goddess of the spring. She was a fundamental deity connected with the Eleusinian Mysteries, and she was sometimes known as Kore. Despite her ancient status as a deity, Collin de Plancy includes Proserpine as a demon in his *Dictionnaire Infernal*. She is named as the Arch-She-Devil and Princess of Mischievous Spirits. These titles for Proserpine were repeated by occultist A. E. Waite in his treatment of the *Grand Grimoire* as presented in his *Book of Black Magic and Pacts*. Although Waite incorrectly cited Wierus for this information, the real source was Charles Berbiguier, the self-styled demonologist and author of *Les Farfadets*. Proserpine does receive a mention in Wierus's larger work, *De Praestigiis Daemonum*. Here she is cited as one of the many ancient gods and goddesses demonized in later times. See also BERBIGUIER, DE PLANCY, KORE, PLUTO, WAITE, WIERUS.

Proxosos: A demon ruled by Oriens, Paimon, Ariton, and Amaimon—the four demonic princes of the cardinal directions. He is named in the *Sacred Magic of Abramelin the Mage*. He appears on the third day of the *Abramelin* working in order to swear his loyalty to the magician. In his translation of the *Abramelin* work, occultist Mathers relates this demon's name to a Greek word meaning "a kid" or "a goat." See also AMAIMON, ARITON, MATHERS, ORIENS, PAIMON.

Pruflas: This is the fourth demon named in the extensive list of infernal entities known as the *Pseu-*

In the Middle Ages, the Devil was thought to appear in the form of a black goat. Traditional image from heraldry. Courtesy of Dover Publications.

domonarchia Daemonum. Reginald Scot, writing in 1584, included a translation of this list of infernal names in his own work *The Discoverie of Witchcraft*. However, he skipped over the entry on Pruflas entirely. How or why this omission occurred is unclear. It is possible that the edition of Wierus's text that Scot was working from had already dropped the demon, and it is equally possible that the error was Scot's. Interestingly, this is also the only spirit included in Wierus's *Pseudomonarchia Daemonum* that fails to appear in the *Lemegeton*—a detail that strongly suggests that this work was based at least in part on Scot's book rather than Wierus's. According to the *Pseudomonarchia*, Pruflas is a great prince and duke who oversees twenty-six legions of lesser spirits. Some of these spirits come from the Order of Thrones and some come from the Order of Angels. Pruflas is said to reside around the Tower of Babylon, where he appears like a flame. A more physical form is implied as well, since he is said to also have a head like that of a nighthawk. He is a demon of war and deceit, having the power to incite wars and quarrels. An alternate spelling of his name is given as *Bufas*. See also *GOETIA*, RUDD, SCOT, WIERUS.

Prziel: An evil angel credited with the power to smite and bind beings of the mortal realm. In a spell outlined in the *Sword of Moses*, he is summoned to torment an enemy by binding throat, mouth, and tongue. He is also called upon to poison the target of the spell and to place a binding upon their mind. All of this together is intended to completely ruin and overcome the enemy who was foolish enough to cross anyone capable of calling upon such puissant powers. See also GASTER, *SWORD OF MOSES*.

Psdiel: A demon named in the *Sword of Moses*, Psdiel is a wicked angel called upon to bind an enemy's tongue, throat, mouth, and mind. He is part of an elaborate curse intended to utterly destroy another human being. The angel, with the help of three of his brethren, is further called upon to place poisonous water in the belly of the victim so that he is filled with disease. See also GASTER, *SWORD OF MOSES*.

Pseudomonarchia Daemonum: The "False Monarchy of Demons." This work, compiled in 1563 by scholar Johannes Wierus, was included as an appendix in his larger work *De Praestigiis Daemonum* ("On Demonic Magick"). The *Pseudomonar-chia* is a list of major demons, including descriptions of their powers and manifest appearances. Notably, the *Pseudomonarchia* includes nearly all of the seventy-two demons named in the *Goetia*, as well as some notes on the proper methods for summoning and compelling these beings. There are some minor differences between the two texts. Notably, Wierus's work does not include the demonic sigils that are such a striking part of the *Goetia*, and the proscribed method for summoning the demons is much simpler, involving only a summoning circle and not an additional triangle.

Other minor differences exist in both the descriptions and order of spirits. The *Pseudomonarchia* is also missing the four Goetic spirits: Seere, Dantalion, Andromalius, and Vassago. These may have been added to the *Goetia* later, or they may have been sourced from an alternate text. Wierus himself claimed to have derived his list of spirits from an earlier work known as the *Liber Officiorum Spirituum*, or the *Book of the Offices of the Spirits*. The publication date of this work is unknown, although grimoiric scholar Joseph Peterson suggests that it significantly predated Wierus's time, owing to the variations in the names and the number of redactions within the text. An English edition of the *Pseudomonarchia* was reproduced in Reginald Scot's *Discoverie of Witchcraft*, published in London 1584. Most modern reproductions of the *Pseudomonar-chia* are based off of Scot's book. See also *GOETIA*, SCOT, WIERUS.

Pumotor: A demon with power to trick all five senses into perceiving things that are not there. According to the *Munich Handbook*, Pumotor is a squire spirit with an affinity for castles. He can help to conjure an entire illusory castle out of thin air. His name is also rendered *Pumiotor*. See also *MUNICH HANDBOOK*.

Purson: One of seventy-two demons traditionally associated with the *Goetia*. In Scot's *Discoverie of Witchcraft*, he is said to have the alias of *Curson*. Wierus's *Pseudomonarchia Daemonum* includes this alias, but gives the demon's primary name as *Pursan*. Both texts say that he appears as a man with a leonine face. He comes forth riding a bear, carrying a ferocious viper in one hand. His appearance is heralded by trumpets. This demon is attributed with the power to discover treasure and give excellent familiars. He can speak on matters occult and divine, even revealing heavenly secrets such as the creation of the world. Additionally, he can take either a body of flesh or an airy body of a more subtle nature. Holding the rank of king, he reputedly governs twenty-two legions of lesser spirits. These are supposedly comprised of beings partly affiliated with the Order of Virtues and partly with the Order of Thrones. He is also named in the *Goetia of Dr. Rudd*, where he is said to be constrained by the angel Pahaliah. See also *GOETIA*, RUDD, SCOT, WIERUS.

Puziel: An evil angel with the power to utterly bind an enemy. He is called upon in the *Sword of Moses* to attack the tongue, mouth, throat, and windpipe of the victim. He also has the power to bind the person's mind. As a final part of this malicious curse, Puziel and the other fallen angels invoked in this spell are asked to afflict the target with disease by putting poison in the person's belly. See also GASTER, *SWORD OF MOSES*.

Pytho: A demonic prince, Pytho is represented as a serpent. He presides over the Second Order of infernal spirits in a nine-tier hierarchy outlined in the *Janua Magica Reserata*. According to this text, the demons of the Second Order serve as the *Spiritus Mendaciorum*, or "Spirits of Lies." Pytho appears to be a mixture of the serpent from the Garden of Eden and the Greek *Python*, a monstrous snake associated with the Delphic Oracle. See also *JANUA MAGICA RESERATA*.

Quartas: A demonic servitor commanded by the infernal ruler Astaroth. In his translation of the *Sacred Magic of Abramelin the Mage*, Mathers suggests that this demon's name is derived from the Latin word for "fourth." However, in all other versions of the *Abramelin* material, the demon's name is given as *Garsas*. See also ASTAROTH, MATHERS.

Quision: A demon ruled by the infernal king Amaimon. Quision's name appears in the *Sacred Magic of Abramelin the Mage*. In the 1898 Mathers translation of this work, the name is spelled *Vision*. Accordingly, Mathers takes the name to refer to an apparition. Due to flaws in the fifteenth-century French manuscript Mathers was working from, it is difficult to say what this demon's name actually means. See also AMAIMON, MATHERS.

Quitta: A demon who serves the infernal king Baruchas in the hierarchy of the north, Quitta holds the rank of duke. He commands lesser spirits numbering in the thousands. According to the *Ars Theurgia*, the demon Quitta is tied to very specific increments of time. If the day is divided into fifteen equal sections, the hours and minutes that fall into the first section belong to Quitta. He will only manifest during this time each day. See also *ARS THEURGIA*, BARUCHAS.

Qulbda: A night-demon with a particularly unpronounceable name, Qulbda serves in the court of the north. According to the *Ars Theurgia*, his immediate superior is the demon-king Raysiel. Qulbda himself holds the rank of chief duke, and he has forty lesser spirits beneath him. He only manifests during the hours of the night, and he is reputed to possess a very evil and stubborn nature. See also *ARS THEURGIA*, RAYSIEL.

Quyron: A demon named in the Peterson translation of the *Sworn Book of Honorius*. According to this text, he ministers to the demon Habaa, king of the spirits of the planet Mercury. As a Mercurial spirit, Quyron is said to manifest in a form that shifts and shimmers like glass or white-hot fire. He has the power to know the secret thoughts and deeds of mortals and spirits alike. He will reveal these secrets to those who know how to appease him. He can also speak on matters concerning the past, present, and future. He provides good-natured spirits as familiars and will volunteer himself as a familiar spirit as well. According to the text, he also possesses some power of mimicry, for it is said that, if commanded, he will do the things that others can do. The angels Michael, Mihel, and Sarapiel, who govern the sphere of Mercury, have power over him. See also HABAA, *SWORN BOOK*.

Rabas: A demon associated with the south. In the *Ars Theurgia*, Rabas is said to serve the demon-king Asyriel. He is a chief duke in the court of Asyriel, and he has forty ministering spirits of his own. He is connected to the hours of the day. See also *ARS THEURGIA*, ASYRIEL.

Rabat: A spirit called upon in an operation known as the *Eye of Abraham*, where the image of an eye is struck until a thief confesses their guilt. The spell appears in the last folio of the grimoire known as the *Book of Oberon*. See also *BOOK OF OBERON*.

Rabdos: A demon from the *Testament of Solomon*. His name reportedly means "staff." Rabdos is said to appear in the form of a hound. He speaks with a loud voice. According to the *Testament of Solomon*, he knows the location of gems hidden within the earth and will reveal these if he is compelled. He is a dangerous demon to work with, however, for he has a bad habit of attacking people, seizing them by the throat and choking the life out of them. He is controlled by the angel Briens, who can put this demon to flight and end his attacks. See also SOLOMON.

Rabidmadar: A being whose name appears near the beginning of the seventeenth-century Venetian grimoire known as the *Secrets of Solomon*. Rabidmadar serves as secretary to Sigambach, an entity in charge of the specific characters or sigils used in forming demonic pacts. Although Sigambach (under the spelling *Singambuth*) also appears in this function in the *Grimorium Verum*, Rabidmadar is not directly named as the secretary. Instead, reference is made to methods for calling, conjuring, and constraining *Rabidanadas*, a clear derivation of *Rabidmadar*. Another variation of his name is *Rabidinadap*. See also *GRIMORIUM VERUM*, *SECRETS OF SOLOMON*, SIGAMBACH.

Rabiel: One of several chief dukes ruled by the demon Malgaras. In the *Ars Theurgia*, Rabiel is said to govern thirty lesser spirits who exist to carry out his commands. He serves this master in the court of the west during the hours of the day. Rabiel is also named as a night-demon in the court of the infernal king Maseriel. Here, he is loyal to the court of the south and has thirty ministering spirits beneath him. See also *ARS THEURGIA*, MALGARAS, MASERIEL, MISIEL.

Rabilon: An evil spirit said to be arrogant and deceitful. Rabilon is named in the *Ars Theurgia*, where he is said to serve Pamersiel, the first and chief spirit of the east under emperor Carnesiel. Rabilon is a mighty duke, and he can be called upon to drive away other evil spirits, particularly those that have chosen to haunt houses. See also *ARS THEURGIA*, CARNESIEL, PAMERSIEL.

Raboc: A demon in the court of king Malgaras, Raboc serves in the region of the west. He is named in the *Ars Theurgia*, where he is said to serve his infernal king during the hours of the night. He has thirty lesser spirits at his command. See also *ARS THEURGIA*, MALGARAS.

Rachiar: In the *Sacred Magic of Abramelin the Mage*, translator S. L. MacGregor Mathers occasionally gets a bit creative with his interpretations of demonic names. In the case of Rachiar, he suggests that the name means "sea breaking on rocks." There is inadequate information to determine whether or not this demon's name actually has anything to do with either rocks or the sea. However, the text is clear on the fact that Rachiar serves in the hierarchy beneath Oriens, Paimon, Ariton, and Amaimon—the four demonic princes connected with the cardinal directions. See also AMAIMON, ARITON, MATHERS, ORIENS, PAIMON.

Raderat: A demon ruled by the arch-fiend Beelzebub. Raderat appears in the *Sacred Magic of Abramelin the Mage*, where he is invoked as part of the

Holy Guardian Angel working central to that text. See also BEELZEBUB, MATHERS.

Ragalim: A demonic servitor of Asmodeus and Astaroth, Ragalim's name appears in the 1898 translation of the *Sacred Magic of Abramelin the Mage* by occultist S. L. MacGregor Mathers. In another version of the *Abramelin* material kept at the Wolfenbüttel library in Germany, the name of this demon appears as *Bagalon*. See also ASTAROTH, ASMODEUS, MATHERS.

Ragaras: A demon whose name appears in an extensive list recorded in the Mathers translation of the *Sacred Magic of Abramelin the Mage*. According to this work, Ragaras serves Oriens, Paimon, Ariton, and Amaimon—the four infernal princes of the cardinal directions. See also AMAIMON, ARITON, MATHERS, ORIENS, PAIMON.

Ramael: A fallen angel listed in the apocryphal *Book of Enoch*, Ramael is named as one of the "chiefs of tens" of the Watcher Angels, or *Grigori*. In this capacity, he was responsible for commanding ten other angels tasked with watching over fledgling humanity. Ramael was one of two hundred Watchers who chose to abandon Heaven in order to couple with mortal women. Ramael's name appears immediately after the name of the fallen angel Ramiel. It is possible that these two names are simply variations upon one another repeated through an error in the text. Later in the same text, the angel *Rumael* appears as one of the Watchers' chiefs. This name is likely a variation on Ramael. See also WATCHER ANGELS.

Ramaratz: In Mathers's edition of the *Sacred Magic of Abramelin the Mage*, Ramaratz appears as a subject of the four infernal princes of the cardinal directions. As such, he can be summoned and compelled in the names of his infernal masters, Oriens, Paimon, Ariton, and Amaimon. See also AMAIMON, ARITON, MATHERS, ORIENS, PAIMON.

Ramblane: Also called *Rombalence*. He is a demon in the court of Paimon, named alongside other powerful demons in that court, including Belial and Basson. The *Book of Oberon*, where he appears, attributes him no formal title or powers. See also *BOOK OF OBERON*.

In the Old Testament, the Heavenly Hosts are often portrayed as a standing army. From an illustrated Bible, by Gustave Doré.

Ramiel: One of the "chiefs of tens" of the Watcher Angels named in the *Book of Enoch*. Before his fall, Ramiel was charged with looking after the human race. Like many of the Watcher Angels, or Grigori, he grew too close to his charges. Eventually he was seduced by the pleasures of the flesh and took a human woman as his wife. His name is listed directly before that of the Watcher Ramael and may in fact simply be a variant upon that name. Further in the *Book of Enoch*, an angel named *Rumjal* appears. This may be a variant spelling of *Ramiel*. In the *Apocalypse of Baruch*, Ramiel is identified as a member of the Heavenly Hosts. Here, he is the angel in charge of true visions. See also RAMAEL, WATCHER ANGELS.

Ramison: "The Creeper." Ramison appears in the *Sacred Magic of Abramelin the Mage* as translated by occultist S. L. MacGregor Mathers. He is governed by the infernal king Amaimon. In the version of the *Abramelin* material kept at the Dresden library in Germany, this name is spelled *Ramyison*. See also AMAIMON, MATHERS.

Ranciel: A demon in service to the infernal king Gediel. Ranciel himself holds the rank of duke and has twenty lesser spirits at his command. According to the *Ars Theurgia*, he serves his master during the hours of the day and is affiliated with the direction south. See also *ARS THEURGIA*, GEDIEL.

Raner: A demonic servitor of the arch-demons Asmodeus and Astaroth. Raner is named in the Mathers edition of the *Sacred Magic of Abramelin the Mage*. See also ASTAROTH, ASMODEUS, MATHERS.

Raphan: A being named in the pseudepigraphal *Testament of Solomon*. According to this work, Raphan was worshipped by the Moabite people as a false god. He was venerated along with Moloch. See also MOLOCH, SOLOMON.

Rapsiel: According to Henson's translation of the *Ars Theurgia*, Rapsiel serves in the hierarchy of the west, underneath the emperor Amenadiel. He holds the rank of duke and commands a total of three thousand eight hundred and eighty lesser spirits. See also AMENADIEL, *ARS THEURGIA*.

Rarnica: A chief duke under the demon Raysiel, a king in the hierarchy of the north. Because Rarnica holds a fair amount of rank, he has fifty lesser spirits beneath him to carry out his commands. According to the *Ars Theurgia*, he is tied to the hours of the day and will only appear between dawn and dusk. See also *ARS THEURGIA*, RAYSIEL.

Rasinet: A demon called upon to procure treasure. He is named in the *Book of Oberon*, an Elizabethan grimoire from England. The spell that invokes him is incredibly specific: it requests that Rasinet and his fellow demons Sylquam and Malcranis produce a total of 100,000 pounds of gold and silver in legal coin. If the demons fail to comply with this demand, their images are thrown into a fire along with cat turds and other foul-smelling substances. His name is also spelled *Rasynet*. See also *BOOK OF OBERON*, MALCRANIS, SYLQUAM.

Rath: In the *Testament of Solomon*, this demon is called the lion-bearer. He is said to come in the form of a great lion, but otherwise his shape is imperceptible to mortals. Like many of the beings named in the *Testament of Solomon*, Rath is a demon of disease. He brings weakness and enfeeblement, especially to those who are already suffering from disease. He commands many legions of spirits and can be called upon to cast out other demons—assuming anyone would want to call upon one demon to drive out another. Allegedly, King Solomon put this demon to work cutting wood and carrying it to the furnace. See also SOLOMON.

Raum: A name alternately given as *Raym* in Wierus's *Pseudomonarchia Daemonum* and as *Raim* in Scot's *Discoverie of Witchcraft*. This demon reportedly manifests in the form of a crow. He can also take the shape of a man, and when he does so, he makes an excellent thief. Scot's *Discoverie of Witchcraft* says that he can steal wonderfully from the house of the king and transport his pilfered goods wherever he is instructed. He can confer dignities and reconcile both friends and foes. The Welsh *Book of Incantations* agrees on these points. Raum is the fortieth of seventy-two demons named in the *Goetia*. Like most of the demons named in this work, he is also knowledgeable about matters concerning the past, present, and future. He has the power to destroy whole cities, though his preferred method of destruction is left unnamed. He formerly belonged to the Order of Thrones and now holds the title of earl among the hierarchies of Hell. Thirty legions of infernal spirits follow his command. In the *Goetia of Dr. Rudd*, he is said to be constrained by the angel Jejazel. See also *BOOK OF INCANTATIONS*, *GOETIA*, RUDD, SCOT, WIERUS.

Rax: The name of this demon is associated with the hierarchy of Astaroth in the Mathers translation of the *Sacred Magic of Abramelin the Mage*. The precise spelling of this demon's name varies greatly between the surviving texts of the *Abramelin* material. It is given variously as *Rak*, *Rah*, and *Pak*. Mathers tries to relate it to the Greek word for "grapeseed." See also ASTAROTH, MATHERS.

Rayma: This demon's name appears in the *Munich Handbook*. He is called upon to discover the identity of a thief. He and his brethren, when properly summoned, have the ability to cause images to appear in human fingernails. See also *MUNICH HANDBOOK*.

Raysiel: According to the *Ars Theurgia*, Raysiel is a mighty king of the north who has one hundred chief dukes beneath him to do his bidding. He is the first spirit in rank directly beneath Demoriel, the Emperor of the North. Raysiel possesses an airy nature and he is not easily perceived with the naked eye. Rather, the *Ars Theurgia* suggests that anyone seeking to interact with Raysiel should summon him into a glass vessel or a scrying crystal. This operation is best carried out in a desolate and remote location, such as a wooded island or a hidden grove. Alternately, a private room of the house can be used for the operation, as long as this room can be kept secret and protected from anyone who might casually wander in to interrupt the work. Raysiel is also found in a list of demons from Johannes Trithemius's *Steganographia*, written around 1499. See also *ARS THEURGIA*, DEMORIEL, TRITHEMIUS.

Reciel: A demon in the service of Gediel, an infernal king in the hierarchy of the south. Reciel is a duke in command of twenty ministering spirits. He serves his master Gediel during the hours of the night. Reciel's name and the sigil that compels him both appear in the *Ars Theurgia*. See also *ARS THEURGIA*, GEDIEL.

Red Dragon Grimoire: Also known as *Le Dragon Rouge* and *Le Veritable Dragon Rouge* (the "True Red Dragon"). This book is almost certainly another version of the *Grand Grimoire*, published in Paris in the early 1800s, although the book itself claims to date back to 1522. The *Red Dragon Grimoire* and the *Grand Grimoire* contain several images in common, most notably a depiction of the demon of pacts known as Lucifuge Rofocale. Perhaps the most significant difference between the two books is their supposed composition. There are claims that the *Grand Grimoire* was written in Rome by Antonio Venitiana del Rabbina, as well as claims that the *Red Dragon Grimoire* was authored by Alibek the Egyptian and first published in Cairo. See also *GRAND GRIMOIRE*.

The so-called Triangle of Pacts, an image from the grimoire known as *Le Dragon Rouge.* From the collection of Grillot de Givry, courtesy of Dover Publications.

Reginon: Also spelled *Regerion*. This name appears in the *Sacred Magic of Abramelin the Mage*, where Mathers suggests that it comes from a Hebrew root meaning "vigorous ones." Reginon is a servitor of the demon-king Ariton, one of four infernal rulers of the cardinal directions named in the *Abramelin* work. See also ARITON, MATHERS.

Remoron: "The Hinderer." This demon is named in the Mathers translation of the *Sacred Magic of Abramelin the Mage*. According to this text, he is governed by the infernal princes of the four cardinal directions. As their dutiful servant, he can be summoned and compelled in the names of Oriens, Paimon, Ariton, and Amaimon. See also AMAIMON, ARITON, MATHERS, ORIENS, PAIMON.

Resbiroth: A demon named in the *Secrets of Solomon*, a seventeenth-century book of magick seized during the Venetian Inquisition. According to this text, Resbiroth serves alongside his fellow demon Serphgathana in the court of Elestor, Count of

The Ranks of Infernal Spirits

In the vast majority of grimoires, demons are typically assigned a rank and royal title to indicate their position in the pecking order of Hell. In the *Testament of Solomon*, which dates to the first few centuries of the Common Era, the demons sometimes present themselves as princes and kings—positions largely in keeping with the concept of royalty that existed at the time. Medieval works, such as the *Pseudomonarchia Daemonum*, expand the demonic hierarchy to include a variety of positions: princes and kings, dukes and earls, counts, presidents, and even knights—positions reflective of the feudal system at work throughout Europe during that time.

The ranks attributed to the infernal legions may tell us more about the time period in which the various books of magick were penned than they do about the actual hierarchy of Hell, but a deeper meaning may also be at work. The *Pseudomonarchia* and later related texts attribute a total of seven titles to the ranks of the infernal spirits. Seven was a number of great significance in medieval and Renaissance Europe. Attributed with magickal potency, it was the number of planets in the sky as well as the number of spheres thought to make up the landscape of the heavens. *The Lesser Key of Solomon* assigns a planet to each of the demonic ranks, and that planet determines the metal, or mixture of metals, that must go into the magickal seal of the spirit. These correspondences have been retained to this day, repeated faithfully in the works of modern occultists such as S. L. MacGregor Mathers and his student Aleister Crowley. Below is a list of the Latin titles that appear in the *Pseudomonarchia*, their English translations as given by Reginald Scot in his 1584 text *The Discoverie of Witchcraft*, as well as the planets and metals associated with each rank in the *Lesser Key of Solomon*:

Latin title	English equivalent	Planet	Metal
Rex	King	Sun	Gold
Princeps	Prince	Jupiter	Tin
Praeses	President	Mercury	Mercury
Dux	Duke	Venus	Copper
Comes	Earl	Mars	Copper & Silver
Marchio	Marquis	Moon	Silver
Miles (soldier)	Knight	Saturn	Lead

Hell. Both Resbiroth and his compatriot are recognized as dukes. See also ELESTOR, *SECRETS OF SOLOMON*, SERPHGATHANA.

Resochin: Also known as *Resochim*, this demon is said to have power over affairs of state. He can give or take away the means for knowing how to proceed in any given situation. This politically minded demon appears in the *True Keys of Solomon*, where he is said to serve beneath chief Sirachi in the hierarchy of Lucifer. Under the name of *Reschin*, he appears in the Venetian *Secrets of Solomon*. Here he is one of eighteen demons reputedly in the service of Duke Syrach, a direct subordinate of Lucifer. If properly approached, he will disclose political secrets for a price. See also LUCIFER, *SECRETS OF SOLOMON*, SIRACHI, SYRACH, *TRUE KEYS*.

Rewboo: A demon who bestows gold and silver. Rewboo appears in the *Book of Oberon*, an Elizabethan magickal text. In rank, he is a great prince with twenty-nine legions under him. When summoned, he takes the form of a knight. See also *BOOK OF OBERON*.

Rewsyn: A curious demon who seems to participate in an unexpected form of demonic possession. According to the *Book of Oberon*, Rewsyn manifests as a beautiful woman who can speak of past, present, and future. When she is bidden to depart from the world, one of Rewsyn's ministering spirits may enter the body in which she was summoned. Once the former body is thus possessed, the new spirit may hold discourse. Ranked a duke in the demonic hierarchies, Rewsyn has ten legions of lesser spirits that serve him. See also *BOOK OF OBERON*.

Richel: A demon of the night that holds the rank of duke. One hundred and twenty lesser spirits attend to his needs. Richel serves beneath the demon Symiel, king of the north by east. According to the *Ars Theurgia*, Richel is reputed to be a troublesome and obstinate spirit. See also *ARS THEURGIA*, SYMIEL.

Rigios: Mathers suggests that the name of this demon is derived from a Greek root meaning "terrible." In his 1898 translation of the *Sacred Magic of Abramelin the Mage*, he identified Rigios as a servitor of the demon Astaroth. His name is given as *Kigios* in other versions of the *Abramelin* material. See also ASTAROTH, MATHERS.

Rigolen: A demon governed by the infernal rulers Amaimon and Ariton. In the *Sacred Magic of Abramelin the Mage*, Rigolen is summoned and forced to swear allegiance to the magician as a part of the Holy Guardian Angel rite central to this text. In the Mathers translation of this work, Rigolen's name is connected to a Hebrew root meaning alternately "foot" and "to drag down." See also AMAIMON, ARITON, MATHERS.

Rimmon: Hell's duly appointed ambassador to Russia, if the early-nineteenth-century French demonologist Charles Berbiguier is to be believed. Rimmon is accorded this curious position in de Plancy's *Dictionnaire Infernal* and Waite's *Book of Black Magic and Pacts* as well. See also BERBIGUIER, DE PLANCY, WAITE.

Rimog: A demon named in the *Sacred Magic of Abramelin the Mage*, Rimog is said to serve the demon Magoth. In the fifteenth-century French manuscript sourced by Mathers, Rimog also serves the demon Kore. See also KORE, MAGOTH, MATHERS.

Risbel: A so-called squire spirit named in the *Munich Handbook*. Risbel has powers of illusion and is called upon to help conjure a castle from thin air.

He must be called in a secluded spot on the tenth night of the moon. An offering of milk and honey is said to help gain his service. His name is also rendered *Ristel*. See also *MUNICH HANDBOOK*.

Rodabell: Also called *Radabelbes*. He is a messenger of the north, serving in the court of the infernal king Egin. He appears in the *Book of Oberon*, a grimoire from Elizabethan England. His name is also spelled *Rodobel* and *Rodybel* at various points in the manuscript. See also ALPHASIS, *BOOK OF OBERON*, EGIN, EMLON, FEMELL.

Roêlêd: The fifteenth of thirty-six demons associated with the decans of the zodiac, Roêlêd is said to cause ailments of the stomach. He may also be known by the name *Iax*. This name appears as part of an incantation to drive Roêlêd away. According to the *Testament of Solomon*, Roêlêd is put to flight, not with a name of God or an angel, but with the name of King Solomon himself. In a later, more accurate translation of this same work, his name instead is *Soubelti*. He causes shivering and numbness and the angel Rizoel holds the power to control him. See also SOLOMON.

Rofanes: One of several demons named in the *Munich Handbook* called before a medium in order to reveal the details of a theft. Rofanes and his brethren can cause human fingernails, made shiny through the proper application of oil, to serve as scrying mirrors. A young virgin boy is typically the medium used in the spell. See also *MUNICH HANDBOOK*.

Roggiol: A servitor of the arch-fiends Astaroth and Asmodeus. According to the Mathers edition of the *Sacred Magic of Abramelin the Mage*, his name may mean "to drag down by the feet." In the edition of the *Abramelin* material published by Peter Hammer in 1725, the name of this demon is given

instead as *Kogiel*. See also ASTAROTH, ASMODEUS, MATHERS.

Roler: One of several demons mentioned in the *Sacred Magic of Abramelin the Mage*, Roler is said to serve the infernal ruler Magoth. Only the Mathers translation contains this spelling of the name. In all other versions of the *Abramelin* material, this demon's name is recorded as *Rotor*. Either way, it is tempting to connect this name in some fashion with wheels or a spinning motion. See also MAGOTH, MATHERS.

Romages: A demon ruled by Oriens, Paimon, Ariton, and Amaimon. In the *Sacred Magic of Abramelin the Mage*, these four demons hold sway over the cardinal directions. As a servant of these great infernal rulers, Romages can be called up and commanded in their names. See also AMAIMON, ARITON, MATHERS, ORIENS, PAIMON.

Romerac: This name may mean "violent thunder" from a Hebrew root identified by occultist S. L. MacGregor Mathers. Romerac is named in the *Sacred Magic of Abramelin the Mage* as one of the servitors of the infernal king Amaimon. See also AMAIMON, MATHERS.

Romiel: A demon of the daylight hours reputed to possess a tractable nature, Romiel is part of the hierarchy of the north, as outlined in the *Ars Theurgia*. He serves the demon-king Symiel, and is one of only ten chief dukes who work for Symiel during the hours of the day. Romiel has a total of eighty attending spirits that carry out his wishes. See also *ARS THEURGIA*, SYMIEL.

Romulon: A demon named in the *Book of Oberon*. According to that grimoire, Romulon is an infernal spirit who can be called upon to find stolen treasure. When he manifests, it is in the guise of a soldier armed with a sword and lance. He is said to be under the power of all other spirits, which places this poor fellow at the absolute bottom rung of a very extensive hierarchy. If anyone ever feels threatened by this demon, they can control him by wielding a cross made of palms blessed on Palm Sunday. See also *BOOK OF OBERON*.

Romyel: A servant of the wandering prince Macariel, Romyel may manifest at any time during the day or night. Although he has the power to appear in whatever form he chooses, he is most fond of appearing as a many-headed dragon with virgins' heads. In this he shares a preference with his infernal prince Macariel. Romyel oversees a total of four hundred ministering spirits. His name and the seal appear in the *Ars Theurgia*. See also *ARS THEURGIA*, MACARIEL.

The seal of the Goetic demon Ronove as depicted in the *Goetia of Dr. Rudd*. It varies slightly from other editions of the *Goetia*. Art by M. Belanger.

Ronove: One of the traditional seventy-two Goetic demons, Ronove is described as both a marquis and an earl. According to Scot's *Discoverie of Witchcraft*, he has command over nineteen legions of lesser spirits, and when he manifests he takes the form of a monster. Exactly what kind of monster is not specified within the text. He reputedly has the power to provide knowledge of foreign languages as well as a gifted understanding of rhetoric. He also procures faithful servants and the favor of friend and foe alike. Wierus's *Pseudomonarchia Daemonum* spells his name *Roneve*. According to the *Goetia of Dr. Rudd*, he is constrained by the angel Jerathel. See also *GOETIA*, RUDD, SCOT, WIERUS.

Roriel: One of twelve infernal dukes in the court of the demon-king Maseriel, Roriel is connected with the hierarchy of the south and he serves his infernal master during the hours of the day. According to the Henson translation of the *Ars Theurgia*, he has command over thirty lesser spirits of his own. See also *ARS THEURGIA*, MASERIEL.

Rosaran: A servant of the demon Ariton, Rosaran is named in the *Sacred Magic of Abramelin the Mage*. His name may be derived from a Hebrew root meaning "evil" or "wicked." See also ARITON, MATHERS.

Royne: A demon of lust who is said to procure sexual indulgence, particularly between a man and his wife. When summoned, he assumes the form of a soldier riding a black horse. His face is like that of a lion, and he carries a serpent in his arms. According to the *Book of Oberon*, he possesses the rank of earl and oversees twenty-six legions of lesser spirits. In addition to his power for procuring sex, Royne is said to be a builder. He can erect great towers and bulwarks of war as well as knock them down. He further consecrates books, reveals hidden treasure, and exposes secrets. See also *BOOK OF OBERON*.

Ruach: A name derived directly from the Hebrew word *ruach*, which means "breath" or "wind," with further connotations of "spirit." *Ruach Ha-Kodesh* is a Hebrew name for God typically translated in the Bible as *the Holy Spirit*. Due to the imperfect syncretization of Jewish mysticism in the medieval grimoiric tradition, several holy words were corrupted into demon names, including *Berith*. Ruach was no exception. In the *Sacred Magic of Abramelin the Mage*, the demon Ruach is mentioned as part of the hierarchy serving beneath the infernal princes of the cardinal directions: Oriens, Amaimon, Ariton, and Paimon. His name is to be scribed upon paper on the second day of the *Abramelin* operation, along with the names of approximately three hundred and twenty other demons. On the third day of the working, which ultimately culminates in the magician's communion with his Holy Guardian Angel, Ruach and the others are supposed to appear in order to swear their service to the magician. See also AMAIMON, ARITON, BERITH, ORIENS, PAIMON.

Ruall: According to the *Book of Incantations*, this demon belonged to the angelic Order of Potentates before his fall. He speaks Egyptian and appears as a muddy dromedary, although he may be compelled to take human form. His office is to procure the love of women. He tells things past, present, and to come and also causes enemies to become friends. Thirty-seven legions follow in his retinue. He appears in the *Book of Oberon* under the variant spelling *Ryall*. He also appears here as a dromedary, but rather than speaking Egyptian, he is said simply to sound as if he is sad. He appears in a list of twelve other demons dedicated to serving Paimon, king of the west. All of his powers in this text are identical to those listed in the *Book of Incantations*. Compare to the Goetic demon *Vuall*.

See also *BOOK OF INCANTATIONS*, *BOOK OF OBERON*, VUALL.

Ruax: A demon who afflicts humans by damaging their intelligence. He is said to have the power to make people slow-witted and confused. He fears the archangel Michael more than any other denizen of Heaven, and he can be put to flight with the name of that powerful being. Ruax appears in the *Testament of Solomon*, where he is named as one of a number of demons of disease. His name may be a variation of the word *Rhyx*, meaning "king." See also SOLOMON.

Rubeus Pugnator: A demon connected with the planet Mars. His name is Latin for the "Red Fighter." In the *Liber de Angelis*, he is named as the king of the demons connected with the sphere of Mars. He is summoned as part of the spell for creating the magickal Ring of Mars, a potent talisman that grants terrible power. The ring can be used to bring destruction down upon any chosen victim. See also *LIBER DE ANGELIS*.

Rudd, Dr. Thomas: The author of several manuscripts on magick and esoteric subjects kept in the Harley collection at the British Museum in London. These manuscripts date to the early 1700s, but they were copied from texts that were much older. Author Adam McLean, founder of Levity .com, appropriately calls these "The Treatises of Dr. Rudd" in his introduction to Rudd's own *Treatise on Angel Magic*. Rudd was a curious fellow with an obvious interest in angels, demons, and ceremonial magick—and a near-obsession on knowing how to tell good spirits from bad. Based on one of his writings, it is clear that he was also a scholar of Hebrew, sympathetic to Jews at a time when such sympathies were hardly in fashion. He was also an avid fan of Dr. John Dee. There is such a huge

The demonic seals in the *Goetia of Dr. Rudd* are often simpler than those found in other versions of the *Goetia*. Compare Rudd's version of the seal of Forcalor on the left to that found in Henson's translation. Art by M. Belanger.

influence of Dee's system of Enochian magick on portions of Rudd's work that Peter Smart, the individual responsible for copying the Harley manuscripts, believed he was copying work that stemmed directly from Dee.

Aside from his manuscripts, little is known about Dr. Rudd. Scholar Frances Yates identifies Dr. Rudd with one Thomas Rudd, an individual responsible for publishing an edition of John Dee's *Mathematical Preface to Euclid* in 1651. If she is correct, we seem to know his first name as well as the general time period during which he lived his life. Both Yates and McLean imply that there is some question as to when precisely Dr. Rudd lived, but in their book, *The Goetia of Dr. Rudd*, authors Steven Skinner and David Rankine give his dates definitely as 1583 to 1656. See also *TREATISE ON ANGEL MAGIC*.

Rukum: The name of this demon may come from a Hebrew term meaning "diversified." Rukum appears in the Mathers translation of the *Sacred Magic of Abramelin the Mage*. According to this work, he is one of several demons ruled by the infernal prince Paimon. In another version of the *Abramelin* material, kept at the Wolfenbüttel library in Germany, the name of this demon is given as *Marku*. See also MATHERS, PAIMON.

Ryon: A demon in the court of Fornnouc, the infernal king of the element of air. With a quick and agile mind, Ryon can serve as an inspiring tutor. In addition, he has the power to cure infirmities and weaknesses. In Driscoll's edition of the *Sworn Book of Honourius*, this demon is described as possessing a lively nature, although he is also somewhat capricious. He can be made to appear by burning the appropriate perfumes. In the Peterson translation of the *Sworn Book*, Ryon is connected with the sphere of Jupiter. He is subordinate to the demonking Formione, who rules over the spirits of Jupiter. This version of Ryon grants joy, gladness, and love to mortals. He can also bestow favors. When he manifests, his form is the color of the heavens. He can be commanded in the names of the angels Satquiel, Raphael, Pahamcocihel, and Asassaiel, who rule the sphere of Jupiter. He bears some connection with the east, possibly the eastern winds. See also FORMIONE, FORNNOUC, *SWORN BOOK*.

Saba: King of the planetary sphere of Mercury, Saba is aided by three infernal ministers: Hanyey, Yron, and Alvedio. When he is near, Saba causes people to shiver with cold. He can appear in many forms, including a king riding a bear, a woman with a distaff, an attractive young man, or a magpie. As he has many forms, he also has many offices. He can help to win court cases or battles. He elevates the poor and casts down the rich and powerful. He teaches all spells and can restore lost knowledge. He can also open locks and release the bindings of spirits. He is named, along with his ministers, in the Elizabethan grimoire known as the *Book of Oberon*. See also ALVEDIO, *BOOK OF OBERON*, HANYEY, SABA, YRON.

Sabas: A servant of the demon Gediel, Sabas holds the rank of duke and governs twenty lesser spirits of his own. According to the *Ars Theurgia*, he is tied to the hours of the day, and, through his association with Gediel, he is also tied to the direction of the south. The name of this demon may be connected to an ancient Egyptian word meaning "star." It is also a variation on *Sheba*, a kingdom mentioned in the Bible. The historian Josephus described a walled Ethiopian city named Saba that may have been the biblical Sheba. See also *ARS THEURGIA*, GEDIEL.

Sabnock: One of the seventy-two demons named in the *Goetia*. In Scot's *Discoverie of Witchcraft*, Sabnock is said to appear in the form of an armed soldier with the head of a lion. He rides a pale horse, as do many of the demons associated with the *Goetia*. Wierus's *Pseudomonarchia Daemonum* spells his name *Sabnac*. In the Welsh *Book of Incantations*, his name is given as *Sabnack*. As his appearance suggests, he is a martial demon. He has the power to build castles, cities, and high towers full of weapons. He can inflict putrid wounds full of maggots that last for a span of thirty days. In addition, he is said to be able to change people's forms and give familiar spirits. Holding the rank of marquis, he commands a total of fifty legions.

Throughout the Middle Ages and the Renaissance, the Devil is described as a black man, and the racist implications of this cannot easily be avoided, as with the demons depicted in this early ninteenth-century engraving by J. Brown. Image courtesy of the Wellcome Collection.

Alternate forms of his name include *Salmac, Sabnacke*, and *Sabnach*. According to the *Goetia of Dr. Rudd*, he is ruled over by the angel Vevaliah. See also *BOOK OF INCANTATIONS, GOETIA*, RUDD, SCOT, WIERUS.

Sachiel: In ceremonial magick, Sachiel is often identified as the angel of the planet Jupiter. He appears in this capacity in both the *Secret Grimoire of Turiel* and the *Grimoire of Armadel*. In Qabbalistic lore, Sachiel is identified as an archangel of the Cherubim. He is the angel of Thursday, and his name is generally taken to mean "the covering of God." As an archangel, he is rarely counted among the fallen. Despite this, however, he makes an appearance in the *Sacred Magic of Abramelin the Mage* as one of a number of demons who serve beneath the infernal princes Oriens, Paimon, Ariton, and Amaimon, who guard the cardinal directions. See also AMAIMON, ARITON, MATHERS, ORIENS, PAIMON.

Sacred Magic of Abramelin the Mage: Sometimes also known simply as the *Book of Abramelin*, this work is powerfully steeped in Jewish esotericism. Aimed at achieving conversation with a heavenly being known as the Holy Guardian Angel, this classic text of ceremonial magick provides the names of literally hundreds of demons who are required to swear their subservience to the operator during the Holy Guardian Angel rite. Attributed to a fourteenth-century Jewish scholar known as Abraham von Worms, the *Abramelin* material was translated into English by occultist Samuel Liddell MacGregor Mathers in 1898. Mathers was working from a fifteenth-century French manuscript, which, at the time, was the only version of the *Abramelin* material available to him. Over the years, Mathers has received some criticism for his translation, but recently *Abramelin* scholar Georg Dehn has discovered that it was the manuscript, and not Mathers's translation, that was flawed. Dehn, in an exhaustive search for the real Abraham von Worms, has brought several other versions of the *Abramelin* material to light. These include a manuscript from 1608 written in cipher and kept at the Wolfenbüttel library, a manuscript dating to 1720 and kept at the Dresden library, and a version of the *Abramelin* material published in 1725 by Peter Hammer in Cologne. In addition to these discoveries, Dehn claims to have traced Abraham von Worms—long thought to be a name crafted to legitimize the *Abramelin* story—to the very real Jewish scholar Rabbi Jacob ben Moses ha Levi Moellin, known in the fourteenth century as *the MaHaRIL*. Dehn's 2006 publication *The Book of*

Abramelin has proven indispensable for its comparison of the surviving manuscripts, especially where the long lists of demon names are concerned. See also MATHERS.

Sadar: A demon whose name and seal appear in the *Ars Theurgia*, Sadar serves beneath the demon-king Raysiel in the court of the north. He is described as a demon of the day, and he will only appear during daylight hours. He holds the rank of duke and has fifty ministering spirits beneath him. See also *ARS THEURGIA*, RAYSIEL.

Saddiel: In the hierarchy of Usiel, Saddiel holds the rank of duke. He is a night-demon tied to the region of the west, and he has forty lesser spirits to serve him. According to the *Ars Theurgia*, he excels at finding hidden things and secreting away treasure, often using enchantments to hide these precious objects. See also *ARS THEURGIA*, USIEL.

Sadiel: A demon from the Henson translation of the *Ars Theurgia*, Sadiel is identified as a member of the hierarchy of the demon Gediel. Gediel is named as the second spirit in the hierarchy of the south, and thus Sadiel is also connected with the direction of the south. He is a duke said to serve his infernal master during the hours of the night. Twenty lesser spirits obey his command. See also *ARS THEURGIA*, GEDIEL.

Saefam: Serving the infernal prince Usiel, Saefam is a duke who commands forty lesser spirits of his own. According to the *Ars Theurgia*, he is tied to the hours of the day and will only manifest during that time. He has the power to hide precious items away, protecting them from discovery and theft. He can also reveal treasures hidden through magickal means. Several of the demons in the *Ars Theurgia* seem to be paired together, with names that closely match. Compare Saefam to *Saefer*, a

demon listed in the same hierarchy. See also *ARS THEURGIA*, USIEL.

Saefer: One of several demons named in the hierarchy of prince Usiel, Saefer has the power to reveal hidden treasure and he is also capable of magickally hiding items away to prevent others from discovering or stealing them. The *Ars Theurgia* gives his rank as chief duke, saying further that forty ministering spirits serve beneath him. This is another demonic name with a match or pairing in the *Ars Theurgia*. Compare to *Saefam*, a demon who is listed in the same hierarchy. See also *ARS THEURGIA*, USIEL.

Saemiet: A demon named in the *Ars Theurgia* from the Henson translation of the complete *Lemegeton*. Saemiet is reputed to serve the demon-king Maseriel, who rules in the west by south. Through Maseriel, Saemiet is affiliated with the hierarchy of the south. He is connected with the hours of the night, serving his infernal master only during this time. His title is duke, and he holds sway over a total of thirty ministering spirits. See also *ARS THEURGIA*, MASERIEL.

Safrit: This demon appears in the thirty-ninth spell of the *Munich Handbook*. He is called upon to assist with general matters of divination. He is also connected with the art of scrying. See also *MUNICH HANDBOOK*.

Sagares: According to occultist Mathers, the name of this demon may be related to the word *sagaris*, a bronze battle-axe used mainly by the ancient people known as the Scythians. Mathers relates the weapon to the double-bladed axe of the Amazons, known as a *labrys*. In the Mathers translation of the *Sacred Magic of Abramelin the Mage*, Sagares is said to serve the demons Astaroth and Asmodeus. He is called upon as a part of the Holy

The Seven Deadlies

The Seven Deadly Sins is a list of major offenses developed by Saint Gregory the Great in 590, during his tenure as pope. The sins are classed as *cardinal sins*, which are the most objectionable vices that can be engaged in by an individual. The sins are: lust, gluttony, avarice, sloth, wrath, envy, and pride. In the Middle Ages, the Seven Deadly Sins were often personified as players in morality plays. By the fourteenth century, these seven major vices had become a popular topic in art and literature. The sins were perhaps most famously treated by Dante Alighieri, in his description of Hell in his epic work *The Divine Comedy*.

In the sixteenth century, a bishop from Trier in Germany, Peter Binsfeld, sought to classify demons according to the Seven Deadly Sins. The way Binsfeld saw it, each demon had a preferred sin that it would use to tempt humanity. The demons could then be loosely arranged in groups according to those sins. He chose a different demonic prince to head each of these seven camps, as follows:

Demon	Deadly Sin
Lucifer	Pride
Leviathan	Envy
Satan	Wrath
Belphegor	Sloth
Mammon	Avarice
Beelzebub	Gluttony
Asmodeus	Lust

The demon Behemoth looks like a good candidate for the sin of gluttony in this image from Collin de Plancy's *Dictionnaire Infernal*. Courtesy of Dover Publications.

Guardian Angel working that is central to the *Abramelin* material. See also ASTAROTH, ASMODEUS, MATHERS.

Salarica: A demon given the rank of senator in the Elizabethan *Book of Oberon*. Salarica, also spelled *Salaryca*, is called upon to compel and control other spirits, rather like pulling rank. Salarica, along with six other infernal senators, serves directly beneath Tantavalerion, a demon named in the same spell. According to the text, Tantavalerion is the supreme ruler of all spirits and they must obey when his name is invoked. See also ASMOO, BOELL, *BOOK OF OBERON*, DANALL, ORYMELL, PASCARY, TANTAVALERION, TYGRA.

Salaul: A demon described as a "squire spirit." In the *Munich Handbook*, Salaul is named in connection with an illusion spell. He is one of several demons presented as having the power to manifest an entire castle out of thin air. The text recommends that Salaul be appeased with an offering of milk and honey. He is to be called upon in a remote and secret location on the tenth day of the moon. See also *MUNICH HANDBOOK*.

Salleos: The nineteenth demon named in the *Goetia*, Salleos is said to manifest as a gallant soldier. He comes riding a crocodile and wearing a ducal crown. According to both Wierus's *Pseudomonarchia Daemonum* and Scot's *Discoverie of Witchcraft*, he holds the rank of earl. In the *Goetia*, however, he is accorded the title of duke. Here, his name is spelled *Saleos*. He reputedly has the power to cause people to fall in love with the opposite sex. He governs thirty legions. His name is also spelled *Zaleos*. In the *Goetia of Dr. Rudd*, his name is spelled *Sallos*. According to this text, he constrained by the

angel Leuviah. See also *GOETIA*, RUDD, SCOT, WIERUS.

Salmatis: A demon named in the sixteenth-century French grimoire *Livre des esperitz*. He is a great marquis who appears in the likeness of an armed knight. He builds strongholds, castles, and even towns. He also commands illusions and transforms people into any appearance that they wish, as well as conjuring grand plays for entertainment. A total of fifty legions of lesser spirits serve beneath him. See also *LIVRE DES ESPERITZ*.

Saltim: For the wizard who has everything, Saltim can be called upon to produce a magnificent flying throne. There is no indication whether or not he possesses the power necessary to cause any other pieces of furniture to perform aerial acrobatics. However, in a pinch, he might also be convinced to enchant a flying rug. According to the *Munich Handbook*, where this curious information can be found, Saltim holds the infernal rank of duke. See also *MUNICH HANDBOOK*.

Salvor: Named in the *Ars Theurgia*, this demon is governed by Maseriel, an infernal king in the court of the west. Salvor holds the title of duke and is said to have thirty ministering spirits at his command. He is connected with the hours of the night, serving only during this time. See also *ARS THEURGIA*, MASERIEL.

Samael: A complicated figure variously identified as both a fallen angel and a loyal member of the heavenly hierarchies. Although he eventually made his way into the demonology of Christian Europe, Samael has his roots planted firmly in Jewish folklore. In the *Chronicles of Jerahmeel*, Samael is described as the "chief of the Satans."[55] Even though this text depicts him as one of the

---

55. Moses Gaster, *The Chronicles of Jerahmeel*, p. 136.

most wicked angels, he is nevertheless presented as an angel in service to the Lord. He is an angel of death, and he is chosen to collect the soul of Moses. In the *Haggadah*, Samael is said to be the guardian of Jacob's brother Esau. In this capacity, Samael is also an evil angel, because the Haggadah presents Esau as a thoroughly wicked person, attached only to the material world and drawn to worship in places of idolatry. In the *Zohar*, a primary text of the Qabbalah, Samael is associated with the evil entity Amalek, the god of the physical world. Here, Samael's name is said to be the occult name of Amalek. According to the *Zohar*, Samael means "poison of God."[56] In his work *The Holy Kabbalah*, occultist A. E. Waite defines Samael as "the severity of God."[57] In this work, Samael is also equated with both Satan and the Serpent. Lilith is his bride. According to Moncure Daniel Conway's *Demonology and Devil-Lore*, Samael is the consort of both the voluptuous maiden Naamah and the arch-she-devil Lilith. He functions as the left hand of God.

In the Gnostic *Apocryphon of John*, found among the Nag Hammadi manuscripts, Samael is given as another name for the evil demiurge of the physical world. This echoes the statements of the *Zohar* concerning Samael's connection to the material realm. Samael, sometimes also spelled *Sammael*, made his way into the grimoiric tradition. In the *Heptameron*, he is described as an angel. He is said to rule over both Monday and Tuesday. He appears in the 1505 *Faustbuch* entitled *Magiae Naturalis et Innatural*, where he is identified with the element of fire. Henry Cornelius Agrippa associates him

The names, figures, and seals of the angels of the seven days of the week, as they appear in Scot's *Discoverie of Witchcraft*. Courtesy of Dover Publications.

with Urieus, another form of Oriens, the demonic guardian of the east. Mathers repeats this association in his edition of the *Sacred Magic of Abramelin the Mage*. Samael also appears in the Mathers translation of the *Grimoire of Armadel*. In keeping with the confusion surrounding this ancient figure, this text also identifies Samael as both a fallen angel and a heavenly being. As a fallen angel, Samael is said to teach magick, necromancy, and the occult sciences. Oddly, he also teaches jurisprudence. According to the *Grimoire of Armadel*, Samael can also reveal what necromantic practices are the most dangerous and should not be abused. Curiously, Samael (spelled *Simiel*) also appears in a list of seven archangels composed by Saint Gregory, who served as Pope Gregory I from 590 until 604. See

56. H. W. Percival, *Sepher Ha-Zohar, or The Book of Light*, p. 148.

57. A. E. Waite, *The Doctrine and Literature of the Kabalah*, p. 77.

also ASAEL, AMALEK, AZAZEL, LILITH, MAC-CATHIEL, NAAMAH, SATAN, WAITE.

Samalo: A demon under the leadership of the greater fiend Beelzebub, Samalo appears in the *Sacred Magic of Abramelin the Mage*. Samalo is one of over three hundred unclean spirits whose names are presented in that work so they can be called upon and bound to the magician's will. See also BEELZEBUB, MATHERS.

Sambas: Connected to the west and southwest winds, Sambas is said to serve king Habaa, ruler of the spirits of the planet Mercury. In the Peterson edition of the *Sworn Book of Honorius*, Sambas is said to gather good spirits to present as familiars. He also has some powers of mimicry, for he can be commanded to perform any task just as it is done by another. He knows all manner of secret thoughts and deeds, and he will reveal these if it is demanded of him. His manifest form shimmers and shifts like the surface of glass or like a dancing, white-hot flame. He can be compelled in the names of the angels Michael, Mihel, and Sarapiel, who command all the spirits of the sphere of Mercury. See also HABAA, *SWORN BOOK*.

Samiel: A benevolent demon who prefers to appear in watery locations, such as wetlands and bogs. Samiel is one of twelve dukes who serve the wandering prince Hydriel. Samiel himself is attended by a total of one thousand three hundred and twenty lesser spirits. According to the *Ars Theurgia*, he manifests as a serpent with a woman's head. Despite this monstrous appearance, he is reputed to behave in a polite and courteous manner. See also *ARS THEURGIA*, HYDRIEL.

Samiet: A demon governed by Armadiel, an infernal king ruling in the northeast. Samiet commands eighty-four lesser spirits and holds the rank of chief duke. According the *Ars Theurgia*, there is a formula to calculate the minutes and hours during which this demon is willing to appear. Divide the day into fifteen equal portions. The eighth portion belongs to Samiet. He is bound to appear only during this time. See also ARMADIEL, *ARS THEURGIA*.

Samon: A great king named in the French *Livre des esperitz* who takes the guise of a beautiful maiden. He holds sway over women and can compel the love of queens. He also inflames the passions of those who think themselves perfect, regardless of their virginity. Twenty-five legions serve under his command. See also *LIVRE DES ESPERITZ*.

Samsapiel: One of the so-called "chiefs of tens" among the Watcher Angels in the *Book of Enoch*. Samsapiel was originally charged with watching over humanity, but he grew too close to those under his care. He fell prey to temptations of the flesh and eventually left Heaven in order to take a human woman as his wife. As one of the chiefs of tens, he led ten other fallen angels in their exodus into the material realm. He answers directly to Azazel and Shemyaza, the leaders of the Watchers. See also AZAZEL, SHEMYAZA, WATCHER ANGELS.

Samyel: A demon in the court of Menadiel, a wandering prince of the air named in the *Ars Theurgia*. Samyel is tied to the eleventh hour of the day. He has a demonic companion, Tharson, who appears after him in the twelfth hour of the day. In addition to his companion, Samyel commands a total of three hundred and ninety subordinate spirits. See also *ARS THEURGIA*, MENADIEL, THARSON.

Sanfrielis: A demon named in the *Munich Handbook*, Sanfrielis is connected with divination and scrying. He is reputed to help a spirit medium see visions of the thief or thieves responsible for a crime. See also *MUNICH HANDBOOK*.

Sapason: A demon in the court of prince Ariton. Sapason appears in the *Sacred Magic of Abramelin the Mage*. According to the Mathers translation of this work, the demon's name comes from a Greek word meaning "to putrefy." The name of this demon is alternately spelled *Sarason*. See also ARITON, MATHERS.

Saphathoraêl: A demon of affliction who plagues humanity by dividing people against one another, Saphathoraêl also causes drunkenness and stumbling. A demon associated with the thirty-six decans of the zodiac, Saphathoraêl appears in the pseudepigraphal text the *Testament of Solomon*. According to this text, Saphathoraêl can be put to flight by invoking the name *Sabaôth*. It should be noted that, while most of the zodiac demons mentioned in the *Testament of Solomon* can be driven away or compelled through the use of specific angel names, Sabaôth is not technically the name of an angel. In the Hebrew tradition, this is one of the titles of God, meaning "Lord of Hosts." See also SOLOMON.

Sarabocres: According to the Peterson translation of the *Sworn Book of Honorius*, Sarabocres is the king of the spirits of the planet Venus. As such, he has the power to inspire love, passion, and pleasure in mortals. He can also cause laughter. His manifest form is exceedingly beautiful, with a countenance that is clear and white as snow. He is controlled and compelled by the angels Hanahel, Raquyel, and Salguyel, who rule over the sphere of Venus. In the Driscoll translation of this same work, Sarabocres is described as one of the "bright demons of the West."[58] His rank is given as king, but since the demon Harthan is established earlier in that same text as the king of the west, Driscoll suggests that Sarabocres's true domain is the air and heavens. This version of Sarabocres is further described as having a nature that is as malleable as pure silver. He is connected with love, lust, and sumptuous earthly pleasures. He is said to have the power to create boundless enjoyment in the opposite sex. He can provide luxurious gifts such as rich perfume and fine cloth, and of course he can inspire love, lust, and all manner of passion between people.

A variation on this demon's name appears in a section of the *Heptameron*. Although the offices and powers of the spirits in this section are extremely similar to those described in the Peterson edition of the *Sworn Book*, in the *Heptameron* Sarabocres is identified as an angel. Under the name *Sarabotres*, he appears in the *Book of Oberon* as the king of the planetary sphere of Venus. According to that text, he encourages harmony, peace, and love through decadence and indulgence. He is served by two ministers, Nasar and Manasa. He can be called upon to arrange marriages, to bring riches in the form of silver, and to remove weakness. He also has the power to gently draw men into the love of women, although whether this power is intended to work against anyone's natural orientation is unclear. His presence is heralded by young girls at play who will call sweetly for mortals to join them. Not creepy at all. See also *BOOK OF OBERON*, HARTHAN, *HEPTAMERON*, MANASA, NASAR, *SWORN BOOK*.

Sarach: An evil-natured and headstrong night-demon named in the hierarchy of the north. Sar-

---

58. Daniel Driscoll, *Sworn Book of Honourius*, p. 101.

ach's immediate superior is the demon-king Raysiel. Sarach himself holds the title of chief duke, and he has twenty lesser spirits beneath him. He appears in the *Ars Theurgia*. Because he is tied to the hours of the night, he will only manifest when darkness holds sway over the land. See also *ARS THEURGIA*, RAYSIEL.

Sarael: According to the *Ars Theurgia*, Sarael is a mighty duke in the hierarchy of the north. He oversees thousands of lesser spirits and answers directly to the infernal king Baruchas. Sarael is bound to only appear during a specific time of the day. Following this formula, divide the day into fifteen equal portions. The second portion is the time when Sarael may appear each day. See also *ARS THEURGIA*, BARUCHAS.

Saranyt: This demon takes the form of a donkey with a woman's face. His chief ability is to raise the dead and allow them to speak. Appearing in the *Book of Oberon*, Saranyt is listed as one of the twelve highest-ranking ministers of Egin, the king in the north. See also *BOOK OF OBERON*, EGIN.

Saraph: In the *Sacred Magic of Abramelin the Mage*, this demon serves beneath the four demonic princes who oversee the cardinal directions. As a servant of Oriens, Paimon, Ariton, and Amaimon, Saraph shares in all of their powers. Mathers suggests that the name of this demon means "to burn" or "to devour with fire," as it comes from the same root as *Seraph*. The Seraphim, or "Fiery Ones," are generally conceived as being the highest order of angels in the heavenly hierarchy. Few people might connect the Seraphim with demons, but biblical scholar W. O. E. Oesterley, in his 1921 work *Immortality and the Unseen World*, points out that the Seraphim, before they were angels, did a stint as demonic entities in early Semitic mythology. Some of this demonic association still lingers, even in biblical passages. In both Numbers 21:6 and Isaiah 14:29, Seraphim are connected with fiery serpents, and not exactly in a positive light. See also AMAIMON, ARITON, MATHERS, ORIENS, PAIMON.

Some Gnostic sects in early Christianity believed that the serpent in Eden was a positive force, bringing wisdom into the world. Image by M. Belanger.

Sargatanas: The Brigadier-General of Hell, at least according to hierarchies attested to in the *Grand Grimoire* and its French knockoff, *Le Dragon Rouge*, or *Red Dragon Grimoire*. If you are interested in spying or thievery, Sargatanas is the demon to call. He is said to have the power to turn anyone invisible and to open any locks. Locks may not be an obstacle anyway, as he has the power to transport people to any place whatsoever. Further, he can reveal anything that takes place in a private house, and he will teach "all the rogueries of the Shepherds."[59] This may allude to a folk belief prevalent in pats of Europe that shepherds typically practiced forms of magick. Among the spirits said to answer to this grand devil of trickery are Loray, Valefar, and Foraii, three demons named in Wierus's *Pseudomonarchia Daemonum*. They also appear in the *Goetia* as Leraie, Valefor, and Morax. See also *GOETIA, GRAND GRIMOIRE,* LERAIE, MORAX, *RED DRAGON GRIMOIRE,* VALEFOR, WIERUS.

Sariel: One of the fallen angels mentioned in the *Book of Enoch.* As one of the Watchers, Sariel was entrusted with knowledge of the phases of the moon. Additionally, he held the knowledge of how to interpret the signs connected with this heavenly body. When he joined the other fallen Watchers to take a wife from the daughters of men, he taught this forbidden knowledge to humanity. Because of his connection to lunar wisdom, Sariel is sometimes presented as the angel of the moon. According to the *Ars Theurgia,* Sariel is a night-demon who serves the infernal king Aseliel, a ruler in the court of the east. In this text, Sariel holds the rank of chief president. He has thirty principal spirits who serve him, with another twenty ministering spirits that also carry out his commands. Sariel appears again in the *Ars Theurgia,* under the rule of the demon Gediel. Here, Sariel is ranked as a duke and he is said to rule by day. He is tied to the region of the south and has only twenty servants to

---

59. Darcy Kuntz, *The Grand Grimoire*, p. 24.

his name. See also *ARS THEURGIA,* ASELIEL, GEDIEL, WATCHER ANGELS.

Saris: A demon whose name may come from a Greek word meaning "pike" or "spear." Saris is named in the *Sacred Magic of Abramelin the Mage.* He is one of several infernal servants of the demonic prince Ariton. See also ARITON, MATHERS.

Sarisiel: A servant of the demon Oriens whose name appears in the *Sacred Magic of Abramelin the Mage.* In his 1898 translation of this work, Mathers suggests that the name of this demon means "minister of God." This would seem to imply that Sarisiel was once a heavenly angel who never bothered to change his name after his fall. See also ORIENS, MATHERS.

Sarra: Mathers relates the name of this demon to a Coptic word meaning "to strike." In the Mathers translation of the *Sacred Magic of Abramelin the Mage,* Sarra appears under the rule of the archdemon Asmodeus. Although several different versions of the *Abramelin* material have survived since the fourteenth-century original was first penned, only the source manuscript for the Mathers edition contains the name of this demon. See also ASMODEUS, MATHERS.

Sartabakim: A demon under the dominion of the infernal rulers Asmodeus and Magoth. This spelling appears in the Mathers translation of the *Sacred Magic of Abramelin the Mage.* In the version kept at the Wolfenbüttel library in Germany, this demon's name is spelled *Sartabachim.* See also ASMODEUS, MAGOTH, MATHERS.

Sarviel: A demon of the night said to flee the light of day. In the *Ars Theurgia,* Sarviel serves the wandering duke Buriel. This same book describes Sarviel and his associates as some of the most evil

The Seventy-Two Names

In a book called *Al-Fihrist*, written in the tenth century by a merchant and scholar named Muhammad ibn Ishaq al-Nadim, mention is made of Solomon and the Jinn he learned to control. To anyone who has read the *Testament of Solomon*, the story is a familiar one: Solomon binds one spirit first and then uses this initial servitor to gain control of the others. The only real difference is the names themselves. In the *Testament of Solomon*, the spirit who gives the others up is *Ornias*. In al-Nadim's work, his name is recorded as *Fuqtus*. Additionally, in the *Al-Fihrist*, the passage about Solomon's Jinn states that there are only seventy—except that, if you count all the names in the passage itself, the text lists *seventy-one*. In at least one version of the text (MS 1934), one of these names is separated into two, bringing the total to seventy-two, a number familiar from the *Goetia*.

If your starting point is the European grimoiric tradition, then that number is the only familiar thing about the names in this document. The translator of this text, Bayard Dodge, warns that while most of the vowel signs are given in the manuscript, some are missing, thus making it impossible to create a perfect transliteration. Direct comparison to the traditional Western demons of the *Goetia* is also difficult, as the *Al-Fihrist* text is only an overview, offering nothing on each spirit beyond its name. Still, the list of names is compelling, and perhaps some future scholar with the ability to navigate both traditions will be able to establish a clearer comparison between the Arabic names and those passed down through European manuscripts.

Solomon's Jinn: Fuqtus, 'Mrd, Kywān, Shimr-āl, Fīrūz, Mhāqāl, Zaynab, Sydūk, Jndrb, Siyyār, Zanbūr, al-Da'ḥs, Kawkab, Hamrān, Dāhir, Qārūn, Shidād, Ṣa'ṣa'sah, Baktān, Harthamah, Takallum, Furūq, Hurmiz, Hamhamah, 'Ayzār, Mazāhim, Murrah, Fatrah, al-Haym, Arhbh, Khyth', Khyfth, Rayāḥ, Zuḥal, Zawba'ah, Mhtūkarā', Hayshab, Ṭq'ytān, Wqāṣ, Qdmnh, Mufarrish, Ayrā'il, Nizār, Shftīl, Dywyd, Ankarā, Khatūfah, Tnkyvvsh, Misalqar, Qādim, Ashja', Nawdar, Tythāmah, 'Uṣar, Thu'bān, Namān, Nmūdrky, Ṭyābūr, Sāhitūn, 'Udhāfir, Mirdās, Shyṭūb, Za'rūsh, Ṣakhr, al-'Aramram, Khashram, Shādhān, al-Ḥarith, al-Ḥurth, 'Udhrah (also spelled 'Adhirah), Faqrūf

---

* In some versions, Ṭyābūr is separated into two names, giving a total of seventy-two names.

and reviled of all demons. They are so evil, in fact, that they are reputed to be hated and despised by all other spirits. Perhaps this is because of Sarviel's monstrous appearance. When Sarviel manifests, he takes the form of a human-headed serpent. The head is female but nevertheless speaks with a rough and masculine voice. Sarviel may be hated by all other spirits outside of his hierarchy, but he is still popular enough within his own hierarchy to hold command over eight hundred and eighty lesser spirits. See also *ARS THEURGIA*, BURIEL.

Satan: This name is derived from a Hebrew word meaning "the adversary." Most instances of the word *Satan* that appear in the Old Testament are intended not as a proper name, but a function. In the *Chronicles of Jerahmeel*, the fallen angel Samael is described as the chief of the Satans, further indicating that this was less a name and more of a function. Nevertheless, over time Satan developed into the Adversary *par excellence*, the infernal Lord of Demons who commands the armies of Hell. He makes a memorable appearance in the *Book of Job*, where he walks right into the court of Heaven and makes a wager with God. Throughout the books of the Old Testament, Satan remains mostly an adversary who tests faith—and one that often does this at the behest of the Lord. In the New Testament, however, Satan becomes the being that stands in direct opposition to Christ and, by extension, God the Father. Later European demonology resoundingly reflects this depiction, where Satan is the head of devils whose sole purpose is the torture and temptation of living human beings. In this, he is equated variously with Lucifer, Beelzebub, and Belial—all demons who have been placed at the head of the infernal hierarchy in various traditions. In Berbiguier's early nineteenth-century work *Les Farfadets*, Satan is depicted as a deposed prince and leader of the opposition, having been ousted by Beelzebub. This hierarchy was taken up and repeated in A. E. Waite's treatment of the *Grand Grimoire*. In Mathers's translation of the *Sacred Magic of Abramelin the Mage*, Satan is identified as one of four principal spirits that oversee all the other demons in the work. He shares this rank with Lucifer, Leviathan, and Belial. Satan is invoked several times in the *Munich Handbook*, although in this text his name is frequently spelled *Sathan*. He is one of three supreme infernal kings named in the *Book of Oberon*. The other two are Bell (short for Bellzebub) and Lucifer. Note that this text (as well as the French *Livre des esperitz*) distinguishes between Satan and Lucifer, treating them as two separate entities. Satan is identified as having belonged to the Order of Thrones and the Cherubim before his fall. Curiously the text says that Satan did not fall of his own will and gives this as the reason for why he, unlike Lucifer, is not bound and inaccessible in Hell. Instead, he abides in the invisible plane of air tangential to our own (a concept strongly reminiscent of the invisible world believed by many Muslims to be inhabited by the Jinn). According to the *Book of Oberon*, he has the power to kill, destroy, make blind, and do many mischiefs. In the sixteenth-century *Livre des esperitz*, he governs the north and all the spirits who fall within that hierarchy, from King Egin on down. See also BEELZEBUB, BERBIGUIER, BELIAL, *BOOK OF OBERON*, EGIN, *GRAND GRIMOIRE*, LEVIATHAN, *LIVRE DES ESPERITZ*, LUCIFER, MATHERS, *MUNICH HANDBOOK*, SAMAEL, WAITE.

Satanachia: In the *Grand Grimoire*, this superior spirit is described as being the Grand General or General in Chief of Hell. His name is derived from *Satan*, which means "Adversary." According to this work, Satanachia is given power over three of the traditional Goetic demons. His subjects are, specifically, Pruslas (usually spelled *Pruflas*), Amon, and Barbatos. In addition to overseeing these three, Satanachia is supposed to hold sway over all women and girls. He has the power to make them do whatever he wishes, which generally comes down to matters of love, lust, and passion. Satanachia is also mentioned in the *Grimorium Verum*, where he holds a similar position of superiority over a number of functionary demons, specifically forty-five. That number rises to fifty-four in the Venetian *Secrets of Solomon*, a text that predates the *Grimorium Verum* and is thought to have influenced it. In both the *True Keys of Solomon* and the *Secrets of Solomon*, his name is spelled *Satanachi*. According to these texts, he serves as a chief spirit to Lucifer, along with his partner-in-crime Syrach, otherwise known as *Sirachi*. See also AMON, BARBATOS, *GRAND GRIMOIRE*, *GRIMORIUM VERUM*, LUCIFER, PRUFLAS, SATAN, *SECRETS OF SOLOMON*, SIRACHI, SYRACH, *TRUE KEYS*.

Satariel: A Watcher Angel named in the *Book of Enoch*. As one of the "chiefs of tens," Satariel was a leader among the Watchers. He and his angelic brethren were seduced by beautiful mortal women and fell as a result of their lust. Satariel and the other Watchers in the *Book of Enoch* were responsible for teaching forbidden knowledge to fledgling humanity. Their descendants were the Nephilim, a race of ambitious and bloodthirsty giants. See also WATCHER ANGELS.

Satifiel: A lesser duke governed by the demon Cabariel in the region of the west, Satifiel is tied to the hours of the day and will not appear at night. According to the *Ars Theurgia*, he should be called forth in a hidden location where no random pass-

LUCIFER, Empereur.

BELZÉBUT, Prince.

ASTAROT, Grand-duc.

LUCIFUGÉ, prem. Ministr.

SATANACHIA, grand général.

AGALIAREPT., aussi général.

FLEURETY, lieutenantgén.

SARGATANAS, brigadier.

NEBIROS, mar. de camp.

This hellish hierarchy, complete with portraits, appears in the *Red Dragon Grimoire*. From the works of Grillot de Givry, courtesy of Dover Publications.

ersby can interfere with the operation. When he appears, he is reputed to have an entourage of fifty lesser spirits who minister to him. He has a basically good nature and will behave respectfully toward those brave enough to call him up. See also *ARS THEURGIA*, CABARIEL.

Schabuach: According to Mathers, this demon's name is derived from an Arabic term and can be taken as meaning "the Soother." In the *Sacred Magic of Abramelin the Mage*, Schabuach appears as part of the demonic hierarchy of the four infernal princes of the cardinal directions. He appears on the third day of the *Abramelin* working in order to swear his service to the magician. See also AMAIMON, ARITON, MATHERS, ORIENS, PAIMON.

Scharak: A demon whose name means "to twine about," perhaps like a snake. In the *Sacred Magic of Abramelin the Mage*, Scharak is said to serve the demon Magoth. According to the Mathers edition of this work, he is also governed by the demon Kore. In the 1608 version of *Abramelin* kept at the Wolfenbüttel library, the name of this demon is presented as *Nearach*. See also KORE, MAGOTH, MATHERS.

Sched: In the Mathers translation of the *Sacred Magic of Abramelin the Mage*, the demon Sched is ranked within the hierarchies of the four demon-princes Oriens, Paimon, Ariton, and Amaimon. These four beings preside over the cardinal directions, and all of the demons who serve beneath them, Sched included, share in their many infernal powers. Mathers suggests that the name of this demon is derived from the Hebrew word *shedim*. This is a term from the Bible typically translated as "demon." It refers to graven images and false gods. See also AMAIMON, ARITON, MATHERS, ORIENS, PAIMON.

Schelagon: An infernal servitor of the arch-fiend Astaroth, Schelagon appears in the Mathers trans-

lation of the *Sacred Magic of Abramelin the Mage*. See also ASTAROTH, MATHERS.

Sclavak: The "torturer" or "pain-bringer." According to Mathers, the name of this demon comes from a Coptic root. In his translation of the *Sacred Magic of Abramelin the Mage*, Sclavak is named as a servant of Asmodeus. In other versions of the *Abramelin* material, his name is spelled *Schaluach*. See also ASMODEUS, MATHERS.

Scot, Reginald: An English author best known for his 1584 work *The Discoverie of Witchcraft*. Scot wrote his book as an argument against the belief in witchcraft, maintaining that most magick was the result of delusion or sleight-of-hand. In the course of his argument, he referenced a number of grimoires and ceremonial techniques. A devout Protestant, his deconstruction of ceremonial magick is rife with anti-Catholic sentiment. He saw what he called a "popish" influence on many of the rites and rituals contained in the magickal grimoires. Scot drew much of his grimoiric material from a book written (or compiled) in 1570 by John Cokars and an individual who gave only the initials T. R. It was from this text that Scot obtained his English translation of Wierus's *Pseudomonarchia Daemonum*. Scot lived from 1538 until 1599. His book was ultimately decried by King James I, who ordered the work to be burned. See also WIERUS.

Sebach: A demon of the night that only appears during the hours between dusk and dawn, Sebach serves as a chief duke to the demon-king Raysiel. He has forty ministering spirits to attend him. According to the *Ars Theurgia*, Sebach is a particularly evil-tempered spirit with a stubborn and headstrong nature. He is affiliated with the north. See also *ARS THEURGIA*, RAYSIEL.

Secrets of Solomon: Or *Clavicula Salomonis de Secretis*, a grimoire originating from Venice, 1636. A copy of the manuscript resides in the Polish *Biblioteka Nurdowa* and another is kept at Leipzig. The original text belonged to one Leonardo Longo, a former Dominican monk from Naples. Longo was tried for witchcraft by the Venetian Inquisition, at which point the book was seized and preserved in the Archivo di Stato di Venezia. This text is noteworthy because its contents bridge a gap between ceremonial magick and the folk traditions that have heavily influenced certain aspects of modern witchcraft. Longo is most likely the scribe of the original version, copying his material from a composite of earlier sources. Interestingly, the *Secrets of Solomon* attributes Demon Princes to specific continents, a tradition that can also be seen in later texts such as the *Red Dragon Grimoire* and the *Grimorium Verum*, as well as the work of the self-styled demonologist Charles Berbiguier. Given their similarities, the *Grimorium Verum* is likely a derivative work of Longo's *Clavicula Salomonis de Secretis*. See also GRIMORIUM VERUM.

Seere: One of the seventy-two demons of the *Goetia*. Seere's name is left out of both Wierus's *Pseudomonarchia Daemonum* and Scot's *Discoverie of Witchcraft*, both texts that otherwise include the majority of the Goetic demons. In the *Goetia*, Seere is said to hold the rank of prince with twenty-six legions under his command. He is tied to the demon Amaimon, who rules as the infernal king of the east. When he manifests, Seere takes the form of a beautiful man. He rides upon a horse with wings. He is a demon of transportation, fetching things from any corner of the globe. He is said to have the power to pass over the whole globe in the twinkling of an eye. He can also reveal thieves and expose hidden treasures.

He further seems able to alter the movement of time, as he is said to bring all things suddenly to pass. According to the *Goetia of Dr. Rudd*, he is constrained by the angel Tabamiah. He can be found in the Welsh *Book of Incantations* under the spelling *Seer*. See also AMAIMON, *BOOK OF INCANTATIONS*, *GOETIA*, RUDD, SCOT, WIERUS.

Segal: In Peterson's definitive *Grimorium Verum*, Segal is the tenth demon serving under Syrach, a grand duke of Hell. An illusionist, Segal can show the magician a wide variety of marvelous visions, conjuring chimeras from the air and revealing things both natural and supernatural. His name is spelled *Segol* in the *Secrets of Solomon*. See also *GRIMORIUM VERUM*, *SECRETS OF SOLOMON*, SYRACH.

Sekabin: A servitor of the infernal prince Ariton, Sekabin is named in the Mathers translation of the *Sacred Magic of Abramelin the Mage*. According to Mathers, the name of this demon comes from a Chaldean term meaning "those that cast down." In the versions of the *Abramelin* material kept in the German libraries at Wolfenbüttel and Dresden, the name of this demon is spelled *Secabim*. See also ARITON, MATHERS.

Selentis: Tied to methods of scrying, this demon appears in the *Munich Handbook*. He is called upon to assist with a process of divination. He helps bring thieves to justice by revealing their identities. See also *MUNICH HANDBOOK*.

Semlin: In Mathers's 1898 translation of the *Sacred Magic of Abramelin the Mage*, Semlin is said to serve beneath the arch-demons Asmodeus and Astaroth. According to occultist S. L. MacGregor Mathers's nineteenth-century translation of this work, Semlin's name means "simulacrum." See also ASTAROTH, ASMODEUS, MATHERS.

The Original Demon Lovers

Few classes of demons have captured the popular imagination with precisely the same allure as the incubus and the succubus. These two infernal seducers were believed to visit mortal men and women while they slept, bringing them wicked and erotic dreams. The very name of the incubus is connected directly to sleep: it is derived from the Latin word *incubare*, meaning to "lie down." Some scholars have suggested that this word was deemed appropriate for the incubus for the fact that this demon was often thought to "lie down" upon its victims, paralyzing them and pressing them into their beds. In this, the incubus may be related to the *mara*, or nighthag, a phenomenon generally thought to be connected with night terrors.

Although the connection between the incubus and the nighthag seems to imply that these demon lovers were merely a product of sleep and dreams, some writers in medieval and Renaissance Europe believed them instead to be very real, physical beings. The Dominican monk Frater Ludovico Sinistrari, writing in the 1600s, suggests that incubus and succubus demons have bodies, but Sinistrari views the "flesh" of the incubus demons to be subtler than the gross physical bodies of human beings. This subtler body allows these creatures to move through the air and enter rooms with locked doors and windows. In his curious text *Demoniality*, Sinistrari argues that these demons are essentially "aerial animals." They are born, reproduce, and die just like living men and women. Despite this, Sinistrari still sees them as agents of Hell rather than wholly natural beings. They exist to tempt and torment human beings—occasionally reproducing with them. In one section of *Demoniality*, Sinistrari describes the offspring of human and demonic unions:

> *The children thus begotten by Incubi are tall, very hardy and bloodily bold, arrogant beyond words and desperately wicked.*[*]

These are all qualities that could be applied with equal accuracy to the human-angel hybrids described in the *Book of Enoch*—believed to be lost to Western civilization during Sinistrari's time.

---

[*] Sinistrari, *Demoniality*, p. 21.

Semper: One of twelve high-ranking servitors of Oriens, king of the east, Semper appears in the *Book of Oberon* and is said to take the form of a comely maiden. This appearance masks a potent and sometimes terrifying power, for Semper can summon great winds and cast illusions of phantom ships upon the seas. He also causes wounds to fester until they are filled with worms. The name of this demon is identical to a word in Latin meaning "always," although it is unclear from the text if this meaning holds any relevance for the demon. His powers and appearance both bear a resemblance to the Goetic demon *Vepar*, whose same is sometimes spelled *Separ*. See also *BOOK OF OBERON*, ORIENS, VEPAR.

A ship being confronted by a sea-devil. Woodcut, 1720. Image courtesy of the Wellcome Collection, London.

Sequiel: In the *Ars Theurgia*, Sequiel is named as a demon in the hierarchy of the north. He serves beneath the demon Raysiel, a mighty king of the north. Sequiel is a demon of the day, and he serves his king only during the hours between dawn and dusk. As befits a demon of his rank, Sequiel has fifty lesser spirits to attend him. See also *ARS THEURGIA*, RAYSIEL.

Seraphius: A tutelary spirit from the *Book of Oberon* with specialized knowledge on the construction of magickal rings. The rings he teaches people to make are used to bind spirits. All of these rings have a little door on them that can be opened or shut, and it is through this that the bound spirit enters or exits as it carries out its tasks. Seraphius's name may be a derivative of the word *Seraphim*, which is simultaneously used to designate an order of angels and dangerous, fiery serpents in the story of Exodus. See also *BOOK OF OBERON*.

Sergulath: A mighty demon who commands several spirits in his own right, Sergulath nevertheless serves under his own master, Nebiros. The second in rank within Nebiros's hierarchy, Sergulath is a martial demon. According to Peterson's *Grimorium Verum*, when summoned he can reveal the perfect methods for destroying one's enemies. He also reveals all the arts and sciences of war. This demon's name also appears in the *True Keys of Solomon* under the spelling *Sergulas*. Here, he is associated with crafting and merchandise. See also *GRIMORIUM VERUM*, NEBIROS, *TRUE KEYS*.

Sergulaf: Alternately, *Sergulath*. A clever and industrious being, Sergulaf is able to supply tools and machines of all kinds. His name appears in the seventeenth-century Venetian grimoire known as the *Secrets of Solomon*, where he is named, along with the demon Hael, as one of two chief ministers to the infernal duke Resbiroth. Hael and Surgulaf also oversee eight demons in their own retinue, each of whom has their own offices and powers. As the *Grimorium Verum* is almost certainly derived from the *Secrets of Solomon*, this demon's name likely gave rise to *Sergulath*, who fulfills similar functions in that tome. See also HAEL, RESBIROTH, *SECRETS OF SOLOMON*, SERGULATH.

Sergurth: One of four principal demons serving under Duke Satanachi. A particularly vile sort of demon, Sergurth gives people power over women and girls for the purpose of using them for sex. He appears in the *Clavicula Salomonis de Secretis*, or *Secrets of Solomon*, a seventeenth-century grimoire from Venice. That text gives *Serguty* as an alternate version of his name, which likely led to the variation *Serguthy* that appears in the derivative *Grimorium Verum*. See also *SECRETS OF SOLOMON*, SATANACHI, SERGUTHY.

Serguthy: This demon can wield power over women, both young and old. This power is most likely turned toward spells of love and lust. According to Peterson's *Grimorium Verum*, he is one of four main spirits who serve beneath Satanachia. See also SATANACHIA. See also *GRIMORIUM VERUM*.

Sermeot: A name reputed to mean "the death of the flesh." Sermeot appears in the Mathers translation of the *Sacred Magic of Abramelin the Mage*. In this text, Sermeot is said to be ruled by the demon Ariton. See also ARITON, MATHERS.

Serphgathana: A demon who serves Elestor, one of the three top-ranking infernal powers, at least according to the *Secrets of Solomon*. In this seventeenth-century Venetian grimoire, Serphgathana is named alongside Resbiroth, where they are both identified as dukes. They are called upon as go-betweens for Elestor. See also ELESTOR, RESBIROTH, *SECRETS OF SOLOMON*.

Seson: One of twelve influential ministers of Oriens, king over the spirits of the east. Seson appears in the *Book of Oberon*, a grimoire dating to Elizabethan England. According to this text, Seson takes the form of a lion-faced man wearing a diadem. He rides upon a wild boar and carries a venomous serpent in his hand. If this appearance is too ferocious, his summoner can compel him to take an airy body (i.e., non-corporeal) in the likeness of an ordinary man. Seson is a demon of prophecy, telling of all things that have been or ever shall be. He can show many things, including the location of hidden treasure, but he is especially good at exposing the secrets of others. See also *BOOK OF OBERON*, ORIENS.

Severion: A spirit that may occupy a marginal existence between demon and faerie. The *Book of Oberon* lists him as the fourth advisor to King Oberion, a being who is simultaneously described as the king of the faeries and a fallen angel. Severion is called upon to assist Oberion's appearance in a scrying vessel. See also *BOOK OF OBERON*, OBERION.

Shamsiel: One of the fallen Watcher Angels who left Heaven to take a mortal wife. Shamsiel is named in the *Book of Enoch*. According to this text, he was entrusted with knowledge of the signs of the sun. After he polluted himself with mortal flesh, he taught this forbidden knowledge to humanity. He is sometimes identified as the angel of the sun. His name may also be connected with Shamash, the Akkadian and Babylonian god of justice and the sun. See also WATCHER ANGELS.

Shax: The forty-fourth demon in the *Goetia*. He also appears in Scot's *Discoverie of Witchcraft*. In Wierus's *Pseudomonarchia Daemonum*, his name is given as *Chax*. He is said to manifest in the form of a stork with a voice that is both hoarse and subtle. He has the power to render people deaf, blind, and dumb. He is both a liar and a thief, stealing horses as well as money from the house of any king. He will not tell the truth unless magickally compelled to do so, and while he gives familiars, the conjuror is cautioned to ensure that these do not share his propensity for deception. He will reveal the locations of things that are hidden, so long as they are not kept by wicked spirits. Another form of his name is given as *Scox*. He is described as a dark and mighty marquis with thirty legions at his command. In the *Goetia of Dr. Rudd*, he is said to appear in the form of a stock dove, as opposed to a stork. According to this text, he is under the power of the angel Jelahiah. He is also described in the *Book of Incantations*. See also *BOOK OF INCANTATIONS*, *GOETIA*, RUDD, SCOT, WIERUS.

Seventeenth-century image of a familiar spirit, from an English woodcut. Familiars were often thought to take the shape of an animal companion, such as a dog, cat, or toad. Courtesy of Dover Publications.

Shemhamphorash: The "Shattered Name" or "Divided Name." This refers to the ineffable name of God, also known as the Tetragrammaton. The *Shemhamphorash* is a Qabbalistic technique for deriving angel names from Holy Scripture. It is based upon a mathematical exercise that derives the number seventy-two from the fourfold name of God. The names of seventy-two angels arise from this technique and they are tied closely with ceremonial and demonic magick. With the *Shemhamphorash*, each of the seventy-two demons described in the *Goetia* has a specific angel set over it that can bind and compel that demon. If the person working the invocation knows the name and seal of this angel, then the angel can be called upon to assist with the control of the demon. Most editions of the *Goetia* merely begin with the word *Shemhamphorash*, and for a while the true significance of this term was lost. In the *Goetia of Dr. Rudd*, however, the angels of the *Shemhamphorash* are applied directly to the seventy-two Goetic demons, erasing any doubt that these forces are meant to work in tandem with one another. Several different spellings of this word can be found scattered throughout the grimoires. It is sometimes corrupted into the name *Semiforas*. See also *GOETIA*, RUDD.

Shemyaza: A fallen angel frequently presented as one of two leaders of the Watcher Angels, along with the angel Azazel. According to the *Book of Enoch*, it was Shemyaza who first had the idea to leave Heaven in order to take wives among the beautiful daughters of men. When two hundred of the other Watcher Angels agreed to engage in this sin, Shemyaza made them all gather on the slopes of Mount Hermon and swear a pact to take joint responsibility for the deed so that the sole responsibility would not fall to him. In addition to polluting his heavenly nature by indulging in sex with mortal women, Shemyaza is also credited with having taught early humanity the art of enchantment and root-cutting. Although he taught this forbidden knowledge, Shemyaza's main sin depicted in the *Book of Enoch* is one of lust.

In Jewish legends surrounding the birth of Noah, Shemyaza appears under the name *Shemhazai*. Here he is again paired with the fallen angel Azazel. In Ginzburg's *Legends of the Jews*, a collection of the Jewish Haggadah, the familiar story of the *Book of Enoch* plays out, with Azazel and Shemhazai leaving Heaven to consort with mortal women. According to this text, Shemhazai sired two angel-human hybrid sons, named Hiwwa and Hiyya. An abbreviation of Shemyaza's name may appear in the collection of Jewish folklore known as the *Chronicles of Jerahmeel*. Here, a passage refers to the angels Azah and Azazel, who fell due to their desires for mortal women. According to this text, they were punished by being suspended forever between Heaven and Earth. The same punishment was meted out in the Haggadah, but Shemhazai is depicted as a willing penitent, while the fallen angel Azazel is said to resist punishment and continue in his wicked ways. See also AZAZEL, WATCHER ANGELS.

Many conjurations were not intended to summon a physical demon but rather an apparition in a mirror or in a scrying crystal, sometimes called a shew-stone. Candles or oil lamps were often set up nearby to aid the vision. Illustration by Catherine Rogers.

Sibilla: A spirit conjured to appear in the light of a candle for the purpose of prognostication. Her name is probably derived from the word *sibyl*, one of several prophetesses at the Oracle of Delphi from ancient Greece. As a spirit, Sibilla is said to reveal the identities of thieves, to discover lost or stolen items, and to divine the location of hidden treasure. She is fair and beautiful, appearing in an angelic form. Her name shows up in the final folio of the grimoire known as the *Book of Oberon*. See also BOOK OF OBERON.

Sibolas: A servant of the demon Ariton, one of the four infernal princes of the cardinal directions. Sibolas appears in the *Sacred Magic of Abramelin the Mage*. According to the Mathers translation of this work, this demon's name is from the Hebrew language and means "a rushing lion." See also ARITON, MATHERS.

Sid: In the grimoire known as the *Clavicula Salomonis*, or *Key of Solomon*, Sid is described as the Great Demon. His name appears alongside a number of names of God in an invocation that also calls upon both the Prince of Darkness and the Angels of Darkness. How the name *Sid* came to be associated with a great demon remains unclear. It may be an abbreviation of *Sidonay*, an alternate name of the demon Asmodeus listed in both Wierus's *Pseudomonarchia* and Scot's *Discoverie of Witchcraft*. See also ASMODEUS, *CLAVICULA SALOMONIS*, SCOT, SINDONAY, WIERUS.

Sidonay: Another name used by the demon Asmoday. Sidonay is the first and chiefest under the power of Amaimon and goes before all others, at least according to the Welsh *Book of Incantations*. He teaches arithmetic, geometry, astronomy, and all handicrafts and business. He can also make people invisible and reveal the location of hidden treasure. Seventy-two legions bow to his command. His seal must be worn on the breast as protection in his presence. See also ASMODAY, *BOOK OF INCANTATIONS*.

Sidragosum: A demon with the power to cause young women to burst irresistibly into dance. According to Peterson's *Grimorium Verum*, he serves as the sixth spirit beneath the demons Hael and Sergulath. In the 1709 *Clavicle of Solomon*, he not only compels people to dance but also inspires them to take off all their clothes. In this text, his name is spelled *Sidragosum*. See also *CLAVICLE OF SOLOMON*, *GRIMORIUM VERUM*, HAEL, SERGULATH.

Sifon: One of several demons ruled by Asmodeus and Magoth in the Mathers translation of the *Sacred Magic of Abramelin the Mage*. This list appears in only one other version of the *Abramelin* material. In the version kept at the Wolfenbüttel library in Germany, the name of this demon appears as *Siphon*. See also ASMODEUS, MAGOTH, MATHERS.

Sigambach: A being—presumably a demon—in charge of arranging, or at least signing off on, demonic pacts. He is also a keeper of demonic sigils, those figures specific to each entity used to summon them and protect against their powers. This demon of pacts and sigils is named in the seventeenth-century Venetian grimoire *Clavicula Salomonis de Secretis*. He also makes an appearance in the *Grimorium Verum* under the alternate spelling *Singambuth*. The *Clavicula* identifies his secretary as Rabidmadar. In that text, the process of forging a pact is described as the "art of Rabidmadar," suggesting that this being has much more power than one might attribute to an ordinary secretary.

See also *GRIMORIUM VERUM*, RABIDMADAR, RESBIROTH, *SECRETS OF SOLOMON*.

Sikastin: According to the Mathers translation of the *Sacred Magic of Abramelin the Mage*, this demon supposedly serves under the dual leadership of Magoth and Kore. The name of this demon appears in all other *Abramelin* texts as *Sikastir*. See also KORE, MAGOTH, MATHERS.

Silitor: In the *Munich Handbook*, Silitor is reputed to have the power to cast a powerful illusion that can convince all viewers that an entire castle, complete with servants and squires, has been conjured from thin air. This work is to take place at night in a remote and secret place on the tenth night of the moon. The text calls for an offering of milk and honey to be made to Silitor, who is described as a "squire spirit." See also *MUNICH HANDBOOK*.

Sirachi: One of two chief spirits said to serve Lucifer in the *True Keys of Solomon*. Along with the demon Satanachi (a variation on *Satanachia*), Sirachi carries out Lucifer's commands in Europe and Asia. The grimoire also contains a long list of demons who serve under Sirachi's rule. The name of this demon is also given as *Sinachi*. He may be a variation of the demon known as Duke Syrach, whose hierarchy is listed in the *Grimorium Verum*. See also *GRIMORIUM VERUM*, LUCIFER, SATANACHIA, SYRACH.

Sirchade: When summoned, this demon can cause the magician to see all manner of beasts. He serves as the ninth demon under Duke Syrach. According to Peterson's *Grimorium Verum*, he should only be conjured on Thursdays. See also *GRIMORIUM VERUM*, SYRACH.

Sirechael: A demon named in the *True Keys of Solomon*. He is one of several demons said to serve beneath chief Sirachi, an agent of Lucifer.

Red Letter Day

In the *Sworn Book of Honorius*, the reader is instructed to construct a magickal symbol using a number of different-colored inks. But what was the scribal significance of the colors? A medieval book was typically written in black ink, and before the ninth century, was block text with little or no spacing between words. That would make a manuscript nearly impossible to read and therefore useless to the owner. So, to introduce a new section of text or distinguish certain words, a scribe would often employ the use of a different-colored ink, thus creating a visual separation from the page.

The use of color assigned status to the word, essentially elevating its importance from the text surrounding it. Red or vermilion were generally used for this purpose, made from red lead or mercuric sulfide. These materials (or similar variants) were commonly available throughout most of Europe and could be made into a smooth-flowing ink. A frequent element of liturgical manuscripts and Books of Hours that depended on the use and status of color was that of the calendar. The Christian calendar listed saint's days, major feast days such as Christmas and Easter, and other days of worship. Early on in book production, red was used to highlight the most important feast days, from which we derive the term *red-letter day*. Blue, green, and yellow ink soon became available, and a complicated hierarchy of color and status developed based on the availability and cost of a pigment. By the fourteenth century, the most important days were illuminated in pure gold or lapis blue (being the most expensive materials), with secondary feast days colored in red or striped red and blues or greens, and the most minor feast days indicated in black.

The use of any of these colors in scribal work—whether it was for sanctioned manuscripts for the Church or for forbidden grimoires—had great symbolic meaning, not the least of which was a symbol of the very value of the manuscript.

—*Jackie Williams, traditional scribe*

Decorative capital done in the Italian Whitevine tradition of illumination by Jackie Williams.

Sirechael is said to influence things that are sentient and animate. He is also said to offer things, but the text provides no insight into the nature or identity of these items. See also LUCIFER, SIRACHI, *TRUE KEYS*.

Sirgilis: A demon said to serve the infernal king Amaimon, Sirgilis is named in the *Sacred Magic of Abramelin the Mage*. In the 1898 Mathers translation of this work, his name is spelled *Scrilis*. Mathers relates the name to the Latin root for *sacrilege*. See also AMAIMON, MATHERS.

Sirkael: One of eighteen demons overseen by Duke Syrach. Sirkael is named in the seventeenth-century Venetian grimoire *Secrets of Solomon*. According to that text, Sirkael can make animals appear. It is unclear whether these are illusory animals or animals that the demon has teleported from far away, but regardless of their provenance, the conjured animals are promised to be fully ambulatory, able to prance or rage or perform any other action demanded of them. See also *SECRETS OF SOLOMON*, SYRACH.

Sirumel: A demon of illusion who can make it seem as if day has changed to night. His name appears in the *True Keys of Solomon*. According to this text, he serves chief Sirachi, an agent of Lucifer. He is also known by the name *Selytarel*. See also LUCIFER, SIRACHI, *TRUE KEYS*.

Sismael: While the *Munich Handbook* freely identifies many of its spirits as demons, only rarely does it specifically describe those demons as being *malignus*, or "wicked." Sismael, however, is one such demon, and he is called upon in a particularly nasty curse. This wicked agent of Hell has the power to rob people of their senses, and when properly summoned, he will afflict any specified enemy. He reputedly has the power to bind the

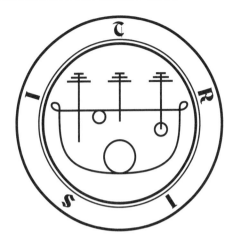

The sigil of the demon Sitri, based on a variant recorded by John Harries in his *Book of Incantations*. Image by Catherine Rogers.

mind, addle the thoughts, and inspire delusions. See also *MUNICH HANDBOOK*.

Sitri: The twelfth demon named in the *Goetia*. Sitri is a great prince of Hell said to manifest with a leopard's face and the wings of a gryphon. When he assumes human form, he is very beautiful, and perhaps in accordance with this beauty, he has power over love, lust, and the pleasures of the flesh. He can make men and women desire one another, inflaming each with love for the other. He is said to laugh at and mock women, willingly revealing their secrets to the magician. He also has the power to render women luxuriously naked. Sixty legions obey his command. According to Wierus's *Pseudomonarchia Daemonum*, his name is spelled *Sytry*, and he is also sometimes known as *Bitru*. In the *Goetia of Dr. Rudd*, he is said to be governed by the angel Hahajah. In the Welsh *Book of Incantations*, Sitri is a great prince. He has the same powers of lust and nakedness as elsewhere, but no mention is made of his mockery. See also *BOOK OF INCANTATIONS*, *GOETIA*, RUDD, SCOT, WIERUS.

Sixth and Seventh Books of Moses: Attributed to Moses, this magickal text was intended to demonstrate how Moses was able to outdo the magicians of the Pharaoh with his own tricks. The *Sixth and Seventh Books of Moses* circulated through Germany in the form a variety of pamphlets in the 1800s. Eventually, it was compiled in 1849 by an antiquarian from Stuttgart by the name of Johann Scheible. This book is a blend of the grimoiric tradition, Talmudic lore, and the essentially German tradition of the *Faustbuch*, which featured the demon Mephistopheles. See also MEPHISTOPHELES.

Skor: In the Elizabethan *Book of Oberon*, Skor is named twice in a list of about eighty demons serving under the infernal kings of the four directions. In the first instance, he is described as having the appearance of a wading bird known as curlew; in the second, he is said to appear as a dog. In both cases, he is a demon of fetching, who steals money from treasuries and houses and brings this back to his master. In the second entry, he is additionally said to take away the sight of enemies, presumably so they cannot see who or what is thieving from them. In the first entry, he is ranked as a king with six legions. In the second, he is a prince served by forty-six legions. In both entries, Skor is said to be very faithful. Note: a curlew is a wading bird native to Great Britain. It has a long, thin, curving beak designed to pluck prey from shallow waters. The bird's name may be derived from the old French word for messenger, *corliu*, which shares roots with *courier*, a play on words very appropriate for a demon described as a carrier. See also *BOOK OF OBERON*.

Sobe: The name of this demon may be derived from a Greek root meaning "horsetail" or "flyswatter." Sobe is supposed to serve the greater demons Magoth and Asmodeus. The name of this demon appears only in the Mathers translation of the *Sacred Magic of Abramelin the Mage* and the version of the *Abramelin* material kept at the Wolfenbüttel library in Germany. This alternate text gives the demon's name as *Sobhe*. See also ASMODEUS, MAGOTH, MATHERS.

Sobel: This is one of several demons whose existence is almost certainly the result of scribal error. In the fifteenth-century French manuscript sourced by Mathers for his translation of the *Sacred Magic of Abramelin the Mage*, this name appears variously as *Sobel* and *Cobel*. In all other surviving manuscripts of this material, the name is actually spelled *Lobel*. See also MATHERS.

Sobronoy: Identified as a *demon malignus* by the *Munich Handbook*, Sobronoy lives up to this wicked reputation by attacking any enemy specified to him as a target. The hapless person who becomes targeted by this being is then struck down and robbed of all faculties. The demon has the power to bind the thoughts and delude the mind, completely addling the senses. See also *MUNICH HANDBOOK*.

Sochas: One of thirty dukes who serve beneath the demon Barmiel. According to the *Ars Theurgia*, Sochas serves during the hours of the day. He is connected with the south. He has twenty ministering spirits to carry out his commands. See also *ARS THEURGIA*, BARMIEL.

Sodiel: A revealer of secrets who can also hide away treasure to protect it from thieves, Sodiel serves the infernal prince Usiel in the court of the west. The *Ars Theurgia* gives his rank as duke and says that he holds sway over a total of forty lesser spirits. He serves his infernal master during the dark hours of the night. See also *ARS THEURGIA*, USIEL.

Sogan: A demon with an unusual skill for retrieving souls from purgatory. Rather than release them fully from their suffering, however, he brings them back to those who summon him so the spirits can be questioned. A regular psychopomp, he also fetches other souls of the dead, particularly those whose bodies rest near the water. The spirits that Sogan retrieves are said to appear as ethereal versions of their former selves, so they will be recognizable to any who knew them in life. In addition to his powers as a psychopomp, this demon is well versed in mathematical sciences, wisdom, and philosophy. According to the *Book of Oberon*, Sogan holds the rank of marquis and oversees thirty-six legions of lesser spirits. When he manifests, he takes the form of a pale horse, which may be an indication of his connection to the dead. An alternate version of his name is *Sogom*. See also *BOOK OF OBERON*.

Soleviel: The seventh wandering prince of the *Ars Theurgia*, Soleviel is reputed to command two hundred infernal dukes in addition to two hundred other demonic companions. Soleviel's court changes places year by year, with half of the demons beneath him serving for one year and the other half serving in the next. Soleviel's court is the only hierarchy described in the *Ars Theurgia* that functions with this arrangement. Under the spelling *Soleuiel*, this demon also appears in Johannes Trithemius's *Steganographia*. See also *ARS THEURGIA*, TRITHEMIUS.

Solomon: The son of David and Bathsheba, Solomon was a biblical monarch renowned for his faith and wisdom. His story appears mainly in 1 Kings and 2 Chronicles, but there are numerous extra-biblical sources that elaborate upon his life and times. Solomon is best known as the Jewish mon-

King Solomon's power over demons is explored in the 1473 work *Das Buch Belial* by Jacobus de Teramo. Here, the demon Belial dances for Solomon.

arch who oversaw the construction and completion of the Holy Temple at Jerusalem. He is credited with having written *Song of Songs*, the *Book of Proverbs*, and *Ecclesiastes*. In Jewish, Christian, and Muslim folklore, King Solomon is known not only for his wisdom but also for his power over evil spirits. The pseudepigraphal *Testament of Solomon* tells how Solomon prayed for the power to protect a young laborer from the demon Ornias. According to the text, God heard Solomon's prayer and awarded him with a special seal, often depicted as a ring, that granted power over demons. Solomon lost no time in putting this powerful talisman to use. He summoned a series of demons, forcing them to reveal their own names as well as the holy names that could control, compel, and bind them. If the *Testament of Solomon* and related legends are to be believed, the Holy Temple was build with the aid of a vast number of demons pressed into service by Solomon himself.

The grimoires of medieval and Renaissance Europe are the direct inheritors of the Solomonic tradition outlined in the *Testament of Solomon*. Although no written line of descent exists to show us how the concepts about demonic invocation recorded in the last few centuries before the Common Era survived to reemerge in the 1100s and beyond, the connection is unmistakable. King Solomon's name comes up frequently in both Christian and Jewish sources, and many of the grimoires are directly attributed to this ancient biblical king. These are of course as pseudepigraphal as the *Testament of Solomon* itself, but that did not stop medieval writers and copyists from putting the old king's name on numerous forbidden tomes. Perhaps the two most famous Solomonic works are the *Clavicula Salomonis*—known as the *Key of Solomon*—and the even more widely circulated *Lemegeton*, also known as the *Lesser Key of Solomon*.

King Solomon plays a significant role in the folklore of Arabia and the Middle East. In the Muslim tradition, the spirits controlled by King Solomon are identified as Jinn, or genies. They are not exactly perceived as demons but are rather thought to be another race of beings entirely, separate and distinct from humanity. There are some correlations between the concept of the Jinn and the semi-divine children of the Watcher Angels. However, because their status as demonic entities is debatable, they have been omitted from this text. See also *CLAVICULA SALOMONIS, LEMEGETON, ORNIAS, WATCHER ANGELS*.

Sonneillon: A demon who oversees the sin of hate. It is through his manipulation of this negative emotion that he supposedly works to lead mortals astray. His adversary is Saint Stephen. Sonneillon is named in the *Admirable History* by Sebastien Michaelis.

Soonek: A demon with the power to undo the curse of the Tower of Babel, Soonek can imbue those who summon him with the ability to understand all voices, including those of wild beasts.

Soonek himself appears in the form of a cruel bear, although he can be compelled to take the shape of a man. In addition to his skill with language, this demon knows the past, present, and future and can reveal the location of hidden treasures. He holds the rank of earl and commands a total of eighteen legions. His name appears in the Elizabethan grimoire known as the *Book of Oberon*. See also *BOOK OF OBERON*.

Soriel: One of several demons ruled by the infernal prince Dorochiel. Soriel serves his master in the capacity of chief duke. He is attached to the hours of the night and the region of the west. In the *Ars Theurgia*, this demon is said to have command over four hundred subordinate spirits. He is said to manifest only at a specific time between midnight and dawn each night. See also *ARS THEURGIA*, DOROCHIEL.

Sorosma: Occultist S. L. MacGregor Mathers thought this demon's name might possibly be derived from a Greek word meaning "funeral urn." Sorosma appears in the *Sacred Magic of Abramelin the Mage*, where he is said to serve the demon Beelzebub. Elsewhere in the same text, this demon also appears as a servitor of Oriens. See also BEELZEBUB, MATHERS, ORIENS.

Sorriolenen: In the Mathers translation of the *Sacred Magic of Abramelin the Mage*, Sorriolenen is said to serve the infernal rulers Magoth and Kore. In the versions of the *Abramelin* material kept at the Dresden and Wolfenbüttel libraries, this name is spelled *Serupolon*. See also KORE, MAGOTH, MATHERS.

Soterion: A demon whose name appears in connection with the four infernal princes of the cardinal directions: Oriens, Paimon, Ariton, and Amaimon. Soterion's name can be found in

Mathers's 1898 translation of the *Sacred Magic of Abramelin the Mage*. See also AMAIMON, ARITON, MATHERS, ORIENS, PAIMON.

Sotheano: One of several dukes loyal to Pamersiel, the first and chief spirit of the east, Sotheano is not a pleasant spirit to deal with. He is an arrogant being, thoroughly evil, and given to deceit. Nevertheless, the *Ars Theurgia* suggests that he can be useful in driving away other spirits of darkness, especially those that haunt houses. His name, seal, and the method for summoning him all appear in this seventeenth-century text. See also *ARS THEURGIA*, PAMERSIEL.

Sowrges: A demon with power over the waters and the seas, particularly in regard to travel. He can give safe passage even through floods. His powers are not limited to seafaring, as he can also assist with speedy transportation by horse. When summoned, he manifests as a knight astride a mount with three heads: that of a bird, that of a fish, and that of a regular horse. Each head may represent a different mode of travel over which Sowrges has authority. According to the *Book of Oberon*, he is a great marquis who governs parts of Africa. He oversees twenty-six legions of lesser spirits and can teach grammar, logic, rhetoric, and divinity. Like many other demons mentioned in the same text, he also has the power to reveal hidden treasure and open any treasures locked away. See also *BOOK OF OBERON*.

Sphandôr: In the *Testament of Solomon*, Sphandôr is a demon of disease, afflicting humanity with terrible ailments. He is said to suck the marrow from the bones, causing his victim to weaken and waste away. He further causes trembling in the hands and the shoulders, and he can paralyze the nerves of the hands. Under threat from King Solomon, Sphandôr reveals that he can be put to flight by invoking the name of the angel Araêl. Sphandôr is connected with the zodiac; and when he manifests, he takes a monstrous, composite form, with the head of an animal and the body of a man. See also SOLOMON.

Sphendonaêl: One of the demons belonging to the thirty-six decans of the zodiac named in the *Testament of Solomon*. In the Conybeare translation of this book, Sphendonaêl is a demon of disease, with the power to afflict humanity with ailments of the throat. He is also credited with the power to cause glandular tumors. The McCown translation connects him additionally with tetanus. He can be put to flight with the name of his governing angel, Sabrael, also spelled *Sabael*. See also SOLOMON.

Star: One of the twelve high-ranking demons in the eastern court of King Oriens. Star can strike people deaf and blind or even addle their wits. Despite these rather vicious powers, the *Book of Oberon* describes him as a good and true spirit. In a related manuscript (known by the designation *Additional MS. 36674, fol 64r number 7*), his name is given as *Scor*, a spelling that might indicate his connection with another spirit named in the *Book of Oberon*, Skor. See also *BOOK OF OBERON*, SKOR.

Steganographia: A book reputed to teach methods for communicating over long distances through the use of spirits. The *Steganographia* was written by the German abbot Johannes Trithemius around 1499. It was not published during his lifetime, and the first posthumous edition was not produced until 1606.

At first glance, the *Steganographia* is simply a book about spirits. The first book contains a list of spirits that is nearly identical to that put forth in the *Ars Theurgia*. There are only minimal variations in the names, and it seems likely that Trithemius's work influenced or inspired the material in the *Ars Theurgia*. This notion is supported by the fact that the invocations given by Trithemius as well as the descriptions of the spirits and their offices are more extensive than those found in the *Ars Theurgia*. The second book concerns itself with a series of angels and the third book addresses matters of astrology, including spirits of the hours and the mansions of the planets. The title of the book itself, a word believed to be coined by Trithemius, gives away the dual nature of this text. *Steganographia* means "secret writing" or "hidden writing," and centuries after its publication, it was discovered to contain an elaborate code. The encrypted book within the *Steganographia* deals with cryptography and the art of steganography itself, which is the insertion of hidden messages within unrelated or misleading cover text. The discovery of the hidden text within this book has led some modern cryptographers to assert that the demons and spirits described within the text were all a part of the ruse and held no real significance to Trithemius. Although it is impossible to definitively establish that Trithemius was or was not a practitioner of the magickal arts, his interest in the occult is undeniable, as he produced several other non-encrypted works pertaining to occult topics, including the *Antipalus Maleficiorum*. See also *ARS THEURGIA*, TRITHEMIUS.

Stephanate: A demon in service to Belzébut, a variation of Beelzebub that appears in the *True Keys of Solomon*. According to this text, Stephanate is one of three chief spirits to serve this infernal king. See also BEELZEBUB, MATHERS, *TRUE KEYS*.

Stolas: The thirty-sixth demon of the *Goetia*, Stolas is a great prince with twenty-six legions of infernal spirits in his service. He appears in both Scot's *Discoverie of Witchcraft* and Wierus's *Pseudomonarchia Daemonum*. According to these texts, he teaches astronomy and has absolute knowledge of the virtues of precious stones and herbs. Although he has the power to take human shape, he first manifests as a night-raven. The *Goetia of Dr. Rudd* gives his name as *Stolus*, saying that he can be constrained in the name of the angel Menadel. According to the *Book of Incantations*, he is a great and powerful prince appearing in the shape of a mighty raven. See also *BOOK OF INCANTATIONS*, *GOETIA*, RUDD, SCOT, WIERUS.

Storax: A spirit identified as the first advisor of Oberion, a being seen as both a fallen angel and king of the faeries. Given Oberion's liminal identity, there is a high chance that Storax treads similar lines between demon and fey. His name appears in the Elizabethan grimoire known as the *Book of Oberon*. Perhaps coincidentally, this demon's name is synonymous with an exotic resin often used in incense to summon and protect from spirits. See also *BOOK OF OBERON*, OBERION.

Sucax: A bold marquis of Hell, Sucax appears as a man with a woman's face. His voice is sweet and his manner is benevolent. According to the fifteenth-century grimoire known as the *Munich Handbook*, he can aid in travel of any sort and gift the magician with the ability to speak any language. Sucax is also able to cast a compulsion on women so that the magician might gain their love. He is especially skilled with inspiring the love of widows, and particularly savvy magicians might seek to point him toward rich ones. In addition to all of this, Sucax oversees twenty-three legions of spirits in the army of Hell. See also *GOETIA*, RUDD, SCOT, WIERUS.

Succor Benoth: A demon credited with being the Chief of the Eunuchs in the hierarchy of Hell. This particular hierarchy appears in A. E. Waite's presentation of the *Grand Grimoire* in his *Book of Black Magic and Pacts*. Succor Benoth is a misspelling of the name *Succoth Benoth*, a god allegedly worshipped by Babylonian captives in Samaria, according to 2 Kings 17:30. This curious interpretation of the "demon" Succor Benoth stems from the early-nineteenth-century work of French demonologist Charles Berbiguier. Succor Benoth also appears in the *Dictionnaire Infernal* of Collin de Plancy. Here, he is said to be a favorite of the demon Proserpine. See also BERBIGUIER, DE PLANCY, *GRAND GRIMOIRE*, PROSERPINE, WAITE.

Suchay: A demon of love and lust who specializes in bespelling widows. His name appears in the Elizabethan grimoire known as the *Book of Oberon*, where he is listed among the twelve highest-ranking ministers of Paimon, king of the west. In addition to acquiring the love of widows, Suchay is also a teacher of languages and a demon of transport. He has the ability to whisk people away so they travel great distances in the blink of an eye. He manifests as a beautiful woman, when he deigns to appear. Compare to Sucax. See also *BOOK OF OBERON*, PAIMON, SUCAX.

Sudoron: A demon whose name is also rendered *Sumuron*. He is ruled by the infernal prince Paimon, one of the four demons associated with the cardinal directions in the *Sacred Magic of Abramelin the Mage*. See also MATHERS, PAIMON.

Suffales: A demon of discord and warfare, Suffales incites arguments and shatters peace. According to the *Book of Oberon*, he is one of twelve high-ranking ministers of King Oriens, the reigning king of the east. That text warns that Suffales is a mendacious demon, rarely telling the truth. With effort, he can be constrained, at which point he appears like a spark of flame. See also *BOOK OF OBERON*, ORIENS.

Suffugiel: A demon named in the Peterson translation of the *Grimorium Verum*, Suffugiel is credited with the curious ability of providing mandrakes. This could prove very useful to an aspiring magician since, according to legend, the mandrake root lets out a bloodcurdling shriek when harvested. The sound of its voice is exceptionally harmful, and it was thought to strike dead any mortal who happened to hear it. In addition to providing risk-free mandragora roots, Suffugiel is said to also

Many superstitions surrounded the poisonous mandrake plant. It was rumored to grow only near the gallows. Image from a medieval woodcut. Courtesy of Dover Publications.

supply familiar spirits. He additionally teaches magick and the dark arts. In the demonic hierarchy, this demon is one of four main spirits serving beneath the infernal king Satanachia. His name appears in the *Secrets of Solomon* under the variation *Suffugruêl*. His name is alternately given as *Suffugrel* or *Sustugriel*. See also *GRIMORIUM VERUM*, SATANACHIA, *SECRETS OF SOLOMON*.

Sugunth: A demon named in the *True Keys of Solomon*. According to this text, Sugunth works as one of five principal spirits in service to chief Satanachi, an agent of Lucifer. Satanachi is a variation on the demon *Satanachia*. See also LUCIFER, SATANANCHIA, *TRUE KEYS*.

Supipas: A name that may mean "relating to swine." Supipas appears in the Mathers translation of the *Sacred Magic of Abramelin the Mage*. In this text, he is reputed to serve the arch-fiends Magoth and Kore. See also KORE, MAGOTH, MATHERS.

Surgatha: A demon from the Peterson translation of the *Grimorium Verum*, Surgatha is credited with the ability to open any lock instantly. According to this work, Surgatha serves as the fifteenth demon under the infernal duke Syrach. Surgatha also appears in the *True Keys of Solomon* and the *Secrets of Solomon*, where he is again attributed with the ability to unlock anything. A variant of his name is *Surgath*. After his duke, he serves Lucifer. See also *GRIMORIUM VERUM*, LUCIFER, SIRACHI, SYRACH.

Suriel: One of a dozen demons said to hold the rank of chief duke beneath the demon-prince Dorochiel. According to the *Ars Theurgia*, Suriel himself commands forty lesser spirits. His name is only one letter off from that of the demon Suriet, who is also said to serve Dorochiel as a chief duke. Suriel owes allegiance to the court of the west. See also *ARS THEURGIA*, DOROCHIEL, SURIET.

Suriet: A demon in the hierarchy of the infernal prince Dorochiel, Suriet holds the rank of chief duke and has a total of forty lesser spirits beneath him. His name is remarkably similar to that of the demon Suriel, who is also said to serve Dorochiel in the capacity of chief duke. Both demons appear in the *Ars Theurgia*. See also *ARS THEURGIA*, DOROCHIEL, SURIEL.

Suvantos: A demon in the service of Almiras, the master of invisibility. Suvantos is said to also serve Almiras's infernal minister Cheros. According to the *Clavicula Salomonis*, Suvantos is a demon of illusion and trickery. He can be called upon to make people invisible. He appears in the same capacity in the *Sacred Magic of Abramelin the Mage*. See also ALMIRAS, CHEROS, MATHERS.

Sword of Moses: A work that claims to have been published from a unique manuscript, presumably in Hebrew. The book was produced by Dr. Moses Gaster in London in 1896. Gaster was a highly respected scholar of Hebrew, responsible for a making a number of works connected to Jewish folklore and beliefs available in English. The *Sword of Moses* is a Jewish magickal text that may date back as far as the ninth century. The book outlines a method of magick with clear Solomonic and Qabbalistic influences. Many of the spells in the book involve curses and aggressive magick. Demons and so-called wicked angels are called upon to carry out most of this dark work. See also GASTER.

Sworn Book of Honorius: Also known as the *Liber Juratus*, or simply the *Sworn Book*. This book was supposedly written by Honorius, son of Euclid, and inspired by the angel Hochmel. The name of the angel is almost certainly derived from the Hebrew word *hochmah* (sometimes also transliterated as *chochmah*), meaning "wisdom." *Hochmah* is also one of the ten Sephiroth on the Qabbalistic Tree of Life. It is called the *Sworn Book* because those individuals chosen to receive a copy were allegedly sworn to have only one copy of the book for themselves and to have this copy buried with them when they died. Secrecy is stressed in the opening passages of the text, and that secrecy is put forward as crucial to the continued survival of the mystic arts contained within the book. The text is comprised primarily of orations and prayers, although it also contains sections on angels and demons. There are similarities between some of the orations found in the *Sworn Book* and orations found in the *Ars Notoria*, indicating a connection between the two texts. There are also similarities between portions of the *Sworn Book* and the *Heptameron*, attributed to Peter de Abano. Several of the demons connected with the spheres of the planets have variations that appear in the *Heptameron*. In the *Heptameron*, however, all of these spirits are identified as angels.

Some of the oldest surviving manuscripts of the *Sworn Book* were written in the fourteenth century. These are kept in the British Museum under the designations Sloane MS 313 and Sloane MS 3854. Of these, Sloane 313 is known to have belonged to the famous English magician Dr. John Dee. Occult scholar Joseph Peterson counts the *Sworn Book* among the oldest and most influential medieval manuscripts on magick, suggesting that it has its origins as far back as the thirteenth century. Most versions of the text are entirely in Latin, although a manuscript exists that contains Latin as well as some English. This is also kept in the collection at the British Museum and is known as Royal MS 17 Axlii.

In 1977, Daniel Driscoll of Heptangle Press undertook one of the first modern English transla-tions of this work. This was published under the title *The Sworn Book of Honourius the Magician*. For many years, this remained the only English version of this Latin text. In 1998, Joseph Peterson produced a translation for his resource site, esotericarchives.com. This translation draws primarily upon Royal MS 17 Axlii. There are significant differences between the Driscoll and the Peterson translations, including changes in nearly all of the demon names recorded in the book. According to Peterson, the discrepancies are partly due to errors on Driscoll's part, but also occur because Driscoll simply failed to use the best manuscripts. Because of the significant differences, not only in the spelling of the names but in the demons' associations, powers, and offices, I have included demons from both texts under separate entries in this work.

Syeonell: A demon whose preferred form is that of a ferocious bear, although he can be compelled to take human form. Upon doing so, he appears as a small child. His name appears in the Elizabethan grimoire known as the *Book of Oberon*, where he is said to teach all kinds of languages and to reveal hidden treasure. That text gives his rank as either count or earl and says that he has eighteen legions of lesser spirits under his command. See also *BOOK OF OBERON*.

Sylquam: Named in an extensive invocation intended to procure 100,000 pounds of lawful coin in gold and silver, Sylquam appears in the *Book of Oberon* along with Malcranis and Rasinet. In the course of the spell, all three are threatened to have their images cast into fire, along with cat turds and other foul-smelling substances as punishment, if they fail in their task. See also *BOOK OF OBERON*, MALCRANIS, RASINET.

Syman Mobris: A rare demon with a first and a last name. He is called upon in the *Book of Oberon* to craft books overnight. He is said to have knowledge of conjuration, alchemy, nigromancy, the sciences, and the arts. He can produce books on any or all of these topics. *Symeam* is a variation of his name. See also *BOOK OF OBERON*.

Symiel: The second spirit under Demoriel, the Emperor of the North. In the *Ars Theurgia*, Symiel rules as a mighty king in the north by east. Only ten dukes serve him during the day, but by night this number increases to one thousand. The demons who serve Symiel by day are all reputed to have good and tractable natures. The demons who serve him by night, however, are stubborn and willful. Symiel can also be found in Johannes Trithemius's *Steganographia*. See also *ARS THEURGIA*, DEMORIEL.

Synoryell: A demon who appears in the form of a bear, possibly rabid. He understands the languages of birds and beasts and can teach the same. Named in the *Book of Oberon*, he is identified among twelve chief ministers of the demon-king of the north, Egin. Like many demons in that grimoire, he can be called upon to reveal the location of hidden treasure. See also *BOOK OF OBERON*, EGIN.

Syrach: A grand duke of Hell named in the Peterson translation of the *Grimorium Verum*. This fierce spirit rules over eighteen other demons, each of whom have different powers and offices. The *True Keys of Solomon* contains a variation of this demon. Instead of Duke Syrach, however, he is called *Chief Sirachi*. He is said to serve directly beneath Lucifer. In the *Secrets of Solomon*, a seventeenth-century grimoire from Venice, he appears along with Lucifer and a demon named Beschard in a spell to bring lightning. He is also called upon in an invisibility spell. See also *GRIMORIUM VERUM*, LUCIFER, *SECRETS OF SOLOMON*, SIRACHI, *TRUE KEYS*.

Syrtroy: A demon who has powerful abilities to deceive the senses. According to the *Munich Handbook*, Syrtroy is one of several demons who can be called upon to help create an illusory castle. This castle will not merely be a glamour that misleads the eyes, but it will appear real in all respects. The magician and any associates will reputedly be able to enter the building and interact with its servants and foot soldiers (all presumably demons themselves). The spell further states that Syrtroy, as well as his infernal companions, can only be called up in a remote and secluded location on the tenth night of the moon in a secret and remote location. The text calls for an offering of milk and honey. The name of this demon may be a variation on *Sitri*, one of the traditional seventy-two Goetic demons. See also *MUNICH HANDBOOK*, SITRI.

Tablat: A demon named in the Mathers translation of the *Sacred Magic of Abramelin the Mage*. He is one of a number of demonic servitors who operate under the authority of the arch-demons Asmodeus and Astaroth. As a servant of these two greater demons, he can be summoned and compelled in their names. See also ASTAROTH, ASMODEUS, MATHERS.

Tachan: A name that may mean "grinding to powder." Tachan appears in the Mathers translation of the *Sacred Magic of Abramelin the Mage*, where it is said that he is ruled by the arch-demon Beelzebub. Other versions of the *Abramelin* material spell his name *Tedeam*. See also BEELZEBUB, MATHERS.

Tagnon: A servitor of the four infernal princes of the cardinal directions: Oriens, Paimon, Ariton, and Amaimon. Tagnon is a demon named in the *Sacred Magic of Abramelin the Mage*. According to this text, he is one of over three hundred unclean spirits summoned and bound to the magician's will as part of the Holy Guardian Angel rite. See also AMAIMON, ARITON, MATHERS, ORIENS, PAIMON.

Tagora: According to Mathers, the name of this demon comes from a Coptic term meaning "assembly." Tagora appears in Mathers's edition of the *Sacred Magic of Abramelin the Mage*, where he is said to serve under the dual leadership of Magoth and Kore. See also KORE, MAGOTH, MATHERS.

Takaros: A demon ruled by the infernal prince Paimon. In his translation of the *Sacred Magic of Abramelin the Mage*, Mathers suggests that the name of this demon comes from a Greek word meaning "soft" or "tender." See also MATHERS, PAIMON.

Tami: A demon of illusion from the fifteenth-century *Munich Handbook*. He is named in connection with an ambitious spell designed to conjure an entire castle out of thin air. This illusion is said to include a moat, battlements, knights, servants, and soldiers. This massive feat is to be undertaken outside in a remote and secluded spot. Tami and his infernal brethren will only answer the call at night on the tenth day of the lunar cycle. His name is also spelled *Tamy*. See also *MUNICH HANDBOOK*.

Tamiel: A fallen angel named in the *Book of Enoch*, Tamiel is depicted as a sort of angelic lieutenant in this extra-biblical text. He is described as one of the "chiefs of tens" put in charge of a small group of the Watchers. He broke his trust with Heaven through sins of the flesh. His immediate superiors were the angels Shemyaza and Azazel. The Watcher Angels are sometimes also called the *Grigori*, from the Greek word meaning "to watch." See also AZA-ZEL, SHEMYAZA, WATCHER ANGELS.

A confrontation between angels on the shores of the Lake of Fire. From an illustration by Gustav Doré.

Tamon: A demon whose preferred form is that of a foul-mouthed goat. According to the *Book of Oberon*, where his name appears, he is not only rude but also incredibly indiscreet in his speech. For those willing to put up with his nasty chatter, this demon can help to find precious stones, minerals, money, and other treasures hidden in the earth. Fifty legions serve him and he holds the rank of king. See also *BOOK OF OBERON*.

Tamor: According to the *Book of Oberon*, when this demon first appears, he manifests as a living flame so bright it is blinding. Although he can be compelled to take human form, he will do so only reluctantly. He is given the rank of prince and is said to have thirty-four legions of lesser spirits beneath him. Among his powers is the ability to make his summoner known to influential people and also gain their favor. Additionally, he can reveal hidden treasure and help his master acquire it, but only if the treasure is not guarded by other spirits. Finally, he can teach astronomy and the liberal arts, assuming one has the patience to deal with him. His name is sometimes written as *Chamor*. See also *BOOK OF OBERON*.

Tangedem: This demon answers to Almiras, the master of invisibility, and his minister, Cheros. According to the *Clavicula Salomonis*, he is a demon of trickery and illusion. He can be called upon in a spell to make someone invisible. Tangedem appears in connection with the same work in Mathers's translation of the *Sacred Magic of Abramelin the Mage*. See also ALMIRAS, CHEROS, MATHERS.

Tantavalerion: In the *Book of Oberon*, this demon is addressed as "emperor and most magnificent ruler of all spirits." The language suggests that he ranks even higher than Lucifer, Satan, and Belzebuth, the unholy trinity who hold lordship over the demon-kings of the cardinal directions and all the spirits that serve them. If this is true, then Tantavalerion is one of the most overlooked infernal beings in history, as his name is barely known outside of the grimoires. The *Book of Oberon* is not the only book of magick to mention Tantavalerion in this capacity. The manuscript known as *e Musaeo 173* from the Bodleian Library and published by Daniel Harms as *Of Angels, Demons & Spirits* also mentions this supreme ruler of all spirits, with only a slight variation on the spelling of the name. In that text, he appears as *Cantivalerion*. In either case, his name is invoked in order to make other spirits submit, be docile, and refrain from harming those who have called upon them. He is invocated along with seven other spirits identified as *senators*, another term fairly unique to demon-kind in the grimoires. These infernal senators serve directly beneath Tantavalerion as Orymell, Tygra, Danall, Salarica, Pascary, Boell, and Asmoo (possibly a variation of the more familiar *Asmoday*). The *Book of Oberon* mentions a second name for Tantavalerion, and it's an interesting one: *Golgathell*. Although there is nothing in the *Book of Oberon* to suggest the origin or meaning of this name, it is nevertheless tempting to connect it to the biblical *Golgotha*. To Christians, this is the site of the Crucifixion. In Aramaic, the word means "skull," and it is the name of a dome-like hill just outside the walls of Jerusalem. The Romans knew the place as *Calvary*. See also ASMOO, BEELZEBUB, BOELL, *BOOK OF OBERON*, DANALL, LUCIFER, ORYMELL, PASCARY, SALARICA, SATAN, TYGRA.

Taob: This bold prince of Hell commands twenty-five legions of devils. When summoned, he appears as nothing more than an ordinary man. According to the fifteenth-century grimoire known as the *Munich Handbook*, Taob is a

Satan, Death, an Angel, and Flesh all contribute to the crucible of human life. In some views, devils are permitted their temptations to strengthen people through adversity. From an illustration by Christoph Murer, 1622. Courtesy of the Wellcome Collection, London.

demon in charge of the affairs of the bedchamber. He can inflame a woman with love for the magician. Should she not race immediately to be by his side, the demon can transform her into another shape entirely, until such time as she relents to her newfound passion. Another potentially desirable ability accorded to this demon is the power to render people sterile. This may come in handy in preventing any illegitimate issue from illicit, demonically inspired affairs. There is no indication in the text as to whether or not Taob's powers also work to compel love in men. See also *MUNICH HANDBOOK*.

Tarados: A servant of the infernal rulers Oriens, Amaimon, Paimon, and Ariton. In the *Sacred Magic of Abramelin the Mage*, these four demons are said to rule over the cardinal directions. Tarados can be summoned and compelled in their names. See also AMAIMON, ARITON, MATHERS, ORIENS, PAIMON.

Taralim: A demonic servant of the infernal king Amaimon. Taralim's name appears in the *Sacred Magic of Abramelin the Mage*. According to the Mathers translation of this work, the name comes

Personal Demons

In the ancient Greek world, demons—or *daimones*, as they were called—were not universally viewed as evil beings. They were instead ambiguous creatures that occupied a state above humanity yet below the gods. Although some of these beings certainly held malevolent designs upon humanity, others could actually be helpful. The idea of a guiding genius comes from the Greek belief in personal demons. Consider that the philosopher Socrates was widely believed to have a *daimones* of his own. According to the philosopher himself, this being provided him with advice throughout his lifetime. Some of Socrates' critics were suspicious of his open admission of daimonic influence, although within the context of his culture, the presence of such a demon was often considered a boon. Still, the question was raised as to whether or not this entity was a good demon or a bad demon. In explaining his relationship with the entity, Socrates described his demon as a guiding voice that often stopped him before he said or did something unwise. The demon was good, he argued, because it had never steered him incorrectly or encouraged him in anything that caused him harm. In his opinion, it was a being both daimonic and heavenly, as shown here in his own words:

> *A divine and daimonic thing comes to me . . . This began in childhood—*
> *a certain voice comes, and whenever it comes, it always turns me away*
> *from what I am about to do, but never urges me to go ahead.**

Although Socrates is viewed by many to be the father of critical thinking, it seems that he often took the advice of his personal demon without question. On the day that Socrates was to be executed for supposedly corrupting the youth of Athens, the great philosopher reported that his personal demon had nothing at all to say to stay his course. For once in his life, the mysterious inner voice was silent, a sign that Socrates interpreted as meaning that his death was neither a bad thing nor a thing to be feared.

---

* Quoted on p. 68 in *Socrates in the Apology: An Essay on Plato's Apology of Socrates* by C. D. C. Reeve.

from a Hebrew root meaning "mighty strongholds." See also AMAIMON, MATHERS.

Taraor: A demon named in the fifteenth-century *Munich Handbook*, Taraor is mentioned as part of an invisibility spell. He is depicted as a guardian of the north. He and three other demons are called upon to provide an enchanted cloak that will render its wearer completely invisible. The cloak is an infernal object, however, so its use comes with some risk. If the proper precautions are not taken, the cloak will kill anyone who wears it within a week and three days. Taraor is called upon in the first hour of the day during a waxing moon. See also *MUNICH HANDBOOK*.

Taret: Named in Mathers's translation of the *Sacred Magic of Abramelin the Mage*, Taret is one of a number of demons ruled by the arch-fiends Astaroth and Asmodeus. See also ASTAROTH, ASMODEUS, MATHERS.

Taros: An infernal duke in the hierarchy of the west. In the Henson edition of the *Ars Theurgia*, he is said to serve the demon Cabariel in the court of the west. Taros oversees an entourage of fifty ministering spirits. He is most likely to appear during the hours of the day and is reputed to be both good-natured and obedient. See also *ARS THEURGIA*, CABARIEL.

Tasma: The name of this demon is purportedly taken from a Chaldean word meaning "weak." This may indicate that the demon himself is weak, but it is more likely to indicate that the demon can visit weakness upon others. Tasma appears in Mathers's translation of the *Sacred Magic of Abramelin the Mage*. Here, he serves beneath Oriens, Paimon, Ariton, and Amaimon, the four demonic princes of the cardinal directions. See also AMAIMON, ARITON, MATHERS, ORIENS, PAIMON.

Tatahatia: A spirit of science and virtue described in Mathers's edition of the *Grimoire of Armadel*. Tatahatia is said to be able to put enemies to flight. He also has power over darkness and can produce a veil of darkness that will blind anyone trapped within. See also MATHERS.

Tediel: A night-demon named in the *Ars Theurgia* from Henson's translation of the complete *Lemegeton*, Tediel is a servant of the infernal prince Camuel. Although he holds the rank of duke, Tediel has no servants at his command. He speaks courteously with those who would seek to converse with him and when he manifests, he assumes a beautiful form. Although he belongs to the hours of the night, he manifests during the day. Through

An image depicting the 1634 execution of Father Urbain Grandier, accused of trafficking with demons in Loudun, France. Courtesy of Dover Publications.

Camuel, he is tied to the region of the east. See also *ARS THEURGIA*, CAMUEL.

Tephras: Called the "spirit of the ashes," this demon manifests in the form of a cloud of dust that nevertheless has a human face. He appears in the *Testament of Solomon*, where it is said that he reaches his full power in the summer. In this, he is essentially the personification of wildfires, for he is credited with burning fields and destroying the habitations of men. He also presides over a disease described only as "hermitertian fever." He answers to the angel Azael and can be put to flight with that angel's name. Solomon allegedly put him to work lifting great stones and throwing these up to the workers at the higher portions of the Temple. See also SOLOMON.

Terath: A demon associated with the hours of the day, Terath holds the rank of duke and has fifty ministering spirits beneath him. He himself serves the infernal king Raysiel, a high-ranking demon in the hierarchy of the north. Terath's name and sigil both appear in the *Ars Theurgia*, the second book of the *Lesser Key of Solomon*. See also *ARS THEURGIA*, RAYSIEL.

Testament of Amram: Probably written in the second century BCE, the *Testament of Amram* is one of the older sectarian writings found among the texts of the Essenes. These writings, discovered in a cave near Qumran, are more popularly known as the Dead Sea Scrolls. The Essenes were a Jewish messianic community whose beliefs may have influenced early Christianity.

Under the designation 4Q543-8 in the collection of the Dead Sea Scrolls, this Aramaic work is pseudonymously attributed to Amram, identified as the father of Moses. The document is sometimes called the *Dream Vision of Amram* because the most striking portion of the text details a vision manifested in a dream. In this dream, the leaders of the Sons of Light and Sons of Darkness appear to Amram to demand his allegiance to one side or the other. The ongoing war between the Sons of Light and the Sons of Darkness figures strongly in the eschatology of the Essenes. In the various writings associated with the war between these two factions, the head of the armies of the Sons of Light is frequently identified as Michael, although sometimes his name is given as Melchizedek. The chief of the armies of the Sons of Darkness is identified as Belial. He is often given the title the Prince of Darkness. In the *Testament of Amram*, he is described as a dark Watcher Angel with a "visage like a viper." In some of the Essene writings, Belial is also known by the name *Melchiresha*. One of the other Qumran manuscripts to discuss these beings and their functions is known as the *War Rule*, or *Rule of the War*. See also BELIAL, WATCHER ANGELS.

Testament of Solomon: An extra-biblical text currently dated to the last few centuries before the Common Era. The *Testament of Solomon* is a pseudepigraphal work, meaning that it is attributed to King Solomon but it was not actually written by the biblical monarch himself. The book lists a number of demons, together with their powers and the best method to control them. According to the text, King Solomon was granted power over these evil spirits as a reward for faith and prayer. With the help of a magickal seal or ring given to him by God, Solomon summoned and compelled a variety of demons and fallen angels, forcing them to work for him toward the completion of his temple. For those demons known to attack humanity, he extracted the name of the angel that could be called upon to drive them away. Interestingly, several of the demons of the *Tes-*

The Ineffable Name

The *Tetragrammaton* is known as the ineffable name of God. The word means, literally, "the four letters." This four-lettered Hebrew name of God is believed by many Jews to be too holy to pronounce. The letters that make up this holiest of names are *Yod He Vah He*, and although no vowels are supplied, this name is generally rendered *Yahweh*. It is one of two primary names of God that appear throughout Genesis and the Old Testament. The other name is *Elohim*—which is notably a plural.

In ceremonial magick, the Tetragrammaton is commonly used to summon, compel, and bind demons, and it can often be found inscribed in sigils intended to assist in these purposes. It may appear in the original Hebrew, but as the grimoiric tradition became more Christianized, it was also frequently written out simply as *Tetragrammaton*.

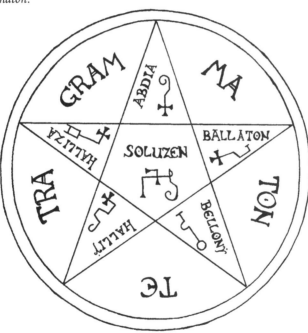

The Pentagram of Solomon as depicted in the *Lemegeton*. The Tetragrammaton, a Hebrew word, is transliterated into English and written around the arms of the star. Image by Jackie Williams.

tament of Solomon claim to be the offspring of angels themselves, a fact that ties this work to the earlier *Book of Enoch*. The *Testament of Solomon* was written during a time when the Essene community at Qumran (known for the Dead Sea Scrolls) was writing extensively about the War in Heaven and the ongoing battle between the Sons of Darkness and the Son of Light. This epic struggle of good versus evil is intricately tied in with the Watcher Angel myth that appears in the *Book of Enoch* and is obliquely referenced in the *Testament of Solomon*.

The notion that King Solomon had power over demons is an old one. The *Apocalypse of Adam*, a first or second century CE Gnostic text from the Nag Hammadi library, depicts King Solomon as a controller of demons. His involvement with both demonic magick and astrology is further established in rabbinical lore. In the Quran, Solomon's power is over the Jinn, and he uses these inhuman spirits to help erect his temple. The *Testament of Solomon* is one of the core texts of the Solomonic tradition, and this tradition powerfully influenced the ceremonial magick of the grimoires sourced throughout this book. Solomon's power to compel demons with the holy names of God and the angels is also intricately connected with aspects of Jewish esotericism, notably the Qabbalah. See also SOLOMON, WATCHER ANGELS.

Thaadas: A minister of Batthan, the king of the spirits of the sun. Thaadas appears in the Peterson translation of the *Sworn Book of Honorius*. He has the power to provide wealth, power, and fame. He can also make people healthy and well loved. His region is the east, and his manifest form is bright, with skin the color of citrus. He is constrained by the angels Raphael, Cashael, Dardyhel, and Hanrathaphael, who oversee the sphere of the sun. See also BATTHAN, *SWORN BOOK*.

Thalbus: A demon of the night reputed to possess an evil and deceitful nature, Thalbus is a mighty duke ruled by the demon-prince Cabariel. As a demon of rank, he has fifty lesser spirits beneath him to carry out his commands. Thalbus's name and the seal that can bind him appear in the *Ars Theurgia*, the second book of the *Lesser Key of Solomon*. According to this text, he is affiliated with the west. See also ARS THEURGIA, CABARIEL.

Thamuz: The demonic ambassador to Spain, Thamuz is attributed with this role in Waite's presentation of the *Grand Grimoire* in his 1910 *Book of Black Magic and Pacts*. This description of Thamuz stems from the work of nineteenth-century demonologist Charles Berbiguier. The name of this demon derives from a Syrian and Phoenician deity, Tammuz, who corresponds closely with the Greek Adonis. Tamuz is also a name of a month in the Hebrew calendar. See also BERBIGUIER, WAITE.

Thanatiel: According to the *Ars Theurgia*, this demon can only appear at a specific time each day. If the day is divided into fifteen sections of time, then Thanatiel's time falls between those hours and minutes measured in the third portion. He serves the wandering prince Icosiel as a mighty duke, and he has a total of two thousand two hundred lesser spirits beneath him. He has a fondness for houses and is most likely to be found in homes and private residences. See also ARS THEURGIA, ICOSIEL.

Tharas: A demon of the daylight hours reputed to appear between dawn and dusk, Tharas holds the title of chief duke and he has fifty lesser spirits to minister to his needs. Tharas himself serves the demon-king Raysiel. Through Raysiel, he is connected with the court of the north. Tharas's name and demonic seal both appear in the *Ars Theurgia*. See also *ARS THEURGIA*, RAYSIEL.

Thariel: A demon of the night ruled by Raysiel, a king in the hierarchy of the north. In the *Ars Theurgia*, Thariel is described as being stubborn and ill-natured. He holds the rank of chief duke and has an entourage of forty ministering spirits to serve him. See also *ARS THEURGIA*, RAYSIEL.

Tharson: An "under duke" who serves the chief duke Samyel in the larger hierarchy of the wandering prince Menadiel. Tharson belongs to the twelfth hour of the day, for he is said to always follow behind Samyel, and Samyel manifests in the eleventh hour. Tharson and his fellow demons are named in the *Ars Theurgia*, a magickal text thought to date mainly to the seventeenth century. See also *ARS THEURGIA*, MENADIEL, SAMYEL.

Thitodens: A demon of scrying and divination. He is called upon in the *Munich Handbook* to lend his power to spells aimed at achieving visions and secret or hidden information. See also *MUNICH HANDBOOK*.

Thoac: An infernal duke in the hierarchy of the north beneath the infernal king Raysiel, Thoac serves his master during the hours of the day. According to the *Ars Theurgia*, he has fifty lesser spirits to attend him. See also *ARS THEURGIA*, RAYSIEL.

Thobar: In the *Munich Handbook*, Thobar is named in a spell concerned with achieving justice after a theft. He is one of several demons conjured to reveal the identity of thieves and the whereabouts of their stolen articles. He accomplishes this through a particular method of divination that requires a young boy to act as intermediary between the demons and the magician. See also *MUNICH HANDBOOK*.

Thurcal: A demon who only manifests during the hours of the night, Thurcal is a chief duke governed by Raysiel, an infernal king of the north. His name and seal appear in the *Ars Theurgia*. According to this text, Thurcal is an evil and stubborn spirit with an entourage of twenty lesser spirits. See also *ARS THEURGIA*, RAYSIEL.

Thuriel: One of twelve dukes named in the court of the infernal prince Macariel. Thuriel reputedly appears in the form of a many-headed dragon, although he has the power to assume a variety of shapes. He is tied to no particular hour of the day or night and may appear whenever he pleases. According to the *Ars Theurgia*, he has a total of four hundred minor spirits at his command. See also *ARS THEURGIA*, MACARIEL.

Tigara: A demon named in the *Ars Theurgia*, Tigara is said to serve Barmiel, the first and chief spirit of the south. Tigara holds the rank of duke and has twenty lesser spirits under his command. He serves his infernal king during the hours of the day. See also *ARS THEURGIA*, BARMIEL.

Tigrafon: Also spelled *Tigraphon*, this demon appears in Mathers's translation of the *Sacred Magic of Abramelin the Mage*. He is said to serve under the dual leadership of the arch-fiends Magoth and Kore. See also KORE, MAGOTH, MATHERS.

Timira: A servitor of the demons Astaroth and Asmodeus, Timira appears in the *Sacred Magic of Abramelin the Mage*. According to Mathers's translation of that work, the name of this demon is from a Hebrew word for "palm." See also ASTAROTH, ASMODEUS, MATHERS.

Tiraim: A demon serving under the joint leadership of Magoth and Kore, at least according to the Mathers translation of the *Sacred Magic of Abramelin the Mage*. In other editions of this work, this

A witch casting spells over a steaming cauldron. Engraving by H. S. Thomassin. Although many of the grimoires seem to assume a male practitioner, some, like the *Book of Oberon*, account for practitioners of any gender. Image courtesy of the Wellcome Collection, London.

demon serves only the arch-fiend Magoth. In the versions of *Abramelin* kept at the Wolfenbüttel and Dresden libraries, this demon's name is spelled *Lotaym*. See also KORE, MAGOTH, MATHERS.

Tirana: This demon loyally serves the four infernal princes of the cardinal directions. As a demon who answers to Oriens, Paimon, Ariton, and Amaimon, Tirana shares all of their powers and can confer these to others when summoned. He appears in the *Sacred Magic of Abramelin the Mage*. See also AMAIMON, ARITON, MATHERS, ORIENS, PAIMON.

Tistator: A demon of lies and deceit, Tistator appears in the *Sacred Magic of Abramelin the Mage*. He is said to be useful in matters pertaining to illusion and trickery, and should also be called upon to assist with invisibility spells. This demon can also be found in the Mathers translation of the *Clavicula Salomonis*, also known as the *Key of Solomon*. See also CLAVICULA SALOMONIS, MATHERS.

Tmsmael: A wicked angel invoked in a spell to separate a husband from his wife, Tmsmael appears in the *Sword of Moses*. He is said to possess a number of malevolent powers, including the ability to inflict sharp pains, inflammation, and dropsy. See also GASTER, *SWORD OF MOSES*.

Torfora: A demon named in the *Sacred Magic of Abramelin the Mage*, Torfora appears in the hierarchy ruled by all four infernal princes of the cardinal directions: Oriens, Paimon, Amaimon, and Ariton. Summoned as part of the Holy Guardian Angel rite, Mathers suggests that this demon's name is derived from a Hebrew term meaning "small knife" or "lancet." See also AMAIMON, ARITON, MATHERS, ORIENS, PAIMON.

Toxai: A demon whose name is taken to mean "the toxic one." In the Mathers edition of the *Sacred Magic of Abramelin the Mage*, Toxai is listed among the demons governed by infernal ruler Astaroth. A variant of this demon's name is *Texai*. See also ASTAROTH, MATHERS.

Tracatat: A minister of the demon Canibores. According to Driscoll's translation of the *Sworn Book*, Tracatat holds sway over passion and voluptuousness in both men and women. He can heighten pleasure and summon luxury items like costly fabric and perfumes. When he manifests, this demon assumes a body that shines like a star. He is compared to malleable silver, and is said to have a moderate stature. He is closely related to the demon Trachathath from the Peterson translation of the *Sworn Book*. See also CANIBORES, *SWORN BOOK*, TRACHATHATH.

Trachathath: A servant of the demon Sarabocres, named as the infernal king of the planet Venus in the Peterson translation of the *Sworn Book of Honorius*. Trachathath has power over passion, lust, and pleasure. He is almost certainly a variation of the demon Tracatat, named in the Driscoll edition of the *Sworn Book*. This demon is also said to be one of four in Sarabocres's court ruled by the east and west winds. See also SARABOCRES, *SWORN BOOK*, TRACATAT.

Trachi: A demon ruled by Oriens, Amaimon, Paimon, and Ariton, the four infernal princes of the cardinal directions, Trachi appears in the *Sacred Magic of Abramelin the Mage*. According to Mathers, his name is from a Greek word meaning "harsh" or "rude." See also AMAIMON, ARITON, MATHERS, ORIENS, PAIMON.

Transidium: According to the *Clavicula Salomonis*, this demon wields power over invisibility. Transidium is one of several demons who answer to the demonic master of invisibility, Almiras, and his infernal minister, Cheros. This demon is also mentioned in connection with invisibility in the *Sacred Magic of Abramelin the Mage*. See also ALMIRAS, CHEROS, *CLAVICULA SALOMONIS*, MATHERS.

Trapisi: A demon whose name may come from a Greek root meaning "turning," Trapisi is governed by the four demonic princes of the cardi-

nal directions. He is named in Mathers's translation of the *Sacred Magic of Abramelin the Mage*. See also AMAIMON, ARITON, MATHERS, ORIENS, PAIMON.

Treatise on Angel Magic: A manuscript in the collection of the British Library filed under the designation Harley MS 6482. It is one of several manuscripts in this collection produced by the same individual. Written at the end of the seventeenth century, the *Treatise on Angel Magic* deals mainly with methods for summoning angels, although it contains the names and descriptions of both demons and fallen angels as well. It bears some techniques in common with the Enochian magick of Dr. John Dee, and it includes a set of seven magickal squares specifically described as the Tables of Enoch. The work is attributed to a scholar by the name of Dr. Rudd, who is thought by writers like Francis Yates to be the individual known as Thomas Rudd. In 1651, this Rudd published an edition of the Euclidean *Mathematical Preface*, originally written by Dr. John Dee, establishing a connection between his work and the writings of Dr. Dee. The Harley manuscripts are not Rudd's originals but are instead copies made by one Peter Smart. Occultist Adam McLean believes that the Rudd manuscripts were never meant for public consumption. Instead, he suggests that they were copies produced for private use or for the use of a small circle of practitioners working closely with Dr. Rudd. See also RUDD.

Triay: The *Munich Handbook* identifies Triay as a demon with a particularly nasty temperament. This malignant demon, carefully conjured, can be set upon an enemy. When he attacks, the victim will be struck senseless with no hope of recovering, unless the magician wills it. He attacks the

Devilish Melodies

The Devil is a fiddle player. At least, that's what we learn in the classic song "The Devil Went Down to Georgia," where the Devil appears to challenge a young fiddle player named Johnny. Johnny, according to the song, is "the best that ever was," and he knows it—so the Devil takes advantage of his sin of pride, betting him a golden violin if Johnny can outplay Old Scratch. The song, covered dozens of times since it was written, is a rousing mix of story and melody. It draws upon a well-established tradition in Southern folklore where the Devil shows up to wage a bet for a boastful person's soul.

The Devil's connection with the violin is much older than this 1979 song by the Charlie Daniels Band, however. Around 1749, the Devil reportedly appeared to a real-life fiddle player and offered a pact. The "fiddle" player was none other than renowned Baroque violinist Guiseppe Tartini. Tartini was a composer as well as a master of the violin, and he created one of his most masterful works after a very peculiar dream.

While Tartini slept, he dreamed that the Devil appeared to him and made a pact. As part of the pact, the Devil did whatever Tartini would bid him. Curious about the Devil's skill on his favorite instrument, Tartini handed Old Scratch his violin and asked him to play. In the dream, the Devil reportedly admitted that he could manage a few tunes and then proceeded to play a sonata that left Tartini utterly dumbfounded. In Tartini's own words recording the event, "Imagine my surprise when I heard a sonata so unusual and so beautiful, performed with such mastery and intelligence, on a level I had never before conceived was possible!"*

Tartini was so overcome by the beauty and mastery of the Devil's violin work in his dream that he awoke gasping for breath. He immediately took up his violin in the waking world and struggled to recreate the infernal melody of his dream. Although Tartini felt that he did not even come close, the resulting sonata is considered a masterwork. Tartini called it the *Devil's Trill* (sometimes also called the *Devil's Trill Sonata*), and anyone who's attempted to play it will admit that it seems almost inhuman in its complexity.

---

* Mario Gómez, "The Legend of Tartini's 'Devil's Trill Sonata.'"

mind, causing delusions and confusing the senses. See also *MUNICH HANDBOOK*.

Trimasel: Skilled in the alchemical arts, the demon Trimasel is reputed to be able to teach how to craft a powder that will transform any base metal into either silver or gold. This demon is further skilled in both chemistry and sleight of hand, and he will teach either of these skills upon request. Named in Peterson's *Grimorium Verum*, Trimasel, whose name can also be rendered *Trimasael*, is one of the four main spirits serving under the demon Satanachia. See also *GRIMORIUM VERUM*, SATANACHIA.

Trinitas: A demon connected with Monday, Trinitas is named in the *Grimoire of Pope Honorius*. His name may be derived from the word *trinity* and is related to the Latin word for "three." See also *GRIMOIRE OF POPE HONORIUS*.

Trisaga: A servitor of the demon-kings Amaimon and Ariton. In his translation of the *Sacred Magic of Abramelin the Mage*, Mathers relates the name of this demon to "three" and "triads." In other versions of the *Abramelin* material, the name of this demon appears as *Trisacha*. See also AMAIMON, ARITON, MATHERS.

Trithemius, Johannes: A German cryptographer and occultist who lived between 1462 and 1516. Born Johann Heidenberg, he was elected abbot of the Benedictine abbey of Sponheim in 1483 at the age of twenty-one. He turned the abbey into a center of learning, significantly increasing the collection of books in its library. However, rumors of his involvement in the occult abounded, ultimately forcing him to resign in 1506. On the recommendation of the Bishop of Würzburg, he became the abbot of Saint James's Abbey and served there until the end of his life.

His most famous work is the *Steganographia*, a book written around 1499 and posthumously published in 1606. On the surface, it seems to be a book on magick and occultism, and its first chapter includes a list of spirits nearly identical to that outlined in the *Ars Theurgia*. *Steganographia*, however, is a word coined by Trithemius from Greek roots meaning "concealed writing." Later studies of this book revealed it to contain hidden material on cryptography and steganography, the art of concealing hidden messages beneath innocuous or misleading cover text. Trithemius's choice of cover text was anything but innocuous, however. The choice of concealing his hidden messages in a work on demons was a curious one, especially in a time when interest in such subjects could earn censure and worse from the church. Despite this, there is some debate among modern scholars as to whether or not Trithemius believed in the spiritual and demonic magick put forth in the *Steganographia*.

Although it may be hard to posthumously prove that he was a practicing magician, it is impossible to deny his long-standing interest in occult topics. One of his other books, the *Antipalus Maleficiorum*, written in 1508, contains a catalogue of necromantic books that remains one of the most complete resources on Renaissance magick to this day. In addition to inventing the art and science of steganography, Trithemius numbered occultists Paracelsus and Agrippa among his students. It was at Trithemius's suggestion that Agrippa held off on the publication of his *Three Books of Occult Philosophy* for nearly two decades after the work was first produced. See also AGRIPPA, *STEGANOGRAPHIA*.

True Keys of Solomon: A text kept in the British Museum under the designation of Lansdowne 1202, with the title *Les Vrais Clavicules du Roi Salomon par Armadel*. Lansdowne 1202 contains three books of Solomonic material. The first two were sourced by Mathers in his 1898 translation of the *Clavicula Salomonis*. The third section, referenced in this work as *Les Vrais Clavicules*, was rejected by Mathers on the grounds that the *Key of Solomon* is traditionally comprised only of two books. Additionally, he felt that this third book bore too much in common with a completely different work known as the *Grimorium Verum*. Joseph Peterson, a modern occult scholar, agrees that *Les Vrais Clavicules* shares material in common with the *Grimorium Verum*. He includes a translation of the *Clavicules* at the end of his own edition of the *Grimorium Verum*, published in 2007. The *True Keys of Solomon* contains a list of demons, their offices, and functions, as well as a few spells and instructions for crafting certain essential magickal tools, such as the wand. One of the most interesting details about this text is that it accounts for female practitioners of magick. In almost all other grimoires, practitioners are assumed to be male. Of course, this should come as no surprise because the grimoiric tradition is a tradition founded in the written word. In the twelfth through the sixteenth centuries, when many of the grimoires were written, few women were taught to read. The vast majority of practitioners tended to be clergy, in part because the clergy were the most widely literate class at the time. See also *CLAVICULA SALOMONIS*, *GRIMORIUM VERUM*, MATHERS.

Tudiras Hoho: A great marquis who appears as a pretty maid. He is one of very few demons with a first and a last name. He makes men wise in all the sciences and can transform a person into the guise of a bird. His rather unique name appears in the French *Book of Spirits*, where it is said that thirty-

Pentagram surrounded by astrological figures. Detail from the *Clavis Inferni*. Image courtesy of the Wellcome Collection, London.

one legions follow his command. See also *LIVRE DES ESPERITZ*.

Tugaros: A demon in the service of Camuel, a king in the hierarchy of the east. According to the *Ars Theurgia*, Tugaros holds the rank of duke, although he has no ministering spirits beneath him. He is tied to the hours of the night, but he manifests during the hours of the day. When he manifests, he is courteous and beautiful to behold. See also *ARS THEURGIA*, CAMUEL.

Tulot: A demon ruled by the four infernal princes of the cardinal directions: Oriens, Paimon, Ariton, and Amaimon. Tulot's name appears as part of the working focused on the Holy Guardian Angel, as described in the 1898 Mathers translation of the *Sacred Magic of Abramelin the Mage*. See also AMAIMON, ARITON, MATHERS, ORIENS, PAIMON.

Turael: A Watcher Angel named in the *Book of Enoch*. He is said to be one of the chiefs of these fallen angels. Compare to the angel Turiel, whose name means "rock of God." Elsewhere in the same text, his name is spelled *Turel*. See also WATCHER ANGELS.

Turitel: According to Mathers, the root of this demon's name comes from a Hebrew term meaning "rock" or "mountain." Turitel is named in the *Sacred Magic of Abramelin the Mage*. According to this text, he is ruled by the infernal prince Oriens. See also MATHERS, ORIENS.

Tuveries: This mighty marquis in the hierarchy of Hell has a full thirty legions under his command. Described in the thirty-fourth spell of the fifteenth-century grimoire known as the *Munich Handbook*, Tuveries appears as a knight riding a black horse. When requested, he has the power to reveal all things hidden, including treasure. He further assists in all travel over bodies of water, causing distances by river or sea to be crossed with alacrity. He will also teach trivium to the magician. This skill may be more important than it seems at first glance. In the modern age, *trivia* has come to mean information of little consequence. However, in the days of the *Munich Handbook*, trivium might well refer to the secrets of the crossroads, otherwise known as the *tri-via*. This was a juncture of three roads, sacred to the goddess Hecate, thought to be a patroness of witches. By the fifteenth century, Hecate had come to be viewed as a dark goddess indeed, and so Tuveries may have it within his power to teach the magician all the secrets of the black arts. See also *MUNICH HANDBOOK*.

Tygra: A demon attributed with the rank of senator, he is one of seven who serve the great emperor Tantavalerion. In the *Book of Oberon*, Tantavalerion and his seven senators are called upon to compel other spirits to appear, as well as to keep them docile and obedient. See also ASMOO, BOELL, *BOOK OF OBERON*, DANALL, ORYMELL, PASCARY, SALARICA, TANTAVALERION.

Tyros: A demon named in the *Munich Handbook*. Tyros has power to assist with divination. He is called upon in a spell connected with the art of scrying. See also *MUNICH HANDBOOK*.

Ubarin: According to the *Sacred Magic of Abramelin the Mage*, Ubarin is a demonic servitor of the archfiend Magoth. In the Mathers translation of this work, Ubarin is said to also serve the demon Kore. Occultist Mathers suggests that this demon's name means "insult" or "outrage." Ubarin is spelled *Ubarim* in other versions of the Abramelin material. See also KORE, MAGOTH, MATHERS.

Udaman: A demonic servitor of both Astaroth and Asmodeus, Udaman appears in the 1898 Mathers translation of the *Sacred Magic of Abramelin the Mage*. The name of this demon may be derived from a Greek word, *eudaimon*, meaning "good demon." See also ASTAROTH, ASMODEUS, MATHERS.

Udiel: One of several demons ruled by the infernal king Malgaras, Udiel holds the rank of chief duke. He is connected with the region of the west and he only serves his demonic master during the hours of the day. The *Ars Theurgia* describes Udiel as having thirty lesser spirits at his command. See also *ARS THEURGIA*, MALGARAS.

Ugales: One of several demons who answer to Astaroth and Asmodeus, Ugales is named in the 1898 translation of the *Sacred Magic of Abramelin the Mage* by occultist S. L. MacGregor Mathers. In the other copies of this work, the name of this demon is spelled *Ugalis*. See also ASTAROTH, ASMODEUS.

Ugirpen: A demon commanded by the infernal ruler Astaroth, Ugirpen appears in the *Sacred Magic of Abramelin the Mage*. He is invoked along with all the other demonic servitors of Astaroth as part of the Holy Guardian Angel rite. See also ASTAROTH, MATHERS.

Urbaniel: The fifteenth duke serving beneath the infernal prince Icosiel, Urbaniel is reportedly drawn to the interior of homes. According to the *Ars Theurgia*, he belongs to the last portion of time if the day is divided into fifteen parts. He may only make an appearance during these specific hours and minutes each day. When he appears, he is likely to be accompanied by at least a few of the two thousand two hundred lesser spirits said to minister to him. His name is likely derived from the Latin word *urbanus*, meaning "city." See also *ARS THEURGIA*, ICOSIEL.

Uriel: In the *Ars Theurgia*, Uriel makes an appearance as one of the so-called "wandering princes." In this capacity he is said to have ten chief dukes and one hundred lesser dukes who serve to carry out his wishes. Those of his hierarchy are described as being truculent and evil by nature. They are also said to be full of trickery, so they are always false in their dealings. Uriel's manifest form is that of a serpent with the head of a beautiful maiden. All of the demons who serve in his court assume the same monstrous shape when they appear to mortals. Uriel also appears as a demon in Trithemius's *Steganographia*.

Uriel, of course, is a name that is not typically associated with demonic entities. He is better known as one of the archangels. Uriel appears in the *Book of Enoch* alongside the archangels Michael, Raphael, and Gabriel. Later in the same text, seven archangels are named, and Uriel is again included among their number. He appears as the fourth of the archangels in Saint Gregory's heavenly hierarchy as well as that composed by Pseudo-Dionysus. Uriel is also identified as an angel in the *Testament of Solomon*. Uriel's name is sometimes rendered *Oriel* or *Auriel*. His name is taken to mean "Light of God" or "Fire of God." See also *ARS THEURGIA*, *BOOK OF ENOCH*, SOLOMON.

Urigo: A name rendered *Urgido* in both the Wolfenbüttel and Dresden versions of the *Sacred Magic of Abramelin the Mage*. In Mathers's widely read translation of this work, Urigo's name is presented as meaning "spoiled" or "rotten." Most of the *Abramelin* texts agree that Urigo is a servant of the demon Magoth. Mathers also lists him as a servant of Kore. See also KORE, MAGOTH, MATHERS.

Ursiel: One of twelve main dukes said to serve the demon-king Caspiel, Emperor of the South. Ursiel is a stubborn and churlish spirit who interacts with humanity only reluctantly. According to the *Ars Theurgia*, Ursiel sometimes appears alongside his master, Caspiel, but he can also be conjured independently. Although no explanation of the meaning of the demon's name is given in the *Ars Theurgia*, there is a possible connection to *Ursa*, the bear. Ursiel reportedly has a total of two thousand two hundred and sixty lesser spirits at his command. See also *ARS THEURGIA*, CASPIEL.

Usiel: In the *Ars Theurgia*, Usiel is named as the third spirit under Amenadiel, Emperor of the West. Usiel rules the region of the northwest. He commands a total of eighty infernal dukes. Half of these serve him during the hours of the day. The other half serve during the hours of the night. Usiel and the infernal dukes in his hierarchy are most often invoked to protect valuables from theft or discovery and to reveal precious objects that have been obscured by others through enchantment. The name of this demon can also be found in the *Steganographia* of Trithemius, written around 1499. See also AMENADIEL, *ARS THEURGIA*, TRITHEMIUS.

Usiniel: A demon in the court of prince Usiel. Usiniel is a revealer of secrets, helping mortals to discover treasure hidden away by magickal means. He can also very adequately hide things through his own magick, preventing their theft or discovery. The *Ars Theurgia* gives his rank as duke and says that he has thirty lesser spirits at his command. See also *ARS THEURGIA*, USIEL.

Nine-Tenths of the Law

In 1630, a group of Ursuline nuns in Loudun, France, accused Father Urbain Grandier of summoning demons to possess them. The nuns threw wild fits, often performing lewd acts and exposing themselves in a demonically inspired frenzy. Grandier was a worldly priest, tall and attractive, with a reputation for anything but celibacy. He made a lot of enemies both through his sexual indiscretions and his political leanings. In 1618, he penned a sarcastic work criticizing Cardinal Richelieu. Richelieu was not a man easily trifled with and may well have manipulated the situation at Loudun to destroy Grandier.

One of Grandier's many enemies, a Father Mignon, first undertook the task of exorcising the nuns. His work produced a number of curious documents allegedly written by the demons in possession of the nuns. Asmodeus, writing in bad French in a delicate woman's hand, apparently penned a contract promising to leave the body of the nun in his possession. A pact between Father Grandier and the Devil was produced under similar circumstances. It was countersigned by a variety of well-known demons, including Baalberith, Astaroth, and Beelzebub. This was later submitted as evidence at his trial. Mignon's efforts at exorcism seemed only to encourage the nuns, and eventually he was forbidden to continue with his work. However, Richelieu still had it in for Grandier. Before the whole thing was over, the cardinal got directly involved, ordering a full investigation. With Richelieu in control of the proceedings, Grandier was arrested, tortured horribly, and then burned at the stake in 1634. The case is recounted in Aldous Huxley's 1952 work *The Devils of Loudun*. The nuns continued to behave as though possessed, even after Grandier's death. Richelieu was the only member of the clergy able to finally drive the devils out of them: he threatened to cut off their funding if they did not cease and desist.

A portion of the pact supposedly signed between seventeenth-century priest Urbain Grandier and the devils. The text of the pact is written backward and in Latin. Courtesy of Dover.

Usyr: One of several spirits called upon in the *Munich Handbook* to create an illusory castle complete with knights and servants and a banquet hall. Usyr is propitiated with an offering of milk and honey. He is described as a "squire spirit" in the text and is supposed to be called upon in a remote and secret place on the tenth day of the moon. See also *MUNICH HANDBOOK*.

Utifa: Named in the Mathers translation of the *Sacred Magic of Abramelin the Mage*, Utifa is said to serve beneath the demon Asmodeus. Although several versions of the *Abramelin* material exist, only the fifteenth-century French manuscript sourced by Mathers contains the name Utifa. See also ASMODEUS, MATHERS.

Vaal: A great king who grants lordships, political favors, and boons. He can make one influential and well respected in society. He is named in the French grimoire *Livre des esperitz*, where it is said

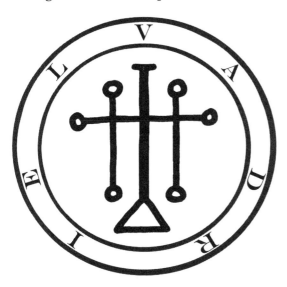

The seal of the demon Vadriel, who serves the Emperor Carnesiel in the *Ars Theurgia*. From a talisman by M. Belanger.

that thirty-nine legions of lesser spirits serve him. See also *LIVRE DES ESPERITZ*.

Vadriel: A demon governed by the infernal emperor Carnesiel, Vadriel is named in the *Ars Theurgia*, where he is said to serve in the court of the east. See also *ARS THEURGIA*, CARNESIEL.

Vadros: A mighty duke in the hierarchy of Amenadiel, the infernal Emperor of the West. Vadros commands an impressive retinue of three thousand eight hundred and eighty lesser spirits. His name and seal appear in the *Ars Theurgia*. See also AMENADIEL, *ARS THEURGIA*.

Valac: The sixty-second demon of the *Goetia*, Valac is also named in both Wierus's *Pseudomonarchia Daemonum* and Scot's *Discoverie of Witchcraft*. He is said to assume the form of a boy with angel's wings. When he is called to appear, he comes riding a two-headed dragon. He is credited with the title of president and is said to hold dominion over thirty legions of infernal spirits. He has a strange power over serpents. He magickally knows the location of these creatures and can deliver them across any distance to his conjuror. He will also reveal the location of hidden treasure. According to the Welsh *Book of Incantations*, in addition to his other powers, he renders serpents harmless so they are safe to handle and study. He appears under the spelling *Volach* in the fifteenth-century grimoire known as the *Munich Handbook*. Here, he is reputed to be a mighty president of Hell with twenty-seven legions under his command. He appears as a beautiful boy with not one but *two* heads, and wings like that of an angel. In the *Goetia of Dr. Rudd*, he is said to be ruled by the angel Jahhael. In this text, his name is spelled *Valu*. Another variation of his name is *Volac*. See also BOOK OF INCANTATIONS, GOETIA, MUNICH HANDBOOK, RUDD, SCOT, WIERUS.

Vale: A mighty duke named in the *Book of Incantations*. Vale appears in the form of a lion with a man's head. He makes a good familiar but tempts those with whom he is familiar to steal. He governs ten legions. His seal is to be worn constantly to keep him under control. His name is likely a variation on the Goetic demon *Valefar*. See also *BOOK OF INCANTATIONS*, VALEFAR.

Valefar: A demon connected with thieves. He is the sixth spirit named among the seventy-two demons of the *Goetia*. In Wierus's *Pseudomonarchia Daemonum*, he is said to be very familiar with those who seek him out, but he ultimately leads these individuals to no greater fate than the gallows. According to this text, he takes the unlikely shape of a lion with the head of a thief. He is a strong duke with ten legions of spirits under his command. An alternate version of his name is given as *Malaphar*. This is rendered *Malephar* in Scot's *Discoverie of Witchcraft*. In the *Goetia of Dr. Rudd*, Valefar is said

to appear as a lion with a man's head, howling. Rather than being specifically attracted to working with thieves, according to this text, Valefar tempts people to steal. Despite this, he is said to make a good familiar. He is constrained with the name of the angel Jelahel. See also *GOETIA*, RUDD, SCOT, WIERUS.

Vapula: The sixtieth demon named in the *Goetia*, Vapula is a teaching demon credited with the power to make people skilled in mechanics, philosophy, and all book-learning. Vapula is said to hold the rank of duke and to rule over a total of thirty-six legions. He manifests as a lion with gryphon's wings. His name appears in both the *Pseudomonarchia Daemonum* of Johannes Wierus and Scot's *Discoverie of Witchcraft*. He also appears in the Welsh *Book of Incantations* and is one of the seventy-two demons named in the *Goetia*. In the *Goetia of Dr. Rudd*, his name is given as *Napula*. Here, he is said to govern only thirty legions of lesser spirits. Instead of the title of duke, he is ascribed the title of president. The *Goetia of Dr. Rudd* also says that the demon can be constrained with the name of a specific angel set over him. According to the text, the name of that angel is *Mizrael*. See also *GOETIA*, RUDD, SCOT, WIERUS.

Varbas: When summoned, this demon arrives in the form of a fierce lion, but he can assume a more pleasing human shape upon request. Varbas is said to be an excellent physician, teaching how to heal the sick. He also teaches nigromancy (the black arts) and can magickally alter people's appearances. He holds the rank of prince or king and has twenty-six legions of lesser spirits to serve him. He appears in the *Book of Oberon*, where his name is alternately given as *Carbas*. Compare this demon in appearance and powers to a similarly leonine

The Hordes of Hell

One of the most compelling treatises on the summoning and binding of demons from the grimoiric tradition is the *Goetia*, a book from the *Lesser Key of Solomon*. Often described as a work of black magick, all of the seventy-two spirits it catalogues are specifically defined as demons. The exact origin of this work is shrouded in mystery, although an early version of it is certainly represented in Wierus's compilation, the *Pseudomonarchia Daemonum*. One of the things that makes the *Goetia* such an interesting text is that it gives specific and often vivid descriptions of how each of these demons is supposed to appear when summoned. Most of the Goetic demons arrive riding a mount of some kind, and frequently this infernal steed is described as "a pale horse."

Readers familiar with the Book of Revelation should immediately recognize this as the steed of the horseman identified as Death in Revelation 6:8. Other demons from the *Goetia* come riding dragons. Some take the form of dragons themselves, and many others are described as soldiers. They are frequently depicted with a lion's head or a serpent's tail. A few are "foul angels," suggesting that they underwent some hideous transformation in the process of their fall from Heaven. The descriptions, too, seem to share some influence from the Book of Revelation. This chilling portion of the Bible, which purports to foretell the end of the world, had a major influence on the iconography of demons. Throughout the text, references are made to dragons, serpents, monsters, and vengeful angels. These beings are both terrible and awesome in their fury. Lions, scorpions, horses, and soldiers armed for battle all contribute attributes to these fearsome composite horrors:

> *The locusts looked like horses prepared for battle. On their heads*
> *they wore something like crowns of gold, and their faces resembled*
> *human faces. Their hair was like women's hair, and their teeth were*
> *like lions' teeth. They had breastplates like breastplates of iron, and*
> *the sound of their wings was like the thundering of many horses and*
> *chariots rushing into battle. They had tails and stings like scorpions...**

There is no denying the impact that these colorful descriptions from Revelation had on later visions of the demonic hordes of Hell, particularly in the *Goetia*. The demons who appear in the form of soldiers or as fierce leonine figures wearing crowns upon their heads all bear echoes of these deadly hosts depicted in this final portion of the Bible.

---

* Revelation 9:7–10, New International Version

demon, Marbas. See also *BOOK OF OBERON*, MARBAS.

Varpiel: One of twelve dukes who serve the wandering prince Macariel. Varpiel's name and seal appear in the *Ars Theurgia*. He holds sway over a total of four hundred lesser spirits and he prefers to take the form of a many-headed dragon. He is tied to no specific hour but may manifest whenever he pleases in the day or the night. See also *ARS THEURGIA*, MACARIEL.

The specter of death. One of the Four Horsemen described in the Book of Revelation. From Doré's *Bible Illustrations*.

Vasenel: A mighty duke with a total of one thousand three hundred and twenty lesser spirits at his command. According to the *Ars Theurgia*, Vasenel himself serves the demon Emoniel, a wandering duke of the air. Vasenel has a fondness for wooded areas and is able to appear during both the day and the night. See also *ARS THEURGIA*, EMONIEL.

Vaslos: A chief duke governed by the demon-king Symiel. Vaslos serves in the hierarchy of the north and has forty ministering spirits under his command. He is connected with the hours of the day and will not manifest at night. According to the *Ars Theurgia*, he possesses a basically good and obedient nature. See also *ARS THEURGIA*, SYMIEL.

Vassago: The third demon named in the *Goetia*, Vassago is a prince with twenty-six legions under his command. He is said to possess the same nature as Agares, another of the seventy-two traditional Goetic demons. Vassago is known as a finder of lost things. In addition, he is able to speak of matters pertaining to the past and the future. Although his name appears in the *Goetia*, he is conspicuously absent from both Wierus's *Pseudomonarchia Daemonum* and Scot's *Discoverie of Witchcraft*. He does, however, appear in the Welsh *Book of Incantations*. In that text, he governs thirty-one legions. In the *Goetia of Dr. Rudd*, his name is spelled *Vasago*. According to this work, he can be constrained in the name of the angel Syrael. See also AGARES, *BOOK OF INCANTATIONS*, *GOETIA*, RUDD, SCOT, WIERUS.

A hideous sea-witch from a medieval woodcut. Mermaids in the Middle Ages were not always attractive, and they were frequently hostile toward sailors and ships. Courtesy of Dover Publications.

Vepar: The forty-second demon of the *Goetia*. According to the *Pseudomonarchia Daemonum* of

Wierus, Vepar takes the form of a siren or mermaid. This appearance is appropriate, for Vepar is a demon connected with the seas. He is said to be a guide of all the waters and especially of ships laden with armor. He can cause the sea to become rough and stormy, and he can further cast an illusion of ships, so the waters seem to be full of oceangoing craft. In addition to all of this, his watery nature allows him to cause wounds to putrefy, filling them with maggots. Through this, he can reputedly kill in three days. He holds the rank of duke and has command over twenty-nine legions. An alternate form of his name is *Separ*. He also appears in Scot's *Discoverie of Witchcraft* and in the *Book of Incantations*. According to the *Goetia of Dr. Rudd*, he is constrained in the name of the angel Michael. This may or may not be the famed archangel Michael. See also *BOOK OF INCANTATIONS*, *GOETIA*, RUDD, SCOT, WIERUS.

Verdelet: A member of the royal household of Hell and the duly appointed Master of Ceremonies. Verdelet appears with these attributions in both Collin de Plancy's *Dictionnaire Infernal* and A. E. Waite's treatment of the *Grand Grimoire*. Verdelet seems to stem entirely from Berbiguier's early-nineteenth-century work *Les Farfadets*. See also BERBIGUIER, DE PLANCY, WAITE.

Verrin: A demon of impatience. Verrin's special adversary is Saint Dominic, who can grant the faithful power to resist the demon's temptations. The name of this fiend is sometimes rendered *Verrine*. The demon Verrin appears in the *Admirable History*, a book by Sebastien Michaelis recounting his exorcism of a nun. See also *ADMIRABLE HISTORY*.

Vessur: According to the Henson translation of the *Ars Theurgia*, Vessur is a demon accorded the title of duke. He is one of twelve infernal dukes said to serve the demon-king Maseriel during the hours of the day. As a demon of rank, thirty lesser spirits obey his command. He is associated with the direction of the south. See also *ARS THEURGIA*, MASERIEL.

Vetearcon: A demon of weakness and disease named in the *Liber de Angelis*, Vetearcon answers to the infernal king Bilet. Under the leadership of this scion of Hell, Vetearcon is conjured to lay a curse upon a hapless victim. The demon then visits terrible suffering upon this person in the form of fever, tremors, and weakness of the limbs. These infernally inspired diseases do not abate until the spell is brought to an end. See also BILETH, *LIBER DE ANGELIS*.

Vijas: A demon connected with visions and scrying, Vijas appears in the fifteenth-century magickal text known as the *Munich Handbook*. He is summoned to assist with a spell of divination that uses a human fingernail to show images of secret things. See also *MUNICH HANDBOOK*.

Vine: The forty-fifth demon of the *Goetia*. According to both Wierus's *Pseudomonarchia Daemonum* and Scot's *Discoverie of Witchcraft*, he first manifests in the strange form of a lion riding upon a black horse and carrying a viper in one hand. Vine is one of the only demons named in the *Pseudomonarchia Daemonum* with no legions of spirits attributed to his rule—a detail that may be an omission from an earlier source. Both the *Pseudomonarchia Daemonum* and Scot's *Discoverie of Witchcraft* agree that this demon is able to magickally build towers and to tear down walls of stone. He can also render waters rough and choppy, making them dangerous for ships. He answers questions concerning the past, present, and future as well as occult matters. He is also very knowledgeable on the subject of witches and will reveal all that he knows. Vine is ascribed the dual rank of king

Princes of the Thumb

Scrying is a divinatory technique that typically makes use of shiny, reflective surfaces to conjure visions. The crystal shew-stone used to summon the spirits of the *Ars Theurgia* is an example of a scrying stone, and the traditional concept of a magick mirror also stems from the practice of scrying—and its use by figures such as Dr. John Dee to conjure not only visions of the future, but also visions of otherwise invisible spirits. While magick mirrors and crystal balls may be relatively familiar to many readers, the idea of scrying in a thumbnail probably sounds a little weird. And yet there are a number of spells devoted to charming spirits into appearing on the reflective surface of a human fingernail.

In the fifteenth-century *Munich Handbook*, there are several variations on this curious divination technique. The magician is told to find a young boy. The boy should be a virgin, usually between eight and ten years old. Oil is rubbed on the child's fingernails so that their surface becomes shiny and reflective. Then the magician stands before the boy and invokes a series of demons. The demons are supposed to appear to the boy on the shiny surface of his fingernails. As the magician asks questions, the boy relates what he sees from the demons.

The use of a boy as an intermediary in spells like this may have given rise to the notion that virgin boys were often sacrificed in the course of the black arts. Although the boy is not directly harmed with this spell, he is a sacrifice, in a way. The magician uses the boy as an intermediary with the infernal spirits so as to better keep himself distant from any harm they may cause. Part of the reasoning behind this is, as an innocent, the child will be less likely to fall to the influence of the evil spirits. This method of divination is far older than the *Munich Handbook*. Nearly identical spells can be found in Hellenic Egyptian magickal texts such as the *Leyden Papyrus*, dating to approximately the third century of the Common Era. The technique is likely older still. The use of the thumbnails specifically in such divination spells led to certain demons being referred to as "princes of the thumb," as in the Jewish magickal text known as *Codex Gaster* 315. According to Professor Richard Kieckhefer, who edited and analyzed the material in the *Munich Handbook*, one Babylonian ritual tablet from approximately 2000 BCE specifically mentions "the master of the nail of this finger" in a ritual that also involves several other elements present in the thumbnail divinations outlined in the Munich Handbook.[*]

---

[*] Richard Kieckhefer, *Forbidden Rites*, p. 116.

and earl. In the *Goetia of Dr. Rudd*, he has thirty-six legions of lesser spirits under his command. He excels at discovering the identities of witches. According to this text, the angel Sealiah has power over him. Variations on his name include *Viné* and *Vinea*. The Welsh *Book of Incantations* also states that he governs thirty-six legions. This text omits any mention of his powers concerning witches, possibly because the book was written by a cunning-man—a profession many at the time equated with *witch*. See also BOOK OF INCANTATIONS, GOETIA, RUDD, SCOT, WIERUS.

Vipos: A great count who appears in the semblance of an angel. He has the power to make people wise and hardy. His name appears in the *Livre des esperitz*, a sixteenth-century French grimoire, where it is said he gives truthful answers on anything asked of him. He holds sway over twenty-five legions of spirits. Compare to the Goetic demon *Ipos*. See also IPOS, *LIVRE DES ESPERITZ*.

A woman consults a sorcerer to spy on her lover through his glass. From a painting by Sir Edward Burne-Jones. Image courtesy of the Wellcome Collection, London.

Virus: In modern times, this word is immediately recognizable: a virus is an infectious agent responsible for everything from AIDS to the common cold. It only seems appropriate, then, that *Virus* also appears as the name of a demon. However, in the fifteenth century the word did not have the same connotations that it does today. Nevertheless, it was not a pleasant word. Originating in Latin, *virus* referred to a slime or a poison. In the case of spell number thirty-nine in the *Munich Handbook*, Virus is a relatively innocuous demon who is summoned to assist the magician with matters of scrying and divination. He is neither infectious nor slimy, despite his name. See also *MUNICH HANDBOOK*.

Virytus: This demon is summoned as part of an elaborate operation for discovering hidden things. He has power over the art of divination, and he is one of several demons mentioned in the *Munich Handbook* in connection with a spell designed to reveal images and hidden information through a process of scrying into a human fingernail. See also *MUNICH HANDBOOK*.

Vm: One of the more peculiar names ascribed to a demon. According to the *Munich Handbook*, Vm is handy with divination spells, and he can help people learn more about hidden and secret things. Although there is no indication whatsoever in the text, it is tempting to presume that Vm bears some relation to the demon Vmon, who also appears in the *Munich Handbook*. Since one appears in spell number thirty-eight and the other appears in the very similar spell number thirty-nine, it is more likely that one of these is a transcription error, and both names reference the same agent of Hell. See also *MUNICH HANDBOOK*, VMON.

Vmon: According to the *Munich Handbook*, Vmon is a demon connected with matters of divination. Vmon's specialty involves a specific method of scrying that allows the magician to obtain information concerning a theft. A variation of Vmon's name may appear one spell later in the guise of the demon Vm. See also *MUNICH HANDBOOK*, VM.

Vnrus: A spirit identified as a demon by the fifteenth-century magickal manual known as the *Munich Handbook*. Although his name sounds vaguely like some unfortunate disease one might not tell one's parents about, Vnrus actually seems relatively harmless. He is summoned in conjunction with a spell concerning divination and the discovery of hidden things. See also *MUNICH HANDBOOK*.

Vom: A demon named in the *Munich Handbook* as part of a spell aimed at scrying and divination. Note the similarities between this name and the demons Vm and Vmon, both named in similar spells. See also *MUNICH HANDBOOK*, VM, VMON.

Vralchim: A fair-minded demon, Vralchim is noted for his ability to help the magician uncover the details of a theft so that the thieves may come to justice and the goods may be recovered. He is summoned as a part of spell number thirty-eight in the fifteenth-century *Munich Handbook*.

Vraniel: An infernal duke who governs forty lesser spirits, Vraniel serves in the hierarchy of the demon-prince Dorochiel. He is connected with the region of the west. His name and seal appear in the *Ars Theurgia*. According to this text, he is bound to the hours of the first half of the night. See also *ARS THEURGIA*, DOROCHIEL.

Vresius: A spirit connected with the art of divination. Although not all of the spirits recorded in the *Munich Handbook* are infernal, Vresius is specifically defined as a demon. He is called to lend his powers to a spell for scrying and visions. See also *MUNICH HANDBOOK*.

Vriel: A duke in the hierarchy of the south under the infernal king Gediel. According to Henson's translation of the *Ars Theurgia*, Vriel is a demon of the night, serving his master only during the hours of darkness. As a duke in the court of the demon-king Gediel, Vriel has dominion over twenty lesser spirits of his own. He is also said to serve the demon-king Raysiel, who rules in the north. Here, Vriel is attended by another fifty ministering spirits of his own, and he appears only during the hours of the day. In the *Book of Oberon*, he is described as a boisterous king who speaks in a hoarse voice. He has powers of transformation, transmuting metals, changing water into wine, and changing fools into wise men. He can also make people invisible. In that text, he is said to be one of the twelve highest-ranking servitors of the king of the north, Egin. His name is given variously as *Vriell* and *Viall*. See also *ARS THEURGIA*, *BOOK OF OBERON*, EGIN, GEDIEL, RAYSIEL.

Vsagoo: This demon, described as a great prince, is purported to have command over twenty legions of lesser spirits. This version of his name appears in the Elizabethan grimoire known as the *Book of Oberon*, where he is said to appear in angelic form. According to that text, he is called upon to give the love of women and also to reveal the location of hidden treasure. His name may be a variation of the more familiar Goetic demon *Vassago*. His name is also incredibly close to that of *Vzago*, another demon named in the *Book of Oberon*, although their offices are different. See also *BOOK OF OBERON*, VASSAGO, VZAGO.

Vual: A demon formerly of the Order of Powers, Vual is one of seventy-two demons named in the *Goetia*. His name also appears in Scot's *Discoverie of Witchcraft*. Vual is said to hold the title of duke. He rules over thirty-seven legions of infernal spirits. He first manifests in the form of a dromedary and he speaks the Egyptian tongue. He procures the love of women as well as the favor of friends and foes. He is also said to speak on matters concerning the past, present, and future. In Wierus's *Pseudomonarchia Daemonum*, his name is spelled *Wal*. In the *Discoverie of Witchcraft*, Scot makes the strange statement that Vual appears as a dromedary in human form. This is likely the result of an error in the translation of Wierus's Latin. In the *Goetia of Dr. Rudd*, Vual is said to appear first as a dromedary and then later in the form of a man. According to this text, he is constrained by the angel Atatiah (this may have been intended to be read *Aliliah*).

The demon *Vua-all*, named in the *Munich Handbook*, may also be a variation of this being. Under the name *Vau-ael*, he may also appear in the Mathers translation of the *Grimoire of Armadel*. Given his treatment in the text, this being is likely a fallen angel. When summoned, he can conjure pleasant visions for the magician. He is said to be a faithful servant with much to teach. His sigil is further reputed to contain secrets for exorcism. See also *GOETIA*, RUDD, SCOT, WIERUS.

Vzago: A demon named in the *Book of Oberon* who appears as an angel. He serves in the court of Egin, king of the north, and his primary office is to gain the favor and esteem of others. He can also change someone's face, make them invisible, or make them wise. His name may be a variant of one of the seventy-two Goetic demons, *Vassago*. The *Book of Oberon* identifies another demon with a very similar name, *Vsagoo*, and while it is tempting to interpret one as a misspelling of the other, the two have very little in common when it comes to their ranks and powers. See also *BOOK OF OBERON*, EGIN, VASSAGO, VSAGOO.

Vzmyas: A demon called upon to bring visions. He has power over the art of divination and can assist those seeking secret or hidden information. In the *Munich Handbook*, he appears in a scrying spell aimed at revealing the culprit in a theft. See also *MUNICH HANDBOOK*.

Waite, Arthur Edward: A writer and student of the occult who lived from 1857 until 1943. American by birth, Waite spent most of his childhood and all of his adult life in Great Britain. He was involved with the Hermetic Order of the Golden Dawn as well as Freemasonry. He authored over seventy books on esoteric subjects, including the *Book of Black Magic and Pacts*, first published in 1910. This work includes partial translations of a number of grimoires, including the *Grand Grimoire*, which Waite viewed as a despicable tome of nefarious magick. His writings were influential in Freemasonry and various aspects of occultism. He is best known for his work with the Tarot. The Rider-Waite Tarot, designed with artist Pamela Colman Smith, has become the most influential Tarot of the twentieth century. Waite's deck redefined much of the Tarot's imagery and interpretation. See also *GRAND GRIMOIRE*.

Watcher Angels: Sometimes also called the *Grigori*, from the Greek word meaning "to watch," the Watcher Angels are heavenly beings believed to have come down to the mortal world in order to mate with human women. They are associated with the Sons of God mentioned in Genesis 6:4. This passage reads: ". . . the sons of God came in unto the daughters of men, and they bare children unto them, the same became mighty men which were of old, men of renown." This story remains a fragment in the Bible, never fully elaborated upon in the canonical text. The full story appears in the *Book of Enoch*, a text that was once considered scripture but was removed from the biblical canon around the third century of the Common Era.

According to the *Book of Enoch*, in the days before the Flood, two hundred Watcher Angels met on the slopes of Mount Hermon and agreed to leave Heaven in order to pursue more human lives. They were led by the angels Azazel and Shemyaza. They took wives from among the daughters of men, siring children and teaching their

In the *Book of Enoch*, the sinful empire of the Watchers is judged and washed away in the Flood. Artwork by Jackie Williams.

new families forbidden knowledge, such as root-cutting, astrology, and the art of cosmetics. The children of the Watchers were giants compared to their mortal mothers, and thus their existence gave rise to the biblical notion of "giants in the earth," translated in the New International Version as *Nephilim*. The plural Nephilim is generally used to refer to these half-angelic offspring. The word is variously translated as meaning "the fallen ones" or, sometimes, "miscarriage"—a reference to the difficult births alleged to accompany the bearing of these giants. The offspring of the Watchers are sometimes also referred to as *Gibborim*, meaning "giants," and *Rephaim*, translated as "heroes" or

"men of renown."[60] The *Anakim*, referenced in Numbers 13:22–33, may also refer to a tribe of descendants from these fallen angels.

The *Book of Enoch* was so thoroughly suppressed once it was cut from the biblical canon that it was lost for over a thousand years. But the legend of the Watchers was a persistent one and it was not limited solely to the *Book of Enoch*. Versions of the tale can be found spread throughout Jewish sources such as the Haggadah and the *Chronicles of Jerahmeel*. References to the Watcher Angels also appear in the *Testament of Solomon*. In this text, many of the demons summoned by the biblical monarch proclaim their status as the offspring of angels. A few claim to be the fallen angels themselves, still walking the earth and causing trouble. The material in the *Testament of Solomon* suggests that the story of the Watchers may in fact lie at the root of the belief that demons and fallen angels reside in the earth seeking to corrupt humanity. In the *Book of Enoch*, the Watchers and all of their children are punished for their transgressions. The angelic fathers are bound hand and foot in the desert, and their half-angelic offspring are wiped from the earth. In Jewish sources like the Haggadah, however, only some of the Watchers are punished. Others, such as Azazel, were thought to remain active in the world. See also AZAZEL, *BOOK OF ENOCH*, SHEMYAZA.

Wierus, Johannes: A humanist scholar with an interest in witchcraft and the occult who lived from 1515 until 1588. His name is sometimes also spelled *Johannes Weyer* or *Wier*. He was a student of occultist Henry Cornelius Agrippa, and he defended Agrippa

---

60. In Reverend W. O. E. Oesterley's *Immortality and the Unseen World*, the word *rephaim* is also presented as a Hebrew term for the dead and sometimes the heroic dead (pp. 63–64).

Inquisitors and Textual Magick

Inquisitors seeking to uncover active witches within the European community spoke out harshly against Pagan charms and folk magick while at the same time employing certain aspects of higher occult magick themselves, such as textual amulets. These protective charms were small slips of parchment inscribed with symbols and phrases from Scripture. Although their magickal formulae were based on phrases from the Bible, textual amulets nevertheless had their roots in similar amulets used widely throughout the ancient world by pre-Christian magicians and occultists.

Despite their Pagan roots, textual amulets were in frequent use throughout Christian Europe in the Middle Ages. Although most of the text on textual amulets was drawn from Scripture, not all of it was recognizable as such. Frequently used phrases were often shortened to sigils that used only the first letter of each key word in the phrase. The same technique of sigil creation is at work with magickal words such as *ALGA*, an abbreviation for *Atah Gibor Le-olam Adonai* ("You, O Lord, are mighty forever").

As textual amulets were part of the magickal tradition that grew up around the written word, these magickal formulae had to be copied by literate individuals trained in the scribal arts—which is to say that nearly all of these amulets were produced by clergy, whether the amulets were sanctioned by the Church or not. Most of the amulets were definitely not sanctioned by the Church, of course, and their very popularity among the peasantry inspired several attempts by the Church to stamp out the practice entirely. Textual amulets proved too popular to completely wipe out, however, and they eventually gained acceptance within the Church instead, giving rise to items such as the now familiar and entirely orthodox St. Benedict medal. This medal started life as a textual amulet, and it was originally rejected as such by the Church, although that shadowy origin has been all but lost in the modern understanding of this amulet's history.

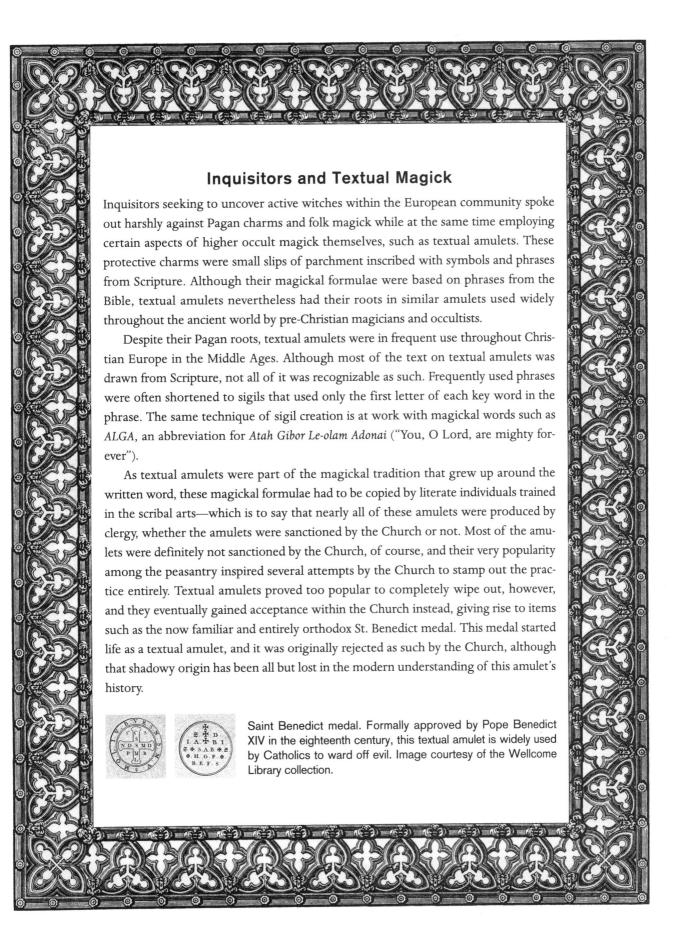

Saint Benedict medal. Formally approved by Pope Benedict XIV in the eighteenth century, this textual amulet is widely used by Catholics to ward off evil. Image courtesy of the Wellcome Library collection.

after allegations of witchcraft and diabolism began to circulate after his death. Wierus's best-known book, *De Praestigiis Daemonum*, was counted among some of the most influential books of all time by Sigmund Freud. Published in 1563, this tome is a humanist approach to the Witchcraze that gripped Europe at the time. Perhaps the most widely recognized portion of this book is an appendix of names entitled *Pseudomonarchia Daemonum*. Wierus faced a good deal of criticism for daring to reproduce these infernal names, and his very interest in compiling such a list raised questions of his own involvement in diabolical matters. Notably, however, Wierus's aim in publishing this material was not to promote the worship of demons but to criticize the gullibility of those individuals who believed wholeheartedly in the practice of witchcraft. The book has been portrayed by some scholars, including Joseph Peterson, as a point-by-point rebuttal of the vitriolic witch-hunter's manual known as the *Malleus Maleficarum*, or "Hammer of Witches," produced in 1486 by Catholic Inquisitors Heinrich Kramer and James Sprenger. See also AGRIPPA, *PSEUDOMONARCHIA DAEMONUM*.

Xaphan: A demon said to hail originally from one of the lower orders of Heaven. According to de Plancy's *Dictionnaire Infernal*, Xaphan was something of an inventor even while he still resided in the heavenly sphere. He was recruited for the rebellion and he devised a plan to blow up the celestial realm. Of course, this plan was never carried out because Xaphan and all his compatriots were overthrown and cast into the Abyss. Residing now in the infernal realms, Xaphan is said to work the forge of Hell itself, fanning the flames for the rest of eternity. His symbol is a bellows. See also DE PLANCY.

Xezbeth: A demon named in the 1853 edition of Collin de Plancy's *Dictionnaire Infernal*, Xezbeth is said to govern illusions, fantasies, and deceit. According to the text, he has so many followers that it is impossible to number them. See also DE PLANCY.

The Power of Names

Names have power. That's something our ancestors firmly believed. Biblically speaking, a single word brought the universe into existence: *In the beginning, there was the Word*. This moment in Genesis strongly echoes a creation myth of the ancient Egyptians, where the utterance of a word is also the catalyst for creation. The power of words—and names—goes back to the very roots of the Western tradition. In addition to having a single word spark creation, the ancient Egyptians placed significant value on a person's name. In order to truly destroy someone, after that person died, every instance of their name was struck from the written record. On papyrus, it was blacked out, and on stone, it was chiseled away until the glyphs were completely unreadable. Unmaking the name was not simply viewed as a symbolic action. If the person was deceased, unmaking the name also unmade the spirit.

In addition to the power held by a person's name, non-human beings had names as well, and these names could summon them, compel them, and bind them. The vast majority of the *Book of What Is in the Duat*, one of the ancient Egyptian manuals of the afterlife, is concerned with names. Every gate that the deceased approaches in the journey through the afterlife has a name, and the dead person is expected to know that name in order to pass through the gate. Names are important both for beneficent guardians that the deceased may encounter and for hungry spirits that may attack the deceased and seek to frustrate this journey. Knowing the names of these beings affords the deceased some protection, for they could then command the spirits—bargaining with the good ones and driving

the evil ones away. The magickal power inherent in names is a theme that repeats throughout ancient Egyptian religious writings, and it most certainly was passed down to the practitioners of Hellenic magick in Egypt's waning years. Magickal papyri found in Egypt, Greece, and Rome all echo this belief in the power of names for commanding gods, demons, and other spirits and for securing their aid in enacting spells.

Ani and his wife in the Egyptian Hall of the Dead. In ancient Egypt, a person was immortal so long as someone remembered their name. Detail from the Papyrus of Ani. 1250 BCE. Image courtesy of the Wellcome Collection, London.

Yaciatal: One of four demons who can empower the Ring of the Sun. The construction of this potent talisman requires animal sacrifice. The finished item is reputed to grant its wielder the power to bind tongues. It can also summon a demon in the form of a great black horse. This infernal steed will convey its master speedily to any destination. Yaciatal is one of the demons invoked to aid in the construction of this item. He appears in the fifteenth-century magickal manual *Liber de Angelis*. See also *LIBER DE ANGELIS*.

Yaffla: A minister of the infernal king Albunalich. According to the Driscoll edition of the *Sworn Book*, Yaffla is associated with the element of earth from the direction of the north. When he manifests, he has a bright and beautiful complexion. In temperament, he is described as being hard-working and patient. He can impart knowledge of the past and future, and he can affect the emotions of other people, inciting rancor and inspiring the baring of swords. He is one of the guardians of all the treasures hidden in the earth. If he considers someone unworthy, he will utterly frustrate them in their search for these buried treasures. For others, he can bestow gold and precious gems in abundance. He also has the power to bring rain. Compare to the demon Yasfla in the Peterson edition of the *Sworn Book*. See also ALBUNALICH, *SWORN BOOK*.

Yasfla: A demon named in the Joseph H. Peterson translation of the *Liber Juratus*, or *Sworn Book of Honorius*. Yasfla is said to serve the demon-king Maymon, who rules the spirits of Saturn. Yasfla is connected to both the planet Saturn and the direction north. He has the power to incite anger and hatred in people. He can also call down snow and ice. He is controlled by the angels Bohel, Cafziel, Michrathon, and Satquiel, who govern all things connected with the sphere of Saturn. Compare Yasfla to the demon Yaffla, who originates from a different version of the same book. See also MAYMON, *SWORN BOOK*, YAFFLA.

Ybarion: A demonic servitor of the infernal ruler Asmodeus. Ybarion is named in the *Sacred Magic of Abramelin the Mage*. In the Mathers translation of this work, this name is rendered *Sbarioat*. Mathers tries to parse this name as something tied to the Coptic tongue. He gives its meaning as "little friend." See also ASMODEUS, MATHERS.

Ycanohl: A demon of war, death, and destruction. In the *Sworn Book of Honorius* as translated by Peterson, Ycanohl is a minister of the demon Iammax, king of the spirits of Mars. He has the power to incite unrest and bloodshed, and when he manifests, he assumes a body that is blood-red and glows like a burning coal. He is constrained by the angels Samahel, Satihel, Ylurahihel, and Amabiel, who control the sphere of Mars. His region is the south. See also IAMMAX, *SWORN BOOK*.

Yconaababur: A demon whose name appears in the Driscoll edition of the *Sworn Book*. Yconaababur is said to serve the infernal king Jamaz, the ruler of the element of fire. He is also connected with the direction south. As a demon of fire, Yconaababur has a nature that is both hot and hasty. He is also described as being energetic, generous, and strong. He will manifest if enticed with the proper perfumes, and when he appears he has a complexion like fire. He is said to have power over decay, either staving it off entirely or reversing its effects. He can also provide familiar spirits that appear in the likeness of soldiers. Additionally, he is said to be able to raise an army of one thousand soldiers. Translator Driscoll suggests that he has the power to call these up from the dead. Finally, Yconaababur is also reputed to be able to cause death at will. See also JAMAZ, *SWORN BOOK*.

Yfasue: According to the fifteenth-century magickal text known as the *Liber de Angelis*, Yfasue serves beneath the infernal king known as the Red Fighter, or *Rubeus Pugnator*. Both he and his master are demons of Mars, and they are called upon to assist in the construction of the enchanted Ring of Mars. Yfasue lends his powers of destruction to this powerful talisman. Once properly charged, the ring can be used to lash out at enemies and utterly destroy them. See also *LIBER DE ANGELIS*, RUBEUS PUGNATOR.

Ygarim: A demonic servant of Beelzebub whose name appears in the *Sacred Magic of Abramelin the Mage*. In Mathers's translation of this work, he gives the demon's name as *Igurim*. Mathers suggests that the name of this demon means "fears." See also BEELZEBUB, MATHERS.

Ygrim: A demon of scrying and divination. He is named in the fifteenth-century *Munich Handbook*, where he is said to aid in the appearance of visions. See also *MUNICH HANDBOOK*.

Ylemlys: According to occultist Mathers, the name of this demon means "the silent lion." Ylemlys appears in connection with the Holy Guardian Angel working in the *Sacred Magic of Abramelin the Mage*. He serves in the court of prince Ariton, one of the four demons said to rule the cardinal directions. His name is alternately spelled *Ilemlis*. See also ARITON, MATHERS.

Ym: In the *Munich Handbook*, Ym appears as a demon of illusion. In this text, he is described as a "squire spirit," and he helps to conjure an illusory castle complete with servants, knights, and a banquet hall. See also *MUNICH HANDBOOK*.

Yobial: A demon named in the *Liber de Angelis*, Yobial is connected with the planet Mars. He answers to the infernal king known as the *Rubeus Pugnator*. Under this fearsome demon's rule, Yobial is summoned to help create the Ring of

Mars with sword and shield and an angel above. Demons associated with Mars took on the bellicose attributes of this ancient god. Engraving by N. Dorigny, 1695. Courtesy of the Wellcome Collection, London.

Mars. This destructive talisman is reputed to give a person the power to strike out at enemies and destroy them. See also *LIBER DE ANGELIS*, RUBEUS PUGNATOR.

Yron: According to the *Liber de Angelis*, a fifteenth-century manual of magick, Yron is one of several demons who serve beneath the infernal king Bilet, also known as *Bileth*. Bilet and his servants can be conjured up by the magician in order to inflict disease. The demons will target any of the magician's enemies, bringing them fevers, tremors, and weakness in their limbs. The demons will not relent unless they are called away from their evil task by the magician himself. The name *Yron* also shows up in the *Book of Oberon*, but here he is one of three demons who minister to King Saba, ruler of Mercury. In this Elizabethan grimoire, he is said to have an attractive appearance and a pleasing voice. His skin is translucent and he wears garments of many shifting colors. He can be called upon to open any lock or loose the bindings of any spirit. He gives victory in both court cases and battles, and can cast down those who have grown too rich and powerful. He raises up the poor, helps regain lost knowledge, and appeases judges. Alvedio and Hanyey are the other two ministers who work with him in the sphere of Mercury. See also ALVEDIO, BILETH, *BOOK OF OBERON*, HANYEY, *LIBER DE ANGELIS*, SABA.

Ythanel: A minister of the infernal king Jamaz, who reigns over the element of fire. According to Driscoll's edition of the *Sworn Book*, Ythanel is a hot-headed, impetuous demon with a complexion like living flame. In addition, he is energetic, strong, and disposed to act generously toward others. He can reverse or prevent decay, and he can cause death at will. He is reputed to be able to raise an army of one thousand soldiers. He also provides familiars. All of these spirits have the appearance of soldiers as well. See also JAMAZ, *SWORN BOOK*.

Zabriel: A demon accorded the title of duke. Zabriel is ruled by Carnesiel, the infernal Emperor of the East. According to the *Ars Theurgia*, Zabriel can be compelled in the name of his master to assume visible form, although a scrying mirror or crystal glass will aid greatly in perceiving this manifestation. See also *ARS THEURGIA, CARNESIEL.*

Zach: This oracular demon can answer all questions concerning matters in the past, present, and future. In the edition of the *Sworn Book* translated by Joseph Peterson, Zach is named as a minister of the demon Habaa, king of the spirits of Mercury. In accordance with his mercurial nature, Zach is said to manifest in a form that shifts and shimmers like glass or white-hot flame. He has a special awareness of all secret thoughts and deeds, and he can reveal the secret affairs of both mortals and spirits. He also provides good-natured familiar spirits. According to the text, he can be compelled in the names of Michael, Mihel, and Sarapiel, the angels thought to govern the sphere of Mercury. See also *HABAA, SWORN BOOK.*

Sigil for the demon Zachariel, as it appears in the *Lemegeton*. Image by M. Belanger.

Zachariel: A demon bound to appear only once per day, Zachariel belongs to the tenth portion of time when the hours and minutes of the day have been divided into fifteen equal parts. According to the *Ars Theurgia*, this demon holds the rank of duke, and he has no fewer than two thousand two hundred ministering spirits to attend to his needs. He is ruled by the demon Icosiel, described as a wandering prince of the air. See also *ARS THEURGIA*, ICOSIEL.

Zaebos: A grand count of Hell, at least according to de Plancy's *Dictionnaire Infernal*, Zaebos is said to have a good and sweet nature. When summoned, he appears riding on the back of a crocodile. He takes the form of a soldier wearing a ducal crown on his head. Given the similarities in their appearances, Zaebos is likely another name for the Goetic demon Sallos. See also DE PLANCY, SALLOS.

Zagal: A demon named in the *Sacred Magic of Abramelin the Mage*. Zagal is said to be a servant of the demon Oriens, one of the four infernal princes of the cardinal directions. In his translation of the *Abramelin* material, Mathers renders this name *Agab*. He suggests that it comes from a Hebrew term meaning "beloved." See also MATHERS, ORIENS.

Zagalo: A servant of the arch-fiend Beelzebub, Zagalo appears in the *Sacred Magic of Abramelin the Mage*. He is one of over three hundred infernal spirits summoned as part of the process of the Holy Guardian Angel rite described in that text. See also BEELZEBUB, MATHERS.

Zagan: The sixty-first demon of the *Goetia*, Zagan is said to manifest like a bull with gryphon's wings. In Scot's *Discoverie of Witchcraft*, he is accorded the dual titles of king and president. In addition to holding dominion over thirty-three legions of lesser spirits, he reputedly has the power of transformation. He can turn water into wine or wine into water. He can also turn blood into wine and wine into blood. In addition, he can turn a fool into a wise man and transform any metal into a valuable coin. In his *Pseudomonarchia Daemonum*, Wierus gives his name as *Zagam*. In the *Goetia of*

Dr. Rudd, he is said to rule over thirty-six legions of lesser spirits. Umabel is the name of the angel that frustrates him. Under the name *Zagam*, he appears in the *Liber de Angelis*. In this text, he is portrayed as a dark spirit conjured at the crossroads at night. He is invoked in the course of a love spell. This is no sweet and delicate spell of amorous love, however. Zagam is tied to a spell of compulsion, intended to rob the will of a woman until she submits to the false passion. According to the text, if a crossroads cannot be easily found, Zagam can instead be summoned in a location where thieves are regularly executed. At this lonely and haunted place, three doves are sacrificed in the name of this demon. Zagam, thus propitiated, will come and leave a symbol or figure in the dust where the working took place. This sign can then be used to compel the love of any woman, forcing her to experience an inextinguishable passion. See also *GOETIA*, RUDD, SCOT, WIERUS.

Zagayne: A demon with powers of transformation, Zagayne can transmute substances and even people. His most useful trick is to change mere dirt into any metal—for example, gold. His name appears in the *Book of Oberon*, a grimoire from Elizabethan England. According to that text, he serves in the court of Paimon, king of the west, as one of twelve principal servitors. He manifests in the form of a wild bull. Compare his name to *Zagan*, one of the seventy-two Goetic demons. See also *BOOK OF OBERON*, PAIMON, ZAGAN.

Zahbuk: A wicked angel invoked in the *Sword of Moses*, Zahbuk is named in association with a curse. This angel, along with several of his malevolent brethren, is called upon to strike an enemy by separating him from his wife. Zahbuk can inspire anger, strife, and infidelity between married couples, but his powers do not stop there. He is also a powerful spirit of disease. He can visit illness and suffering on people, causing sharp pains and terrible inflammations. See also GASTER, *SWORD OF MOSES*.

Zainael: Although this spirit may well be a fallen angel, the *Grimoire of Armadel* identifies him as the spirit that taught magick to Moses himself. According to the text, Zainael was the being that enabled the biblical Patriarch to transform his rod into a live serpent in the contest with the wizards of Pharaoh's court. Zainael is also said to have the power to make people rich. His sigil contains knowledge of divination and can help those who can decode it to obtain the wisdom of the Magi. See also MATHERS.

Zalanes: "The Trouble-Bringer." This demon appears in the Mathers translation of the *Sacred Magic of Abramelin the Mage*. According to the text, Zalanes is ruled by the demon Paimon, one of the four infernal princes of the cardinal directions. In the version of the *Abramelin* material kept in the library at Dresden, this name is spelled *Bulanes*. See also MATHERS, PAIMON.

Zambas: In the Driscoll translation of the *Sworn Book*, Zambas serves as a minister to the demon Zobha. Zambas has the power to tear down buildings and other structures, likely through the use of earthquakes. He is connected with the subterranean regions of the earth, and because of this he is also cognizant of the location of hidden ores and precious metals. If a mortal knows the proper offerings to appease this demon, it is said that he will provide gold and silver in great abundance in response. He is also said to confer honors and dignities, helping those he favors to gain power and influence in the earthly realm. See also *SWORN BOOK*, ZOBHA.

Zamor: In the *Ars Theurgia*, Zamor is said to serve the demon-king Malgaras. Through Malgaras, he is attached to the court of the west. A night-demon allowed only to appear during the hours of darkness, he is said to command a total of thirty subordinate spirits. See also *ARS THEURGIA*, MALGARAS.

Zanno: A demon of illusion with the power to completely deceive the senses. He appears in the *Munich Handbook* in connection with an illusion spell intended to create an entire castle out of thin air. The text describes Zanno as a "squire spirit." To properly call him up, an offering of milk and honey is recommended. He must be called in a remote and secluded location on the tenth night of the moon. His name is also given as *Zaimo* within the text. See also *MUNICH HANDBOOK*.

Zaquiel: One of the Watcher Angels condemned for their sins in the *Book of Enoch*. According to this apocryphal text, Zaquiel and his compatriots were seduced by sins of the flesh. Charged with watching over humanity, they instead indulged in worldly pleasures and took wives from among the daughters of mankind. Zaquiel is named as one of the "chiefs of tens." These were lieutenants of the fallen angels, responsible for leading the others astray. In addition to their sin of lust, the Watchers also taught forbidden knowledge, such as curses and enchantments, to humanity. See also WATCHER ANGELS.

Zaragil: A demon named in the *Sacred Magic of Abramelin the Mage*, Zaragil appears in an extensive list of demons identified as servants of the infernal princes of the four cardinal directions. As such, he can be called in the names of Oriens, Paimon, Ariton, and Amaimon. In 1898, occultist S. L. MacGregor Mathers attempted a translation

A Demon in the Making

If you are a modern aficionado of the paranormal, there is one demon whose name you may feel is missing from this extensively sourced dictionary: *Zozo*.

Known to many as a demon who manifests primarily through Ouija boards, Zozo is portrayed as an ancient and powerful evil. Sometimes he is erroneously equated with the Mesopotamian dingir *Pazuzu*. However, prior to the late 2000s, Zozo didn't exist.

Zozo cannot be found in Mesopotamian lore. His name is absent from biblical and extra-biblical texts. He is not named in Jewish or Muslim sources. No variation of Zozo appears in any of the known grimoires—which is quite a trick, given the number and variety of names recorded in those texts. But if he is absent from all of these sources, then where does the name Zozo even come from?

The answer can be found in the Ouija board he is believed to inhabit.

Ouija boards, patented in 1891, are devices for spirit communication that work primarily through the ideomotor effect. Sitters place their fingers on a pointer, or *planchette*, and the board spells out messages through their collective and largely unconscious micromotions.

When there is no clear direction, or if the group is conflicted about potential answers, the planchette can begin to swing idly from side to side, typically following the arcs of the letters. Those letters are traditionally arranged in two rows: from *A* to *M* and from *N* to *Z*. If the planchette's swing is interpreted as communication, then this arrangement presents a very limited range of possible words: *Mama*, *Nana*, *No-no*, and, of course, *Zozo*. Interestingly, those who believe fervently in the reality of *Zozo* insist that he will give both *Mama* and *No-no* as alternate names—never once questioning how the very layout of the letters could be tied to this perceived communication.

Born from unconscious action and the very human impulse to seek meaning in otherwise random information, Zozo is not a demon but a living element of modern folklore evolving before our eyes. In that respect, he would hardly be the first being fabricated through a mix of fiction, expectation, and belief.

Ouija boards have been used throughout the nineteenth and twentieth centuries to communicate with spirits. Thanks in large part to their representation in the 1973 movie *The Exorcist*, they have become equated with demonic possession. Art by Catherine Rogers.

of this work, and he suggests that this demon's name may mean "Scatterer." In another manuscript of the *Abramelin* material, written in code and kept at the Wolfenbüttel library in Germany, the name of this demon is given as *Haragil*. See also AMAIMON, ARITON, MATHERS, ORIENS, PAIMON.

Zath: A minister of the demon Abas, the infernal king of the subterranean realms. Named in the *Sworn Book* translated by Daniel Driscoll, Zath is said to be able to convey gold, silver, and all manner of metals to those who properly appease him. His connection with the earth also gives this demon an affinity for earthquakes. With this power, he can tear down great buildings by causing the ground beneath them to tremble and shake. He and his infernal brethren also have some power over earthly positions of power. Thus, Zath can help people to gain favor and achieve influence in the mortal world. See also ABAS, *SWORN BOOK*.

Zayme: One of twelve high-ranking ministers to the king of the west, Paimon. Zayme takes the form of a raven and can carry money from place to place. Additionally, he grants visions of distant locations, particularly buildings, serving as a kind of palantir. He can also bestow honor and esteem. His name appears in the *Book of Oberon*, a grimoire from Elizabethan England. See also *BOOK OF OBERON*, PAIMON.

Zelentes: According to the *Munich Handbook*, Zelentes has power over matters of divination. He can lend his skills to spells that involve scrying by inspiring visions of secret and hidden things. See also *MUNICH HANDBOOK*.

Zepar: A demon associated with love and lust, Zepar is the sixteenth demon of the *Goetia*. Ac-

cording to both Wierus's *Pseudomonarchia Daemonum* and Scot's *Discoverie of Witchcraft*, this demon has the ability to inflame women with the love of men. Apparently, if his power to inspire love fails, he also has the ability to transform his targets into different shapes, keeping them thus transformed until such time as they give in to the love spell. He also makes women barren. A grand duke of Hell, Zepar appears in the form of a soldier and has twenty-six legions of lesser spirits beneath him. In the *Goetia of Dr. Rudd*, he appears as a man in red apparel, armed like a soldier. According to this text, the angel Hakamiah has power to control and compel him. See also *GOETIA*, RUDD, SCOT, WIERUS.

Zeriel: According to the Henson translation of the *Ars Theurgia*, Zeriel is a demon in the court of the infernal king Maseriel. Through Maseriel, he is affiliated with the direction of the south. He is one of twelve infernal dukes said to serve Maseriel during the hours of the day. Thirty lesser spirits owe allegiance to him. See also *ARS THEURGIA*, MASERIEL.

Zhsmael: One of several angels named as part of a curse in the *Sword of Moses*, Zhsmael is included with a list of evil angels who possess the power to visit pain and disease upon mortals. The magician invokes this angel and his brethren as part of a spell intended to separate a man from his wife. Zhsmael can inspire distrust and infidelity in the marriage. See also GASTER, *SWORD OF MOSES*.

Zobha: An infernal president of the subterranean realms. According to Daniel Driscoll's edition of the *Sworn Book*, Zobha cannot be conjured directly to appear to mortals. Instead, he relies upon his three ministers, Drohas, Palas, and Zambas, to carry out his will. Serving directly beneath the demon-king

Abas, Zobha has the power to tear down buildings, presumably by causing temblors and earthquakes. He also knows the location of gold and other precious metals hidden deep within the ground, and he will bring great quantities of both silver and gold to those who gain his favor. He has some sway over earthly titles and dignities, and can help mortals to gain honors and influence within the world. In the Peterson translation of the *Sworn Book*, the name of this demon remains the same, but many of his attributions change. Instead of ruling in the subterranean realms, Zobha is a demon tied to the planet Mercury that is also connected to the west and southwest winds. His infernal master is the demon Habaa, the king of the spirits of the planet Mercury. In this version of the *Sworn Book*, Zobha is a demon of secrets, and he is privy to the hidden dealings and thoughts of spirits and mortals alike. He will reveal these secrets to those who consult him, also providing those individuals with good and loyal familiars. See also ABAS, DROHAS, PALAS, *SWORN BOOK*, ZAMBAS.

Zoeniel: One of the demonic servants of Amenadiel, the infernal Emperor of the West. Zoeniel appears in the Henson's translation of the *Ars Theurgia*. According to this text, Zoeniel is a grand duke of Hell, and he has three thousand eight hundred and eighty lesser spirits that carry out his commands. See also AMENADIEL, *ARS THEURGIA*.

Zombar: An infernal king named in the *Liber de Angelis*, he has the power to sow hatred and discord among the living. According to the text, if an image of lead is fashioned in this demon's name, that image will then have the power to inspire strife and hatred in all who pass by it. When it is buried beneath a road near a city or town, the inhabitants will soon become divided by their anger, endlessly fighting amongst themselves. See also *LIBER DE ANGELIS*.

Zosiel: A mighty duke said to command two thousand two hundred lesser spirits. Zosiel serves the wandering prince Icosiel, whose name and seal appear in the seventeenth-century magickal text known as the *Ars Theurgia*. Zosiel will only appear during the hours and minutes of the fourth portion of the day, when the day has been divided up into fifteen equal portions. Zosiel is attracted to people's homes and is most likely to appear in private houses. See also *ARS THEURGIA*, ICOSIEL.

Zsniel: This angel is called upon to go forth and separate a man from his wife in a curse described in the *Sword of Moses*. Zsniel appears in a list of several evil and wicked angels alleged to wield the power to sow strife and infidelity within a marriage. In addition to having the ability to set loved ones against one another, Zsniel is a demon of disease. He can afflict his victims with pain, dropsy, and inflammations. See also GASTER, *SWORD OF MOSES*.

Zugola: A demon named in the *Sacred Magic of Abramelin the Mage*. Zugola is a demonic servant, and he bows to the leadership of Paimon, one of the infernal princes of the cardinal directions. See also MATHERS, PAIMON.

Zynextyur: A demon who serves in the hierarchy of Albunalich, king of the element of earth. Zynextyur is a hard-working demon reputed to help guard the gold and precious stones in the earth. According to the Driscoll translation of the *Sworn Book*, he is described as an even-tempered and patient being whose manifest form is large, with a bright and beautiful complexion. He is known for greedily guarding the precious things buried in the earth. He can wear down and utterly frustrate anyone seeking such treasures if he does not feel that they are worthy to possess them. For those he deems worthy, however, he can bestow gifts of gems and precious metals. He has the power to summon gentle rains, and he is also known for his ability to inspire rancor between people. He has a predilection for certain types of incense and perfumes, and he is more likely to manifest if these are burned for his benefit. See also ALBUNALICH, *SWORN BOOK*.

APPENDIX I:
THE BIBLICAL HOSTS
OF HELL

For as much as the very concept of demons is perceived as being tied to the Abrahamic faiths, the Bible identifies surprisingly few demons by proper names. There are, of course, a few that are familiar: Beelzbub, Bael, Belial, Mammon, Lucifer, Astaroth, Behemoth, Leviathan, and Satan. This brief list reads like a regular who's who in Hell—right up until you actually research where these names came from and what they originally were intended to be.

Many of the names that we widely accept as demons presented in the Bible were not always intended as such by the people who wrote the book in the first place. *Mammon*, for example, is a word that means "riches," and it was originally used to personify the evils of greed. *Belial* was synonymous with wickedness, and when a group of people were referred to as the "children of Belial," it was not always literally intended that they were the children of the demon. Rather, the phrase indicated that they were a wicked people, set

Angels sent to bring pestilence to Rome. Wood engraving by P. Noël, in *Les Merveilles de l'Art et de l'Industrie*, 1869. Image courtesy of the Wellcome Collection, London.

apart from the righteous children of Israel by their improper values and behavior. (This usage appears frequently in the *Testament of the Twelve Patriarchs*, for example.) Eventually, however, names such as Mammon and Belial were taken to represent real, literal beings of evil and not merely concepts. Astaroth, Bael (more properly called *Baal*), Moloch, and even Beelzebub all started life as gods in other cultures. They are demonized in the Bible because they competed directly with the children of Israel's devotion to their one God.

Satan and Lucifer are even more complicated when their origins are compared to what they have come to mean in Western culture. In many ways, our modern understanding of these two names represents an evolution from their original biblical presentation. This transformation can be used to eloquently demonstrate how archetypes change and grow over time. The adversary, *Satan* or *Shaitan*, makes appearances in the Old Testament, but he's not the major player in the Old Testament that he becomes in the New Testament. He plays a direct role in the *Book of Job*, appearing as a specific individual who walks into the court of Heaven and essentially enters into a wager with God over the faith of God's servant Job. But in most other places in the Old Testament, *Satan* is not presented as a unique being. The *adversary* is more of a title or a job description, and it is a role typically taken up by a variety of angels.[61] In the collection of extra-biblical Jewish folklore known as the *Chronicles of Jerahmeel*, for example, the so-called "wicked angel" Samael is described as the "chief of the Satans."[62] In this text, Samael is chosen by God to collect the soul of Moses. Although Samael is depicted in negative terms within the text, he is simultaneously presented as a being subordinate to and subject to the will of God—although he is clearly a wicked angel, he nevertheless still takes his orders from the Lord. This is an idea of Satan, or any satan, that modern Christians often have a hard time conceptualizing: Satan, like any other angel, works according to God's will.

Our modern understanding of Lucifer also has grown well beyond his biblical origins. At this point in our popular mythology, Lucifer is the Light-Bearer, the first and best angel who fell through the sin of pride against God. Or, perhaps, like the Muslim Ibliss, Lucifer is that one prideful being who, when commanded to bow down before humanity, flatly refused and thus turned away from the Almighty. We see these Luciferian tropes reiterated again and again in books, movies, television, and even games, yet very little of this is stated directly about Lucifer in the Bible. Lucifer's most famous biblical appearance can be found in Isaiah 14:12, and as explicit a reference as this may seem, many biblical scholars argue that Isaiah was talking about a mortal ruler and not a celestial being: "How art thou fallen from heaven, O Lucifer, son of the morning! how art thou cut down to the ground, which didst weaken the nations!"[63]

The name *Lucifer* here is the Latin word for "morning star," hence the two have become conflated, particularly in the Latin vulgate (the Latin version of the Bible). Literal interpretations of the Bible often parse this section as referring to Lucifer's expulsion from Heaven, a catastrophic descent that puts the "fall" in "fallen angel." Most biblical scholars, on the other hand, assert that this passage refers to an ancient leader antagonistic to the early Israelites.[64]

Most of the other instances where Lucifer "appears" in the Bible—from the temptation of Eve in Genesis onward—are *implied* appearances, some-

---

61. Elaine Pagels. *The Origin of Satan*, pp. 40–44.

62. Moses Gaster, *The Chronicles of Jerahmeel, or The Hebrew Bible Historiale*, p. 136.

63. Isaiah 14:12, King James Version.

64. Common interpretation tells us this leader was Nebuchadnezzar, the king of Babylon, although there are dissenters to this reading. See Albert Barnes, *Notes, Critical, Explanatory, and Practical on the Book of the Prophet Isaiah, Volume 1*, p. 297.

times where a *shaitan* or adversary is mentioned and sometimes only as an earthly ruler being presented in highly florid terms. Consider the passages in Ezekiel 28: 13–19. These appear to speak of a cherub who was "perfect in thy ways from the day that thou wast created, till iniquity was found in thee"(Ezekiel 28:15). These passages are often cited for the argument that Lucifer originally belonged to the angelic Order of the Cherubim. And yet, the passage as popularly quoted typically omits the lines that give context to Ezekiel's criticism of this "cherub." A few lines earlier, Ezekiel is instructed to prophesize to the prince of Tyrus (Ezekiel 28:2), and when that crucial detail is included, it is clear the cherub refers to the prince and no one else.

As we have come widely to identify the king of fallen angels as *Lucifer Morningstar*, you might expect that the Bible simply codes him as such, using *Morning Star* in place of Lucifer when expounding upon his evil. The morning star in Latin is just Lucifer, after all.

The passage in Isaiah 14:12 is not the only occasion in the Bible where the Morning Star is equated with a living person. The other significant instance, however, has little to do with the fallen angel Lucifer. The New International Version of the Bible has the following statement in Revelation 22:16: "I, Jesus, have sent my angel to give you this testimony for the churches. I am the Root and the Offspring of David, and the bright Morning Star." Isaiah's earlier passage clearly does not use the morning star as a reference to Jesus, but its use in Revelation indicates how dangerous it can be to assume that all references to the Morning Star are referential to Lucifer.

Over and over again, we fill in the blanks with the name of our expectation. The majority of our modern depictions of Lucifer owe less to biblical canon and more to literature adjacent to or inspired by biblical texts: from the many sectarian documents discovered at Qumran on down to the work of the blind poet Milton, whose *Paradise Lost* defined the perceptions of demons, Lucifer, and Hell for most of the English-speaking world.

APPENDIX II: WHERE DEMONS COME FROM

Part One: Visions of Hell

Most discourses on demonic entities approach them as beings that inhabit a realm separate from that of ordinary reality. Frequently, the realm of demons is depicted as being both adjacent to and underneath the mortal realm—a chthonic empire of shadow and flame that serves as a kind of dungeon for fallen souls. This vision of the underworld echoes Sumerian ideas of the afterlife as expressed in documents like the *Epic of Gilgamesh*. Here, the realm of the dead is a subterranean land of darkness where the souls of the departed huddle like mournful birds amid squalor and dust: "There is the house whose people sit in darkness; dust is their food and clay their meat. They are clothed like birds with wings for covering, they see no light, they sit in darkness. I entered the house of dust and I saw the kings of the earth, their crowns put away forever."[65]

This dismal realm of the dead is perhaps influenced by early Sumerian burial practices: the dead were often interred under the dirt floors of their own homes, and their spirits were thought to continue in some semblance of life, residing in the space beneath the earthly home they inhabited in life.[66] Notably, the squalid unpleasantness of the Sumerian underworld is not explicitly intended as a place of punishment or remediation. As far as their mythology indicates, death was simply viewed as an unpleasant state of affairs.

A more familiar Christian vision of Hell often involves a fiery underworld in which the souls of the damned face eternal torture for their transgressions. Christianity's fiery visions of the underworld may have been influenced by very real perceptions of volcanoes, where deep places in the earth are

---

65. N. K. Sandars, *The Epic of Gilgamesh*, p. 92.

66. Paul Collins, "Everyday Life in Sumer," *The Sumerian World*, p. 355.

clearly associated with magma and steam.[67] But an ancient Egyptian influence may also be posited. In the collection of documents known widely as the *Egyptian Book of the Dead*, one of the punishments of undeserving souls involves immersion in a lake of fire.[68] The idea that the underworld—or at least the shadowy realm of the dead that lies beyond our more familiar mortal world—contains a lake of fire as a place of suffering and torment is several thousand years older than the religion that inspired Milton's poetic depiction of Lucifer.

Christianity is not the only belief system to present a place in the afterlife dedicated to punishment for the unworthy, although it is certainly one of the few to present that punishment as eternally retributive as opposed to remedial. The *Garuda Purana*, a Hindu holy text and one of the Vishnu Puranas, details the experiences of the soul after death. Of particular interest to our purposes are the descriptions of the states between death and rebirth, where the souls of sinners are tortured in the realm of Yama, god of death:

"Some of the sinful are cut with saws, like firewood, and others thrown flat on the ground, are chopped into pieces with axes. Some, their bodies half-buried in a pit, are pierced in the head with arrows. Others, fixed in the middle of a machine, are squeezed like sugar-cane. Some are surrounded closely with blazing charcoal, enwrapped with torches, and smelted like a lump of ore."[69]

The pain and misery visited upon unworthy souls in Yama's realm would be perfectly at home in any Christian vision of Hell, with one salient exception: Yama's torture is reparative, meaning that it is intended to help souls let go of their flaws before they are subsequently released for rebirth. Unlike the Christian concept of damnation, the suffering inflicted in this Hindu vision of Hell is temporary.

Betwixt and Between

Other depictions of the realm of demons present it not as a place of punishment but merely as an existence different from our own (albeit one that is often full of horrors). In his collection *Strange Stories from a Chinese Studio*, author Pu Songling describes people who are chosen from birth to move between the earthly realm and the Hell realm, functioning essentially as tax collectors for the damned.[70] Based in Taoist concepts of a Yin world of spirits and a Yang world of flesh, the "space" occupied by demons in Songling's work is separate from and yet contiguous with our own—as proved by the tremendous amount of traffic carried out between the two realms. The Islamic belief in Jinn similarly places these non-human beings in an "invisible world" that is both distinct from and adjacent to the material realm populated by humanity.[71] All of this suggests that the realm of spirits—whether those spirits are classed as Jinn, yokai, or demons—exists in tandem with our mortal realm. Our worlds are two aspects of a larger whole, and despite being inhabited by beings of a different substance, interlocution is possible between these realms.

---

67. In the *Aeneid*, Virgil places the entrance to the underworld in a volcanic cave near Lake Avernus. The Roman poet was drawing upon a much older tradition. According to Strabo, when Odysseus went to commune with the dead, he did so on the shores of Avernus. See Eleanor Winsor Leach, "Viewing the Spectacula of Aeneid 6," in *Reading Vergil's Aeneid*, p. 115.

68. R. O. Faulkner. *The Ancient Egyptian Book of the Dead*, pp. 68–69, 118–119.

69. *Garuda Purâna*: Chapter III: 49–51, translated by Ernest Wood and S. V. Subrahmanyam.

70. Pu Songling, *Strange Stories from a Chinese Studio*.

71. Amira El-Zein, *Islam, Arabs, and the Intelligent World of the Jinn*.

Demons, flying through the air, torment Saint Anthony. Reproduction of an engraving by M. Schongauer, circa 1470–1475. Image courtesy of the Wellcome Collection, London.

Although it is not often expressly stated, this interconnected model was also at work throughout the Middle Ages and Renaissance in Europe. There, witchfinders, Inquisitors, and theologians all posited a world populated by evil spirits, any of which could be called up by mortals willing to formulate a pact with dark powers. This placed demons simultaneously separate from yet adjacent to the mortal realm—and able to move into that realm, despite doctrinal belief that demons were bound effectively as prisoners in Hell.

In works like the *Malleus Maleficarum*, the infamous "Hammer of Witches" written to educate on their powers and habits, demons are often depicted as spirit-beings, invisible and intangible to all save those to whom they wish to appear. This holds true within the grimoiric tradition as well, where demons are often described as having ethe-real, or "airy," bodies[72]—language that at once acknowledges some consistent form yet distinguishes that form from mortal clay. And yet, airy as they are, they can also assume a completely tangible form, appearing as a black dog or goat at the Witches' Sabbat. According to reports in both the *Malleus Maleficarum* and the *Compendium Maleficarum*, these proxy forms encountered by witches were physical enough to allow for the consummation of sex acts.

Nowhere was this physicality of spirits clearer than in the writings on incubus and succubus demons. Reports of incubus and succubus attacks were related to folk traditions of the night hag, or mara.[73] These beings were thought to appear to mortals in their sleep, often pressing them down upon their bed to suffocate them. One distinct difference separating the myths of the incubus and succubus demons from those of the night hags is the explicitly erotic element of the incubus and succubus reports. Simply put, these demons appeared expressly to have sex. The incubus appeared as a male demon and typically approached women in their sleep. The succubus was the female counterpart of this demon,

---

72. This concept has its roots in the theological writings of St. Augustine. Aquinas, writing in the thirteenth century, argued instead that angels (and, by extension, demons) must have no bodies at all. Proponents of both positions debated throughout the Medieval and Renaissance periods. See Benjamin W. McCraw, "Augustine and Aquinas on the Demonic," *Philosophical Approaches to Demonology*, pp. 24–25.

73. Carl Lindahl, John McNamara, and John Lindow, *Medieval Folklore: A Guide to Myths, Legends, Tales, Beliefs, and Customs*, pp. 291–292.

and she would make nightly visits to slumbering men.[74]

Frater Ludovico Sinistrari, writing in the late seventeenth century, drafted what has become the definitive source on incubus and succubus beliefs of his day.[75] As Sinistrari recounts, some theologians believed that these beings were spirits only and simply assumed an illusory form that appeared male or female. As Sinistrari himself says in this approach to the phenomenon, it is seen as "nothing but phantasmagoria, glamour, and diabolical spells."[76] This illusion could nevertheless trick men into giving up their seed to the demons through nocturnal emissions, which the demons essentially harvested as succubi, later appearing as incubi to women and using the stolen sperm to impregnate them.

That incubus demons were responsible for impregnating women—particularly nuns who claimed to have had no congress with mortal men—was accepted as true in Sinistrari's day. The emission and retention of seed was then used to explain why, for example, the child thus begotten just so happened to resemble the local bishop. Rather than impugn the honor and celibacy of either the bishop or the nun, incubus and succubus demons were blamed, for these demons were particularly notorious for visiting holy men and women in the night in an attempt to tempt and torment them.

Sinistrari himself rejected the idea that incubus and succubus demons were beings purely of spirit, positing instead a kind of halfway point between spirit and flesh. In this, he saw them as beings that occupied both worlds, capable of moving between them at will (much like the Islamic Jinn). Sinistrari based this conclusion on a number of points that made sense to him in his day, not the least of which was his assertion that incubi and succubi did not merely steal other people's seed, but were capable of reproducing with humans in their own right. The proofs he offers for this reproduction reveal a deeper thread in the complicated tapestry of Medieval and Renaissance demonology. First, let us take a look at what Sinistrari says. Then, in the next section, we'll delve into how and why this is so significant.

Sinistrari states: "Now, it is undoubted by Theologians and philosophers that carnal intercourse between mankind and the Demon sometimes gives birth to human beings ... They further observe that, from a natural cause, the children thus begotten by Incubi are tall, very hardy, and bloodily bold, arrogant beyond words, and desperately wicked."[77]

This description is very specific but, presented without further context, is hardly a convincing argument that these tall, bold, and arrogant children are undisputedly the hybrids of demons. Clearly, Sinistrari is writing with more information in mind—something more profound than merely a personal observation regarding one or two children supposedly sired by a visit from an incubus.

A little later in his treatise, Sinistrari cites the main inspiration for his argument. He believes that children can be born of mixed human and de-

---

74. Incubi and succubi could and would cross gender lines. The distinction between the two types of demon was less a matter of perceived gender and more a matter of preferred sexual positions. *Incubus* is from the Latin verb *incubare*, which means "to lie down upon." *Succubus* evolved from the Latin *sub-cubare*, meaning "to lie beneath."

75. Ludovico Sinistrari, *Demoniality.*

76. Ludovico Sinistrari, *Demoniality*, p. 6.

77. Ludovico Sinistrari, *Demoniality*, p. 21.

monic heritage because of the Bible. At one point, he mentions the example of the Antichrist, but his biblical source is even older than *Revelation*:

"We also read in the Bible, Genesis, ch. vi., v. 4, that giants were born when the sons of God went in to the daughters of men; this is the actual text. Now, those giants were men of great stature, says Baruch, ch. iii, v. 26, and far superior to other men. Not only were they distinguished by their huge size, but also their physical powers, their rapine, and their tyranny."[78]

Sinistrari is referencing a tradition woven within the canonical biblical narrative as well as throughout Apocryphal texts adjacent to accepted Scripture. It is the story of the Watcher Angels, and even though its primary testament, the *Book of Enoch*, was lost to Western Christendom for nearly a thousand years, this tale profoundly influenced the demonology of Western Europe. Several concepts key to the Solomonic tradition rely upon the Watcher narrative, so it behooves us to take a closer look at this story.

PART TWO:
THE WATCHERS OF ENOCH

Scattered throughout what Christians know as the Old Testament, there are fragments of an unfinished tale. It is a tale of love, lust, betrayal, and divine retribution. These fragments hint at the existence of angelic beings who abandoned their place in Heaven in order to cohabit with the daughters of men. Often referred to as Watchers, or *yryn*,[79] these beings are connected with the Flood story

in Genesis, where they are described as "sons of God," or *bene ha Elohim*:[80]

"And it came to pass, when men began to multiply on the face of the earth, and daughters were born unto them, that the sons of God saw the daughters of men that they were fair; and they took them wives of all which they chose...There were giants in the earth in those days; and also after that, when the sons of God came in unto the daughters of men, and they bare children to them, the same became mighty men which were of old, men of renown."[81]

The story of these Watcher Angels is never fully elaborated upon in the Bible as it has come down to people today. Instead, the lines that do exist merely hint at a much bigger story for which there is little context.

Biblical scholars, ancient and modern alike, have had mixed feelings about this enigmatic passage in Genesis, sometimes seeking to explain away its meaning and sometimes seeking to gloss over the lines entirely.[82] The story of the Watchers is theologically problematic for a number of reasons, not the least of which being its presentation of angels as corporeal beings capable of begetting children—a quality that flies in the

---

78. Ludovico Sinistrari, *Demoniality*, pp. 25–26.

79. Ida Fröhlich, "The Figure of the Watchers in the Enochic Tradition (1–3 Enoch)," *Henoch*, p. 9.

80. *Elohim* is one of the words in the Bible translated into English as *God* (the other main one being *YHWH*). Notably, Elohim is a form that is plural. Nevertheless, in translation, it is represented as singular. The implications that this word could be a linguistic artifact pointing to a pre-monotheistic time are difficult to ignore.

81. Genesis 6:1–4, King James Version.

82. Alternate theological positions interpret the so-called "sons of God" as either human men figuratively identified as *bene ha elohim* due to their position as judges or as the righteous sons of Seth, as opposed to the wicked children of Cain. For further elaboration on these points, see Jeremy Hultin, "Jude's Citation of 1 Enoch," in *Jewish and Christian Scriptures: The Function of "Canonical" and "Non-Canonical" Religious Texts*, pp. 113–28.

face of key articles of faith established during the development of Christian doctrine and codified with the Fourth Lateran Council.[83] Despite the apparent contradictions in a story of angels commingling with humanity, the tale of the Watchers as told in the *Book of Enoch* was widely influential throughout the ancient world, with evidence of this influence in the sacred writings of both Christians and Jews (and, arguably, Muslims, in later tales of Jinn).[84]

Finding Enoch

The story of the *Book of Enoch* begins, at least as far as we are able to verify through primary materials, in a remote settlement in the inhospitable reaches of the Judean desert on the northern shore of the Dead Sea. The settlement of Khirbet Qumran, established by a sectarian movement of Second Temple Jews known as the Essenes,[85] is best known in modern history as the site of the discovery of the *Dead Sea Scrolls*.[86] Better known to scholars as the *Qumran manuscripts*, these scrolls represent an unprecedented trove of scripture that

sheds light both on Second Temple Judaism and on the earliest development of Christianity. For context, before the discovery of the Dead Sea Scrolls, the oldest known version of the Hebrew Bible was dated to the tenth century of the Common Era. The Qumran manuscripts—which contain, among other things, every book of the Hebrew Bible except for the Books of Esther and Nehemiah—push that date back by 1,200 years.

The Dead Sea Scrolls are important not only because of all the versions of traditional biblical texts they contain; these texts also shed light on the books that either never made it into the formal biblical canon or got lost along the way.[87] Among these are multiple copies of texts concerned with the Watcher Angels and their children, the Giants, all of which are fragments of the broader Enochic material.

The *Book of Enoch*, which is actually a composite of several works, is officially labeled a *pseudepigraphal* text. These extra-biblical writings are attributed to an ancient author, while their true authors remain anonymous. Generally, the name of a famous patriarch was adopted in order to give the book more apparent authority. Such texts were typically cut from the biblical canon when their authorship was called into question or because they contained heterodox views. Often, one reason engendered the other.

In the case of the *Book of Enoch*, Church fathers still exuberantly accepted the book as Scripture

---

83. George J. Marshall, *Angels: An Indexed and Partially Annotated Bibliography of Over 4,300 Scholarly Books and Articles Since the Seventh Century B.C.*, p. 2.

84. Jeremy Hultin, "Jude's Citation of 1 Enoch," in *Jewish and Christian Scriptures*, p. 114.

85. Not all scholars agree that the Essenes wrote the Dead Sea Scrolls. See Hillel Newman, *Proximity to Power and Jewish Sectarian Groups of the Ancient Period*.

86. The Dead Sea Scrolls were first discovered by a trio of Bedouins between November 1946 and February 1947. Excavation continued through the 1950s, ultimately revealing no fewer than ten caves, each filled with jars packed with scrolls. Since the initial discovery of seven scrolls, nearly a thousand texts, in various states of disrepair, have been recovered from the caves of Qumran. Many have been translated. See Michael O. Wise, Martin G. Abegg Jr., and Edward M. Cook, *The Dead Sea Scrolls: A New Translation*.

87. The official term for such lost books of the Bible is *Apocrypha*, from a Greek word meaning "hidden," "concealed," or "obscured." Some Bibles contain apocryphal texts, typically including them at the end so it is clear that they are separate from the canon. Other Bibles omit them entirely. Choices made about the inclusion or exclusion of apocryphal texts vary widely across the many sects of Christianity.

up through the first and second centuries of the Common Era. (At that point, it had already dwindled in popularity among Jews, in part because of its influence on early Christianity.[88]) Clement, Athenagoras, Irenaeus, and Tertullian all accepted the book as canon. Tertullian, in fact, identifies Enoch as the "oldest prophet."[89] Notably, the *Book of Enoch* is referenced as an authentic book in the Bible itself: the prophecy of Enoch is quoted in the Epistle of Jude 14–15. Other Christian and Jewish texts contain references to the *Book of Enoch* as well, including the *Book of Jubilees*, the *Testament of the Twelve Patriarchs*, the *Apocalypse of Peter*, and the *Epistle of Barnabas*, attesting to its influence.[90]

Despite his own fervent opinions of the *Book of Enoch*, Tertullian, who lived between 155 and 220, acknowledged that some Christians had begun to question its authenticity. Writing at the end of the second century CE, he was the first to make this observation. From Tertullian onward, it is possible to trace the trajectory of opinion on the *Book of Enoch* through the developing works of Church fathers. Origen, who lived from 184 to 253, demonstrates a devolution in Enoch's favor across his career. While Origen's earlier writings refer to the *Book of Enoch* as Scripture, by the end he changes his opinion, ultimately stating that *Enoch* is accepted as Scripture only by a Christian minority.[91]

Adam and Eve Expelled from the Garden. Line engraving by Raphael Sadeler, 1583. Courtesy of the Wellcome Collection, London.

St. Augustine, who lived between 354 and 440 CE, rejects the book entirely, offering the excuse that it is simply too ancient to verify—although it probably didn't hurt that its depiction of angels went against his assertion that spiritual beings cannot have fleshly bodies.[92]

By the ninth century CE, Nicephorus, patriarch of Constantinople from 806 to 815, was one of the last to mention the *Book of Enoch* in a way that suggested he had actually read the text. He discusses it in his list of canonical and uncanonical books at the conclusion of his *Chronographiae Compendium*. Around the same time, the book is included in the chronology of George Syncellus. After that, nothing but rumors about the *Book of*

88. Tertullian specifically declares that Jewish opinion on the *Book of Enoch* dwindled in direct response to the text's importance among Christians. See James Drummond, *The Jewish Messiah: A Critical History of the Messianic Idea Among the Jews from the Rise of the Maccabees to the Closing of the Talmud*, p. 72.

89. Jeremy Hultin, "Jude's Citation of 1 Enoch," in *Jewish and Christian Scriptures*, p. 115.

90. Jeremy Hultin, "Jude's Citation of 1 Enoch," in *Jewish and Christian Scriptures*, 113–114.

91. Jeremy Hultin, "Jude's Citation of 1 Enoch," in *Jewish and Christian Scriptures*, p. 117.

92. Benjamin W. McCraw, "Augustine and Aquinas on the Demonic," *Philosophical Approaches to Demonology*, pp. 24–25.

Enoch remained throughout Europe and the Western world.

At the beginning of the seventeenth century in Europe, one of those rumors became persistent: the *Book of Enoch* had survived in Ethiopia. In conversation with the French astronomer Nicolas-Claude Fabri de Peiresc, a Capuchin monk from Egypt insisted that he had read the by-then fabled *Book of Enoch* in the Ethiopian language of *Ge'ez*.[93] Peiresc, who lived between 1580 and 1637 and had a passion for collecting antiquarian curiosities, became immediately obsessed. He did not rest until he had acquired something sold to him as the *Book of Enoch*. It was, of course, in Ge'ez, and while Peiresc was an incredibly learned man, there is great doubt that he could read it, for, although the title page declared the little vellum manuscript the *Book of Enoch*, later inquiries proved that it most decisively was not.[94] When this disappointing fact was revealed, most stopped looking for the *Book of Enoch*, although stories about it continued to circulate. In 1703, J. A. Fabricus curated a collection of quotations, allusions, and references to the *Book of Enoch*, drawing mainly from the works of Greek and Latin writers of the first four centuries, fanning the flames of interest even more.[95] But it was not until the late 1700s that anyone in Europe managed to lay their hands upon the near-mythic tome.

---

93. John Kitto, *The Cyclopaedia of Biblical Literature*, vol. 1, p. 629.

94. Instead, the book, which remained in Peiresc's library until his death, was a collection of biblical retellings mixed liberally with uniquely Ethiopic folk beliefs. It can be read in a modern translation under the title *The Book of the Mysteries of the Heavens and the Earth* by E. A. Wallis Budge, with a foreword by R. A. Gilbert.

95. See J. T. Milik, *The Books of Enoch: Aramaic Fragments of Qumran Cave 4*, p. v.

The Ethiopian Adventure

James Bruce was a huge red-headed Scot who proudly traced his heritage back to none other than Robert the Bruce, the famous fourteenth-century Scottish king. A Freemason of the Scottish Rite, Bruce's main occupation was exploration. In the 1770s, he took it upon himself to discover the source of the Blue Nile, a journey that took him deep into the country then known as *Abyssinia* (modern-day Ethiopia). As recounted in Bruce's travelogue of his adventures, pragmatically entitled *Travels to Discover the Source of the Nile*, he acquired three copies of the *Book of Enoch* from a monastery at Gondar.[96] Bruce seems to have had some idea about the importance of the text (and there are conspiracy theories that suggest the real incentive for his trip down the Nile was to recover this and other religious texts for the Freemasons), but once he had it, it wasn't translated out of Ge'ez for nearly thirty years. In 1800, a version of Bruce's *Book of Enoch*, sometimes termed the *Ethiopic Enoch* or *I Enoch*, was translated into Latin by Silvestre de Sacy.[97] The text wasn't widely available in an English translation for several more decades, although once it was, the book was reprinted copiously.[98]

How (and why) did the Church in Ethiopia preserve a piece of Scripture lost to the rest of Christendom? This is a complicated question, and while the full answer requires a good deal of backstory, there is a simple, if superficial, response: that piece

---

96. James Bruce, *Travels to Discover the Source of the Nile*.

97. Silvestre de Sacy, "Notice sur le livre d'Enoch," *Magazin Encyclopedique*, p. 382.

98. I delve further into the *Book of Enoch*'s creative legacy in the nineteenth century (including its influence on the poet Lord Byron) in my work the *Watcher Angel Tarot Guidebook*.

Detail of an Ethiopian protective amulet with prayers written in Ge'ez. The figure striking down the demon is Susenyos, a seventeenth-century Ethiopian emperor and folk hero. Image courtesy of the Wellcome Collection, London.

ing these teachings into their own language from probably the fifth century onward.[100]

Ethiopian Christianity had followed its own path from the very beginning. The faith developed a vibrant and distinct expression due to the unique geographical and cultural milieu of the country.[101] Following the Council of Chalcedon in 451, both Rome and Byzantium sought control over the Christians in Ethiopia, but the country remained staunchly tied to the Coptic Church of Alexandria, which had distinguished itself as separate from both. In the seventh century, when Islam overtook Alexandria, Ethiopia had no further guidance from Christian authority beyond what they maintained for themselves. Despite internal conflicts, the country resisted Muslim invasion, retaining its own unique religious character and continuing to develop in relative isolation for the next five hundred years. As a result, the Ethiopian biblical canon developed a very different character from what became familiar throughout Europe. To this day, the only complete version of the *Book of Enoch* is in Ge'ez, preserved under the title *Mäshafä Henok*, and until the discovery of the Dead Sea Scrolls, scholars thought it was the oldest example to survive.

of Scripture was part of the Bible when the Ethiopians adopted the text. Whether it came along with Christianity or Judaism is up for debate, as both religions made converts in Ethiopia,[99] but at no point did the *Book of Enoch* stop being viewed as canon by the Ethiopians as they began translat-

---

99. Saheed A. Adejumobi, *The History of Ethiopia*, p. 171.

100. Nickelsburg and VanderKam assert that the original *I Enoch* was composed in Aramaic and then translated into Greek. Thus, the document in Ge'ez is the translation of a translation. See George W. E. Nickelsburg and James C. VanderKam, *1 Enoch*, p. 13.

101. The same can be said of Ethiopian Judaism. "The ceremonies & observances of the [Ethiopian] church, however, were drawn from many sources and framed an amalgam unique to itself." Some of these influences included Coptic Christianity, heterodox Judaism practiced among native Axumite tribes, and Axumite paganism (which itself was imported from Saudi Arabia and was derived from the religion of the Sabaeans). See R. A. Gilbert's foreword to *The Book of the Mysteries of the Heaven and the Earth*, edited by E. A. Wallis Budge, p. x.

An Ancient Tale

The texts stored in the caves of Qumran vary in age across several centuries. Some were written as recently as the first century CE, while others date as far back as the third century BCE.[102] The Enochic fragments at Qumran are among some of the oldest texts in the caves, particularly the portions of the first section known to scholars as the *Book of the Watchers*.[103] Of its thirty-six chapters, 1 Enoch 6–11 and 1 Enoch 12–16 represent the oldest stratum of Enochic material.[104] The full text that we know as the *Book of Enoch* is a composite of several works edited over time,[105] and even the *Book of the Watchers* shows signs of redaction and addition, suggesting that the versions stored at Qumran developed from an even older tradition.

Could this mean the Watcher story preserved in the Enochic material gave rise to the story in *Genesis*? Current scholarly opinion suggests that the *Book of the Watchers* arose in response to the fragmented tale in Genesis 4:1–6 and is intended to elaborate on that story. By this reasoning, the document is essentially a *Midrash*, a type of Jewish religious writing that provides exposition on the underlying meaning or significance of an established biblical text.[106]

Whether *Genesis* or *Enoch* came first is less significant to our current line of inquiry than the fact that I Enoch is a pre-Christian text that existed in a place and a time that hugely impacted developing Christian views (and, by extension, Western notions of demonology). The Essenes stood at the ideological crux between Second Temple Judaism and early Christianity, and their literature is reflective of this tumultuous and liminal time. They were a sectarian group: Due to ideological differences (primarily a growing dualism incompatible with strict Jewish monotheism),[107] they had split from the orthodoxy of their day. In modern terms, we would think of them as a doomsday cult, because they were wholly convinced that a war was coming for which they had to prepare. This was not a worldly war, although they believed its ultimate expression would play out in the physical realm, but a spiritual war between the opposing forces of Darkness and Light.[108]

Many of the texts gathered by the Essenes at their settlement in the desert are what biblical scholars call *apocalyptic* texts: these texts speak of

---

102. These dates are still debated by scholars. Notably, Gregory L. Doudna writes: "In fact, existing radiocarbon data, while confirming second and first century BCE dates of scribal activity among the Qumran cave finds, do not confirm scribal activity in the first century CE." See Doudna, "The Legacy of an Error in Archaeological Interpretation," in *Qumran: The Site of the Dead Sea Scrolls*, p. 153.

103. Chapters 1–36 in the *Book of Enoch* are identified as the *Book of the Watchers*. These may date as far back as 300 BCE. See Marianne Dacy, "The Fallen Angels in the Book of 1 Enoch Reconsidered," *Henoch*, p. 28.

104. According to Annette Yoshiko Reed, "These and other factors have led scholars to propose that 1 En. 6–11 represents one of the most ancient strata in the *Book of the Watchers*, possibly even preserving a 'literary unit of distinct origin' or a part of 'an independent midrashic source.'" See Reed, *Fallen Angels and the History of Judaism and Christianity*, p. 25.

105. Loren T. Stuckenbruck actually identifies at least nineteen distinct literary traditions within *I Enoch*. See Stuckenbruck, "The Book of Enoch: Its Reception in Second Temple Judaism and in Christianity," *Early Christianity*, p. 8.

106. Notably, Annette Yoshiko Reed disagrees: "In my view, it is likely that 1 En. 6–11 was shaped by oral traditions about angelic descent and specific fallen angels, and it is significant that these traditions reflect far more than mere exegesis of Gen. 6:1–4." See Reed, *Fallen Angels and the History of Judaism and Christianity*, p. 29.

107. "Dualism is evident throughout the works of the Qumran Community and, in fact, is considered central to Qumran belief." From Miryam T. Brand, *Spirited Evil: Persian Influence and Its Limits in Qumran Texts*, p. 32.

108. Liora Goldman, "Dualism in the 'Visions of Amram,'" *Revue de Qumran*, pp. 421–432.

the end of the world, or at least world-changing events, and how the righteous may triumph. The *Book of Enoch*, notably, is classed as an apocalypse, and this is likely one of the reasons it appealed so strongly to the Essenes. (They kept multiple copies of the text at Qumran.) The eschatology of the Essenes, their growing interest in a war between the factions of Darkness and Light, their belief that angels headed the armies on both sides—these same ideas influenced early Christianity and had an indelible impact on demonology as it is currently understood in the Western world.[109]

The Watchers' Tale

The story begins with the "Rebellion of the Watchers."[110] Here, a figure named Shemihazah[111] addresses a company of two hundred Watcher Angels and encourages them to join him in the "great sin"[112] of choosing wives from among the daughters of men. The rebel Watchers[113] are described with language that clearly relates this story to Genesis 6: 1–4. Spurred both by Shemihazah's words and their own desire for these beautiful

women, the Watchers swear an oath together that binds them to the enterprise.[114] I Enoch 6:7 contains a list of twenty names in addition to Shemihazah, describing these as "their chiefs of tens."[115]

In the next section, we learn that the Watchers took wives and began having sex with them. As they joined with their mortal wives, they also taught them "sorcery and charms" and "the cutting of roots and plants."[116] This knowledge is presumably forbidden, or at least ordinarily reserved only for the sons of God. At this point, however, the text does not explicitly decry this instruction in magick as sinful, but it becomes important later.

Many of the Watchers' wives conceived and "bore to them great giants."[117] Most retellings of this tale equate the giants with the Nephilim, but that is not precisely the case. The text actually defines three distinct generations proceeding from the Watchers. First are the giants. From the giants come the Nephilim,[118] and from the Nephilim are born beings called *Elioud*, an obscure term not used outside of the Enochic material. All of these hybrid children share qualities with the giants, as I Enoch 7:2 says, "And they were growing in accordance with their greatness."[119]

In the very next passage, the text states that these hybrid children had appetites that out-stripped

109. It's important to note, however, that these ideas were not exclusive to the Essenes but represented a developing stream of dualism in the broader cultural milieu. See Shaul Shaked, "Iranian Influence on Judaism: First Century BCE to Second Century CE," in *The Cambridge History of Judaism*.

110. George W. E. Nickelsburg and James C. VanderKam, *1 Enoch*, p. 23.

111. Variants of this name include Shemyaza, Semihaz, and Shemhazai.

112. I Enoch 6:3. See George W. E. Nickelsburg and James C. VanderKam, *1 Enoch*, p. 23.

113. In the *Midrash of Shemhazai and Asael*, the Watchers actually ask permission of God to go down to the earth. Their purpose is to redeem humanity from wickedness. Although God warns them against this plan, he also does not stop them. In this version, the corruption comes from a quality inherent in the earthly plane itself, not from the heavenly Watchers. See Moses Gaster. *The Chronicles of Jerahmeel, or The Hebrew Bible Historiale*.

114. I Enoch 6:4–5. See George W. E. Nickelsburg and James C. VanderKam, *1 Enoch*, p. 24.

115. I Enoch 6:7, See George W. E. Nickelsburg and James C. VanderKam, *1 Enoch*, p. 24.

116. I Enoch 7:1, See George W. E. Nickelsburg and James C. VanderKam, *1 Enoch*, p. 24.

117. I Enoch 7:1–2.

118. This word *Nephilim* is often used interchangeably with the giants in other biblical writings. Notably, in Bereshit 6:1–4 of the Tanakh, the Hebrew version of Genesis 6: 1–4, the phrase rendered *giants in the earth* in the King James version instead refers to the Nephilim.

119. George W. E. Nickelsburg and James C. VanderKam, *1 Enoch*, p. 24.

the world into which they were born. They ate everything the sons of men could produce, and when that food ran out, they began to kill and eat people. These appetites, combined with the children's size, should sound familiar from the work of Ludovico Sinistrari.

The children's impossible appetites may have been seen as an inevitable result of their hybrid nature, or at least one symptom of this. Among the many prohibitions of the ancient Jews was something called *kilayim*, a rule against mixing different kinds of animals, plants, and even fibers in clothing. The Watchers commit this sin by mixing their heavenly stock with earthly women. By this reasoning, the very existence of the Watchers' children was an affront to the divinely mandated order of nature.[120]

For the rest of this passage, the children of the Watchers engage in a demonic rendition of *The Very Hungry Caterpillar*. They go after birds, beasts, creeping things, and fish, finally escalating to devouring one another's flesh and drinking the blood.[121] The detail about drinking blood further highlights the unnatural appetite of the Watchers' descendants. A key part of the Jewish kosher laws is founded on the biblical admonition against the drinking of blood.[122] After all of this wickedness,

An angel looks on, impassive, as men, women, children, and animals all drown in the Flood. Etching by c, 1800s. Courtesy of the Wellcome Collection, London.

I Enoch 7:6 tells us, "Then the earth brought accusation against the lawless ones."[123]

We know from the fragment in *Genesis* that all of this ultimately leads up to the Flood, but the text takes a detour to further explore the issue of forbidden knowledge. Nickelsburg and others identify this section as an interpolation, a portion of the story added in the early evolution of the text to enlarge upon the Watchers' narrative.[124] A new angelic leader is introduced under the name of *Asael*.[125] Asael teaches weaponsmithing and "every instrument of war."[126] Asael's arts of the forge are not limited to weapons of destruction. He teaches gold and silversmithing, the crafting of jewelry, and the secrets of precious stones. In

120. Ida Fröhlich, "The Figure of the Watchers in the Enochic Tradition (1–3 Enoch)," *Henoch*, p. 11.

121. I Enoch 7:3. See George W. E. Nickelsburg and James C. VanderKam, *1 Enoch*, p. 25.

122. This is recorded in Leviticus 17:12: "Therefore I say to the Israelites, 'None of you may eat blood, nor may any foreigner residing among you eat blood.'" Bible, New International Version. Notably, blood contains the spirit of an animal, and that substance is reserved for God alone.

123. George W. E. Nickelsburg and James C. VanderKam, *1 Enoch*, p. 25.

124. Reed, *Fallen Angels*, p. 28; Fröhlich, p. 9; et al.

125. Significantly, this name is rendered *Azazel* in a related Qumran text, the *Book of the Giants*. Many comparisons have been made between this figure and the similarly named figure from Leviticus related to the Jewish Day of Atonement. See Reed, *Fallen Angels and the History of Judaism and Christianity*, pp. 97–98.

126. I Enoch 8:1. See George W. E. Nickelsburg and James C. VanderKam, *1 Enoch*, p. 25.

a detail that connects him firmly to traditional depictions of Azazel, he also teaches cosmetics and dye-making, so the Watchers' wives can make many-colored clothes.[127]

Asael is not the sole instructor in new and forbidden knowledge. Shemihazah reappears in the next line at the top of a list of tutelary Watchers. According to the passage, Shemihazah teaches spells and root-cutting, details that directly echo I Enoch 7:1. Other Watchers teach the signs of the earth, sun, moon, lightning, and stars. The names of these Watchers each reflect the knowledge they impart. I Enoch 8:3 explicitly states, "And they all began to reveal mysteries to their wives and to their children." Then, in a line parallel to the hungry children story, I Enoch 8:4 says, "As men were perishing, the cry went up to heaven."[128]

There is a lot to unpack here. First, in Shemihazah's portion of the tale, the main sins revolve around lust and improper mixing of peoples. Forbidden knowledge is touched upon in the Shemihazah material but not directly identified as a cause of destruction. In Shemihazah's tale, the real problem ends up being the Watchers' children themselves, who are simply not meant to exist on the mortal plane. They are effectively monsters (the Qumran text known as the *Book of Giants* explicitly describes them as such), and it is in response to their very existence that the earth cries out.

Asael's section frames the tale instead around issues of forbidden revelations. The Watchers teach their wives and children information that has dangerous implications. With Asael's weapons of war, the danger is overt: war hurts people.

But Asael's other gifts are less obviously problematic: eye makeup, "ornaments for women,"[129] and dye for clothes. Here, the threat seems to revolve around temptation. Women who wear makeup and jewelry and clothes of many colors are more enticing, and from the perspective of this text, that enticement leads to wickedness.

The litany of natural signs imparted by the other Watchers is harder to reconcile as inherently detrimental. The transgression here seems to revolve more around the improper transmission of otherwise sacred (or at least heavenly) mysteries. The same can be said of Shemihazah's spells and root-cutting, unless these were intended to be used for cursing and poisoning. Basically, in this section, Shemihazah and the other Watchers teach humanity magick, and everyone is punished for it.

The Punishment

The rest of the passages associated with the *Book of the Watchers* tell about the repercussions of the Watchers' sins. Whether those sins involve lust or knowledge, the result is the same: death and destruction. The earth and its people suffer at the hands of the Watchers' progeny, and eventually the complaints reach God. God decides that the Watchers and the empires they've built with their children have spread wickedness throughout the earth and enough is enough. After sending his angels out to inflict some serious retribution,[130] he plans for the whole planet to be wiped clean. All of this tracks pretty closely with the biblical account of the Flood, with elaborations to account for the two leaders of the Watchers and the numerous children.

---

127. I Enoch 8:2. See George W. E. Nickelsburg and James C. VanderKam, *1 Enoch*, p. 25.

128. George W. E. Nickelsburg and James C. VanderKam, *1 Enoch*, pp. 25–26.

129. I Enoch 8:1. See George W. E. Nickelsburg and James C. VanderKam, *1 Enoch*, p. 25.

130. As a sidenote, this is one of the first places that we see the names of all four archangels appear in a biblical text.

One archangel is dispatched to warn Noah about the impending Flood. (The angel is called *Sariel* in the Nickelsburg translation, a name curiously close to that of the Watcher who teaches the signs of the moon.[131]) Raphael gets the job of capturing Asael. God instructs him to "bind Asael hand and foot, and cast him into the darkness. And make an opening in the wilderness that is in Doudael. Throw him there, and lay beneath him sharp and jagged stones. And cover him with darkness, and let him dwell there for an exceedingly long time."[132]

Gabriel gets the job of killing all the giants and other half-breeds (or, more specifically, arranging for them to kill one another). If there was any question about whether or not their existence was seen as a violation of the *kilayim* prohibition, the language of this passage clears that right up: "Go, Gabriel, to the bastards, to the half-breeds, to the sons of miscegenation; And destroy the sons of the watchers from among the sons of men; Send them against one another in a war of destruction."[133]

Michael is sent after Shemihazah and the others. First, they are forced to watch their children die. Then, "[once] they see the destruction of their beloved ones, bind them for seventy generations in the valleys of the earth, until the day of their judgment and consummation, until the everlasting judgment is consummated. Then they will be led away to the fiery abyss, and to the torture, and to the prison where they will be confined forever."[134]

Writing at least in the second century BCE and probably much earlier, the author of this section establishes a vision of Hell and damnation that has haunted Western civilization ever since. Consider that, prior to this, the Jews had a vision of the underworld that was ambiguous at best. Neither Heaven nor Hell precisely, *Sheol* was a place of dust and darkness, very clearly influenced by the Babylonian and Sumerian visions of the afterlife.[135]

In the Enochic material, the place of punishment is directly referred to as an abyss—at least three centuries before the *Book of Revelation* was even penned. It is a dark and fiery pit in which sinners are bound, to be released only upon the day of final judgment. The tradition represented by *I Enoch* is almost certainly where we get this familiar vision of Hell. The only difference is in the names of the fallen angels first bound there. In later centuries, we would name the first to fall Lucifer or Satan. In the Enochic tradition, the leaders of the Watchers are the first bound in Hell: Azazel and Shemihazah.

Other concepts foundational both to Western demonology and Western magick are established in this text. The knowledge transmitted by the Watchers to their wives and children is echoed in every grimoire that has come down to us where an angel—fallen or otherwise—is conjured for the purpose of instructing the sorcerer in some forbidden art. Consider the amount of ink spilled in the lists of spirits recounting not only their rank but also their areas of expertise. Angels (holy or fallen) teach philosophy, sciences, mathematics, alchemy, magick, and other mysteries not simply because their otherworldly status grants

131. George W. E. Nickelsburg and James C. VanderKam, *1 Enoch*, p. 27.

132. I Enoch 10: 4–5. See George W. E. Nickelsburg and James C. VanderKam, *1 Enoch*, p. 28.

133. I Enoch 10:9. See George W. E. Nickelsburg and James C. VanderKam, *1 Enoch*, p. 29.

134. I Enoch 10:11–12. See George W. E. Nickelsburg and James C. VanderKam, *1 Enoch*, p. 29.

135. *The Epic of Gilgamesh* translated by N. K. Sandars, p. 92.

Jacob wrestles the angel. He wins only because the angel must flee before dawn, an acknowledgment of the liminal nature of this being. Illustration of Genesis 32:24–32 by Salvator Rosa, 1766. Courtesy of the Wellcome Collection, London.

them access to divine knowledge but because a precedent was set portraying them as willing purveyors of such information.

Another concept influenced by the Watchers' tale is the magickal notion of *Witchblood*. This is a supernatural heritage that predisposes a person to more-than-human powers, specifically revolving around witchcraft.[136] While *Enoch* is certainly not the only document to record the idea, it has nevertheless been one of the most influential in Western society. It also establishes the notion that otherwise spiritual beings, angels, can manifest physically in the world and even take up regular residence within it. Variously throughout Western folklore, the legacy of the Watchers has been

identified as a source of supernatural beings in the world, from faeries to vampires.[137]

Finally, and most pertinently to our current inquiry, the Watchers' tale establishes the nature and reason for the demons that haunt the mortal world. In a section that describes the fate of the Watchers' doomed children, we learn:

"The spirits that have gone forth from the body of their flesh are evil spirits, for from humans they came into being, and from the holy watchers was the origin of their creation. Evil spirits they will be on the earth, and evil spirits they will be called. The spirits of heaven, in heaven is their dwelling; but the spirits begotten on the earth, on earth is their dwelling. And the spirits of the giants lead astray, do violence, make desolate, and attack and wrestle and hurl upon the earth and cause illnesses.... These spirits will rise up against the sons of men and against the women, for they have come forth from them."[138]

They're demons. The progeny of the Watchers all become demons bound to the earth.

In case there is any uncertainty about this, a passage from *Jubilees* that scholars agree is directly inspired by the Enochic texts,[139] tells us that, in the days after the Flood, Noah's sons were led astray by "unclean demons."[140] The Watchers are specifically named as "the fathers

---

137. For the far-reaching impact of myths of the Watchers, consider Lady Wilde's matter-of-fact observation that all faeries are fallen angels and their kin. See Lady Wilde, *Legends, Charms, and Superstitions of Ireland*, p. 89.

138. I Enoch 15: 9–11. See George W. E. Nickelsburg and James C. VanderKam, *1 Enoch*, p. 37.

139. Loren T. Stuckenbruck, *The Myth of Rebellious Angels: Studies in Second Temple Judaism and New Testament Texts*, p. 84.

140. R. H. Charles, *The Book of Jubilees, or The Little Genesis*, 2005, 10:1.

---

136. Michael Howard explicitly identifies the Witchblood as an inheritance from the Watchers. See Michael Howard, *The Book of Fallen Angels*.

of these spirits,"[141] and translator R. H. Charles confirms that these are "the spirits which issued from the children of angels and the daughters of men."[142] Asael/Azazel and Shemihazah/Shemyaza are not named in this text, however. Instead, the leader of these earth-bound spirits is called *Mastema*, and a few passages later, he is equated with Satan.[143]

This idea that demons are the angry spirits of disembodied giants—a class of being related to, yet categorically different from, fallen angels—would come to play a significant role in Western demonology. First and foremost, it established a clear reason for demonic possession: robbed of their own flesh, these powerful angelic hybrids sought to overtake the bodies of humans. By any means necessary, they wanted to live again.

In this, the spirits of the Watchers' children are not motivated merely by an evil nature. They are jealous, angry, and committed to reclaiming some taste of the existence that was stolen from them. This represents a shift in attitude toward demons and demonic possession that can be felt down to the present day. Demons were hardly a new concept at the time of the Enochic material. Judaism had inherited a wealth of demons from the Babylonians, who had in their turn inherited most of their demonology from the Sumerians.[144] But these demons afflicted humanity primarily because their nature made them agents of destruction and disease. There was nothing complicated or personal about it; they were just bad. With the "unclean spirits" that issued from the slain children of the Watchers, things became personal.

And now it was war.[145]

---

141. R. H. Charles, *The Book of Jubilees, or The Little Genesis*, 2005, 10:5.

142. R. H. Charles, *The Book of Jubilees, or The Little Genesis*, 2005, p. 79.

143. R. H. Charles, *The Book of Jubilees, or The Little Genesis*, 2005, 10:8–11.

144. I explore this more fully in my book *Sumerian Exorcism*.

145. For those gathered at Qumran, this war was literal, one that they fully anticipated to play out upon the earth, as evidenced in texts like the *War Rule*: "For the Instructor, the Rule of War. The first attack of the Sons of Light shall be against the forces of the Sons of Darkness, the army of Belial." Col. 1, The War Scroll.

APPENDIX III:
THE TESTAMENT OF SOLOMON

In a previous section, we explored how the tale of the Watcher Angels linked the children of the Watchers with demons. According to these beliefs, the children of the fallen angels remained bound to the earth, typically in the form of restless spirits. Because so much had been taken away from them, these restless spirits were thought to delight in the torment and destruction of humanity.[146] We might not have a written record linking this belief to the later European beliefs in demons if not for a curious text dating to some point between the first and third centuries of the Common Era. Known as the *Testament of Solomon*, this book is significant to our study for a number of reasons, not the least of which being the fact that it establishes a direct line between the tradition of the Watcher Angels and later European demonology.

The *Testament of Solomon*, like the *Book of Enoch* before it, is a pseudepigraphal text. It was not written by the biblical King Solomon. Instead, his name was used to lend the text greater credibility. Additionally, his name was attached to this particular text because of a legend that had come to surround King Solomon. Although there is no reference to this whatsoever in the Bible, a persistent belief developed in the ancient world that Solomon, because of his great faith and wisdom, was given the power to command and control demons.[147] When exactly this belief came into play is uncertain, but it enjoyed a colorful existence in the Talmudic tradition of the Jews, and by the writing of the *Testament of Solomon* it was firmly established among Christians as well. Notably, the Solomonic tradition, which often involved the binding of demons into vessels of brass, lies also at the

---

146. In the *Book of Jubilees*, a tenth of the spirits of the dead giants are allowed to harrow the children of earth. See R. H. Charles, *The Book of Jubilees, or The Little Genesis*, 2005, 10: 8–13.

147. In Islamic lore, Solomon controls not demons but Jinn. See Amira El-Zein, *Islam, Arabs, and the Intelligent World of the Jinn*.

heart of many Arabian myths concerning genies, or Jinn. Although they exist a long way down the line of transmission, the tales of *The Thousand and One Arabian Nights* show a strong influence from this same belief in Solomon's power over spirits.

So how did the people of the early Christian world come to believe that Solomon could command demons? According to biblical stories, King Solomon was the wisest of men. The successor of the much-loved King David (who slew the giant Goliath with a single well-placed stroke from his slingshot), King Solomon is credited with many wonders. It was Solomon who designed and built the Temple of Jerusalem, which ultimately housed the famed Ark of the Covenant.

An artist's vision of Solomon's Temple. According to the *Testament of Solomon*, demons aided in its construction. Woodcut possibly based on work by the Jesuit Villalpandus (1552–1608). Courtesy of the Wellcome Collection, London.

Many myths have grown up around King Solomon's work with the temple. The Knights Templar, first established in 1118 CE, took their name from Solomon's Temple. They made their base upon the Temple Mount and were rumored to be seeking lost treasures and artifacts hidden beneath the ruins of the temple. The Freemasons claim connections to the Templars but also to the masons who labored to complete King Solomon's Temple. Their mythic figure, Hiram Abif, may have historic roots in King Hiram of Tyre, a foreign ruler who provided money and materials to Solomon for the construction of his costly and elaborate temple.

If an extra-biblical text is to be believed, King Hiram of Tyre wasn't the only person helping Solomon build his legendary temple. According to the Testament of Solomon, a text dating to around the third century of the Common Era, King Solomon conscripted demons as slave labor for the temple project. The document, written in Greek with a style reminiscent of the New Testament, describes how a young worker, favored by King Solomon, was beset by a demon. The demon, whose name was Ornias, preyed upon the young laborer, slowly causing the boy to waste away. When King Solomon learned of this unnatural predation, he prayed day and night for the Lord God to deliver the demon unto his power. According to the *Testament of Solomon*, an Archangel finally appeared and delivered to Solomon a ring bearing a special seal. Through this finger-ring, the Lord God gave Solomon power over the demons that dwelled in the earth. The *Testament of Solomon*, supposedly written by Solomon himself for future generations, claims to record the names and offices of these demons, as well as the angels that have the power to command and bind them.

With such a heavenly gift, Solomon wasted no time gaining influence over the demons in the world. Ornias was the first to be bound. Solomon not only stopped Ornias from preying upon the young worker but also saw fit to punish the demon by commanding him to perform menial labor for the construction of the temple. With Ornias's help, Solomon then called up demon after demon, including Asmodeus, Beelzebub, and even a form of Lilith. He questioned each, learned the angel that held power over them, and then commanded them in the name of his God to bend their powers to lowly tasks such as cutting Theban marbles, mixing clay for bricks, and cutting and carrying wood. The demons weren't too thrilled with this slave labor, but they were powerless to resist as long as Solomon had the ring conferred by God.

Although it is highly doubtful that the Temple of Jerusalem was actually constructed with the aid of demons, the *Testament of Solomon* remains a compelling tale, and its treatment of demonic entities, in particular the methods of calling and binding them, laid the foundation for traditions of ceremonial magick that developed later in Western Europe. For our purposes, one of the most intriguing pieces the *Testament of Solomon* has to offer to our puzzle of the development of Western demonology and the connection of fallen angels is a series of statements directly relating to the Watchers.

When King Solomon calls several of the demons up, they tend to puff themselves up and make all manner of threats before realizing that they have no hope of resisting the power conferred to Solomon in the form of the heavenly seal. When Solomon calls Asmodeus to bind him, the demon rebukes the ancient king, saying, "But how shall I answer thee, for thou art a son of man; whereas I was born an angel's seed by a daughter of man."[148]

Later in the same text, Beelzeboul, identified as the prince of demons, declares himself the last of the angels of Heaven who came down. Then he talks about his son who haunts the Red Sea, just in case there was any question that he was referencing the Enochic tradition.[149] These statements alone reveal the close connection between the *Testament of Solomon* and the tradition of the Watcher Angels.

The *Testament of Solomon* establishes a number of concepts upon which are built the very foundations of Solomonic magick. First, there is a significance given to the decans of the zodiac. These number thirty-six, and accordingly, Solomon is presented a demon for each one.[150] There is the magickal seal given to Solomon in the form of a ring. The demons must obey whoever wields this. This "Seal of Solomon" later gives rise to a profusion of images passed along through the grimoires, many of which are designed to control individually named demons. Some of these seals are scribed on parchment or etched in metal and held or worn as a lamen. Others, like Solomon's, are worn as a ring.

The names themselves were also talismanic. Knowledge of a demon's name was one part of their control, and that control was completed with knowledge of the angel who presided over them. In a few rare cases, this "angel" actually turns out to be one of the many secret names of God, but for the most part, every demon has an angel in

---

148. F. C. Conybeare, Aleister Crowley, and S. L. MacGregor Mathers, *The Three Magical Books of Solomon*, p. 271.

149. F. C. Conybeare, Aleister Crowley, and S. L. MacGregor Mathers, *The Three Magical Books of Solomon*, p. 273.

150. In later iterations of the Solomonic tradition, the number of demons rises to seventy-two. This number, significant throughout the grimoires, also appears in connection with Solomon and the Jinn in Muslim traditions. Notably, thirty-six, if doubled, yields seventy-two.

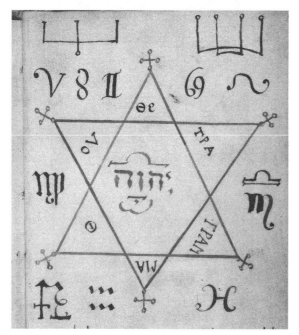

The Star of Solomon surrounded by astrological symbols. Detail of a page from the eighteenth-century grimoire *Clavis Inferni*. Image courtesy of the Wellcome Collection, London.

counterpart. Although the text is rarely clear on the precise relationship entwining these beings, given what we know of the Watchers, it is tempting to conjecture that at least some of the angels hold sway over their demons as parent to child.

APPENDIX IV:
THE STAR OF
BAPHOMET

Perhaps the most widely recognizable symbol of the black arts is the so-called *Sabbatic Goat*, a five-pointed inverted pentagram with the head of a goat depicted within the star. This image is frequently also associated with the demon Baphomet, and in some systems, it is called the *Goat of Mendes*. The use of this inverted star in connection with LaVeyan Satanism and other antinomian traditions has led to a certain amount of confusion concerning five-pointed stars in general, and their association with magick and the occult.

The five-pointed star, when transcribed point-up within a circle, is a symbol used widely by modern Pagans to represent the four elements of earthly existence bound and overseen by spirit, magick, or Will. This use of the five-pointed star is in no way infernal or demonic. Similarly, the five-pointed star has a positive use in Pennsylvania Dutch hexes and can be found in use as a good luck charm on private residences across the state of Pennsylvania, where it is so ubiquitous that the

From Satanists to heavy metal bands, the Star of Baphomet is a popular antinomian icon. Art by Catherine Rogers.

vast majority of individuals who hang this symbol on the outside of their houses are likely ignorant of its origin as a hex.[151] The five-pointed star is also used within the iconography of Freemasonry.

---

151. Pennsylvania has a colorful history of magick and hexenkraft, thanks to its Pennsylvania Dutch population. See William W. Neifert, "Witchcraft," in *The Pennsylvania-German: A Popular Magazine of Biography, History, Genealogy, Folklore, Literature, Etc.*, pp. 114–121.

In particular, it is used to represent the women's branch of Freemasonry, known as the Order of the Eastern Star.

The five-pointed star, point-up or otherwise, was not always a symbol associated with demons or the Devil. So when did its association with the black arts begin? The following quote is taken from a journal published by a London-based Masonic lodge, the Quatuor Coronati, in 1902:

"From old Greek times the Pentagram has been the symbol of Hygeia and Health, and is mentioned by Pythagoras. We may here observe that when it is erect, i.e., with one point vertical it is the Christian symbol, or the talisman, or the Masonic Star; but the Kabalists also use it in an inverted position and then it refers to the Devil and Black Magic, and has the names of the 'Witch's Foot' or the 'Head of the Evil Goat.'"[152]

This quote demonstrates that, at least by the early 1900s, the association of the inverted five-pointed star with the Sabbatic Goat had been established. This statement from Eliphas Levi is slightly older:

"The star of the microcosm or the magic Pentagram, that star wherein the human figure was sketched by Agrippa with the head in the ascending point...The Burning Star which, when inverted, is the hieroglyphic sign of the goat of black magic.[153]

Notably, Levi, whose work Waite is compiling in this book, lived between 1810 and 1875. His books were published around the 1850s. So the association of the pentagram with the black arts in general and the Sabbatic Goat (Baphomet) goes back at least to Levi and the mid-1800s.

The five-pointed star and talismans specifically called *pentacles* and *pentagrams* appear in works on ceremonial magick such as the *Clavicula Salomonis* (*Key of Solomon*). Most surviving copies of these works date to the sixteenth and seventeenth centuries, but Johannes Trithemius, who lived in the 1400s, includes several manuscripts by this name in a list of books on magick. This list, along with several of the relevant works, are available for public perusal on Joseph H. Peterson's informative site, EsotericArchives.com.

Although these pentacles are certainly associated with ceremonial magick, it's important to note that they are not expressly associated with black magick or Satanic imagery. That association seems to be largely a nineteenth-century construct—though it may have its roots in the dilettante Satanism that grew popular in France near the end of the 1700s.

---

152. J. W. Horsley, "Solomon's Seal and the Shield of David Traced to Their Origin," *Ars Quatuor Corontorum, 1902,* p. 52.

153. A. E. Waite, *The Mysteries of Magic: A Digest of the Writings of Eliphas Levi,* p. 323.

APPENDIX V:
A PAGAN PERSPECTIVE ON ANGELS

Throughout the biblical tradition, the angels—messengers of God—occupy a curious space beneath God but above humanity. Not expressly depicted as divine themselves, they are nevertheless otherworldly beings who, though capable of assuming the form of men, are clearly not mortal men themselves. The ambiguous nature of angels as they appear in the biblical tradition proved so problematic during the age of the Reformation that the Protestant branches of Christianity chose to abandon the veneration of these heavenly beings entirely. Most Protestant arguments against the inclusion of angels in Christian iconography suggested that the veneration of these beings tread dangerously into the territory of idolatry. There may be more truth to this than anyone suspected at the time.

The angels that appear in the biblical tradition were almost certainly gods and goddesses belonging to a polytheistic religion that predated and ul-timately evolved into Jewish monotheism.[154] If the *Book of Job* is any indication, this angelic pantheon was overseen by a chief deity[155] in much the same way that Zeus presided over the gods of Olympus. According to scholarly interpretations, Psalm 82 records the radical split of this chief deity from his pantheon of gods (for ease of reference, the original word being translated variously as *God* and *the gods* in the Psalm appears in brackets):

"God [Elohim] takes his place in the court of the mighty, to pronounce judgment among the gods [also Elohim]: How much longer will you judge unjustly?...This is my sentence: Though you

---

154. "One subject on which there is now widespread, though not universal, agreement is the identity of the sons of God. It is now generally held that they denote God's heavenly court, what were originally seen as gods but later, with the emergence of absolute monotheism, became regarded as angels." In John Day, *From Creation to Babel: Studies in Genesis 1–11*, p. 77.

155. "Yahweh was identified with the original patriarchal god, El Shaddai." In Avner Falk, *Psychoanalytic History of the Jews*, p. 74.

447

are gods, all sons of the Most High [Elyon], yet you shall die as mortals die, and fall as any prince does. Arise, O God [Elohim], and judge the Earth, for all the nations are yours."[156]

In this passage, which remains in the Bible to this day, the chief deity, who is equated with the biblical God, sentences all the other gods beneath him to death as he asserts his supremacy. But, when it comes to folk beliefs, it is not that easy to topple a preexisting pantheon. Even when the empowered priesthood declares that the old gods are dead, their worship continues—whether overtly or in secret. Many religious systems will seek to demonize the gods and goddesses that have fallen out of favor, but, in the case of particularly entrenched pantheons, assimilation is often a more effective route.

This seems to have been the case with the angels.

Once the idea of this chief deity's supremacy began taking root, over time, the other gods and goddesses took progressively more subordinate roles to him. Eventually, the chief of the gods became *the* God—specifically the one Western civilization is acquainted with through the Bible. Once this occurred, rather than abandoning the other gods entirely, the people from whom we have inherited this belief system essentially demoted the lesser gods. The other members of the pantheon retained their place in the heavenly council, only they were no longer officially viewed as gods. Rather, they became something akin to immortal assistants. Higher in the cosmological pecking order than simple humans but necessarily ranked beneath the now Supreme Deity, these beings developed into the angels as we know them today.

---

156. Frank Moore Cross, *Canaanite Myth and Hebrew Epic*, pp. 71–72.

An angel appears to a man as he dreams. Woodcut, sixteenth–seventeenth century. Image courtesy of the Wellcome Collection, London.

This evolution—or devolution, rather—is suggested by the retention of the term *Elohim* throughout early portions of the Bible (and, notably, the passage from *Psalms* quoted above). This term is translated in almost every instance as God—meaning *Lord God*—but it is a plural word. As we can see clearly from Psalm 82, it could be used interchangeably to indicate the gods and goddesses of the pantheon, and this is almost certainly where the term originates. When the chief deity ultimately equated with Yahweh in the Bible came to be viewed as the one and only God, the term for the entire pantheon was simply integrated into his name.

In an attempt to reconcile the absolute monotheism of the Bible, many theologians assert that the word *Elohim* is intended as a "singular plural." (It is frequently used with singular verbs.) In this sense, it is supposedly intended as a kind of biblical "royal we." Van Wolde distinguishes it as the common, as opposed to familiar, name for God within the Bible.[157] The dubious nature of these defenses is undermined by the consistent use of Yahweh as a singular term, as well as the different strata in which these two distinct names for God see use.[158] A critical reading of the biblical record reveals an evolution of Jewish monotheism that involved the reframing, rejection, and occasional integration of multiple gods into the One.

The early deific status of the angels echoes most feelingly in the *Book of Job*. In Job 1:6–12, Satan, the adversary, walks into the heavenly council on the day "the angels came to present themselves before the Lord."[159] In this scene, God presides over what amounts to a heavenly board meeting, and while he occupies the biggest seat at the table, it is by far not the *only* seat. The other beings that appear on this council of gods are generally taken to be angels, but it's important to note that this is an interpretive reading of the text. The original text itself is not precisely clear on the

godly status—or lack thereof—of the other beings present on the council. The word used in the passage is *bene ha Elohim*, typically translated as "sons of God" and, notably, identical to the term used to designate the Watchers in Genesis 6:1–4.

If the idea that angels actually started out as gods in their own right seems difficult to accept, consider that angel names are typically translated to mean "of God" or "like God." Their subordination to the supreme deity is taken to be inherent in their very names. And yet, if we look at the name of a standard angel, such as Raphael, we see that there could be a very different reading of that name.

The root *raph* means "healing." The root *el* means "lord" or "god." (God and lord—deity and kingship—were virtually synonymous in the ancient biblical world.) The combination of these two words is generally rendered "healing of God." This, of course, suggests that the angel is in some fashion either an extension of God or some subordinate representative of God's healing power. And yet, consider the possibility that the name Raphael could actually be read "God of healing." For modern Pagans who feel drawn to the concept of angels—often guiltily, since the angels are seen as such a solidly Judeo-Christian concept—it may be useful to approach this older identity of angels not as servants of a supreme God but as rightful members of their own pantheon.

---

157. Ellen van Wolde, "Chance in the Hebrew Bible: Views in Job and Genesis 1," in *The Challenge of Chance*.

158. Many biblical scholars see these two words, both of which are translated as *God* in biblical passages, as remnants of two different phases in the emerging beliefs of the Israelites and subsequent development of the biblical material itself. The terms themselves are used to identify the work of distinct writers of the biblical material, typically designated the J writer, or Yahwist, and the P, or Priestly, writer. See John Romer, *Testament: The Bible and History*, pp. 73–90.

159. Job 1:6, New International Version.

APPENDIX VI:
A CURIOUS GENESIS:
EARLY ROOTS OF THE
DICTIONARY OF DEMONS

I've had a fascination with names ever since I was little. I think it happens to most kids. You start asking why your parents gave you the name that they did, and eventually you find out that your name means something. Then you learn that all names mean something. I was captivated by this notion, and as a writer, it never lost its allure. I would buy baby name books just to read through all the different names and their meanings, dreaming up characters to go with certain names. I kept lists of names on hand for creating characters on the fly with different creative projects, and around 2002 or so, I started keeping a spreadsheet of some of the more obscure, rare, and unusual names, along with their meanings and origins. Demons and angels were a part of this list, mainly because you just don't find names like that in baby name books. And what if you want a perfectly sinister name for that villain in a short story?

I got my angel names from Gustav Davidson's classic *Dictionary of Angels*. He's got some fallen angels in that work as well, but most of them were the old familiar ones: Satan, Lucifer, Beelzebub, Belial. For really unusual names, I collected grimoires. The first book of this type that I ever owned was Francis Barrett's *The Magus*, though I find it hard to class it strictly as a grimoire. It's mostly a compilation of other people's work, and Barrett isn't always clear about when he's borrowing something from a much older source. Still, I was excited to own it. I think it may have been the first occult book I ever bought with my own money. I remember feeling very naughty about buying it and sneaking it into the house so my grandmother wouldn't catch sight of it and ask me what on earth it was. It probably says something about me that, at an age when other kids were buying copies of *Playboy* and hiding them under their beds, I was sneaking around with nineteenth-century grimoires. But if you've kept up with any of my other books, you already know that I'm at least a little strange.

The Magus was only the start of the collection. I bought a number of other books over the years, amassing a pretty sizable library. I have to admit, the magickal system outlined in the grimoires never really appealed to me. When I bought *The Magus*, I picked it up with all the intentions of a teenager seeking a scary book of black magick for a thrill. (Don't judge me too harshly; I was fourteen.) I was expecting eye of newt and toe of frog, but instead I got astrological charts and angels assigned to every hour of the day, not to mention complicated magickal circles that had more to do with Hebrew names of God than the nefarious antics of the witches in *Macbeth*. But it did add a wealth of weird and curious names to my collection—which served in part to inspire me to seek out other grimoires and magickal tomes, if only to add to my growing compilation of weird, unusual, and off-the-wall names.

I started the spreadsheet that would eventually become the *Dictionary of Demons* back in 2002. The date sticks out to me because I was in Chicago, working with URN, the new incarnation of a band I'd helped found back in college. I remember sitting in the practice space in the finished basement of our drummer, jotting down notes from various sources in between songs. I took the notes and spreadsheet with me when we went on tour that year, and I worked on my little personal resource during that interminably long period that always seems to exist between the time at which a band shows up at a venue and the time when the band actually takes the stage to play. I know some folks who perform in metal bands usually use that period of time to enjoy the venue, drink, and otherwise blow off some of the steam built up from spending however many hours crammed in the touring van with instruments, swag, and fellow musicians, but I've never been much of a party animal. Give me a nice, quiet corner where I can sit with my nose stuck in a book, occasionally looking up and observing the crowd,

and I will be happier than I could ever possibly be in a loud and smoke-filled bar, rubbing elbows with people I've never met before.

I'm not an extrovert, really. I just play one on TV.

Of course, let me state clearly that I was not working on a collection of demon names while touring with a metal band because heavy metal music is in any way demonic. Heavy metal music may often play with dark and even infernal imagery, but it does so largely from an artistic perspective. The demons, at the time, were only part of a larger reference work I was compiling for my own personal use. What did I want an alphabetized collection of demon names for, might you ask? Don't laugh, but in its first incarnation, the spreadsheet was a gaming reference.

For those of you who've followed my writing for a little while now, you probably already know that I'm an old-school gamer. I was introduced to the role-playing game *Dungeons & Dragons* in fourth grade by a very progressive school system that felt the game was a perfect mix of math and creativity for its newly founded program of gifted students. Now, I'm not connecting D&D to demons any more than I'm trying to connect demons with heavy metal music (although during the early '80s when I was first learning to game, there were plenty of people who connected them both, rather erroneously, thanks to the Satanic Panic). Gaming did not lead me to demons, but gaming certainly led me to read more about world mythology. The carefully constructed fantasy worlds necessitated by gaming also inspired me to make a concerted effort to compile, compare, and categorize the various entities found within world myths—sometimes to weave novels and short stories and sometimes to add color to elaborate game worlds of my own, created for the various gaming groups I was involved in from fourth grade onward.

Demons became an object of fascination for a variety of reasons, not the least of which was my Catholic upbringing. Catholicism retains the colorful collection of saints and angels from the early Church that was rejected by other Protestant faiths during the period of the Reformation. And, where there are angels, there are also inevitably their fallen counterparts, demons. My early exposure to the concept of demons was not exclusively a religious one, however. An early and avid reader, I very quickly demonstrated a fascination with dark and macabre topics. I was reading Poe's *Tales of Mystery and Imagination* long before my school had me playing D&D, so we really can't blame the early exposure to roleplaying for my curious tastes. I just liked dark and weird stuff, and I liked it from a pretty early age. I didn't like it because I found it scary; I liked it because it was neat. I don't think I can explain it better than that. The minute I heard about anything unusual or bizarre, I wanted to know more about it, and this led me to delve into topics like ghosts, demons, psychic phenomena, werewolves, and vampires (and everything else under the dark side of the moon) at an age when other children were more likely to be playing with dolls or watching cartoons. Magick, witches (of the folkloric variety—it took me until college to discover that there were living, modern people who practiced a different type of witchcraft), spirit conjurations, and spells were also a part of this fascination. For this, you might be able to blame Shakespeare, because when I read *Macbeth* at age ten, I launched into a years-long fixation on witches, witchcraft, and the period of American and European history that involved the Witch Trials and the Inquisition.

Long story short, I was a weird kid, and I read widely and voraciously on a number of fairly un-usual topics. So perhaps it comes as no surprise that by the age of fourteen, I had managed to obtain my first Tarot deck, and a few years later, I was working hard to find real books on magick and witchcraft in that lonely corner of the bookstore with all the volumes on crystals, astral projection, and similar topics. The trick at the time, of course, was to get out from under the watchful eye of whatever potentially disapproving parent or guardian might have been responsible for taking me to the mall at the time. Driving myself around was still a couple of years off.

In my readings on magick and witchcraft in the various encyclopedias and other reference books I had managed to find at the public library, I had already encountered the concept of the *grimoire*. This was a book of magick incantations and spells, and one source suggested that it was written in red or silver ink on black pages. Another source suggested that some of the rarest and most evil of these tomes had been bound in human skin. All of this was sensationalistic and most of it was bunk, but that didn't make it any less interesting to me at the time. At fourteen, the notion of a forbidden book of black magick that could summon up all manner of bizarre and outré entities was endlessly intriguing. And it would be the coolest thing ever to pull out at a slumber party right about the time when everyone started thinking about playing "Light as a Feather." So I went on a search for one, and eventually I found it in *The Magus*—although in finding that tome, I learned that most of what I'd read about grimoires up till that point had been misleading at best and outright fabricated at worst.

That simply inspired me to search harder for the real story behind such tomes, a search that, in its own way, also led me to my work with the *Dictionary of Demons*.

DEMONS
AND THE DECANS
OF THE ZODIAC

According to Eliphas Lévi, the Goetic demons of the Solomonic tradition are associated with the decans of the zodiac—thirty-six measurements of ten degrees each. In *Mysteries of Magic: a Digest of the Writings of Eliphas Lévi*, Lévi quotes what he claims is an old edition of the *Lesser Key*: "Thou shalt write these names in thirty-six talismans, two on each talisman, one on each side. Thou shalt divide these talismans into four series of nine each, according to the number of the letters of the Schema [Hamphorash]. On the first series thou shalt engrave the letter *Jod* represented by the Blossoming Rod of Aaron, on the second the letter *He*, represented by the cup of Joseph, on the third the *Vau*, represented by the sword of David my father; and on the fourth the final *He*, represented by the golden shekel. The thirty-six talismans shall be a book containing all natural secrets,

and angels and demons shall speak to thee in its diverse combinations."[160]

Interestingly, the *Testament of Solomon*, which predates any known editions of the *Lesser Key*, also associates demons with the decans of the zodiac. There is one key difference, however. The *Testament of Solomon* relates only one demon to each decan, rather than assigning two demons, one for night and one for day. On the next page is a chart showing the zodiac demons as they are defined in the *Testament of Solomon*. I have also included the names of the constraining angels and other agents of exorcism provided by the text to put each demon to flight. The list starts with the Ram, which is the sign of Aries.

---

160. Quoted in A. E. Waite, The *Mysteries of Magic*, p. 113.

NEW EDITION MATERIAL

Two key compilations of the *Testament of Solomon* are widely available, and each sources a slightly different collection of texts. The first, which is the most commonly reprinted one due to its being in the public domain, is a translation into English initially published by F. C. Conybeare in the October 1898 edition of the *Jewish Quarterly Review*. The other, which is widely accepted as the more complete and accurate of the two, was compiled by McCown in Greek. Like Conybeare's version, Mc-Cown's Greek translation is in the public domain, but the language provides a significant barrier for accessibility. At the time when I was writing the first edition of the *Dictionary of Demons*, I had only Conybeare's *Testament* to work from. I have since tracked down an English translation of McCown's work, as published in *The Old Testament Pseudepigrapha, Volume 1: Apocalyptic Literature and Testaments* (1983) by D. C. Duling.

McCown was working with a much more complete selection of manuscripts than was Conybeare. Most notably, Conybeare's primary source had several lacunae in the text, which led to er-rors and omissions (decans 4 and 22 are missing entirely). McCown's more complete selection of sources allows for these to be corrected, and the missing decans are also addressed. The two men additionally made different choices in the transliteration of a few of the names, and for that reason, I have created the following chart to help readers better navigate the different versions.

As is evident, the two versions start out identical and then begin with slight deviations from the fourth decan onward. By the eighteenth decan, however, the two diverge significantly, particularly at decan 20 of the McCown version, where each of the demons' names is preceded by the title *Rhyx*, meaning "Lord" or "King." The appearance of Zeus as a "constraining angel" in McCown's translation may strike some readers as odd, but it is perfectly in keeping with the magickal milieu of the time period from which the *Testament of Solomon* grew. The Greek and Roman magickal papyri, dating to the same period, similarly make use of a polyglot assembly of gods, goddesses, and spiritual powers cobbled together from the various cultures that mixed and mingled in the Hellenic world.

Translator	Decan	Demon	Constraining Power
Conybeare	1st	Ruax	Michael
McCown	1st	Ruax	Michael
Conybeare	2nd	Barsafael	Gabriel
McCown	2nd	Barsafel	Gabriel
Conybeare	3rd	Arôtosael	Uriel
McCown	3rd	Artosael	Ouriel
Conybeare	4th	[omitted]	——
McCown	4th	Oropel	Raphael
Conybeare	5th	Iudal	Uruel
McCown	5th	Kairoxanondalon	Ourouel
Conybeare	6th	Sphendonaêl	Sabrael
McCown	6th	Sphendonael	Sabael
Conybeare	7th	Sphandôr	Araêl
McCown	7th	Sphandor	Arael
Conybeare	8th	Belbel	Araêl
McCown	8th	Belbel	Karael
Conybeare	9th	Kurtaêl	Iaôth
McCown	9th	Kourtael	Iaoth
Conybeare	10th	Metathiax	Adônaêl
McCown	10th	Metathiax	Adonael
Conybeare	11th	Katanikotaêl	Iae, Ieô, (sons of Sabaôth)
McCown	11th	Katanikotael	Angel; Eae; Ieo; Sabaoth
Conybeare	12th	Saphathoraél	Iealô, Iôelet, Sabaôth, Ithoth & Bae
McCown	12th	Saphthorael	Iae; Ieo; sons of Sabaoth
Conybeare	13th	Bobêl	Adonaêl
McCown	13th	Phobothel	Adonai
Conybeare	14th	Kumeatêl	Zôrôêl
McCown	14th	Leroel	Iax, Solomon
Conybeare	15th	Roêlêd	Iax, Solomon
McCown	15th	Soubelti	Rizoel
Conybeare	16th	Atrax	Throne of the Most High
McCown	16th	Katrax	Zeus (!)
Conybeare	17th	Ieropaêl	Iudarizo, Sabunê & Denôê
McCown	17th	Ieropa	Iouda Zizabou
Conybeare	18th	Buldumêch	The God of Abram, Isaac & Jacob
McCown	18th	Modebel	"The Eight Fathers"

Translator	Decan	Demon	Constraining Power
Conybeare	19th	Naôth (also Nathath)	Phnunoboêol
McCown	19th	Mardero	his own name
Conybeare	20th	Marderô	Sphênêr, Rafael
McCown	20th	Rhyx Nathotho	Phounebiel
Conybeare	21st	Alath	Rorêx
McCown	21st	Rhyx Alath	Rarideris
Conybeare	22nd	[omitted]	——
McCown	22nd	Rhyx Audameoth	Raiouoth
Conybeare	23rd	Nefthada	Iathôth & Uruêl
McCown	23rd	Rhyx Manthado	Iaoth, Ouriel
Conybeare	24th	Akton	Marmaraôth & Sabaôth
McCown	24th	Rhyx Aktonme	Marmaraoth of mist
Conybeare	25th	Anatreth	Arara & Charara
McCown	25th	Rhyx Anatreth	Arara, Arare
Conybeare	26th	Enenuth	Allazoôl
McCown	26th	Rhyx, the Enautha	Kalazael
Conybeare	27th	Phêth	The Eleventh Aeon
McCown	27th	Rhyx Axesbuth	his name
Conybeare	28th	Harpax	Kokphnêdismos
McCown	28th	Rhyx Harpax	Kok, Phedisomos
Conybeare	29th	Anostêr	Marmaraô
McCown	29th	Rhyx Anoster	Marmaroath
Conybeare	30th	Alleborith	a fishbone
McCown	30th	Rhyx Physikoreth	Cheribum, Seraphim
Conybeare	31st	Hephesimireth	Seraphim & Cherubim
McCown	31st	Rhyx Aleureth	a fish bone
Conybeare	32nd	Ichthion	Adonaêth
McCown	32nd	Rhyx Ichthnon	Adonai malthē
Conybeare	33rd	Agchoniôn	Lycurgos
McCown	33rd	Rhyx Achoneōth	Leikourgos
Conybeare	34th	Autothith	Alpha & Omega
McCown	34th	Rhyx Authoth	Alpha & Beta
Conybeare	35th	Phthenoth	the "Evil Eye"
McCown	35th	Rhyx Phtheneoth	"Evil Eye"
Conybeare	36th	Bianakith	Mêltô, Ardu & Anaath
McCown	36th	Rhyx Mianeth	Melto, Ardad, Anaath

INFERNAL CORRESPONDENCES

Air*

Azazel
Bealphares
Camory
Fornnouc
Gutly
Harex
Iesse
Nesachnaadob
Niagutly

*All demons in the *Ars Theurgia* are described as "spirits of the air."

Anger/Strife

Albunalich
Alchibany
Alflas
Andras
Asflas

Assaibi
Assalbi
Autothith
Balidcoh
Beelzebub
Buldumêch
Carmehal
Carmox
Darial
Faccas
Haibalidech
Katanikotaêl
Klothod
Maymon
Mextyura
Pasfran
Pathophas
Saphathoraêl
Yaffla
Yasfla
Ycanohl

Zombar
Zynextyur

Blindness

Arôtosael
Shax
Tatahatia

Crib Death

Agchoniôn
Amitzrapava
Kawteeah
Khailaw
Khavaw Reshvunaw
Lilith
Mitruteeah
Obizuth
Paritesheha

Darkness

Almadiel
Arepach
Aspar
Ayylalu
Budar
Bufiel
Buriel
Camiel
Casbriel
Cazul
Cugiel
Cupriel
Drubiel
Drusiel
Furtiel
Habnthala
Harthan
Hebethel
Hekesha
Kawteeah
Khailaw
Khavaw Reshvunaw
Lazaba
Lilith
Lucifer
Lyut
Merosiel
Mitruteeah
Morlas
Nastros
Nedriel
Paritesheha
Qulbda
Sarviel
Tatahatia

Death

Atranrbiabil
Carnax
Carnical
Jamaz
Kasdeja
Minal
Pasfran
Pathophas
Yconaababur
Ythanel

Decay

Atranrbiabil
Carnax
Carnical
Jamaz
Minal
Yconaababur
Ythanel

Deceit

Abas
Abrulges
Aldal
Aldrusy
Amaimon
Aonyr
Apilki
Berith
Brymiel
Cazul
Chabri
Cugiel
Curtnas
Derisor

Destatur
Drabos
Dragon
Draplos
Dubiel
Flauros
Frasmiel
Furfur
Gomeh
Guthac
Guthor
Hamorphiel
Hemostophilé
Hermon
Hudac
Iat
Itrasbiel
Itules
Ladiel
Mador
Madriel
Morlas
Nadriel
Nartniel
Ormenu
Otim
Pandor
Pithius
Pruflas
Rabilon
Shax
Sotheano
Thalbus
Tistator
Uriel
Xezbeth

Destruction

Abaddon
Aglasis
Apolhun
Atraurbiabilis
Aym
Burasen
Flauros
Hyachonaababur
Hyiciquiron
Iachadiel
Iammax
Innyhal
Malphas
Mayrion
Meririm
Milion
Proathophas
Raum
Rubeus Pugnator
Sergulath
Vine
Ycanohl
Yfasue
Yobial

Disease

Akton
Alath
Anatreth
Anostêr
Arôtosael
Artenegelun
Ataf
Atrax
Axiôphêth
Barsafael

Bianakith
Bileth
Bothothêl
Drsmiel
Enenuth
Gartiraf
Guland
Guziel
Harpax
Hephesimireth
Iabiel
Iax
Ichthion
Ieropaêl
Iudal
Kumeatêl
Kurtaêl
Laftalium
Marbas
Marderô
Merihem
Metathiax
Naôth
Nephthada
Nymgarraman
Obizuth
Ocel
Oclachanos
Oreoth
Rath
Roêlêd
Ruax
Sabnock
Sphandôr
Sphendonaêl
Tephras
Tmsmael
Vetearcon

Yron
Zahbuk
Zhsmael
Zsniel

Earth

Aledep
Aliybany
Assalbi
Balidcoh
Hali
Hyiciquiron
Mahazael
Turitel
Zambas
Zath
Zynextyur
Yaffla
Zobha

Earthquakes

Aledep
Hyiciquiron
Khil
Khleim
Zambas
Zath

Fever

Artenegelun
Atrax
Marderô
Oclachanos
Vetearcon
Yron

Fire

Atranrbiabil
Bonoham
Buriol
Carnax
Carnical
Haristum
Jamaz
Meririm
Minal
Pasfran
Pathophas
Pruflas
Samael
Saraph
Tephras
Yconaabaur
Ythanel

Gives Familiars

Alocer
Amaimon
Ariton
Belial
Betor
Drohas
Eladeb
Gaap
Hanni
Hemostophilé
Jamaz
Malutens
Mephistopheles
Oriens
Paimon
Palas
Pasfran
Pathophas

Phalet
Purson
Quyron
Sabnock
Sambas
Shax
Suffugiel
Yconaababur
Ythanel
Zach
Zobha

Hidden Treasure

Abariel
Adan
Aledep
Aliybany
Almoel
Amen
Ameta
Ansoel
Ariel
Ariton
Asflas
Asmoday
Assalbi
Asuriel
Avnas
Aziel
Balidcoh
Barbarus
Barbatos
Barfos
Barsu
Burfa
Claunech
Ethiel
Fabariel

Foras
Gamasu
Godiel
Hali
Hissain
Las Pharon
Magni
Marae
Ossidiel
Pathier
Potiel
Rabdos
Saddiel
Saefam
Saefer
Sodiel
Tuveries
Usiel
Usiniel
Valac
Zambas
Zath
Zobha

Illusions

Asmodeus
Castumi
Cutroy
Dabuel
Dantalion
Demor
Derisor
Destatur
Fegot
Glitia
Gomeh
Guthac
Guthor

Hemostophilé
Hepoth
Hudac
Iat
Klepoth
Lytay
Magoth
Maitor
Moloy
Morail
Onor
Oor
Pumotor
Risbel
Salaul
Silitor
Sirchade
Sirumel
Syrtroy
Tami
Tangedem
Tistator
Transidium
Usyr
Vepar
Xezbeth
Ym
Zanno

Infidelity

Asmodeus
Buldumêch
Drsmiel
Iabiel
Tmsmael
Zahbuk
Zhsmael
Zsniel

Invisibility

Abas
Aldal
Almiras
Apelout
Asmoday
Bael
Belamith
Chemosh
Enarkalê
Firiel
Foras
Glasya Labolas
Melemil
Menail
Morail
Sargatanas
Taraor
Transidium

Jupiter

Aycolaytoum
Dominus Penarum
Formione
Guth
Guthryn
Iesse
Magog
Marastac
Naadob
Nesaph
Ryon
Sachiel

Knowledge

Anael
Andrealphus

Apolin
Bathin
Buer
Dantalion
Drohas
Eladeb
Fornnouc
Gaap
Glasya Labolas
Gutly
Harex
Heramael
Hethatia
Iesse
Maraloch
Maralock
Mephistopheles
Morax
Nesachnaadob
Niagutly
Paimon
Phoenix
Procell
Vapula

Languages

Agares
Barbatos
Caim
Forneus
Hael
Ronove
Sucax

Love/Lust

Abdalaa
Abelaios
Aycolaytoum

Badalam
Batthan
Baxhathau
Baysul
Brulefer
Cambores
Canibores
Caudes
Chaudas
Cynassa
Dominus Penarum
Ebal
Ebuzoba
Formione
Frimoth
Furfur
Gaap
Gaeneron
Gahathus
Galant
Guth
Guthryn
Ialchal
Iarabal
Magog
Marastac
Maylalu
Naadob
Naasa
Naassa
Nassar
Nesaph
Nessar
Ornias
Ryon
Salleos
Sarabocres

Satanachia
Serguthy
Shemyaza
Sitri
Sucax
Taob
Tracatat
Trachathath
Vual
Zagan
Zepar

Magick/Sorcery

Agaliarept
Baalberith
Baphomet
Leonard
Lucifuge Rofocale
Shemyaza
Suffugiel
Tuveries
Vine
Zainael

Mars

Atraurbiabilis
Carmehal
Carmox
Hyachonaababur
Iammax
Innyhal
Karmal
Mayrion
Pasfran
Pathophas
Proathophas

Rubeus Pugnator
Ycanohl
Yfasue
Yobial

Mercury

Budarim
Drohas
Eladeb
Habaa
Hyyci
Larmol
Palas
Quyron
Sambas
Zach
Zobha

Moon

Abuchaba
Arnochap
Asmoday
Bileth
Enêpsigos
Harthan
Hebethel
Lassal
Milalu
Milau
Onoskelis
Sariel

Murder

Atraurbiabilis
Andras

Carmehal
Carmox
Glasya Labolas
Hyachonaababur
Iammax
Innyhal
Proathophas

Necromancy

Ariton
Bifrons
Bileth
Frastiel
Gamigin
Iachadiel
Magoth
Malutens
Murmur
Nebiros
Phalet
Samael

Nightmares/Sleep

Apolin (dreams)
Fegot
Huictugaras
Marae
Maraloch (dreams)
Maras
Proculo

Poison

Keteb
Penemuê
Prziel
Psdiel

Puziel
Samael

Riches

Anituel
Albunalich
Alchibany
Aledep
Alepta
Alflas
Aliybany
Asflas
Aziabelis
Balidcoh
Ialchal
Iarabal
Lucifuge Rofocale
Raum

Saturn

Albunalich
Alchibany
Alflas
Assaibi
Haibalidech
Harith
Maymon
Marion
Mextyura
Yasfla

Storms

Albunalich
Alchibany
Alflas
Arnochap

Assaibi
Bechar
Bechaud
Fleurèty
Furfur
Haibalidech
Maymon
Mextyura
Milalu
Milau
Yasfla

Sun

Barchan
Batthan
Baxhathau
Caudes
Chatas
Chaudas
Gahathus
Ialchal
Iarabal
Shamsiel
Yaciatal

Transformation

Andrealphus
Asmodeus
Beelzebub
Berith
Clisthert
Haniel
Hemostophilé
Magoth
Orias
Ornias
Ose

Sabnock
Taob
Trimasel
Zagan
Zepar

Transportation

Abbnthada
Aglasis
Ayylalu
Barchan
Bathin
Chatas
Feremin
Gimela
Habnthala
Harthan
Hebethel
Hepoth
Hiepacth
Humet
Lautrayth
Lyut
Merfide
Mertiel
Oliroomin
Raum
Sargatanas
Seere
Sucax
Tuveries
Vepar
Yaciatal

Venus

Cambores
Cynassa
Naasa
Nassar
Pamersiel
Sarabocres

Warfare

Atraurbiabilis
Azazel
Carmehal
Carmox
Chemosh
Eligor
Gadriel
Halphas
Hyachonaababur
Iammax
Innyhal
Karmal
Klothod
Leraie
Pasfran
Pathophas
Proathophas
Pruflas
Sergulath
Ycanohl

Water

Abbnthada
Arbiel
Ayylalu
Azael
Barchiel
Chamoriel
Chariel
Dusiriel
Elelogap
Focalor
Habnthala
Hebethel
Hydriel
Kunos Paston
Lameniel
Lyut
Mermo
Mortoliel
Musuziel
Pelariel
Procell
Samiel
Vepar
Vine

PLANETARY & ELEMENTAL CORRESPONDENCES

Air*

Azazel

Bealphares

Camory

Fornnouc

Gutly

Harex

Iesse

Nesachnaadob

Niagutly

* All demons in the *Ars Theurgia* are
  described as "spirits of the air."

Earth

Aledep

Aliybany

Assalbi

Balidcoh

Hali

Hyiciquiron

Mahazael

Turitel

Yaffla

Zambas

Zath

Zobha

Zynextyur

Fire

Atranrbiabil

Bonoham

Buriol

Carnax

Carnical

Haristum

Jamaz

Meririm

Minal

Pasfran

Pathophas

Pruflas

Samael

Saraph

Tephras

Yconaababur

Ythanel

Jupiter

Aycolaytoum

Dominus Penarum

Formione

Guth

Guthryn

Harith

Iesse

Magog

Marastac

Naadob

Nesaph

Ryon

Sachiel

Mars

Atraurbiabilis
Carmehal
Carmox
Hyachonaababur
Iammax
Innyhal
Karmal
Mayrion
Pasfran
Pathophas
Proathophas
Rubeus Pugnator
Ycanohl
Yfasue
Yobial

Mercury

Budarim
Drohas
Eladeb
Habaa
Hyyci
Larmol
Palas
Quyron
Sambas
Zach
Zobha

Moon

Abuchaba
Arnochap
Asmoday
Bileth
Enêpsigos

Harthan
Hebethel
Lassal
Milalu
Milau
Onoskelis
Sariel

Saturn

Albunalich
Alchibany
Alflas
Assaibi
Haibalidech
Maymon
Marion
Mextyura
Yasfla

Sun

Barchan
Batthan
Baxhathau
Caudes
Chatas
Chaudas
Gahathus
Ialchal
Iarabal
Shamsiel
Yaciatal

Venus

Cambores
Cynassa
Naasa

Nassar
Pamersiel
Sarabocres

Water

Abbnthada
Arbiel
Ayylalu
Azael
Barchiel
Chamoriel
Chariel
Dusiriel
Elelogap
Focalor
Habnthala
Hebethel
Hydriel
Kunos Paston
Lameniel
Lyut
Mermo
Mortoliel
Musuziel
Pelariel
Procell
Samiel
Vepar
Vine

GOETIC DEMONS AND CONSTRAINING ANGELS

The *Goetia of Dr. Rudd* stands out among early manuscripts of the *Goetia* in that it assigns each of the seventy-two Goetic demons an angel from the Shemhamphorash. The demons are invoked in tandem with the angels, and the angels are thought to control the infernal spirits. Such assignments are considered a relatively new development, dating primarily to the work of late-nineteenth and early-twentieth-century occultists such as S. L. Mac-Gregor Mathers and Aleister Crowley.

Rudd's manuscript demonstrates that the tradition is much older. Additionally, Rudd's work contains errors suggestive that Rudd himself was copying his information from an even earlier source. From this it would seem that the correla-tion between the seventy-two Goetic demons and the seventy-two angels of the Shemhamphorash dates well before the nineteenth century and may have been an integral part of the Goetic tradition from the start. However, there seems to be no standard system by which the demons are paired with the angels.

The following chart details Rudd's attributions and compares them against the attributions used widely by modern occultists as compiled by Lon Milo DuQuette. Rudd's manuscript also attributes a specific biblical passage (in all but one case a psalm) to the angels, and I have included these as well, as they seem to be part of the mechanism used to control the demons.

Demon	Angel (Rudd)	Angel (DuQuette)	Psalm
Bael	Vehujal	Vehuel	3:5
Agares	Jeliel	Heahziah	21:20
Vassago	Syrael	Heahziah	90:2
Gamigin	Elemiah	Mebehiah	6:4
Marbas	Mahasiah	Nemamiah	33:4
Valefor	Jelahel	Harahel	9:11
Amon	Achasiah	Umabel	102:8
Barbatos	Cahetal	Annauel	94:6
Paimon	Hasiel	Damabiah	24:6
Buer	Aladiah	Eiael	32:22
Gusoin	Laviah	Rochel	17:50
Sitri	Hahajah	Haiaiel	9:22
Beleth	Jezaliel	Vehurah	97:6
Leraie	Mebahel	Sitael	9:9
Eligos	Haziel	Mahashiah	93:22
Zepar	Hakamiah	Aehaiah	87:1
Botis	Loviah	Haziel	8:1
Bathin	Caliel	Lauiah	9:9[1]
Sallos	Leuviah	Ieiazel	39:1
Purson	Pahaliah	Hariel	119:2
Marax	Nelchael	Leviah	30:18
Ipos	Jejael	Leuuiah	120:5
Aim	Melabel	Nelchael	120:8
Naberius	Haiviah	Melahel	32:18
Glasia-Labolas	Nithhajah	Nithhaiah	9:1
Bime	Haajah	Ieathel	118:145
Ronove	Jerathel	Reiiel	139:1
Berith	Seechiah	Lecabel	70:15
Astaroth	Reiajel	Iehuiah	53:4
Forneus	Omael	Chavakiah	70:6
Forcas	Lectabal	Aniel	70:16
Asmodeus	Vasariah	Rehnel	32:4
Gaap	Jehujah	Hahael	33:11
Furfur	Lehahiah	Vevaliah	130:5
Marchosias	Chajakiah	Saliah	114:1
Stolas	Menadel	Asaliah	25:8
Phenix	Aniel	Daniel	79:8

---

1. This text in this angelic seal is actually from Psalm 51:1, although Rudd incorrectly identifies it as 9:9.

Demon	Angel (Rudd)	Angel (DuQuette)	Psalm
Halphas	Hamiah	Amamiah	90:9
Malphas	Rehael	Nithael	29:13
Raum	Jejazel	Poiel	87:15
Forcalor	Hahahel	Ieilael	119:2
Vepar	Michael	Mizrael	120:7
Sabnock	Vevaliah	Iahhel	87:14
Shax	Jelahiah	Mekekiel	118:108
Vine	Sealiah	Meniel	93:18
Bifrons	Ariel	Habuiah	114:9
Vuall	Alaliah	Iabamiah	103:25
Haagenti	Mihael	Mumiah	97:3
Procel/Crocell	Vehuel	Ieliel	144:3
Furcas	Daniel	Elemiah	102:8
Balam	Hahasiah	Lelahel	103:32
Alloces	Imamiah	Cahethel	7:18
Camio	Nanael	Aladiah	118:75
Murmus	Nithael	Hahiah	102:19
Orobas	Nanael (repeat)	Mebahel	101:13
Gemori	Poliah	Hakamiah	144:5
Ose	Nemamiah	Caliel	113:19
Amy/Auns	Jejalel	Pahliah	6:3
Orias	Hazahel	Ieiaiel	112:3
Vapula/Napula	Mizrael	Hahuiah	144:18
Zagan	Umabel	Haaiah	112:2
Vulac/Volac	Jahhael	Sahiiah	118:159
Andras	Anavel	Amael	2:11
Haures/Havres	Mehiel	Vasariah	32:18
Andrealphas	Damabiah	Lehahiah	89:15
Cimeries	Marakel	Monadel	37:22
Amducias	Eiael	Haamiah	36:4
Belial	Habujah	Ihiazel	105:1
Deccarabia	Roehel	Michael	15:5
Seere	Tabamiah	Ielahiah	Genesis 1:1[2]
Dantalion	Hajajel	Ariel	108:29
Andromalius	Mumiah	Mihael	114:7

---

2. This is the only angelic seal in Rudd's manuscript that includes a biblical passage from a source other than the Psalms.

BIBLIOGRAPHY

Abegg, Jr., Martin G. "The Linguistic Analysis of the Dead Sea Scrolls: More Than (Initially) Meets the Eye." In *Rediscovering the Dead Sea Scrolls: An Assessment of the Old and New Approaches and Methods*. Edited by Maxine L. Grossman. Grand Rapids, MI: William B. Eerdmans Publishing, 2010.

Adejumobi, Saheed A. *The History of Ethiopia*. The Greenwood Histories of the Modern Nations series. Westport, CT: Greenwood Press, 2006.

Agrippa, Henry Cornelius. (Donald Tyson, ed.) *Three Books of Occult Philosophy*. St. Paul, MN: Llewellyn, 1993.

Ainsworth, Theresa. "A Timeline of the Decans." Research essay, Queen's University in Ontario, Canada, September 2018. http://hdl.handle.net/1974/24821.

Allegro, John M. *The Dead Sea Scrolls and the Christian Myth*. Buffalo, NY: Prometheus Books, 1992.

Allison, Dale C. *Testament of Abraham*. Commentaries on Early Jewish Literature series. Edited by L. Stuckenbruck. Berlin: Walter de Gruyter, 2003.

Al-Nadim. *The Fihrist of al-Nadim: A Tenth-Century Survey of Muslim Culture, Vols. I and II*. Edited and translated by Bayard Dodge. New York: Columbia University Press, 1970.

Ankarloo, Bengt, and Stuart Clark. *Witchcraft and Magic in Europe: Ancient Greece and Rome*. Philadelphia: University of Pennsylvania Press, 1999.

———. *Witchcraft and Magic in Europe: Biblical and Pagan Societies*. Philadelphia, PA: University of Pennsylvania Press, 2001.

———. *Witchcraft and Magic in Europe: The Middle Ages*. Philadelphia: University of Pennsylvania Press, 2001.

The Apocrypha. (Edgar J. Goodspeed, ed.) New York: Random House, 1959.

Ashe, Steven. *The Testament of Solomon*. Oxford: Glastonbury Books, 2006.

Bailey, Michael D. *Fearful Spirits, Reasoned Follies: The Boundaries of Superstition in Late Medieval Europe*. Ithaca, NY: Cornell University Press, 2013.

Barnes, Albert. *Notes, Critical, Explanatory, and Practical on the Book of the Prophet Isaiah, Volume 1*. New York: Leavitt & Allen Bros., 1860.

Barnes, T. D. "Proconsuls of Africa, 337–92." *Phoenix*, vol. 39, no. 2 (Summer, 1985), pp. 144–53.

Barrett, Francis. *The Magus: A Complete System of Occult Philosophy*. New York: Citadel Press, 1989.

Ben Joseph, Rabbi Akiba. (Knut Stenring, trans.) *The Book of Formation, or Sepher Yetzirah*. Berwick, ME: Ibis Press, 2004.

Benedict XIV. *Heroic Virtue: A Portion of the Treatise of Benedict XIV on the Beatification and Canonization of the Servants of God, Vol. III*. Translator not recorded. London: Thomas Richardson and Son, 1852.

Berbiguier, Charles. *Les Farfadets*, vols. 1–3. Paris: P. Gueffier, 1821.

Berrios, German E. *The History of Mental Symptoms: Descriptive Psychopathology Since the Nineteenth Century*. Cambridge, UK: Cambridge University Press, 1996.

Betz, Hans Dieter. *The Greek Magical Papyri in Translation*, vol. 1. Chicago: University of Chicago Press, 1992.

Blair, Leonard. "Rome Opens Up Exorcism Course to All Major Christian Faiths to Fight Rising Demonic Force." *Christian Post*. May 9, 2019. https://www.christian post.com/news/rome-opens-up-exorcism-course-to-all-major-christian-faiths-to -fight-rising-demonic-forces.html.

Bodin, Jean. *De Magorum Daemonomania*. Book Four. Frankfurt, Germany, 1586.

Book of Jasher. Salt Lake City, UT: J. H. Parry Publishers, 1887.

Boudet, Jean-Patrice. "Les who's who démonologiques de la Renaissance et leurs ancêtres médiévaux." *Médiévales*. Vol. 44, Spring 2003. Published online Dec. 9, 2005. http://journals.openedition.org/medievales/1019.

Brand, Miryam T. "Iranian Influence at Qumran: Texts and Beliefs." In *Iran, Israel, and the Jews Symbiosis and Conflict from the Achaemenids to the Islamic Republic*. Edited by Aaron Koller and Daniel Tsadik. Eugene, OR: Pickwick Publications, 2018.

———. *Spirited Evil: Persian Influence and Its Limits in Qumran Texts.* Eighth Symposium of the Melammu Project. Conference volume. 2014.

Brann, Noel L. *The Debate Over the Origin of the Genius During the Italian Renaissance.* Boston: Brill Academic Publishers, 2001.

Bruce, James. *Travels to Discover the Source of the Nile.* London: J. Ruthven, 1790.

Butler, Elizabeth M. *The Fortunes of Faust.* Magic in History Series. University Park, PA: Penn State Press, 1998.

———. *Ritual Magic.* Magic in History Series. University Park, PA: Penn State Press, 1998.

Calmet, Augustin. *The Phantom World.* Ware, UK: Wordsworth Editions, 2001.

Chamberlin, E. R. *The Bad Popes.* New York: Dorset Press, 1969.

Charles, R. H. *The Apocalypse of Baruch.* New York: Macmillan, 1918.

———. *The Book of Enoch the Prophet.* York Beach, ME: Weiser Books, 2003.

———. *The Book of Jubilees, or The Little Genesis.* Berwick, ME: Ibis Press, 2005.

———. *The Book of Jubilees, or The Little Genesis.* London: Adam and Charles Black, 1902.

Charlesworth, J. H., ed. *Caves of Enlightenment: Proceedings of the American Schools of Oriental Research Dead Sea Scrolls Jubilee Symposium (1947–1997).* North Richland Hills, TX: Bibal Press, 1998.

Cohen, Abraham. *Everyman's Talmud.* New York: Schocken Books, 1975.

Collerton, Daniel, Elaine Perry, and Urs Peter Mosimann, eds. *The Neuroscience of Visual Hallucinations.* West Sussex, UK: John Wiley & Sons, 2015.

Collins, Andrew. *From the Ashes of Angels: The Forbidden Legacy of a Forgotten Race.* Rochester, VT: Bear & Co., 2001.

Collins, Paul. "Everyday Life in Sumer." *The Sumerian World.* Edited by Harriet Crawford. Abingdon, Oxfordshire, UK: Routledge, 2013.

Cone, Steven D., and Robert F. Rea. *A Global Church History: The Great Tradition Through Cultures, Continents and Centuries.* London: Bloomsbury Publishing, 2019.

Conway, Moncure Daniel. *Demonology and Devil-Lore,* vols. 1 and 2. New York: Henry Holt and Company, 1879.

———. *Solomon and Solomonic Literature.* London: Trench, Trubner & Co., 1899.

Conybeare, F. C., Aleister Crowley, and S. L. MacGregor Mathers. *The Three Magical Books of Solomon: The Testament of Solomon & His Greater & Lesser Keys in One Volume.* Mockingbird Press: 2017.

Cross, Frank Moore. *The Ancient Library of Qumran*, third edition. Sheffield, UK: Sheffield Academic Press, 1995.

———. *Canaanite Myth and Hebrew Epic*. Cambridge, MA: Harvard University Press, 1973.

Dacy, Marianne. "The Fallen Angels in the Book of 1 Enoch Reconsidered." *Henoch* 33, 1 (2011).

Davidson, Gustav. *A Dictionary of Angels, Including the Fallen Angels*. New York: The Free Press, 1967.

Day, John. *From Creation to Babel: Studies in Genesis 1–11*. New York: Bloomsbury. 2013.

De Abano, Peter. (Joseph H. Peterson, trans.) *The Heptameron, or Magical Elements*. Esoteric Archives: 1998. Online at http://esotericarchives.com/solomon/heptamer.htm.

De Hamel, Christopher. *The British Library Guide to Manuscript Illumination History and Techniques*. Toronto: University of Toronto Press, 2001.

De Laurence, L. W. (S. L. MacGregor Mathers, trans.) *The Lesser Key of Solomon Goetia, the Book of Evil Spirits*. Chicago: De Laurence, Scot & Co. 1916.

De Plancy, Collin. *Dictionnaire Infernal: Recherches et Anecdotes sur les Démons*, first edition. Paris: P. Mongie, 1818.

———. *Dictionniare Infernal*. Revised Edition. Paris: Sagnier et Bray, 1853.

Dehn, Georg, ed. (Steven Guth, trans.) *The Book of Abramelin*. Lake Worth, FL: Ibis Press, 2006.

Dionysius the Areopagite. *Caelestis Hierarchia*. Venice, Italy: Johannes Tacuinus de Tridino, 1502.

Doré, Gustav. *The Doré Bible Illustrations*. Mineola, NY: Dover Publications, 1974.

———. *Doré's Illustrations for Milton's "Paradise Lost."* New York: Dover Publications, 1993.

Doresse, Jean. *The Secret Books of the Egyptian Gnostics*. Rochester, VT: Inner Traditions International, 1986.

Doudna, Gregory L. "The Legacy of an Error in Archaeological Interpretation: The Dating of the Qumran Cave Scroll Deposits." In *Qumran: The Site of the Dead Sea Scrolls: Archaeological Interpretations and Debates*. Edited by Katharina Galor, Jean-Baptiste Humbert, and Jürgen Zangenberg. Leiden: Brill, 2006.

Driscoll, Daniel, trans. *Sworn Book of Honourius the Magician*. Gillette, NJ: Heptangle Books, 1977.

Drummond, James. *The Jewish Messiah: A Critical History of the Messianic Idea Among the Jews from the Rise of the Maccabees to the Closing of the Talmud.* London: Longmans Green & Co., 1877.

Duling, Dennis C. "The Testament of Solomon." *The Old Testament Pseudepigrapha, Volume One: Apocalyptic Literature and Testaments.* Edited by James H. Charlesworth. Hendrickson Publishers, Peabody, MA: 1983.

DuQuette, Lon Milo. *Angels, Demons and Gods of the New Millennium.* York Beach, ME: Weiser Books, 1997.

El-Zein, Amira. *Islam, Arabs, and the Intelligent World of the Jinn.* Contemporary Issues in the Middle East series. Syracuse University Press. Syracuse, NY: 2009.

Falk, Avner. *Psychoanalytic History of the Jews.* Cranbury, NJ: Associated University Presses, 1996.

Fanger, Claire. *Conjuring Spirits: Texts and Traditions of Medieval Ritual Magic.* University Park, PA: Penn State Press, 1998.

Faulkner, R. O. *The Ancient Egyptian Book of the Dead.* Edited by Carol Andrews. Austin, TX: University of Texas Press, 1972.

Fekkes, Jan. *Isaiah and Prophetic Traditions in the Book of Revelation: Visionary Antecedents and Their Development.* Journal for the Study of the New Testament Supplement series 93. Sheffield, England: Sheffield Academic Press, 1994.

Flint, Valerie I. J. *The Rise of Magic in Early Medieval Europe.* Princeton, NJ: Princeton University Press, 1991.

Friedman, Richard Elliott. *Who Wrote the Bible?* New York: Harper & Row, 1989.

Fröhlich, Ida. "The Figure of the Watchers in the Enochic Tradition (1–3 Enoch)." *Henoch* vol. 33, issue 1 (2011). Accessed via Academia.edu, October 10, 2019.

Gager, John G. *Curse Tablets and Binding Spells from the Ancient World.* Oxford: Oxford University Press, 1992.

Gaster, Moses, trans. *The Chronicles of Jerahmeel, or The Hebrew Bible Historiale.* Oriental Translation Fund New series, IV, 1899.

———. *The Sword of Moses.* New York: Cosimo Publishing, 2005.

Geller. M. J. "Freud and Mesopotamian Magic." *Mesopotamian Magic: Textual, Historical, and Interpretative Perspectives.* Edited by I. Tzvi Abusch and Karel Van Der Toorn. Groningen, Netherlands: Styx Publications, 1999.

Gilbert, R. A. Foreword to *The Book of the Mysteries of the Heaven and the Earth. The Book of the Mysteries of the Heaven and the Earth and Other Works of Bakhayla Mîkâ'êl.* Edited by E. A. Wallis Budge. Berwick, ME: Ibis Press, 2004.

———. *The Golden Dawn Scrapbook*. York Beach, ME: Weiser, 1997.

Gilmore, George William. *The New Schaff-Herzog Encyclopedia of Religious Knowledge*. New York: Funk & Wagnalls, 1914.

Ginzberg, Louis. (Henrietta Szold, trans.) *The Legends of the Jews: From Joseph to the Exodus*, volume II. Philadelphia: The Jewish Publication Society of America, 1920.

———. (Paul Radin, trans.) *The Legends of the Jews: Bible Times and Characters from the Exodus to the Death of Moses*, vol. III. Philadelphia: The Jewish Publication Society of America, 1911.

Goldman, Liora. "Dualism in the 'Visions of Amram.'" *Revue de Qumran* vol. 24, no. 3 (May 2010).

Gómez, Mario. "The Legend of Tartini's 'Devil's Trill Sonata.'" *The Violinist*. Published online October 2, 2008.

The Grand Grimoire. (Kuntz, Darcy, ed., A. E. Waite, trans.) Edmonds, WA: Holmes Publishing Group, 2001.

Grillot de Givry, Émile (J. Courtenay Locke, trans.) *Illustrated Anthology of Sorcery, Magic, and Alchemy*. New York: Causeway Books, 1973.

Guazzo, Francesco Maria. (Montague Summers, trans.) *Compendium Maleficarum*. Dover, Mineola, NY: 1988.

Harms, Daniel, James R. Clark, and Joseph H. Peterson. *The Book of Oberon: A Sourcebook of Elizabethan Magic*. Woodbury, MN: Llewellyn Publications, 2016.

Harries, John. *The Book of Incantations*. NLW MS 11117B. National Library of Wales. Accessed online: https://www.library.wales/discover/digital-gallery/manu-scripts/modern-period/john-harries-book-of-incantations/.

Hayman, Henry. "The Book of Enoch in Reference to the New Testament and Early Christian Antiquity." *The Biblical World* vol. 12, no. 1 (1898), pp. 37–46. www.jstor.org/stable/3137165.

Henson, Mitch, trans. *Lemegeton: The Complete Lesser Key of Solomon*. Jacksonville, FL: Metatron Books, 1999.

Horsley, J. W. "Solomon's Seal and the Shield of David Traced to Their Origin." *Ars Quatuor Corontorum, 1902* vol. 15 (1902). Edited by W. H. Rylands.

Howard, Michael. *The Book of Fallen Angels*. Somerset, UK: Capall Bann, 2004.

Huber, Richard. *Treasury of Fantastic and Mythological Creatures*. Mineola, NY: Dover, 1981.

Hultin, Jeremy. "Jude's Citation of 1 Enoch." *Jewish and Christian Scriptures: The Function of "Canonical" and "Non-Canonical" Religious Texts*. Edited by James H.

Charlesworth and Lee Martin McDonald. T&T Clark Jewish and Christian Text series. Vol. 7. London: T&T Clark International, 2010.

Humphreys, W. Lee. *Crisis and Story: Introduction to the Old Testament*. Second edition. Mountain View, CA: Mayfield Publishing, 1990.

Jacobs, Joseph, Alfred Trübner Nutt, Arthur Robinson Wright, and William Crooke. *Folk-Lore: A Quarterly Review*. Vol. 7. London: David Nutt, 1896.

Josephus. *The Life and Works of Flavius Josephus*. Philadelphia: John C. Winston Company, 1957.

Juste, David. "MS Florence, Biblioteca Medicea Laurenziana, Plut. 89 sup. 38" (update: 14.08.2018), *Ptolemaeus Arabus et Latinus. Manuscripts*. http://ptolemaeus.badw.de/ms/357.

Kaczynski, Richard. *Perdurabo: The Life of Aleister Crowley*. Tempe, AZ: New Falcon, 2002.

Kieckhefer, Richard. *Forbidden Rites: A Necromancer's Manual of the Fifteenth Century*. University Park, PA: Penn State Press, 1997.

———. *Magic in the Middle Ages*. Cambridge: Cambridge University Press, 1993.

King James. *Daemonologie*. New Bern, NC: Godolphin House, 1996.

Kitto, John, ed. *The Cyclopaedia of Biblical Literature*. Vol. 1. Tenth edition. New York: Ivison & Phinney, 1854.

Kohl, Benjamin G., and H. C. Erik Midelfort, eds. *On Witchcraft: An Abridged Translation of Johann Weyer's De Praestigiis Daemonum*. Asheville, NC: Pegasus Press, 1998.

Kramer, Samuel Noah. *Gilgamesh and the Huluppa-Tree. A Reconstructed Sumerian Text*. Chicago: University of Chicago Press, 1938.

Lacoste, Jean-Yves. *Encyclopedia of Christian Theology*. Vol. 1. New York: Routledge, 2004.

Leach, Eleanor Winsor. "Viewing the Spectacula of Aeneid 6." In *Reading Vergil's Aeneid: An Interpretive Guide*. Edited by Christine Perkell. Norman, OK: University of Oklahoma Press, 1999.

LeCouteux, Claude. *The Book of Grimoires*. Translated by John. E. Graham. Rochester, VT: Inner Traditions, 2013.

Lehner, Ernst, and Johanna Lehner. *The Picture Book of Devils, Demons and Witchcraft*. Mineola, NY: Dover, 1971.

Leitch, Aaron. *Secrets of the Magickal Grimoires: The Classical Texts of Magick Deciphered*. Woodbury, MN: Llewellyn, 2005.

Lévi, Eliphas. *The Book of Splendors*. York Beach, ME: Weiser, 1984.

———. *The History of Magic.* (A. E. Waite, trans.) York Beach, ME: Weiser, 1999.

Levy, B. Barry. *Planets, Potions, and Parchments: Scientifica Herbarica from the Dead Sea Scrolls to the Eighteenth Century.* Montreal: McGill-Queens University Press, 1990.

Lindahl, Carl, John McNamara, and John Lindow. *Medieval Folklore: A Guide to Myths, Legends, Tales, Beliefs, and Customs.* New York: Oxford University Press, 2002.

Luck, Georg. *Arcana Mundi: Magic and the Occult in the Greek and Roman Worlds.* Baltimore, MD: Johns Hopkins University Press, 1985.

Lurker, Manfred. *Dictionary of Gods and Goddesses, Devils and Demons.* New York: Routledge & Kegan Paul, 1987.

Lutz, Henry Frederick. *Selected Sumerian and Babylonian Texts.* Philadelphia, PA: University of Pennsylvania Press, 1919.

Mack, Carol K., and Dinah Mack. *A Field Guide to Demons, Fairies, Fallen Angels & Other Subversive Spirits.* New York: Arcade Publishing, 1998.

Marshall, George J. *Angels: An Indexed and Partially Annotated Bibliography of Over 4,300 Scholarly Books and Articles Since the Seventh Century B.C.* Jefferson, NC: McFarland, 2015.

Masello, Robert. *Raising Hell: A Concise History of the Black Arts.* New York: Berkley, 1996.

Mathers, S. L. MacGregor, trans. *The Book of the Sacred Magic of Abramelin the Mage.* Mineola, NY: Dover, 1975.

———. *The Grimoire of Armadel.* York Beach, ME: Weiser, 1995.

———. *The Key of Solomon the King.* York Beach, ME: Weiser, 1989.

McCraw, Benjamin W. "Augustine and Aquinas on the Demonic." *Philosophical Approaches to Demonology.* Edited by Benjamin W. McCraw and Robert Arp. Routledge Studies in the Philosophy of Religion. Oxford: Routledge, 2017.

McDonald, Lee Martin. *The Formation of Biblical Canon: Volume 1: The Old Testament: Its Authority and Canonicity.* London: Bloomsbury T&T Clark, 2017.

McLean, Adam, ed. *A Treatise on Angel Magic.* York Beach, ME: Weiser, 2006.

McRobbie, Linda Rodriguez. "The Strange and Mysterious History of the Ouija Board." Smithsonian.com. October 27, 2013. https://www.smithsonianmag.com /history/the-strange-and-mysterious-history-of-the-ouija-board-5860627/.

Milik, J. T. *The Books of Enoch: Aramaic Fragments of Qumran Cave 4.* Oxford: Clarendon Press, 1976.

Murtaugh, Stephen. *Authentication of "The Secret Grimoire of Turiel" in Comparison with Frederick Hockley's "A Complete Book of Magic Science."* July 19, 2013. Academia.edu.

Neifert, William W. "Witchcraft." In *The Pennsylvania-German: A Popular Magazine of Biography, History, Genealogy, Folklore, Literature, Etc.* Edited by H. W. Kriebel. Vol. IX, Jan.–Dec. East Greenville, PA: Kriebel Publishing, 1908.

Newman, Hillel. *Proximity to Power and Jewish Sectarian Groups of the Ancient Period.* Leiden, Netherlands: Brill, 2006.

Newman, Robert, C. "The Council of Jamnia and the Old Testament Canon." *Westminster Theological Journal* 38, 4 (Spring 1976), 319–348.

Nickelsburg, George W. E., and James C. VanderKam. *1 Enoch.* Minneapolis, MN: Fortress Press, 2004.

Oesterley, W. O. E. *Immortality and the Unseen World.* New York: Macmillan, 1921.

Pagels, Elaine. *The Origin of Satan.* New York: Random House, 1995.

Paton, Lewis Bayles. *Spiritism and the Cult of the Dead in Antiquity.* New York: Macmillan, 1921.

Payne-Towler, Christine. "Eros Magic and the Magical Image." Tarot University Arkletters. January 21, 2006. https://noreah.typepad.com/tarot_arkletters/2006/01/eros_magic_.html.

Percival, H. W. *Sepher Ha-Zohar, or The Book of Light.* New York: Theosophical Publishing Company, 1914.

Perrin, Andrew B. *The Dynamics of Dream-Vision Revelation in the Aramaic Dead Sea Scrolls.* Bristol, CT: Vandenhoeck & Ruprecht, 2015.

Peterson, Joseph H, ed. *Arbatel: Concerning the Magic of the Ancients.* Lake Worth, FL: Ibis Press, 2009.

———. *Ars Notoria: The Notory Art of Solomon.* Online at http://www.esotericarchives.com/notoria/notoria.htm.

———. *Clavicules du Roi Salomon, par Armadel. Livre Troisième. Concernant les Esprits & Leurs Pouvoirs.* Esoteric Archives, 2003. Online at http://www.esotericarchives.com/solomon/ksol3.htm.

———. *Grand Grimoire.* Esoteric Archives, 1998. Online at http://esotericarchives.com/solomon/grand.htm.

———. *Gremoire du Pape Honorius.* Esoteric Archives, 1999. Online at http://esotericarchives.com/solomon/grimhon2.htm.

———. *Grimorium Verum.* Scotts Valley ,CA: CreateSpace, 2007.

———. *The Key of Knowledge, or Clavicula Salomonis*. Esoteric Archives, 1999. Online at http://esotericarchives.com/solomon/ad36674.htm.

———. *The Secrets of Solomon: A Witch's Handbook from the Trial Records of the Venetian Inquisition*. Kasson, MN: Twilit Grotto Press, 2018.

———. *Sworn Book of Honorius*. Esoteric Archives, 1998. Online at http://esotericarchives.com/juratus/juratus.htm.

———. *The Sworn Book of Honorius: Liber Iuratus Honorii*. Lake Worth, FL: Ibis Press, 2016.

Pinches, Theophilus G. *Religion of Babylonia and Assyria*. London: Archibald Constable & Co., 1906.

Platt, Rutherford H. *The Forgotten Books of Eden: Lost Books of the Old Testament*. New York: Bell Publishing, 1980.

Pliny. *Natural History*, vol. 2. (John Bostock and H. T. Riley, trans.) London: George Bell & Sons, 1890.

Reed, Annette Yoshiko. *Fallen Angels and the History of Judaism and Christianity*. New York: Cambridge University Press, 2005.

Reed, Annette Yoshiko, and John C. Reeves. *Enoch from Antiquity to the Middle Ages: Sources From Judaism, Christianity, and Islam*. Volume I. Oxford: Oxford University Press, 2018.

Reeve, C. D. C. *Socrates in the Apology: An Essay on Plato's Apology of Socrates*. Indianapolis, IN: Hackett, 1990.

Reimer, Stephen R. *Manuscript Studies: Medieval and Early Modern*. IV–VI. Paleography: Scribal Abbreviations. Online at http://www.ualberta.ca/~sreimer/ms-course/course/abbrevtn.htm.

Remy, Nicolas. (Montague Summers, ed.) *Demonolatry: An Account of the Historical Practice of Witchcraft*. Mineola, NY: Dover, 2008.

Roberts, Alexander, and James Donaldson, eds. *The Ante-Nicene Fathers: Translations of the Writings of the Fathers Down to AD 325*. Vol. IV. New York: Charles Scribner's Sons, 1926.

Romer, John. *Testament: The Bible and History*. New York: Henry Holt and Co., 1988.

Rudwin, Maximilian. *The Devil in Legend and Literature*. La Salle, IL: Open Court Publishing, 1959.

Ruelle, C. E. "Hermès Trismégiste: Le Livre Sacré Sur les Décans." *Revue de Philologie de Littérature et D'Histoire Anciennes* vol. 32, no. 1 (January 1908): 227–277.

Russell, Jeffrey Burton. *The Devil: Perceptions of Evil from Antiquity to Primitive Christianity*. Ithaca, NY: Cornell University Press, 1987.

———. *A History of Witchcraft*. New York: Thames and Hudson, 1980.

———. *Mephistopheles: The Devil in the Modern World*. Ithaca, NY: Cornell University Press, 1986.

———. *The Prince of Darkness: Radical Evil and the Power of Good in History*. Ithaca, NY: Cornell University Press, 1988.

Sandars, N. K., trans. *The Epic of Gilgamesh*. London: Penguin Books, 1960.

Savedow, Steve. *Goetic Evocation*. Chicago: Eschaton Productions, 1996.

Schrire, T. *Hebrew Magic Amulets: Their Decipherment and Interpretation*, second edition. New York: Behrman House, 1982.

Scot, Reginald. *The Discoverie of Witchcraft*. Mineola, NY: Dover, 1972.

The Secret Grimoire of Turiel. (Kuntz, Darcy, ed., Marius Malchus, trans.) Edmonds, WA: Holmes Publishing, 2000.

Sepher ha-Zohar, Le Livre de la Spleneur. (Jean de Pauly, trans.) Paris: Ernest Leroux, 1908.

Sepher ha-Zohar, or the Book of Light. (H. W. Percival, ed.) New York: Theosophical Publishing Company, 1914.

Shaked, Shaul. "Iranian Influence on Judaism: First Century BCE to Second Century CE." In *The Cambridge History of Judaism*. Edited by W. D. Davies and L. Finkelstein. Vol. 1. Cambridge: Cambridge University Press, 1984.

Silvestre de Sacy, Antoine Isaac. "Notice sur le livre d'Enoch." *Magazin Encyclopedique* vol. VI, issue I (1800).

Sinistrari, Ludovico Maria. (Montague Summers, trans.) *Demoniality*. Mineola, NY: Dover, 1989.

The Sixth and Seventh Books of Moses. Lake Worth, FL: Ibis Press, 2008.

Skemer, Don C. *Binding Words: Textual Amulets in the Middle Ages*. University Park, PA: Penn State Press. 2006.

Skinner, Stephen, and David Rankine. *Clavis Inferni: The Grimoire of St. Cyprian*. Sourceworks of Ceremonial Magic series. Singapore: Golden Hoard Press, 2009.

———. *The Goetia of Dr. Rudd*. London: Golden Hoard Press, 2007.

———. *The Keys to the Gateway of Magic: Summoning the Solomonic Archangels and Demon Princes*. Sourceworks of Ceremonial Magic series. Singapore: Golden Hoard Press, 2011.

Skjaervo, P. O. "Zoroastrian Dualism." In *Light Against Darkness: Dualism in Ancient Mediterranean Religion and the Contemporary World*. Journal of Ancient Judaism Supplements series, book 2. Gottingen: Vandenhoeck & Ruprecht, 2011.

Smeaton, Oliphant. *The Medici and the Italian Renaissance*. World's Epoch-Makers series. New York: Charles Scribner's Sons, 1901.

Smith, William. *Dictionary of Greek and Roman Antiquities*, vol. 3. London: Little & Brown, 1870.

Songling, Pu. *Strange Stories from a Chinese Studio*. London: Penguin Books, 2006.

Spence, Lewis. *An Encyclopedia of Occultism*. Mineola, NY: Dover. 2003.

Stafford, Tom. "How the Ouija Board Really Moves." BBC Future. July 29, 2013. https://www.bbc.com/future/article/20130729-what-makes-the-ouija-board-move.

Strayer, Joseph R. *The Reign of Phillip the Fair*. Princeton, NJ: Princeton University Press, 1980.

Stuckenbruck, Loren T. "The Book of Enoch: Its Reception in Second Temple Judaism and in Christianity." *Early Christianity* vol. 4 (2013). Edited by Clare K. Rothschild, Jens Schröter, and Francis Watson.

———. *The Myth of Rebellious Angels: Studies in Second Temple Judaism and New Testament Texts*. Tübingen: Mohr Siebeck, 2014.

Suster, Gerald. *The Legacy of the Beast: The Life, Work, and Influence of Aleister Crowley*. York Beach, ME: Weiser, 1989.

Thompson, Reginald Campbell. *The Devils and Evil Spirits of Babylonia*. Vol. 1. London: Luzac and Co., 1903.

———. *Semitic Magic: Its Origins and Development*. London: Luzac & Co., 1908.

Thomson, Ian. "The Divine Comedy: The Greatest Single Work of Western Literature." *Irish Times*. Sept. 8, 2018 https://www.irishtimes.com/culture/books/the-divine-comedy-the-greatest-single-work-of-western-literature-1.3619042.

Thorndike, Lynn. *A History of Magic and Experimental Science During the First Thirteen Centuries of Our Era*. Vol. II. New York: MacMillan Company, 1923.

Trithemius, Johannes. (Joseph H. Peterson, ed.) *Antipalus Maleficiorum*. First published in 1605 but written in 1508. Esoteric Archives. Online at http://esotericarchives.com/tritheim/antipalus.htm.

———. *Steganographia*. (Joseph H. Peterson, ed.) First published in 1621. Esoteric Archives, 1997. Online at http://esotericarchives.com/tritheim/stegano.htm.

Trump, Robert W. *A Brief Encyclopaedia of the Materials and Techniques of Manuscript Illumination.* Fayette, MO: Potboiler Press, 1999.

Van Der Toorn, Karel, Bob Becking, and Pieter W. Van Der Horst, eds. *Dictionary of Deities and Demons in the Bible.* Second edition. Leiden, Netherlands: Brill Academic Publishers, 1999.

Van Wolde, Ellen. "Chance in the Hebrew Bible: Views in Job and Genesis 1." In *The Challenge of Chance. The Frontiers Collection.* May 14, 2016. https://doi.org/10.1007/978-3-319-26300-7_7.

VanderKam, James C., and William Adler, eds. *Jewish Apocalyptic Heritage in Early Christianity.* Jewish Traditions in Early Christian Literature series, vol 4. Minneapolis, MN: Fortress Press, 1996.

Vermes, Geza, trans. *The Complete Dead Sea Scrolls in English.* Fourth edition, revised. New York: Penguin Books, 2004.

Waite, Arthur Edward. *The Book of Black Magic.* York Beach, ME: Weiser, 1993.

———. *The Book of Black Magic and Pacts.* (L. W. De Laurence, ed.) Chicago: De Laurence Co., 1910.

———. *The Doctrine and Literature of the Kabalah.* London: Theosophical Publishing Society, 1902.

———. *The Mysteries of Magic: A Digest of the Writings of Eliphas Lévi.* London: George Redway, 1886.

Walker, D. P. *Spiritual and Demonic Magic from Ficino to Campanella.* University Park, PA: Penn State Press, 2000.

Walters, Henry Beauchamp. *The Art of the Greeks.* New York: Macmillan, 1906.

Walther, Ingo F. *Codices Illustres: The World's Most Famous Illuminated Manuscripts.* New York: Taschen, 2001.

The War Scroll (1QM). https://www.qumran.org/js/qumran/hss/1qm.

Welburn, Andrew. *The Beginnings of Christianity: Essene Mystery, Gnostic Revelation, and the Christian Vision.* Edinburgh, UK: Floris Books, 1995.

Wierus, Johannes. *De Praestigiis Daemonum.* Basel, Switzerland: Ionnem Oporinum, 1564.

———. *De Praestigiis Daemonum.* Fourth edition. Basel, Switzerland: Ionnem Oporinum, 1566.

Wilde, Lady Speranza. *Legends, Charms, and Superstitions of Ireland.* Mineola, NY: Dover Publications, 2006.

Winston, David. "The Iranian Component in the Bible, Apocrypha, and Qumran: A Review of the Evidence." *History of Religions* vol. 5, no. 2 (Winter 1966).

Wise, Michael O., Martin G. Abegg Jr., and Edward M. Cook. *The Dead Sea Scrolls: A New Translation.* New York: HarperCollins, 2005.

Wood, Ernest, and S. V. Subrahmanyam, trans. Garuda Purâna. Allahabad, Uttar Pradesh, India: Indian Press, 1911.

Yates, Frances Amelia. *Giordano Bruno and the Hermetic Tradition.* Volume 2. Chicago, IL: University of Chicago Press, 1979.

———. *The Occult Philosophy in the Elizabethan Age.* London: Routledge & Kegan Paul, 1979.

Zohar: The Book of Enlightenment. (Daniel Chanan Matt, trans.) Ramsey, NJ: Paulist Press, 1983.

ART CREDITS

Image: Alphabet letters on the chapter openers
Artist: Jackie Williams

Page 4: Seven Heavens
Source: St. Dionysius's *Celestial Hierarchy*
Artist/Credit: Merticus Collection, used with permission

Page 6: Tree of Life, from the Llewellyn art department

Page 8: Gates of Hell
Source: Lehner, Ernst & Johanna: *The Picture Book of Devils, Demons, and Witchcraft*, p. 5
Artist/Credit: Jacobus de Teramo, *Das Buch Belial*, printed at Augsburg, 1473
Permission: Dover Publications

Page 10: Satan and Minions
Source: Richard Huber, *Treasury of Fantastic and Mythological Creatures*. Plate 21, fifteenth-century image
Permission: Dover Publications

Page 17: Mesopotamian Demon Bowl
Artist/Source: Anonymous, 6th–7th century
Permission: Wellcome Collection, London

Page 24: Grimoire, Interior Pages with JHS
Source: *Clavis Inferni*, 18th century
Permission: Wellcome Collection, London

Page 28: Grimoire, Interior Pages with Holy Spirit
Source: *Clavis Inferni*, 18th century
Permission: Wellcome Collection, London

Page 33: Angel Binding the Devil
Source: *Encyclopaedia of Occultism* by Lewis Spence, between pages 124 and 125
Permission: Dover Publications

Page 36: Abraxas Seals
Source: *Encyclopaedia of Occultism* by Lewis Spence, between pages 184 and 185
Permission: Dover Publications

Page 41: *AGLA* Knife
Source: *The Discoverie of Witchcraft* by Reginald
  Scot, p. 243
Permission: Dover Publications

Page 42: Conjuring Angels (Abramelin Technique)
Artist/Source: William Charlton Wright, 19th
  century
Permission: Wellcome Collection, London

Page 46: Squatting Devil
Source: Richard Huber, *Treasury of Fantastic and
  Mythological Creatures*. Plate 21,
  medieval print
Permission: Dover Publications

Page 49: Punishments of Hell
Artist/Source: A. Collaert, 17th century
Permission: Wellcome Collection, London

Page 55: Amaimon, King of the South
Source: *Clavis Inferni*, 18th century
Permission: Wellcome Collection, London

Page 58: Seal of Andromalius
Artist/Credit: M. Belanger

Page 63: Satyr, 2002
Artist/Source: Joseph Vargo

Page 64: Warrior Angels
Artist/Credit: Gustav Doré
Source: Gustav Doré, *Doré's Illustrations for
  Paradise Lost*, p. 23
Permission: Dover Publications

Page 69: John Dee's Crystal, 17th century
Artist: Attributed to the angel Uriel
Permission: Wellcome Collection, London

Page 74: Astaroth
Artist/Credit: Collin de Plancy
Source: *Dark Realms Magazine* archives
Permission: Joseph Vargo, used with permission

Page 77: Seal of Asyriel
Artist/Credit: M. Belanger

Page 86: The Demon Bael
Artist/Credit: Collin de Plancy
Source: *Dark Realms Magazine* archives
Permission: Joseph Vargo

Page 88: Baphomet
Artist/Credit: Eliphas Lévi, *La Magie Noire*
Source: Lehner, Ernst & Johanna: *The Picture Book
  of Devils, Demons, and Witchcraft*, p. 24
Permission: Dover Publications

Page 92: Seal of Barmiel
Artist/Credit: M. Belanger

Page 97: Mithras & Bull
Source: *Encyclopaedia of Occultism* by Lewis
  Spence. Between pp. 280 & 281.
Permission: Dover Publications

Page 100: Seal of Belial
Artist/Credit: M. Belanger

Page 105: Saul Consults Samuel
Artist/Source: J. Taylor, 1813
Permission: Wellcome Collection, London

Page 110: Sigil of Baal
Artist/Source: Catherine Rogers

Page 120: English Devil
Source: Richard Huber, *Treasury of Fantastic and
  Mythological Creatures*. Plate 23, woodcut
Permission: Dover Publications

Page 122: Locusts in Revelation
Artist/Source: Anonymous, 16th century
Permission: Wellcome Collection, London

Page 124: Masked Angel
Artist/Source: Kirsten Brown

Page 128: Scribal Arts II
Artist/Credit: Jackie Williams

Page 132: Gate to Hell
Artist/Source: T. Stothard, 1792
Permission: Wellcome Collection, London

Page 134: Hell's Angels
Artist/Credit: Gustav Doré
Source: Gustav Doré, *Doré's Illustrations for Paradise Lost*, p. 4
Permission: Dover Publications

Page 136: Woman Conjured from Mirror
Artist/Source: F. Rops, 19th century
Permission: Wellcome Collection, London

Page 141: Saint Michael Fighting the Dragon
Artist/Source: Albrecht Dürer, 1498
Permission: Wellcome Collection, London

Page 146: Seal of Decarabia
Artist/Credit: M. Belanger

Page 150: Witch & Demon
Source: *Witchcraft, Magic and Alchemy*, Grillot de Givry, p. 122
Permission: Dover Publications

Page 153: John Dee and Edward Kelley, Necromancing
Source: *Encyclopaedia of Occultism* by Lewis Spence. Between pp. 288 & 289
Permission: Dover Publications

Page 155: Balaam's Vision
Artist/Credit: Gustav Doré
Source: Gustav Doré, *Doré's Bible Illustrations*, p. 45
Permission: Dover Publications

Page 158: Egyn, King of the North
Artist/Source: *Clavis Inferni*, 18th century
Permission: Wellcome Collection, London

Page 159: Horned Demon
Artist/Credit: Joseph Vargo

Page 163: Witches' Pact
Source: *Compendium Maleficarum*, Francesco Maria Guazzo, p. 16
Permission: Dover Publications

Page 174: Seal of Foras
Artist/Credit: M. Belanger

Page 178: Four Horsemen
Artist/Credit: Hans Burgkmair woodcut
Source: Lehner, Ernst & Johanna: *The Picture Book of Devils, Demons, and Witchcraft*, p. 55
Permission: Dover Publications

Page 180: Sigil of Gaap
Artist/Source: Catherine Rogers

Page 186: Smoke
Artist/Source: Kirsten Brown

Page 189: Scribal Art
Artist/Credit: Jackie Williams

Page 193: Book of Magick
Source: *Witchcraft, Magic and Alchemy* by Grillot de Givry, p. 113
Permission: Dover Publications

Page 197: Marbas/Mithras
Artist/Source: Catherine Rogers

Page 200: Zodiac Angel Mercury
Artist/Source: N. Dorigny, 1695
Permission: Wellcome Collection, London

Page 201: Tree of Life, from the Llewellyn art department

Page 207: Devils and Child
Artist/Credit: Geoffrey Landry
Source: Lehner, Ernst & Johanna, *The Picture Book of Devils, Demons, and Witchcraft*, p. 7
Permission: Dover Publications

Page 213: Rapture
Artist/Source: Kirsten Brown

Page 218: St. Cado & the Devil
Source: Grillot de Givry, *Witchcraft, Magic and Alchemy*, p. 150
Permission: Dover Publications

Page 220: Seal of Ipos
Artist/Credit: M. Belanger

Page 221: Lilit Amulet
Artist/Source: Anonymous, traditional
Permission: Wellcome Collection, London

Page 223: Seal of Itrasbiel
Artist/Credit: M. Belanger

Page 228: Angel of Death
Artist/Credit: Gustav Doré
Source: Gustav Doré, *Doré's Bible Illustrations*, p. 35
Permission: Dover Publications

Page 230: Tobias's Nuptial Night
Artist/Source: S. F. Ravenet after a painting by Le Seuer

Page 232: Witches' Dance
Source: Francesco Maria Guazzo, *Compendium Maleficarum*, p. 37
Permission: Dover Publications

Page 234: Rites of Eleusis
Source: *Encyclopaedia of Occultism* by Lewis Spence, between pp. 280 & 281
Permission: Dover Publications

Page 235: St. Catherine Battles a Demon
Artist/Source: Woodcut, anonymous
Permission: Wellcome Collection, London

Page 241: Seal of God
Artist/Credit: Jackie Williams

Page 242: Christ Casts Out the Demon

Artist/Source: Johann Daniel de Montalegre
Permission: Wellcome Collection, London

Page 245: Berbiguier
Source: Grillot de Givry, *Witchcraft, Magic and Alchemy*, p. 142
Permission: Dover Publications

Page 246: The Shameful Kiss
Source: *Compendium Maleficarum*, Francesco Maria Guazzo, p. 35
Permission: Dover Publications

Page 249: Lilith
Artist/Credit: Sumerian bas-relief
Source: Richard Huber, *Treasury of Fantastic and Mythological Creatures*. Plate 4.
Permission: Dover Publications

Page 252: Lucifer and the Serpent
Artist/Credit: Gustav Doré
Source: *Doré's Illustrations for Paradise Lost*, p. 19
Permission: Dover Publications

Page 257: Tomb of the Demon Queen
Artist/Source: Joseph Vargo

Page 259: Punishment of the Gluttonous
Source: Lehner, Ernst & Johanna: *The Picture Book of Devils, Demons, and Witchcraft*, p. 47
Permission: Dover Publications

Page 262: Sigil of Malphas
Artist/Source: Catherine Rogers

Page 266: Seal of Marchosias
Artist/Credit: M. Belanger

Page 269: Witch Conjuring
Artist/Source: J. Dixon, 1773
Permission: Wellcome Collection, London

Page 272: Dr. Faustus
Artist/Credit: published by John Wright, 1631

Source: Lehner, Ernst & Johanna: *The Picture Book of Devils, Demons, and Witchcraft*
Permission: Dover Publications

Page 277: Death and the Raven
Artist/Source: Walter Appleton Clark
Permission: Wellcome Collection, London

Page 280: The Devil in Hell
Artist/Source: Buonamico di Martino, 15th century
Permission: Wellcome Collection, London

Page 281: Seal of Murmus
Artist/Credit: M. Belanger

Page 283: Indulgences
Artist/Source: Anonymous, circa 15th century
Permission: Wellcome Collection, London

Page 286: Summoning Circle
Source: Reginald Scot, *The Discoverie of Witchcraft*, p. 244
Permission: Dover Publications

Page 289: Two Men Summoning a Devil
Artist/Source: Woodcut, 1720, anonymous
Permission: Wellcome Collection, London

Page 291: Hexagram of Solomon
Artist/Credit: Jackie Williams

Page 295: Angelic Hierarchy
Artist/Credit: Merticus Collection
Source: *Celestial Hierarchy*

Page 300: Devil Holding Court
Source: *Compendium Maleficarum*, Francesco Maria Guazzo, p. 36
Permission: Dover Publications

Page 302: Seal of Oriel
Artist/Credit: M. Belanger

Page 307: Persian Angel
Artist/Source: Illuminated manuscript, 1750, anonymous
Permission: Wellcome Collection, London

Page 311: Paimon, King of the West
Artist/Source: *Clavis Inferni*, 18th century
Permission: Wellcome Collection, London

Page 313: Satan Cast Out
Artist/Credit: Gustav Doré
Source: Gustav Doré, *Doré's Illustrations for Paradise Lost*, p. 19
Permission: Dover Publications

Page 314: Oriens, King of the East
Artist/Source: *Clavis Inferni*, 18th century
Permission: Wellcome Collection, London

Page 321: Demonic Grotesque
Artist/Credit: Joseph Vargo

Page 323: Seal of Procel
Artist/Credit: M. Belanger

Page 324: Dancing Goat
Artist/Credit: traditional heraldry
Source: Richard Huber, *Treasury of Fantastic and Mythological Creatures*. Plate 66.
Permission: Dover Publications

Page 331: Heavenly Chariots
Artist/Credit: Gustav Doré
Source: Gustav Doré, *Doré's Bible Illustrations*, p. 129
Permission: Dover Publications

Page 333: Triangle of Pacts
Source: Grillot de Givry, *Witchcraft, Magic and Alchemy*, p. 106
Permission: Dover Publications

Page 337: Seal of Ronove
Artist/Credit: M. Belanger

Page 339: Forcalor Comparison
Artist/Credit: M. Belanger

Page 342: Conjuror with Demons
Artist/Source: J. Brown, 1813
Permission: Wellcome Collection, London

Page 344: The Demon Behemoth
Source: Grillot de Givry, *Witchcraft, Magic and Alchemy*, p. 137
Permission: Dover Publications

Page 346: Seven Angels & Symbols
Source: Scot's *Discoverie of Witchcraft*, p. 231
Permission: Dover Publications

Page 349: Gnostic Revelation
Artist/Credit: M. Belanger

Page 353: Infernal Hierarchy
Source: *Witchcraft, Magic and Alchemy*, by Grillot de Givry, p. 130
Permission: Dover Publications

Page 357: Sea-Devil
Artist/Source: Woodcut, 1720, anonymous
Permission: Wellcome Collection, London

Page 359: Witch's Familiar
Source: Richard Huber, *Treasury of Fantastic and Mythological Creatures*. Plate 23.
Permission: Dover Publications

Page 360: Scrying Table
Artist/Source: Catherine Rogers

Page 362: Italian Whitevine Capital
Artist/Credit: Jackie Williams

Page 363: Seal of Sitri
Artist/Credit: Cathrine Rogers

Page 365: Solomon and Belial
Artist/Credit: Jacobus de Teramo, *Das Buch Belial*, printed at Augsburg, 1473
Source: Lehner, Ernst & Johanna: *The Picture Book of Devils, Demons, and Witchcraft*, p. 5
Permission: Dover Publications

Page 369: European Mandrake
Source: Richard Huber, *Treasury of Fantastic and Mythological Creatures*. Plate 56.
Permission: Dover Publications

Page 374: Lake of Fire
Artist/Credit: Gustav Doré
Source: Gustav Doré, *Doré's Illustrations for Paradise Lost*, p. 2
Permission: Dover Publications

Page 375: Life's Crucible
Artist/Source: Christoph Murer, 1622
Permission: Wellcome Collection, London

Page 377: Death of Grandier
Source: Lehner, Ernst & Johanna: *The Picture Book of Devils, Demons, and Witchcraft*, p. 80
Permission: Dover Publications

Page 379: Pentagram of Solomon
Artist/Credit: Jackie Williams

Page 382: Witch Summoning from Cauldron
Artist/Source: H. S. Thomassin (1687–1741)
Permission: Wellcome Collection, London

Page 386: Pentagram
Artist/Source: *Clavis Inferni*, 18th century
Permission: Wellcome Collection, London

Page 391: Pact of Urbain Grandier
Source: Lehner, Ernst & Johanna: *The Picture Book of Devils, Demons, and Witchcraft*, p. 80
Permission: Dover Publications

Page 393: Seal of Vadriel
Artist/Credit: M. Belanger

Page 396: Specter of Death
Artist/Credit: Gustav Doré
Source: Gustav Doré, *The Doré Bible Illustrations*,
    p. 237
Permission: Dover Publications

Page 396: Sea-Witch
Artist/Credit: Woodcut from I. I. Shipper
Source: Richard Huber, *Treasury of Fantastic and
    Mythological Creatures*
Permission: Dover Publications

Page 399: Wizard
Artist/Source: Sir Edward Burne-Jones,
    19th century
Permission: Wellcome Collection, London

Page 404: Judgment
Artist/Credit: Jackie Williams

Page 405: Saint Benedict Medal
Permission: Wellcome Collection, London

Page 408: Ani and His Wife
Artist/Source: Papyrus of Ani, 1250 BCE
Permission: Wellcome Collection, London

Page 411: Zodiac Angel Mars
Artist/Source: N. Dorigny, 1695
Permission: Wellcome Collection, London

Page 413: Seal of Zachariel
Artist/Credit: M. Belanger

Page 416: Spirit Board
Artist/Source: Catherine Rogers

Page 421: Plague Angels
Artist/Source: P. Noël, 1869
Permission: Wellcome Collection, London

Page 427: Temptation of Saint Anthony
Artist/Source: M. Schongauer, 1470–1475
Permission: Wellcome Collection, London

Page 431: Adam and Eve Expelled
Artist/Source: Raphael Sadeler, 1583
Permission: Wellcome Collection, London

Page 433: Ethiopian Charm with Susenyos
Artist/Source: Anonymous, traditional
Permission: Wellcome Collection, London

Page 436: Biblical Flood
Artist/Source: L. Friedrich after W. Kaulbach
Permission: Wellcome Collection, London

Page 439: Jacob Wrestles the Angel
Artist/Source: Salvator Rosa, 1766
Permission: Wellcome Collection, London

Page 442: Temple of Solomon
Artist/Source: Woodcut, possibly Villalpandus,
    16th century
Permission: Wellcome Collection, London

Page 444: Star of Solomon
Artsit/Source: *Clavis Inferni*, 18th century

Page 445: Baphomet
Artist/Source: Catherine Rogers

Page 448: Angelic Messenger
Artist/Source: Woodcut, anonymous, 16th–17th
    century
Permission: Wellcome Collection, London

TO WRITE TO THE AUTHOR

If you wish to contact the author or would like more information about this book, please write to the author in care of Llewellyn Worldwide and we will forward your request. Both the author and the publisher appreciate hearing from you and learning of your enjoyment of this book and how it has helped you. Llewellyn Worldwide cannot guarantee that every letter written to the author can be answered, but all will be forwarded. Please write to:

M. Belanger
℅ Llewellyn Worldwide Ltd.
2143 Wooddale Drive
Woodbury, MN 55125-2989
Please enclose a self-addressed stamped envelope for reply,
or $1.00 to cover costs. If outside the U.S.A., enclose
an international postal reply coupon.

Many of Llewellyn's authors have websites with additional information and resources. For more information, please visit our website at http://www.llewellyn.com.